INTERNATIONAL CRIMINAL LAW:

CASES AND MATERIALS

By

Edward M. Wise

Professor of Law & Director
Comparative Criminal Law Project
Wayne State University Law School

Ellen S. Podgor

Professor of Law
Georgia State University
College of Law

LEXIS Publishing™

LEXIS®NEXIS®• MARTINDALE-HUBBELL®
MATTHEW BENDER®• MICHIE™• SHEPARD'S®

Library of Congress Cataloging-in-Publication Data

Wise, Edward M.
  International criminal law / Edward M. Wise, Ellen S. Podgor.
    p. cm. – (Casebook series)
  Includes index.
  ISBN 0-8205-4830-8 (softbound)
    1. International offenses—Cases. 2. Criminal jurisdiction—United States—Cases. I.
Podgor, Ellen S., 1952- II. Title. III. Casebook series (New York, N.Y.)

K5165 .W57 2000
345.73'01—dc21

00-063576

This publication is designed to provide accurate and authoritative information in regard to the subject matter covered. It is sold with the understanding that the publisher is not engaged in rendering legal, accounting, or other professional services. If legal advice or other expert assistance is required, the services of a competent professional should be sought.

Editorial Offices
2 Park Avenue, New York, NY 10016-5675 (212) 448-2200
201 Mission Street, San Francisco, CA 94105-1831 (415) 908-3200
701 East Water Street, Charlottesville, VA 22902-7587 (804) 972-7600
www.lexis.com

(Pub.3141)

To –

Sandra F. Van Burkleo

&

Cheryl L. Segal

PREFACE

This book contains a collection of cases, materials, notes, and questions concerning international criminal law. It is designed for use as a teaching tool, not as a reference work, although it does try to provide an overview of most of the topics that fall within the scope of international criminal law. Apart from the occasional citations on specific points that occur throughout, we have included at the end of the book a short list of general reference works to serve as a preliminary guide for further reading.

We have tried to keep the book short, as casebooks go, and to make it useable both by teachers who want to emphasize the increasingly important transnational dimension of U.S. criminal law and by those who want to explore the increasingly important use of criminal sanctions to enforce norms of international law. These two developments are interrelated and it is more and more difficult, in any event, to keep them separate.

The book is divided into four parts. The first part contains a brief introduction to the field of international criminal law and a chapter on the general jurisdictional principles, of both national and international law, that govern efforts to extend U.S. criminal law to foreign crimes and foreign criminals. The second part contains materials dealing with the specific application of those principles in cases involving the Foreign Corrupt Practices Act, antitrust and securities regulation, export controls, computer crimes, narcotics and money laundering, piracy and terrorism, and torture. The third part deals with procedural aspects of trying such cases in the U.S. courts and covers the extraterritorial application of the U.S. Constitution, immunities from jurisdiction, mutual assistance in criminal cases, extradition, alternatives to extradition, prisoner transfer treaties, recognition of foreign criminal judgments, and the bearing of international human rights instruments on criminal procedure. The fourth and final part of the book deals with the prosecution of international crimes; it takes up the question of what crimes constitute international crimes, the Nuremberg and Tokyo precedents, the *ad hoc* tribunals for the former Yugoslavia and for Rwanda, the statute that will likely establish in the not too distant future a permanent international criminal court, and the substantive law of the international crimes of aggression, genocide, crimes against humanity, and conventional war crimes.

Our main focus, at least in the first three parts, is on relatively recent decisions of the United States courts and the effect of contemporary globalization on U.S. criminal law. We have tried, above all, to convey a sense of the "international flavor" that is developing in federal prosecutions.[*] As a result of this particular focus, some topics have been slighted that might figure more prominently in a longer, more comprehensive work on international

---

[*] For a preliminary sketch, *see* Ellen S. Podgor, Essay, *Globalization and the Federal Prosecution of White Collar Crime*, 34 AM. CRIM. L. REV. 325 (1997).

criminal law.

Our basic aim has been to construct a set of teaching materials that will provide students with a grounding in the transnational issues likely to arise in federal criminal cases and also in the law that has been produced as a consequence of international efforts to impose criminal responsibility on the perpetrators of human rights atrocities.

This book tries to provide a picture of the present state of a rapidly expanding and changing field. Events no doubt will quickly overtake much of what we present. We only hope that, in the meanwhile, teachers and students will be persuaded through using this book to regard international criminal law as an ·exciting field, worthy of their continuing attention as it grows and develops, as it inevitably will, in new directions.

We thank the American Law Institute for permission to reprint sections from the Restatement (Third) of the Foreign Relations Law of the United States, © 1987, The American Law Institute; and other copyright holders including the Virginia Journal of International Law, Jack L. Goldsmith & Eric Posner (quotation on p. 25); the American Society of International Law (excerpt on p. 290 from 94 AJIL 535-36 (2000), © The American Society of International Law); the Academy of Political Science (excerpt on pp. 530-31 from the Political Science Quarterly, 1947); and Alfred P. Rubin (quotation on p. 678).

Edward Wise acknowledges the support provided for work on this book by both the Law School and the Humanities Center of Wayne State University. He specifically thanks Dean Joan Mahoney and the Director of the Humanities Center, Professor Walter F. Edwards. He also would be remiss in not acknowledging the significant influence of Gerhard O. W. Mueller, who first introduced him to the problems of international criminal law, defined in the most comprehensive possible fashion, decades ago.[*]

Ellen S. Podgor expresses appreciation to Georgia State University College of Law and University of Georgia School of Law and to the students from these schools and from the Temple Tel- Aviv and Rome Summer Abroad Programs who used portions of these materials prior to their publication. She specifically thanks Librarian Rhea Ballard-Thrower, Dean Janice Griffith, Associate Dean Steven Kaminshine, Associate Dean Paul Kurtz, Professor Molly O'Brien, and Dean David Shipley.

Edward M. Wise
Ellen S. Podgor

---

[*] *See* Edward M. Wise, *Gerhard O. W. Mueller and the Foundations of International Criminal Law*, in CRIMINAL SCIENCE IN A GLOBAL SOCIETY: ESSAYS IN HONOR OF GERHARD O. W. MUELLER 45 (Edward M. Wise ed., 1994).

SUMMARY TABLE OF CONTENTS

PART FOUR. THE PROSECUTION OF INTERNATIONAL CRIMES

TABLE OF CONTENTS

PART THREE. PROCEDURE

Part 1
GENERAL PRINCIPLES

Chapter 1
INTRODUCTION

§ 1.01 The Scope of International Criminal Law

What is meant by "international criminal law"? In a broad sense, the subject covers all of the problems lying in the area where criminal law and international law overlap and interact. It is a field that has undergone an enormous expansion in recent years. This expansion is a result both of (a) increasing "globalization" of criminal conduct and consequently of national criminal law, and (b) increasing reliance on criminal sanctions to enforce norms of international law, especially norms of international human rights and humanitarian law.

International criminal law can be subdivided into three main sets of topics. These are: [A] International Aspects of National Criminal Law, [B] Criminal Aspects of International Law: International Standards of Justice, and [C] Criminal Aspects of International Law: International Criminal Law *Stricto Senso*. The term "international criminal law" sometimes has been used to refer to one or another of these three sets of topics standing alone. It is more usually understood nowadays in its broad sense to designate a field that includes all three. (The following discussion of these three subfields is based, in part, on Edward M. Wise, *Terrorism and the Problems of an International Criminal Law*, 19 CONN. L. REV. 799, 801-08 (1987).)

[A] International Aspects of National Criminal Law

The first set of topics comprising international criminal law includes at its core questions concerning the extent to which national courts are permitted to assume jurisdiction over extraterritorial crime, the choice of the applicable law (usually the forum's) in cases involving such crimes, and the recognition of foreign penal judgments. These are all questions about how the courts of one country should act in criminal cases involving a foreign component. They are the counterpart on the criminal side of the questions dealt with in civil cases under the heading "conflict of laws" or "private international law." Taken together, they constitute international criminal law more or less in the original meaning of the term.

1

The term "international law" was coined by Jeremy Bentham in 1780 (to describe what older usage called the "law of nations"); the term "private international law" was invented by Joseph Story in 1834. An equivalent of the term "international criminal law" appeared in German in 1862. Similar cognates came into use in other European languages (but not English) during the 1870s, to designate the branch of law concerned with topics such as jurisdiction, choice of law, and the effect of foreign judgments in criminal cases.

In subsequent years, continental jurists debated the exact nature of the relationship between international criminal law, so defined, and private international law. Earlier writers, from the fourteenth century on, had treated questions arising in connection with divergent criminal laws as a problem of conflict of laws. Story devoted a chapter of his treatise on the conflict of laws to "penal laws and offenses." Yet he also thought of private international law as a "branch of public law." For nineteenth-century continental jurists preoccupied with the "scientific" or systematic arrangement of the law, private international law was a part of private law, criminal law was a part of public law, and the division between private and public law was too sharply drawn to permit anything connected with public law to be treated as part of private international law. Since international criminal law, as first conceived, was primarily a matter of national dispositions regarding the power and competence of a particular country's criminal courts, neither could it be classified as part of public international law. Assertions of power over events taking place abroad might ultimately be subject to limiting principles derived from international law; but the more immediate concern was with the antecedent question of what national law provided that judges should do in cases involving foreign crime. Since national rules regarding such questions did not seem to fit under any other legal rubric, they came, by a process of elimination, to be regarded as occupying a field of their own, which was designated "international criminal law." Some scholars rejected the view that this new field was wholly separate from private international law. Nonetheless, that it was separate came to be the commonly held view in Europe, and implicitly in the United States where, absent standard texts on the subject, international criminal law largely fell into a kind of legal limbo.

International criminal law in its original sense also can be regarded as including, by extension, on the one hand, exceptions from criminal jurisdiction, such as diplomatic immunity and asylum, and, on the other, forms of transnational cooperation, such as extradition, that enable states to circumvent the ordinary restrictions on their power to enforce criminal law outside their own borders. These subjects do not fit exactly within international criminal law as originally defined. Immunities from jurisdiction derive, in large part, from principles of public international law, whereas international criminal law was supposed to be primarily a matter of a state's own rules governing the exercise of its power to punish foreign crimes and crimes committed by foreigners. Extradition, likewise, is not so much a matter of national rules governing the exercise of penal powers, as it is a matter of international obligation, or at least an "international legal transaction" falling rather more clearly within the realm of international law.

Yet it is hard, once one starts talking about a state's jurisdiction over foreigners and foreign crime, to avoid questions of immunity and extradition and other forms of international cooperation in criminal matters. These are connected topics that almost naturally have to be discussed together. There are other instances as well in which it seems inadequate to insist on a crisp distinction between national and international law; hence the tendency to attenuate the distinction and to speak instead about "transnational law." In dealing with problems of criminal law that cut across national boundaries, it is particularly difficult to keep questions of national and international law apart. As a result, international criminal law, practically from the beginning, has been treated as including virtually the whole gamut of problems connected with transnational aspects and applications of domestic systems of criminal law.

[B] Criminal Aspects of International Law: International Standards of Criminal Justice

A second distinct group of topics that also has been designated as "international criminal law" concerns international standards of criminal justice, that is, principles or rules of public international law that impose obligations on states with respect to the content of their domestic criminal law. International standards may require states to respect the rights of persons accused or suspected of crime, or to prosecute and punish certain so-called "international offenses." Both kinds of standards appear in the older body of international law on state responsibility for injury to aliens. More recently, guarantees for persons accused of crime generally have been cast in the form of treaty provisions on human rights; indeed, a large part of contemporary law on the international protection of human rights is directed at setting standards of performance for domestic criminal procedure. Likewise, obligations to prosecute specific types of offenders through the medium of local criminal law have tended to be imposed more and more by general conventions – those dealing, for instance with piracy, the slave trade, traffic in narcotics, war crimes, genocide, torture, hijacking of aircraft, crimes against diplomats, hostage-taking, and other forms of terrorism. By virtue of these treaty obligations, states are required to cooperate in specified ways in suppressing certain kinds of conduct supposedly reprehended by the world at large. The conduct on the part of individuals which states are required to suppress is not necessarily itself a violation of international law; these so-called "international crimes" or "offenses of international concern" generally are tried by national courts applying national law which has been enacted in order to implement a state's international obligations. But they are prosecuted in conformity with international rules stipulating that persons who commit these offenses should be tried and punished.

This second group of topics, unlike the first, falls largely within the domain of public international law. A part of it – the part concerned with holding states to observe certain basic procedural safeguards in administering criminal justice

– usually is assigned to the separate subfield of international human rights law. The other part – the part concerned with international rules requiring states to cooperate in suppressing certain international offenses – sometimes is referred to simply as international criminal law. The effort to suppress such offenses may give rise, in turn, to questions of jurisdiction, extradition, and other forms of interstate cooperation. Indeed, contemporary treaties requiring states to suppress particular offenses typically contain provisions regarding jurisdiction and extradition and mandate that any state in whose territory an offender is found must itself exercise jurisdiction over the offense if it does not extradite to another state which is prepared to prosecute. In this respect, the topics comprising international criminal law, in the sense of a law of international offenses, have definite functional ties to, and more and more overlap with, the topics comprising international criminal law in its original sense of a body of rules concerned with the transnational applications of domestic criminal law. Nonetheless, these are two conceptually distinct sets of topics, or at least have different starting points: the one is concerned with what have been called the "criminal aspects of international law," the other with "international aspects of national criminal law."

[C] Criminal Aspects of International Law: International Criminal Law *Stricto Sensu*

A third group of topics concerns questions of international criminal law in the "strict," "true," "proper," or "material" sense of the term. At one time it was possible to argue that international criminal law "in the material sense of the word" does not exist. *See* Georg Schwarzenberger, *The Problem of an International Criminal Law*, 3 CURRENT LEGAL PROBS. 263 (1950), *reprinted in* INTERNATIONAL CRIMINAL LAW 3 (Gerhard O. W. Mueller & Edward M. Wise, eds. 1965). That is a much less plausible argument today. But exactly what should be included under this heading remains controversial.

In its strictest possible sense, international criminal law would refer to the law applicable in an international criminal court having the power to impose specifically penal sanctions on offenders. Until recently, international criminal law in this sense seemed to be, for the most part, despite the Nuremberg and Tokyo precedents [*see* chap. 18], a purely hypothetical body of law, to be applied by an even more hypothetical court. However, with the creation of *ad hoc* tribunals for the trial of international offenses committed in the former Yugoslavia and in Rwanda [*see* chap. 19], and with the treaty establishing a permanent international criminal court about to come into force in a couple of years [*see* chap. 20], this body of law has begun to look much less hypothetical. It is now generally agreed that there are certain offenses – such as genocide, crimes against humanity, and war crimes – which are directly proscribed by international law; that international law itself imposes criminal responsibility on those who commit these crimes; and that individuals who commit them are potentially triable not only before national courts but also before an international tribunal having jurisdiction over these offenses.

For the most part, these so-called "crimes under international law" (for which rules of international law impose criminal liability directly on individuals) also constitute what have been called "offenses of international concern" (as to which rules of international law impose an obligation on states to prosecute and punish those who commit such offenses). In this respect, the two categories overlap. But they are not coextensive. Not all "offenses of international concern" are "crimes under international law." While states are bound, for instance, by a network of contemporary international treaties to cooperate in repressing certain forms of terrorism and narcotics trafficking, whether terrorism or narcotics trafficking are or should be offenses triable before an international criminal court is a question about which there has been considerable debate.

Nonetheless, much current writing on the scope and nature of international criminal law tends to collapse the distinction between these two types of international crimes – those for which international law does and those for which it does not impose direct criminal liability on individuals. Both types of offenses are said to have a "common denominator," namely, "the preservation of certain interests which represent commonly shared values in the world community." M. Cherif Bassiouni, *Introduction to Symposium on the Teaching of International Criminal Law*, 1 TOURO J. TRANSNAT'L L. 129, 130 (1988). International criminal law is assumed to be ideally, although not entirely in practice, a more or less coherent system founded on a combination of some or all of the following premises: (1) Certain conduct is so reprehended by the world at large that it can be considered to amount to an international crime. (2) An authentic guide to the kind of conduct that amounts to an international crime is a multilateral treaty requiring its repression. (3) Conduct condemned in a widely ratified multilateral treaty also can be regarded as a violation of customary international law. (4) Individuals who engage in such conduct violate international law. (5) In prosecuting individuals who commit international crimes, states enforce international law as organs of the international community. (6) These crimes are the concern of all states. (7) All states therefore have "universal jurisdiction" to prosecute those who commit these crimes. (8) All states, indeed, are bound to prosecute or at least to assist in bringing to justice those who commit these crimes. *See* M. CHERIF BASSIOUNI & EDWARD M. WISE, AUT DEDERE AUT JUDICARE: THE DUTY TO EXTRADITE OR PROSECUTE IN INTERNATIONAL LAW 49-50 (1995). In this view, the existing body of international rules requiring states to prosecute various kinds of criminal conduct already constitutes a body of international criminal law properly so-called; whether it is enforced "directly" before an international tribunal or "indirectly" before national courts depends partly on questions of convenience, partly on contingent political factors.

§ 1.02 The Sources of International Criminal Law

International criminal law is an amalgam of rules and principles drawn from both national and international law. In national legal systems, legal rules and principles are identified and validated by reference to formal "sources of law" such as the constitution, statutes, case law, etc. What are the equivalent "sources" of international law rules and principles?

THE RESTATEMENT (THIRD) OF THE FOREIGN RELATIONS LAW OF THE UNITED STATES (1986)

§ 102 SOURCES OF INTERNATIONAL LAW

(1) A rule of international law is one that has been accepted as such by the international community of states

(a) in the form of customary law;
(b) by international agreement; or
(c) by derivation from general principles common to the major legal systems of the world.

(2) Customary international law results from a general and consistent practice of states followed by them from a sense of legal obligation.

(3) International agreements create law for the states parties thereto and may lead to the creation of customary international law when such agreements are intended for adherence by states generally and are in fact widely accepted.

(4) General principles common to major legal systems, even if not incorporated or reflected in customary law or international agreement, may be invoked as supplementary rules of international law where appropriate.

THE CASE OF THE S.S. LOTUS (FRANCE v. TURKEY)

Permanent Court of International Justice
P.C.I.J., Ser. A, No. 10 (1927)

. . . . On August 2nd, 1926, just before midnight, a collision occurred between the French mail steamer *Lotus*, proceeding to Constantinople, and the Turkish collier *Boz-Kourt*, between five and six nautical miles to the north of

Cape Sigri (Mitylene). The *Boz-Kourt*, which was cut in two, sank, and eight Turkish nationals who were on board perished. After having done everything possible to succour the shipwrecked persons, of whom ten were able to be saved, the *Lotus* continued on its course to Constantinople, where it arrived on August 3rd.

At the time of the collision, the officer of the watch on board the *Lotus* was Monsieur Demons, a French citizen, lieutenant in the merchant service and first officer of the ship, whilst the movements of the *Boz-Kourt* were directed by its captain, Hassan Bey, who was one of those saved from the wreck.

As early as August 3d the Turkish police proceeded to hold an enquiry into the collision on board the *Lotus*; and on the following day, August 4th, the captain of the *Lotus* handed in his master's report at the French Consulate-General, transmitting a copy to the habour master.

On August 5th, Lieutenant Demons was requested by the Turkish authorities to go ashore to give evidence. The examination, the length of which incidentally resulted in delaying the departure of the *Lotus*, led to the placing under arrest of Lieutenant Demons – without previous notice being given to the French Consul-General – and Hassan Bey, amongst others. This arrest, which has been characterized by the Turkish agent as arrest pending trial (*arrestation préventive*), was effected in order to ensure that the criminal prosecution instituted against the two officers, on a charge of manslaughter, by the Public Prosecutor of Stamboul, on the complaint of the families of the victims of the collision should follow its normal course.

The case was first heard by the Criminal Court of Stamboul on August 28th. On that occasion, Lieutenant Demons submitted that the Turkish Courts had no jurisdiction; the Court, however, overruled his objection. When the proceedings were resumed on September 11th, Lieutenant Demons demanded his release on bail; this request was complied with on September 13th, the bail being fixed at 6,000 Turkish pounds.

On September 15th, the Criminal Court delivered its judgment. . . . [I]t sentenced Lieutenant Demons to eighty days' imprisonment and a fine of twenty-two pounds, Hassan Bey being sentenced to a slightly more severe penalty. . . .

[The French government protested the action of the Turkish authorities in subjecting Lieutenant Demons to prosecution. It contended that only the state under whose flag a vessel sails has jurisdiction under international law to prosecute persons on board that vessel for actions leading to a collision on the high seas. France and Turkey were both parties to the Convention of Lausanne of July 24, 1923; under Article 15 of that Convention "all questions of jurisdiction shall, as between Turkey and other contracting Powers, be decided in accordance with the principles of international law." By a special agreement, the French and Turkish governments submitted to the Permanent Court of International Justice two questions: (1) whether Turkey had, contrary to Article

15 of the Convention of Lausanne, acted in conflict with the principles of international law – and, if so, what principles – when it instituted criminal proceedings against M. Demons; and (2) should the reply to (1) be in the affirmative, what pecuniary reparation, if any, was due to M. Demons.]

I

. . . . The prosecution was instituted in pursuance of Turkish legislation. The special agreement does not indicate what clause or clauses of that legislation apply. No document has been submitted to the Court indicating on what article of the Turkish Penal Code the prosecution was based; the French Government, however, declares that the Criminal Court claimed jurisdiction under Article 6 of the Turkish Penal Code, and far from denying this statement, Turkey, in submissions of her Counter-Case, contends that that article is in conformity with the principles of international law. It does not appear from the proceedings whether the prosecution was instituted solely on the basis of that article.

Article 6 of the Turkish Penal Code, Law No. 765 of March 1st, 1926 (Official Gazette No. 320 of March 13th, 1926), runs as follows:

> Any foreigner who, apart from the cases contemplated by Article 4, commits an offense abroad to the prejudice of Turkey or of a Turkish subject, for which offence Turkish law prescribes a penalty involving loss of freedom for a minimum period of not less than one year, shall be punished in accordance with the Turkish Penal Code provided that he is arrested in Turkey. The penalty shall however be reduced by one third and instead of the death penalty, twenty years of penal servitude shall be awarded.
>
> Nevertheless, in such cases, the prosecution will only be instituted at the request of the Minister of Justice or on the complaint of the injured Party. . . .

Even if the Court must hold that the Turkish authorities had seen fit to base the prosecution of Lieutenant Demons upon the above-mentioned Article 6, the question submitted to the Court is not whether that article is compatible with the principles of international law; it is more general. The Court is asked to state whether or not the principles of international law prevent Turkey from instituting criminal proceedings against Lieutenant Demons under Turkish law. Neither the conformity of Article 6 in itself with the principles of international law nor the application of that article by the Turkish authorities constitutes the point at issue; it is the very fact of the institution of proceedings which is held by France to be contrary to those principles. . . .

III

The Court, having to consider whether there are any rules of international law which may have been violated by the prosecution in pursuance of Turkish law of Lieutenant Demons, is confronted in the first place by a question of principle which, in the written and oral arguments of the two Parties, has proved to be a fundamental one. The French Government contends that the Turkish courts, in order to have jurisdiction, should be able to point to some title to jurisdiction recognized by international law in favour of Turkey. On the other hand, the Turkish Government takes the view that Article 15 allows Turkey jurisdiction whenever such jurisdiction does not come into conflict with a principle of international law.

The latter view seems to be in conformity with the special agreement itself, No. 1 of which asks the Court to say whether Turkey has acted contrary to the principles of international law and, if so, what principles. According to the special agreement, therefore, it is not a question of stating principles which would permit Turkey to take criminal proceedings, but of formulating the principles, if any, which might have been violated by such proceedings.

This way of stating the question is also dictated by the very nature and existing conditions of international law. . . . International law governs relations between independent States. The rules of law binding upon States therefore emanate from their own free will as expressed in conventions or by usages generally accepted as expressing principles of law and established in order to regulate the relations between these co-existing independent communities or with a view to the achievement of common aims. Restrictions upon the independence of States cannot therefore be presumed.

Now the first and foremost restriction imposed by international law upon a State is that – failing the existence of a permissive rule to the contrary – it may not exercise its power in any form in the territory of another state. In this sense jurisdiction is certainly territorial; it cannot be exercised by a State outside its territory except by virtue of a permissive rule derived from international custom or from a convention.

It does not, however, follow that international law prohibits a State from exercising jurisdiction in its own territory, in respect of any case which relates to acts which have taken place abroad, and in which it cannot rely on some permissive rule of international law. Such a view would only be tenable if international law contained a general prohibition to states to extend the application of their laws and the jurisdiction of their courts to persons, property and acts outside their territory, and if, as an exception to this general prohibition, it allowed States do so in certain specific cases. But this is certainly not the case under international law as it stands at present. Far from laying down a general prohibition to the effect that States may not extend the application of their laws and the jurisdiction of their courts to persons, property and acts outside their territory, it leaves them in this respect a wide measure of discretion which is only limited in certain cases by prohibitive rules; as regards other cases, every State remains free to adopt the principles which it regards as best and most suitable. . . .

In these circumstances, all that can be required of a State is that it should not overstep the limits which international law places upon its jurisdiction; within these limits, its title to exercise jurisdiction rests in its sovereignty.

It follows from the foregoing that the contention of the French Government to the effect that Turkey must in each case be able to cite a rule of international law authorizing her to exercise jurisdiction, is opposed to the generally accepted international law to which Article 15 of the Convention of Lausanne refers. Having regard to the terms of Article 15 and to the construction which the Court has just placed upon it, this contention would apply in regard to civil as well as to criminal cases, and would be applicable on conditions of absolute reciprocity as between Turkey and the other contracting Parties; in practice, it would therefore in many cases result in paralyzing the action of the courts, owing to the impossibility of citing a universally accepted rule on which to support the exercise of their jurisdiction.

Nevertheless, it has to be seen whether the foregoing considerations really apply as regards criminal jurisdiction or whether this jurisdiction is governed by a different principle; this might be the outcome of the close connection which for a long time existed between the conception of supreme criminal jurisdiction and that of a State, and also by the especial importance of criminal jurisdiction from the point of view of the individual.

Though it is true that in all systems of law the principle of the territorial character of criminal law is fundamental, it is equally true that all or nearly all these systems of law extend their action to offenses committed outside the territory of the State which adopts them, and they do so in ways which vary from State to State. The territoriality of criminal law, therefore, is not an absolute principle of international law and by no means coincides with territorial sovereignty. . . .

This situation may be considered from two different standpoints corresponding to the points of view respectively taken up by the Parties. According to one of these standpoints, the principle of freedom, in virtue of which each State may regulate its legislation at its discretion, provided that in so doing it does not come in conflict with a restriction imposed by international law, would also apply as regards law governing the scope of jurisdiction in criminal cases. According to the other standpoint, the exclusively territorial character of law relating to this domain constitutes a principle which, except as otherwise expressly provided, would, *ipso facto*, prevent States from extending the criminal jurisdiction of their courts beyond their frontiers; the exceptions in question, which include for instance extraterritorial jurisdiction over nationals and over crimes directed against public safety, would therefore rest on special permissive rules forming part of international law.

Adopting, for the purposes of the argument, the standpoint of the latter of these two systems, it must be recognized that, in the absence of a treaty provision, its correctness depends upon whether there is a custom having the force of law establishing it. The same is true as regards the applicability of this system – assuming it to have been recognized as sound – in the particular case.

It follows that, even from this point of view, before ascertaining whether there may be a rule of international law expressly allowing Turkey to prosecute a foreigner for an offense committed by him outside Turkey, it is necessary to begin by establishing both that the system is well-founded and that it is applicable in the particular case. Now, in order to establish the first of these points, one must, as has just been seen, prove the existence of a principle of international law restricting the discretion of States as regards criminal legislation.

Consequently, whichever of the two systems described above be adopted, the same result will be arrived at in this particular case; the necessity of ascertaining whether or not under international law there is a principle which would have prohibited Turkey, in the circumstances of the case before the Court, from prosecuting Lieutenant Demons. . . .

The Court therefore must, in any event, ascertain whether or not there exists a rule of international law limiting the freedom of States to extend the criminal jurisdiction of their courts to a situation uniting the circumstances of the present case. . . .

IV

. . . . The arguments advanced by the French Government, other than those considered above, are, in substance, the three following:

(1) International law does not allow a state to take proceedings with regard to offenses committed by foreigners abroad, simply by reason of the nationality of the victim; and such is the situation in the present case because the offense must be regarded as having been committed on board the French vessel.

(2) International law recognizes the exclusive jurisdiction of the State whose flag is flown as regards everything which occurs on board a ship on the high seas.

(3) Lastly, this principle is especially applicable in a collision case. . . .

As has already been observed, the characteristic features of the situation of fact are as follows: there has been a collision on the high seas between two vessels flying different flags, on one of which was one of the persons alleged to be guilty of the offense, whilst the victims were on board the other.

This being so, the Court does not think it is necessary to consider the contention that a State cannot punish offenses committed abroad by a foreigner simply by reason of the nationality of the victim. For this contention only relates to the case where nationality of the victim is the only criterion on which the criminal jurisdiction of the state is based. Even if that argument were correct generally speaking – and in regard to this the Court reserves its opinion – it could only be used in the present case if international law forbade Turkey to take into consideration the fact that the offense produced its effects on the

Turkish vessel and consequently in a place assimilated to Turkish territory in which the application of Turkish criminal law cannot be challenged, even in regard to offenses committed there by foreigners. But no such rule of international law exists. No argument has come to the knowledge of the Court from which it could be deduced that States recognize themselves to be under an obligation towards each other only to have regard to the place where the author of the offense happens to be at the time of the offense. On the contrary, it is certain that the courts of many countries, even of countries which have given their criminal legislation a strictly territorial character, interpret criminal law in the sense that offenses, the authors of which at the moment of commission are in the territory of another State, are nevertheless to be regarded as having been committed in the national territory, if one of the national territory, if one of the constituent elements of the offense, and more especially its effects, have taken place there. French courts have, in regard to a variety of situations, given decisions sanctioning this way of interpreting the territorial principle. Again, the Court does not know of any cases in which governments have protested against the fact that the criminal law of some country contained a rule to this effect or that the courts of a country construed their criminal law in this sense. Consequently, once it is admitted that the effects of the offense were produced on the Turkish vessel, it becomes impossible to hold that there is a rule of international law which prohibits Turkey from prosecuting Lieutenant Demons because of the fact that the author of the offense was on board the French ship. Since, as has already been observed, the special agreement does not deal with the provision of Turkish law under which the prosecution was instituted, but only with the question whether the prosecution should be regarded as contrary to the principles of international law, there is no reason preventing the Court from confining itself to observing that, in this case, a prosecution may also be justified from the point of view of the so-called territorial principle. . . .

The second argument put forward by the French Government is the principle that the State whose flag is flown has exclusive jurisdiction over everything which occurs on board a merchant ship on the high seas.

It is certainly true that – apart from special cases which are defined by international law – vessels on the high seas are subject to no authority except that of the State whose flag they fly. In virtue of the principle of the freedom of the seas, that is to say, the absence of any territorial sovereignty upon the high seas, no State may exercise any kind of jurisdiction over foreign vessels upon them. Thus, if a war vessel, happening to be at the spot where a collision occurs between a vessel flying its flag and a foreign vessel, were to send on board the latter an officer to make investigations or to take evidence, such an act would undoubtedly be contrary to international law.

But it by no means follows that a State can never in its own territory exercise jurisdiction over acts which have occurred on board a foreign ship on the high seas. A corollary of the principle of the freedom of the seas is that a ship on the high seas is assimilated to the territory of the State the flag of which it flies, for, just as in its own territory, that State exercises its authority upon it, and no other State may do so. All that can be said is that by virtue of the principle of the freedom of the seas, a ship is placed in the same position as national territory, but there is nothing to support the claim according to which the rights of the State under whose flag the vessel sails may go farther than the rights which it exercises within its territory properly so called. It follows that what occurs on board a vessel upon the high seas must be regarded as if it occurred on the territory of the State whose flag the ship flies. If, therefore, a guilty act committed on the high seas produces its effects on a vessel flying another flag or in foreign territory, the same principles must be applied as if the territories of two different States were concerned, and the conclusion must therefore be drawn that there is no rule of international law prohibiting the State to which the ship on which the effects of the offense have taken place belongs, from regarding the offense as having been committed in its territory and prosecuting, accordingly, the delinquent.

This conclusion could only be overcome if it were shown that there was a rule of customary international law which, going further than the principle stated above, established the exclusive jurisdiction of the State whose flag was flown. The French Government has endeavored to prove the existence of such a rule, having recourse for this purpose to the teachings of publicists, to decisions of municipal and international tribunals, and especially to conventions which, whilst creating exceptions to the principle of the freedom of the seas by permitting the war and police vessels of a State to exercise a more or less extensive control over the merchant vessels of another State, reserve jurisdiction to the courts of the country whose flag is flown by the vessel proceeded against.

In the Court's opinion the existence of such a rule has not been conclusively proved. . . . In the first place, as regards teachings of publicists, and apart from the question as to what their value may be from the point of view of establishing the existence of a rule of customary law, it is no doubt true that all or nearly all writers teach that ships on the high seas are subject exclusively to the jurisdiction of the State whose flag they fly. But the important point is the significance attached by them to this principle; now it does not appear that in general, writers bestow upon this principle a scope differing from or wider than that explained above and which is equivalent to saying that the jurisdiction of a State over vessels on the high seas is the same in extent as its jurisdiction in its own territory. On the other hand, there is no lack of writers who, upon a close study of the special question whether a State can prosecute for offenses committed on board a foreign ship on the high seas, definitely come to the conclusion that such offenses must be regarded as if they had been committed in the territory of the State whose flag the ship flies, and that consequently the general rules of each legal system in regard to offenses committed abroad are applicable.

In regard to precedents, it should first be observed that, leaving aside the collision cases which will be alluded to later, none of them relates to offenses affecting two ships flying the flags of different countries, and consequently they are not of much importance in the case before the Court. . . .

On the other hand, there is no lack of cases in which a State has claimed a right to prosecute for an offense, committed on board a foreign vessel, which it regarded as punishable under its legislation. . . .

The cases in which the exclusive jurisdiction of the State whose flag was flown has been recognized would seem rather to have been cases in which the foreign State was interested only by reason of the nationality of the victim, and in which, according to the legislation of that State itself or the practice of its courts, that ground was not regarded as sufficient to authorize prosecution for an offense committed abroad by a foreigner.

Finally, as regards conventions expressly reserving jurisdiction exclusively to the State whose flag is flown, it is not absolutely certain that this stipulation is to be regarded as expressing a general principle of law rather than as corresponding to the extraordinary jurisdiction which these conventions confer on the state-owned ships of a particular country in respect of ships of another country on the high seas. Apart from that, it should be observed that these conventions relate to matters of a particular kind, closely connected with the policing of the seas, such as the slave trade, damage to submarine cables, fisheries, etc., and not to common-law offenses. Above all it should be pointed out that the offenses contemplated by the conventions in question only concern a single ship; it is impossible therefore to make any deduction from them in regard to matters which concern two ships and consequently the jurisdiction of two different States. . . . The Court therefore has arrived at the conclusion that the second argument put forward by the French Government does not, any more than the first, establish the existence of a rule of international law prohibiting Turkey from prosecuting Lieutenant Demons.

It only remains to examine the third argument advanced by the French Government and to ascertain whether a rule specially applying to collision cases has grown up, according to which criminal proceedings regarding such cases come exclusively within the jurisdiction of the State whose flag is flown. . . . In this connection, the Agent of the French Government has drawn the Court's attention to the fact that questions of jurisdiction in collision cases, which frequently arise before civil courts, are but rarely encountered in the practice of criminal courts. He deduces from this that, in practice, prosecutions only occur before the courts of the State whose flag is flown and that that circumstance is proof of a tacit consent on the part of States and, consequently, shows positive international law in collision cases.

In the Court's opinion, this conclusion is not warranted. Even if the rarity of the judicial decisions to be found among the reported cases were sufficient to prove in point of fact the circumstance alleged by the Agent for the French Government, it would merely show that States had often, in practice, abstained from instituting criminal proceedings, and not that they recognized themselves as being obliged to do so; for only if such abstention were based on their being conscious of having a duty to abstain would it be possible to speak of an international custom. The alleged fact does not allow one to infer that States have been conscious of having such a duty. On the other hand, as will presently be seen, there are other circumstances calculated to show that the contrary is true.

So far as the Court is aware there are no decisions of international tribunals in this matter; but some decisions of municipal courts have been cited. Without pausing to consider the value to be attributed to the judgments of municipal courts in connection with the establishment of the existence of a rule of international law, it will suffice to observe that the decisions sometimes support one view and sometimes the other. . . . [A]s municipal jurisprudence is thus divided, it is hardly possible to see in it an indication of the existence of the restrictive rule of international law which alone could serve as a basis for the contention of the French Government.

On the other hand, the Court feels called upon to lay stress upon the fact that it does not appear that the States concerned have objected to criminal proceedings in respect of collision cases before the courts of a country other than that the flag of which was flown, or that they have made protests: their conduct does not appear to have differed appreciably from that observed by them in all cases of concurrent jurisdiction. This fact is directly opposed to the existence of a tacit consent on the part of States to the exclusive jurisdiction of the State whose flag is flown. . . .

The conclusion at which the Court has therefore arrived is that there is no rule of international law in regard to collision cases to the effect that criminal proceedings are exclusively within the jurisdiction of the State whose flag is flown. . . .

The offense for which Lieutenant Demons appears to have been prosecuted was an act – of negligence or imprudence – having its origin on board the *Lotus*, whilst its effects made themselves felt on board the *Boz-Kourt*. These two elements are, legally, entirely inseparable so much so that their separation renders the offense non-existent. Neither the exclusive jurisdiction of either State, nor the limitations of the jurisdiction of each to the occurrences which took place on the respective ships would appear calculated to satisfy the requirements of justice and effectively to protect the interests of the two States. It is only natural that each should be able to exercise jurisdiction and to do so in respect of the incident as a whole. It is therefore a case of concurrent jurisdiction. . . .

. . . . It must therefore be held that there is no principle of international law, within the meaning of Article 15 of the Convention of Lausanne of July 24th, 1923, which precludes the institution of the criminal proceedings under consideration. Consequently, Turkey, by instituting, in virtue of the discretion which international law leaves to every sovereign state, the criminal proceedings in question, has not, in the absence of such principles, acted in a manner contrary to the principles of international law within the meaning of the special agreement. . . .

V

Having thus answered the first question submitted by the special agreement in the negative, the Court need not consider the second question, regarding the pecuniary reparation which might have been due to Lieutenant Demons. . . .

————

NOTES AND QUESTIONS

(1) The report of the *Lotus* case says that the court was evenly divided, 6–6; it was the president's double vote in the case of a tie that resulted in judgment for Turkey. The judges who joined in the opinion of the court were the president, Max Huber (Switzerland), Bustamante (Cuba), Oda (Japan), Anzilotti (Italy), Pessôa (Brazil), and Feïzi-Daïm Bey, the Turkish national judge. Judges Loder (Netherlands), Lord Finlay (Great Britain), Weiss (France), Altamira (Spain), Nyholm (Denmark), and Moore (United States) all delivered separate dissenting opinions. Judge Moore's separate opinion stated, however, that his

> dissent was based solely on the connection of the pending case with Article 6 of the Turkish Penal Code. In the judgment of the Court that there is no rule of international law by virtue of which the penal cognizance of a collision at sea, resulting in the loss of life, belongs exclusively to the country of the ship by or by means of which the wrong was done, I concur, thus making for the judgment on that question, as submitted by the *compromis*, a definitely ascertained majority of seven to five.

(2) The *Lotus* case was decided by the Permanent Court of International Justice, which was created in 1921. It was the predecessor of the present International Court of Justice (ICJ), established in 1945 as "the principal judicial organ of the United Nations" (ICJ Statute, art. 1). Only states may be parties before this court. It has no jurisdiction over individuals and therefore no criminal jurisdiction. But, as in the *Lotus* case, disputes before the ICJ may raise questions of international criminal law involving the respective rights or obligations of the states which are parties to the dispute. In addition, the court can render advisory opinions at the request of the General Assembly, Security Council, and other authorized organs of the United Nations. These too may touch on questions of international criminal law. *See, e.g., Reservations to the Genocide Convention*, 1951 I.C.J. REP. 15.

(3) The judgment in the *Lotus* case is said to epitomize an "extreme positivism" in international law. "Positivism" has various meanings; in an international law context it usually refers to the proposition that international law depends on the consent of states and is to be determined by looking at what states have agreed to be the law. Is that an adequate and workable view of the nature of international law? What are the alternatives? What precisely is the

"source" of the principle enunciated in the *Lotus* opinion that "restrictions on the independence of states cannot be presumed"? How far was this principle really determinative of the result in the *Lotus* case?

(4) How far is the *Lotus* decision good law today? Its specific result has been "reversed" by several multilateral treaties. For instance, Article 11(1) of the Convention on the High Seas, Apr. 29, 1958, 13 U.S.T 2312, 450 U.N.T.S. 82, provides:

> In the event of collision or of any other incident of navigation concerning a ship on the high seas, involving the penal or disciplinary responsibility of the master or of any other person in the service of the ship, no penal or disciplinary proceedings may be instituted against such persons except before the judicial or administrative authorities either of the flag State or of the State of which such person is a national.

Identical language appears in Article 97 of the Law of the Sea Convention, Dec. 10, 1982, U.N. A/CONF. 62/122, *reprinted in* 21 I.L.M. 1261 (1982).

What about the "positivistic" premises of the judgment? How far do those have any residual validity today? We will return to this question in the next section.

§ 1.03 "New" Directions

FILARTIGA v. PENA-IRALA

United States Court of Appeals, Second Circuit
630 F.2d 876 (1980)

KAUFMAN, CIRCUIT JUDGE:

. . . . Implementing the constitutional mandate for national control over foreign relations, the First Congress established original district court jurisdiction over "all causes where an alien sues for a tort only [committed] in violation of the law of nations." Judiciary Act of 1789, ch. 20, § 9(b), 1 Stat. 73, 77 (1789), codified at 28 U.S.C. § 1350. Construing this rarely-invoked provision, we hold that deliberate torture perpetrated under color of official authority violates universally accepted norms of the international law of human rights, regardless of the nationality of the parties. Thus, whenever an alleged torturer is found and served with process by an alien within our borders, § 1350 provides federal jurisdiction. Accordingly, we reverse the judgment of the district court dismissing the complaint for want of federal jurisdiction.

I

The appellants, plaintiffs below, are citizens of the Republic of Paraguay. Dr. Joel Filartiga, a physician, describes himself as a longstanding opponent of the government of President Alfredo Stroessner, which has held power in Paraguay since 1954. His daughter, Dolly Filartiga, arrived in the United States in 1978 under a visitor's visa, and has since applied for permanent political asylum. The Filartigas brought this action in the Eastern District of New York against Americo Norberto Pena-Irala (Pena), also a citizen of Paraguay, for wrongfully causing the death of Dr. Filartiga's seventeen-year old son, Joelito. Because the district court dismissed the action for want of subject matter jurisdiction, we must accept as true the allegations contained in the Filartigas' complaint and affidavits for purposes of this appeal.

The appellants contend that on March 29, 1976, Joelito Filartiga was kidnapped and tortured to death by Pena, who was then Inspector General of Police in Asuncion, Paraguay. Later that day, the police brought Dolly Filartiga to Pena's home where she was confronted with the body of her brother, which evidenced marks of severe torture. As she fled, horrified, from the house, Pena followed after her shouting, "Here you have what you have been looking for for so long and what you deserve. Now shut up." The Filartigas claim that Joelito was tortured and killed in retaliation for his father's political activities and beliefs.

Shortly thereafter, Dr. Filartiga commenced a criminal action in the Paraguayan courts against Pena and the police for the murder of his son. As a result, Dr. Filartiga's attorney was arrested and brought to police headquarters where, shackled to a wall, Pena threatened him with death. This attorney, it is alleged, has since been disbarred without just cause.

During the course of the Paraguayan criminal proceeding, which is apparently still pending after four years, another man, Hugo Duarte, confessed to the murder. Duarte, who was a member of the Pena household, claimed that he had discovered his wife and Joelito in flagrante delicto, and that the crime was one of passion. The Filartigas have submitted a photograph of Joelito's corpse showing injuries they believe refute this claim. Dolly Filartiga, moreover, has stated that she will offer evidence of three independent autopsies demonstrating that her brother's death "was the result of professional methods of torture." Despite his confession, Duarte, we are told, has never been convicted or sentenced in connection with the crime.

In July of 1978, Pena sold his house in Paraguay and entered the United States under a visitor's visa. He was accompanied by Juana Bautista Fernandez Villalba, who had lived with him in Paraguay. The couple remained in the United States beyond the term of their visas, and were living in Brooklyn, New York, when Dolly Filartiga, who was then living in Washington, D. C., learned of their presence. Acting on information provided by Dolly the Immigration and Naturalization Service arrested Pena and his companion, both of whom were subsequently ordered deported on April 5, 1979 following a hearing. They had then resided in the United States for more than nine months.

Almost immediately, Dolly caused Pena to be served with a summons and civil complaint at the Brooklyn Navy Yard, where he was being held pending deportation. The complaint alleged that Pena had wrongfully caused Joelito's death by torture and sought compensatory and punitive damages of $ 10,000,000. . . .

II

Appellants rest their principal argument in support of federal jurisdiction upon the Alien Tort Statute, 28 U.S.C. § 1350, which provides: "The district courts shall have original jurisdiction of any civil action by an alien for a tort only, committed in violation of the law of nations or a treaty of the United States." Since appellants do not contend that their action arises directly under a treaty of the United States, a threshold question on the jurisdictional issue is whether the conduct alleged violates the law of nations. In light of the universal condemnation of torture in numerous international agreements, and the renunciation of torture as an instrument of official policy by virtually all of the nations of the world (in principle if not in practice), we find that an act of torture committed by a state official against one held in detention violates established norms of the international law of human rights, and hence the law of nations.

The Supreme Court has enumerated the appropriate sources of international law. The law of nations "may be ascertained by consulting the works of jurists, writing professedly on public law; or by the general usage and practice of nations; or by judicial decisions recognizing and enforcing that law." *United States v. Smith*, 18 U.S. (5 Wheat.) 153, 160-61(1820). . . . In *Smith*, a statute proscribing "the crime of piracy (on the high seas) as defined by the law of nations," was held sufficiently determinate in meaning to afford the basis for a death sentence. The *Smith* Court discovered among the works of Lord Bacon, Grotius, Bochard and other commentators a genuine consensus that rendered the crime "sufficiently and constitutionally defined."

The Paquete Habana, 175 U.S. 677(1900), reaffirmed that

> where there is no treaty, and no controlling executive or legislative act or judicial decision, resort must be had to the customs and usages of civilized nations; and, as evidence of these, to the works of jurists and commentators, who by years of labor, research and experience, have made themselves peculiarly well acquainted with the subjects of which they treat. Such works are resorted to by judicial tribunals, not for the speculations of their authors concerning what the law ought to be, but for trustworthy evidence of what the law really is.

Id. at 700. Modern international sources confirm the propriety of this approach.[8]

Habana is particularly instructive for present purposes, for it held that the traditional prohibition against seizure of an enemy's coastal fishing vessels during wartime, a standard that began as one of comity only, had ripened over the preceding century into "a settled rule of international law" by "the general assent of civilized nations." Thus it is clear that courts must interpret international law not as it was in 1789, but as it has evolved and exists among the nations of the world today. . . .

The requirement that a rule command the "general assent of civilized nations" to become binding upon them all is a stringent one. Were this not so, the courts of one nation might feel free to impose idiosyncratic legal rules upon others, in the name of applying international law. . . . [But] there are few, if any, issues in international law today on which opinion seems to be so united as the limitations on a state's power to torture persons held in its custody.

The United Nations Charter (a treaty of the United States, see 59 Stat. 1033 (1945)) makes it clear that in this modern age a state's treatment of its own citizens is a matter of international concern. It provides:

---

[8] The Statute of the International Court of Justice, Arts. 38 & 59, June 26, 1945, 59 Stat. 1055, 1060 (1945) provides:

Art. 38

1. The Court, whose function is to decide in accordance with international law such disputes as are submitted to it, shall apply:

(a) international conventions, whether general or particular, establishing rules expressly recognized by the contesting states;

(b) international custom, as evidence of a general practice accepted as law;

(c) the general principles of law recognized by civilized nations;

(d) subject to the provisions of Article 59, judicial decisions and the teachings of the most highly qualified publicists of the various nations, as subsidiary means for the determination of the rules of law.

2. This provision shall not prejudice the power of the Court to decide a case *ex aequo et bono*, if the parties agree thereto.

Art. 59.

The decision of the Court has no binding force except between the parties and in respect of that particular case.

> With a view to the creation of conditions of stability and well-being which are necessary for peaceful and friendly relations among nations . . . the United Nations shall promote . . . universal respect for, and observance of, human rights and fundamental freedoms for all without distinctions as to race, sex, language or religion.

Id. Art. 55. And further:

> All members pledge themselves to take joint and separate action in cooperation with the Organization for the achievement of the purposes set forth in Article 55.

Id. Art. 56.

While this broad mandate has been held not to be wholly self-executing, this observation alone does not end our inquiry. For although there is no universal agreement as to the precise extent of the "human rights and fundamental freedoms" guaranteed to all by the Charter, there is at present no dissent from the view that the guaranties include, at a bare minimum, the right to be free from torture. This prohibition has become part of customary international law, as evidenced and defined by the Universal Declaration of Human Rights, General Assembly Resolution 217 (III)(A) (Dec. 10, 1948) which states, in the plainest of terms, "no one shall be subjected to torture." The General Assembly has declared that the Charter precepts embodied in this Universal Declaration "constitute basic principles of international law."

Particularly relevant is the Declaration on the Protection of All Persons from Being Subjected to Torture, General Assembly Resolution 3452 (1975). The Declaration expressly prohibits any state from permitting the dastardly and totally inhuman act of torture. Torture, in turn, is defined as "any act by which severe pain and suffering, whether physical or mental, is intentionally inflicted by or at the instigation of a public official on a person for such purposes as . . . intimidating him or other persons." The Declaration goes on to provide that "[w]here it is proved that an act of torture or other cruel, inhuman or degrading treatment or punishment has been committed by or at the instigation of a public official, the victim shall be afforded redress and compensation, in accordance with national law." This Declaration, like the Declaration of Human Rights before it, was adopted without dissent by the General Assembly.

These U.N. declarations are significant because they specify with great precision the obligations of member nations under the Charter. Since their adoption, "[m]embers can no longer contend that they do not know what human rights they promised in the Charter to promote." Moreover, a U.N. Declaration is, according to one authoritative definition, "a formal and solemn instrument, suitable for rare occasions when principles of great and lasting importance are being enunciated." Accordingly, it has been observed that the Universal Declaration of Human Rights "no longer fits into the dichotomy of 'binding treaty' against 'non-binding pronouncement,' but is rather an authoritative statement of the international community." Thus, a Declaration creates an expectation of adherence, and "insofar as the expectation is gradually justified by State practice, a declaration may by custom become recognized as laying down rules binding upon the States." Indeed, several commentators have concluded that the Universal Declaration has become, in toto, a part of binding, customary international law.

Turning to the act of torture, we have little difficulty discerning its universal renunciation in the modern usage and practice of nations. The international consensus surrounding torture has found expression in numerous international treaties and accords. *E. g.*, American Convention on Human Rights, Art. 5 ("No one shall be subjected to torture or to cruel, inhuman or degrading punishment or treatment"); International Covenant on Civil and Political Rights (Dec. 16, 1966) (identical language); European Convention for the Protection of Human Rights and Fundamental Freedoms, Art. 3 (semble). The substance of these international agreements is reflected in modern municipal, *i.e.* national law as well. Although torture was once a routine concomitant of criminal interrogations in many nations, during the modern and hopefully more enlightened era it has been universally renounced. According to one survey, torture is prohibited, expressly or implicitly, by the constitutions of over fifty-five nations, including both the United States and Paraguay. Our State Department reports a general recognition of this principle:

> There now exists an international consensus that recognizes basic human rights and obligations owed by all governments to their citizens . . . . There is no doubt that these rights are often violated; but virtually all governments acknowledge their validity.

We have been directed to no assertion by any contemporary state of a right to torture its own or another nation's citizens. Indeed, United States diplomatic contacts confirm the universal abhorrence with which torture is viewed:

> In exchanges between United States embassies and all foreign states with which the United States maintains relations, it has been the Department of State's general experience that no government has asserted a right to torture its own nationals. Where reports of torture elicit some credence, a state usually responds by denial or, less frequently, by asserting that the conduct was unauthorized or constituted rough treatment short of torture.

Having examined the sources from which customary international law is derived the usage of nations, judicial opinions and the works of jurists, we conclude that official torture is now prohibited by the law of nations. The prohibition is clear and unambiguous, and admits of no distinction between treatment of aliens and citizens. . . . The treaties and accords cited above, as well as the express foreign policy of our own government, all make it clear that international law confers fundamental rights upon all people vis-a-vis their own governments. While the ultimate scope of those rights will be a subject for continuing refinement and elaboration, we hold that the right to be free from torture is now among them. . . .

III

Appellee submits that even if the tort alleged is a violation of modern international law, federal jurisdiction may not be exercised consistent with the dictates of Article III of the Constitution. The claim is without merit. Common law courts of general jurisdiction regularly adjudicate transitory tort claims between individuals over whom they exercise personal jurisdiction, wherever the tort occurred. Moreover, as part of an articulated scheme of federal control over external affairs, Congress provided, in the first Judiciary Act, § 9(b), 1 Stat. 73, 77 (1789), for federal jurisdiction over suits by aliens where principles of international law are in issue. The constitutional basis for the Alien Tort Statute is the law of nations, which has always been part of the federal common law.

. . . . A case properly "aris[es] under the . . . laws of the United States" for Article III purposes if grounded upon statutes enacted by Congress or upon the common law of the United States. . . . The law of nations forms an integral part of the common law, and a review of the history surrounding the adoption of the Constitution demonstrates that it became a part of the common law of the United States upon the adoption of the Constitution. Therefore, the enactment of the Alien Tort Statute was authorized by Article III.

During the eighteenth century, it was taken for granted on both sides of the Atlantic that the law of nations forms a part of the common law. 1 BLACKSTONE, COMMENTARIES 263-64 (1st ed. 1765-69); 4 *id.* at 67. Under the Articles of Confederation, the Pennsylvania Court of Oyer and Terminer at Philadelphia, per McKean, Chief Justice, applied the law of nations to the criminal prosecution of the Chevalier de Longchamps for his assault upon the person of the French Consul-General to the United States, noting that "[t]his law, in its full extent, is a part of the law of this state . . . ." *Respublica v. DeLongchamps,* 1 U.S. (1 Dall.) 113, 119 (1784). Thus, a leading commentator has written:

> It is an ancient and a salutary feature of the Anglo-American legal tradition that the Law of Nations is a part of the law of the land to be ascertained and administered, like any other, in the appropriate case. This doctrine was originally conceived and formulated in England in response to the demands of an expanding commerce and under the influence of theories widely accepted in the late sixteenth, the seventeenth and the eighteenth centuries. It was brought to America in the colonial years as part of the legal heritage from England. It was well understood by men of legal learning in America in the eighteenth century when the United Colonies broke away from England to unite effectively, a little later, in the United States of America.

Dickenson, *The Law of Nations as Part of the National Law of the United States,* 101 U. PA. L. REV. 26, 27 (1952).

Indeed, Dickenson goes on to demonstrate that one of the principal defects of the Confederation that our Constitution was intended to remedy was the central government's inability to "cause infractions of treaties or of the law of nations, to be punished." . . . .

As ratified, the judiciary article contained no express reference to cases arising under the law of nations. Indeed, the only express reference to that body of law is contained in Article I, sec. 8, cl. 10, which grants to the Congress the power to "define and punish . . . offenses against the law of nations." Appellees seize upon this circumstance and advance the proposition that the law of nations forms a part of the laws of the United States only to the extent that Congress has acted to define it. This extravagant claim is amply refuted by the numerous decisions applying rules of international law uncodified in any act of Congress. A similar argument was offered to and rejected by the Supreme Court in *United States v. Smith, supra,* and we reject it today. As John Jay wrote in The Federalist No. 3, "Under the national government, treaties and articles of treaties, as well as the laws of nations, will always be expounded in one sense and executed in the same manner, whereas adjudications on the same points and questions in the thirteen states will not always accord or be consistent." Federal jurisdiction over cases involving international law is clear.

Thus, it was hardly a radical initiative for Chief Justice Marshall to state in *The Nereide,* 13 U.S. (9 Cranch) 388 (1815), that in the absence of a congressional enactment, United States courts are "bound by the law of nations, which is a part of the law of the land." These words were echoed in *The Paquete Habana, supra*: "international law is part of our law, and must be ascertained and administered by the courts of justice of appropriate jurisdiction, as often as questions of right depending upon it are duly presented for their determination."

The Filartigas urge that 28 U.S.C. § 1350 be treated as an exercise of Congress's power to define offenses against the law of nations. While such a reading is possible, we believe it is sufficient here to construe the Alien Tort Statute, not as granting new rights to aliens, but simply as opening the federal courts for adjudication of the rights already recognized by international law. The statute nonetheless does inform our analysis of Article III, for we recognize that questions of jurisdiction "must be considered part of an organic growth part of an evolutionary process," and that the history of the judiciary article gives meaning to its pithy phrases. The Framers' overarching concern that control over international affairs be vested in the new national government to safeguard the standing of the United States among the nations of the world therefore reinforces the result we reach today. . . . .

IV

. . . . In the twentieth century the international community has come to recognize the common danger posed by the flagrant disregard of basic human rights and particularly the right to be free of torture. Spurred first by the Great War, and then the Second, civilized nations have banded together to prescribe acceptable norms of international behavior. From the ashes of the Second

World War arose the United Nations Organization, amid hopes that an era of peace and cooperation had at last begun. Though many of these aspirations have remained elusive goals, that circumstance cannot diminish the true progress that has been made. In the modern age, humanitarian and practical considerations have combined to lead the nations of the world to recognize that respect for fundamental human rights is in their individual and collective interest. Among the rights universally proclaimed by all nations, as we have noted, is the right to be free of physical torture. Indeed, for purposes of civil liability, the torturer has become like the pirate and slave trader before him *hostis humani generis*, an enemy of all mankind. Our holding today, giving effect to a jurisdictional provision enacted by our First Congress, is a small but important step in the fulfillment of the ageless dream to free all people from brutal violence.

NOTES AND QUESTIONS

(1) Compare the decision in *Filartiga* with that in the *Lotus* case. To what extent do the two decisions rest on different understandings of the nature of customary international law? Consider the following statement:

> Every two hundred years, it seems, the jurisprudence of customary international law ("CIL") changes. Beginning in the seventeenth century, natural law was said to be the source of CIL. Beginning in the early nineteenth century, positivism was in the ascendency. The positivist view, according to which CIL results from the practice of nations acting out of a sense of legal obligation, was later endorsed by the United States Supreme Court in *The Paquete Habana*. Approximately two centuries after the rise of the positivist view, a new theory is beginning to take hold in some quarters. This theory derives norms of CIL in a loose way from treaties (ratified or not), U.N. General Assembly resolutions, international commissions, and academic commentary – but all colored by a moralism reminiscent of the natural law view. The Second Circuit's decision in *Filartiga v. Pena-Irala* is the most famous United States case to embrace this new understanding of CIL.

Jack L. Goldsmith & Eric A. Posner, *Understanding the Resemblance Between Modern and Traditional Customary International Law*, 40 VA. J. INT'L L. 639 (2000).

(2) What are the implications of the *Filartiga* decision, which was not a criminal case, for federal criminal law? Does it follow from Judge Kaufman's opinion that the federal courts could entertain *criminal* prosecutions for torture in violation of international law, relying for jurisdiction on 18 U.S.C. § 3231,

which provides: "The district courts of the United States shall have original jurisdiction, exclusive of the courts of the States, of all offenses against the laws of the United States"? Like the Alien Tort Statute (also known as the Alien Tort Claims Act), 18 U.S.C. § 3231 derives from Section 9 of the Judiciary Act of 1789. If international law is part of the law of the United States, and if torture is prohibited by international law, why should torture not be considered a federal offense? In this connection, consider the relevance of the holding in *United States v. Hudson & Goodwin*, 11 U.S. (7 Cranch) 32 (1812), that federal jurisdiction does not extend to common law crimes.

Does it follow from *Filartiga* that it would be "sufficient and constitutional" for Congress to give the federal courts blanket jurisdiction over any prosecution for "a crime committed in violation of the law of nations"? What about a statute giving the district courts jurisdiction over "the crime of torture committed in violation of international law"? How would such a statute differ from the piracy statute (codified at 18 U.S.C. § 1651) which, as *Filartiga* observes, was upheld in 1820 in *United States v. Smith*? In its entirety that statute now reads: "Whoever, on the high seas, commits the crime of piracy as defined by the law of nations, and is afterwards brought into or found in the United States, shall be imprisoned for life." Is the piracy statute significantly different because it specifies a particular penalty for the crime? Suppose Congress were to enact that "Whoever commits the crime of torture as defined by international law, and is afterwards found in the United States, shall be imprisoned not more than 20 years"? Would this be "sufficient and constitutional"?

(3) *Filartiga* was decided in 1980, four years before the U.N. General Assembly adopted the 1984 Convention Against Torture and Other Cruel, Inhuman or Degrading Treatment or Punishment [*see* chap. 9]. The Convention entered into force in 1987 and was ratified by the United States in 1994. In 1994, Congress did make torture committed in other countries a federal offense, defining the crime in terms taken more or less from the Torture Convention. *See* 18 U.S.C. §§ 2340–2340B. Earlier, in 1992, Congress enacted the Torture Victim Protection Act (codified at 28 U.S.C. § 1350 note), which placed on a statutory basis the civil cause of action for torture (and for extrajudicial killing) perpetrated "under actual or apparent authority, or color of law, of any foreign nation," and extended it to plaintiffs who are U.S. citizens. We will come back to these statutes in chapter 9. As we will see, cases in which victims seek civil redress under the Alien Tort Claims Act or the Torture Victim Protection Act may serve as a proxy for criminal prosecution and, insofar as they involve determining what international law prohibits, also have an influence on the development of international criminal law. A notable example is *Kadic v. Karadzic*, 70 F.3d 232 (2d Cir. 1995), *cert. denied*, 518 U.S. 1005 (1996), a civil suit alleging "various atrocities, including brutal acts of rape, forced prostitution, forced impregnation, torture, and summary execution, carried out by Bosnian-Serb military forces as part of a genocidal campaign conducted in the course of the Bosnian civil war" (70 F.3d at 236-37); Judge Newman's opinion in the case opens with the words: "Many Americans would probably be surprised to learn that victims of atrocities committed in Bosnia are suing the leader of the insurgent Bosnian-Serb forces in a United States District Court in

Manhattan."

(4) As suggested in note 1, *supra*, the *Filartiga* case also epitomizes a "new" approach that appears to have had a significant effect on the way in which rules of international law, including international criminal law, are established. This approach tends to downplay the importance of actual state practice. It focuses instead on normative utterances, on so-called "soft law." Or rather state practice is taken to include what states sometimes say as well as what they sometimes do. One manifestation of this development is the ascription of quasi-legislative effect to resolutions of the U.N. General Assembly. Another is a readiness to find that the provisions of multilateral conventions have become customary international law and thus bind states which have not become parties to those conventions. Especially in connection with humanitarian and human rights norms, expressions of principles deemed deserving of recognition as the positive law of the "international community" are assumed to have become the law, even in the face of inconclusive or contrary practice. This is a realm of acute controversy. Some commentators are skeptical about this "new" approach. *See, e.g.,* G. M. DANILENKO, LAW-MAKING IN THE INTERNATIONAL COMMUNITY (1993); J. SHAND WATSON, THEORY AND REALITY IN THE INTERNATIONAL PROTECTION OF HUMAN RIGHTS (1999). But it has been quite influential, particularly in the development of human rights and international criminal law.

Chapter 2
GENERAL PRINCIPLES OF JURISDICTION

§ 2.01 Extraterritorial Application of United States Statutes

When does the United States have jurisdiction to prosecute criminal conduct that occurs outside its borders? The answer to this question depends on examination of two further questions: (1) whether a statute should be read as having extraterritorial effect, and (2) whether international law permits the United States to apply its law to particular conduct?

In some instances explicit Congressional language allows for an easy resolution in favor of extraterritorial application. For example, the Foreign Corrupt Practices Act focuses on bribery occurring outside the United States. [see chap. 3]. The Act's focus on international bribery offers a clear basis for finding jurisdiction to prosecute the illegal activity in the United States despite the fact that the actual bribery may have occurred outside the borders of the United States. Statutes also can have extraterritoriality provisions that explicitly allow for the prosecution of certain activities occurring outside the United States. For example, a key perjury statute provides that "[t]his section is applicable whether the statement or subscription is made within or without the United States." 18 U.S.C. § 1621.

In many instances, however, courts are left to interpret whether the statute and conduct warrant extraterritorial application. Legislative intent may be difficult to discern in these instances. *See* Ellen S. Podgor, Essay, *Globalization and the Federal Prosecution of White Collar Crime*, 34 AM. CRIM. L. REV. 325 (1997).

It is also necessary to resolve whether international law permits the application of U.S. law abroad. International law recognizes certain theories or bases of jurisdiction that have been used to resolve questions concerning the extraterritorial application of criminal law [see § 2.03]. Contemporary treaties sometimes provide an additional basis for extraterritorial jurisdiction.

UNITED STATES v. BOWMAN

Supreme Court of the United States
260 U.S. 94, 43 S. Ct. 39, 67 L. Ed. 149 (1922)

MR. CHIEF JUSTICE TAFT delivered the opinion of the Court:

This is a writ of error under the Criminal Appeals Act . . . . to review the ruling of the District Court sustaining a demurrer of one of the defendants to an indictment for a conspiracy to defraud a corporation in which the United States was and is a stockholder, ...

During the period covered by the indictment, i.e., between October, 1919, and January, 1920, the steamship Dio belonged to the United States. The United States owned all the stock in the United States Shipping Board Emergency Fleet Corporation. The National Shipping Corporation agreed to operate and manage the Dio for the Fleet Corporation, which under the contract was to pay for fuel, oil, labor and material used in the operation. The Dio was on a voyage to Rio de Janeiro under this management. Wry was her master, Bowman was her engineer, Hawkinson was the agent of the Standard Oil Company at Rio de Janeiro, and Millar was a merchant and ship repairer and engineer in Rio. Of these four, who were the defendants in the indictment, the first three were American citizens, and Millar was a British subject. Johnston & Company were the agents of the National Shipping Corporation at Rio. The indictment charged that the plot was hatched by Wry and Bowman on board the Dio before she reached Rio. Their plan was to order, through Johnston & Company, and receipt for, 1000 tons of fuel oil from the Standard Oil Company, but to take only 600 tons aboard, and to collect cash for a delivery of 1000 tons through Johnston & Company, from the Fleet Corporation, and then divide the money paid for the undelivered 400 tons among the four defendants. This plan was to be, and was, made possible through the guilty connivance of the Standard Oil agent Hawkinson and Millar the Rio merchant who was to, and did collect the money. Overt acts charged included a wireless telegram to the agents, Johnston & Company, from the Dio while on the high seas ordering the 1000 tons of oil. The Southern District of New York was the district into which the American defendants were first brought and were found, but Millar, the British defendant, has not been found.

The first count charged a conspiracy by the defendants to defraud the Fleet Corporation in which the United States was a stockholder, by obtaining and aiding to obtain the payment and allowance of a false and fraudulent claim against the Fleet Corporation. It laid the offense on the high seas, out of the jurisdiction of any particular State and out of the jurisdiction of any district of the United States, but within the admiralty and maritime jurisdiction of the United States. The second count laid the conspiracy on the Dio on the high seas and at the port of Rio de Janeiro as well as in the city. The third count laid it in the city of Rio de Janeiro. The fourth count was for making and causing to be made in the name of the Standard Oil Company, for payment and approval, a false and fraudulent claim against the Fleet Corporation in the form of an invoice for 1000 tons of fuel oil, of which 400 tons were not delivered. This count laid the same crime on board the Dio in the harbor of Rio de Janeiro. The fifth count laid it in the city and the sixth at the port and in the city.

No objection was made to the indictment or any count of it for lack of precision or fullness in describing all the elements of the crimes denounced in § 35 of the Criminal Code as amended. The sole objection was that the crime was committed without the jurisdiction of the United States or of any State thereof and on the high seas or within the jurisdiction of Brazil. The District Court considered only the first count, which charged the conspiracy to have been committed on the Dio on the high seas, and having held that bad for lack of jurisdiction, a fortiori it sustained the demurrer as to the others.

The court in its opinion conceded that under many authorities the United States as a sovereign may regulate the ships under its flag and the conduct of its citizens while on those ships, ... The court said, however, that while private and public ships of the United States on the high seas were constructively a part of the territory of the United States, indeed peculiarly so as distinguished from that of the States, Congress had always expressly indicated it when it intended that its laws should be operative on the high seas. The court concluded that because jurisdiction of criminal offenses must be conferred upon United States courts and could not be inferred, and because § 35, like all the other sections of c. 4, contains no reference to the high seas as a part of the locus of the offenses defined by it, as the sections in cc. 11 and 12 of the Criminal Code do, § 35 must be construed not to extend to acts committed on the high seas. It confirmed its conclusion by the statement that § 35 had never been invoked to punish offenses denounced if committed on the high seas or in a foreign country.

We have in this case a question of statutory construction. The necessary locus, when not specially defined, depends upon the purpose of Congress as evidenced by the description and nature of the crime and upon the territorial limitations upon the power and jurisdiction of a government to punish crime under the law of nations. Crimes against private individuals or their property, like assaults, murder, burglary, larceny, robbery, arson, embezzlement and fraud of all kinds, which affect the peace and good order of the community, must of course be committed within the territorial jurisdiction of the government where it may properly exercise it. If punishment of them is to be extended to include those committed outside of the strict territorial jurisdiction, it is natural for Congress to say so in the statute, and failure to do so will negative the purpose of Congress in this regard. We have an example of this in the attempted application of the prohibitions of the Anti-Trust Law to acts done by citizens of the United States against other such citizens in a foreign country. *American Banana Co. v. United Fruit Co.*, 213 U.S. 347. That was a civil case, but as the statute is criminal as well as civil, it presents an analogy.

But the same rule of interpretation should not be applied to criminal statutes which are, as a class, not logically dependent on their locality for the Government's jurisdiction, but are enacted because of the right of the Government to defend itself against obstruction, or fraud wherever perpetrated, especially if committed by its own citizens, officers or agents. Some such offenses can only be committed within the territorial jurisdiction of the Government because of the local acts required to constitute them. Others are such that to limit their locus to the strictly territorial jurisdiction would be greatly to curtail the scope and usefulness of the statute and leave open a large immunity for frauds as easily committed by citizens on the high seas and in foreign countries as at home. In such cases, Congress has not thought it necessary to make specific provision in the law that the locus shall include the high seas and foreign countries, but allows it to be inferred from the nature of the offense. Many of these occur in c. 4, which bears the title "Offenses against the operations of the Government." Section 70 of that chapter punishes whoever as consul knowingly certifies a false invoice. Clearly the locus of this crime as intended by Congress is in a foreign country and certainly the foreign country in which he discharges his official duty could not object to the trial in a United States court of a United States consul for crime of this sort committed within its borders. Forging or altering ship's papers is made a crime by § 72 of c. 4. It would be going too far to say that because Congress does not fix any locus it intended to exclude the high seas in respect of this crime. The natural inference from the character of the offense is that the sea would be a probable place for its commission. Section 42 of c. 4 punishes enticing desertions from the naval service. Is it possible that Congress did not intend by this to include such enticing done aboard ship on the high seas or in a foreign port, where it would be most likely to be done? Section 39 punishes bribing a United States officer of the civil, military or naval service to violate his duty or to aid in committing a fraud on the United States. It is hardly reasonable to construe this not to include such offenses when the bribe is offered to a consul, ambassador, an army or a naval officer in a foreign country or on the high seas, whose duties are being performed there and when his connivance at such fraud must occur there. So, too, § 38 of c. 4 punishes the wilfully doing or aiding to do any act relating to the bringing in, custody, sale or other disposition of property captured as prize, with intent to defraud, delay or injure the United States or any captor or claimant of such property. This would naturally often occur at sea, and Congress could not have meant to confine it to the land of the United States. Again, in § 36 of c. 4, it is made a crime to steal, embezzle, or knowingly apply to his own use ordinance, arms, ammunition, clothing, subsistence, stores, money or other property of the United States furnished or to be used for military or naval service. It would hardly be reasonable to hold that if any one, certainly if a citizen of the United States, were to steal or embezzle such property which may properly and lawfully be in the custody of army or naval officers either in foreign countries, in foreign ports or on the high seas, it would not be in such places an offense which Congress intended to punish by this section.

What is true of these sections in this regard is true of § 35, under which this indictment was drawn. . . . It is directed generally against whoever presents a false claim against the United States, knowing it to be such, to any officer of the civil, military or naval service or to any department thereof, or any corporation in which the United States is a stockholder, or whoever connives at the same by the use of any cheating device, or whoever enters a conspiracy to do these things. The section was amended in 1918 to include a corporation in which the United States owns stock. This was evidently intended to protect the Emergency Fleet Corporation in which the United States was the sole stockholder, from fraud of this character. That Corporation was expected to engage in, and did engage in, a most extensive ocean transportation business and its ships were seen in every great port of the world open during the war.

The same section of the statute protects the arms, ammunition, stores and property of the army and navy from fraudulent devices of a similar character. We can not suppose that when Congress enacted the statute or amended it, it did not have in mind that a wide field for such frauds upon the Government was in private and public vessels of the United States on the high seas and in foreign ports and beyond the land jurisdiction of the United States, and therefore intend to include them in the section.

Nor can the much quoted rule that criminal statutes are to be strictly construed avail. As said in *United States v. Lacher*, 134 U.S. 624, 629, quoting with approval from SEDGWICK, STATUTORY AND CONSTITUTIONAL LAW, 2d ed., 282: "penal provisions, like all others, are to be fairly construed according to the legislative intent as expressed in the enactment." They are not to be strained either way. It needs no forced construction to interpret § 35 as we have done.

Section 41 of the Judicial Code provides that "the trial of all offenses committed upon the high seas, or elsewhere out of the jurisdiction of any particular State or district, shall be in the district where the offender is found, or into which he is first brought." The three defendants who were found in New York were citizens of the United States and were certainly subject to such laws as it might pass to protect itself and its property. Clearly it is no offense to the dignity or right of sovereignty of Brazil to hold them for this crime against the government to which they owe allegiance. The other defendant is a subject of Great Britain. He has never been apprehended, and it will be time enough to consider what, if any, jurisdiction the District Court below has to punish him when he is brought to trial.

The judgment of the District Court is reversed, with directions to overrule the demurrer and for further proceedings. . . .

NOTES AND QUESTIONS

(1) Can the United States prosecute for theft of government property when the alleged criminal acts occur outside the United States? In *United States v. Cotton*, 471 F.2d 744, 749-50 (9th Cir. 1973), the court stated that "[t]his nation has a paramount interest in protecting its property, wherever located, by assertion of its penal laws." Applying *Bowman*, the court noted that "[i]t is inconceivable that Congress, in enacting Section 641, would proscribe only the theft of government property located within the territorial boundaries of the nation."

(2) How should *Bowman* be applied when the alleged criminal acts are not committed by United States citizens? In *United States v. Pizzarusso*, 388 F.2d 8 (2d Cir. 1968), Judge Medina stated:

> This case is of interest because it brings before this Court for the first time the question of the jurisdiction of the District Court to indict and convict a foreign citizen of the crime of knowingly making a false statement under oath in a visa application to an American consular official located in a foreign country, in violation of 18 U.S.C. Section 1546. . . . The indictment charges that on March 4, 1965 Jean Philomena Pizzarusso wilfully made under oath a number of false statements in her "Application for Immigrant Visa And Alien Registration" at the American Consulate, Montreal, Canada. Each of these false statements was patently material to the matter in hand. For example: she falsely swore that since her sixteenth birthday her only places of residence for six months or more had been London, England and Montreal, Canada; she falsely swore that she had been in the United States only for short visits for pleasure; she falsely swore that she had never been arrested, and so on. Although at all times pertinent to this case she was a citizen of Canada, she was taken into custody in the Southern District of New York on April 18, 1966. . . .

> 18 U.S.C. Section 1546 is a significant and integral part of the pattern of immigration laws, including those affecting passports and visas. We think the Congress by the enactment of this law contemplated that it would be applied extraterritorially. Visas are documents issued to aliens permitting them to enter the country. In the ordinary course of events we would naturally expect false statements in visa applications to be made outside the territorial limits of the United States. This would seem to overcome the strong presumption that the Congress did not intend the statute to apply extraterritorially. . . . The utterance by an alien of a "false statement with respect to a material fact" in a visa application constitutes an affront to the very sovereignty of the United States. These false statements must be said to have a deleterious influence on valid governmental interests. Therefore, 18 U.S.C. Section 1546, as applied to an alien's perjurious statements before a United States consular officer in a foreign country, represents a law which is "necessary and proper for carrying into Execution," U.S.Const. Art. I, Section 8, the Congressional power over the conduct of foreign relations.

> . . . . Statutes imposing criminal liability on aliens for committing perjury in United States Consulates in foreign countries have been in existence for over one hundred years, *see, e.g.*, 22 U.S.C. Section 1203, which was derived from an act of 1856, and oftentimes courts have routinely sustained convictions without even considering the jurisdictional question. . . . Only one court has ever held that the United States did not have jurisdiction to proceed against an alien under the legislation governing this case. *United States v. Baker*, 136 F. Supp. 546 (S.D.N.Y.1955). In *Baker* it was conceded that there was

authority for deporting an alien for making perjurious statements to a United States Consul, *United States ex rel. Majka v. Palmer*, 67 F.2d 146 (7th Cir. 1933), but the court thought the imposition of criminal sanctions was "far different" from deportation and dismissed the indictment. We would have sustained jurisdiction in *Baker* had the case been before us, and in this view we are apparently joined by the judge who decided *Baker*, since he presided over the instant case in the court below. . . .

(3) In *Bowman*, the Court distinguishes between crimes against private individuals and property, and crimes that are "not logically dependent on their locality for the government's jurisdiction." Is this distinction valid in light of globalization? *See* Gary B. Born, *A Reappraisal of the Extraterritorial Reach of U.S. Law*, 24 LAW & POL'Y INT'L BUS. 1 (1992) ("the rationale for the territoriality presumption has become obsolete"). Is the United States increasing prosecution of acts occurring outside its borders? Is this indicated by an increase in the number of statutes in the United States calling for extraterritorial prosecution, or by an increase in existing statutes being interpreted to include extraterritoriality? *See, e.g., Stegeman v. United States*, 425 F.2d 984 (9th Cir. 1970) (interpreting 18 U.S.C. § 152, a criminal bankruptcy statute, to have extraterritorial application); Michael J. Calhoun, Comment, *Tension on the High Seas of Transnational Securities Fraud: Broadening the Scope of United States Jurisdiction*, 30 LOY. U. CHI.L.J. 679 (1999). Are there other ways to assess an increase in extraterritorial application, such as in the deployment of agents overseas? *See* David Johnston, *Strength Is Seen In a U.S. Export: Law Enforcement*, N.Y.TIMES, Apr. 17, 1995, at A1, A8 ("American law enforcement agencies are rapidly expanding oversees, deploying agents to dozens of countries in scores of joint investigations."); R. Jeffrey Smith & Thomas W. Lippman, *FBI Plans to Double Overseas Offices*, ATL. J. CONST., Aug. 20, 1996, A1 ("The Federal Bureau of Investigation is planning to nearly double its presence overseas during the next four years, opening offices in 23 cities to cope with what officials say is a dramatic expansion of international terrorism, organized crime and narcotics trafficking affecting U.S. citizens.").

(4) Questions can also arise as to whether specific provisions within a statute can be applied extraterritorially. For example, in *United States v. Parness*, 503 F.2d 430 (2d Cir. 1974), the court examined the question of whether the "enterprise" element of the Racketeer Influenced and Corrupt Organization Act (RICO) included enterprises outside the United States. The court stated:

> Parness claims that, in enacting Title IX of the Organized Crime Control Act of 1970, 18 U.S.C. § 1961 et seq. (1970), of which § 1962(b) is a part, Congress did not intend to proscribe the acquisition of foreign businesses by means of criminal conduct committed in the United States despite the impact on domestic commerce. Specifically, he argues that his take-over of Hotel Corp., an Antillean corporation, cannot be said to constitute an offense under § 1962(b) because Hotel Corp. is not an "enterprise" within the meaning of the Act. This argument is predicated

upon an unreasonably narrow interpretation of the statute and is refuted by the language and legislative history of § 1962(b).

Section 1962(b) proscribes the acquisition of "any interest in or control of any enterprise which is engaged in, or the activities of which affect, interstate or foreign commerce." "Enterprise" is defined in § 1961(4) to include "any . . . corporation". On its face the proscription is all inclusive. It permits no inference that the Act was intended to have a parochial application. The legislative history, moreover, strongly indicates the intent of Congress that this provision be broadly construed.

. . . . We find Parness' claim unpersuasive for yet another reason. It presupposes that in enacting § 1962(b) Congress intended to focus exclusively upon the enterprise acquired and sought to protect only American institutions. There is no indication that the statute was meant to have such a limited remedial scope. On the contrary, its legislative history leaves no room for doubt that Congress intended to deal generally with the influences of organized crime on the American economy and not merely with its infiltration into domestic enterprises.

In its Statement of Findings and Purpose, by way of preface to Title IX, Congress made clear its concern for American investors and businessmen, as well as American institutions . . . . Moreover, the provisions of §§ 1963 and 1964 for broad civil remedies to victims of such infiltration further indicate the intent of Congress to protect the individual, as well as the "enterprise".

In short, we find no indication that Congress intended to limit Title IX to infiltration of domestic enterprises. On the contrary, the salutary purposes of the Act would be frustrated by such construction. It would permit those whose actions ravage the American economy to escape prosecution simply by investing the proceeds of their ill-gotten gains in a foreign enterprise. We reject any such construction. . . .

But see Jose v. M/V Fir Grove, 801 F. Supp. 349 (D. Oregon 1991) (RICO found not to have extraterritorial application).

(5) What concerns do courts have in considering whether a statute should have an extraterritorial *application*? Consider this question as raised in the case of *United States v. Boots*, 80 F.3d 580 (1st Cir. 1996):

. . . . [T]he object of the scheme here was exclusively to defraud a foreign government, rather than our own, of customs and tax revenues imposed under foreign law. We believe this added factor pushes defendants' scheme beyond the parameters of the frauds cognizable under section 1343 [wire fraud statute].

The prosecution, relying on cases upholding wire and mail fraud convictions for schemes to evade domestic taxes, argues that customs and tax revenues, even though owed solely to a foreign governmental body under laws of the latter's making, constitute money and property for purposes of the wire and mail fraud statutes. . . .

But none of the prosecution's cited wire fraud cases have involved a scheme to deprive a foreign government of its own taxes and similar exactions. The prosecution urges that section 1343 should apply, because it does not describe any particular type of victim of a scheme to defraud. It punishes use of the wires in interstate or foreign commerce in furtherance of "any scheme or artifice to defraud." If domestic tax fraud falls under section 1343, why not foreign revenue frauds as well, it is contended. Federal wire prosecutions have been based on frauds against private foreign businesses and individuals. . . .

However, schemes aimed at depriving a foreign government of duties and taxes are not the same as domestic tax frauds, nor are they even the same as private commercial frauds aimed at foreign business entities or individuals. At issue is not only whether "money or property," as such, is being targeted, but more importantly here, the extent to which constitutional and prudential considerations factor into our analysis. Foreign customs and tax frauds are intertwined with enforcement of a foreign sovereign's own laws and policies to raise and collect such revenues – laws with which this country may or may not be in sympathy and over which, in any event, we have no authority. In recognition of this, our courts have traditionally been reluctant to enforce foreign revenue laws. The "revenue rule"– a firmly embedded principle of common law, traced to an opinion by Lord Mansfield, *Holman v. Johnson*, 98 Eng. Rep. 1120 (K.B. 1775) – holds that courts generally will not enforce foreign tax judgments, just as they will not enforce foreign criminal judgments, although they will enforce foreign non-tax civil judgments unless due process, jurisdictional, or fundamental public policy considerations interfere. . . . The rationale of the revenue rule has been said to be that revenue laws are positive rather than moral law; they directly affect the public order of another country and hence should not be subject to judicial scrutiny by American courts; and for our courts effectively to pass on such laws raises issues of foreign relations which are assigned to and better handled by the legislative and executive branches of government.

Although this case does not require us to enforce a foreign tax judgment as such, upholding defendants' section 1343 conviction would amount functionally to penal enforcement of Canadian customs and tax laws. The scheme to defraud at issue – proof of which is essential to conviction – had as its sole object the violation of Canadian revenue laws. To convict, therefore, the district court and this court must determine whether a violation of Canadian tax laws was intended and, to the extent implemented, occurred. In so ruling, our courts would have to pass on defendants' challenges to such laws and any claims not to have violated or intended to violate them. Where a domestic court is effectively passing on the validity and operation of the revenue laws of a foreign country, the important concerns underlying the revenue rule are implicated. Of particular concern is the principle of noninterference by the federal courts in the legislative and executive branches' exercise of their foreign policymaking powers. National policy judgments made pursuant to that authority could be undermined if federal courts were to give general effect to wire fraud prosecutions for schemes of this type aimed at violating the revenue laws of any country. It is noteworthy that the federal statute criminalizing the smuggling of goods into foreign countries punishes such activities only if the foreign government has a reciprocal law. *See* 18 U.S.C. § 546. A decision to uphold the present convictions would have the effect of licensing prosecutions against persons who use the wires to engage in smuggling schemes against foreign governments irrespective of whether a particular government had the reciprocal arrangement called for in section 546.

In the case of Canada, to be sure, we cannot say that this specific legislative judgment would be undermined by affirming the instant wire fraud conviction. We do not condone defendants' smuggling activities, nor do we question Canada's revenue laws or the desirability of cooperation in respect to our mutual border. But application of the wire fraud statute to a scheme of this type does not, and cannot, turn upon our attitude towards Canada alone. The revenue rule has not risen or fallen over the centuries based on country-by-country judicial assessments of the potential for a foreign relations conflict. Courts are neither equipped nor constitutionally empowered to make such assessments. Prosecutors, who operate within the executive branch, might of course be expected not to pursue wire fraud prosecutions based on smuggling schemes aimed at blatantly hostile countries, but whether conduct is criminal cannot be a determination left solely to prosecutorial discretion. Rather, the longstanding rule instructs the courts to leave this area alone, so that the legislative and executive branches may exercise their authority and bargaining power to deal with such issues, and also so that a foreign government's revenue laws are not subjected to intrusive scrutiny by the courts of this country. . .

But see United States v. Trapilo, 130 F.3d 547 (2d Cir. 1997) (permitted prosecution under wire fraud of a scheme to defraud a foreign government of tax revenue).

(6) Congress also uses the term "foreign commerce" in criminal statutes. In *United States v. Braverman,* 376 F.2d 249, 251 (2d Cir. 1967), the court stated, "There would seem to be no logical reason for holding that Congress intended to punish those who cause the violation of a law regulating and protecting foreign commerce only when they act within the borders of the United States or that Congress is powerless to protect foreign commerce and those who engage in foreign commerce from intentionally injurious acts, simply because those acts occur outside our borders." *See also United States v. Kaplan,* 171 F.3d 1351 (11th Cir. 1999) (transfer of funds from Panama to the United States for

extortion found to be sufficient evidence of effecting commerce for the Hobbs Act).

(7) The constitutional basis upon which the federal statute is premised may influence a court's determination of whether there is a basis for federal criminal prosecution within the United States. In *United States v. Lewis*, 67 F.3d 225 (9th Cir. 1995), the Ninth Circuit reversed bank fraud convictions finding that, "[U]nlike §§ 1341 and 1343, federal jurisdiction is predicated not upon the use of the mails or wire communications in interstate commerce without regard to the victim bank's status, but upon the 'strong Federal interest' in the financial integrity of a 'federally controlled or insured institution,' defined as a 'federally chartered or insured financial institution,' which is in turn defined as a bank 'operating under the laws of the United States.'. Although the legislative history does not answer the ultimate question whether a non-federally insured, state chartered branch of a foreign bank is 'federally controlled' for purposes of the bank fraud statute, the jurisdictional distinction between the mail and wire fraud statutes on the one hand and § 1344 on the other suggests that the latter's reach is more limited than that of its sister statutes."

(8) Would a general statute authorizing extraterritoriality assist in prosecuting crimes occurring outside the United States? Consider § 208 of the FINAL REPORT OF THE NATIONAL COMMISSION ON REFORM OF THE FEDERAL CRIMINAL LAWS:

> Except as otherwise expressly provided by statute or treaty, extraterritorial jurisdiction over an offense exists when:
>
> (a) one of the following is a victim or intended victim of a crime or violence: the President of the United States, the president-elect, the Vice-President, or, if there is no Vice-President, the officer next in the order of succession to the office of President of the United States, the Vice-President-elect, or any individual who is acting as President under the Constitution and laws of the United States, a candidate for President or Vice-President or any member or member designate of the President's cabinet, or a member of Congress, or a federal judge;
>
> (b) the offense is treason, or is espionage or sabotage by a national of the United States;
>
> (c) the offense consists of a forgery or counterfeiting, or an uttering of forged copies or counterfeits, of the seals, currency, instruments of credit, stamps, passports, or public documents issued by the United States; or perjury or a false statement in an official proceeding of the United States; or a false statement in a matter within the jurisdiction of the government of the United States; or other fraud against the United States, or a theft of property in which the United States has an interest, or, if committed by a national or resident of the United States, any other obstruction of or interference with United States government function;

(d) the accused participates outside the United States in a federal offense committed in whole or in part within the United States, or the offense constitutes an attempt, solicitation, or conspiracy to commit a federal offense within the United States;

(e) the offense is a federal offense involving entry of persons or property into the United States;

(f) the offense is committed by a federal public servant who is outside the territory of the United States because of his official duties or by a member of his household residing abroad or by a person accompanying the military forces of the United States;

(g) such jurisdiction is provided by treaty; or

(h) the offense is committed by or against a national of the United States outside the jurisdiction of any nation.

FINAL REPORT OF THE NATIONAL COMMISSION ON REFORM OF FEDERAL CRIMINAL LAW §208 (1971); *see also* Kenneth R. Feinberg, *Extraterritorial Jurisdiction and the Proposed Federal Criminal Code*, 72 J.CRIM. L. & CRIM. 385 (1981).

(9) Treaties can also play a significant role in promoting the prosecution by criminal acts outside the borders of the United States. *See* Ethan A. Nadelmann, *The Role of the United States in the International Enforcement of Criminal Law*, 31 HARV. INT'L L.J. 37, 44 (1990) ("Today international law enforcement relations increasingly are governed by a multiplicity of bilateral treaties and regional and international conventions dealing with both particular types of criminal activity and different types of cooperation."); *see also* Edward M. Wise, *International Crimes and Domestic Criminal Law*, 38 DEPAUL L. REV. 923 (1989) (Appendix includes a list of "Provisions of the United States Laws Implementing International Obligations to Prosecute Under Multilateral Conventions").

§ 2.02　Jurisdictional Bases

THE RESTATEMENT (THIRD) OF THE FOREIGN RELATIONS LAW OF THE UNITED STATES (1986)

§ 401 CATEGORIES OF JURISDICTION

Under international law, a state is subject to limitations on

(a) jurisdiction to prescribe, *i.e.*, to make its law applicable to the activities, relations, or status of persons, or the interests of persons in things, whether by legislation, by executive act or order, by administrative rule or regulation, or by determination of a court;

(b) jurisdiction to adjudicate, *i.e.*, to subject persons or things to the process of its courts or administrative tribunals, whether in civil or in criminal proceedings, whether or not the state is a party to the proceedings;

(c) jurisdiction to enforce, *i.e.*, to induce or compel compliance or to punish noncompliance with its laws or regulations, whether through the courts or by use of executive, administrative, police, or other nonjudicial action.

UNITED STATES v. LAYTON*

United States District Court for the Northern District of California
509 F. Supp. 212 (1981)

PECKHAM, CHIEF JUDGE:

Laurence J. Layton, a.k.a. Larry Layton, has been indicted on four criminal counts arising from the events which occurred at the Port Kaituma airport in the nation of Guyana on November 18, 1978. Those events resulted in the death of Congressman Leo J. Ryan, then a member of the United States House of Representatives from the 11th Congressional District of California, and the wounding of Richard Dwyer, the Deputy Chief of Mission for the United States in the Republic of Guyana. The four counts of the indictment charge Mr. Layton with (1) conspiracy to murder a Congressman, under 18 U.S.C. § 351(d); (2) aiding and abetting in the murder of a Congressman, under 18 U.S.C. §§ 351(a), 2; (3) conspiracy to murder an internationally protected person, under 18 U.S.C. § 1117; and (4) aiding and abetting in the attempted murder of an internationally protected person, under 18 U.S.C. §§ 1116(a), 2.

. . . . The main contention pressed by defense counsel, is that this court lacks subject matter jurisdiction over these charges because the events on which these charges are based all occurred outside the territorial limits of the United States. The court holds that there is proper subject matter jurisdiction over all the counts of the indictment and therefore denies the motion to dismiss for the reasons discussed below.

---

* *See also* United States v. Layton, 855 F.2d 1388 (9th Cir. 1988). – Eds.

Despite some suggestion by defense counsel that they questioned the constitutional authority of Congress to reach these crimes if committed outside the territorial boundaries of the United States, the courts of the United States have repeatedly upheld the power of Congress to attach extraterritorial effect to its penal statutes, particularly where they are being applied to citizens of the United States, as is the case in this instance. . . .

There are five principles under which the law of nations permits the exercise of criminal jurisdiction by a nation: territorial jurisdiction based on the location where the alleged crime was committed, and including "objective" territorial jurisdiction, which allows countries to reach acts committed outside territorial limits but intended to produce, and producing, detrimental effects within the nation; nationality jurisdiction based on the nationality of the offender; protective jurisdiction based on the protection of the interests and the integrity of the nation; universality jurisdiction for certain crimes where custody of the offender is sufficient; and passive personality jurisdiction based on the nationality of the victim. . . . [*] The fact that Congress in the past may have favored or disfavored any particular ground for asserting extra-territorial jurisdiction is irrelevant to the consideration of Congress's constitutional power to assert that jurisdiction.

> The mere fact that, in the past, Congress may not have seen fit to embody in legislation the full scope of its authorized powers is not a basis for now finding that those powers are lacking. Disuse, or even misuse of power inherent in the federal government, or given it by the Constitution, is not a valid basis for us to hold that this power may not later be employed in a proper manner. . . .

The power of Congress to authorize extra-territorial jurisdiction over the alleged crimes in this matter can be located in at least four of these principles: protective, territorial, passive personality and nationality jurisdiction. The alleged crimes certainly had a potentially adverse effect upon the security or governmental functions of the nation, thereby providing the basis for jurisdiction under the protective principle. The charges also suggest that the alleged offenses were intended to produce and did produce harmful effects within this nation, allowing a claim of jurisdiction under the "objective" territorial principle. The nationality of the alleged victims would also support an assertion of jurisdiction under the passive personality principle. Finally, since Mr. Layton is a citizen of the United States, "American authority over (him) could be based upon the allegiance (he) owe(s) this country and its laws...." . . . . . We therefore see no difficulty in upholding the authority of Congress, under the Constitution, to apply these statutes extra-territorially to the events charged in the indictment.

---

[*] *See also* Harvard Research in International Law, *Jurisdiction With Respect to Crime*, 29 AM. J. INT'L L. 437 (Supp. 1935); THE RESTATEMENT (THIRD) OF THE FOREIGN RELATIONS LAW OF THE UNITED STATES (1986) § 402 (Bases of Jurisdiction to Prescribe). – Eds.

The question facing this court is one of statutory interpretation. For Congress did not explicitly state in any of the statutes relied on in this indictment that they were to apply extra-territorially, at least in the circumstances of this action. The issue then is whether it is proper to infer such an intent and to hold that extra-territorial jurisdiction is implicit in the respective statutes. We hold that such an inference is appropriate under each of the statutes in question....

While it remains true that legislation of Congress is generally to be construed to apply only within the territorial jurisdiction of the United States. . . . courts have not hesitated to invoke the language of *Bowman* in support of an inference of extra-territorial application where the purposes and nature of the statute appear to so warrant. Courts have generally inferred such jurisdiction for two types of statutes: (1) statutes which represent an effort by the government to protect itself against obstructions and frauds; and (2) statutes where the vulnerability of the United States outside its own territory to the occurrence of the prohibited conduct is sufficient, because of the nature of the offense, to infer reasonably that Congress meant to reach those extra-territorial acts. Because this court believes that the statute at issue here fits within both of those categories, an inference of extra-territorial application in the circumstances of this case is not only proper, but compelled. . . .

Certainly the Congress was addressing as important a problem threatening the integrity of the government when it moved to protect Congressmen from assault and murder as it was when it passed laws protecting government property, government checks, or bankruptcy proceedings, or as was the State of Florida when it passed legislation restricting the taking of commercial sponges. . . . .

Nor is the danger to which this statute is addressed "logically dependent on the locality of the violation for jurisdiction," . . . but reaches out to wherever a representative of the national government may travel, for an attack upon a member of Congress, wherever it occurs, equally threatens the free and proper functioning of the government. The concern of this statute is not simply with protecting the peace and order of the community, as with a normal murder, assault, or robbery statute; Congressmen were singled out for protection because of the position they hold in our constitutional government, because their protection is important to the integrity of the national government and therefore serves an important interest of the government itself. . . .

To limit this statute to violations within the territorial limits would also "greatly curtail the scope and usefulness of the statute and leave open a large immunity for (crimes) as easily committed by citizens . . . in foreign countries as at home." . . .

Recent decades have seen Congress playing an increasingly active role in the formulation, implementation, and oversight of foreign affairs and international relations, and by necessity increasing international travel by legislators. This is particularly true of members of the foreign affairs committees of each house of Congress, but it is not limited to those committee members. For instance, increased trade in agriculture and other commodities and an increased understanding of the role of commerce in foreign relations means that many members of Congress have the need to travel outside the territorial limits of the United States in the course of their official duties. Given this widespread travel, to limit the scope of a statute designed to protect the lives and well-being of Congressmen to attacks within the territorial limits of the United States would greatly curtail the scope and usefulness of the statute, and create an obvious means of evasion. . . . It is reasonable to infer that Congress was well aware that its members, who were to be protected by this legislation, are often overseas, just as other courts have made similar inferences concerning Congress's knowledge of the presence overseas of government property, . . . and military units, . . . It is therefore also reasonable to infer that Congress meant to protect its members not only while in this country, but also when outside the territorial limits of the United States, at least when the attack is by a United States citizen and when the Congressman is acting in his or her official capacity. . . .

. . . . The court therefore finds that the counts of the indictment in this case brought under 18 U.S.C. § 351 are properly within the subject matter jurisdiction of this court. . . .

[The court also found that 18 U.S.C. § 1116 and 1117 were properly within the jurisdiction of the court.]

NOTES AND QUESTIONS

(1) Would there be a basis for jurisdiction if the defendant in Layton had been a foreign national? *See* Mark Peterson, Note, *The Extraterritorial Effect of Federal Criminal Statutes: Offenses Directed at Members of Congress*, 6 HASTINGS INT'L & COMP. L. REV. 773 (1983) (argues that a federal court would be justified in this scenario in asserting subject matter jurisdiction over a foreign defendant).

(2) As indicated in the introductory note to this chapter, in deciding whether statutes have extraterritorial effect, courts often consider two questions: (1) whether it was the purpose of Congress to have the statute apply to acts occurring abroad; (2) whether international law permits the United States to exercise extraterritorial jurisdiction with respect to such acts. Which of these two questions should be considered first?

Courts have not followed a consistent approach. For example, in *United States v. Velasquez-Mercado*, 697 F. Supp. 292 (S.D. Texas 1988), the Southern District of Texas dismissed an indictment by examining first the extraterritorial application as intended by Congress. The court stated, "before exploring whether any theory of international law supports a congressional effort to apply our criminal laws extraterritorially, the initial question is whether the Congress even intended such an application. Criminal statutes are given extraterritorial application only if 'the nature of the law permits it and Congress intends it.'"

In *United States v. Felix-Gutierrez*, 940 F.2d 1200 (9th Cir. 1991), Circuit Judge Reinhardt considered international legal principles stating, "Prior to giving extraterritorial effect to any penal statute, we must consider whether extraterritorial application would violate international law. The law of nations permits the exercise of criminal jurisdiction by a nation under five general principles: territorial, national, protective, universality, and passive personality."

(3) In *Layton*, as well as in other cases throughout this section, the courts do not always rely on a single basis of jurisdiction. Because the five jurisdictional bases overlap, more than one may be applicable in the same case. For example in *United States v. Felix-Gutierrez*, *supra* note 2, the court stated:

> Here, three of the international law principles permitting extraterritorial jurisdiction have application: (i) territorial, (ii) protective, and (iii) passive personality. Under the first two of these, jurisdiction is based on the nature of the conduct or offense. Courts have defined the "territorial" principle to include not only acts occurring within the United States, but acts occurring outside the United States' borders that have effects within the national territory. . . . Under the "protective" principle, jurisdiction is based on whether the national interest or national security is threatened or injured by the conduct in question. Under the "passive personality" principle, courts may assert extraterritorial jurisdiction on the basis of the nationality of the victim.

Consider the limitations to categorizing all jurisdictional questions in terms of five principles noted in Edward M. Wise, *Jurisdiction, Theories of Punishment, and the Idea of Community* (Paper presented at a Special Session organized by the Committee on Philosophy and Law, at the Annual Meeting of the American Philosophical Association, Eastern Division, Boston, December 30, 1999).

> There are difficulties with analyzing all jurisdictional questions in terms of these five categories. In the first place, these "principles" or categories originated as generalizations from a mass of national legislative provisions about the competence of criminal courts to act in certain kinds of cases. These empirical generalizations about state practice have been translated into permissive or limiting normative rules, on the assumption that international law is indeed what states in fact do. But state practice does not always come clearly labeled. As a result, these five categories overlap and interweave. Their contours are not entirely settled. For instance: does objective territoriality, based on the crime having had an effect within the territory, require intent to have such effect as well as an actual effect within the territory, or is one or the other sufficient? Who counts as a national? To what kinds of crimes does the protective principle extend? To what kinds of crimes

does the universal principle extend? Moreover, there are cases in which states assert and are admitted to have jurisdiction that do not fit within the accepted contours of these five categories.

(4) Are the five bases of jurisdiction the exclusive methodology for resolving jurisdiction questions? Consider this question in the context of District Judge Weinstein's decision in the *United States v. Georgescu*, 723 F. Supp. 912 (E.D. N.Y. 1989), case:

> Over the mid-Atlantic on a Scandinavian Airlines flight from Copenhagen, Denmark to John F. Kennedy International Airport in Queens, the defendant, a Romanian national, allegedly accosted a nine year old girl who is a national of Norway by placing his hand on her genitals. He was indicted for committing a criminal sexual act while in the special aircraft jurisdiction of the United States. . . . In this case of first impression, he moves to dismiss, claiming lack of jurisdiction in United States courts. His motion must be denied for the reasons stated below. . . .

> The special aircraft jurisdiction statute was originally created to comply with treaty obligations under the Tokyo Convention. While the Tokyo Convention was intended primarily to deal with the punishment of air piracy, it was also designed to cover any other criminal offense. . . . The Tokyo Convention's primary goal was to encourage nations to exercise jurisdiction over crimes committed aboard aircraft registered in that nation. Nevertheless, the Tokyo Convention explicitly provides for jurisdiction over crimes committed aboard aircraft of foreign registry. Article 3(3) provides, "This Convention does not exclude any criminal jurisdiction exercised in accordance with national law." . . .

> Defendant contends that jurisdiction over foreign aircraft is limited by article 4 of the Tokyo Convention. The limitations of article 4 apply to attempts to "interfere with an aircraft in flight to exercise . . . criminal jurisdiction." . . . Interference means forcing the aircraft to land, or unduly delaying the flight. . . .

> The Tokyo Convention's concurrent jurisdiction provisions reflect the international legal community's acceptance of broad bases for jurisdiction over criminal offenses occurring on aircraft. *See generally* RESTATEMENT [(THIRD) OF THE FOREIGN RELATIONS LAW OF THE UNITED STATES] § 402 Comment h, at 240-41, § 403 Reporters' Note 9, at 253-54 (suggesting that acts aboard aircraft be considered a basis of jurisdiction independent of traditional bases in international law, and approving the exercise of criminal jurisdiction over an offense committed on foreign aircraft, especially if the offense involved the use of force). . . . Numerous other signatories to the Tokyo Convention have passed statutes conferring jurisdiction over crimes committed aboard foreign aircraft. . . .

Extension of jurisdiction to include criminal acts committed against foreign nationals aboard a foreign airliner bound for, and actually landing, at a United States airport makes good sense. The pilot can radio ahead for assistance, federal agents can be present to take the culprit into custody at once and the witnesses to the crime will be immediately available. If the United States did not exercise its jurisdiction, there is no guarantee that any other country would do so, since the Tokyo Convention does not oblige a state to prosecute alleged offenders. Mendelsohn, *In-Flight Crime: The International and Domestic Picture Under the Tokyo Convention*, 53 VA.L. REV. 509, 516 (1967). For would-be criminals, it may have an inhibiting effect to know that upon landing they may be immediately apprehended and prosecuted.

Even if Congress's criminalization of defendant's alleged acts and its exercise of jurisdiction were counter to international law, this fact does not lessen the validity of the statutes as superseding domestic legislation. International law is "subject to the Constitution, and is also subject to 'repeal' by other law of the United States." RESTATEMENT, *supra* ch. 2, Introductory Note, at 40; *id.* § 111 (2), at 42. While the courts must make a fair effort to interpret domestic law in a way consistent with international obligations,. . . . in the event of irreconcilable conflict, the courts are bound to apply domestic law if it was passed more recently. . . . The statutory provisions under which defendant is being prosecuted were passed subsequent to the development of the traditional notions of international law jurisdiction to which defendant argues this court is confined. They were also passed subsequent to the Tokyo Convention. The domestic statutes are controlling. . . .

Consistent with the Tokyo Convention, other interested countries could prosecute the defendant for his alleged acts. Since the defendant is Romanian and the victim is Norwegian, Romania and Norway would be the most likely countries to have an interest in this case. Both countries are party to the Tokyo Convention. . . .

It is unclear whether the domestic criminal statutes of Norway and Romania would apply to this case. This court's requests that the United States provide this information have been unavailing. It does appear, however, that the Norwegian Criminal Code makes punishable sexual molestation of a Norwegian national by a foreigner abroad. . . . Thus it is possible that defendant can be extradited to Norway to stand trial.

While extradition can be a complex process, prosecution in Norway may place less of a burden on the alleged victim, who has returned to Norway and must now be brought back to the United States for a trial, where she is likely to face further trauma on the witness stand.

In a case such as this one, the United States' initial exercise of jurisdiction may have been reasonable in order to detain the alleged criminal and gather evidence. Further prosecution in this country under these circumstances may create logistical problems involving the location of witnesses, and evidentiary obstacles involving the testimony of the alleged victim. Evidentiary issues in the taking of the child's testimony will be the subject of a subsequent memorandum. . . .

Despite this court's reservations about the wisdom of further prosecution in this country, it lacks the power to refuse jurisdiction on equitable grounds. . . . In this case, where jurisdiction exists, the indictment properly charges an offense, and the prosecution is timely, the court must allow the case to proceed. The decision on whether to prosecute or refrain and leave prosecution to another country is entirely one for the prosecutor, guided by the Departments of Justice and State. . . .

§ 2.03 Jurisdiction to Prescribe

[A] Territorial Principle

CHUA HAN MOW v. UNITED STATES

United States Court of Appeals for the Ninth Circuit
730 F.2d 1308 (1984)

HUG, CIRCUIT JUDGE:

On May 16, 1973, Chua Han Mow, a Malaysian citizen, was charged along with six others with violating United States laws against importation and distribution of controlled substances. Chua was in Malaysia at this time. Two of Chua's codefendants who were in the United States were arrested and eventually pled guilty to one count each. They each received a 10-year sentence, and they each served approximately three years before being deported.

On August 4, 1975, Chua was arrested by Malaysian authorities and incarcerated in Malaysia until October 1, 1977, pursuant to the Malaysian Emergency Ordinance of 1969. On November 2, 1977, a superseding indictment in the United States was returned against Chua and others. Chua was charged with violating 21 U.S.C. §§ 846 and 963 (Count I – conspiracy to import heroin) and 21 U.S.C. § 959 (Counts II and III – distribution of heroin). Chua was arrested by Malaysian authorities a second time on December 21, 1977. He remained incarcerated in Malaysia until he was extradited to the United States on November 28, 1979.

. . . . On April 20, 1980, Chua withdrew his plea of not guilty and pled guilty to Counts I and III. Count II was dismissed along with a separate indictment from New York. Chua was sentenced to thirty years imprisonment – 15 years each on Counts I and III to run consecutively . . . . On August 30, 1982, Chua filed a petition for writ of habeas corpus in the District Court for the District of Kansas. He raised the same issues which are raised in the current motion. That court dismissed the habeas corpus action without prejudice on the grounds that the *pro se* motion pursuant to section 2255 filed with the sentencing court had not exhausted the section 2255 remedy. On November 22, 1982, Chua filed a second section 2255 motion in the sentencing court. The court denied the motion and this appeal followed. . . .

Chua argues that the United States lacked subject-matter jurisdiction to prosecute him because all the unlawful acts he committed were done in Malaysia. We disagree. There is no constitutional bar to the extraterritorial application of penal laws. *United States v. King*, 552 F.2d 833, 850 (9th Cir. 1976), *cert. denied*, 430 U.S. 966, 52 L. Ed. 2d 357, 97 S. Ct. 1646 (1977). Although courts have been reluctant to give extraterritorial effect to penal statutes, they have done so when congressional intent to give extraterritorial effect is clear. *United States v. Bowman*, [p. 28]. Section 959 specifically states that it is intended to reach prohibited acts committed outside the territorial jurisdiction of the United States. Sections 846 and 963, the statutory basis for the conspiracy count in this case, do not specifically provide for extraterritorial application. This court, however, has regularly inferred extraterritorial reach of conspiracy statutes on the basis of a finding that the underlying substantive statutes reach extraterritorial offenses. . . . Thus, the inference that Congress intended sections 846 and 963 to have extraterritorial application is readily made.

Before giving extraterritorial effect to penal statutes, courts have considered whether international law permits the exercise of jurisdiction. . . . International law recognizes five general principles whereby a sovereign may exercise this prescriptive jurisdiction: (1) territorial, wherein jurisdiction is based on the place where the offense is committed; (2) national, wherein jurisdiction is based on the nationality or national character of the offender; (3) protective, wherein jurisdiction is based on whether the national interest is injured; (4) universal, which amounts to physical custody of the offender; and (5) passive personal, wherein jurisdiction is based on the nationality or national character of the victim. . . . Many cases involve the prosecution of United States citizens for acts committed abroad, but extraterritorial authority is not limited to cases involving the nationality principle. Extraterritorial application of penal laws may be justified under any one of the five principles of extraterritorial authority. . . .

In *King*, this court upheld the authority of the United States to prosecute United States citizens for distribution of heroin in violation of section 959, the same statute involved in the present case. The distribution occurred in Japan, but the heroin was intended for importation into the United States. The court noted that the nationality principle applied because the appellants were United

States citizens. However, the court stated that "appellants" prosecution for violating § 959 could also be justified under the territorial principle, since American courts have treated that as an 'objective' territorial principle." . . . Under the "objective" territorial principle,

> Acts done outside a jurisdiction, but intended to produce and producing detrimental effects within it, justify a State in punishing the cause of the harm as if he had been present at the effect, if the State should succeed in getting him within its power.

Strassheim v. Daily, 221 U.S. 280, 285, 55 L. Ed. 735, 31 S. Ct. 558 (1911). This rule applies to nations as well as states. *Rocha v. United States*, 288 F.2d 545, 549 (9th Cir. 1961). In the present case, Chua intended to create a detrimental effect in the United States and committed acts which resulted in such an effect when the heroin unlawfully entered the country. Chua's section 959 prosecution is therefore justified under the "objective" territorial principle. . .

Other courts have relied on the protective principle to justify jurisdiction over extraterritorial crimes involving the unlawful importation of controlled substances. . . . Noting that drug smuggling compromises a sovereign's control of its own borders, the Seventh Circuit has suggested that it might uphold extraterritorial criminal jurisdiction over alien drug smugglers even if the territorial principle did not apply. . . . We are persuaded that the protective principle also justifies Chua's section 959 prosecution.

The objective territorial principle and the protective principle are equally applicable to the conspiracy count. Furthermore, the Supreme Court has held that extraterritorial jurisdiction over aliens exists when a conspiracy had for its object crime in the United States and overt acts were committed in the United States by co-conspirators. . . . In the present case, Chua's co-conspirators committed acts in furtherance of the conspiracy inside the United States. Co-conspirator Tang was arrested at the San Francisco Airport as he attempted to retrieve suitcases containing heroin. Therefore, the United States does have jurisdiction to prosecute Chua. . . .

Chua argues that the 1970 Drug Act under which he was convicted and sentenced incorporates the Single Convention on Narcotic Drugs, which limits the extraterritorial jurisdiction of the United States. Chua points to Article 36(a)(2)(iv) of the Single Convention which states:

> (iv) Serious offenses heretofore referred to committed either by nationals or by foreigners shall be prosecuted by the Party in whose territory the offense was committed, or by the Party in whose territory the offender is found *if extradition is not acceptable* in conformity with the law of the Party to which application is made, and if such offender has not already been prosecuted and judgment given.

18 U.S.T. 1407, 1425 (emphasis added).

Chua cites no authority supporting the proposition that the Single Convention limits the extraterritorial jurisdiction of the United States. The plain language of the cited provision does not limit the jurisdiction of the United States. The only effect of the provision is that Malaysia would have been required to prosecute Chua if extradition had not been acceptable to Malaysia. The provision is not applicable in this case because extradition was acceptable to Malaysia. . . . AFFIRMED.

NOTES AND QUESTIONS

(1) Does the territoriality principle require an act within the territorial jurisdiction of the United States? See *United States v. Noriega* [p. 421]. Will the intent to commit an act within the territorial jurisdiction of the United States, be sufficient in cases where a drug conspiracy is charged? In *United States v. Ricardo*, 619 F.2d 1124 (5th Cir. 1980), the Fifth Circuit affirmed a conviction stating:

> Appellants were convicted of two marijuana counts, stemming from the seizure of a shrimp boat, the SINCERE PROGRESS I, in the Gulf of Mexico, on the late evening and early morning of November 4-5, 1978. . . . The circumstances of the case reveal that the plan commenced outside the United States. Charts confiscated during the investigation indicate that the voyage originated in Colombia. According to the Americans, they left in their sailboat from Miami, Florida. Assuming their version is correct, the only nexus to the United States is indirect because they were not the masterminds behind the scheme. When the PROGRESS was intercepted, it was approximately 125-150 miles from the Texas Coast. From these facts alone, it is apparent that the Government failed to prove the existence of an overt act committed within the United States. The Government did prove, however, that the PROGRESS intended to rendezvous with another vessel off the coast of Texas, in order to unload their cargo. Given this proof, along with the proximity to the United States coast and the general heading of the ship, we are convinced that the object of appellants' plan had consequences within the United States. Under these circumstances, the question we now address is whether, pursuant to either conspiracy statute, a territorial act must be committed within the United States and in furtherance of the conspiracy before jurisdiction attaches.

> Under the conspiracy statutes in question, §§ 846 and 963, it is not incumbent upon the Government to allege or prove an overt act in order to obtain a conviction. . . . While it is now settled law that proof of an overt act is not required under the conspiracy statutes, the jurisdictional requisites are not settled. The United States and this Circuit have traditionally adhered to the objective principle of territorial jurisdictional, which attaches criminal consequences to extraterritorial

acts that are intended to have effect in the sovereign territory, at least where overt acts within the territory can be proved. . . . Implicit in these statutes is the notion that the prescribed prohibitions apply extraterritorially. . . . It seems somewhat anomalous, however, that Congress intended these statutes to apply extraterritorially, but that jurisdiction attaches only after an act occurred within the sovereign boundaries. Thus, even though the statutes were designed to prevent one type of wrong ab initio, under the traditional approach, the courts were without power to act. This dichotomy directly contravenes the purpose of the enabling legislation.

As a result, it is now settled in this Circuit that when the statute itself does not require proof of an overt act, jurisdiction attaches upon a mere showing of intended territorial effects. . . . The fact that appellants intended the conspiracy to be consummated within the territorial boundaries satisfies jurisdictional requisites. . . .

(2) Can a statute grant "special territorial jurisdiction" in the United States? 18 U.S.C. § 7(3) provides that "special maritime and territorial jurisdiction of the United States" includes "(3) [a]ny lands reserved or acquired for the use of the United States, and under the exclusive or concurrent jurisdiction thereof, or any place purchased or otherwise acquired by the United States by consent of the legislature of the State in which the same shall be, for the erection of a fort, magazine, arsenal, dockyard, or other needful building." *See United States v. Erdos*, 474 F.2d 157 (4th Cir. 1973) (court found "special" territorial jurisdiction for a manslaughter prosecution of an American citizen who was an embassy employee in the Republic of Equatorial Guinea, for killing of another embassy employee who was also an American citizen, where the killing took place within a U.S. embassy in a foreign country).

[B] Nationality Principle

UNITED STATES v. WALCZAK

United States Court of Appeals for the Ninth Circuit
783 F.2d 852 (1986)

PER CURIAM:

Following his conviction for making false statements on a Customs declaration form, Walczak appeals the denial of four pretrial motions. He argues that the district court did not have jurisdiction, that the Customs officials' search of his person and luggage violated the fourth amendment, that he should have been granted an evidentiary hearing on the suppression issue, and that he should have been permitted access to transcripts of the grand jury proceedings. We affirm the judgment of the district court. . . .

On October 10, 1984, Walczak, a United States citizen, was at the International Airport in Vancouver, British Columbia, Canada, about to board a non-stop flight to the United States. He completed Customs form 6059B, answering "no" to the statement "I am * * * carrying currency or monetary instruments over $5000 U.S. * * *." U.S. Customs officials searched him and found over $52,000 in U.S. currency in his carry-on luggage. After questioning by U.S. Customs officials and by the Royal Canadian Mounted Police, he was released. Several days later, he voluntarily surrendered to U.S. Customs officials in Blaine, Washington.

A grand jury at Seattle, Washington indicted Walczak under 18 U.S.C. § 1001 (1982) (False Statements) and 18 U.S.C. § 3238 (1982) (Extraterritorial Jurisdiction). He pled not guilty, and moved to suppress the evidence of his false statement on the grounds that the search was not a valid border search and that the United States customs officials lacked authority to search him at the Vancouver airport in Canada. He requested an evidentiary hearing on the suppression issue. He also moved to discover transcripts of the grand jury proceedings, and to dismiss the indictment on the grounds that the district court lacked jurisdiction over the offense on foreign soil. The court denied all the motions. Walczak then entered a conditional plea of guilty, was fined $5000, given a three year sentence, which was suspended except for thirty days, and placed on probation.

The jurisdiction of the district court over an offense is a question of law to be reviewed *de novo*. . . . Walczak argues that a false statement made outside the borders is not punishable by a court of the United States. This argument fails for several reasons. First, section 1001 states that

> Whoever, in any matter *within the jurisdiction of any department or agency of the United States* knowingly and wilfully falsifies, conceals or covers-up by any trick, scheme or device a material fact, or makes any false, fictitious or fraudulent statements or representations, or makes or uses any false writing or document knowing the same could contain any false, fictitious or fraudulent statement or entry, shall be fined not more than $10,000 or imprisoned not more than five years, or both.

(Emphasis added.) The preclearance procedure is within the jurisdiction of the United States Customs Service, Department of the Treasury. Since the Department of the Treasury is a "department * * * of the United States," the language of § 1001 literally applies to false statements made on Customs forms without regard to the place where the offense occurred.

Second, the rationale of the decision in *United States v. Bowman,* [p.28] extends the reach of certain laws such as § 1001 to cover acts committed outside the United States by United States citizens. *Bowman* stated that some offenses

> are such that to limit their *locus* to the strictly territorial jurisdiction would be greatly to curtail the scope and usefulness of the statute and leave open a large immunity for frauds as easily committed on the high

seas and in foreign countries as at home. In such cases, Congress has not thought it necessary to make specific provisions in the law that the *locus* shall include the high seas and foreign countries, but allows it to be inferred from the nature of the offense.

. . . . In the context of false statements on Customs declarations, § 1001 is such a law.

Third, at least as to Walczak, a United States citizen, the nationality principle of extraterritorial jurisdiction would apply: "American authority over [United States citizens] could be based upon the allegiance they owe this country and its laws if the statute concerned * * * evinces a legislative intent to control actions within and without the United States." *United States v. King*, 552 F.2d 833, 851 (9th Cir. 1976). Therefore the federal court system had jurisdiction to entertain the prosecution of Walczak for a violation of § 1001 committed in Canada.

Section 3238 states, "the trial of all offenses begun or committed upon the high seas, or elsewhere out of the jurisdiction of any particular state or district, shall be in the district where the offender * * * is arrested or first brought." Walczak surrendered to custom officials in the Western District of Washington, and therefore, that district court was the proper court in which to try him. Walczak's argument to the contrary therefore fails. . . . For the foregoing reasons, the district court's denial of appellant's motions is AFFIRMED.

NOTE AND QUESTIONS

What situations warrant use of the nationality principle? *See, e.g.,* 18 U.S.C. § 175 (Prohibitions with respect to biological weapons). How might diplomatic immunity play a factor in where a person may be prosecuted? Should a member of the United States armed forces, who commits a crime abroad, be prosecuted in the United States? *See* Geoffrey R. Watson, *Offenders Abroad: The Case for Nationality-Based Criminal Jurisdiction*, 17 YALE J. INT'L L. 41 (1992).

[C] Protective Principle

UNITED STATES v. GONZALEZ

United States Court of Appeals for the Eleventh Circuit
776 F.2d 931 (1985)

KRAVITCH, CIRCUIT JUDGE:

In this case, six defendants appeal the denial of their motion to dismiss an indictment charging them with knowingly and intentionally possessing, with intent to distribute, marijuana on board a vessel within the customs waters of the United States, 21 U.S.C. § 955a(c). They contend that the operation of section 955a(c), under which the United States may extend its customs waters to specific foreign vessels through arrangements with foreign nations violates their constitutional right to due process. They also claim that no "arrangement" within the meaning of the statute existed in this case.

This court already has held that by adopting the term "customs waters," Congress intended section 955a(c) to apply extra-territorially, and that Congress contemplated executive arrangements with foreign nations which would designate specific vessels as within "customs waters." *United States v. Romero-Galue*, 757 F.2d 1147 (11th Cir. 1985). We now hold that designating "customs waters" around a specific vessel on the high seas, thereby subjecting persons on board to United States prosecution, does not violate due process. We also hold that the arrangements regarding specific vessels may be informal, as long as there is a clear indication of consent by the foreign nation. Accordingly, we affirm the district court's refusal to dismiss the indictment. . . .

The six defendants, all foreign nationals, were crew members aboard the ROSANGEL, a Honduran vessel. On May 24, 1984, the United States Coast Guard cutter V. LYPAN intercepted the ROSANGEL approximately 125 miles due east of Fort Lauderdale, Florida. A Coast Guard officer observed "bale type objects" on the main deck of the ROSANGEL. Coast Guard personnel boarded and searched the vessel, finding 114 bales of marijuana on the main deck and in the forward hold.

After a documentation check revealed that the vessel was of Honduran registry, the Coast Guard contacted the Honduran government by telephone and, with Captain Barrios' permission, waited on board the ROSANGEL for a response. When the Honduran government subsequently issued a statement of "no objection" to the boarding, search, seizure, and prosecution of the crew members of the ROSANGEL under United States law, the six defendants were arrested and transported to Miami for indictment and prosecution. . . .

The defendants were indicted under the Marijuana on the High Seas Act of 1980, 21 U.S.C. § 955a-955d. Congress adopted the Act in an effort "to prohibit all acts of illicit trafficking in controlled substances on the high seas which the

United States can reach under international law." . . . . To achieve this goal, Congress created four different criminal offenses. Congress forbade possession with intent to distribute by any person on board United States vessels or vessels subject to United States jurisdiction, 21 U.S.C. § 955a(a), and on board any vessel by a citizen of the United States. 21 U.S.C. § 955a(b). Neither of these provisions require intent to distribute within the United States. Section 955a(d) proscribed possession with intent to distribute in the United States. These three provisions left a serious gap in Congress' effort to reach "all acts of illicit trafficking": possession with intent to distribute by foreign nationals on board foreign vessels, in cases where intent to distribute within the United States could not be shown. Congress filled the gap with section 955a(c), which states:

> It is unlawful for any person on board any vessel within the customs waters of the United States to knowingly or intentionally manufacture or distribute, or to possess with intent to manufacture or distribute, a controlled substance.

"Customs Waters" is defined in 19 U.S.C. § 1401(j):

> The term "customs waters" means, in the case of a foreign vessel subject to a treaty or other arrangement between a foreign government and the United States enabling or permitting the authorities of the United States to board, examine, search, seize, or otherwise to enforce upon such vessel upon the high seas the laws of the United States, *the waters within such distance of the coast of the United States as the said authorities are or may be so enabled or permitted by such treaty or arrangement* and, in the case of every other vessel, the waters within four leagues of the coast of the United States.

Id. (emphasis added).

The appellants' vessel was well beyond four leagues from the coast of the United States, and therefore we must consider whether a "treaty or other arrangement" had expanded this nation's "customs waters" to include those surrounding the vessel. . . . In enacting section 955a(c), Congress contemplated that the Coast Guard would seek permission from foreign governments to prosecute foreign nationals found on foreign vessels on the high seas. Obviously, Congress did not intend that the United States negotiate formal treaties with respect to each vessel; rather Congress contemplated the precise type of consent shown in the present case. . . .

Requiring execution of a formal agreement would defeat the purpose of the statute, which is to allow enforcement against particular vessels found hovering off the coast. Obviously, a vessel laden with marijuana would not leisurely lay at anchor just beyond four leagues from our shore while United States diplomats journeyed to Honduras, or other appropriate nation, negotiated an agreement, and awaited the approval of the proper bodies within the party nations. It is doubtful that the pride of our diplomats would be offended by this court's observation that during the course of obtaining such an agreement, convoys of vessels could journey back and forth laden with contraband. Once an agreement was in force, the smugglers could simply obtain a different vessel.

Nor would a formal agreement serve any useful purpose. All that the law contemplates is that the foreign nation give express consent to the enforcement of United States laws with respect to the particular vessel. The consenting nation's rights under international law or treaty remain unchanged, as the consent applies only to the particular vessel involved. Consent is a simple notion; it can be granted or refused, and no formal agreement is necessary to understand either option.

Finally, in the legislative history Congress noted that "the time required to obtain prior consent to board 'mother ships' on the high seas has apparently been significantly reduced," indicating that it intended to take advantage of such consent. . . . The record in this case demonstrates that such an arrangement existed. Honduras specifically consented to the United States asserting jurisdiction over the ROSANGEL.

The appellants also argue that even if the consent of Honduras satisfies the statutory requirement for an "arrangement," the statute only authorizes arrangements with "treaty nations." Accordingly, they argue that because no treaty between Honduras and the United States authorizes arrangements, no arrangement existed within the meaning of section 955a(c). . . . This contention also fails. First it runs contrary to the statutory language. The definition of "customs waters" refers to "treaty *or* other arrangement." 19 U.S.C. § 1401(j) (emphasis added). The appellants' argument would amend the definition to read "treaty or other arrangement executed pursuant to a treaty." We decline to rewrite the work of Congress. . . . Appellants advance no congressional purpose, and we can think of none that such a treaty requirement would serve; if the United States can achieve its goal of arrangements without a treaty, then why would Congress require one? Such a requirement would be directly contrary to the express statement of Congress that it intended to reach "all acts of illicit trafficking." . . . Accordingly we hold that nothing in the Marijuana on the High Seas Act requires a treaty before the United States may seek an arrangement.

. . . . Section 955a(c) requires consent by the foreign nation before enforcement of the United States law. Even absent consent, however, the United States could prosecute foreign nationals on foreign vessels under the "protective principle" of international law, . . . which permits a nation to assert jurisdiction over a person whose conduct outside the nation's territory threatens the nation's security or could potentially interfere with the operation of its governmental functions. Congress grounded section 955a(c) on this principle...

Reliance on the protective principle is not a novel idea in American law. Indeed, the protective principle was the basis Congress cited for the Anti-Smuggling Act. S.Rep. No. 1036, 74th Cong. 1st Sess. 5 (1935). The Senate Report to that legislation noted that "there is no fixed rule among the customs and usages of nations which prescribes the limits of jurisdictional waters other than the rule of reasonableness, that a nation may exercise authority upon the high seas to such an extent and to so great a distance as is reasonable and necessary to protect itself and its citizens from injury." *Id.* The Senate Report also noted the opinion of Chief Justice Marshall in *Church v. Hubbart*, 6 U.S. (2 Cranch) 187, 2 L. Ed. 249 (1804), which observed that "if this right be extended too far it will be resisted." *Id.* at 235. The Chief Justice was discussing enforcement of a common type of law in the days of mercantilism, a colonial power's prohibition against trade with its colonies by other nations. He stated that:

> Thus in the channel, where a very great part of the commerce to and from all the north of Europe, passes through a very narrow sea, the seizure of vessels on suspicion of attempting an illicit trade, must necessarily be restricted to very narrow limits; but on the coast of South America, seldom frequented by vessels but for the purpose of illicit trade, the vigilance of the government may be extended somewhat further and foreign nations subject to such regulations as are reasonable in themselves and are really necessary. . . .

Id. at 235. Chief Justice Marshall's words are no less vital today. In the waters between certain areas of Latin America and our nation, nations judge what is reasonable in light of the massive drug trade in those waters. One need only glance at a map of the region and compare the vast length of United States coast to the narrow straits between Yucatan and Cuba . . . and the other narrow passages through the West Indies to understand the reasonableness of enforcing our drug laws outside of our territorial sea. Apparently, foreign nations such as Honduras recognize the reasonableness of current United States enforcement efforts, for consent has been given.

Congress' purpose in enacting section 955a was clearly stated. The Act was "designed to prohibit all acts of illicit trafficking in controlled substances on the high seas which the United States can reach under international law." . . . Congress adopted section 955a(c) and relied on the protective principle because it is often difficult to prove beyond a reasonable doubt that a vessel seized on the high seas carrying contraband was headed for the United States. . . . The protective principle does not require that there be proof of an actual or intended effect inside the United States. The conduct may be forbidden if it has a potentially adverse effect and is generally recognized as a crime by nations that have reasonably developed legal systems. . . . Congress has determined, therefore, that distribution of marijuana and other narcotics meets these criteria. Appellants do not contest the determination of Congress, nor do we believe there would be any basis to attack it. As noted above, that reasonable nations accept the authority advanced by Congress in section 955a(c) is demonstrated by the consent that has been given.

Congress faced a difficulty, however, in flexing fully its legal authority under the protective principle. Although Congress' planned extension of authority was reasonable, there was no need to risk unnecessary friction with foreign nations.

Such friction would not stem from the extension of the United States' drug laws to foreign nationals on the high seas, but from the stopping and seizing of foreign vessels on the high seas. The legislative history reflects Congress' ambivalence between its respect for exclusive state flag jurisdiction on the one hand, and the long history of extra-territorial United States jurisdiction on the other. In light of the fact that nations already were giving consent before passage of the law, and considering the reasonableness of the law, Congress likely believed that obtaining consent would not unduly hinder enforcement efforts; it could achieve its enforcement goal and at the same time minimize any foreign objections. Accordingly, Congress borrowed the notion of "customs waters" and "customs enforcement areas" from the Anti-Smuggling Act; section 955a(c) would not be enforced without the consent of the foreign nation. The "customs waters" approach was adopted for these reasons and not because of any limitations on the authority of the United States in either international law or treaties. *It is misleading, therefore, to consider that consent an element of the offense*; rather, it is a diplomatic requisite illustrating the international partnership that ensures the rule of law on the high seas. The law will not be enforced on the high seas against a foreign nation's vessels without that nation's consent.

Our review of the basis and purpose of section 955a(c) convinces us that the appellants' due process contentions are illusory. There is nothing vague about the statute. Congress has provided clear notice of what conduct is forbidden: any possession of marijuana on the high seas with intent to distribute. The United States will enforce this law to the full extent of its ability under international law. Congress has afforded a legislative grace to our fellow nations by conditioning enforcement of the law upon their consent. This grace, however, does not create a notice problem. Both the offense and the intent of the United States are clear. Those embarking on voyages with holds laden with illicit narcotics, conduct which is contrary to laws of all reasonably developed legal systems, do so with the awareness of the risk that their government may consent to enforcement of the United States' laws against the vessel. Due process does not require that a person who violates the law of all reasonable nations be excused on the basis that his own nation *might* have requested that he not be prosecuted by a foreign sovereign. Accordingly we hold that appellants' challenge to the constitutionality of section 955a(c) is without merit. . . . On the basis of the foregoing discussion, the denial of the appellants' motion to dismiss the indictment is AFFIRMED.

HATCHETT, Circuit Judge, specially concurring: . . .

NOTES AND QUESTIONS

(1) In *Gonzalez* does the court use the protective principle exclusively? Is this also an illustration of "ceded jurisdiction?"

(2) Is it proper for a court to apply the protective principle in cases involving drugs abroad vessels on the high seas? In *United States v. Robinson*, 843 F.2d 1 (1st Cir. 1988), the defendant questioned "how can this principle justify prohibiting foreigners on foreign ships 500 miles offshore from possessing drugs that, as far as the statute (and clear proof here) are concerned, might be bound for Canada, South America, or Zanzibar?" The First Circuit rejected defendant's argument, noting that "appellants' arguments are beside the point, for there is another, different, by perfectly adequate basis in international law for the assertion of American jurisdiction. Panama agreed to permit the United States to apply its law on her ship." The court also stated, "[i]t is clear, under international law's 'territorial principle,' that a 'state has jurisdiction to prescribe and enforce a rule of law in the territory of another state to the extent provided by international agreement with the other state.'"

(3) What kinds of conduct is encompassed within the protective principle? In *United States v. Birch*, 470 F.2d 808 (4th Cir. 1972), the court stated: "[t]he basis found in international law for extraterritorial application of § 499 is the principle of protective jurisdiction. The protective principle determines jurisdiction 'by reference to the national interest injured by the offense.' It provides an appropriate jurisdictional base for prosecuting a person who, acting beyond the territorial boundaries of the United States, falsifies its official documents. Because the national interest is injured by the falsification of official documents no matter where the counterfeit is prepared, we conclude that Congress intended § 499 to apply to persons who commit its proscribed acts abroad." *See also* IAIN CAMERON, THE PROTECTIVE PRINCIPLE OF INTERNATIONAL CRIMINAL JURISDICTION (1994).

[D] Passive Personality Principle

UNITED STATES v. ROBERTS

United States District Court for the Eastern District of Louisiana
1 F.Supp.2d 601 (1998)

VANCE, DISTRICT JUDGE:

. . . . Defendant Roberts was indicted by a federal grand jury on December 11, 1997 and charged with one count of sexual abuse of a minor, 18 U.S.C. § 2243(a), and one count of abusive sexual contact with a minor, 18 U.S.C. § 2244(a). The crimes allegedly occurred on board a cruise ship, the Carnival Cruise Lines' vessel M/V CELEBRATION. Roberts is a national of St. Vincent & the Grenadines, and he was employed by the M/V CELEBRATION at the time the alleged incident took place. The victim is a United States citizen. The United States alleges that the crimes were committed "in an area within the special maritime and territorial jurisdiction of the United States" and that jurisdiction is proper under 18 U.S.C. §§ 7(1) or (8).

It is not disputed that the alleged incident occurred while the cruise ship was "in international waters approximately 63 miles off the coast of Puna Mols, Mexico.". . . The following facts are also uncontested: Carnival Corporation ("Carnival") owns the M/S CELEBRATION, and the company is incorporated under the laws of the Republic of Panama . . . The M/V CELEBRATION is registered in Liberia and flies a Liberian flag. Carnival is a public company, its stock is traded on the New York Stock Exchange, and some of its shareholders are United States citizens. . . . Further, the M/S CELEBRATION begins and ends its cruises in the United States, and the majority of its passengers are United States citizens. . . . It is also undisputed that neither Panama nor Liberia has taken any steps to prosecute the defendant.

The defendant moves this Court to dismiss the indictment on the grounds that the United States does not have jurisdiction over the alleged incident. Roberts contends that jurisdiction is not proper under § 7(1) because the M/V CELEBRATION is not an American vessel. The defendant also states that jurisdiction under 18 U.S.C. § 7(8) is limited "to the extent permitted by international law," and, in this case, jurisdiction is not proper under accepted principles of international law. The government argues that jurisdiction is proper because the M/V CELEBRATION is owned in part by American citizens, and international law permits this exercise of jurisdiction under the objective territorial and the passive personality theories. . . .

In this case, Congress intended for § 2243 and 2244 to reach beyond the strict territorial jurisdiction of the United States because the statutes provide that the laws operate within the "special maritime and territorial jurisdiction of the United States.". . . The question in this case is whether the alleged crimes occurred within the special maritime and territorial jurisdiction of the United States as set forth in 18 U.S.C. §§ 7(1) and 7(8). . . .Given the apparent conflict in Fifth Circuit authority over whether § 7(1)'s special maritime jurisdiction covers prohibited acts committed on foreign flag vessels on the high seas, and the fact that the Court finds jurisdiction under 18 U.S.C. § 7(8), . . . the Court finds it unnecessary to resolve whether jurisdiction likewise lies under § 7(1). . . .

The Court concludes that jurisdiction over this case is proper pursuant to 18 U.S.C. § 7(8). Section 7(8) was added to the United States' special maritime and territorial jurisdiction in 1994 as part of the Violent Crime Control and Law Enforcement Act of 1994, Pub. L. No. 103-322, § 120002, 108 Stat. 2021 (Sept. 13, 1994). The statute expressly states that the special maritime jurisdiction of the United States is extended to include "to the extent permitted by international law, any foreign vessel during a voyage having a scheduled departure from or arrival in the United States with respect to an offense committed by or against a national of the United States." 18 U.S.C. § 7(8).

Defendant Roberts argues that international treaties and principles of international law do not permit this Court to exercise jurisdiction over this matter. First, Roberts contends that several international treaties prohibit the United States from asserting its jurisdiction because the treaties state that foreign vessels are subject to the exclusive jurisdiction of the country whose flag they fly under. Second, Roberts insists that this case does not fall under any of the recognized exceptions to the principle of the "law of the flag."

The treaties relied upon by the defendant do not prevent this Court from exercising jurisdiction over the offensive acts. Defendant has failed to show that any of the treaties are self-executing, and treaties "may act to deprive the United States, and hence its courts, of jurisdiction over property and individuals that would otherwise be subject to that jurisdiction" only if the treaties are self-executing. *United States v. Postal*, 589 F.2d 862, 875 (5th Cir. 1979). It is also well established that unless a treaty is self-executing, "that is, unless it expressly creates privately enforceable rights – an individual citizen does not have standing to protest when one nation does not follow the terms of such agreement." . . .

International law recognizes five theories of jurisdiction, under which a country is permitted to exercise extraterritorial criminal jurisdiction: . . . In this case, the prosecution . . . . is a valid exercise of both passive personality jurisdiction and objective territorial jurisdiction. The principle of passive personality "asserts that a state may apply law – particularly criminal law – to an act committed outside its territory by a person not its national where the victim of the act was its national." RESTATEMENT § 402 cmt. g. Although courts are reluctant to embrace passive personality jurisdiction for ordinary torts or crimes,. . . . international law does not prohibit Congress from incorporating this principle into its legislation. Indeed, prior to the enactment of § 7(8), Congress applied the passive personality principle in the Omnibus Diplomatic Security and Antiterrorism Act of 1986, 18 U.S.C. § 2231, which makes it a crime to kill, or attempt or conspire to kill, or to cause serious bodily injury, to a national of the United States outside the territory of the United States. Moreover, some courts have recently expressed approval of passive personality jurisdiction. . . . In addition, Congress is moving towards accepting passive personality jurisdiction outside the realm of terrorism, as evidence by several pieces of legislation. . . .

This move towards accepting passive personality jurisdiction continued with the passage of § 7(8), which authorizes the United States to exercise its jurisdiction over "any foreign vessel during a voyage having a scheduled departure from or arrival in the United States with respect to an offense committed by or against a national of the United States." 18 U.S.C. § 7(8). Given the specific requirement that the vessel have a scheduled departure from or arrival in the United States, this statute expresses concern for United States nationals but limits jurisdiction to vessels that are most likely to have a connection to America. Indeed, in this case, the M/V CELEBRATION originates and terminates its voyage in the United States, and the majority of its passengers are American citizens. Further, Carnival Corporation has its corporate headquarters in this country and some of its shareholders are United States citizens. The Court must also add that the country whose flag the cruise ship flies under, Liberia, has little to no interest in the alleged offense because neither the victim nor the defendant are Liberian, the vessel does not operate in or around Liberian territory, and the vessel's owners center their corporate operations in the United States. In short, the Court finds that jurisdiction is reasonable in this case pursuant to § 7(8), and it is permitted by international law because it does not intrude upon another sovereign's interest, and it serves to protect America's nationals abroad.

The objective territorial principle also supports jurisdiction over this matter. Jurisdiction under this principle is asserted over foreigners for an act committed outside the United States that produces substantial and detrimental effects within the United States. . . . IT IS ORDERED that defendant's motion to dismiss is DENIED.

NOTE AND QUESTIONS

The use of the passive personality principle in the United States is relatively new. Is there a constitutional basis for this principle? Should the use of the passive personality principle be limited to situations where the defendant is not prosecuted by the state where the crime is alleged to have been committed? *See* Geoffrey R. Watson, *The Passive Personality Principle*, 28 TEX. INT'L L.J. 1 (1993).

[E] Universality Principle

UNITED STATES v. YUNIS

United States Court of Appeals for the District of Columbia Circuit
924 F.2d 1086 (1991)

MIKVA, CHIEF JUDGE:

Appellant Fawaz Yunis challenges his convictions on conspiracy, aircraft piracy, and hostage-taking charges stemming from the hijacking of a Jordanian passenger aircraft in Beirut, Lebanon. He appeals from orders of the district court denying his pretrial motions relating to jurisdiction, illegal arrest, alleged violations of the Posse Comitatus Act, and the government's withholding of classified documents during discovery. Yunis also challenges the district court's jury instructions as erroneous and prejudicial.

Although this appeal raises novel issues of domestic and international law, we reject Yunis' objections and affirm the convictions. . . .

On June 11, 1985, appellant and four other men boarded Royal Jordanian Airlines Flight 402 ("Flight 402") shortly before its scheduled departure from Beirut, Lebanon. They wore civilian clothes and carried military assault rifles, ammunition bandoleers, and hand grenades. Appellant took control of the cockpit and forced the pilot to take off immediately. The remaining hijackers tied up Jordanian air marshals assigned to the flight and held the civilian passengers, including two American citizens, captive in their seats. The hijackers explained to the crew and passengers that they wanted the plane to fly to Tunis, where a conference of the Arab League was under way. The hijackers further explained that they wanted a meeting with delegates to the conference and that their ultimate goal was removal of all Palestinians from Lebanon.

After a refueling stop in Cyprus, the airplane headed for Tunis but turned away when authorities blocked the airport runway. Following a refueling stop at Palermo, Sicily, another attempt to land in Tunis, and a second stop in Cyprus, the plane returned to Beirut, where more hijackers came aboard. These reinforcements included an official of Lebanon's Amal Militia, the group at whose direction Yunis claims he acted. The plane then took off for Syria, but was turned away and went back to Beirut. There, the hijackers released the passengers, held a press conference reiterating their demand that Palestinians leave Lebanon, blew up the plane, and fled from the airport.

An American investigation identified Yunis as the probable leader of the hijackers and prompted U.S. civilian and military agencies, led by the Federal Bureau of Investigation (FBI), to plan Yunis' arrest. After obtaining an arrest warrant, the FBI put "Operation Goldenrod" into effect in September 1987. Undercover FBI agents lured Yunis onto a yacht in the eastern Mediterranean Sea with promises of a drug deal, and arrested him once the vessel entered international waters. The agents transferred Yunis to a United States Navy munitions ship and interrogated him for several days as the vessel steamed toward a second rendezvous, this time with a Navy aircraft carrier. Yunis was flown to Andrews Air Force Base from the aircraft carrier, and taken from there to Washington, D.C. In Washington, Yunis was arraigned on an original indictment charging him with conspiracy, hostage taking, and aircraft damage. A grand jury subsequently returned a superseding indictment adding additional aircraft damage counts and a charge of air piracy.

Yunis filed several pretrial motions, among them a motion to suppress statements he made while aboard the munitions ship. In *United States v. Yunis (Yunis I)*, 859 F.2d 953 (D.C. Cir. 1988), this court reversed a district court order suppressing the statements, and authorized their introduction at trial. We revisited the case on a second interlocutory appeal relating to discovery of classified information, reversing the district court's disclosure order. *United States v. Yunis (Yunis II)*, 867 F.2d 617 (D.C. Cir. 1989).

Yunis admitted participation in the hijacking at trial but denied parts of the government's account and offered the affirmative defense of obedience to military orders, asserting that he acted on instructions given by his superiors in Lebanon's Amal Militia. The jury convicted Yunis of conspiracy, 18 U.S.C. § 371 (1988), hostage taking, 18 U.S.C. § 1203 (1988), and air piracy, 49 U.S.C. App. § 472(n) (1988). However, it acquitted him of three other charged offenses that went to trial: violence against people on board an aircraft, 18 U.S.C. § 32(b)(1) (1988), aircraft damage, 18 U.S.C. § 32(b)(2) (1988), and placing a destructive device aboard an aircraft, 18 U.S.C. § 32(b)(3) (1988). The district court imposed concurrent sentences of five years for conspiracy, thirty years for hostage taking, and twenty years for air piracy. Yunis appeals his conviction and seeks dismissal of the indictment. . . .

Yunis argues that the district court lacked subject matter and personal jurisdiction to try him on the charges of which he was convicted, that the indictment should have been dismissed because the government seized him in violation of the Posse Comitatus Act and withheld classified materials useful to his defense, and that the convictions should be reversed because of errors in the jury instructions. . . .

Yunis appeals first of all from the district court's denial of his motion to dismiss for lack of subject matter and personal jurisdiction. *See United States v. Yunis*, 681 F. Supp. 896 (D.D.C. 1988). Appellant's principal claim is that, as a matter of domestic law, the federal hostage taking and air piracy statutes do not authorize assertion of federal jurisdiction over him. Yunis also suggests that a contrary construction of these statutes would conflict with established principles of international law, and so should be avoided by this court. Finally, appellant claims that the district court lacked personal jurisdiction because he was seized in violation of American law. . . .

The Hostage Taking Act provides, in relevant part:

> (a) Whoever, whether inside or outside the United States, seizes or detains and threatens to kill, to injure, or to continue to detain another person in order to compel a third person or a governmental organization to do or to abstain from any act . . . shall be punished by imprisonment by any term of years or for life.
>
> (b)(1) It is not an offense under this section if the conduct required for the offense occurred outside the United States unless –
>
> (A) the offender or the person seized or detained is a national of the United States;
>
> (B) the offender is found in the United States; or
>
> (C) the governmental organization sought to be compelled is the Government of the United States.

18 U.S.C. § 1203. Yunis claims that this statute cannot apply to an individual who is brought to the United States by force, since those convicted under it must

be "found in the United States." But this ignores the law's plain language. Subsections (A), (B), and (C) of section 1203(b)(1) offer *independent* bases for jurisdiction where "the offense occurred outside the United States." Since two of the passengers on Flight 402 were U.S. citizens, section 1203(b)(1)(A), authorizing assertion of U.S. jurisdiction where "the offender or the person seized or detained is a national of the United States," is satisfied. The statute's jurisdictional requirement has been met regardless of whether or not Yunis was "found" within the United States under section 1203(b)(1)(B).

Appellant's argument that we should read the Hostage Taking Act differently to avoid tension with international law falls flat. Yunis points to no treaty obligations of the United States that give us pause. Indeed, Congress intended through the Hostage Taking Act to execute the International Convention Against the Taking of Hostages, which authorizes any signatory state to exercise jurisdiction over persons who take its nationals hostage "if that State considers it appropriate." . . .

Nor is jurisdiction precluded by norms of customary international law. The district court concluded that two jurisdictional theories of international law, the "universal principle" and the "passive personal principle," supported assertion of U.S. jurisdiction to prosecute Yunis on hijacking and hostage-taking charges. . . . Under the universal principle, states may prescribe and prosecute "certain offenses recognized by the community of nations as of universal concern, such as piracy, slave trade, attacks on or hijacking of aircraft, genocide, war crimes, and perhaps certain acts of terrorism," even absent any special connection between the state and the offense. *See* RESTATEMENT (THIRD) OF THE FOREIGN RELATIONS LAW OF THE UNITED STATES §§ 404, 423 (1987). Under the passive personal principle, a state may punish non-nationals for crimes committed against its nationals outside of its territory, at least where the state has a particularly strong interest in the crime. . . .

Relying primarily on the RESTATEMENT, Yunis argues that hostage taking has not been recognized as a universal crime and that the passive personal principle authorizes assertion of jurisdiction over alleged hostage takers only where the victims were seized because they were nationals of the prosecuting state. Whatever merit appellant's claims may have as a matter of international law, they cannot prevail before this court. Yunis seeks to portray international law as a self-executing code that trumps domestic law whenever the two conflict. That effort misconceives the role of judges as appliers of international law and as participants in the federal system. Our duty is to enforce the Constitution, laws, and treaties of the United States, not to conform the law of the land to norms of customary international law. . . .

To be sure, courts should hesitate to give penal statutes extraterritorial effect absent a clear congressional directive. . . . Similarly, courts will not blind themselves to potential violations of international law where legislative intent is ambiguous. . . . But the statute in question reflects an unmistakable congressional intent, consistent with treaty obligations of the United States, to authorize prosecution of those who take Americans hostage abroad no matter where the offense occurs or where the offender is found. Our inquiry can go no further. . . .

The Antihijacking Act provides for criminal punishment of persons who hijack aircraft operating wholly outside the "special aircraft jurisdiction" of the United States, provided that the hijacker is later "found in the United States." 49 U.S.C. App. § 1472(n). Flight 402, a Jordanian aircraft operating outside of the United States, was not within this nation's special aircraft jurisdiction. . . . Yunis urges this court to interpret the statutory requirement that persons prosecuted for air piracy must be "found" in the United States as precluding prosecution of alleged hijackers who are brought here to stand trial. But the issue before us is more fact-specific, since Yunis was indicted for air piracy while awaiting trial on hostage-taking and other charges; we must determine whether, once arrested and brought to this country on those other charges, Yunis was subject to prosecution under the Antihijacking Act as well.

The Antihijacking Act of 1974 was enacted to fulfill this nation's responsibilities under the Convention for the Suppression of Unlawful Seizure of Aircraft (the "Hague Convention"), which requires signatory nations to extradite or punish hijackers "present in" their territory. . . . This suggests that Congress intended the statutory term "found in the United States" to parallel the Hague Convention's "present in [a contracting state's] territory," a phrase which does not indicate the voluntariness limitation urged by Yunis. Moreover, Congress interpreted the Hague Convention as requiring the United States to extradite or prosecute "offenders in its custody," evidencing no concern as to how alleged hijackers came within U.S. territory. . . . From this legislative history we conclude that Yunis was properly indicted under section 1472(n) once in the United States and under arrest on other charges.

The district court correctly found that international law does not restrict this statutory jurisdiction to try Yunis on charges of air piracy. . . . Aircraft hijacking may well be one of the few crimes so clearly condemned under the law of nations that states may assert universal jurisdiction to bring offenders to justice, even when the state has no territorial connection to the hijacking and its citizens are not involved. . . . But in any event we are satisfied that the Antihijacking Act authorizes assertion of federal jurisdiction to try Yunis regardless of hijacking's status vel non as a universal crime. Thus, we affirm the district court on this issue. . . .

NOTES AND QUESTIONS

(1) Does *Yunis* really rely on the universality principle? Is there a proper basis in the United States Constitution to proceed against Yunis? *See* Andreas F. Lowenfeld, *U.S. Law Enforcement Abroad: The Constitution and International Law*, 83 AM. J. INT'L 880 (1989). Was the method used by the FBI

in arresting Yunis proper? *Id. see also* Abraham Abramovsky, *Extraterritorial Jurisdiction: The United States Unwarranted Attempt to Alter International Law in* United States v. Yunis, 15 YALE J. INT'L. L. 121 (1990).

(2) As to what crimes does international law permit the exercise of universal jurisdiction? To what extent should the United States rely on the universality principle to assert jurisdiction over war crimes and crimes against humanity committed by non-nationals abroad? *See* Kenneth C. Randall, *Universal Jurisdiction Under International Law*, 66 TEX. L. REV. 785 (1988). These questions will recur in connection with our discussion of the national prosecution of "international offenses" in subsequent chapters. *See* especially chaps. 9, 11, 17, 18.

§ 2.04 Limitations to Jurisdiction to Prescribe

THE RESTATEMENT (THIRD) OF THE FOREIGN RELATIONS LAW OF THE UNITED STATES (1986)

§ 402   BASES OF JURISDICTION TO PRESCRIBE

Subject to § 403, a state has jurisdiction to prescribe law with respect to

(1) (a) conduct that, wholly or in substantial part, takes place within its territory;

(b) the status of persons, or interests in things, present within its territory;

(c) conduct outside its territory that has or is intended to have substantial effect within its territory;

(2) the activities, interests, status, or relations of its nationals outside as well as within its territory; and

(3) certain conduct outside its territory by persons not its nationals that is directed against the security of the state or against a limited class of other state interests.

§ 403   LIMITATIONS ON JURISDICTION TO PRESCRIBE

(1) Even when one of the bases for jurisdiction under § 402 is present, a state may not exercise jurisdiction to prescribe law with respect to a person or activity having connections with another state when the exercise of such jurisdiction is unreasonable.

(2) Whether exercise of jurisdiction over a person or activity is unreasonable is determined by evaluating all relevant factors, including, where appropriate:

(a) the link of the activity to the territory of the regulating state, *i.e.*, the extent to which the activity takes place within the territory, or has substantial, direct, and foreseeable effect upon or in the territory;

(b) the connections, such as nationality, residence, or economic activity, between the regulating state and the person principally responsible for the activity to be regulated, or between that state and those whom the regulation is designed to protect;

(c) the character of the activity to be regulated, the importance of regulation to the regulating state, the extent to which other states regulate such activities, and the degree to which the desirability of such regulation is generally accepted;

(d) the existence of justified expectations that might be protected or hurt by the regulation;

(e) the importance of the regulation to the international political, legal, or economic system;

(f) the extent to which the regulation is consistent with the traditions of the international system;

(g) the extent to which another state may have an interest in regulating the activity; and

(h) the likelihood of conflict with regulation by another state.

(3) When it would not be unreasonable for each of two states to exercise jurisdiction over a person or activity, but the prescriptions by the two states are in conflict, each state has an obligation to evaluate its own as well as the other state's interest in exercising jurisdiction, in light of all the relevant factors, Subsection (2); a state should defer to the other state if that state's interest is clearly greater.

§ 404 UNIVERSAL JURISDICTION TO DEFINE AND PUNISH CERTAIN OFFENSES

A state has jurisdiction to define and prescribe punishment for certain offenses recognized by the community of nations as of universal concern, such as piracy, slave trade, attacks on or hijacking of aircraft, genocide, war crimes, and perhaps certain acts of terrorism, even where none of the bases of jurisdiction indicated in § 402 is present.

NOTES AND QUESTIONS

(1) When might the exercise of jurisdiction be considered unreasonable? In *In re Grand Jury Proceedings (Marsoner)*, 40 F.3d 959 (9th Cir. 1994), the court stated:

. . . In the past, courts have used section 40 of the Restatement (Second) of Foreign Relations Law (1965) to evaluate whether international comity precludes enforcement of an order compelling a witness to sign a consent authorizing disclosure of foreign bank records. . . . Section 40 of the Restatement has been revised and is now encompassed within section 403 of the Restatement (Third). Under the revised Restatement, reasonableness is "an essential element in determining whether, as a matter of international law, the state may exercise jurisdiction to prescribe." Restatement (Third) of Foreign Relations Law § 403 reporter's note 10 (1987).

Applying these factors to the situation presented here, we hold that international comity does not preclude enforcement of the district court's order. Marsoner is suspected of using his Austrian bank accounts to evade taxes in the United States. The grand jury seeks Austrian bank information in an effort to link Marsoner to alleged illegal activities that occurred in the United States between 1989 and 1991. Although Marsoner is an Austrian citizen, he a United States resident and his economic activity, which includes tax liabilities, involves the United States. The United States has a strong interest in collecting taxes, ... and in prosecuting individuals for tax evasion, . . .

In *United States v. MacAllister*, 160 F.3d 1304 (11th Cir. 1998), the court stated:

Macallister asserts that extraterritorial application of § 963 is unreasonable based on the principles set forth in § 403(2) of the Restatement (Third) of the Foreign Relations Law of the United States. We conclude otherwise. "[D]rug smuggling is a serious and universally condemned offense," and therefore, "no conflict is likely to be created by extraterritorial regulation of drug traffickers."

(2) How does the United States determine what will be considered unreasonable in international criminal law. Comment (a) to section 403 makes the following observation:

a. Reasonableness in international law and practice. The principle that an exercise of jurisdiction on one of the bases indicated in § 402 is nonetheless unlawful if it is unreasonable is established in United States law, and has emerged as a principle of international law as well. There is wide international consensus that the links of territoriality or nationality, § 402, while generally necessary, are not in all instances sufficient conditions for the exercise of such jurisdiction. Legislatures and administrative agencies, in the United States and in other states, have generally refrained from exercising jurisdiction where it would be unreasonable to do so, and courts have usually interpreted general language in a statute as not intended to exercise or authorize the exercise of jurisdiction in circumstances where application of the statute would be unreasonable.

Some United States courts have applied the principle of reasonableness as a requirement of comity, that term being understood not merely as an act of discretion and courtesy but as reflecting a sense of obligation among states. This section states the principle of reasonableness as a rule of international law. The principle applies regardless of the status of relations between the state exercising jurisdiction and another state whose interests may be affected. While the term "comity" is sometimes understood to include a requirement of reciprocity, the rule of this section is not conditional on a finding that the state affected by a regulation would exercise or limit its jurisdiction in the same circumstances to the same extent. Some elements of reciprocity may be relevant in considering the factors listed in Subsection (2). . . .

§ 2.05 New Approaches

Can jurisdiction be examined from other perspectives? Consider the approach to jurisdiction in terms of theories of punishment suggested in a report of the Committee on International Terrorism of the American Branch of the International Law Association:

> Debate in terms of the propriety of abstract "principles of jurisdiction" is likely to lead to a dead-end. THE RESTATEMENT (THIRD) OF FOREIGN RELATIONS LAW has tried to rephrase the debate in terms of whether it is unreasonable to exercise jurisdiction over a particular person or activity. But by what criteria should reasonableness be gauged? Prevailing fashion seeks to derive criteria of accommodation or priority from an analysis of relevant "state interests." Yet the usual mode of analysis tends to overlook "the criminological aspects of the problem" – the need to justify its extraterritorial applications in terms of the same purposes or "theories of punishment" (retribution, deterrence, etc.) that are used to justify criminal law generally. Fitzgerald, *The Territorial Principle in Penal Law: An Attempted Justification*, 1 GA. J. INT'L & COMP. L. 29 (1970).
>
> It may be fruitful to reexamine questions of extraterritorial jurisdiction in terms of criminal law theory and the "boundary assumptions" implicit in particular "theories of punishment." Lea Brilmayer has recently proposed generally considering all government coercion across borders in terms of the political theories that are supposed to justify a state's monopoly of legitimate violence within its borders. L. BRILMAYER, JUSTIFYING INTERNATIONAL ACTS (1989). "Theories of punishment" are,

in a way, a special kind of political theory serving to justify and explain why it makes sense for government to use criminal law to exercise coercion against individuals. At least when extraterritorial coercion takes the form of prosecution in an ordinary domestic court, it seems obviously pertinent to ask whether it can be justified in terms of the purposes which criminal law generally is supposed to subserve.

Suppose debate over the legitimacy of extraterritorial jurisdiction were recast in these terms. The idea of deterrence provides one superficially easy answer: punishing those who injure a state or its nationals will serve to discourage others from perpetrating like injuries in the future. But this ignores the "boundary assumptions" implicit in any well-developed theory of deterrence. An adequate theory of deterrence has to cope with the Kantian objection that we are never justified in using one individual solely as a means to influence the conduct of others. The individual has to have done something to invite punishment; and that something usually reduces to a breach of the ground rules tacitly accepted by members of a particular community. Where the offender is not a member of the community inflicting punishment, the ultimate basis for punishment is not the same as it is in a purely domestic context. . . .

An alternate line of argument extends the relevant community to include all humanity. . . .

This line of argument gives rise to a nest of questions. How far does it depend on recent treaties dealing with particular aspects of terrorism that permit a state to exercise jurisdiction over an offender found in its territory? What is the actual language in these treaties that is supposed to authorize the exercise of universal jurisdiction? Can such provisions confer jurisdiction over nationals of non-ratifying states? Does it make a difference if the offense occurred in the territory of a party? To what extent can such provisions be said to have created or to have become customary law? To what extent is the argument for universal jurisdiction independent of existing treaties? What precisely is there in state practice to support assertions of universal jurisdiction as a matter of customary law? How far does it really make sense to say that jurisdiction asserted by a self-appointed police force has been exercised on behalf of the international community? Does the international community sufficiently resemble a national community so as to permit enlarging the "boundary assumptions" implicit in particular "theories of punishment" to embrace the entire world?

Report of the Committee on International Terrorism, in PROCEEDINGS AND COMMITTEE REPORTS OF THE AMERICAN BRANCH OF THE INTERNATIONAL LAW ASSOCIATION 1989-1990, at 86, 92-94.

Part 2
SPECIFIC APPLICATIONS

Chapter 3
FOREIGN CORRUPT PRACTICES ACT

§3.01 Introduction

[A] Overview of Act

The Foreign Corrupt Practices Act (FCPA) was passed in 1977 with the purpose of criminalizing conduct relating to the bribing of foreign government officials. In 1988 there were amendments to the Act which "changed the focus of illegality from the status of the recipient to the purpose or nature of the payment." DONALD R. CRUVER, COMPLYING WITH THE FOREIGN CORRUPT PRACTICES ACT 16 (1994). The International Anti-Bribery and Fair Competition Act of 1998 again revisited this Act. Discussing the need for the initial legislation, as well as the recent modifications, House Report 105-802 states:

> Investigations by the Securities and Exchange Commission (SEC) in the mid-1970s revealed that over 400 U.S. companies admitted making questionable or illegal payments in excess of $300 million to foreign government officials, politicians, and political parties. Many public companies maintained cash "slush funds" from which illegal campaign contributions were being made in the United States and illegal bribes were being paid to foreign officials. Scandals involving payments by U.S. companies to public officials in Japan, Italy, and Mexico led to political repercussions within those countries and damaged the reputation of American companies throughout the world.

> In the wake of these disclosures, Congress enacted the Foreign Corrupt Practices Act of 1977 (the FCPA). . . . The FCPA amended the Securities Exchange Act of 1934, 15 U.S.C. § 78 et seq., to require issuers of publicly traded securities to institute adequate accounting controls and to maintain accurate books and records. Civil and criminal penalties were enacted for the failure to do so. In addition, the FCPA required both issuers and all other U.S. nationals or residents, as well as U.S. business entities and foreign entities with their primary place of business in the United States (defined as "domestic concerns") to refrain from making any unlawful payments to public officials, political parties, party officials, or candidates for public office, directly or through others, for the purpose of causing that person to make a decision or take an

action, or refrain from taking an action, for the purpose of obtaining or retaining business.

Since the passage of the FCPA, American businesses have operated at a disadvantage relative to foreign competitors who have continued to pay bribes without fear of penalty. . . . Such bribery is estimated to affect international contracts valued in the billions of dollars each year. Some of our trading partners have explicitly encouraged and subsidized such bribes by permitting businesses to claim them as tax-deductible business expenses.

Beginning in 1989, the U.S. government began an effort to convince our trading partners at the OECD to criminalize the bribery of foreign public officials. Achieving comparable prohibitions in other developed countries and combating corruption generally has been a major priority of the U.S. business community, the U.S. Congress, and successive Administrations since the late 1970s.

International bribery and corruption continue to be problems worldwide. They undermine the goals of fostering economic development, trade liberalization, and achieving a level playing field throughout the world for businesses. It is impossible to calculate with certainty the losses suffered by U.S. businesses due to bribery by foreign competitors. The Commerce Department has stated that it has learned of significant allegations of bribery by foreign firms in approximately 240 international commercial contracts since mid-1994 valued at nearly $108 billion. This legislation, coupled with implementation of the OECD Convention by our major trading partners, is designed to result in a substantial leveling of the playing field for U.S. businesses. . . .

Fortunately, in the 1990s the international community has made a concerted effort in the fight against corruption. Gradually, as awareness of the effects of transnational bribery became more apparent, progress was made in efforts to combat bribery overseas. After almost four years of substantial work in the OECD's Working Group on Bribery, on May 27, 1994, the OECD Council approved a Recommendation on Bribery in International Business Transactions (the Recommendation). The 29 OECD member states agreed that bribery distorts international competitive conditions; that all countries share a responsibility to combat bribery in international business transactions, however their nationals may be involved; and that further action is needed on the national and international level. Member states agreed to "take concrete and meaningful steps" to meet the goal of deterring, preventing, and combating bribery of foreign officials. However, the Recommendation did not require each member state to criminalize the bribery of officials of another country.

These efforts ultimately culminated in the signing of the Organization for Economic Cooperation and Development Convention on Combating

Bribery of Foreign Public Officials in International Business Transactions (the OECD Convention). Thirty-three countries, composed of most of the world's largest trading nations, signed the OECD Convention on December 17, 1997. For twenty years after the passage of the Foreign Corrupt Practices Act, the United States was virtually alone in criminalizing foreign bribery. Now, thirty-four other countries have taken a step in this direction. Twenty-eight of the twenty-nine OECD member countries along with five other countries, Argentina, Bulgaria, Brazil, Chile, and the Slovak Republic, signed the OECD Convention. . . .

Under the OECD Convention: The U.S. and its trading partners agreed to criminalize bribery of foreign public officials, including officials in all branches of government, and to criminalize payments to officials of public agencies and public international organizations; The OECD Convention also calls for criminal penalties for those who bribe foreign public officials. If a nation's legal system lacks the concept of corporate criminal liability, the nation must provide for equivalent non-criminal sanctions, such as fines; Parties to the agreement pledged to work to provide legal assistance in investigations and proceedings within the scope of the OECD Convention and to make bribery of foreign public officials an extraditable offense; and The OECD Convention requires the Parties to cooperate in an OECD follow-up program to monitor and promote full implementation. . . .

NOTES AND QUESTIONS

(1) Do bans on extraterritorial anti-bribery place United States corporations at a disadvantage in competing in the global market? Should the United States use "persuasion" or "coercion" in promoting anti-corruption laws? *See* Steven R. Salbu, Colloquy, *Are Extraterritorial Restrictions on Bribery a Viable and Desirable International Policy Goal Under the Global Conditions of the Late Twentieth Century?*, 24 YALE J. INT'L L. 223 (1999) ("global attitudes about what comprises bribery are so varied that extraterritorial application of anti-corruption laws creates two kinds of perils: a moral peril and a political peril").

(2) On November 18, 1998, President Clinton signed into law the International Anti-Bribery and Fair Competition Act of 1998. At the time of the signing he stated that the Act "makes certain changes in existing law to implement the Convention on Combating Bribery of Foreign Public Officials in International Business Transactions which was negotiated under the auspices of the Organization for Economic Cooperation and Development (OECD). The United States continues to press signatories to take action within their countries to implement the Convention. *See Effort to Implement OECD Anti-Corruption Convention Continues*, 16 INT. ENFORCEMENT L. RPTR. 753 (2000).

(3) The Department of Justice assists companies and nationals in complying with the FCPA through a Foreign Corrupt Practices Act Opinion Procedures. *See* 28 C.F.R. Part 80. "Under this procedure, the Attorney General will issue an opinion in response to a specific inquiry from a person or firm within thirty days of the request. . . . Conduct for which the Department of Justice has issued an opinion stating that the conduct conforms with current enforcement policy will be entitled to a presumption, in any subsequent enforcement action, of conformity with the FCPA." *Foreign Corrupt Practice Act – DOJ Brochure*, <http://www/usdoj.gov/criminal/fraud/fcpa/dojdocb.htm>.

[B] Key Statutory Provisions

§ 78dd-1. Prohibited foreign trade practices by issuers

(a) Prohibition. It shall be unlawful for any issuer which has a class of securities registered pursuant to section 12 of this title [15 U.S.C. § 78l] or which is required to file reports under section 15(d) of this title [15 U.S.C. § 78o(d)], or for any officer, director, employee, or agent of such issuer or any stockholder thereof acting on behalf of such issuer, to make use of the mails or any means or instrumentality of interstate commerce corruptly in furtherance of an offer, payment, promise to pay, or authorization of the payment of any money, or offer, gift, promise to give, or authorization of the giving of anything of value to–

(1) any foreign official for purposes of–

(A)(i) influencing any act or decision of such foreign official in his official capacity, (ii) inducing such foreign official to do or omit to do any act in violation of the lawful duty of such official, or (iii) securing any improper advantage; or

(B) inducing such foreign official to use his influence with a foreign government or instrumentality thereof to affect or influence any act or decision of such government or instrumentality, in order to assist such issuer in obtaining or retaining business for or with, or directing business to, any person;

(2) any foreign political party or official thereof or any candidate for foreign political office for purposes of–

(A)(i) influencing any act or decision of such party, official, or candidate in its or his official capacity, (ii) inducing such party, official, or candidate to do or omit to do an act in violation of the lawful duty of such party, official, or candidate, or (iii) securing any improper advantage; or

(B) inducing such party, official, or candidate to use its or his influence with a foreign government or instrumentality thereof to affect or influence any act or decision of such government or instrumentality, in order to assist such issuer in obtaining or retaining business for or with, or directing business to, any person; or

(3) any person, while knowing that all or a portion of such money or thing of value will be offered, given, or promised, directly or indirectly, to any foreign official, to any foreign political party or official thereof, or to any candidate for foreign political office, for purposes of–

(A)(i) influencing any act or decision of such foreign official, political party, party official, or candidate in his or its official capacity, (ii) inducing such foreign official, political party, party official, or candidate to do or omit to do any act in violation of the lawful duty of such foreign official, political party, party official, or candidate, or (iii) securing any improper advantage; or

(B) inducing such foreign official, political party, party official, or candidate to use his or its influence with a foreign government or instrumentality thereof to affect or influence any act or decision of such government or instrumentality,

in order to assist such issuer in obtaining or retaining business for or with, or directing business to, any person.

(b) Exception for routine governmental action. Subsections (a) and (g) shall not apply to any facilitating or expediting payment to a foreign official, political party, or party official the purpose of which is to expedite or to secure the performance of a routine governmental action by a foreign official, political party, or party official.

(c) Affirmative defenses. It shall be an affirmative defense to actions under subsection (a) or (g) that–

(1) the payment, gift, offer, or promise of anything of value that was made, was lawful under the written laws and regulations of the foreign official's, political party's, party official's, or candidate's country; or

(2) the payment, gift, offer, or promise of anything of value that was made, was a reasonable and bona fide expenditure, such as travel and lodging expenses, incurred by or on behalf of a foreign official, party, party official, or candidate and was directly related to–

(A) the promotion, demonstration, or explanation of products or services; or

(B) the execution or performance of a contract with a foreign government or agency thereof.

(d) Guidelines by the Attorney General. . . .

(e) Opinions of the Attorney General. . . .

(f) Definitions. For purposes of this section:

(1) (A)The term "foreign official" means any officer or employee of a foreign government or any department, agency, or instrumentality thereof, or of a public international organization, or any person acting in an official capacity for or on behalf of any such government or department, agency, or instrumentality, or for or on behalf of any such public international organization.

(B) For purposes of subparagraph (A), the term "public international organization" means–

(i)an organization that is designated by Executive order pursuant to section 1 of the International Organizations Immunities Act (22 U.S.C. 288); or

(ii) any other international organization that is designated by the President by Executive order for the purposes of this section, effective as of the date of publication of such order in the Federal Register.

(2)(A) A person's state of mind is "knowing" with respect to conduct, a circumstance, or a result if–

(i) such person is aware that such person is engaging in such conduct, that such circumstance exists, or that such result is substantially certain to occur; or

(ii) such person has a firm belief that such circumstance exists or that such result is substantially certain to occur.

(B) When knowledge of the existence of a particular circumstance is required for an offense, such knowledge is established if a person is aware of a high probability of the existence of such circumstance, unless the person actually believes that such circumstance does not exist.

(3)(A) The term "routine governmental action" means only an action which is ordinarily and commonly performed by a foreign official in–

(i) obtaining permits, licenses, or other official documents to qualify a person to do business in a foreign country;

(ii) processing governmental papers, such as visas and work orders;

(iii) providing police protection, mail pick-up and delivery, or scheduling inspections associated with contract performance or inspections related to transit of goods across country;

(iv) providing phone service, power and water supply, loading and unloading cargo, or protecting perishable products or commodities from deterioration; or

(v) actions of a similar nature.

(B) The term "routine governmental action" does not include any decision by a foreign official whether, or on what terms, to award new business to or to continue business with a particular party, or any action taken by a foreign official involved in the decisionmaking process to encourage a decision to award new business to or continue business with a particular party.

(g) Alternative jurisdiction. . . .

---

§ 78dd-2. Prohibited foreign trade practices by domestic concerns

(a) Prohibition. It shall be unlawful for any domestic concern, other than an issuer which is subject to section 30A of the Securities Exchange Act of 1934 [15 U.S.C. § 78dd-1], or for any officer, director, employee, or agent of such domestic concern or any stockholder thereof acting on behalf of such domestic concern, to make use of the mails or any means or instrumentality of interstate commerce corruptly in furtherance of an offer, payment, promise to pay, or authorization of the payment of any money, or offer, gift, promise to give, or authorization of the giving of anything of value to—

(1) any foreign official for purposes of—

(A)(i) influencing any act or decision of such foreign official in his official capacity, (ii) inducing such foreign official to do or omit to do any act in violation of the lawful duty of such official, or (iii) securing any improper advantage; or

(B) inducing such foreign official to use his influence with a foreign government or instrumentality thereof to affect or influence any act or decision of such government or instrumentality,

in order to assist such domestic concern in obtaining or retaining business for or with, or directing business to, any person;

(2) any foreign political party or official thereof or any candidate for foreign political office for purposes of—

(A)(i) influencing any act or decision of such party, official, or candidate in its or his official capacity, (ii) inducing such party, official, or candidate to do or omit to do an act in violation of the lawful duty of such party, official, or candidate, or (iii) securing any improper advantage; or

(B) inducing such party, official, or candidate to use its or his influence with a foreign government or instrumentality thereof to affect or influence any act or decision of such government or instrumentality,

in order to assist such domestic concern in obtaining or retaining business for or with, or directing business to, any person; or

(3) any person, while knowing that all or a portion of such money or thing of value will be offered, given, or promised, directly or indirectly, to any foreign official, to any foreign political party or official thereof, or to any candidate for foreign political office, for purposes of–

(A)(i) influencing any act or decision of such foreign official, political party, party official, or candidate in his or its official capacity, (ii) inducing such foreign official, political party, party official, or candidate to do or omit to do any act in violation of the lawful duty of such foreign official, political party, party official, or candidate, or (iii) securing any improper advantage; or

(B) inducing such foreign official, political party, party official, or candidate to use his or its influence with a foreign government or instrumentality thereof to affect or influence any act or decision of such government or instrumentality,

in order to assist such domestic concern in obtaining or retaining business for or with, or directing business to, any person.

(b) Exception for routine governmental action. Subsections (a) and (i) shall not apply to any facilitating or expediting payment to a foreign official, political party, or party official the purpose of which is to expedite or to secure the performance of a routine governmental action by a foreign official, political party, or party official.

(c) Affirmative defenses. It shall be an affirmative defense to actions under subsection (a) or (i) that–

(1) the payment, gift, offer, or promise of anything of value that was made, was lawful under the written laws and regulations of the foreign official's, political party's, party official's, or candidate's country; or

(2) the payment, gift, offer, or promise of anything of value that was made, was a reasonable and bona fide expenditure, such as travel and lodging expenses, incurred by or on behalf of a foreign official, party, party official, or candidate and was directly related to–

(A) the promotion, demonstration, or explanation of products or services; or

(B) the execution or performance of a contract with a foreign government or agency thereof.

(d) Injunctive relief. . . .

(e) Guidelines by the Attorney General. . . .

(f) Opinions of the Attorney General. . . .

(g) Penalties . . . .

(h) Definitions. For purposes of this section:

(1) The term "domestic concern" means–

(A) any individual who is a citizen, national, or resident of the United States; and

(B) any corporation, partnership, association, joint-stock company, business trust, unincorporated organization, or sole proprietorship which has its principal place of business in the United States, or which is organized under the laws of a State of the United States or a territory, possession, or commonwealth of the United States.

(2)(A) The term "foreign official" means any officer or employee of a foreign government or any department, agency, or instrumentality thereof, or of a public international organization, or any person acting in an official capacity for or on behalf of any such government or department, agency, or instrumentality, or for or on behalf of any such public international organization.

(B) For purposes of subparagraph (A), the term "public international organization" means–

(i) an organization that is designated by Executive order pursuant to section 1 of the International Organizations Immunities Act (22 U.S.C. 288); or

(ii) any other international organization that is designated by the President by Executive order for the purposes of this section, effective as of the date of publication of such order in the Federal Register.

(3)(A) A person's state of mind is "knowing" with respect to conduct, a circumstance, or a result if–

(i) such person is aware that such person is engaging in such conduct, that such circumstance exists, or that such result is substantially certain to occur; or

(ii) such person has a firm belief that such circumstance exists or that such result is substantially certain to occur.

(B) When knowledge of the existence of a particular circumstance is required for an offense, such knowledge is established if a person is aware of a high probability of the existence of such circumstance, unless the person actually believes that such circumstance does not exist.

(4)(A) The term "routine governmental action" means only an action which is ordinarily and commonly performed by a foreign official in–

(i) obtaining permits, licenses, or other official documents to qualify a person to do business in a foreign country;

(ii) processing governmental papers, such as visas and work orders;

(iii) providing police protection, mail pick-up and delivery, or scheduling inspections associated with contract performance or inspections related to transit of goods across country;

(iv) providing phone service, power and water supply, loading and unloading cargo, or protecting perishable products or commodities from deterioration; or

(v) actions of a similar nature.

(B) The term "routine governmental action" does not include any decision by a foreign official whether, or on what terms, to award new business to or to continue business with a particular party, or any action taken by a foreign official involved in the decision-making process to encourage a decision to award new business to or continue business with a particular party.

(5) The term "interstate commerce" means trade, commerce, transportation, or communication among the several States, or between any foreign country and any State or between any State and any place or ship outside thereof, and such term includes the intrastate use of–

(A) a telephone or other interstate means of communication, or

(B) any other interstate instrumentality.

(i) Alternative jurisdiction. . . .

---

§ 78dd-3. Prohibited foreign trade practices by persons other than issuers or domestic concerns[*]

(a) Prohibition. It shall be unlawful for any person other than an issuer that is subject to section 30A of the Securities Exchange Act of 1934 [15 USCS § 78dd-1] or a domestic concern (as defined in section 104 of this Act [15 USCS § 78dd-2]), or for any officer, director, employee, or agent of such person or any stockholder thereof acting on behalf of such person, while in the territory of the United States, corruptly to make use of the mails or any means or instrumentality of interstate commerce or to do any other act in furtherance of an offer, payment, promise to pay, or authorization of the payment of any money, or offer, gift, promise to give, or authorization of the giving of anything of value to–

---

[*] Originally the FCPA limited prosecutions of employees when the government first convicted the employer. *See* United States v. McClain, 738 F.2d 655 (5th Cir. 1984).

(1) any foreign official for purposes of–

(A)(i) influencing any act or decision of such foreign official in his official capacity, (ii) inducing such foreign official to do or omit to do any act in violation of the lawful duty of such official, or (iii) securing any improper advantage; or

(B) inducing such foreign official to use his influence with a foreign government or instrumentality thereof to affect or influence any act or decision of such government or instrumentality,

in order to assist such person in obtaining or retaining business for or with, or directing business to, any person;

(2) any foreign political party or official thereof or any candidate for foreign political office for purposes of–

(A)(i) influencing any act or decision of such party, official, or candidate in its or his official capacity, (ii) inducing such party, official, or candidate to do or omit to do an act in violation of the lawful duty of such party, official, or candidate, or (iii) securing any improper advantage; or

(B) inducing such party, official, or candidate to use its or his influence with a foreign government or instrumentality thereof to affect or influence any act or decision of such government or instrumentality,

in order to assist such person in obtaining or retaining business for or with, or directing business to, any person; or

(3) any person, while knowing that all or a portion of such money or thing of value will be offered, given, or promised, directly or indirectly, to any foreign official, to any foreign political party or official thereof, or to any candidate for foreign political office, for purposes of–

(A)(i) influencing any act or decision of such foreign official, political party, party official, or candidate in his or its official capacity, (ii) inducing such foreign official, political party, party official, or candidate to do or omit to do any act in violation of the lawful duty of such foreign official, political party, party official, or candidate, or (iii) securing any improper advantage; or

(B) inducing such foreign official, political party, party official, or candidate to use his or its influence with a foreign government or instrumentality thereof to affect or influence any act or decision of such government or instrumentality,

in order to assist such person in obtaining or retaining business for or with, or directing business to, any person.

(b) Exception for routine governmental action. Subsection (a) of this section shall not apply to any facilitating or expediting payment to a foreign official, political party, or party official the purpose of which is to expedite or to secure the performance of a routine governmental action by a foreign official, political party, or party official.

(c) Affirmative defenses. It shall be an affirmative defense to actions under subsection (a) of this section that–

(1) payment, gift, offer, or promise of anything of value that was made, was lawful under the written laws and regulations of the foreign official's, political party's, party official's, or candidate's country; or

(2) the payment, gift, offer, or promise of anything of value that was made, was a reasonable and bona fide expenditure, such as travel and lodging expenses, incurred by or on behalf of a foreign official, party, party official, or candidate and was directly related to–

(A) the promotion, demonstration, or explanation of products or services; or

(B) the execution or performance of a contract with a foreign government or agency thereof.

(d) Injunctive relief. . . .

(e) Penalties

(1)(A) Any juridical person that violates subsection (a) of this section shall be fined not more than $ 2,000,000.

(B) Any juridical person that violates subsection (a) of this section shall be subject to a civil penalty of not more than $ 10,000 imposed in an action brought by the Attorney General.

(2)(A) Any natural person who willfully violates subsection (a) of this section shall be fined not more than $ 100,000 or imprisoned not more than 5 years, or both.

(B) Any natural person who violates subsection (a) of this section shall be subject to a civil penalty of not more than $ 10,000 imposed in an action brought by the Attorney General.

(3) Whenever a fine is imposed under paragraph (2) upon any officer, director, employee, agent, or stockholder of a person, such fine may not be paid, directly or indirectly, by such person.

(f) Definitions. For purposes of this section:

(1) The term "person", when referring to an offender, means any natural person other than a national of the United States (as defined in section 101 of the Immigration and Nationality Act (8 U.S.C. 1101) or any corporation,

partnership, association, joint-stock company, business trust, unincorporated organization, or sole proprietorship organized under the law of a foreign nation or a political subdivision thereof.

(2)(A) The term "foreign official" means any officer or employee of a foreign government or any department, agency, or instrumentality thereof, or of a public international organization, or any person acting in an official capacity for or on behalf of any such government or department, agency, or instrumentality, or for or on behalf of any such public international organization.

(B) For purposes of subparagraph (A), the term "public international organization" means–

(i) organization that is designated by Executive order pursuant to section 1 of the International Organizations Immunities Act (22 U.S.C. 288); or

(ii) any other international organization that is designated by the President by Executive order for the purposes of this section, effective as of the date of publication of such order in the Federal Register. . . .

§ 78ff. Penalties

(a) Willful violations; false and misleading statements. Any person who willfully violates any provision of this title (other than section 30A [15 U.S.C. § 78dd-1]), or any rule or regulation thereunder the violation of which is made unlawful or the observance of which is required under the terms of this title, or any person who willfully and knowingly makes, or causes to be made, any statement in any application, report, or document required to be filed under this title or any rule or regulation thereunder or any undertaking contained in a registration statement as provided in subsection (d) of section 15 of this title [15 U.S.C. § 78o(d)], or by any self-regulatory organization in connection with an application for membership or participation therein or to become associated with a member thereof, which statement was false or misleading with respect to any material fact, shall upon conviction be fined not more than $ 1,000,000, or imprisoned not more than 10 years, or both, except that when such person is a person other than a natural person, a fine not exceeding $ 2,500,000 may be imposed; but no person shall be subject to imprisonment under this section for the violation of any rule or regulation if he proves that he had no knowledge of such rule or regulation.

(b) Failure to file information, documents, or reports. Any issuer which fails to file information, documents, or reports required to be filed under subsection (d) of section 15 of this title [15 U.S.C. § 78o(d)] or any rule or regulation thereunder shall forfeit to the United States the sum of $ 100 for each and every day such failure to file shall continue. Such forfeiture, which shall be in lieu of any criminal penalty for such failure to file which might be deemed to arise under subsection (a) of this section, shall be payable to the Treasury of the United States and shall be recoverable in a civil suit in the name of the United States.

(c) Violations by issuers, officers, directors, stockholders, employees, or agents of issuers.

(1) (A) Any issuer that violates subsection (a) or (g) of section 30A [15 U.S.C. § 78dd-1] shall be fined not more than $ 2,000,000.

(B) Any issuer that violates subsection (a) or (g) of section 30A [15 U.S.C. § 78dd-1] shall be subject to a civil penalty of not more than $ 10,000 imposed in an action brought by the Commission.

(2) (A) Any officer, director, employee, or agent of an issuer, or stockholder acting on behalf of such issuer, who willfully violates subsection (a) or (g) of section 30A of this title [15 U.S.C. § 78dd-1] shall be fined not more than $ 100,000, or imprisoned not more than 5 years, or both.

(B) Any officer, director, employee, or agent of an issuer, or stockholder acting on behalf of such issuer, who violates subsection (a) or (g) of section 30A of this title [15 U.S.C. § 78dd-1] shall be subject to a civil penalty of not more than $ 10,000 imposed in an action brought by the Commission.

(3) Whenever a fine is imposed under paragraph (2) upon any officer, director, employee, agent, or stockholder of an issuer, such fine may not be paid, directly or indirectly, by such issuer.

§ 3.02 Scope of the FCPA

[A] Individuals Liable

UNITED STATES v. CASTLE

United States Court of Appeals for the Fifth Circuit
925 F.2d 831 (1991)

PER CURIAM:

In this case, we are called upon to consider the Foreign Corrupt Practices Act of 1977 (hereinafter "FCPA"), 15 U.S.C. §§ 78dd-1, 78dd-2, and determine whether "foreign officials," who are excluded from prosecution under the FCPA itself, may nevertheless be prosecuted under the general conspiracy statute, 18 U.S.C. § 371, for conspiring to violate the FCPA.

We hold that foreign officials may not be prosecuted under 18 U.S.C. § 371 for conspiring to violate the FCPA. The scope of our holding, as well as the rationale that undergirds it, is fully set out in Judge Sanders's memorandum opinion of June 4,1990, 741 F. Supp. 116, which we adopt and attach as an appendix hereto. . . .

APPENDIX

. . . . Defendants Castle and Lowry have moved to dismiss the indictment against them on the grounds that as Canadian officials, they cannot be convicted of the offense charged against them. The two other defendants, Blondek and Tull, are U.S. private citizens, and they do not challenge their indictment on this ground. . . .

The indictment charges all four defendants with conspiring to bribe foreign officials in violation of the FCPA. Blondek and Tull were employees of Eagle Bus Company, a U.S. concern as defined in the FCPA. According to the indictment, they paid a $ 50,000 bribe to Defendants Castle and Lowry to ensure that their bid to provide buses to the Saskatchewan provincial government would be accepted.

There is no question that the payment of the bribe by Defendants Blondek and Tull is illegal under the FCPA, and that they may be prosecuted for conspiring to violate the Act. Nor is it disputed that Defendants Castle and Lowry could not be charged with violating the FCPA itself, since the Act does not criminalize the receipt of a bribe by a foreign official. The issue here is whether the Government may prosecute Castle and Lowry under the general conspiracy statute, 18 U.S.C. § 371, for conspiring to violate the FCPA. Put more simply, the question is whether foreign officials, whom the Government concedes it cannot prosecute under the FCPA itself, may be prosecuted under the general conspiracy statute for conspiring to violate the Act. . . .

The principle enunciated by the Supreme Court in *Gebardi* [*v. United States*, 287 U.S. 112, 53 S. Ct. 35, 77 L. Ed. 206 (1932)] squarely applies to the case before this Court. Congress intended in both the FCPA and the Mann Act to deter and punish certain activities which necessarily involved the agreement of at least two people, but Congress chose in both statutes to punish only one party to the agreement. In *Gebardi* the Supreme Court refused to disregard Congress' intention to exempt one party by allowing the Executive to prosecute that party under the general conspiracy statute for precisely the same conduct. Congress made the same choice in drafting the FCPA, and by the same analysis, this Court may not allow the Executive to override the Congressional intent not to prosecute foreign officials for their participation in the prohibited acts.

. . . . [T]he exclusive focus was on the U.S. companies and the effects of their conduct within and on the United States.

First, Congress was concerned about the domestic effects of such payments. In the early 1970 's, the Watergate affair and resulting investigations revealed that the payment of bribes to foreign officials was a widespread practice among U.S. companies. In the House Report accompanying an earlier version of the Act, it was noted that more than 400 companies had admitted making such payments, distributing well over 300 million dollars in corporate funds to foreign officials. . . . Such massive payments had many negative domestic effects, not the least of which was the distortion of, and resulting lack of confidence in, the free market system within the United States.

> The payment of bribes to influence the acts or decision of foreign officials . . . is unethical. It is counter to the moral expectations and values of the American public. But not only is it unethical, it is bad business as well. It erodes public confidence in the integrity of the free market system. . . . In short, it rewards corruption instead of efficiency and puts pressure on ethical enterprises to lower their standards or risk losing business.

. . . . The House Committee further noted that many of the payments were made not to compete with foreign companies, but rather to gain an edge over a competitor in the United States.

Congress' second motivation was the effect of such payments by U.S. companies on the United States' foreign relations. The legislative history repeatedly cited the negative effects the revelations of such bribes had wrought upon friendly foreign governments and officials. Yet the drafters acknowledged, and the final law reflects this, that some payments that would be unethical or even illegal within the United States might not be perceived similarly in foreign countries, and those payments should not be criminalized. For example, grease payments, those payments made "to assure or to speed the proper performance of a foreign official's duties," are not illegal under the Act since they were often a part of the custom of doing business in foreign countries. . . . Additionally, the Act was later amended to permit an affirmative defense on the grounds that the payment was legal in the country in which it was made. 15 U.S.C. § 78dd-2(c)(1). These exclusions reinforce the proposition that Congress had absolutely no intention of prosecuting the foreign officials involved, but was concerned solely with regulating the conduct of U.S. entities and citizens.[2]

---

[2] Congress considered, and rejected, the idea that a demand for a payment by a foreign official would be a valid defense to a criminal prosecution under the Act, because

> at some point the U.S. company would make a conscious decision whether or not to pay a bribe. That the payment may have been first proposed by the recipient rather than the U.S. company does not alter the corrupt purpose on the part of the person paying the bribe.

. . . . The very fact that Congress considered this issue underscores Congress' exclusive focus on the U.S. companies in *making* the payment. If the drafters were concerned that a demand by a foreign official might be considered a defense to a prosecution, they clearly were expecting that only the payors of the bribes, and not the foreign officials demanding and/or receiving the bribes, would be prosecuted.

[The Government argued that a statement in a House Report showed congressional intent to allow conspiracy prosecutions of foreign officials.] . . . .

This language [in the House Report] does not refute the overwhelming evidence of a Congressional intent to exempt foreign officials from prosecution for receiving bribes, especially since Congress knew it had the power to reach foreign officials in many cases, and yet declined to exercise that power. . . . (United States has power to reach conduct of noncitizens under international law). Congress' awareness of the extent of its own power reveals the fallacy in the Government's position that only those classes of persons deemed by Congress to need protection are exempted from prosecution under the conspiracy statute. The question is not whether Congress could have included foreign officials within the Act's proscriptions, but rather whether Congress intended to do so, or more specifically, whether Congress intended the general conspiracy statute, passed many years before the FCPA, to reach foreign officials.

The drafters of the statute knew that they could, consistently with international law, reach foreign officials in certain circumstances. But they were equally well aware of, and actively considered, the "inherent jurisdictional, enforcement, and diplomatic difficulties" raised by the application of the bill to non-citizens of the United States. . . . In the conference report, the conferees indicated that the bill would reach as far as possible, and listed all the persons or entities who could be prosecuted. The list includes virtually every person or entity involved, including foreign nationals who participated in the payment of the bribe when the U.S. courts had jurisdiction over them. But foreign officials were not included.

It is important to remember that Congress intended that these persons would be covered by the Act itself, without resort to the conspiracy statute. Yet the very individuals whose participation was required in every case – the foreign officials accepting the bribe – were excluded from prosecution for the substantive offense. Given that Congress included virtually every possible person connected to the payments except foreign officials, it is only logical to conclude that Congress affirmatively chose to exempt this small class of persons from prosecution.

Most likely Congress made this choice because U.S. businesses were perceived to be the aggressors, and the efforts expended in resolving the diplomatic, jurisdictional, and enforcement difficulties that would arise upon the prosecution of foreign officials was not worth the minimal deterrent value of such prosecutions. Further minimizing the deterrent value of a U.S. prosecution was the fact that many foreign nations already prohibited the receipt of a bribe by an official. . . . In fact, whenever a nation permitted such payments, Congress allowed them as well. See 15 U.S.C. § 78dd-2(c)(1).

Based upon the language of the statute and the legislative history, this Court finds in the FCPA what the Supreme Court in *Gebardi* found in the Mann Act:

an affirmative legislative policy to leave unpunished a well-defined group of persons who were necessary parties to the acts constituting a violation of the substantive law. The Government has presented no reason why the prosecution of Defendants Castle and Lowry should go forward in the face of the congressional intent not to prosecute foreign officials. If anything, the facts of this case support Congress' decision to forego such prosecutions since foreign nations could and should prosecute their own officials for accepting bribes. . . .

[B] Private Parties

LAMB v. PHILLIP MORRIS, INC.

United States Court of Appeals for the Sixth Circuit
915 F.2d 1024 (1990)

GUY, CIRCUIT JUDGE:

. . . . On May 14, 1982, a Phillip Morris subsidiary known as C.A. Tabacalera National and a B.A.T. subsidiary known as C.A. Cigarrera Bigott, SUCS. entered into a contract with La Fundacion Del Nino (the Children's Foundation) of Caracas, Venezuela. The agreement was signed on behalf of the Children's Foundation by the organization's president, the wife of the then President of Venezuela. Under the terms of the agreement, the two subsidiaries were to make periodic donations to the Children's Foundation totaling approximately $ 12.5 million dollars. In exchange, the subsidiaries were to obtain price controls on Venezuelan tobacco, elimination of controls on retail cigarette prices in Venezuela, tax deductions for the donations, and assurances that existing tax rates applicable to tobacco companies would not be increased. According to the plaintiffs' complaint, the defendants have arranged similar contracts in Argentina, Brazil, Costa Rica, Mexico, and Nicaragua.

In the plaintiffs' view, the donations promised by the defendants' subsidiaries amount to unlawful inducements designed and intended to restrain trade. . . . The plaintiffs filed their complaint alleging violations of federal antitrust laws on August 21, 1985, in the United States District Court for the Eastern District of Kentucky. Both defendants promptly moved for dismissal on several grounds. The plaintiffs then sought leave to amend their complaint to add a claim under the FCPA. On June 28, 1989, the district court dismissed the plaintiffs' antitrust claims as barred by the act of state doctrine, and dismissed the FCPA claim as an impermissible private action. This appeal followed. . . .

[The court reversed the order insofar as the antitrust claims are concerned and remanded it for further consideration].

Although the Foreign Corrupt Practices Act was enacted more than a decade ago, the question of whether an implied private right of action exists under the FCPA apparently is one of first impression at the federal appellate level.* Thus, we must analyze the FCPA, which generally forbids issuers of registered securities and other "domestic concerns" (as well as their agents) to endeavor to influence foreign officials by offering, promising, or giving "anything of value," see 15 U.S.C. §§ 78dd-1(a), 78dd-2(a), to ascertain whether the plaintiffs may assert a private cause of action. . . .

In determining whether to infer a private cause of action from a federal statute, our focal point is Congress' intent in enacting the statute. As guides for discerning that intent, we have relied on the four factors set out in *Corded v. Ash*, 422 U.S. 66, 78, 45 L. Ed. 2d 26, 95 S. Ct. 2080 (1975), along with other tools of statutory construction. Our focus on congressional intent does not mean that we require evidence that Members of Congress, in enacting the statute, actually had in mind the creation of a private cause of action. . . . The intent of Congress remains the ultimate issue, however, and "unless this congressional intent can be inferred from the language of the statute, the statutory structure, or some other source, the essential predicate for implication of a private remedy simply does not exist." *Thompson v. Thompson*, 484 U.S. 174, 179, 108 S. Ct. 513, 98 L. Ed. 2d 512 (1988) (citations omitted). Thus, as *Thompson* makes clear, our central focus is on congressional intent, ... "with an eye toward" the four *Corded* factors: (1) whether the plaintiffs are among "the class for whose especial benefit" the statute was enacted; (2) whether the legislative history suggests congressional intent to prescribe or proscribe a private cause of action; (3) whether "implying such a remedy for the plaintiff would be 'consistent with the underlying purposes of the legislative scheme' "; and (4) whether the cause of action is " 'one traditionally relegated to state law, in an area basically the concern of States, so that it would be inappropriate to infer a cause of action.' "

. . . The defendants contend, and we agree, that the FCPA was designed with the assistance of the Securities and Exchange Commission (SEC) to aid federal law enforcement agencies in curbing bribes of foreign officials. . . [From] the general tenor of the FCPA itself, which requires the Attorney General to participate actively in encouraging and supervising compliance with the Act, . . . we find that the FCPA was primarily designed to protect the integrity of American foreign policy and domestic markets, rather than to prevent the use of foreign resources to reduce production costs. The plaintiffs, as competitors of foreign tobacco growers and suppliers of the defendants, cannot claim the status of intended beneficiaries of the congressional enactment under scrutiny . . .

Despite the paucity of authority in the legislative history for their position, the plaintiffs assert that Congress fully intended to permit private rights of

---

*Other courts have since ruled that there is no private cause of action under the FCPA. *See* J.S.D. Service Center Corporation v. General Electric Technical Services Company, Inc., 937 F. Supp. 216, 226 (S.D. N.Y. 1996). – Eds.

action under the FCPA. We disagree. The plaintiffs have identified only one reference in a House report to a private right of action: "The committee intends that courts shall recognize a private cause of action based on this legislation, as they have in cases involving other provisions of the Securities Exchange Act, on behalf of persons who suffer injury as a result of prohibited corporate bribery." . . . . Unlike the House, the Senate initially included a provision that expressly conferred a private right of action under the FCPA on competitors. Significantly, the Senate committee deleted that provision. . . . The availability of a private right of action apparently was never resolved (or perhaps even raised) at the conference that ultimately produced the compromise bill passed by both houses and signed into law; neither the FCPA as enacted nor the conference report mentions such a cause of action. . . . Because the conference report accompanying the final legislative compromise makes no mention of a private right of action, we infer that Congress intended no such result. Accordingly, we reject the plaintiffs' assertion that one isolated comment in an earlier House report mandates recognition of a private right of action.

. . . . Recognition of the plaintiffs' proposed private right of action, in our view, would directly contravene the carefully tailored FCPA scheme presently in place. Congress recently expanded the Attorney General's responsibilities to include facilitating compliance with the FCPA. Specifically, the Attorney General must "establish a procedure to provide responses to specific inquiries" by issuers of securities and other domestic concerns regarding "conformance of their conduct with the Department of Justice's [FCPA] enforcement policy . . . . " Moreover, the Attorney General must furnish "timely guidance concerning the Department of Justice's [FCPA] enforcement policy . . . to potential exporters and small businesses that are unable to obtain specialized counsel on issues pertaining to [FCPA] provisions.". . . Because this legislative action clearly evinces a preference for compliance in lieu of prosecution, the introduction of private plaintiffs interested solely in post-violation enforcement, rather than pre-violation compliance, most assuredly would hinder congressional efforts to protect companies and their employees concerned about FCPA liability. . . .

. . . . Because the potential for recovery under federal antitrust laws in this case belies the plaintiffs' contention that an implied private right of action under the FCPA is imperative, we attach no significance to the absence of state laws proscribing bribery of foreign officials. More importantly, since none of the *Corded* factors supports the plaintiffs' private right of action theory, we AFFIRM the district court's dismissal of the FCPA claim. . . .

NOTES AND QUESTIONS

(1) In an effort to deter bribery of foreign officials, Congress also included accounting provisions as part of the FCPA. These require record-keeping and

internal controls. "Congress believed that almost all such bribery was covered up in the corporation's books, and that to require proper accounting methods and internal accounting controls would discourage corporations from engaging in illegal payments." *Lewis v. Spock*, 612 F. Supp. 1316 (N.D. Cal. 1985). Like the anti-bribery provisions, the accounting provisions have been held not to provide a private cause of action. Enforcement is through "the SEC or the Department of Justice." *Id.* *See also Shields v. Erickson*, 710 F. Supp. 686, 688 (N.D. Ill. 1989) ("We find no convincing evidence in the legislative history to support plaintiff's contention that Congress intended this provision, which requires the corporation to use proper accounting methods and internal accounting controls, to create a private right of action.").

(2) When does an individual act corruptly for purposes of the FCPA? *See United States v. Liebo*, 923 F.2d 1308 (8th Cir. 1990) (discussing whether a gift of honeymoon tickets was given "corruptly").

Chapter 4
ANTITRUST AND SECURITIES REGULATION

Should the United States be permitted to proceed against individuals and companies that violate securities and antitrust laws outside the United States? The Securities Exchange Commission (SEC) and the Antitrust Division of the Department of Justice pursue violations occurring extraterritorially. Congress has assisted by providing new legislation for international enforcement of securities and antitrust violations. What issues arise when enforcing these laws internationally?

§ 4.01 Antitrust

UNITED STATES v. NIPPON PAPER INDUSTRIES CO., LTD.

United States Court of Appeals for the First Circuit
109 F.3d 1 (1997)

SELYA, CIRCUIT JUDGE:

This case raises an important, hitherto unanswered question. In it, the United States attempts to convict a foreign corporation under the Sherman Act, a federal antitrust statute, alleging that price-fixing activities which took place entirely in Japan are prosecutable because they were intended to have, and did in fact have, substantial effects in this country. The district court, declaring that a criminal antitrust prosecution could not be based on wholly extraterritorial conduct, dismissed the indictment. . . . We reverse. . . .

In 1995, a federal grand jury handed up an indictment naming as a defendant Nippon Paper Industries Co., Ltd. (NPI), a Japanese manufacturer of facsimile paper. The indictment alleges that in 1990 NPI and certain unnamed coconspirators held a number of meetings in Japan which culminated in an agreement to fix the price of thermal fax paper throughout North America. NPI and other manufacturers who were privy to the scheme purportedly accomplished their objective by selling the paper in Japan to unaffiliated trading houses on condition that the latter charge specified (inflated) prices for the paper when they resold it in North America. The trading houses then shipped and sold the paper to their subsidiaries in the United States who in turn sold it to American consumers at swollen prices. The indictment further relates that, in 1990 alone, NPI sold thermal fax paper worth approximately $ 6,100,000 for eventual import into the United States; and that in order to ensure the success of the venture, NPI monitored the paper trail and confirmed that the prices charged to end users were those that it had arranged. These activities, the indictment posits, had a substantial adverse effect on commerce in the United States and unreasonably restrained trade in violation of Section One of the Sherman Act, 15 U.S.C. § 1 (1994).

NPI moved to dismiss because, inter alia, if the conduct attributed to NPI occurred at all, it took place entirely in Japan, and, thus, the indictment failed to limn an offense under Section One of the Sherman Act. The government opposed this initiative on two grounds. First, it claimed that the law deserved a less grudging reading and that, properly read, Section One of the Sherman Act applied criminally to wholly foreign conduct as long as that conduct produced substantial and intended effects within the United States. Second, it claimed that the indictment, too, deserved a less grudging reading and that, properly read, the bill alleged a vertical conspiracy in restraint of trade that involved overt acts by certain coconspirators within the United States. Accepting a restrictive reading of both the statute and the indictment, the district court dismissed the case. . . .

Our law has long presumed that "legislation of Congress, unless a contrary intent appears, is meant to apply only within the territorial jurisdiction of the United States." *EEOC v. Arabian American Oil Co.*, 499 U.S. 244, 248, 113 L. Ed. 2d 274, 111 S. Ct. 1227 (1991). In this context, the Supreme Court has charged inquiring courts with determining whether Congress has clearly expressed an affirmative desire to apply particular laws to conduct that occurs beyond the borders of the United States. . . .

The earliest Supreme Court case which undertook a comparable task in respect to Section One of the Sherman Act determined that the presumption against extraterritoriality had not been overcome. In *American Banana Co. v. United Fruit Co.*, 213 U.S. 347, 53 L. Ed. 826, 29 S. Ct. 511 (1909), the Court considered the application of the Sherman Act in a civil action concerning conduct which occurred entirely in Central America and which had no discernible effect on imports to the United States. Starting with what Justice Holmes termed "the general and almost universal rule" holding "that the character of an act as lawful or unlawful must be determined wholly by the law of the country where the act is done," . . . . and the ancillary proposition that, in cases of doubt, a statute should be "confined in its operation and effect to the territorial limits over which the lawmaker has general and legitimate power," . . . the Court held that the defendant's actions abroad were not proscribed by the Sherman Act.

Our jurisprudence is precedent-based, but it is not static. By 1945, a different court saw a very similar problem in a somewhat softer light. In *United States v. Aluminum Co. of Am.*, 148 F.2d 416 (2d Cir. 1945) (*Alcoa*), the Second Circuit, sitting as a court of last resort, ... mulled a civil action brought under Section One against a Canadian corporation for acts committed entirely abroad which, the government averred, had produced substantial anticompetitive effects within the United States. The *Alcoa* court read *American Banana* narrowly; that case, Judge Learned Hand wrote, stood only for the principle that "we should not impute to Congress an intent to punish all whom its courts can catch, for conduct which has no consequences within the United States." . . . But a sovereign ordinarily can impose liability for conduct outside its borders that produces consequences within them, and while considerations of comity argue against applying Section One to situations in which no effect within the United States has been shown – the *American Banana* scenario – the statute, properly interpreted, does proscribe extraterritorial acts which were "intended to affect imports [to the United States] and did affect them." . . . On the facts of *Alcoa*, therefore, the presumption against extraterritoriality had been overcome, and the Sherman Act had been violated. . . .

Any perceived tension between *American Banana* and *Alcoa* was eased by the Supreme Court's most recent exploration of the Sherman Act's extraterritorial reach. In *Hartford Fire Ins. Co. v. California*, 509 U.S. 764, 125 L. Ed. 2d 612, 113 S. Ct. 2891 (1993), the Justices endorsed *Alcoa's* core holding, permitting civil antitrust claims under Section One to go forward despite the fact that the actions which allegedly violated Section One occurred entirely on British soil. While noting *American Banana's* initial disagreement with this proposition, the *Hartford Fire* Court deemed it "well established by now that the Sherman Act applies to foreign conduct that was meant to produce and did in fact produce some substantial effect in the United States." . . . The conduct alleged, a London-based conspiracy to alter the American insurance market, met that benchmark. . . .

To sum up, the case law now conclusively establishes that civil antitrust actions predicated on wholly foreign conduct which has an intended and substantial effect in the United States come within Section One's jurisdictional reach. . . .

Were this a civil case, our journey would be complete. But here the United States essays a criminal prosecution for solely extraterritorial conduct rather than a civil action. This is largely uncharted terrain; we are aware of no authority directly on point, and the parties have cited none.

Be that as it may, one datum sticks out like a sore thumb: in both criminal and civil cases, the claim that Section One applies extraterritorially is based on the same language in the same section of the same statute: "Every contract, combination in the form of trust or otherwise, or conspiracy, in restraint of trade or commerce among the several States, or with foreign nations, is declared to be illegal." 15 U.S.C. § 1. Words may sometimes be chameleons, possessing different shades of meaning in different contexts, . . . but common sense suggests that courts should interpret the same language in the same section of the same statute uniformly, regardless of whether the impetus for interpretation is criminal or civil. . . .

NPI and its amicus, the Government of Japan, urge that special reasons exist for measuring Section One's reach differently in a criminal context. We have reviewed their exhortations and found them hollow. We discuss the five most promising theses below. The rest do not require comment.

1. *Lack of Precedent.* NPI and its amicus make much of the fact that this appears to be the first criminal case in which the United States endeavors to extend Section One to wholly foreign conduct. We are not impressed. There is a first time for everything, and the absence of earlier criminal actions is probably more a demonstration of the increasingly global nature of our economy than proof that Section One cannot cover wholly foreign conduct in the criminal milieu.

Moreover, this argument overstates the lack of precedent. There is, for example, solid authority for applying a state's criminal statute to conduct occurring entirely outside the state's borders. . . .

2. *Difference in Strength of Presumption.* The lower court and NPI both cite *United States v. Bowman* [p. 28], for the proposition that the presumption against extraterritoriality operates with greater force in the criminal arena than in civil litigation. This misreads the opinion. To be sure, the *Bowman* Court, dealing with a charged conspiracy to defraud, warned that if the criminal law "is to be extended to include those [crimes] committed outside of the strict territorial jurisdiction, it is natural for Congress to say so in the statute, and failure to do so will negative the purpose of Congress in this regard." . . . But this pronouncement merely restated the presumption against extraterritoriality previously established in civil cases like *American Banana* . . . . The *Bowman* Court nowhere suggested that a different, more resilient presumption arises in criminal cases. . . .

3. *The Restatement.* NPI and the district court, . . . both sing the praises of the RESTATEMENT (THIRD) OF FOREIGN RELATIONS LAW (1987), claiming that it supports a distinction between civil and criminal cases on the issue of extraterritoriality. The passage to which they pin their hopes states:

> In the case of regulatory statutes that may give rise to both civil and criminal liability, such as the United States antitrust and securities laws, the presence of substantial foreign elements will ordinarily weigh against application of criminal law. In such cases, legislative intent to subject conduct outside the state's territory to its criminal law should be found only on the basis of express statement or clear implication.

Id. at § 403 cmt. f. We believe that this statement merely reaffirms the classic presumption against extraterritoriality – no more, no less. After all, nothing in the text of the Restatement proper contradicts the government's interpretation of Section One. . . . What is more, other comments indicate that a country's decision to prosecute wholly foreign conduct is discretionary. . . .

4. *The Rule of Lenity.* The next arrow which NPI yanks from its quiver is the

rule of lenity. The rule itself is venerable; it provides that, in the course of interpreting statutes in criminal cases, a reviewing court should resolve ambiguities affecting a statute's scope in the defendant's favor. . . . But the rule of lenity is inapposite unless a statutory ambiguity looms, and a statute is not ambiguous for this purpose simply because some courts or commentators have questioned its proper interpretation. . . . Put bluntly, the rule of lenity cannot be used to create ambiguity when the meaning of a law, even if not readily apparent, is, upon inquiry, reasonably clear. . . . In view of the fact that the Supreme Court deems it "well established" that Section One of the Sherman Act applies to wholly foreign conduct, *Hartford Fire*, 509 U.S. at 796, we effectively are foreclosed from trying to tease an ambiguity out of Section One relative to its extraterritorial application. Accordingly, the rule of lenity plays no part in the instant case.

5. *Comity.* International comity is a doctrine that counsels voluntary forbearance when a sovereign which has a legitimate claim to jurisdiction concludes that a second sovereign also has a legitimate claim to jurisdiction under principles of international law. . . . Comity is more an aspiration than a fixed rule, more a matter of grace than a matter of obligation. . . .

In this case the defendant's comity-based argument is even more attenuated. The conduct with which NPI is charged is illegal under both Japanese and American laws, thereby alleviating any founded concern about NPI being whipsawed between separate sovereigns. And, moreover, to the extent that comity is informed by general principles of reasonableness, *see* Restatement (Third) of Foreign Relations Law § 403, the indictment lodged against NPI is well within the pale. In it, the government charges that the defendant orchestrated a conspiracy with the object of rigging prices in the United States. If the government can prove these charges, we see no tenable reason why principles of comity should shield NPI from prosecution. We live in an age of international commerce, where decisions reached in one corner of the world can reverberate around the globe in less time than it takes to tell the tale. Thus, a ruling in NPI's favor would create perverse incentives for those who would use nefarious means to influence markets in the United States, rewarding them for erecting as many territorial firewalls as possible between cause and effect.

We need go no further. *Hartford Fire* definitively establishes that Section One of the Sherman Act applies to wholly foreign conduct which has an intended and substantial effect in the United States. We are bound to accept that holding. Under settled principles of statutory construction, we also are bound to apply it by interpreting Section One the same way in a criminal case. The combined force of these commitments requires that we accept the government's cardinal argument, reverse the order of the district court, reinstate the indictment, and remand for further proceedings.

Reversed and remanded.

LYNCH, CIRCUIT JUDGE (concurring):

. . . . While courts, including this one, speak of determining congressional intent when interpreting statutes, the meaning of the antitrust laws has emerged through the relationship among all three branches of government. In this criminal case, it is our responsibility to ensure that the executive's interpretation of the Sherman Act does not conflict with other legal principles, including principles of international law.

That question requires examination beyond the language of Section One of the Sherman Act. It is, of course, generally true that, as a principle of statutory interpretation, the same language should be read the same way in all contexts to which the language applies. But this is not invariably true. New content is sometimes ascribed to statutory terms depending upon context. . . . Where Congress intends that our laws conform with international law, and where international law suggests that criminal enforcement and civil enforcement be viewed differently, it is at least conceivable that different content could be ascribed to the same language depending on whether the context is civil or criminal. . . .

NOTES AND QUESTIONS

(1) Would the United States have still been able to prosecute extraterritorial antitrust conduct if the First Circuit Court of Appeals had not reversed the district court decision? *See* John R. Wilke, *Appeals Court Says U.S. Antitrust Laws Cover Actions Abroad by Foreign Firms*, WALL ST. JRL., March 19, 1997, B7. ("Had the appeals court's decision gone the other way, 'executives could simply charter a cruise outside the territorial jurisdiction of the U.S. to fix and raise prices for American consumers without fear of prosecution,' said Gary Spratling, deputy assistant attorney general.").

(2) When does foreign conduct have "an intended and substantial effect in the United States"? Should the same standard be used in civil and criminal cases? What, if any, jurisdictional base is the court using in allowing an extraterritorial application? [*see* chap. 2].

(3) In 1994, Congress enacted the International Antitrust Enforcement Assistance Act. 15 U.S.C. §§ 6201-6212. The Act allows for mutual assistance in enforcing antitrust violations. Implementation of the Act is through the Foreign Commerce Section of Antitrust Division of the Department of Justice. U.S. ATTYS. MAN. 7-3.600 (1997). There have been successful prosecutions where foreign governments have assisted the United States. "[I]n cases where

foreign governments provide no cooperation in obtaining evidence, or where none of the overt acts of the conspiracy occur within the United States, results have been less favorable for the DOJ." Meredith E. B. Bell & Elena Laskin, Note, *Antitrust Violations*, 36 AM. CRIM. L. REV. 357, 388 (1999).

§ 4.02 Securities Regulation

Jurisdiction to prosecute securities violations is most commonly found in the Securities Act of 1933 and the Securities Exchange Act of 1934. "The preamble to both the 1933 and 1934 Acts provide that they are intended to apply to 'interstate and foreign commerce.'" Bruce Zagaras, *Avoiding Criminal Liability in the Conduct of International Business*, 21 WM. MITCHELL L. REV. 749, 770 (1996). "Courts have held that nearly any securities violation, occurring within or outside United States borders, and having a real impact on investors or the markets in the United States, is subject to the federal securities laws." Jason Anthony, Amani Harrison, Patrick Linehan, & Jeffery Palker, Note, *Securities Fraud*, 36 AM. CRIM. L. REV. 1095, 1145 (1999). Prosecutors have also used 18 U.S.C. § 1341 (mail fraud statute), 18 U.S.C. § 1343 (wire fraud statute), and 18 U.S.C. § 371 (conspiracy), in the prosecution of securities violations.

In *Tamari v. Bache & Co. (Lebanon) S.A.L.*, 730 F.2d 1103, 1107-08 (7th Cir. 1984), the court considered issues of jurisdiction in the context of actions under the Commodity Exchange Act ("CEA"), 7 U.S.C. §§ 6b and 6c, for damages resulting from alleged fraud and mismanagement of commodity futures trading accounts. Circuit Judge Swygert stated:

> Finding nothing in the Act or its legislative history to indicate that Congress did not intend the CEA to apply to foreign agents, but recognizing there also is no direct evidence that Congress intended such application, we believe it is appropriate to rely on the "conduct" and "effects" tests in discerning whether subject matter jurisdiction exists over this dispute. Both tests were developed in cases brought under the antifraud provisions of the federal securities laws and have recently been applied in similar cases arising under the Commodity Exchange Act. . . . When the conduct occurring in the United States is material to the successful completion of the alleged scheme, jurisdiction is asserted based on the theory that Congress would not have intended the United States to be used as a base for effectuating the fraudulent conduct of foreign companies. . . . Under the effects test, courts have looked to whether conduct occurring in foreign countries had caused foreseeable and substantial harm to interests in the United States. . . . The underlying theory is that Congress would have wished domestic markets and domestic investors to be protected from improper foreign transactions. . . .

But see Mak v. Wocom Commodities Limited, 112 F.3d 287 (7th Cir. 1997) (declined to extend *Tamari* to "distant and uncertain circumstances").

[A] Effects Test

SCHOENBAUM v. FIRSTBROOK

United States Court of Appeals for the Second Circuit
405 F.2d 200 (1968)

LUMBARD, CHIEF JUDGE:

Plaintiff, an American shareholder of Banff Oil Ltd., a Canadian corporation, brought this shareholder derivative action to recover under Section 10(b) of the Securities Exchange Act of 1934, 15 U.S.C. 78j(b) and Rule 10b-5, 17 CFR § 240.10b-5 (1967), for damages to the corporation resulting from the sales, in Canada, of Banff treasury stock to defendants Aquitaine of Canada, Ltd., and Paribas Corporation. Plaintiff alleged that the defendant corporations and Banff's directors, who are the individual defendants in this action, conspired to defraud Banff by making Banff sell treasury shares at the market price which the defendants, who had inside information not yet disclosed to the public, knew did not represent the true value of the shares.

Defendants moved pursuant to Rules 12(c) and 56, Fed.R.Civ.P., for summary judgment, and under Rule 12(b) to dismiss the complaint on the ground that the Court lacked jurisdiction over the subject matter. Judge Cooper, refusing to permit plaintiff to carry out a program of discovery, entered judgment for defendants, holding that the Court lacked jurisdiction because the Securities and Exchange Act does not have extraterritorial application, and that plaintiff failed to state a cause of action under § 10(b) and Rule 10b-5. . . .

We find that the district court had subject matter jurisdiction but affirm the judgment below because, while plaintiff's complaint alleges a breach of fiduciary duty by Banff's directors in authorizing sales of treasury shares at too low a price, these allegations fail to state a cause of action under § 10(b) of the Exchange Act. . . .

We believe that Congress intended the Exchange Act to have extraterritorial application in order to protect domestic investors who have purchased foreign securities on American exchanges and to protect the domestic securities market from the effects of improper foreign transactions in American securities. In our view, neither the usual presumption against extraterritorial application of legislation nor the specific language of Section 30(b) show Congressional intent to preclude application of the Exchange Act to transactions regarding stocks traded in the United States which are effected outside the United States, when extraterritorial application of the Act is necessary to protect American investors.

Section 2 of the Exchange Act, 15 U.S.C. § 78b, states that because transactions in securities are affected with "a national public interest" it is "necessary to provide for regulation and control of such transactions and of practices and matters related thereto, * * * necessary to make such regulation and control reasonably * * * complete state commerce and to insure the maintenance of fair and honest markets in such transactions."

The Act seeks to regulate the stock exchanges and the relationships of the investing public to corporations which invite public investment by listing on such exchanges. . . .

Banff common stock is registered and traded on the American Stock Exchange. To protect United States shareholders of Banff common stock, Banff is required to comply with the provisions of the Securities Exchange Act concerning financial reports to the SEC, § 13, 15 U.S.C. § 78m; proxy solicitation, § 14, 15 U.S.C. § 78n, and reports of insider holdings, § 16, 15 U.S.C. § 78p. Similarly, the anti-fraud provision of § 10(b), which enables the Commission to prescribe rules "necessary or appropriate in the public interest or for the protection of investors" reaches beyond the territorial limits of the United States and applies when a violation of the Rules is injurious to United States investors. "Acts done outside a jurisdiction, but intended to produce and producing detrimental effects within it, justify a state in punishing the cause of the harm as if [the actor] had been present at the [time of the detrimental] effect, if the state should succeed in getting him within its power." . . .

The Commission has recognized the broad extraterritorial applicability of the Act and has specifically exempted certain foreign issuers from the operation of Sections 14 and 16 of the Act, when enforcement would be impractical. . . . The Commission has applied Section 15(a), 15 U.S.C. § 78o, to foreign brokerdealers who transact business through use of the mails. . . . Although it has the power to grant exemptions from rules under § 10(b), ... the Commission has not promulgated a rule exempting foreign transactions from Rule 10b-5.

The provision contained in Section 30(b) does not alter our conclusion that the Exchange Act has extraterritorial application. In our view, while section 30(b) was intended to exempt persons conducting a business in securities through foreign securities markets from the provisions of the Act, it does not preclude extraterritorial application of the Exchange Act to persons who engage in isolated foreign transactions.

Section 30, entitled "Foreign Securities Exchanges," deals with the extent to which the Act applies to persons effecting securities transactions through foreign exchanges. Section 30(a) empowers the SEC to regulate all brokers and dealers who use the mails or interstate commerce, for the purpose of effecting a transaction in American securities on exchanges outside the United States. . . . It was intended to prevent evasion of the Act through transactions on foreign exchanges. . . .

We hold that the district court has subject matter jurisdiction over violations of the Securities Exchange Act although the transactions which are alleged to violate the Act take place outside the United States, at least when the transactions involve stock registered and listed on a national securities exchange, and are detrimental to the interests of American investors. . . .

However, the district court found that the only harm alleged was to the foreign corporation on whose behalf plaintiff brought the action. We do not agree. A fraud upon a corporation which has the effect of depriving it of fair compensation for the issuance of its stock would necessarily have the effect of reducing the equity of the corporation's shareholders and this reduction in equity would be reflected in lower prices bid for the shares on the domestic stock market. This impairment of the value of American investments by sales by the issuer in a foreign country, allegedly in violation of the Act, has in our view, a sufficiently serious effect upon United States commerce to warrant assertion of jurisdiction for the protection of American investors and consideration of the merits of plaintiff's claim. . . . .

Since we conclude that the district court had subject matter jurisdiction we must go on to examine plaintiff's second claim: that defendants were not entitled to summary judgment under Rules 12(c) and 56, Fed.R.Civ.Pro. We agree with the trial court that on motion for summary judgment plaintiff's unsupported allegations based upon information and belief cannot be credited where they are contradicted by the affidavits on personal knowledge which defendants submitted in support of their motion. We further agree that on the record, plaintiff has shown at most a breach of fiduciary duty by Banff's directors and that this is insufficient to constitute a cause of action under § 10(b) of the Exchange Act. . . . .[*]

The judgment is affirmed.

HAYS, CIRCUIT JUDGE (concurring in part and dissenting in part):

I concur in Judge Lumbard's distinguished opinion on the issue of jurisdiction. I am constrained to dissent on the point of the applicability to the facts of this case of the provisions of Section 10(b) and, more particularly, Rule 10b-5. . . .

[B] Conduct Test

KAUTHAR SDN BHD v. STERNBERG

United States Court of Appeals for the Seventh Circuit
149 F.3d 659 (1998)

RIPPLE, CIRCUIT JUDGE:

. . . . This case centers on a $ 38 million investment made by Kauthar in a company called Rimsat, Ltd. Kauthar is a Malaysian corporation with its

---

[*] A rehearing *en banc* was granted and heard on the issue of whether defendants were entitled to summary judgment under Rules 12 (c) and 56 of the Federal Rules of Civil Procedure. *See* Schoenbaum v. United States, 405 F.2d 215 (2d Cir. 1968). – Eds.

principal place of business in Kuala Lumpur, Malaysia. Rimsat, whose principal place of business is in Fort Wayne, Indiana, was incorporated in the Caribbean island nation of Nevis for the purpose of providing satellite communications services to customers within the Pacific Rim region. These satellite communications were to be provided using satellites that Rimsat had contracted to purchase from a Russian satellite company. The satellites were to be placed in geosynchronous (or geostationary) orbit positions ("GSOs") that were leased to Rimsat by a company called Friendly Islands Satellite Communications, Ltd., doing business as "Tongasat." Tongasat is incorporated in the Pacific Rim Kingdom of Tonga.

Apparently, there is a limited number of GSOs available in the world because satellites may not be put in too close proximity to one another or else communications interference occurs. Satellites in geosynchronous orbit, by definition, stay essentially in the same spot over the earth and on the same equatorial plane. Consequently, the number of these spots in space is finite and, as with all scarce resources for which there is demand, they are valuable. The International Telecommunications Union ("ITU") and the International Frequency Registration Board, agencies of the United Nations, coordinate the registration and regulation of GSO positions. Only sovereign nations may apply to the ITU for rights to a GSO position for operation of a satellite. In this case, the Kingdom of Tonga obtained seven GSOs which it leased out to others through its company Tongasat. Rimsat's apparent plan was to make its fortune by buying relatively inexpensive Russian communications satellites, leasing GSOs from Tongasat and selling satellite communications services.

Not surprisingly, such a venture is highly capital-intensive. Rimsat and various of the individual defendants involved in forming Rimsat and Tongasat sought investors for this project. Kauthar allegedly was convinced, on the basis of various communications and meetings, that Rimsat was a worthy investment, and it sank $ 38 million into the venture through a purchase of Rimsat stock. Kauthar effected this purchase by wiring funds to Rimsat's bank in Fort Wayne, Indiana.

In January 1995, several of Rimsat's creditors forced Rimsat into bankruptcy by filing a petition for involuntary bankruptcy in the United States Bankruptcy Court for the Northern District of Indiana. Six weeks later, when Kauthar realized that its equity stake in Rimsat was worthless, it brought this suit. Essentially, Kauthar alleged in its complaint that all of the parties involved in soliciting its investment in Rimsat intentionally misled Kauthar about the investment. Kauthar specifically points to a document that it terms a "prospectus" that was disseminated by Rimsat to outline the company's investment and business plans. In its 113-page amended complaint, Kauthar identifies alleged misrepresentations contained in the prospectus in addition to other misrepresentations and omissions it alleges were made in the course of dealings. . . .

Kauthar alleged in Counts I and II of its complaint violations of § 10(b) of the 1934 Act, 15 U.S.C. § 78j(b), and Rule 10b-5, 17 C.F.R. § 240.10b-5, which relate to fraud in the purchase or sale of a security. In Counts III and IV of its complaint, Kauthar alleged additional securities fraud claims predicated on violations of § 17(a) of the 1933 Act, 15 U.S.C. § 77q, and of § 12(2) of the 1933 Act, 15 U.S.C. § 77l. Before we address the specifics of each claim, we first consider a problem common to all of them. . . .

The district court determined that the securities violations alleged by Kauthar in Counts I-IV of its complaint were beyond the ambit of statutory protection because they involved transnational securities transactions without a sufficient connection to the United States. Specifically, the district court held that Kauthar's allegations satisfied neither the "effects" nor the "conduct" analyses employed by federal courts to decide whether the securities acts cover a particular transnational securities transaction. We review this question of law de novo.

Courts have struggled for many years to define with meaningful precision the extent to which the antifraud provisions of the securities laws apply to securities transactions that are predominantly extraterritorial in nature but have some connection to the United States. The courts that have addressed the issue have noted that the question is a difficult one because Congress has given little meaningful guidance on the issue.[5] In addition, resort to the legislative history of the securities acts does little to illuminate Congress' intent in this area. *See, e.g., Zoelsch v. Arthur Andersen & Co.,* 824 F.2d 27, 30 (D.C. Cir. 1987) ("If the text of the 1934 Act is relatively barren, even more so is the legislative history. Fifty years ago, Congress did not consider how far American courts should have jurisdiction to decide cases involving predominantly foreign securities transactions with some link to the United States. The web of international connections in the securities market was then not nearly as extensive or complex as it has become."). In fact, some courts have admitted candidly that, in fashioning an approach to the issue of extraterritorial application of the securities laws, policy considerations and the courts' best judgment have been utilized to determine the reach of the federal securities laws.

In dealing with this difficult area we begin, as we always do in matters of

---

[5]*See, e.g.,* Robinson v. TCI/US West Communications, Inc., 117 F.3d 900, 904-05 (5th Cir. 1997) ("With one small exception the Exchange Act does nothing to address the circumstances under which American courts have subject matter jurisdiction to hear suits involving foreign transactions."); Itoba Ltd. v. Lep Group PLC, 54 F.3d 118, 121 (2d Cir. 1995) ("It is well recognized that the Securities Exchange Act is silent as to its extraterritorial application."), *cert. denied,* 516 U.S. 1044 (1996); Zoelsch v. Arthur Andersen & Co., 824 F.2d 27, 30 (D.C. Cir. 1987) (stating that provisions of 1934 Act furnish "no specific indications of when American federal courts have jurisdiction over securities law claims arising from extraterritorial transactions"). *But see* SEC v. Kasser, 548 F.2d 109, 114 (3d Cir. 1977) ("The anti-fraud laws suggest that such [extraterritorial] application is proper. The securities acts expressly apply to 'foreign commerce,' thereby evincing a Congressional intent for a broad jurisdictional scope for the 1933 and 1934 Acts." . . .)

statutory interpretation, with the words of the statute. Although the statutory language gives us little guidance, it does give us some clue of the direction we must take. Congress did leave some indication in the language of the securities laws about their intended application to foreign commerce. Section 10(b) prohibits fraud by the "use of any means or instrumentality of interstate commerce or of the mails" in "connection with the purchase or sale of any security." 15 U.S.C. § 78j & (b). "Interstate commerce" is defined to include "trade, commerce, transportation, or communication . . . between any foreign country and any State." 15 U.S.C. § 78c(a)(17). A single passage in the statute addresses foreign transactions explicitly. As the District of Columbia Circuit noted in *Zoelsch,* . . . . § 30(b) states that the 1934 Act "shall not apply to any person insofar as he transacts a business in securities without the jurisdiction of the United States, unless he transacts such business in contravention of such rules and regulations as the Commission may prescribe as necessary or appropriate to prevent the evasion of this chapter." 15 U.S.C. § 78dd(b). The Supreme Court has said that "it is a longstanding principle of American law 'that legislation of Congress, unless a contrary intent appears, is meant to apply only within the territorial jurisdiction of the United States.'" *EEOC v. Arabian Am. Oil Co.,* 499 U.S. 244, 248, 113 L. Ed. 2d 274, 111 S. Ct. 1227 (1991) (*quoting Foley Bros., Inc. v. Filardo,* 336 U.S. 281, 285, 93 L. Ed. 680, 69 S. Ct. 575 (1949)). But, as some courts have noted, this statutory language suggests that the antifraud provisions were intended to apply to some transnational securities transactions.

Although the circuits that have confronted the matter seem to agree that there are some transnational situations to which the antifraud provisions of the securities laws are applicable, agreement appears to end at that point. Identification of those circumstances that warrant such regulation has produced a disparity in approach, to some degree doctrinal and to some degree attitudinal, as the courts have striven to implement, in Judge Friendly's words, "what Congress would have wished if these problems had occurred to it." *Bersch v. Drexel Firestone, Inc.,* 519 F.2d 974, 993 (2d Cir.), *cert. denied,* 423 U.S. 1018 (1975).

These efforts have produced two basic approaches to determining whether the transaction in question ought to be subject to American securities fraud regulation. These two approaches (we think that "test" is too inflexible a term to characterize the present state of the case law) focus on whether the activity in question has had a sufficient impact on or relation to the United States, its markets or its citizens to justify American regulation of the situation. Specifically, one approach focuses on the domestic conduct in question, and the other focuses on the domestic effects resulting from the transaction at issue.[8]

---

[8]The general approach of the courts has been to assume that the securities laws are applicable if either approach so indicates. . . . We note, however, that the Second Circuit, from which these analytical approaches of conduct and effects originated, has recently stated that they need not "be applied separately and distinctly from each other" and that, in fact, "an admixture or combination of the two often gives a better picture of

When focusing on the effects, the courts seek to determine whether actions " 'occurring in foreign countries have caused foreseeable and substantial harm to interests in the United States.' " . . . Several cases have examined the type and severity of the harm that must be suffered domestically in order to enable an exercise of jurisdiction. This case, however, affords us no occasion to explore this approach; the record does not reveal sufficient effect on domestic interests to justify its invocation here.

In contrast with the effects analysis, which examines actions occurring outside of the United States, the conduct analysis focuses on actions occurring in this country as they "relate[ ] to the alleged scheme to defraud." . . . . The chronic difficulty with such a methodology has been describing, in sufficiently precise terms, the sort of conduct occurring in the United States that ought to be adequate to trigger American regulation of the transaction. Indeed, the circuits that have confronted the matter have articulated a number of methodologies.

The predominant difference among the circuits, it appears, is the degree to which the American-based conduct must be related causally to the fraud and the resultant harm to justify the application of American securities law. At one end of the spectrum, the District of Columbia Circuit appears to require that the domestic conduct at issue must itself constitute a securities violation. . . . At the other end of the spectrum, the Third, Eighth and Ninth Circuits, although also focusing on whether the United States-based conduct caused the plaintiffs' loss, to use the Fifth Circuit's words, "generally require some lesser quantum of conduct." . . . In *SEC v. Kasser,* 548 F.2d 109, 114 (3d Cir.), *cert. denied,* 431 U.S. 938 (1977), the Third Circuit stated that the conduct came within the scope of the statute if "at least some activity designed to further a fraudulent scheme occurs within this country." The Eighth Circuit, in *Continental Grain (Australia) Pty. Ltd. v. Pacific Oilseeds, Inc.,* 592 F.2d 409, 421 (8th Cir. 1979), held that the antifraud provisions were applicable when the domestic conduct "was in furtherance of a fraudulent scheme and was significant with respect to its accomplishment." The Ninth Circuit adopted the Continental Grain approach in *Grunenthal GmbH v. Hotz,* 712 F.2d 421, 425 (9th Cir. 1983).

Our colleagues in the Second and Fifth Circuits have set a course between the two extremes that we have just discussed. That approach requires a higher quantum of domestic conduct than do the Third, Eighth and Ninth Circuits. . . . The Second Circuit has stated that foreign plaintiffs' suits under the antifraud provisions of the securities laws, such as Kauthar's, will be "heard only when substantial acts in furtherance of the fraud were committed within

---

whether there is sufficient United States involvement to justify the exercise of jurisdiction by an American court." Since the aim of this inquiry is to measure the degree of United States involvement in the transaction in question, the joint assessment of conduct and effects seems appropriate because it permits a more comprehensive assessment of the overall transactional situation.

the United States." Furthermore, if the United States-based activities were merely preparatory in nature, or if the " 'bulk of the activity was performed in foreign countries,' " jurisdiction will not exist. . . . In addition, only "where conduct 'within the United States directly caused' the loss will a district court have jurisdiction over suits by foreigners who have lost money through sales abroad." . . .

Although this court has not had occasion to articulate an approach to the extraterritorial application of the securities laws, we have employed these concepts with respect to analogous actions brought under the Commodity Exchange Act. . . . In that context, we have stated that "when the conduct occurring in the United States is material to the successful completion of the alleged scheme, jurisdiction is asserted based on the theory that Congress would not have intended the United States to be used as a base for effectuating the fraudulent conduct of foreign companies." We think that our approach under the Commodities Act ought to be followed with respect to the securities laws and, although stated more generally, that it represents the same midground as that identified by the Second and Fifth Circuits. In our view, the absence of all but the most rudimentary Congressional guidance counsels that federal courts should be cautious in determining that transnational securities matters are within the ambit of our antifraud statutes. Nevertheless, we would do serious violence to the policies of these statutes if we did not recognize our Country's manifest interest in ensuring that the United States is not used as a "base of operations" from which to "defraud foreign securities purchasers or sellers." . . . This interest is amplified by the fact that we live in an increasingly global financial community. The Second and Fifth Circuit's iterations of the test embody a satisfactory balance of these competing considerations. This analytical pattern will enable the courts to address situations in which the United States is being used as a launching pad for fraudulent international securities schemes. At the same time, it will cause us to refrain from adjudicating disputes which have little in the way of a significant connection to the United States.

We believe, therefore, that federal courts have jurisdiction over an alleged violation of the antifraud provisions of the securities laws when the conduct occurring in the United States directly causes the plaintiff's alleged loss in that the conduct forms a substantial part of the alleged fraud and is material to its success. This conduct must be more than merely preparatory in nature; however, we do not go so far as to require that the conduct occurring domestically must itself satisfy the elements of a securities violation.

We turn now to an application of these principles to Kauthar's allegations. Kauthar argues that a host of alleged general activities undertaken by various of the defendants constitutes conduct that was part of the scheme to defraud Kauthar and to solicit Kauthar's investment in Rimsat. Kauthar alleges that various documents containing fraudulent misrepresentations and omissions were prepared in the United States and were sent to it by wire and by the United States mail in an effort to obtain Kauthar's investment. Kauthar also alleges that phone calls were made from Fort Wayne, Indiana, and from San Diego, California, for the same purpose. Kauthar further alleges that the defendants had meetings and phone conversations in the United States to discuss the deceptive information contained in the prospectus and to "ultimately agree upon a plan to obtain equity funding from Kauthar by means of false and deceptive statements of fact." . . . Thus, according to the complaint, the United States was utilized as a base of operations from which to launch the defendants' fraudulent scheme to defraud Kauthar. Moreover, Kauthar also alleges a set of specific acts that, in combination with those already mentioned, satisfy the conduct analysis. Specifically, Kauthar alleges that it wired the payment for the Rimsat securities, over $ 38 million, in six installments to Rimsat's bank account in Fort Wayne, Indiana. Therefore, Kauthar has alleged that the defendants conceived and planned a scheme to defraud Kauthar in the United States, that they prepared materials in support of the scheme to solicit the payment in the United States and sent those materials from the United States via the United States mail, and that they received in the United States the fraudulently solicited payment for the securities – the final step in the alleged fraud. We think these allegations sufficient to bring the alleged conduct within the ambit of the securities laws. We are therefore constrained to disagree respectfully with the district court's contrary conclusion. . . .

Because we have determined that the court did have jurisdiction to consider the securities violations claims alleged in Counts I-IV of Kauthar's complaint (to the extent that the conduct analysis is satisfied), we must determine whether those claims survive the alternative holdings upon which the district court also based its decision to dismiss the action. . . .

[The court found claims these waived and also that the "10 (b) and Rule 10b-5 violations alleged in Counts I and II of the complaint" were "time barred."]

For these reasons, the judgment of the district court is affirmed.

NOTES AND QUESTIONS

(1) Which of the approaches discussed above should a court use in deciding whether there is federal jurisdiction to proceed on a securities matter within the United States? Should the approach be consistent in both civil and criminal cases? In determining whether there is sufficient "conduct" to pursue a securities fraud case in the United States, do principles of comity suggest a preference for a particular approach? *See* Michael J. Calhoun, Comments, *Tension on the High Seas of Transnational Securities Fraud: Broadening the Scope of United States Jurisdiction*, 30 LOY. U. CHI. L.J. 679 (1999) ("Principles of international comity do not impose any absolute obligations on courts to deny jurisdiction since comity concerns are a matter of courtesy and good will.")

(2) Are there limits to extraterritorial application under the "effects" and "conduct" tests? In *Leasco Data Processing Equipment Corporation v. Maxwell*,

468 F.2d 1326 (2d Cir. 1972), Chief Judge Friendly stated:

> If all the misrepresentations here alleged had occurred in England, we would entertain most serious doubt whether, despite *United States v. Aluminum Co. of America,* 148 F.2d 416, 443-444 (2d Cir. 1954), and *Schoenbaum,* § 10(b) would be applicable simply because of the adverse effect of the fraudulently induced purchases in England of securities of an English corporation, not traded in an organized American securities market, upon an American corporation whose stock is listed on the New York Stock Exchange and its shareholders. . . . It is true, as Judge L. Hand pointed out in the *Aluminum* case, ... that if Congress has expressly prescribed a rule with respect to conduct outside the United States, even one going beyond the scope recognized by foreign relations law, a United States court would be bound to follow the Congressional direction unless this would violate the due process clause of the Fifth Amendment. However, the language of § 10(b) of the Securities Exchange Act is much too inconclusive to lead us to believe that Congress meant to impose rules governing conduct throughout the world in every instance where an American company bought or sold a security. When no fraud has been practiced in this country and the purchase or sale has not been made here, we would be hard pressed to find justification for going beyond *Schoenbaum.* . . .

(3) In determining whether Congress intended extraterritorial application of a securities statute, what factors should be considered? *See Bersch v. Drexel Firestone, Incorporated,* 519 F.2d 974, 985 (2d Cir. 1975) ("When, as here, a court is confronted with transactions that on any view are predominantly foreign, it must seek to determine whether Congress would have wished the precious resources of United States courts and law enforcement agencies to be devoted to them rather than leave the problem to foreign countries.") Do the "effects" and "conduct" tests operate in the alternative, or does the existence of one prong permit extraterritoriality? Consider the *Besch* case, which states:

> We have thus concluded that the anti-fraud provisions of the federal securities laws:
>
> (1) Apply to losses from sales of securities to Americans resident in the United States whether or not acts (or culpable failures to act) of material importance occurred in this country; and
>
> (2) Apply to losses from sales of securities to Americans resident abroad if, but only if, acts (or culpable failures to act) of material importance in the United States have significantly contributed thereto; but
>
> (3) Do not apply to losses from sales of securities to foreigners outside the United States unless acts (or culpable failures to act) within the United States directly caused such losses.

Id. at 992. *See also* INTERNATIONAL CRIMINAL LAW 218-22 (Ved P. Nanda & M. Cherif Bassiouni eds. 1987).

(4) Should extraterritorial application differ depending upon whether the securities violation involves allegations of fraud? Consider the following statement from *Securities and Exchange Commission v. Kasser*, 548 F.2d 109, 114-16 (3d Cir. 1977):

> . . . . In our view, the federal securities laws do grant jurisdiction in transnational securities cases where at least some activity designed to further a fraudulent scheme occurs within this country. . .
>
> From a policy perspective, and it should be recognized that this case in a large measure calls for a policy decision, we believe that there are sound rationales for asserting jurisdiction. First, to deny such jurisdiction may embolden those who wish to defraud foreign securities purchasers or sellers to use the United States as a base of operations. By sustaining the decision of the district court as to the lack of jurisdiction, we would, in effect, create a haven for such defrauders and manipulators. We are reluctant to conclude that Congress intended to allow the United States to become a "Barbary Coast," as it were, harboring international securities "pirates."
>
> We also are concerned that a holding of no jurisdiction might induce reciprocal responses on the part of other nations. Some countries might decline to act against individuals and corporations seeking to transport securities frauds to the United States. Such parties may well be outside the ambit of the power of our courts. For foreign nations to adopt the position that the defendants are urging this Court to take would enable defrauders beyond the reach of our courts to escape with impunity. By finding jurisdiction here, we may encourage other nations to take appropriate steps against parties who seek to perpetrate frauds in the United States. Accordingly, our inclination towards finding jurisdiction is bolstered by the prospect of reciprocal action against fraudulent schemes aimed at the United States from foreign sources.
>
> As a final policy justification for asserting jurisdiction here, we register the opinion that the antifraud provisions of the 1933 and 1934 Acts were designed to insure high standards of conduct in securities transactions within this country in addition to protecting domestic markets and investors from the effects of fraud. By reviving the complaint in this case, this Court will enhance the ability of the SEC to police vigorously the conduct of securities dealings within the United States. Such a result would appear to comport with the basic purposes of the federal statutes. . . .

How might the jurisdiction question differ when the matter does not involve an aspect of fraud? Consider the following passage from *Europe and Overseas Commodity Traders v. Banque Paribas London*, 147 F.3d 118, 125 (2d Cir. 1998):

> [B]ecause it is well-settled in this Circuit that "the anti-fraud provisions

of American securities laws have broader extraterritorial reach than American filing requirements," . . . the extent of conduct or effect in the United States needed to invoke U.S. jurisdiction over a claimed violation of the registration provisions must be greater than that which would trigger U.S. jurisdiction over a claim of fraud. To adapt the conduct and effects test for use in interpreting the registration provisions, we must take into account Congress's distinct purpose in drafting the registration laws.

See also Plessey Company PLC v. General Electric Company, 628 F. Supp. 477, 494 (D. Del. 1986) ("[a]lthough the Second Circuit has developed a substantial jurisprudence on the extraterritorial effect of the Exchange Act, its cases have focused largely on adjudicating acts of fraud . . . As Judge Friendly has said, '[t]he problem of conflict between our laws and that of a foreign government is much less when the issue is the enforcement of the anti-fraud sections of the securities laws than with such provisions as those requiring registration of persons or securities.' " *ITT v. Cornfeld*, 619 F.2d at 921).

(5) Should parallel investigations, by the Securities Exchange Commission and a grand jury acting under the Department of Justice, be permitted to occur? *See Securities and Exchange Commission v. Dresser Industries, Inc.*, 628 F.2d 1368, 1377 (D.C. Cir. 1980) ("The SEC cannot always wait for Justice to complete the criminal proceedings if it is to obtain the necessary prompt civil remedy; neither can Justice always await the conclusion of the civil proceeding without endangering its criminal case. Thus we should not block parallel investigations by these agencies in the absence of 'special circumstances' in which the nature of the proceedings demonstrably prejudices substantial rights of the investigated party or of the government."). *See also* ELLEN S. PODGOR & JEROLD H. ISRAEL, WHITE COLLAR CRIME IN A NUTSHELL 298-319 (1997).

(6) Are investigations of securities fraud always initially investigated by the Securities Exchange Commission? *See* R. Robin McDonald, *International Securities Fraud probe Targets Marietta Woman*, ATL. J. CONST., May 27, 1996, at D1 (describes U.S. Bureau of Alcohol, Tobacco & Firearms investigation of an individual being investigated for possible international securities fraud "for making 'straw purchases' of firearms for her fiancé, a convicted felon, to sell in South Africa.")

(7) The International Securities Enforcement Cooperation Act of 1990 allowed for increased enforcement of securities violations. "In 1997, the SEC made 240 requests to foreign governments for enforcement assistance. In some cases, the SEC used the foreign governments to help secure incriminating documents, in others, they used assistance to help prosecute the violators overseas." Jason Anthony, Amani Harrison, Patrick Linehan & Jeffery Palker, Note, *Securities Fraud*, 36 AM. CRIM. L. REV. 1095, 1146 (1999).

Chapter 5
EXPORT CONTROLS

The United States government places restrictions on international trade through criminal statutes that control transfers on certain goods. Key among the statutes is the Export Administration Act that requires licenses when certain goods are shipped. 50 U.S.C.App. §§ 2401-2420. Military related items are also subject to restrictions found in the Arms Export Control Act (22 U.S.C. §§ 2751-2796(d). Other Acts have also restricted trade between the United States and other countries. (*e.g.*, Trading with the Enemy Act). Considerations that can factor into criminalizing violations of export controls are national security and protection of technology. [*See also* chap. 6 for a discussion regarding computer crimes.]

§ 5.01   Export Administration Act

UNITED STATES v. SHETTERLY

United States Court of Appeals for the Seventh Circuit
971 F.2d 67 (1992)

KANNE, CIRCUIT JUDGE:

After a jury trial, Donald Shetterly was convicted of attempting to export a controlled microwave amplifier to (then) West Germany without an export license in violation of § 2410(a) of the Export Administration Act of 1979, 50 U.S.C. § 2401, et seq., and was sentenced to 41 months imprisonment. He now appeals his conviction and sentence and we affirm.

In 1987, Mr. Shetterly owned and operated Stoney Creek Limited, Inc., d/b/a Anderson Honda, a motorcycle sales and service dealership in Anderson, Indiana. Mr. Shetterly was introduced to Karl Mann, a West German businessman, by a business partner. From 1987 through 1989, Mr. Shetterly sent electronic equipment, including microwave amplifiers and computer software, to Mr. Mann in West Germany. Mr. Mann had told Mr. Shetterly that he could obtain the equipment less expensively in the United States than in West Germany.

In October 1988, Mr. Mann sent a letter to Mr. Shetterly requesting him to purchase an amplifier from Berkshire Technologies, Inc., of Oakland, California, "model no. BTL-1.6-30 H1," with a 20 degrees Kelvin operating temperature.

. . . On November 10, 1988, Mr. Shetterly faxed an order to Berkshire for "one amplifier model number L-1.6-30 HI at a cost of $ 6,500.00." The amplifier was on the Department of Commerce's commodity control list and therefore a validated license was required for its exportation out of the United States.[2] Berkshire, which had previously sold only one HI amplifier, contacted the Department of Commerce and agreed to cooperate in an investigation of Mr. Shetterly.

As part of the investigation, Maureen Barnato, a Berkshire employee, called Mr. Shetterly on November 14, 1988, concerning the order. Ms. Barnato informed Mr. Shetterly that the HI amplifier was a controlled item and therefore an export license was required for its shipment out of the country. Mr. Shetterly told Ms. Barnato that the amplifier would not be exported. . . . Mr. Shetterly received the amplifier, isolator and a power supply on March 17, 1989. . . . Mr. Shetterly's sale price of the amplifier to Mr. Mann was $ 7,150.00. . . .

Mr. Shetterly argues that the evidence is insufficient to support his conviction. . . . Mr. Shetterly asserts that the government failed to establish that the amplifier shipped to him had a net value in excess of $ 5,000.00 and therefore required a validated license for its exportation. "Net value" is defined as the larger of the actual selling price of the commodity or its current market price, to the same type of purchaser in the United States. . . . In fact, he submits that the testimony of his expert witnesses established that the amplifier had a net value below $ 5,000.00. . . . However, this evidence merely conflicts with evidence presented by the government. Mr. Shetterly intended to purchase the amplifier at a price of $ 6,500.00. Any modification of the amplifier would only have affected its market price and is not relevant because the actual selling price was greater than $ 5,000.00. . . . There was sufficient evidence submitted to show that the net value of the amplifier was greater than $ 5,000.00. The conflicting testimony concerning the value of the isolator was for the jury to consider; the jury apparently found Mr. Lum's testimony more credible.

Mr. Shetterly contends that even if the net value of the amplifier exceeded

---

[2]Export licenses are required for exporting certain commodities under the Export Administration Act. . . . A general license merely requires that the commodity meet certain standards – no license application is necessary and no license document is issued. . . . A validated license requires the exporter to file a license application before exporting commodities which cannot be exported under a general license or with other authorization by the Office of Export Licensing. . . . Such commodities are included in the Department of Commerce's commodity control list. . . . At the time of the offense, a validated license was required for exportation of the Berkshire amplifier because its value exceeded $ 5,000.00. . . . However, the Berkshire amplifier was exempted from the control list, effective July 1, 1990; therefore, a validated license is no longer needed for its exportation. The district court granted the government's pre-trial motion in limine prohibiting Shetterly from making any reference to this change as it occurred after the date of the offense.

$ 5,000.00, the government failed to prove that he was aware of its value. . . . Although Mr. Shetterly asserts that at most he knew that the amplifier and isolator together cost $ 6,500.00, he ordered "one amplifier model number L-1.6-30 HI at a cost of $ 6,500.00" . . . from Berkshire. In addition, Ms. Barnato had warned Mr. Shetterly that the amplifier was a controlled item and that a license was needed for its exportation out of the country. . . .

An agent for the Department of Commerce testified that he had checked the government's records of export license applications and had found no record for an application by either Mr. Shetterly or Mr. Mann. On cross-examination, the agent testified that Mr. Mann's name was not on the Department's "black list" of end users for whom export licenses should not be granted and that the West German government had given him information about Mr. Mann's business. On redirect, the agent was asked about the information he had received from the West German government. Mr. Shetterly takes issue with the agent's response that he was told Mr. Mann was in the business of reselling electronic equipment to various places, including the People's Republic of China and Hong Kong. The agent's testimony responded to an issue raised during cross-examination; there was no plain error. . . .

The government introduced a letter from the Director of the Office of Technology and Policy Analysis for the Bureau of Export Administration, which stated that the Berkshire amplifier was a controlled item at the time of the offense. Mr. Shetterly contends that the letter is hearsay, testimonial, and was produced for purposes of litigation. Any error was harmless considering that other evidence was admitted which indicated that the amplifier was a controlled item at the time when Mr. Shetterly attempted to export it to West Germany without a license. . . .

Mr. Shetterly contends that Instruction No. 8 failed to properly set forth the essential element of knowledge in the charged offense. *See United States v. Jamil,* 707 F.2d 638, 642 (2d Cir. 1983) (knowledge is an essential element of proving a violation of the Export Administration Act, 50 U.S.C. § 2410(a)). In general, failure to instruct the jury on an essential element of the offense constitutes plain error. . . .

Instruction No. 8 reads in relevant part as follows:

To sustain the charge of unlawful exportation of a controlled commodity, as charged in Count 1 of the indictment, the government must prove the following propositions:

First: That [Mr. Shetterly] exported, or attempted to export, the [Berkshire amplifier];

Second: That [Mr. Shetterly] did so without first having obtained a validated export license from the United States Department of Commerce;

Third: That the exportation of the [Berkshire amplifier] required a validated export license; and

Fourth: That [Mr. Shetterly] did so knowingly.

Mr. Shetterly contends that the instruction failed to indicate whether "knowingly" modifies only the first element, that he exported or attempted to export the amplifier, and therefore removed the issue whether he knew that an export license was needed from the jury. . . .

50 U.S.C. § 2410(a) states that one who "knowingly violates or conspires to or attempts to violate any provision of [the Export Administration Act], or any regulation, order or license issued thereunder" commits a crime. Mr. Shetterly contends that an exportation or attempted exportation of a controlled commodity without a license becomes a crime under § 2410(a) only when the exporter knows that a license is required. We agree with the government's assertions that Mr. Shetterly's reading of the statute would require the government to prove a "willful" violation, which is prohibited by § 2410(b) and carries a stiffer penalty, and that specific intent is not required for a violation of § 2410(a).

In order to establish that Mr. Shetterly violated § 2410(a), the government was required to prove beyond a reasonable doubt that Mr. Shetterly knowingly exported or attempted to export a controlled commodity, without obtaining the appropriate export license, in violation of 15 C.F.R. § 799.1 Supp.1 (the commodities control list). . . . Instruction No. 8 properly set forth the government's burden. Any ambiguity in the instruction was to Shetterly's benefit as he would have been held to a higher standard than was required by § 2410(a), the statute under which he was charged. There was no plain error.

Mr. Shetterly contends that Instruction No. 15 was an incomplete description of "net value." He acknowledges that the instruction was a verbatim recital of the regulation defining "net value," 15 C.F.R. § 771.5, but contends that it was insufficient. He asserts that the jury should have been instructed to subtract the value of the isolator in calculating the net value of the amplifier, and informed about shipping charges, nonreusable containers, and how certain terms in the regulation are determined. We disagree. The evidence indicated that the isolator was a separate and uncontrolled item. Therefore, the jury could have inferred that the value of the isolator should not be included in a determination of the value of the amplifier. Moreover, the other matters were not material issues at trial. Instruction No. 15 was properly given to the jury; there was no plain error. The district court did not err in instructing the jury. . . .

Finally, Mr. Shetterly argues that the district court misapplied the Sentencing Guidelines by refusing to depart below the Guidelines. See 18 U.S.C. § 3742(a)(2). The district court sentences a defendant within the range of the Sentencing Guidelines unless the court finds aggravating or mitigating factors of a kind or to a degree not adequately considered by the Commission in formulating the Guidelines. . . . In determining whether a circumstance was adequately considered by the Commission, a court can consider only the Guidelines themselves, along with its policy statements and the official

:ommentary of the Commission. . . .

Mr. Shetterly was sentenced pursuant to Guideline § 2M5.1, which provides for a base offense level of 22 "if national security or nuclear proliferation controls were invaded." One of the bases of the Export Administration Act is to protect national security. *See* 50 U.S.C. § 2402. Accordingly, the district judge sentenced Mr. Shetterly to 41 months of imprisonment, the minimum sentence in the applicable Guideline range. Mr. Shetterly alleges that trial counsel's petition to depart downward from the Guidelines was inadequate, and that the district court erred in failing to consider the implication of Application Note 2 of Guideline § 2M5.1, whereby a court can consider the degree to which the violation threatened a security interest of the United States, the volume of commerce involved, the extent of planning or sophistication, and whether there were multiple occurrences in determining a sentence within the Guidelines. The Note also provides that where such factors are present in an extreme form, a departure from the Guidelines may be warranted. . . . In sentencing Mr. Shetterly, the district judge stated:

> In this case it is fairly obvious, exporting these kinds of things outside the United States is something that Congress decided would be a threat to national security. What is a threat to national security in 1985, may not be a threat to national security in 1990. Technology changes, everybody catches up, Congress doesn't move very quickly. In any case, what you did, what you were found guilty of, was a crime at the time, and I don't know why it is not a crime today. . . . If I see something that [Congress didn't] consider [in the Guidelines], then I bring that up. . . . All of the things that [Mr. Shetterly has] urged in this case are taken into account by the Guidelines . . . . And in this case I specifically don't see any reason to depart from these Guidelines.

The district judge's statements indicate he considered that it would no longer be illegal to export the Berkshire amplifier out of the country without a license. The record does not indicate that the district judge believed he lacked authority to depart from the Guidelines; rather it is clear that the judge used his discretion in refusing to depart. Therefore, we have no jurisdiction to review his refusal to depart. . . .

We AFFIRM Mr. Shetterly's conviction and sentence.

CONGRESSIONAL FINDINGS AND POLICY

50 App. U.S.C. § 2401   Congressional findings

The Congress makes the following findings:

(1) The ability of United States citizens to engage in international commerce is a fundamental concern of United States policy.

(2) Exports contribute significantly to the economic well-being of the United States and the stability of the world economy by increasing employment and production in the United States, and by earning foreign exchange, thereby contributing favorably to the trade balance. The restriction of exports from the United States can have serious adverse effects on the balance of payments and on domestic employment, particularly when restrictions applied by the United States are more extensive than those imposed by other countries.

(3) It is important for the national interest of the United States that both the private sector and the Federal Government place a high priority on exports, consistent with the economic, security, and foreign policy objectives of the United States.

(4) The availability of certain materials at home and abroad varies so that the quantity and composition of United States exports and their distribution among importing countries may affect the welfare of the domestic economy and may have an important bearing upon fulfillment of the foreign policy of the United States.

(5) Exports of goods or technology without regard to whether they make a significant contribution to the military potential of individual countries or combinations of countries may adversely affect the national security of the United States.

(6) Uncertainty of export control policy can inhibit the efforts of United States business and work to the detriment of the overall attempt to improve the trade balance of the United States.

(7) Unreasonable restrictions on access to world supplies can cause worldwide political and economic instability, interfere with free international trade, and retard the growth and development of nations.

(8) It is important that the administration of export controls imposed for national security purposes give special emphasis to the need to control exports of technology (and goods which contribute significantly to the transfer of such technology) which could make a significant contribution to the military potential of any country or combination of countries which would be detrimental to the national security of the United States.

(9) Minimization of restrictions on exports of agricultural commodities and products is of critical importance to the maintenance of a sound agricultural sector, to a positive contribution to the balance of payments, to reducing the level of Federal expenditures for agricultural support programs, and to United States cooperation in efforts to eliminate malnutrition and world hunger.

(10) It is important that the administration of export controls imposed for foreign policy purposes give special emphasis to the need to control exports of goods and substances hazardous to the public health and the environment which are banned or severely restricted for use in the United States, and which, if exported, could affect the international reputation of the United States as a responsible trading partner.

(11) Availability to controlled countries of goods and technology from foreign sources is a fundamental concern of the United States and should be eliminated through negotiations and other appropriate means whenever possible.

(12) Excessive dependence of the United States, its allies, or countries sharing common strategic objectives with the United States, on energy and other critical resources from potential adversaries can be harmful to the mutual and individual security of all those countries. . . .

50 App. U.S.C. § 2402   Congressional declaration of policy

The Congress makes the following declarations:

(1) It is the policy of the United States to minimize uncertainties in export control policy and to encourage trade with all countries with which the United States has diplomatic or trading relations, except those countries with which such trade has been determined by the President to be against the national interest.

(2) It is the policy of the United States to use export controls only after full consideration of the impact on the economy of the United States and only to the extent necessary–

   (A) to restrict the export of goods and technology which would make a significant contribution to the military potential of any other country or combination of countries which would prove detrimental to the national security of the United States;

   (B) to restrict the export of goods and technology where necessary to further significantly the foreign policy of the United States or to fulfill its declared international obligations; and

   (C) to restrict the export of goods where necessary to protect the domestic economy from the excessive drain of scarce materials and to reduce the serious inflationary impact of foreign demand.

(3) It is the policy of the United States (A) to apply any necessary controls to the maximum extent possible in cooperation with all nations, and (B) to

encourage observance of a uniform export control by all nations with which the United States has defense treaty commitments or common strategic directives.

(4) It is the policy of the United States to use its economic resources and trade potential to further the sound growth and stability of its economy as well as to further its national security and foreign policy objectives.

(5) It is the policy of the United States–

(A) to oppose restrictive trade practices or boycotts fostered or imposed by foreign countries against other countries friendly to the United States or against any United States person;

(B) to encourage and, in specified cases, require United States persons engaged in the export of goods or technology or other information to refuse to take actions, including furnishing information or entering into or implementing agreements, which have the effect of furthering or supporting the restrictive trade practices or boycotts fostered or imposed by any foreign country against a country friendly to the United States or against any United States person; and

(C) to foster international cooperation and the development of international rules and institutions to assure reasonable access to world supplies.

(6) It is the policy of the United States that the desirability of subjecting, or continuing to subject, particular goods or technology or other information to United States export controls should be subjected to review by and consultation with representatives of appropriate United States Government agencies and private industry.

(7) It is the policy of the United States to use export controls, including license fees, to secure the removal by foreign countries of restrictions on access to supplies where such restrictions have or may have a serious domestic inflationary impact, have caused or may cause a serious domestic shortage, or have been imposed for purposes of influencing the foreign policy of the United States. In effecting this policy, the President shall make reasonable and prompt efforts to secure the removal or reduction of such restrictions, policies, or actions through international cooperation and agreement before imposing export controls. No action taken in fulfillment of the policy set forth in this paragraph shall apply to the export of medicine or medical supplies.

(8) It is the policy of the United States to use export controls to encourage other countries to take immediate steps to prevent the use of their territories or resources to aid, encourage, or give sanctuary to those persons involved in directing, supporting, or participating in acts of international terrorism. To achieve this objective, the President shall make reasonable and prompt efforts to secure the removal or reduction of such assistance to international terrorists through international cooperation and agreement before imposing export controls.

(9) It is the policy of the United States to cooperate with other countries with which the United States has defense treaty commitments or common strategic objectives in restricting the export of goods and technology which would make a significant contribution to the military potential of any country or combination of countries which would prove detrimental to the security of the United States and of those countries with which the United States has defense treaty commitments or common strategic objectives, and to encourage other friendly countries to cooperate in restricting the sale of goods and technology that can harm the security of the United States.

(10) It is the policy of the United States that export trade by United States citizens be given a high priority and not be controlled except when such controls (A) are necessary to further fundamental national security, foreign policy, or short supply objectives, (B) will clearly further such objectives, and (C) are administered consistent with basic standards of due process.

(11) It is the policy of the United States to minimize restrictions on the export of agricultural commodities and products.

(12) It is the policy of the United States to sustain vigorous scientific enterprise. To do so involves sustaining the ability of scientists and other scholars freely to communicate research findings, in accordance with applicable provisions of law, by means of publication, teaching, conferences, and other forms of scholarly exchange.

(13) It is the policy of the United States to control the export of goods and substances banned or severely restricted for use in the United States in order to foster public health and safety and to prevent injury to the foreign policy of the United States as well as to the credibility of the United States as a responsible trading partner.

(14) It is the policy of the United States to cooperate with countries which are allies of the United States and countries which share common strategic objectives with the United States in minimizing dependence on imports of energy and other critical resources from potential adversaries and in developing alternative supplies of such resources in order to minimize strategic threats posed by excessive hard currency earnings derived from such resource exports by countries with policies adverse to the security interests of the United States.

UNITED STATES v. GREGG

United States Court of Appeals for the Eighth Circuit
829 F.2d 1430 (1987)

DUMBAULD, SENIOR DISTRICT JUDGE:

Appellants, Werner Ernst Gregg and his wife Roswitha Gregg, operated an export business known as Gregg International, handling avionics devices. Both defendants appeal from denial of their motion to suppress evidence. Werner Gregg also alleges various trial errors. We affirm the judgments of conviction.

The curious feature of this case is that the customs agents investigating defendants' possible violation of export prohibitions first scrutinized trash collected from defendants' residence and place of business, and "found gold" in the form of discarded telex communications between defendants and customers. On the basis of these telexes the agents prepared affidavits which convinced Magistrate Calvin Hamilton that a search warrant should issue authorizing interception of current telex communications of Gregg International. Details of the investigation are described in the opinion of the District Court denying the motion to suppress. *U.S. v. Gregg,* 629 F. Supp. 958 at 959-61 (W.D.Mo. W.D. 1986). As a result of the telex materials, together with subsequent searches of the Greggs' residence and business, customs searches when Werner Gregg was personally attempting to carry merchandise out of the country, and statements taken from the defendants, an indictment containing thirteen counts was returned against both defendants. Werner Gregg was convicted on Counts I-IV, and VII-IX, both inclusive and was sentenced, in the aggregate, to three years custody, followed by five years' probation, and a $ 200,000 fine. Roswitha Gregg was fined $ 4000 and three years confinement, suspended except for six months. A proviso ordered that husband and wife not be incarcerated simultaneously.
. . .

Counts I-IV charged violations of section 38 of the Foreign Military Sales Act of October 22, 1968, 82 Stat. 1320, as added by Section 212 (a) (1) of the International Security Assistance and Arms Export Control Act of 1976, 90 Stat. 729, 744-45, section 201 (a) of which changed the name of the Foreign Military Sales Act to the Arms Export Control Act [90 Stat. 734], 22 U.S.C. § 2778, ... It will be noted that allegations of willfulness are contained in every count under which Werner Gregg was convicted. It is also noteworthy that the prosecutors did not utilize the false representation provisions of 22 U.S.C. § 2778 (c), but relied on 18 U.S.C. §§ 1001 and 1002.

Count VII involved items for which a license from the Commerce Department was required, and alleged violation of section 11(b) of the Export Administration Act of 1979, 93 Stat. 503, 529, 50 U.S.C. App. § 2410, which provides:

(a) Except as provided in subsection (b) of this section, whoever knowingly violates or conspires to or attempts to violate any provision of this Act [sections 2401 to 2420 of this Appendix] or any regulation, order, or license issued thereunder shall be fined not more than five times the value of the exports involved or $ 50,000, whichever is greater, or imprisoned not more than 5 years, or both. (b) (1) Whoever willfully violates or conspires to or attempts to violate any provision of this Act [sections 2401 to 2420 of this Appendix] or any regulation, order, or license issued thereunder, with knowledge that the exports involved will be used for the benefit of, or that the destination or intended destination of the goods or technology involved is, any controlled country or any country to which exports are controlled for foreign policy purposes –

* * *

(B) in the case of an individual, shall be fined not more than $ 250,000, or imprisoned not more than 10 years, or both.

It will be noted that conviction under this statute requires proof of (1) willfulness; (2) violation of the Act or a regulation issued thereunder; (3) knowledge that the exports involved will be used for the benefit of, or that the destination or intended destination of the goods or technology involved is, any controlled country or any country to which exports are controlled for foreign policy purposes.

The Court's charge clearly covered these requisites:

The crime of attempted unlawful export of an item on the Commodity Control List as charged in Count VII of the indictment has two essential elements which are:

One: That the defendant intended to commit the crime of unlawful export of an item on the Commodity Control List; and

Two: That on or about June 25, 1984, the defendant intentionally carried out some act which was a substantial step towards the commission of the unlawful export of an item on the Commodity Control List.

To convict the defendant of an attempted unlawful export of an item on the Commodity Control List, the government must prove each of these essential elements beyond a reasonable doubt . . .

To assist you in determining whether the defendant intended to commit the crime of unlawful export of an item on the Commodity Control List, as required by element one above, you are advised that the elements of the offense alleged in Count VII are as follows:

First, that the defendant attempted to export the item alleged in the indictment;

Second, that the item was listed on the Department of Commerce Commodity Control List;

Third, that the defendant did so with knowledge that such item would be used for the benefit of a country to which exports are restricted for foreign policy purposes;

Fourth, that in so doing the defendant did not possess or have issued to him a validated license or other authorization for such export as required by law; and

Fifth, the defendant did such acts knowingly and willfully. . . .

Counts VIII and IX charged violations of 18 U.S.C. §§ 1001 and 1002. . . .

Appellant Werner Gregg strenuously contends that it was error not to admit as exhibits for consideration by the jury the Arms Export Control Act, the Export Administration Act, and the voluminous regulations thereunder. The argument is that they are relevant to the question whether specific intent was proved. Like questions of evidence generally, this was a matter for the trial court's discretion.

Strictly speaking, this material would be irrelevant since the crucial issue is not whether the jury would be confused by these massive legislative and bureaucratic artifacts (or even whether the courts would be confused thereby) but *whether Werner Gregg was confused* by them. There was evidence that Gregg possessed considerable expertise on the subject. Indeed he gave lectures and published newsletters on the subject. The trial court's charge admirably sifted out the portions of the statutes and regulations applicable to each count, and the pertinent references to the Munitions List and the Commodity Control List. The court's instructions likewise made it perfectly clear that the Government must prove beyond a reasonable doubt that the defendant acted knowingly and willfully, and with specific intent, and particular knowledge, as required by the respective counts involved. Construction of the statutes and regulations so as to determine with precision what was required for conviction on a particular count was a matter of law for the court to decide. There was no harmful error in not cluttering the record unnecessarily with additional voluminous and complex exhibits, which might indeed have distracted and unduly burdened or confused the jury.

Appellant also argues that the statutes and regulations are unconstitutionally vague. It is true that Congress enumerated various policies requiring conflicting factors to be weighed. Twenty points are specified in sections 2 and 3 of the Export Administration Act of 1979.

Thus Congress declares that exports contribute to national well-being, but some exports might be detrimental to national security by contributing to the military potential of unfriendly countries. Hence export controls should be imposed to restrict such exports, but only to the extent necessary, or to prevent drain of scarce materials, or to discourage restrictions imposed by foreign countries, or to encourage other countries to act against terrorism. There may be ambiguities and vagueness in these policy objectives, but the task of weighing and balancing the conflicting factors is committed by Congress to Executive discretion. As explained clearly by Judge Zobel in *U.S. v. Moller-Butcher*, 560 F. Supp. 550, 552-553 (D. Mass. 1983), Congress enumerated the factors which are to guide the discretion of the executive department, but "also clearly expressed its desire that the executive branch, not the courts, have the final word on which items should be restricted."

The policy factors specified by Congress are not elements of the criminal offense of unlawful export. When the case gets to court, all that the Government needs to prove is that the item exported appears on the Munitions List or the Commodity Control List, as the case may be (and, of course, that the defendant knowingly and willfully exported it, with the necessary intent and knowledge, and without an appropriate license). There is no unconstitutional vagueness. It is as simple a matter as forbidding a passenger to ride on a train without a valid ticket. . . .

What evidence does the record contain that appellant Gregg had such knowledge? The Government's brief is not helpful in pointing to any. . . . It would not be necessary to scrutinize the entire record (although we have done so) in order to conclude that there is plainly sufficient circumstantial evidence from which the jury might infer that Gregg knew that the destination of the Laser Nav was Japan, a country exports to which required a license.

It will be remembered that the Laser Nav was the item part of which was found in Gregg's hand-carried luggage at the Los Angeles airport when he was about to board Singapore Airlines flight 11 for the Tokyo international airport. The other portion of the Laser Nav had been checked through to Tokyo. The fact that Gregg had two sets of paperwork in his possession for the shipment, stating different values, is also indicative of devious guilty knowledge. This inference is corroborated by the fact that Gregg concocted a fictitious "lease" in an effort to get back the seized equipment. It is likewise significant that Honeywell jealously guards the Laser Nav against the possibility of "reverse engineering" and that Gregg resorted to subterfuge in procuring the device. Honeywell's sales agent was informed that it was to be used in an airplane owned by Jetex.

The contention that there was insufficient evidence to support a verdict of guilty cannot be accepted. . . .

AFFIRMED.

§ 5.02　　Arms Export Control Act

UNITED STATES v. BECK

United States Court of Appeals, Seventh Circuit
615 F.2d 441 (1980)

BAUER, CIRCUIT JUDGE:

Defendant-appellee Richard Beck was found guilty by a jury of one count of aiding and abetting the illegal export of arms in violation of 22 U.S.C. § 2778, 22 C.F.R. § 127.01, and 18 U.S.C. § 2, and five counts of aiding and abetting the filing of false customs export declarations in violation of 18 U.S.C. § 1001, 22 C.F.R. § 127.02 and 18 U.S.C. § 2. He was acquitted of a conspiracy count. . . . On May 29, 1979, six weeks after the verdict, the trial court granted the defendant's post-trial motion for a judgment of acquittal. On May 31, 1979, the court denied the Government's motion for reconsideration of the judgment of acquittal. . . . The Government appeals the trial court's ruling on several grounds. It asserts first that the trial court applied the wrong standard for ruling on a motion for acquittal; second, that the ruling was based on improper considerations; and third, that the evidence was sufficient to support the verdict. The Government also urges us to reassign the case to another district judge for sentencing in the event of a reversal. . . . Because we believe that the evidence was sufficient to sustain the jury's verdict as to each of the counts upon which the defendant was convicted, we reverse. . . .

The commercial export of arms and ammunition from the United States is governed by the Arms Export Control Act, 22 U.S.C. § 2778, and the International Traffic in Arms Regulations (ITAR), 22 C.F.R. §§ 121-30. Persons desiring to export arms from the United States must first register with the State Department's Office of Munitions Control (OMC) and then obtain individual export licenses for each shipment of arms abroad. 22 C.F.R. §§ 122, 123.

Licenses for specific shipments are granted or withheld by the OMC on the basis of a number of considerations, principally the foreign policy of the United States toward the country of the arms' destination. 22 C.F.R. § 123.05. Since 1963, the United States, as a matter of its foreign policy, has prohibited the commercial sale of arms to the Republic of South Africa.

Richard Beck, a South African citizen, owned and operated an importing business with a partner, Roland Whiteing. The business, as described by Beck, imported sporting goods, firearms, photographic equipment and radio equipment. . . . In April 1977, Whiteing contacted Seymour Freilich, the main operating officer of Concealable Body Armour of America (CBA), a police equipment distributor in Detroit. Freilich indicated that he was willing to supply Beck with a variety of munitions. CBA was an OMC registrant, but had never applied for any arms export licenses.

Beck wrote to Freilich after Whiteing returned to South Africa. Beck's first letter of April 25, 1977 outlined what became the framework for his future arrangements with Freilich and detailed the shipping, labelling and means of payment for each shipment. Beck requested that his orders be filled in small parcels (only two or three guns to a package) in order "to make it less conspicuous from your side and also have a less chance of being confiscated en route." Beck stated that payment would be by international letter of credit. . . .

At the same time, Beck asked Freilich to send a separate invoice by mail listing all firearms by serial numbers for use by Beck's customs clearing agent, Freight Services. The import of American weapons into South Africa is legal under South African law; South African customs law is, however, quite strict. In order to clear through customs, Freight Services had to demonstrate that the weapons' serial numbers corresponded with invoices.

A series of letters followed, detailing orders by Beck to Freilich for various munitions. Several shipments were made pursuant to the international letters of credit established by Beck. In each case, CBA usually Freilich personally delivered the goods directly to the air freight forwarding company. The air freight company then prepared certain shipping documents based on the information Freilich provided.

Among the documents prepared were United States Customs Export Declarations, which inform the Customs Service of the contents, ultimate consignee and ultimate destination of export shipments. Freilich told each air freight forwarding company to label the cartons as sporting goods. An employee of the forwarding company then looked to the United States Commodity Schedule B and picked the number corresponding to that description. The CBA cartons were designated number 735.1500, which covers underwater breathing devices and game, sport, gymnastic, athletic or playground equipment. This designation was repeated on every CBA shipment.

On October 27, 1977, President Carter announced at a news conference that the United States would support a mandatory arms embargo against the Republic of South Africa to be instituted by all countries of the United Nations. The President said that the United States would intensify its existing embargo on South Africa arms sales by extending the embargo beyond firearms to include a number of categories of police and military equipment and by forbidding the sale of spare weapons parts. While the Carter announcement did not alter the existing U.S. ban on arms sales to South Africa, it focused considerable public attention on United States arms policy toward South Africa both here and in that country. As a measure of the widespread attention the Carter announcement received in South Africa, clippings were introduced at trial from three South African papers showing that the United Nations embargo, the Carter announcement and related events had provoked extensive most often front page coverage every day from October 26 through November 1.

On November 1, four days after the Carter announcement, Beck wrote Freilich with a new order. His letter opened:

It is very sad that our mutual friend Mr. Carter is making our business as difficult as possible but I am sure we will circumvent his best intentions somehow.

Starting with the very next shipment on November 19, 1977, letters of credit were abandoned as the means of payment in favor of international wire transfers. A wire transfer is a direct movement of funds from buyer to seller. Unlike a letter of credit, payment by these means gives no indication to the various bank intermediaries of any details destination, purchaser, nature of goods involved in the underlying transaction.

While the November 19 shipment was sent directly to South Africa, the next shipment on November 23 was sent to a "Werner Saneli [sic], Gondrand Bros., Ltd., Schoneggstrasse # 5, 8021 Zurich, Switzerland." Werner Sameli is the air freight manager of Gondrand Bros., a Swiss customs brokerage firm. Shipping documents reflected Zurich to be the ultimate destination. . . . Gondrand Bros. sent the goods on to South Africa on November 29. A wire transfer for the value of the shipment and shipping costs to Zurich was sent to CBA by Aimcom the same day.

On December 28, 1977, Beck sent Freilich an extensive order. On January 23, 1978, CBA packed 140 weapons and 5,000 rounds of ammunition in ten cartons. On January 25 Freilich delivered the cartons, along with seventeen cartons of flashlights, to Pandair, his new freight forwarding company. The five shipper's export declarations, prepared at Freilich's direction, described the commodities as 27 cartons of "Sporting Equipment" with Schedule B Commodity Number 735.1500 listed on the form.

Subsequently, the shipment was sent on an American Airlines flight to Chicago, where the boxes were to be transferred to a Swissair flight to Zurich. Buckley-Jones then sent several cables to Sameli again detailing the airway bill numbers and transshipment instructions.

The shipment, however, did not leave O'Hare; it was delayed, first, because of snow, and then because one box in the shipment was misplaced. Then on February 11 an American Airlines freight handler noticed ammunition through a tear in one of the boxes. He informed his supervisor, who in turn notified federal law enforcement agencies. On Monday, February 13, the boxes were inspected by United States Customs Service agents. After examining the export declarations and confirming that OMC showed no export license covering the shipment, the agents seized the ten boxes containing the firearms and ammunition.

Unaware of the Government's seizure in Chicago, the various parties to the shipment attempted to locate the guns and ammunition. On February 21, 1978, Werner Sameli phoned Pandair in Detroit at Buckley-Jones' urging. He then telexed South Africa, informing Buckley-Jones that the cartons were still in Chicago due to snow but that they would be shipped out on the next flight to Zurich. The same day Beck sent a wire transfer for $ 26,532.77 to CBA covering the cost of the shipment and freight charges to Zurich.

Meanwhile in Chicago, the Customs agents loaded the Aimcom shipment onto the Swissair flight that Sameli had promised. The agents retained all of the firearms and ammunition, except one revolver which was sent on with the shipment. They filled the original cartons with old books.

The next day at 9 a. m. (Zurich time), Sameli informed Buckley-Jones that the sporting goods were on their way and requested shipping instructions. Buckley-Jones telexed back that Sameli should send the shipment on the first available Johannesburg flight. . . . Later that day, however, after the flight arrived, Sameli refused to ship out the goods. He discovered that he was listed, not as the consignee, but as the buyer on all the documents accompanying the cartons. He therefore had full financial responsibility for the shipment. He also found a clause on the commercial invoice prohibiting diversion of the goods beyond Switzerland. Sameli telexed Johannesburg that he would not do "illegal business" and that he would not ship the goods out of Switzerland.

Buckley-Jones responded the next day, February 23, and asked Sameli to hold the goods while the importer contacted the U.S.A. The next morning, February 24, Freight Services telexed Sameli that the invoices were in error and that new ones would be sent from the United States. The amended invoices never arrived.

On March 15, the shipment was seized by Swiss customs. Sameli, cooperating with Swiss customs, waited nearly two weeks to see what actions the South Africans would take before advising them of the results. Finally, on March 28, he telexed:

> [attention] mr buckley jones x re sporting goods x on the occasion of the transfer of the goods to the bonded warehouse customs ordered the shipment to be physically examined x the following contents was found x 17 cartons containing flashlights x 10 cartons containing sales boxes for revolvers filled with old books and one sales box for revolver containing a revolver x this gun was seized by customs authorities on behalf of the swiss federal attorney x since it is illegal to import weapons of any kind aneee [sic] or handle weapons of any kind in transit we face prosecution and since shipment was addressed to mr sameli any measures taken will be against this person x we await your comments and we mainly are interested in who is to cover the cost accumulated x regards x w h sameli.

Buckley-Jones replied that "we are shocked and amazed to hear the news especially when you advise us of what [the] contents were."

On August 3, 1978, the instant indictment was returned against Beck, Freilich and CBA. Beck was charged with conspiracy and with aiding and abetting the commission by Freilich of two offenses involving the seized shipment: (1) the attempted export of arms without an export license and (2) the making of false statements in export declarations. Three false statements were charged in each of the five other counts: (1) that the cartons contained commodities corresponding to Customs Schedule B Commodity No. 735.1500, namely underwater breathing devices and game, sport, gymnastic, athletic or playground equipment; (2) that the goods were ultimately destined for Zurich, Switzerland; and (3) that the goods were destined for an ultimate consignee named Mr. Werner Sameli, c/o Gondrand Bros. Ltd., Zurich, Switzerland. The news immediately reached South Africa where it was reported in a number of South African papers and where Beck read of his indictment. . . . On November 16, 1978, Richard Beck left South Africa for the United States and was arrested when he arrived in Chicago on November 17 by U.S. customs agents. . . .

Criminal intent is often difficult to demonstrate by direct proof; it may be inferred from the attendant facts and circumstances. . . . Conviction under 22 U.S.C. § 2778(a) and (c) and 22 C.F.R. § 127.01 requires proof that the defendant (1) exported or attempted to export (2) goods that are on the United States Munitions List (3) without first having obtained a license for the export (4) willfully. The trial court found the evidence insufficient to prove Beck's participation in the attempted export. In ruling on the motion for acquittal, the trial court said Beck did nothing more than order and buy the merchandise.

Unless every purchaser is an aider and abettor of every seller in anything the seller does in connection with the sale, there is nothing in this situation which indicates that Mr. Beck was any more than a purchaser of Mr. Freilich's merchandise, and that Mr. Freilich was the one who was responsible. Beck adds that he did not aid an illegal export, but only arranged a legal import.

The buyer-seller, importer-exporter labels tend to lead the arguments down the road of semantics rather than substance. A purchaser of stolen goods is not liable as an aider and abettor of the theft because of his status as a buyer, but because he enters the plan too late. . . . The gravamen of the offense is the theft, not what happens to the goods afterwards. If the defendant does not aid the theft itself, he does not commit an act that aids the commission of the offense.

The illegal act required in a § 2778 prosecution is an export or attempted export that is, the movement of goods across the international border. Beck did not merely purchase guns in South Africa which had already been exported. He worked actively with Freilich in developing the export plan. He gave specific packaging instructions so that there would be less chance of confiscation and said the goods should be shipped via direct South African flights for the same reason. He later arranged for a different freight forwarding company to call

Freilich; Freilich changed shippers. He sent Freilich a copy of his import permits so that Freilich could tailor his invoices to Beck's needs. Beck consciously assisted the transportation of the goods across the international border. He did not enter the plan too late, but did so right on time. . . . Since Beck consciously assisted the attempted export, he committed the act required to be held liable as an aider and abettor.

Beck next asserts that even if he assisted the export, he lacked the requisite intent. Beck testified at trial that he did not know that Freilich lacked an export license; he further testified that he thought the export of the guns, which he characterized as sporting goods, was perfectly legal in the United States.

Beck's first contention has already been rejected as a basis for overturning a guilty verdict. In *United States v. Lizarraga-Lizarraga,* 541 F.2d 826 (9th Cir. 1976), the Ninth Circuit held that the defendant need not know that he is specifically required to have an export license. Rather, "the "willfully' requirement of § 1934 (the predecessor statute to § 2778) indicates that the defendant must know that his conduct in exporting from the United States articles proscribed by the statute is violative of the law." . . . The government must "prove that the defendant voluntarily and intentionally violated a known legal duty not to export the proscribed articles." Since the aider and abettor must have the same state of mind as the principal, an aider and abettor need not know that the principal needs or lacks an export license. The prosecution must only show that the defendant was aware of a legal duty not to export the articles.

Evidence adduced at trial showed that Beck had been in the arms business since 1972 and that he was a well-educated, knowledgeable businessman. Beck admitted that he knew about the arms embargo on South Africa but said he thought it was "on military weapons, military hardware and not directly on sporting rifles and sporting handguns."

The jury could have easily disbelieved Beck's story that the guns were sporting goods. The seized shipment, for example, contained 5 Armalite rifles described by Beck on the witness stand as sporting goods. . . . The jury certainly could have drawn the inference that Beck read about or heard about the intensification of the arms embargo.

Beck testified that he thought the intensification would make it more difficult, but not impossible, to get weapons. He admitted, however, that he understood "Mr. Carter's intention was to intensify (the export ban to) include all sporting weapons of any type." Beck also admitted that he had "no way" of circumventing Carter's intentions. It was soon after the announcement that the mode of payment was switched to a less conspicuous method, wire transfer, and a little later that the shipping route was switched. Beck's earlier letters also indicated that Freilich was to pack guns a few at a time to avoid confiscation. All of this is circumstantial evidence of a desire to avoid detection and thus also evidence of his knowledge of a duty not to export. Knowledge that the principal engages in subterfuges in order to export arms supports the inference that the alleged aider and abettor knows of a legal duty not to export the arms. . . .

Evidence that Beck came to the United States voluntarily was admitted to support Beck's claim that he did not know the export of the guns was illegal. . . . Beck also testified that he believed the indictment was the result of some kind of mixup; that Freilich had presented an arms license to the court and that the court had in turn dropped the indictment. . . . The events surrounding Beck's decision to come to the United States do not necessarily exonerate Beck. The jury could have easily decided that Beck came to the United States only because he believed that the charges had been dropped. . . .

Admittedly there was some evidence that Beck did not have the requisite intent. When evidence conflicts, however, the trial judge must let the jury perform its historic function. . . . There was enough evidence to require jury consideration, and there was support for the verdict in the record. It was therefore error for the trial court to grant the motion for acquittal as to this count. . . . REVERSED AND REMANDED WITH DIRECTIONS.

NOTES AND QUESTIONS

(1)   What level of wilfulness is required by the Arms Export Control Act? In *United States v. Murphy*, 852 F.2d 1 (1st Cir. 1988), the court stated:

> To sustain a conviction under sec. 2778, the government must prove that the defendant (1) willfully (2) engaged in the business of exporting (3) defense articles (4) that are on the United States Munitions List (5) without a license. *See United States v. Beck,* 615 F.2d 441, 450 (7th Cir. 1980). Murphy would like to escape conviction because the prosecution did not present evidence that Murphy knew he had to register with the United States government and that the arms were on the Munitions List before sending them to Ireland. While the act does require proof of specific intent, willfulness means that "defendant must know that his conduct in exporting from the United States articles proscribed by the statute is violative of the law." *United States v. Lizarraga-Lizarraga,* 541 F.2d 826, 828-29 (9th Cir. 1976) (requiring specific intent under 22 U.S.C. § 1934, the predecessor statute to sec. 2778). In other words, the "government must prove that the defendant voluntarily and intentionally violated a known legal duty not to export the proscribed articles." . . . Therefore, it is sufficient that the government prove that Murphy knew he had a legal duty not to export the weapons. . . .
>
> The prosecution proved beyond a reasonable doubt that Murphy knew it was illegal to send the weapons out of the country. Evidence of these

year-long clandestine efforts, covert acts, and subterfuges to purchase weapons for shipment to Ireland for the IRA's use supports the jury's verdict that Murphy was aware of that duty. . . .

The court's instruction incorporated all the elements of the offense and made clear that conviction would not require evidence that defendants knew of the licensing requirement or were aware of the munitions list. The instruction was as follows:

> an act is done willfully if it is committed with the knowledge that it was prohibited by law and with the purpose of disobeying or disregarding the law . . . Thus, while the government must show that a defendant knew that the exportation of firearms and munitions in this case was illegal, it is not necessary for the government to show that the defendants were aware of or had consulted the United States Munitions List or the licensing and registration provisions of the Arms Export Control Act and its regulations or the National Registration & Transfer Record or the Federal Firearms Law involved in count 2 . . . Ignorance of the law in this respect, in this case, is not an excuse. In this case, what is required is proof that the defendants acted knowingly and willfully with the specific intent to violate the law, and that's what I said to you.

The jury charge was proper under the statute and caselaw.

(2) "Willful" is a "word of many meanings" "often . . . influenced by its context." *Spies v. United States*, 317 U.S. 492, 497 (1943). Should wilfulness under the Arms Export Control Act be redefined as a result of the Supreme Court decision in *Ratzlaf v. United States*, 114 S.Ct. 655 (1994), where the Court stated, "We do not dishonor the venerable principle that ignorance of the law generally is no defense to a criminal charge. . . . In particular contexts, however, Congress may decree otherwise." *See also Cheek v. United States*, 498 U.S. 192 (1991) (complex tax statute).

(3) Do defendants have the right to contest whether an item is properly on the munitions list? Consider this issue as presented in the following case.

UNITED STATES v. MARTINEZ

United States Court of Appeals for the Eleventh Circuit
904 F.2d 601(1990)

RONEY, SENIOR CIRCUIT JUDGE:

Elizabeth Martinez and her fiance Mario Valladares were convicted of conspiring to violate and on six occasions violating the Arms Export Control Act

(AECA), 22 U.S.C.A. § 2778, based on their non-licensed exports of video signal descramblers which are included on the United States Munitions List, 22 C.F.R. § 121. The sole point asserted on this appeal is that such devices are not military in character and therefore do not belong on the Munitions List. Holding that the political question doctrine renders the propriety of an item's placement on the Munitions List a non-justiciable issue in Federal court, we affirm.

Defendants formed Pan-American Import Export, Inc. in Miami, Florida and began to export electronic systems designed to permit reception of television programming via satellite through the descrambling of pay television signals in conjunction with a home satellite receiver. They knew that the Videocipher II was a controlled item whose export required proper licensing, which they did not obtain, and they employed false invoicing and other schemes to avoid detection. They argue, nevertheless, that the inclusion of "cryptographic devices and software (encoding and decoding)" on the list is overbroad because this heading includes items already in the public domain whose dissemination would pose no security threat, and which lack any characteristic that is inherently or predominantly military.

The Arms Export Control Act authorizes the President of the United States to control the export of articles affecting the national security. . . . The regulations implementing this authority provide that the designation of items for the Munitions List be "made by the Department of State with the concurrence of the Department of Defense." 22 C.F.R. § 120.2. Such designations are to be "based primarily on whether an article . . . is deemed to be inherently military in character." 22 C.F.R. § 120.3.

Relying principally upon the constitutional framework of the separation of powers between the coordinate branches of Government, the Supreme Court has recognized that some questions are so inherently political as to be excluded from judicial review. *Baker v. Carr,* 369 U.S. 186, 210, 82 S. Ct. 691, 706, 7 L. Ed. 2d 663 (1962). Where, as here, the controversy involves Presidential and Congressional handling of a foreign affairs matter, the political question doctrine routinely precludes judicial scrutiny. . . . The Supreme Court has, for example, declined to evaluate the credentials of a foreign diplomat, *In re Baiz,* 135 U.S. 403, 10 S. Ct. 854, 34 L. Ed. 222 (1890), or to determine whether one ratifying a treaty in behalf of a foreign nation had the power to do so, *Doe v. Braden,* 57 U.S. (16 How.) 635, 14 L. Ed. 1090 (1854), or whether a new nation should be recognized, *United States v. Palmer,* 16 U.S. (3 Wheat.) 610, 4 L. Ed. 471 (1818), or whether a state of war exists, *The Divina Pastora,* 17 U.S. (4 Wheat.) 52, 4 L. Ed. 512 (1819), or whether a treaty was broken, *Ware v. Hylton,* 3 U.S. (3 Dall.) 199, 1 L. Ed. 568 (1796), or whether the President properly refused to grant a foreign air flight license, *Chicago & Southern Air Lines v. Waterman SS. Corp.,* 333 U.S. 103, 68 S. Ct. 431, 92 L. Ed. 568 (1948), because the conduct of foreign affairs lay at the heart of each case.

The question whether a particular item should have been placed on the Munitions List possesses nearly every trait that the Supreme Court has enumerated traditionally renders a question "political." . . . No satisfactory or manageable standards exist for judicial determination of the issue, as defendants themselves acknowledge the disagreement among experts as to whether Videocipher II belongs on the List. . . . Neither the courts nor the parties are privy to reports of the intelligence services on which this decision, or decisions like it, may have been based. . . . The consequences of uninformed judicial action could be grave. Questions concerning what perils our nation might face at some future time and how best to guard against those perils

> are delicate, complex, and involve large elements of prophecy. They are and should be undertaken only by those directly responsible to the people whose welfare they advance or imperil. They are decisions of a kind for which the Judiciary has neither aptitude, facilities nor responsibility and which has long been held to belong in the domain of political power not subject to judicial intrusion or inquiry. . . .

Indeed, Congress has recently amended AECA to shield the contents of the Munitions List from judicial review. Although it is unclear whether the statutory amendment applies to this case, it is clear that the amendment supports the judicially developed doctrine here applied.

Defendants do not assert that Congress lacks power to place restrictions on exports. They do not contend that the statute under which they were prosecuted violates any right secured to them by the Constitution. They interpose no defense of justification. They do not question that administrative and congressional avenues were available to them for securing removal of Videocipher II from the Munitions List. Instead, they ask the Judicial Branch of Government to excuse conduct which they knew to be criminal, based on their disagreement with a political decision made by the Executive Branch of Government.

The political decision concerning the defense of this country is not judicially reviewable.

AFFIRMED.

NOTE

Applying the Federal Sentencing Guidelines to convictions under the Arms Control Act can present unique issues. For example, in *United States v. Johnson*, 952 F.2d 565 (1st Cir. 1991), appellants argued the propriety of using a "threat to national security and the potential for death and destruction by appellants' conduct as 'aggravating circumstances.' " If these factors were included in formulating the actual guideline, then an upward departure under the guidelines would not be warranted. In rejecting appellants' arguments, the court stated, "[t]heir logic would require that an internationally trained terrorist bent on murdering scores of innocent civilians be sentenced no more severely than an unlicenced arms dealer, and that one who would provide arms to a body of insurgents be sentenced no more harshly than one who would supply them with drug paraphernalia."

Courts have also faced questions of what constitutes "sophisticated weaponry" allowing for a higher base sentencing level. For example, in *United States v. Tsai*, 954 F.2d 155 (3d Cir. 1992), the court affirmed a district court holding that "optical receivers and infra-red domes constituted sophisticated weaponry."

§ 5.03 Executive Export Restrictions and Trade Embargos

UNITED STATES v. EHSAN

United States Court of Appeals for the Fourth Circuit
163 F.3d 855 (1998)

WILKERSON, CHIEF JUDGE:

Mohammad Reza Ehsan was indicted for shipping equipment in violation of a ban on exports to Iran. See Exec. Order No. 12959, 60 Fed. Reg. 24757 (1995). Ehsan claimed that Executive Order 12959 and its implementing regulations, 31 C.F.R. §§ 560.203-.205, .406, were ambiguous. The district court agreed and, applying the rule of lenity, dismissed two counts of Ehsan's indictment. We hold that the Executive Order and the Iranian Transactions Regulations are not ambiguous. We therefore reverse the judgment of the district court and remand this case with instructions to reinstate counts two and three of Ehsan's indictment. . . .

On March 15, 1995, President Clinton announced "that the actions and policies of the Government of Iran constitute an unusual and extraordinary threat to the national security, foreign policy, and economy of the United States." Exec. Order No. 12957, 60 Fed. Reg. 14615 (1995). Invoking the authority of the International Emergency Economic Powers Act, 50 U.S.C. § 1701 et seq., the President declared a national emergency to deal with that threat. Two months later the President issued Executive Order 12959, which bans most importation, exportation, and reexportation of goods between the United States and Iran. 60 Fed. Reg. 24757 (1995).

To implement these Executive Orders the Office of Foreign Assets Control (OFAC) promulgated the Iranian Transactions Regulations, 31 C.F.R. Part 560. With regard to exports and reexports, the regulations declare that:

> Except as otherwise authorized . . . the exportation from the United
> States to Iran or the Government of Iran, or the financing of such

exportation, of any goods, technology, or services is prohibited.

31 C.F.R. § 560.204.

Except as otherwise authorized . . . the reexportation to Iran or the Government of Iran of any goods or technology exported from the United States, the exportation of which to Iran was subject to export license application requirements under any United States regulations in effect immediately prior to May 6, 1995, is prohibited, unless the reexportation is of goods that have been substantially transformed outside the United States, or incorporated into another product out side the United States and constitute less than 10 percent by value of that product exported from a third country.

Id. § 560.205.

Any transaction by any United States person or within the United States that evades or avoids, or has the purpose of evading or avoiding, or attempts to violate, any of the prohibitions contained in this part is hereby prohibited.

Id. § 560.203. These regulations largely track the language of Executive Order 12959. OFAC also issued a number of interpretive regulations, including one as to transshipments:

The prohibitions in § 560.204 apply to the exportation from the United States, for transshipment or transit, of goods which are intended or destined for Iran.

Id. § 560.406(b).

This case presents a challenge to an indictment for violations of the Iranian Transactions Regulations and Executive Order 12959. According to the indictment, Mohammad Reza Ehsan made two attempts between May 1995 and May 1996 to order Transformer Oil Gas Analysis Systems (TOGAS) from Shimadzu Scientific Instruments, Inc., for shipment directly or through third countries to Iran. Shimadzu rebuffed Ehsan, citing the Iranian export ban.

In May 1996 Ehsan again attempted to order two TOGAS from Shimadzu, this time to be sent to Dubai, United Arab Emirates (U.A.E.). He presented Shimadzu two checks in October 1996 in payment for the two TOGAS and asked Shimadzu to ship the systems to his agent in Newark, New Jersey. According to the government, customs agents then created a dummy package and caused the shipment to be sent to Rome, Italy. When Shimadzu informed Ehsan that the package had been sent to Rome, Ehsan had it forwarded to Dubai. After the package arrived in the U.A.E. federal agents arrested Ehsan.

Ehsan was indicted for violating Executive Order 12959 and 31 C.F.R. §§ 560.203, 560.204, and 560.406(b), as well as for conspiracy and for making false statements to an agency of the United States. Ehsan challenged the indictment, claiming that the Executive Order and its implementing regulations were ambiguous. Noting that neither the Executive Order nor the regulations define "export," "reexport," or "transshipment," Ehsan argued that his shipment to Dubai and his planned shipment on to Iran was a permissible "reexport," not an impermissible "export" and "transshipment." The district court agreed that the Executive Order and its implementing regulations were ambiguous and, applying the rule of lenity, adopted Ehsan's proposed definitions. The district court then dismissed counts two and three of the indictment, which charged violations of the export ban, leaving only the conspiracy and false statement counts. The government appeals. . . .

In dismissing Ehsan's indictment, the district court thought itself bound to select the narrowest of the proffered definitions of "export" and "transship," since "ambiguity concerning the ambit of criminal statutes should be resolved in favor of lenity." *United States v. Bass,* 404 U.S. 336, 347, 30 L. Ed. 2d 488, 92 S. Ct. 515 (1971) (internal quotation marks omitted). It is not the case, however, that a provision is "'ambiguous' for purposes of lenity merely because it [is] possible to articulate a construction more narrow than that urged by the Government." . . . Rather, there must be a "grievous ambiguity or uncertainty in the language and structure of the Act, such that even after a court has seized every thing from which aid can be derived, it is still left with an ambiguous statute." . . . Courts must exhaust the tools of statutory construction in this search for statutory meaning. . . . The rule of lenity is a last resort, not a primary tool of construction; it ought to be employed only where a provision's language, structure, and purpose fail to illuminate its meaning. In this case, these traditional interpretive tools resolve any ambiguity in the Executive Order and Iranian Transactions Regulations. . . .

We begin with the language of the Executive Order and the Iranian Transactions Regulations. The embargo prohibits "the exportation from the United States to Iran" of any goods, technology, or services, Exec. Order No. 12959; 31 C.F.R. § 560.204, including "the exportation . . . for transshipment or transit, of goods which are intended or destined for Iran," 31 C.F.R. § 560.406(b). "Export" is the critical term. This single word gives notice of what behavior the regulations prohibit.

"Export" is also a clear term. The Executive Order and regulations do not define "export" or "exportation," but their ordinary meaning is manifest. "Exportation" has been defined as "the act of exporting; the sending of commodities out of a country, typically in trade," The RANDOM HOUSE DICTIONARY OF THE ENGLISH LANGUAGE 682 (2d ed. 1987), "the act of sending or carrying goods and merchandise from one country to another," BLACK'S LAW DICTIONARY 579 (6th ed. 1990), and "a severance of goods from [the] mass of things belonging to [the] United States with [the] intention of uniting them to [the] mass of things belonging to some foreign country," *id.* The verb "export" itself means "to ship (commodities) to other countries or places for sale, exchange, etc.," RANDOM HOUSE at 682, "to carry or send abroad," BLACK'S at 579, and "to send, take, or carry an article of trade or commerce out of the country," *id.* These definitions vary in specificity, but all make clear that exportation involves the transit of goods from one country to another for the purpose of trade.

Common-law usage confirms this ordinary definition. Nearly a century ago the Supreme Court declared that "the word 'export' as used in the Constitution and laws of the United States, generally means the transportation of goods from this to a foreign country." *Swan & Finch Co. v. United States,* 190 U.S. 143, 145, 47 L. Ed. 984, 23 S. Ct. 702 (1903). More specifically, the meaning "of exportation is a severance of goods from the mass of things belonging to this country with an intention of uniting them to the mass of things belonging to some foreign country or other." . . . Courts have applied similar definitions in those rare cases joining issue on the meaning of the term – not only in the customs and duties arena, . . . but also in a context directly analogous here – the interpretation of a congressional weapons embargo, . . .

Throughout this history "exportation" has consistently meant the shipment of goods to a foreign country with the intent to join those goods with the commerce of that country. "The intent characterizes the act, and determines its legal complexion." . . . If Ehsan's bona fide purpose was to seek a market in Dubai, then this was an exportation to the U.A.E. . . . If, however, he intended to seek a market in Iran, then the shipment fits the plain meaning of an "exportation" to Iran. . . .

This is consistent with the purpose of the Executive Order. The President issued the order "to deal with [Iran's] unusual and extraordinary threat to the national security, foreign policy, and economy of the United States." . . . The order is clothed with the most serious of purposes, and it is couched in the broadest of terms. It prohibits, with only limited exceptions, the exportation "of any goods, technology . . . , or services," the reexportation "of any goods or technology," the entering into "any transaction . . . by a United States person relating to goods or services of Iranian origin," and "any new investment by a United States person in Iran." . . . Moreover, it bars "any transaction . . . that evades or avoids" its restrictions. The obvious purpose of the order is to isolate Iran from trade with the United States.

Consistent with the plain meaning of the term "export," the Executive Order intended to cut off the shipment of goods intended for Iran. This broad export ban reflected the President's appraisal of the nation's interest in sanctioning Iran's sponsorship of international terrorism, its frustration of the Middle East peace process, and its pursuit of weapons of mass destruction. . . . In the absence of a "grievous ambiguity," to apply the rule of lenity would be to take this important foreign policy decision out of the hands of the Executive and put it in those of the courts. . . .

Ehsan makes several arguments for the dismissal of his indictment. First, he maintains that the TOGAS shipment was not an impermissible export to Iran, but rather a permissible export to the U.A.E. and reexport to Iran. Ehsan insists that the government may not prosecute him for an export to Iran when he reasonably could have thought he was engaged in reexportation. Although Ehsan labors mightily to manufacture a textual ambiguity, his reading of the regulations is not a reasonable one. "Reexport" simply means "to export again." RANDOM HOUSE at 1619. Ehsan's transaction may indeed have constituted a reexport, if he shipped the TOGAS with the purpose of joining them with the commerce of the U.A.E. and then shipped them from the U.A.E. with the intent to join them with the commerce of Iran. Or it may not, if the stop in Dubai was merely an intermediate step – or transshipment – in the TOGAS' intended journey to Iran. This, however, is a question for the jury, not an ambiguity in the regulatory scheme.

Ehsan also places great weight on the fact that the TOGAS cleared customs in Dubai. Once the shipment cleared customs, he argues, the "export" to the U.A.E. was complete. Customs clearance, however, is simply another fact for the jury to weigh in determining whether Ehsan intended to export the goods to Dubai or to Iran – just as his bills of lading, his purchase orders, and the situs of his ultimate customer certainly will be. *See United States v. Hercules Antiques,* 44 C.C.P.A. 209, 213-15 (1957).

Finally, Ehsan claims that Executive Order 13059 – issued in 1997 "to clarify the steps taken in Executive Orders 12957 . . . and 12959" – demonstrates that the earlier order is ambiguous. 62 Fed. Reg. 44531 (1997). It is true that Executive Order 13059 states its prohibitions in a more comprehensive manner than does Executive Order 12959. It also imposes a more comprehensive embargo – for instance, by eliminating the safe harbor for non-sensitive reexports. *See* Exec. Order No. 13059 § 2. To that end, the 1997 order restates and expands the embargo to include all exportation and reexportation, direct and indirect, with the specific destination of Iran. This rephrasing of the language and scope of the export ban, however, does not undermine the simple, unambiguous bar in Executive Order 12959 of all "exportation . . . to Iran." To so hold would be to discourage the President and Congress from rephrasing or updating their regulations. . . .

Because Executive Order 12959 and the Iranian Transactions Regulations are not ambiguous, the district court erred in applying the rule of lenity to narrow their scope. Ehsan's due process and vagueness challenges fail for the same reason. We therefore reverse the judgment of the district court and remand the case with instructions to reinstate counts two and three of the indictment. . . . REVERSED AND REMANDED

NOTES AND QUESTIONS

(1) What level of intent is necessary for proving a violation of a trade embargo? Consider the court's discussion of this issue in *United States v.*

Macko, 994 F.2d 1526, 1532-35 (11th Cir. 1993):

> Congress has authorized the President to declare and enforce comprehensive trade embargoes under certain circumstances. . . . The Cuban Assets Control Regulations (the "regulations"), promulgated in 1963, establish such an embargo. . . . Subject to narrow exceptions, the regulations prohibit all commercial transactions with Cuba or Cuban nationals. . . .

> At the time Macko and Van Ameringen engaged in the activities at issue here, an individual who willfully violated the TWEA or the regulations faced a possible fine of up to $ 50,000 and imprisonment for as long as ten years. . . . Because the regulations proscribe activity that is not generally perceived to be wrong, we have held that "willfulness" in this context requires a finding of specific intent to violate the trade provisions. . . . To establish that Macko and Van Ameringen acted with the requisite specific intent, the Government must prove that they actually knew of the prohibition against dealings with Cuba or Cuban nationals and deliberately violated it. . . .

> The facts and circumstances of this case, viewed in the light most favorable to the Government, show that Macko and Van Ameringen attempted to conceal the location of the cigarette factory. Macko actively misled his suppliers about the destination of equipment and goods, and he did not tell freight forwarders that Cuba was the final stop. He and Van Ameringen traveled to Cuba through Panama in a manner that left no reference to Cuba on their passports. Both were in possession of Department of the Treasury brochures that mention the Cuban embargo, albeit in relation to imports rather than exports. Macko initially lied to U.S. Customs agents about traveling and sending equipment to Cuba. Van Ameringen's correspondence about the project with other participants scrupulously avoided mentioning Cuba by name. Macko had experience in exporting machinery from the United States and Van Ameringen was involved in international sales of various goods. Also, their conduct occurred against the backdrop of a longstanding and widely publicized trade embargo against Cuba.

> Van Ameringen contends that his "secretive or covert behavior [falls] short of evidence of actual knowledge of the specific regulations at issue." . . . Such behavior may prove a general awareness of illegality but not specific intent, he says. In other contexts, however, we have acknowledged that juries may consider devious conduct along with other circumstantial evidence to infer specific intent. . . .

> After reviewing the record in this case, we conclude that the evidence was sufficient for a reasonable jury to find beyond a reasonable doubt that Macko and Van Ameringen knew about the Cuban trade embargo and deliberately violated it through their own conduct or by aiding and abetting other individuals. Consequently, the district court erred in granting Macko's and Van Ameringen's motions for a judgment of

acquittal on the TWEA charges. . . .

(2) Can a state impose a trade restriction on companies doing business with a particular company? In *Crosby v. National Foreign Trade Council*, 120 S.Ct. 2288 (2000), the Supreme Court found "the Burma law of the Commonwealth of Massachusetts, restricting the authority of its agencies to purchase goods or services from companies doing business with Burma, is invalid under the Supremacy Clause of the National Constitution owing to its threat of frustrating federal statutory objectives." The Court found "that the state law undermines the intended purpose and 'natural effect' of at least three provisions of the federal Act, that is, its delegation of effective discretion to the President to control economic sanctions against Burma, its limitation of sanctions solely to United States persons and new investment, and its directive to the President to proceed diplomatically in developing a comprehensive, multilateral strategy towards Burma."

Chapter 6
COMPUTER CRIMES

Computers provide increased accessability and speed in communications. The abuse and misuse of this technology, however, can present unique issues in international criminal law. Unlike most criminal acts, the perpetrator of a computer crime can remain at home while the victims of the crime are in another country. Questions can arise as to which country has jurisdiction to prosecute the crime. Differing criminal laws may offer different resolutions. In some cases a jurisdiction may have no applicable criminal statute for the particular computer misuse. Should the case in these instances be prosecuted in the jurisdiction with the strongest legal support? Should the location of the perpetrator, the computer, the victim, or the investigation be the proper place for prosecution? These are some of the questions that need to be resolved in international criminal law. *See also* Richard W. Aldrich, *Cyberterrorism and Computer Crimes: Issues Surrounding the Establishment of an International Regime*, Institute for National Securities Studies, Occasional Paper 32 (April 2000).

The speed with which technology develops can result in having legal issues lag behind the scientific developments. As quickly as new laws are enacted to check an abuse of computers, new technology develops that can require changing the legal process. The breadth of computer crimes make the possibility of a single criminal statute problematic. For example, computer crimes can entail theft of trade secrets, pornography, terrorism, and financial institution fraud.

In the United States there are several statutes that are employed to prosecute computer misuses. A key piece of legislation is found in 18 U.S.C. § 1030, a statute initially passed as the Counterfeit Access Device and Computer Fraud and Abuse Act of 1984. The Electronic Communications Privacy Act and the Economic Espionage Act also provide for prosecution of computer crimes. Statutes that are applicable to a wide array of conduct may also be useful in prosecuting crimes related to computers. For example, money laundering, securities fraud, and illegal gambling may be scrutinized under a wide array of criminal statutes that are not specifically focused on computer activity.

At the international level, there are several international initiatives focusing on how best to curtail international computer crimes. The Council of Europe ("COE"), an international organization with membership in excess of forty countries, has been an advocate for international cooperation in combating computer crimes. In May 1998, the G-8 countries (United States, United Kingdom, France, Germany, Italy, Canada, Japan, and Russia) adopted a set of principles pertaining to computer crimes. The United Nations has also been concerned with computer crimes and developed a manual on the prevention and control of computer-related crime. The consensus of most is that international cooperation is needed to combat international crimes involving computers. *See, e.g.*, David M. Cielusniak, *You Cannot Fight What You Cannot See: Securities Regulation on the Internet*, 22 FORDHAM L. REV. 612 (1998).

Securing necessary information for a prosecution while maintaining individual and business privacy remains a concern. In this regard encryption has presented a growing controversy. In *Berstein v. United States*, 922 F. Supp. 1426 (N.D. Cal. 1996) encryption was described as follows:

> Encryption basically involves running a readable message known as "plaintext" through a computer program that translates the message according to an equation or algorithm into unreadable "ciphertext." Decryption is the translation back to plaintext when the message is received by someone with an appropriate "key." The message is both encrypted and decrypted by common keys. The uses of cryptography are far-ranging in an electronic age, from protecting personal messages over the Internet and transactions on bank ATMs to ensuring the secrecy of military intelligence.

Id. The propriety of using statutes such as the Arms Export Control Act and the International Traffic in Arms regulations to monitor encryption remains uncertain. *See Berstein v. United States*, 192 F.3d 1308 (9th Cir. 1999) (granting rehearing *en banc*).

The Economic Espionage Act, passed by Congress in 1996, focuses on both domestic and international related activity. *See* Kent B. Alexander & Kristen L. Wood, *The Economic Espionage Act: Setting the Stage for a New Commercial Code of Conduct*, 15 GA. ST. U. L. REV. 907 (1999). Specifically 18 U.S.C. § 1831 prohibits the misappropriation of trade secrets that benefit any foreign government and 18 U.S.C. § 1832 focuses on domestic trade secrets. The Economic Espionage Act includes extraterritorial application in certain circumstances. Why did Congress pass a statute prohibiting the theft of trade secrets? How does one prosecute the theft of a trade secret without revealing the trade secret. Consider these as well as other issues as presented in the following case:

UNITED STATES v. HSU

United States Court of Appeals for the Third Circuit
155 F.3d 189 (1998)

RENDELL, CIRCUIT JUDGE:

In this appeal we explore for the first time the relationship between the confidentiality provisions of the newly-enacted Economic Espionage Act of 1996, 18 U.S.C. § 1831, et seq., and principles of criminal law regarding discovery and disclosure of material evidence. The district court ordered the government to disclose alleged corporate trade secrets based upon a theory that we find does not apply. It also held that the defense of legal impossibility does not pertain to the attempt and conspiracy crimes with which the defendants are charged. We will affirm the court's holding regarding the applicability of the defense of legal impossibility, but will reverse its discovery order and remand for a review of other asserted defenses to the crimes in the indictment. . . .

On July 10, 1997, a federal grand jury indicted Kai-Lo Hsu, Chester S. Ho, and Jessica Chou (collectively, "the defendants") for their involvement in an alleged conspiracy to steal corporate trade secrets from Bristol-Myers Squibb. The indictment alleges that the defendants sought to obtain the processes, methods, and formulas for manufacturing Taxol, an anti-cancer drug produced by Bristol-Myers and regarded by the company as a highly valuable trade secret.

According to the indictment, the defendants' conspiracy began on June 7, 1995, when Chou, the Manager of Business Development for Yuen Foong Paper Company in Taiwan ("YFP"), requested information about Taxol from John Hartmann, an undercover FBI agent whom Chou mistakenly believed to be a technological information broker in the United States. From August 28, 1995, until January 12, 1996, Chou allegedly contacted Hartmann repeatedly to obtain information about Taxol manufacturing techniques and distribution. These contacts led to a meeting in Los Angeles on February 27, 1996, between Hartmann and Hsu, the Technical Director for YFP's operations. Hsu purportedly told Hartmann at that meeting that YFP wanted to diversify into biotechnology and to introduce technology from advanced countries into Taiwan. When Hartmann responded that Bristol-Myers would be unlikely to share its secret technology with YFP, Hsu allegedly responded, "We'll get [it] another way," and told Hartmann to pursue paying Bristol-Myers employees for the confidential Taxol formulas.

The indictment asserts that Hsu and Chou then "communicated many times" with Hartmann over the next fourteen months to discuss the transfer of Taxol technology and to negotiate a specific price for the acquisition of Bristol-Myers's trade secrets. In response, Hartmann told the defendants that a corrupt Bristol-Myers scientist would be willing to sell Taxol information to YFP. The "corrupt" scientist was actually a Bristol-Myers employee cooperating with the FBI. Intrigued by such a prospect, Chou allegedly sent an e-mail to Hartmann on March 13, 1997, outlining the "core technology" that YFP would need to complete a deal, . . . Chou also allegedly told Hartmann that she would offer $400,000 in cash, stock, and royalties to the Bristol-Myers scientist in exchange for his disclosure of the Taxol secrets. In addition, Chou and Hsu purportedly began making arrangements for a 1997 meeting between the parties, the purpose of which was for YFP to establish the authenticity of the "corrupt" scientist and to determine whether Hartmann really could produce the Taxol trade secrets that Chou and Hsu had requested.

Hartmann agreed to a meeting, and on June 14, 1997, he and the Bristol-Myers scientist met with three representatives from YFP, including Hsu, Ho, and another unidentified scientist, at the Four Seasons Hotel in Philadelphia. Ho was a professor of biotechnology and the Director of the Biotechnology Innovation Center at the National Chiao Tung University in Taiwan, and he had apparently been asked to evaluate the Taxol technology at the meeting as a favor to YFP.

The indictment alleges that the bulk of the June 14 meeting consisted of detailed discussions regarding the manufacturing processes for Taxol. The Bristol-Myers scientist explained the background and history of Taxol production, and displayed copies of Bristol-Myers documents outlining specific technological processes and scientific data pertaining to the manufacture of the drug. According to the indictment, these documents contained trade secrets and were "clearly marked with Bristol-Myers identification as well as the block stamped word 'CONFIDENTIAL.' " Hsu, Ho, and the other YFP employee reviewed the documents during the meeting and purportedly asked the Bristol-Myers scientist "numerous" questions regarding specific areas of Taxol technology. Finally, after Hartmann and the Bristol-Myers scientist left the room, the FBI rushed in and arrested Hsu and Ho at the hotel.

The indictment returned by the grand jury charged Hsu, Ho, and Chou with six counts of wire fraud in violation of 18 U.S.C. § 1343, one count of general federal conspiracy in violation of 18 U.S.C. § 371, two counts of foreign and interstate travel to facilitate commercial bribery in violation of 18 U.S.C. § 1952(a)(3), one count of aiding and abetting in violation of 18 U.S.C. § 2, and, most importantly for our purposes, two counts of criminal activity under the Economic Espionage Act of 1996 ("the EEA"), including attempted theft of trade secrets, and a conspiracy to steal trade secrets, in violation of 18 U.S.C. §§ 1832 (a)(4) and (a)(5). . . .

Shortly after the indictment was returned, the defense requested in discovery a copy of the Bristol-Myers documents disclosed to Hsu and Ho at the June 14 meeting. However, on August 12, 1997, the government filed a motion pursuant to 18 U.S.C. § 1835 and Fed. R. Crim. P. 16(d)(1) for a protective order to prevent the disclosure of the Bristol-Myers trade secrets allegedly contained in those documents. The government proposed that the district court enter an order under which the trial judge would review the documents and the proposed redactions by Bristol-Myers in camera, and would then permit redactions of proprietary secret information. The documents as redacted would be used at trial. The gravamen of the government's contention was that the defendants had no need for the actual trade secrets themselves, because they had been charged only with attempt and conspiracy to steal trade secrets, rather than with the actual theft of trade secrets, under the EEA.

The defendants maintained, though, that unique constitutional and procedural requirements of criminal prosecutions dictated full access to the documents shown to them during the investigation. The defendants also contended that they needed the documents to establish the defense of legal impossibility, arguing that they could not be convicted of attempting to steal trade secrets if the documents did not actually contain trade secrets. Therefore, they proposed an order under which the proprietary information in the Bristol-Myers documents would be disclosed, but only to select members of the defense team, such as the defendants' attorneys and trial experts, and under which the documents would be filed under seal and returned or destroyed at the end of the case.

The district court agreed with the defendants and adopted their version of the proposed protective order. *See United States v. Hsu*, 982 F. Supp. 1022 (E.D. Pa. 1997). The court held that legal impossibility is not a viable defense to the crime of attempted theft of trade secrets under the EEA, and it thus rejected the defendants' argument that they needed the documents to establish that claim. . . . Nevertheless, it ordered the government to divulge the alleged trade secrets, because it found that the existence of a trade secret is an essential element of the crime of the theft of trade secrets, and that the existence of a trade secret in that prosecution is "a question of fact which the defendants have the right to have a jury decide." . . . Believing the defendants to be charged both with actual theft and attempted theft of trade secrets, the court concluded that "if during discovery we deny to the defendants complete access to the Taxol technology, we inhibit their constitutional right to effective cross-examination as well as their right to have a jury, rather than a judge, determine whether a 'trade secret' exists." . . . Therefore, the court held, the defendants "are entitled to review the June 14th documents to the extent of their constitutional rights." . . . The district court's opinion "encouraged" the government to file an interlocutory appeal to clarify the "unsettled and important questions of law" raised by this case. . . .

We note at the outset that we disagree with the district court as to the offenses charged. The indictment is limited to charging the defendants with attempt and conspiracy and contains no charge of actual theft of trade secrets. As we will discuss below, we believe this changes the analysis greatly. We begin, though, with an overview of the EEA and an analysis of the relevant statutory provisions. . . .

The EEA became law in October 1996 against a backdrop of increasing threats to corporate security and a rising tide of international and domestic economic espionage. The end of the Cold War sent government spies scurrying to the private sector to perform illicit work for businesses and corporations, ... and by 1996, studies revealed that nearly $ 24 billion of corporate intellectual property was being stolen each year. . . .

The problem was augmented by the absence of any comprehensive federal remedy targeting the theft of trade secrets, compelling prosecutors to shoehorn economic espionage crimes into statutes directed at other offenses. . . . For example, the government often sought convictions under the National Stolen Property Act ("NSPA"), 18 U.S.C. § 2314, or the mail and wire fraud statutes, 18 U.S.C. §§ 1341 and 1343. However, the NSPA "was drafted at a time when computers, biotechnology, and copy machines did not even exist," . . . . and industrial espionage often occurred without the use of mail or wire. Consequently, it soon became clear to legislators and commentators alike that a new federal strategy was needed to combat the increasing prevalence of espionage in corporate America. Congress recognized "the importance of developing a systematic approach to the problem of economic espionage," . . . and stressed that "only by adopting a national scheme to protect U.S. proprietary economic information can we hope to maintain our industrial and economic edge and thus safeguard our national security." . . . The House and Senate thus passed the Economic Espionage Act, and the President signed the bill into law on October 11, 1996.

The EEA consists of nine sections which protect proprietary information from misappropriation. Three sections are of particular import to our analysis: what acts are penalized by the statute, how the law defines a "trade secret," and when trade secrets are to remain confidential.

A. Criminal activities

The EEA criminalizes two principal categories of corporate espionage, including "Economic espionage" as defined by 18 U.S.C. § 1831, and the "Theft of trade secrets" as defined by § 1832. The former provision punishes those who knowingly misappropriate, or attempt or conspire to misappropriate, trade secrets with the intent or knowledge that their offense will benefit a foreign government, foreign instrumentality, or foreign agent. The legislative history indicates that § 1831 is designed to apply only when there is "evidence of foreign government sponsored or coordinated intelligence activity." . . . By contrast, § 1832, the section under which the defendants are charged, is a general criminal trade secrets provision. It applies to anyone who knowingly engages in the theft of trade secrets, or an attempt or conspiracy to do so, "with intent to convert a trade secret, that is related to or included in a product that is produced for or placed in interstate or foreign commerce, to the economic benefit of anyone other than the owner thereof, and intending or knowing that the offense will, injure any owner of that trade secret." Section 1832(a) makes clear that attempt and conspiracy are distinct offenses, and it lists them separately from those acts that constitute completed crimes under the statute.

Section 1832 also contains at least three additional limitations not found in § 1831. First, a defendant charged under § 1832 must intend to convert a trade secret "to the economic benefit of anyone other than the owner thereof," including the defendant himself. This "economic benefit" requirement differs from § 1831, which states merely that the offense "benefit," in any manner, a foreign government, instrumentality, or agent. Therefore, prosecutions under § 1832 uniquely require that the defendant intend to confer an economic benefit on the defendant or another person or entity. Second, § 1832 states that the defendant must intend or know that the offense will injure an owner of the trade secret, a restriction not found in § 1831. The legislative history indicates that this requires "that the actor knew or was aware to a practical certainty that his conduct would cause such a result." . . . Finally, unlike § 1831, § 1832 also requires that the trade secret be "related to or included in a product that is produced for or placed in interstate or foreign commerce." . . .

The EEA defines a "trade secret" to expressly extend protection to the misappropriation of intangible information for the first time under federal law. 18 U.S.C. § 1839(3) provides that a "trade secret" means:

all forms and types of financial, business, scientific, technical, economic, or engineering information, including patterns, plans, compilations, program devices, formulas, designs, prototypes, methods, techniques, processes, procedures, programs, or codes, whether tangible or intangible, and whether or how stored, compiled, or memorialized physically, electronically, graphically, photographically, or in writing if –

(A) the owner thereof has taken reasonable measures to keep such information secret; and

(B) the information derives independent economic value, actual or potential, from not being generally known to, and not being readily ascertainable through proper means by, the public.

The EEA's definition of a "trade secret" is similar to that found in a number of state civil statutes and the Uniform Trade Secrets Act ("UTSA"), a model ordinance which permits civil actions for the misappropriation of trade secrets. There are, though, several critical differences which serve to broaden the EEA's scope. First, and most importantly, the EEA protects a wider variety of technological and intangible information than current civil laws. Trade secrets are no longer restricted to formulas, patterns, and compilations, but now include programs and codes, "whether tangible or intangible, and whether or how stored." Second, the EEA alters the relevant party from whom proprietary information must be kept confidential. Under the UTSA, information classified as a "trade secret" cannot be generally known by businesspersons or competitors of the trade secret owner. UTSA § 1(4). The EEA, however, indicates that a trade secret must not be generally known to, or readily ascertainable by, the general public, rather than simply those who can obtain economic value from the secret's disclosure or use. Finally, the EEA contains a definition crafted to reach only illicit behavior. Although legislators eliminated language providing that general knowledge, skills, and experience are not "trade secrets," . . . . it is clear that Congress did not intend the definition of a trade secret to be so broad as to prohibit lawful competition such as the use of general skills or parallel development of a similar product. . . .

The EEA also contains a provision designed to preserve the confidentiality of trade secrets during criminal prosecutions. 18 U.S.C. § 1835 states that a court:

shall enter such orders and take such other action as may be necessary and appropriate to preserve the confidentiality of trade secrets, consistent with the requirements of the Federal Rules of Criminal and Civil Procedure, the Federal Rules of Evidence, and all other applicable laws. An interlocutory appeal by the United States shall lie from a decision or order of a district court authorizing or directing the disclosure of any trade secret. . . .

This section does not, of course, abrogate existing constitutional and statutory protections for criminal defendants. It does, however, represent a clear indication from Congress that trade secrets are to be protected to the fullest extent during EEA litigation. Moreover, it further encourages enforcement actions by protecting owners who might otherwise "be reluctant to cooperate in prosecutions for fear of further exposing their trade secrets to public view, thus further devaluing or even destroying their worth." . . . Therefore, as with the definition of trade secrets, the confidentiality provision aims to strike a balance between the protection of proprietary information and the unique considerations inherent in criminal prosecutions. . . .

With this statutory framework in mind, we turn our attention to determining whether the district court properly ordered the government to disclose the alleged trade secrets in this case. We begin by recognizing that the defendants are charged only with attempting to steal, and conspiring to steal, trade secrets under § 1832. The district court believed that the defendants were charged with both attempted theft of trade secrets as well as with "the completed offense of unauthorized conveyance of a trade secret under 18 U.S.C. § 1832(2)." . . . It thus found that the defendants' constitutional rights to cross-examination and a fair trial would be violated absent full disclosure of the Bristol-Myers documents.

However, the district court's analysis represents an incorrect reading of the indictment and a mistaken view of the charges lodged under the EEA. For one thing, there is no § 1832(2) in the statute. More importantly, the defendants are not charged with the completed offense of theft of trade secrets. They have been indicted only for attempting to steal, and conspiring to steal, trade secrets pursuant to §§ 1832(a)(4) and (a)(5). Therefore, our task is to examine the defendants' entitlement to the information they seek, as defending against the attempt and conspiracy provisions of the EEA, rather than the completed theft provisions. We need not decide, as the district court did, whether a failure to disclose trade secrets would undermine the constitutional rights of defendants charged with a completed offense under the statute.

The defendants argue that unfettered access to confidential documents is required even in EEA prosecutions for attempt and conspiracy. They assert that documents containing trade secrets are "material to the preparation of the defendant's defense," and therefore, that they must be disclosed consistent with the terms of Fed. R. Crim. P. 16(a)(1)(C). In particular, they contend that disclosure is warranted by (1) the availability of a legal impossibility defense, and (2) their need for access to the proprietary information as it relates to their defense of the allegations of the indictment and other defenses to the crimes charged. . . . After reviewing the legislative history of the EEA, we conclude that Congress did not intend to allow legal impossibility to be asserted as a defense to attempt crimes created by its terms. Congress never spoke directly as to why it used the term "attempt," or as to the issue of legal impossibility, in any of the reports or debates on the statute. We find, however, that, . . . the underlying purposes of the law provide substantial evidence of a congressional intent that the defense of legal impossibility should not apply. . . .

Just as the Drug Control Act embraced a "comprehensive" solution for drug trafficking, so too does the EEA attempt to provide a "comprehensive" mechanism for curtailing the escalating threat of corporate espionage. The Senate Report includes an entire section entitled "Need for a Comprehensive Federal Law," and "underscores the importance of developing a systematic approach to the problem of economic espionage." . . . The Report notes that "a Federal criminal statute will provide a comprehensive approach to [the theft of trade secrets] – with clear extraterritoriality, criminal forfeiture, and import-export sanction provisions." . . . Likewise, the House Report states that the EEA is designed to provide a "systematic approach" to trade secret theft, and asserts that "a comprehensive federal criminal statute will better facilitate the investigation and prosecution of this crime." . . . The House also explained that the EEA was crafted to punish virtually every form of illegal industrial espionage, "from the foreign government that uses its classic espionage apparatus to spy on a company, to the two American companies that are attempting to uncover each other's bid proposals, or to the disgruntled former employee who walks out of his former company with a computer diskette full of engineering schematics." . . . We believe that the great weight of the EEA's legislative history evinces an intent to create a comprehensive solution to economic espionage, and we find it highly unlikely that Congress would have wanted the courts to thwart that solution by permitting defendants to assert the common law defense of legal impossibility. . . . [G]iven the strong indicia of legislative intent, and given the practical import of a contrary finding, we conclude that Congress could not have intended EEA attempt crimes to be subject to the somewhat obscure and rarely used common law defense of legal impossibility. . . .

We agree with the district court's conclusion that a charge of "attempt" under the EEA requires proof of the same elements used in other modern attempt statutes, including the Model Penal Code. A defendant is guilty of attempting to misappropriate trade secrets if, "acting with the kind of culpability otherwise required for commission of the crime, he . . . purposely does or omits to do anything that, under the circumstances as he believes them to be, is an act or omission constituting a substantial step in a course of conduct planned to culminate in his commission of the crime." Model Penal Code § 5.01(1)(c) (1985). Thus, the defendant must (1) have the intent needed to commit a crime defined by the EEA, and must (2) perform an act amounting to a "substantial step" toward the commission of that crime. . . .

It naturally follows that the government need not prove that an actual trade secret was used during an EEA investigation, because a defendant's culpability for a charge of attempt depends only on "the circumstances as he believes them to be," not as they really are. The government can satisfy its burden under § 1832(a)(4) by proving beyond a reasonable doubt that the defendant sought to acquire information which he or she believed to be a trade secret, regardless of whether the information actually qualified as such. Consequently, in the instant case, the defendants have no arguable constitutional or statutory right to view the unredacted portion of the Taxol documents in order to defend against charges of attempt on the basis of legal impossibility. . . . We also hold that the defendants have no need for the Taxol documents to defend against the government's charges of conspiracy, because we conclude that legal impossibility is not a defense to conspiracy. . . .

Having concluded that the defendants' right to access actual trade secrets is not required in order to defend against an element of the government's case, the question remains whether the defendants' right of access to the information as it relates to other defenses passes muster under the test of materiality. The defendants argue that the unredacted documents are also material to the preparation of the potential defenses of entrapment, outrageous government conduct, and jurisdiction, and contend that the documents are needed to defend against the elements of attempt and conspiracy, the allegations of the indictment, and the evidence that the government intends to introduce at trial. . . . Thus, while we might be skeptical of the defendants' asserted need for this information, we will not decide whether they have a right to access documents that could conceivably reveal information needed to preserve their rights to a fair trial. Only defense counsel know the precise contours of the defendants' case, and we are not in a position to make judgments about the impact of the redacted material without having seen the material ourselves.

Accordingly, we will remand this action to the district court. If the defendants raise before the district court the additional arguments that they have urged on appeal, we would expect the district court to conduct an in camera review to determine whether the documents have been properly redacted to exclude only confidential information and to assess whether what was redacted is "material" to the defense.

In such event, because "public policy requires protection of portions of a document, . . . in camera inspection by the trial judge or magistrate is unavoidable." . . . The district court's Order dated October 27, 1997, will be reversed, and the cause will be remanded for further proceedings consistent with this opinion.

Chapter 7
NARCOTICS AND MONEY LAUNDERING

§ 7.01 Jurisdiction Over Narcotics Prosecutions

UNITED STATES v. LARSEN

United States Court of Appeals for the Ninth Circuit
952 F.2d 1099 (1991)

T.G. NELSON, CIRCUIT JUDGE:

Charles Edward Larsen was convicted for his involvement in an international marijuana smuggling operation in violation of 18 U.S.C. §§ 2, 371, 1952(a)(3) and 21 U.S.C. §§ 841(a)(1), 846, 963, 952. Larsen challenges the legality of his conviction on numerous grounds, including the court's extraterritorial application of 21 U.S.C. § 841(a)(1). We affirm.

Larsen's conviction was based on evidence which established that he, along with codefendants and numerous other individuals, conspired to import shipments of Southeast Asian marijuana into the United States from 1985 to 1987, and to distribute the marijuana in the United States. The profits from these ventures were concealed by a fictitious partnership created by the defendant and others. This partnership was used to purchase the shipping vessel intended to transport the marijuana. During some of the smuggling operations, Larsen served as captain of the vessel.

Under Count Eight, Larsen was convicted of aiding and abetting codefendant Walter Ulrich in the crime of knowing and intentional possession with intent to distribute marijuana in violation of 21 U.S.C. § 841(a)(1). The marijuana was seized by customs inspectors from a ship on the high seas outside of Singapore. Larsen claims that the district court erred when it denied his motion to dismiss Count Eight because 21 U.S.C. § 841(a)(1) does not have extraterritorial jurisdiction. A district court's jurisdiction is a matter of law, and reviewed de novo. . . .

Congress is empowered to attach extraterritorial effect to its penal statutes so long as the statute does not violate the due process clause of the Fifth Amendment. . . . There is a presumption against extraterritorial application when a statute is silent on the matter. . . . However, this court has given extraterritorial effect to penal statutes when congressional intent to do so is clear. . . . Since 21 U.S.C. § 841(a)(1) is silent about its extraterritorial application, we are "faced with finding the construction that Congress intended." . . .

The Supreme Court has explained that to limit the *locus* of some offenses "to the strictly territorial jurisdiction would be greatly to curtail the scope and usefulness of the statute and leave open a large immunity for frauds as easily committed by citizens on the high seas and in foreign countries as at home." *United States v. Bowman* [p. 28]. Congressional intent to attach extraterritorial application " 'may be inferred from the nature of the offenses and Congress' other legislative efforts to eliminate the type of crime involved.' ". . .

Until now, the Ninth Circuit has not applied this "intent of congress/nature of the offense test" to 21 U.S.C. § 841(a)(1); however, four other circuits have. They all held that Congress did intend the statute to have extraterritorial effect.

The Fifth Circuit held that Congress intended that 841(a)(1) have extraterritorial effect because it was a part of the Comprehensive Drug Abuse Prevention and Control Act of 1970, and the power to control illegal drug trafficking on the high seas was an essential incident to Congress' intent to halt drug abuse in the United States. . . .

The Third Circuit held that Congressional intent to apply 841(a)(1) extraterritorially could be implied because "Congress undoubtedly intended to prohibit conspiracies to [distribute] controlled substances into the United States . . . . as part of its continuing effort to contain the evils caused on American soil by foreign as well as domestic suppliers of illegal narcotics. . . . To deny such use of the criminal provisions 'would be greatly to curtail the scope and usefulness of the statute[ ].' ". . .

The First Circuit concluded that the district court had jurisdiction over a crime committed on the high seas in violation of 841(a)(1) because "[a] sovereign may exercise jurisdiction over acts done outside its geographical jurisdiction which are intended to produce detrimental effects within it." . . .

The Second Circuit similarly held that "because section 841(a)(1) properly applies to schemes to distribute controlled substances within the United States," its extraterritorial application was proper. . . .

Extraterritorial application of a drug possession/distribution statute comports with the reasoning behind the Supreme Court's *Bowman* decision, since such a statute is "not logically dependent on [its] locality for the Government's jurisdiction, but [was] enacted because of the right of the government to defend itself against obstruction, or fraud wherever perpetrated" and "it would be going too far to say that because Congress does not fix any locus it intended to exclude the high seas in respect of this crime." . . .

Defendant claims that Congress intended to limit section 841(a)(1) to only territorial crimes, as demonstrated by its later enactment of 21 U.S.C. § 955(a), recodified at 46 U.S.C. § 1903, which expressly confers jurisdiction over the high seas in cases dealing with controlled substance possession and distribution. Defendant implies that in providing a separate statute which expressly governs the high seas, Congress acknowledged that the former statute did not.

If the two statutes had precisely the same provisions, beyond the extraterritoriality issue, defendant's argument might have some merit. However, there are other differences between the statutes that can explain Congress' intent in enacting § 1903. For example, § 1903 does not require *intent* to distribute, as does § 841(a)(1). Recognizing this, the Second Circuit held that Congress did not enact § 1903 to fill a void left by the silence in § 841(a)(1) as to its extraterritorial effect but, rather, to extend drug possession/distribution laws to those cases where it was not possible to show intent to distribute. . .

Furthermore, as the Eleventh Circuit pointed out in a case dealing with a related matter, there is an enhanced penalty available for crimes charged under § 841(a)(1) which is not available under 1903. . . .

Larsen cites to a passing reference in *Hayes* [653 F.2d 8, 15-16 (1st Cir. 1981)] which stated that Congress accepted the views of representatives from the Department of Justice and the DEA who testified that the Comprehensive Drug Abuse Prevention and Control Act of 1970 did not apply to American ships on the high seas. While the *Hayes* court acknowledged that some might conclude that § 841(a)(1) does not apply extraterritorially because of this Congressional testimony, the court nevertheless held that § 841(a)(1) did have extraterritorial application. . . .

In affirming Larsen's conviction, we now join the First, Second, Third, and Fifth Circuit Courts in finding that 21 U.S.C. § 841(a)(1) has extraterritorial jurisdiction. We hold that Congress' intent can be implied because illegal drug trafficking, which the statute is designed to prevent, regularly involves importation of drugs from international sources.

AFFIRMED.

NOTES AND QUESTIONS

(1) In some cases the statute may specifically include language of extraterritoriality. For example, 21 U.S.C. § 959 specifically provides for extraterritoriality within the statute as follows:

§ 959. Possession, manufacture or distribution of controlled substance

(a) Manufacture or distribution for purpose of unlawful importation. It shall be unlawful for any person to manufacture or distribute a controlled substance in schedule I or II or flunitrazepam or listed chemical-

(1) intending that such substance or chemical be unlawfully imported into the United States or into waters within a distance of 12 miles of the coast of the United States; or

(2) knowing that such substance or chemical will be unlawfully imported into the United States or into waters within a distance of 12 miles of the coast of the United States.

(b) Possession, manufacture, or distribution by person on board aircraft. It shall be unlawful for any United States citizen on board any aircraft, or any person on board an aircraft owned by a United States citizen or registered in the United States, to–

(1) manufacture or distribute a controlled substance or listed chemical; or

(2) possess a controlled substance or listed chemical with intent to distribute.

(c) Acts committed outside territorial jurisdiction of United States; venue. This section is intended to reach acts of manufacture or distribution committed outside the territorial jurisdiction of the United States. Any person who violates this section shall be tried in the United States district court at the point of entry where such person enters the United States, or in the United States District Court for the District of Columbia.

(2) Who gets to decide whether there is sufficient jurisdiction? Is this a question of law or fact? Will it make a difference whether jurisdiction is a specific element of the statute? Consider how the court resolved this issue in the case of *United States v. Medjuck*, 48 F.3d 1107 (9th Cir. 1995):

Medjuck, a Canadian citizen, and Sotirkys, an American citizen, were members of an extensive international conspiracy to smuggle drugs. The conspirators owned and operated a ship, the Saratoga Success, in which they attempted to transport 28 tons of hashish from Pakistan to Canada. The Saratoga Success never reached Canada. After a series of incidents, the ship beached in the Philippines. Sotirkys thereafter met with other conspirators in Amsterdam, the Philipines, and Singapore. They agreed to secure the Lucky Star, a vessel registered in St. Vincent, a sovereign island nation in the British West Indies. They arranged to have the Lucky Star loaded with the 28 tons of hashish from the Saratoga Success and an additional 42 tons of hashish from Pakistan.

Meanwhile, Medjuck and others were responsible for securing a ship to rendezvous with the Lucky Star approximately 800 miles northwest of

Midway Island, in order to offload and transport the hashish to Canada. Medjuck financed the hiring of the Barbara H., and her American captain and crew. Unknown to Medjuck, the captain and crew of the Barbara H. were U.S. Customs and FBI undercover agents.

On June 23, 1991, the two ships met, but due to inclement weather and rough seas, only 2.4 tons of hashish were offloaded. The captain of the Lucky Star refused to attempt a second rendezvous, and despite the coconspirators' objections, proceeded back to Asia. After tracking the Lucky Star for several days, two United States Navy destroyers intercepted the vessel. A Coast Guard officer assigned to one of the destroyers sought permission to board the Lucky Star. The captain of the Lucky Star consented, and the vessel was boarded, secured, and directed to proceed to Hawaii while the Coast Guard awaited the flag nation's consent to the assertion of United States jurisdiction. Ten days later, as the Lucky Star neared Hawaii, St. Vincent, the flag nation, gave its consent. When the ship arrived in Honolulu, the cargo was seized and the crew incarcerated.

During this time, the Barbara H., still controlled by undercover agents, sailed toward Hawaii, where the 2.4 tons of hashish were offloaded and flown to California. Agents thereafter met with two coconspirators and agreed to transfer the drugs to a location in California. Five individuals were arrested when they arrived to take possession. Medjuck was arrested in Seattle; Sotirkys surrendered to U.S. officials in Singapore.

All seven were charged with violating the MDLEA, 46 U.S.C. App.§ 1903(a), conspiring to violate the Act, 46 U.S.C. App. § 1903(j), conspiring to import 70 tons of hashish into the United States, 21 U.S.C. § 846, and possessing 2.4 tons of hashish with intent to distribute, 21 U.S.C. § 841(a)(1). Medjuck was also charged with obstructing justice, 18 U.S.C. § 1512, and Sotirkys was charged with fraudulently using a passport, 18 U.S.C. § 1544, and making false customs declarations, 18 U.S.C. § 1001. The captain and crew of the Lucky Star were prosecuted in separate proceedings. . . .

In pretrial proceedings, Medjuck and Sotirkys challenged the jurisdiction of the United States to prosecute them under section 1903. The court ruled that it would instruct the jury as a matter of law that the jurisdictional requirements of section 1903 were satisfied, and that no proof of nexus to the United States was required. The court also ruled as a matter of law that flag nation consent may be obtained after law enforcement agents board and control a vessel, and that the Navy's participation in the seizure of the Lucky Star did not violate the Posse Comitatus Act, 18 U.S.C. § 1385.

Based on these rulings, Medjuck conditionally pleaded guilty to violating section 1903, and reserved the right to appeal the trial court's rulings on jurisdiction and flag nation consent. Sotirkys was tried before a jury and found guilty of the counts alleging violations of section 1903, the use of a fraudulent passport, and making false customs declarations. With respect to section 1903, the jury was instructed that "it is not for you to determine . . . . the jurisdiction of the United States, ... those issues are for the court to decide and I hereby instruct you, as a matter of law, that the Lucky Star was subject to the jurisdiction of the United States." . . .

Defendants contend that the district court erred by determining as a matter of law that the statutory and constitutional requirements for assertion of subject matter jurisdiction were satisfied in this case. . . The MDLEA prohibits drug activity by "any person on board a vessel of the United States, or on board a vessel subject to the jurisdiction of the United States, or who is a citizen of the United States or a resident alien of the United States on board any vessel." 46 U.S.C. App. § 1903(a). A "vessel subject to the jurisdiction of the United States" includes "a vessel registered in a foreign nation where the flag nation has consented or waived objection to the enforcement of United States law by the United States." . . .

We agree with defendants that the district court erred by not submitting to the jury the question whether the Lucky Star was a vessel subject to the jurisdiction of the United States. There is general agreement that the jurisdiction requirement found in section 1903(a) is an element of the crime charged and therefore must be decided by the jury. . . . We have noted in dictum that an element of the offense is that the vessel must be "subject to the jurisdiction of the United States." . . .

The district court's error of improperly instructing the jury cannot be deemed harmless error. . . . The MDLEA was intended by Congress to provide for the extraterritorial enforcement of United States drug laws. . . . There is generally no constitutional bar to such extraterritorial application of domestic penal laws. . . . We require only that Congressional intent of extraterritorial scope be clear and that application of the statute to the acts in question not violate the due process clause of the Fifth Amendment. . . . Due process is not offended as long as there is a sufficient nexus between the conduct condemned and the United States. . . .

We agree with defendants that the district court erred by ruling as a matter of law that the government need not demonstrate nexus in this case. We have recognized that such proof is necessary for the prosecution of crew members aboard a foreign flag vessel. . . . We agree with defendants that the government has the burden of demonstrating such a nexus and that defendants should have the opportunity for rebuttal on remand. Medjuck entered a conditional plea after the district court ruled that no nexus was required and had denied

Medjuck's request for an evidentiary hearing. Sotirkys went to trial but evidence of nexus was precluded by the court's pretrial ruling. Thus, neither defendant has had the opportunity to rebut the evidence relied upon by the district court in its clarification order. . . .

(3) Statutes concerning drug offenses often receive extraterritorial application. How far outside the confines of drug statutes will courts go in permitting extraterritoriality? Will extraterritorial jurisdiction be found in cases of violence that may be influenced by drug trafficking? Consider this question as raised in the following case.

UNITED STATES v. VASQUEZ-VELASCO

United States Court of Appeals for the Ninth Circuit
15 F.3d 833 (1994)

FLETCHER, CIRCUIT JUDGE:

Javier Vasquez-Velasco was convicted in a jury trial of committing violent crimes in aid of a racketeering enterprise in violation of 18 U.S.C. § 1959. Vasquez-Velasco appeals the district court's denial of his motion to dismiss for lack of subject matter jurisdiction. He also argues that his trial was improperly joined, and appeals the district court's denial of his motions for severance. Finally, he appeals the district court's imposition of a sentence greater than ten years in the absence of a special verdict. We affirm. . . .

The circumstances underlying this trial occurred in January and February, 1985. At that time, an American citizen named John Walker was living in Guadalajara, Mexico and writing a novel. In December 1984, Alberto Radelat, a legal resident alien in the United States, travelled to Guadalajara to visit his friend Walker. Radelat was a photographer. Neither Walker nor Radelat had any apparent association with the DEA or with any drug-related activities.

On the night of January 30, 1985, members of the "Guadalajara Narcotics Cartel" gathered at a Guadalajara restaurant known as "La Langosta." The cartel members at this gathering included Rafael Caro-Quintero, Ernesto Fonseca-Carillo, and Javier Barba-Hernandez, all well-known drug dealers in Guadalajara, the appellant Vasquez-Velasco, and other members of the cartel.

That night Walker and Radelat went to the La Langosta restaurant at approximately 7:00 p.m. Soon after they entered, they were grabbed by ten to fifteen members of the cartel and beaten with fists and guns. They were subsequently carried to a storage room in the back of the restaurant while the beating continued. Vasquez-Velasco assisted in carrying and beating the two men. The two men were tortured until one of them admitted that they were police. Both were later killed in a field outside of Guadalajara. The next day

Vasquez-Velasco informed Barba-Hernandez that both tourists had died. In June 1985, the bodies of Walker and Radelat were found in Primavera Park outside of Guadalajara.

A grand jury returned a Sixth Superseding Indictment charging nineteen persons associated with the cartel with various crimes performed in 1984 and 1985. Counts One and Two of the indictment charged Vasquez-Velasco with committing violent crimes in aid of a racketeering enterprise in violation of 18 U.S.C. § 1959. Specifically, the indictment alleged that Vasquez-Velasco, as a member of the cartel, participated in the murders of Walker and Radelat for the purpose of maintaining and increasing his position in the drug trafficking activities of the cartel. . . . Vasquez-Velasco was convicted under both counts on August 6, 1990. On May 23, 1991 he was sentenced to two consecutive terms of life imprisonment. . . .

Vasquez-Velasco raises four issues on appeal. First, he argues that the district court erred in ruling that § 1959 applies extraterritorially. . . .

"Generally there is no constitutional bar to the extraterritorial application of United States penal laws." . . . To determine whether a given statute should have extraterritorial application in a specific case, courts look to congressional intent. *Bowman* [p. 28]. When faced with a criminal statute such as § 1959, we may infer that extraterritorial application is appropriate from "'the nature of the offenses and Congress' other legislative efforts to eliminate the type of crime involved.'" . . . Where "the *locus* of the conduct is not relevant to the end sought by the enactment" of the statute, and the statute prohibits conduct that obstructs the functioning of the United States government, it is reasonable to infer congressional intent to reach crimes committed abroad.

In determining whether a statute applies extraterritorially, we also presume that Congress does not intend to violate principles of international law. Thus, in the absence of an explicit Congressional directive, courts do not give extraterritorial effect to any statute that violates principles of international law.

. . . . In general, international law recognizes several principles whereby the exercise of extraterritorial jurisdiction may be appropriate. These principles include the objective territorial principle, under which jurisdiction is asserted over acts performed outside the United States that produce detrimental effects within the United States, and the protective principle, under which jurisdiction is asserted over foreigners for an act committed outside the United States that may impinge on the territorial integrity, security, or political independence of the United States. . . . Nevertheless, an exercise of jurisdiction on one of these bases still violates international principles if it is "unreasonable". . . .

Our circuit has applied this analysis to find that the extraterritorial application of the precursor to § 1959 in circumstances similar to those presented by this case is consistent with Congressional intent. In *Felix-Gutierrez,* the defendant was charged as an accessory after the fact to the commission of a violent crime, the kidnapping and murder of Enrique Camarena, in aid of a racketeering enterprise. The defendant was charged under 18 U.S.C. § 1952B, the predecessor to § 1959. . . . We held that because drug trafficking by its nature involves foreign countries and because DEA agents often work overseas, the murder of a DEA agent in retaliation for drug enforcement activities is a crime against the United States regardless of where it occurs. Thus, we found that Congress would have intended that § 1959 be applied extraterritorially to cases involving the murder of DEA agents abroad. . . .

We have also held that extraterritorial application of a statute such as § 1959 to the murder of a DEA agent is consistent with principles of international law, particularly the objective territorial and the protective principles. Our circuit has repeatedly approved extraterritorial application of statutes that prohibit the importation and distribution of controlled substances in the United States because these activities implicate national security interests and create a detrimental effect in the United States. . . .

Finally, we are convinced that extraterritorial application of § 1959 to violent crimes associated with drug trafficking is reasonable under international law principles. Because drug smuggling is a serious and universally condemned offense, no conflict is likely to be created by extraterritorial regulation of drug traffickers. . . .

Although the violent crime in which Vasquez-Velasco participated was the murder of an American citizen, and not the murder of a DEA agent, extraterritorial application of § 1959 is still appropriate in this case. According to the government's theory, the cartel members mistook Walker and Radelat for DEA agents and killed them in retaliation for the losses inflicted on the cartel by the DEA. . . . The murders of Walker and Radelat . . . . were performed to further the cartel's drug smuggling activities by intimidating the DEA from continuing its enforcement activities against the cartel's drug trafficking. Such actions could also intimidate local police and drug agencies, thereby inhibiting them from cooperating with the DEA. In this context, the murder of American citizens has an equally direct and adverse impact on our nation's security interest in combatting the importation and trafficking of illegal narcotics. . .

Vasquez-Velasco argues that even if § 1959 may be applied extraterritorially if the murders were committed with the purpose of retaliating against the DEA, in this case there is insufficient evidence to establish such a nexus between the murder of the two American tourists and the DEA's activities in Mexico.

If the evidence at trial only suggested that two tourists were randomly murdered, extraterritorial application of § 1959 would be inappropriate. We therefore must decide whether there is sufficient evidence in the record to indicate that the murders of Walker and Radelat were in fact performed with the intention of adversely affecting DEA activities and thus of promoting the cartel's drug trafficking activities.

In considering the evidence, it is helpful to remember that Vasquez-Velasco was charged with committing a violent crime in aid of a racketeering enterprise. In order to convict Vasquez-Velasco of this crime, the government was required to prove (1) that the Guadalajara Narcotics Cartel exists; (2) that the cartel is a racketeering enterprise engaged in drug smuggling; (3) that Vasquez-Velasco participated in the murders of Walker and Radelat; and (4) that Vasquez-Velasco acted for the purpose of promoting his position in the cartel. *See* 18 U.S.C. § 1959. Given the facts that the government was required to establish at trial to prove the elements of the crime charged, we find it appropriate to consider both the direct testimony as to Vasquez-Velasco's participation in the murders and the broader circumstantial evidence of the events that occurred around the time of the murders.

When viewed in its entirety, the record clearly supports the government's contention that Walker and Radelat were murdered in retaliation for the DEA's activities in Mexico. At trial, the government presented evidence that the Guadalajara Narcotics Cartel became a powerful drug trafficking organization in the early 1980's. By 1983 and 1984, large amounts of cocaine were being distributed by members of the cartel in the United States, and the cartel controlled extensive marijuana fields in Mexico. In 1984 and 1985, the cartel suffered from losses amounting to billions of dollars as a result of investigations by American authorities. For example, in May 1984, as a result of American inspections, the Mexican authorities raided several marijuana ranches in the Zacatecas area, destroying over ten tons of processed marijuana, hashish oil and marijuana seeds. In June 1984, several million dollars worth of cocaine proceeds were seized in a California hotel. And in November, over 10,000 tons of marijuana worth approximately $ 5 billion were destroyed in raids in Chihuahua.

As a result of these raids, the cartel engaged in a series of retaliatory actions against DEA agents in Mexico and against people suspected of cooperating with the DEA. . . .

Vasquez-Velasco argues that there is insufficient evidence supporting the government's theory because no one at trial specifically testified that Walker and Radelat were murdered because they were mistaken for DEA agents. While Vasquez-Velasco is correct in arguing that no one at trial specifically testified that Walker and Radelat were mistaken for DEA agents, there clearly is sufficient evidence in the record to support this theory. As we have already indicated, at the time the murders took place the cartel was suffering from serious economic setbacks. Cartel members had identified the DEA as responsible for their losses and had already planned to "pick up" agent Camarena. They were aware that they were being followed by DEA agents and had actively threatened some who came too close. In this context, it is wholly reasonable to believe that when fifteen cartel members beat and killed two American tourists who were caught "spying" on them, they did so in the belief that the tourists were DEA agents. The fact that Camarena was captured, tortured and murdered one week later only strengthens the government's case by suggesting a pattern of retaliatory activity by the cartel. In light of the extensive evidence as to the cartel's knowledge and behavior during the time of the murders, the only logical explanation for the cartel's murders of Walker and Radelat is that supplied by the government. We therefore conclude that there is sufficient evidence in the record to support the extraterritorial application of § 1959 given the facts of this case. . . .

§ 7.02 International Narcotics Trafficking

"The international trade of illicit drugs is estimated to exceed $300 billion per year, making illicit drugs the third most valuable internationally-traded commodity after oil and arms." Joseph J. Duffy & John A. Hedges, *United States Money Laundering Statutes: The Business Executive's Conundrum,* INTERNATIONAL TRADE: AVOIDING RISKS 14-3 (William M.Hennay ed., 1991). Because of the magnitude of narcotics trafficking, it has become a major focus of criminal law on both the national and international level.

On the national level, there are drug-related statutes with extraterritorial application. For example, 21 U.S.C. § 959(c) allows for the prosecution of acts outside the United States [*see* p.155]. There are also statutes specifically focused on international narcotics trafficking. The Foreign Narcotics Kingpin Designation Act which went into effect in the United States on December 3, 1999, "provide[s] authority for the identification of, and application of sanctions on a worldwide basis to, significant foreign narcotics traffickers, their organizations, and the foreign persons who provide support to those significant foreign narcotics traffickers and their organizations, whose activities threaten the national security, foreign policy, and economy of the United States ." *See* 18 U.S.C. § 1902. The policy underlying this Act provides:

§ 1901. Findings and policy

(a) Findings. Congress makes the following findings:

(1) Presidential Decision Directive 42, issued on October 21, 1995, ordered agencies of the executive branch of the United States Government to, inter alia, increase the priority and resources devoted to the direct and immediate threat international crime presents to national security, work more closely with other governments to develop a global response to this threat, and use aggressively and creatively all legal means available to combat international crime.

(2) Executive Order No. 12978 of October 21, 1995 [50 U.S.C. § 1701 note], provides for the use of the authorities in the International Emergency Economic Powers Act (IEEPA) (50 U.S.C. 1701 et seq.) to target and apply sanctions to four international narcotics traffickers and their organizations that operate from Colombia.

(3) IEEPA was successfully applied to international narcotics traffickers in Colombia and based on that successful case study, Congress believes similar authorities should be applied worldwide.

(4) There is a national emergency resulting from the activities of international narcotics traffickers and their organizations that threatens the national security, foreign policy, and economy of the United States.

(b) Policy. It shall be the policy of the United States to apply economic and other financial sanctions to significant foreign narcotics traffickers and their organizations worldwide to protect the national security, foreign policy, and economy of the United States from the threat described in subsection (a)(4).

On June 2, 2000, President Clinton issued the first list of drug kingpins under the Act.

There are also international initiatives focused on narcotics trafficking. The three conventions that form the cornerstone of curbing international narcotics trafficking are the Single Convention on Narcotics Drugs, March 30, 1961; the Protocol Amending the Single Convention on Narcotics Drugs, March 25, 1972; and the United Nations [Vienna] Convention Against Illicit Traffic in Narcotic Drugs and Psychotropic Substances, December 20, 1988. *See* M. Cherif Bassiouni & Jean Francois Thony, *The International Drug Control System, in* 1 INTERNATIONAL CRIMINAL LAW 905 (M. Cherif Bassiouni ed., 2d ed. 1999). These conventions make elaborate provision for international cooperation in suppressing the traffic in illicit drugs. They allow parties to exercise extraterritorial jurisdiction over offenders who are "found" within their territory and whose extradition is refused; but, unlike recent anti-terrorism conventions [*see* chap. 8], do not make it mandatory to do so with respect to non-nationals. *See* M. CHERIF BASSIOUNI & EDWARD M. WISE, AUT DEDERE AUT JUDICARE: THE DUTY TO EXTRADITE OR PROSECUTE IN INTERNATIONAL LAW 14 (1995).

"The [United States] Department of State's Bureau of International Narcotics and Law Enforcement Affairs (INL) is responsible for managing more than $200 million a year in narcotics control and anti-crime assistance to foreign countries." *See International Narcotics Control Strategy Report, 1999* (Released by the Bureau for International Narcotics and Law Enforcement Affairs, U.S. Department of State Washington, D.C., March 2000) <http://www.state.gov/www/global/narcotics_law/1999_narc_report/legis99.html> A report is required to be filed "on the extent to which each country that received INL assistance in the past two fiscal years has 'met the goals and objectives of the United Nations Convention Against Illicit Traffic in Narcotic Drugs and Psychotropic Substances.'" *Id.* "Although the Convention does not contain a list of goals and objectives, it does set forth a number of obligations that the parties agree to undertake. Generally speaking, it requires the parties to take legal measures to outlaw and punish all forms of illicit drug production, trafficking, and drug money laundering, to control chemicals that can be used

to process illicit drugs, and to cooperate in international efforts to these ends."
Id.

§ 7.03   Money Laundering

Money laundering serves as an integral aspect of drug trafficking. In the
United States, the two key money laundering statutes are 18 U.S.C. § 1956 and
18 U.S.C. § 1957. These money laundering statutes were initially enacted "to
prevent organized crime from concealing the proceeds of drug trafficking by
converting 'cash into manageable form.'" *Trujillo v. Banco Central Del Ecuador*,
35 F. Supp. 2d 908, 913 (S.D. Fl. 1998). Section 1956 of title 18 allows for
prosecution when funds are going into or outside the United States. 18 U.S.C.
§ 1956(a)(2) provides:

> (2) Whoever transports, transmits, or transfers, or attempts to transport,
> transmit, or transfer a monetary instrument or funds from a place in the
> United States to or through a place outside the United States or to a
> place in the United States from or through a place outside the United
> States–
>
> (A) with the intent to promote the carrying on of specified unlawful
> activity; or
>
> (B) knowing that the monetary instrument or funds involved in the
> transportation represent the proceeds of some form of unlawful
> activity and knowing that such transportation, transmission, or
> transfer is designed in whole or in part–
>
> (i) to conceal or disguise the nature, the location, the source, the
> ownership, or the control of the proceeds of specified unlawful activity;
> or
>
> (ii) to avoid a transaction reporting requirement under State or
> Federal law, shall be sentenced to a fine of not more than $ 500,000
> or twice the value of the monetary instrument or funds involved in
> the transportation, transmission, or transfer, whichever is greater,
> or imprisonment for not more than twenty years, or both. For the
> purpose of the offense described in subparagraph (B), the
> defendant's knowledge may be established by proof that a law
> enforcement officer represented the matter specified in
> subparagraph (B) as true, and the defendant's subsequent
> statements or actions indicate that the defendant believed such
> representations to be true.

Both sections 1956 and 1957 provide for extraterritorial jurisdiction in limited
circumstances.

Department of Justice Guidelines restrict prosecutors from individually making the decision to bring international prosecutions under sections 1956 and 1957. The United States Attorneys Manual, 9-105.300 provides:

> There are four categories of money laundering prosecutions which require prior authorization from the Criminal or Tax Division:
>
> 1. Extraterritorial Jurisdiction. Criminal Division (Asset Forfeiture & Money Laundering Section) (AFMLS) approval is required before the commencement of any investigation where jurisdiction to prosecute is based solely on the extraterritorial jurisdiction provisions of §§ 1956 and 1957. Due to the potential international sensitivities, as well as proof problems, involved in using these extraterritorial provisions, no grand jury investigation may be commenced, no indictment may be returned, and no complaint may be filed without the prior approval of AFMLS, Criminal Division when jurisdiction to prosecute these offenses exists only because of these extraterritorial provisions. . . .

In recent years money laundering has been extended beyond drug trafficking. *See United States v. Piervinanzi*, 23 F.3d 670 (2d Cir. 1994) (defendant charged with international money laundering in alleged bank fraud scheme). The use of a money laundering charge as an appendage to white collar offenses has raised issues regarding both the appropriateness of charging money laundering and the sentencing guideline that should be applied to these convictions. *See United States v. Powers*, 168 F.3d 741 (5th Cir. 1999) (court grouped money laundering and fraud offense but sentenced under money laundering since this produced a higher offense guideline).

Enormous sums of money can be involved in money laundering schemes. *See* Larry Neumeister, *Couple Admit Laundering Russian Money*, ATL. J. CONST., Feb. 17, 2000, at A8 (discussing the laundering of seven billion dollars). The prosecution of international money laundering schemes raises issues not only with respect to which country should serve as the law enforcer, but there can also be issues of which agency within the United States should be responsible for a prosecution. *See* Timothy L. O'Brien & Lowell Bergman, *Law-Enforcement Rivalry in U.S. Slowed Inquiry on Russian Funds*, N.Y. TIMES, Sept. 29, 1999, at A1 (discussing rivalries between the Manhattan DA and FBI New York office).

The Clinton Administration has placed a high priority on combatting international money laundering and economic crime. *See Clinton Administration Proposes International Crime Fighting Legislation,* 63 CRIM. L. REP. 208 (May 20, 1998). "Western Union and thousands of storefront operations" are now required to register with the Treasury Department in efforts "to choke off illicit drug profits flowing to Columbia and other trafficking centers." *New Net Cast for Drug Cash*, ATL. J. CONST., Aug. 19, 1999, at B2. Other countries have also joined in the efforts with comparable money laundering statutes. William M. Hennay & John A. Hedges, *International Trends in the Criminalization of Money Laundering*, INTERNATIONAL TRADE:

AVOIDING RISKS 5-1 to 5-12 (W. M. Hennay ed., 1991). Cooperative efforts can also be seen in the international sphere. *Id.* at 5-12 to 5-22. For example, "[t]he United Nations Convention against Illicit Traffic in Narcotic Drug and Psychotropic Substances, adopted in 1988 in Vienna, includes significant money laundering control measures." *Id.* at 5-15. Likewise, the Financial Action Task Force (FATF), an inter-governmental body with twenty-six participating countries, has as its purpose "the development and promotion of policies to combat money laundering." The FATF issued forty recommendations that include recommendations on how to strengthen international cooperation. *See* FATC Recommendations, <http://www.oecd.org/fatf/recommenations.htm>.

NOTES AND QUESTIONS

(1) To what extent does the defendant's conduct have to occur in the United States to apply the money laundering statute 18 U.S.C. § 1956(a)(2)? Can requiring presence in the United States preclude prosecutions premised upon electronic transfers? District Judge Clement considered this issue in an order issued in *United States v. Stein,* 1994 U.S. Dist. LEXIS 8471 stating, "[i]t is plain from both the purpose of section 1956 and its legislative history that Congress did not intend to limit section 1956 so that it would only apply to defendants who are actually present in the United States."

(2) Do these same principles apply in forfeiture claims premised upon money laundering? In *United States v. Approximately $ 25,829,681.80 in Funds (Plus Interest),* 1999 U.S. Dist. LEXIS 18499, District Judge McKenna of the Southern District of New York denied a motion to dismiss stating in part:

> The Government makes two claims for forfeiture in this case: one based on alleged acts of wire fraud and the other based on alleged acts of money laundering. . . . Turning to the Government's second claim, the forfeiture statute makes subject to forfeiture "any property, real or personal, involved in a transaction or attempted transaction in violation of . . . section 1956 or 1957 of this title, or any property traceable to such property." . . . Thus, the underlying allegations of wire fraud and money laundering are of crucial importance to the Government's case. . . . The language of the forfeiture statute does not condition forfeiture on the involvement of a claimant in the underlying violations of law. Rather, the proper focus is on the defendant-*in-rem* funds and their connection to the wire fraud and money laundering. . . .

> Clemente does not dispute that the Government has *in rem* jurisdiction over the funds in this case. Instead, Clemente argues that jurisdiction is lacking here "because applying the forfeiture statute to the instant facts would impermissibly give it extraterritorial effect." . . .

> Concerning the allegations of money laundering, Clemente notes that the language of 18 U.S.C. § 1956 limits its application to situations where (1) the accused is a U.S. citizen or (2) "the conduct occurs in part

in the United States." 18 U.S.C. § 1956(f). . . . Clemente argues that the "conduct" demanded by the statute must involve actual physical activity within the United States, ... This Court, finding convincing precedent in *United States v. Stein,* [*supra* note 1] disagrees with Clemente. In *Stein,* the defendant, who was accused of money laundering, initiated a transfer of funds from New Orleans to London while he was in the United Kingdom. Because he was not physically present in the United States, he argued that jurisdiction was lacking. Judge Clement rejected his argument, holding that the term "conduct" in 18 U.S.C. § 1956 does not demand a physical presence within the United States. . . . Judge Clement reasoned that "the defendant . . . acted, *albeit electronically or otherwise*, within the borders of the United States." *Id.* (emphasis added). Similarly, a lack of physical activity in the United States in this case is not fatal to jurisdiction. As in *Stein,* the parties initiating the fund transfers "acted electronically" within the United States, and such action is sufficient to constitute "conduct" for purposes of 18 U.S.C. § 1956. Thus, this Court finds that it would have subject matter jurisdiction over the money laundering claim.

Clemente argues that even if this Court would have jurisdiction over the wire fraud and money laundering claims, that does not necessarily mean that it has jurisdiction over the forfeiture claim. Rather, Clemente frames the question as "whether permitting forfeiture would impermissibly give [the forfeiture statute] extraterritorial effect." . . . Clemente contends that the "conduct" and/or "effects" tests commonly used in RICO and securities fraud cases should be used to determine whether jurisdiction is proper.

This Court has found no precedent addressing the proper focus of inquiry regarding jurisdiction under the forfeiture statute when transnational conduct is involved. However, guidance is found in analogous RICO case law holding that if the predicate acts are sufficient to confer jurisdiction upon a court, then the "conduct" or "effects" tests need not be employed. For example, in *Alfadda v. Fenn,* 935 F.2d 475 (2d Cir. 1991), the plaintiffs alleged as RICO predicate acts securities fraud violations consummated by securities sales which occurred primarily in the United States. . . . The Second Circuit held that these "predicate acts . . . serve as a basis of subject matter jurisdiction for the RICO claims." . . . Subsequent case law from this District confirms that if RICO predicate acts occurred in the United States, then jurisdiction over the RICO claim itself is proper. . . .

This Court concludes that, as with RICO, a finding that the predicate violations underlying the forfeiture action occurred in the United States is sufficient to support a finding of subject matter jurisdiction over the forfeiture action itself. Here, the Government alleges key acts of wire fraud and money laundering involving use of the wires in the United States. Thus, this Court has subject matter jurisdiction over the Government's forfeiture action.

(3) The electronic transfer of funds, outside a money laundering context, also raise similar jurisdiction issues. Consider the court's resolution of this issue in *United States v. Gilboe*, 684 F.2d 235 (2d Cir. 1982):

> Defendant's massive fraud on the international shipping industry left victims on the continents of Asia, North America and Europe. The scheme involved several other apparently fraudulent transactions but the charges against defendant in this case stem from two shipments of grain arranged by defendant to the People's Republic of China, one from Argentina and the other from the United States. . . .
>
> Appellant argues that the district court did not have jurisdiction over the offenses charged because he was a nonresident alien whose acts occurred outside the United States and had no detrimental effect within the United States. In connection with the Argentina and New Orleans transactions, defendant was charged with both wire fraud under 18 U.S.C. § 1343 and transportation of funds obtained by fraud under 18 U.S.C. § 2314.
>
> Turning first to the former charges, defendant was convicted on four counts of wire fraud under § 1343, . . . Defendant admitted that, in negotiating with the Manhattan shipowner for the shipment from Argentina, he had telephone and telex conversations with a ship broker in Bayshore, Long Island and that he caused other telex and telephone negotiations to occur between Manhattan and Hong Kong. These negotiations were to obtain ships to transport the grain, a key element of the fraud. The evidence was clearly sufficient to sustain jurisdiction on this offense, which forms the basis for count one. . . . With respect to the shipments from New Orleans, defendant also admitted that he caused the payments received from the Chinese corporation to be electronically transferred through Manhattan banks to accounts in the Bahamas, the basis for counts three, four and five. This evidence was sufficient to justify asserting jurisdiction over defendant. . . .
>
> With respect to the conviction on counts charging violations of § 2314, defendant's jurisdictional argument depends on his premise that the section applies only to the transportation of tangible items and does not cover "electronic crediting and debiting," the means by which the funds in defendant's scheme moved from one bank to another. However, if such transfers of money are covered by § 2314, defendant's attack on jurisdiction fails because the evidence clearly showed that defendant had aided and abetted the transportation in foreign commerce through banks in Manhattan of "securities or money . . . . taken by fraud." The question whether the section covers electronic transfers of funds appears to be one of first impression, but we do not regard it as a difficult one. Electronic signals in this context are the means by which funds are transported. The beginning of the transaction is money in one account and the ending is money in another. The manner in which the funds were moved does not affect the ability to obtain tangible paper dollars or

a bank check from the receiving account. Indeed, we suspect that actual dollars rarely move between banks, particularly in international transactions. If anything, the means of transfer here were essential to the success of the fraudulent scheme. Defendant depended heavily on his ability to move funds rapidly out of reach of disgruntled shipowners who were to receive payment within days of loading the grain. And it was not until the funds, through a series of bank transfers, came to rest in the Bahamas that defendant's scheme was complete. . . . The record amply shows that the direct transfers of precise amounts received through fraud were in a manner clearly indicating that the fraud and transfer were a single transaction. The primary element of this offense, transportation, "does not require proof that any specific means of transporting were used." . . . Therefore, since fraudulently obtained funds were transported within the meaning of the section and banks in Manhattan were utilized, there was sufficient evidence to support jurisdiction under § 2314.

(4) What happens when the government charges separate counts of domestic and international money laundering for the same financial transaction? In *United States v. Zvi*, 168 F.3d 49, 57 (2d Cir. 1999), the Second Circuit found it "multiplicitous" to charge both "domestic and international money laundering based on the same funds transfers."

§ 7.04 Currency Transaction Reports

18 U.S.C. § 1956 and § 1957 are not the only United States statutes that can be attributed to efforts to decrease national and international drug activity. There are also an array of reporting statutes that are directed at curtailing money laundering. For example, the Bank Secrecy Act requires banks to file currency transactions reports with the Internal Revenue Service for certain monetary transactions. In certain circumstances individuals transporting money into and out of the United States are required to report the currency on a customs form. Businesses have also been subject to Internal Revenue reporting requirements for certain monetary transactions. What happens when the government decides to use a currency transaction reporting statute in a situation that does not involve drugs or money laundering?

UNITED STATES v. BAJAKAJIAN

Supreme Court of the United States
524 U.S. 321, 118 S. Ct. 2028, 141 L. Ed. 2d 314 (1998)

JUSTICE THOMAS delivered the opinion of the Court:

Respondent Hosep Bajakajian attempted to leave the United States without reporting, as required by federal law, that he was transporting more than $10,000 in currency. Federal law also provides that a person convicted of willfully violating this reporting requirement shall forfeit to the government "any property . . . involved in such offense." 18 U.S.C. § 982(a)(1). The question in this case is whether forfeiture of the entire $ 357,144 that respondent failed to declare would violate the Excessive Fines Clause of the Eighth Amendment. We hold that it would, because full forfeiture of respondent's currency would be grossly disproportional to the gravity of his offense. . . .

On June 9, 1994, respondent, his wife, and his two daughters were waiting at Los Angeles International Airport to board a flight to Italy; their final destination was Cyprus. Using dogs trained to detect currency by its smell, customs inspectors discovered some $230,000 in cash in the Bajakajians' checked baggage. A customs inspector approached respondent and his wife and told them that they were required to report all money in excess of $10,000 in their possession or in their baggage. Respondent said that he had $8,000 and that his wife had another $ 7,000, but that the family had no additional currency to declare. A search of their carry-on bags, purse, and wallet revealed more cash; in all, customs inspectors found $357,144. The currency was seized and respondent was taken into custody.

A federal grand jury indicted respondent on three counts. Count One charged him with failing to report, as required by 31 U.S.C. § 5316(a)(1)(A),[1] that he was transporting more than $10,000 outside the United States, and with doing so "willfully," in violation of § 5322(a).[2] Count Two charged him with making a

---

[1]The statutory reporting requirement provides:

"[A] person or an agent or bailee of the person shall file a report . . . when the person, agent, or bailee knowingly –

"(1) transports, is about to transport, or has transported, monetary instruments of more than $ 10,000 at one time –

"(A) from a place in the United States to or through a place outside the United States . . . ." *31 U.S.C. § 5316*(a).

[2]Section 5322(a) provides: "A person willfully violating this subchapter . . . shall be fined not more than $ 250,000, or imprisoned for not more than five years, or both." § 5322(a).

false material statement to the United States Customs Service, in violation of 18 U.S.C. § 1001. Count Three sought forfeiture of the $ 357,144 pursuant to 18 U.S.C. § 982(a)(1), which provides:

> "The court, in imposing sentence on a person convicted of an offense in violation of section . . . 5316, . . . shall order that the person forfeit to the United States any property, real or personal, involved in such offense, or any property traceable to such property." 18 U.S.C. § 982(a)(1).

Respondent pleaded guilty to the failure to report in Count One; the Government agreed to dismiss the false statement charge in Count Two; and respondent elected to have a bench trial on the forfeiture in Count Three. After the bench trial, the District Court found that the entire $ 357,144 was subject to forfeiture because it was "involved in" the offense. The court also found that the funds were not connected to any other crime and that respondent was transporting the money to repay a lawful debt. . . . The District Court further found that respondent had failed to report that he was taking the currency out of the United States because of fear stemming from "cultural differences": Respondent, who had grown up as a member of the Armenian minority in Syria, had a "distrust for the Government." . . .

Although § 982(a)(1) directs sentencing courts to impose full forfeiture, the District Court concluded that such forfeiture would be "extraordinarily harsh" and "grossly disproportionate to the offense in question," and that it would therefore violate the Excessive Fines Clause. The court instead ordered forfeiture of $15,000, in addition to a sentence of three years of probation and a fine of $ 5,000 – the maximum fine under the Sentencing Guidelines – because the court believed that the maximum Guidelines fine was "too little" and that a $ 15,000 forfeiture would "make up for what I think a reasonable fine should be."

The United States appealed, seeking full forfeiture of respondent's currency as provided in § 982(a)(1). The Court of Appeals for the Ninth Circuit affirmed. 84 F.3d 334 (1996). Applying Circuit precedent, the Court held that, to satisfy the Excessive Fines Clause, a forfeiture must fulfill two conditions: The property forfeited must be an "instrumentality" of the crime committed, and the value of the property must be proportional to the culpability of the owner. . . . A majority of the panel determined that the currency was not an "instrumentality" of the crime of failure to report because " 'the crime [in a currency reporting offense] is the withholding of information, . . . not the possession or the transportation of the money.' ". . . The majority therefore held that § 982(a)(1) could never satisfy the Excessive Fines Clause in cases involving forfeitures of currency and that it was unnecessary to apply the "proportionality" prong of the test. Although the panel majority concluded that the Excessive Fines Clause did not permit forfeiture of *any* of the unreported currency, it held that it lacked jurisdiction to set the $ 15,000 forfeiture aside because respondent had not cross-appealed to challenge that forfeiture. . . .

Judge Wallace concurred in the result. He viewed respondent's currency as an instrumentality of the crime because "without the currency, there can be no offense," and he criticized the majority for "striking down a portion of" the statute. He nonetheless agreed that full forfeiture would violate the Excessive Fines Clause in respondent's case, based upon the "proportionality" prong of the Ninth Circuit test. Finding no clear error in the District Court's factual findings, he concluded that the reduced forfeiture of $15,000 was proportional to respondent's culpability.

Because the Court of Appeals' holding – that the forfeiture ordered by § 982(a)(1) was *per se* unconstitutional in cases of currency forfeiture – invalidated a portion of an act of Congress, we granted certiorari. . . .

The Eighth Amendment provides: "Excessive bail shall not be required, nor excessive fines imposed, nor cruel and unusual punishments inflicted." U.S. Const., Amdt. 8. This Court has had little occasion to interpret, and has never actually applied, the Excessive Fines Clause. We have, however, explained that at the time the Constitution was adopted, "the word 'fine' was understood to mean a payment to a sovereign as punishment for some offense." . . . The Excessive Fines Clause thus "limits the government's power to extract payments, whether in cash or in kind, 'as punishment for some offense.' ". . . Forfeitures – payments in kind – are thus "fines" if they constitute punishment for an offense.

We have little trouble concluding that the forfeiture of currency ordered by § 982(a)(1) constitutes punishment. The statute directs a court to order forfeiture as an additional sanction when "imposing sentence on a person convicted of" a willful violation of § 5316's reporting requirement. The forfeiture is thus imposed at the culmination of a criminal proceeding and requires conviction of an underlying felony, and it cannot be imposed upon an innocent owner of unreported currency, but only upon a person who has himself been convicted of a § 5316 reporting violation. . . .

The United States argues, however, that the forfeiture of currency under § 982(a)(1) "also serves important remedial purposes." . . . The Government asserts that it has "an overriding sovereign interest in controlling what property leaves and enters the country." It claims that full forfeiture of unreported currency supports that interest by serving to "deter illicit movements of cash" and aiding in providing the Government with "valuable information to investigate and detect criminal activities associated with that cash." Deterrence, however, has traditionally been viewed as a goal of punishment, and forfeiture of the currency here does not serve the remedial purpose of compensating the Government for a loss. . . . Although the Government has asserted a loss of information regarding the amount of currency leaving the country, that loss would not be remedied by the Government's confiscation of respondent's $ 357,144. . . . The United States also argues that the forfeiture mandated by § 982(a)(1) is constitutional because it falls within a class of historic forfeitures of property tainted by crime. . . .

Traditional *in rem* forfeitures were thus not considered punishment against the individual for an offense. . . . The forfeiture in this case does not bear any of the hallmarks of traditional civil *in rem* forfeitures. The Government has not proceeded against the currency itself, but has instead sought and obtained a criminal conviction of respondent personally. The forfeiture serves no remedial purpose, is designed to punish the offender, and cannot be imposed upon innocent owners.

Section 982(a)(1) thus descends not from historic *in rem* forfeitures of guilty property, but from a different historical tradition: that of *in personam*, criminal forfeitures. Such forfeitures have historically been treated as punitive, being part of the punishment imposed for felonies and treason in the Middle Ages and at common law. . . . It was only in 1970 that Congress resurrected the English common law of punitive forfeiture to combat organized crime and major drug trafficking. . . .

The Government specifically contends that the forfeiture of respondent's currency is constitutional because it involves an "instrumentality" of respondent's crime. According to the Government, the unreported cash is an instrumentality because it "does not merely facilitate a violation of law," but is " 'the very *sine qua non* of the crime.' ". . . The Government reasons that "there would be no violation at all without the exportation (or attempted exportation) of the cash."

Acceptance of the Government's argument would require us to expand the traditional understanding of instrumentality forfeitures. This we decline to do. Instrumentalities historically have been treated as a form of "guilty property" that can be forfeited in civil *in rem* proceedings. In this case, however, the Government has sought to punish respondent by proceeding against him criminally, *in personam*, rather than proceeding *in rem* against the currency. It is therefore irrelevant whether respondent's currency is an instrumentality; the forfeiture is punitive, and the test for the excessiveness of a punitive forfeiture involves solely a proportionality determination. . . .

Because the forfeiture of respondent's currency constitutes punishment and is thus a "fine" within the meaning of the Excessive Fines Clause, we now turn to the question of whether it is "excessive." . . . The touchstone of the constitutional inquiry under the Excessive Fines Clause is the principle of proportionality: The amount of the forfeiture must bear some relationship to the gravity of the offense that it is designed to punish. . . . Until today, however, we have not articulated a standard for determining whether a punitive forfeiture is constitutionally excessive. We now hold that a punitive forfeiture violates the Excessive Fines Clause if it is grossly disproportional to the gravity of a defendant's offense. . . .

Under this standard, the forfeiture of respondent's entire $ 357,144 would violate the Excessive Fines Clause. Respondent's crime was solely a reporting offense. It was permissible to transport the currency out of the country so long as he reported it. Section 982(a)(1) orders currency to be forfeited for a "willful"

violation of the reporting requirement. Thus, the essence of respondent's crime is a willful failure to report the removal of currency from the United States. Furthermore, as the District Court found, respondent's violation was unrelated to any other illegal activities. The money was the proceeds of legal activity and was to be used to repay a lawful debt. Whatever his other vices, respondent does not fit into the class of persons for whom the statute was principally designed: He is not a money launderer, a drug trafficker, or a tax evader. . . . And under the Sentencing Guidelines, the maximum sentence that could have been imposed on respondent was six months, while the maximum fine was $ 5,000.
. . .

The harm that respondent caused was also minimal. Failure to report his currency affected only one party, the Government, and in a relatively minor way. There was no fraud on the United States, and respondent caused no loss to the public fisc. Had his crime gone undetected, the Government would have been deprived only of the information that $ 357,144 had left the country. The Government and the dissent contend that there is a correlation between the amount forfeited and the harm that the Government would have suffered had the crime gone undetected. . . . We disagree. There is no inherent proportionality in such a forfeiture. It is impossible to conclude, for example, that the harm respondent caused is anywhere near 30 times greater than that caused by a hypothetical drug dealer who willfully fails to report taking $ 12,000 out of the country in order to purchase drugs.

Comparing the gravity of respondent's crime with the $ 357,144 forfeiture the Government seeks, we conclude that such a forfeiture would be grossly disproportional to the gravity of his offense. It is larger than the $ 5,000 fine imposed by the District Court by many orders of magnitude, and it bears no articulable correlation to any injury suffered by the Government. . . .

The early monetary forfeitures . . . . were considered not as punishment for an offense, but rather as serving the remedial purpose of reimbursing the Government for the losses accruing from the evasion of customs duties. They were thus no different in purpose and effect than the *in rem* forfeitures of the goods to whose value they were proportioned. . . . By contrast, the full forfeiture mandated by § 982(a)(1) in this case serves no remedial purpose; it is clearly punishment. The customs statutes enacted by the First Congress, therefore, in no way suggest that § 982(a)(1)'s currency forfeiture is constitutionally proportional.

For the foregoing reasons, the full forfeiture of respondent's currency would violate the Excessive Fines Clause. The judgment of the Court of Appeals is Affirmed.

JUSTICE KENNEDY, with whom THE CHIEF JUSTICE, JUSTICE O'CONNOR, and JUSTICE SCALIA join, dissenting.

For the first time in its history, the Court strikes down a fine as excessive under the Eighth Amendment. The decision is disturbing both for its specific holding and for the broader upheaval it foreshadows. At issue is a fine Congress fixed in the amount of the currency respondent sought to smuggle or to transport without reporting. If a fine calibrated with this accuracy fails the Court's test, its decision portends serious disruption of a vast range of statutory fines. The Court all but says the offense is not serious anyway. This disdain for the statute is wrong as an empirical matter and disrespectful of the separation of powers. The irony of the case is that, in the end, it may stand for narrowing constitutional protection rather than enhancing it. To make its rationale work, the Court appears to remove important classes of fines from any excessiveness inquiry at all. This, too, is unsound; and with all respect, I dissent. . . .

The majority justifies its evisceration of the fine because the money was legal to have and came from a legal source. . . . This fact, however, shows only that the forfeiture was a fine, not that it was excessive. As the majority puts it, respondent's money was lawful to possess, was acquired in a lawful manner, and was lawful to export. It was not, however, lawful to possess the money while concealing and smuggling it. Even if one overlooks this problem, the apparent lawfulness of the money adds nothing to the argument. If the items possessed had been dangerous or unlawful to own, for instance narcotics, the forfeiture would have been remedial and would not have been a fine at all. . . . If respondent had acquired the money in an unlawful manner, it would have been forfeitable as proceeds of the crime. As a rule, forfeitures of criminal proceeds serve the nonpunitive ends of making restitution to the rightful owners and of compelling the surrender of property held without right or ownership. . . . Most forfeitures of proceeds, as a consequence, are not fines at all, let alone excessive fines. Hence, the lawfulness of the money shows at most that the forfeiture was a fine; it cannot at the same time prove that the fine was excessive. . . .

The crime of smuggling or failing to report cash is more serious than the Court is willing to acknowledge. The drug trade, money laundering, and tax evasion all depend in part on smuggled and unreported cash. Congress enacted the reporting requirement because secret exports of money were being used in organized crime, drug trafficking, money laundering, and other crimes. . . . Likewise, tax evaders were using cash exports to dodge hundreds of millions of dollars in taxes owed to the Government.

The Court does not deny the importance of these interests but claims they are not implicated here because respondent managed to disprove any link to other crimes. Here, to be sure, the Government had no affirmative proof that the money was from an illegal source or for an illegal purpose. This will often be the case, however. By its very nature, money laundering is difficult to prove; for if the money launderers have done their job, the money appears to be clean. The point of the statute, which provides for even heavier penalties if a second crime can be proved, is to mandate forfeiture regardless. . . . It is common practice, of course, for a cash courier not to confess a tainted source but to stick to a well-rehearsed story. The kingpin, the real owner, need not come forward to make a legal claim to the funds. He has his own effective enforcement measures to ensure delivery at destination or return at origin if the scheme is thwarted. He is, of course, not above punishing the courier who deviates from the story and informs. The majority is wrong, then, to assume *in personam* forfeitures cannot affect kingpins, as their couriers will claim to own the money and pay the penalty out of their masters' funds. Even if the courier confessed, the kingpin could face an *in personam* forfeiture for his agent's authorized acts, for the kingpin would be a co-principal in the commission of the crime. . . .

In my view, forfeiture of all the unreported currency is sustainable whenever a willful violation is proven. The facts of this case exemplify how hard it can be to prove ownership and other crimes, and they also show respondent is far from an innocent victim. For one thing, he was guilty of repeated lies to Government agents and suborning lies by others. Customs inspectors told respondent of his duty to report cash. He and his wife claimed they had only $ 15,000 with them, not the $ 357,144 they in fact had concealed. He then told customs inspectors a friend named Abe Ajemian had lent him about $ 200,000. Ajemian denied this. A month later, respondent said Saeed Faroutan had lent him $ 170,000. Faroutan, however, said he had not made the loan and respondent had asked him to lie. Six months later, respondent resurrected the fable of the alleged loan from Ajemian, though Ajemian had already contradicted the story. As the District Court found, respondent "has lied, and has had his friends lie.". . . He had proffered a "suspicious and confused story, documented in the poorest way, and replete with past misrepresentation.". . .

Respondent told these lies, moreover, in most suspicious circumstances. His luggage was stuffed with more than a third of a million dollars. All of it was in cash, and much of it was hidden in a case with a false bottom.

The majority ratifies the District Court's see-no-evil approach. The District Court ignored respondent's lies in assessing a sentence. It gave him a two-level downward adjustment for acceptance of responsibility, instead of an increase for obstruction of justice. . . . It dismissed the lies as stemming from "distrust for the Government" arising out of "cultural differences." . . . While the majority is sincere in not endorsing this excuse, . . . it nonetheless affirms the fine tainted by it. This patronizing excuse demeans millions of law-abiding American immigrants by suggesting they cannot be expected to be as truthful as every other citizen. Each American, regardless of culture or ethnicity, is equal before the law. Each has the same obligation to refrain from perjury and false statements to the Government.

In short, respondent was unable to give a single truthful explanation of the source of the cash. The multitude of lies and suspicious circumstances points to some form of crime. Yet, though the Government rebutted each and every fable respondent proffered, it was unable to adduce affirmative proof of another crime in this particular case.

Because of the problems of individual proof, Congress found it necessary to enact a blanket punishment. . . . One of the few reliable warning signs of some serious crimes is the use of large sums of cash. So Congress punished all cash smuggling or non-reporting, authorizing single penalties for the offense alone and double penalties for the offense coupled with proof of other crimes. . . . The requirement of willfulness, it judged, would be enough to protect the innocent. The majority second-guesses this judgment without explaining why Congress' blanket approach was unreasonable.

Money launderers will rejoice to know they face forfeitures of less than 5% of the money transported, provided they hire accomplished liars to carry their money for them. Five percent, of course, is not much of a deterrent or punishment; it is comparable to the fee one might pay for a mortgage lender or broker. . . . It is far less than the 20-26% commissions some drug dealers pay money launderers. . . . Since many couriers evade detection, moreover, the average forfeiture per dollar smuggled could amount, courtesy of today's decision, to far less than 5%. In any event, the fine permitted by the majority would be a modest cost of doing business in the world of drugs and crime.

Given the severity of respondent's crime, the Constitution does not forbid forfeiture of all of the smuggled or unreported cash. . . .

The Court's holding may in the long run undermine the purpose of the Excessive Fines Clause. . . . Under the Court's holding, legislators may rely on mandatory prison sentences in lieu of fines. Drug lords will be heartened by this, knowing the prison terms will fall upon their couriers while leaving their own wallets untouched. . . . The majority's holding may not only jeopardize a vast range of fines but also leave countless others unchecked by the Constitution. Non-remedial fines may be subject to deference in theory but overbearing scrutiny in fact. So-called remedial penalties, most *in rem* forfeitures, and perhaps civil fines may not be subject to scrutiny at all. I would not create these exemptions from the Excessive Fines Clause. I would also accord genuine deference to Congress' judgments about the gravity of the offenses it creates. I would further follow the long tradition of fines calibrated to the value of the goods smuggled. In these circumstances, the Constitution does not forbid forfeiture of all of the $ 357,144 transported by respondent. I dissent.

Chapter 8
PIRACY AND TERRORISM

§ 8.01 Terrorism in General

Fighting terrorism is a priority of the United States Department of Justice. This includes both domestic and international terrorism. Terrorism is not, however, an easily defined term. *See* CHRISTOPHER L. BLAKESLEY, TERRORISM, DRUGS, INTERNATIONAL LAW, AND THE PROTECTION OF HUMAN LIBERTY (1992).

Absent agreement on a comprehensive international anti-terrorism treaty, several multilateral conventions have been concerned with specific forms of terrorism. The Tokyo Convention on Offenses and Certain Other Acts Committed on Board Aircraft, Sept. 14, 1963, 20 U.S.T. 2941, T.I.A.S. No. 6768, 704 U.N.T.S. 219, dealt generally with jurisdiction over crimes committed on aircraft, although it actually antedates the first big wave of aircraft hijacking that began around 1968. International concern with hijacking then led to adoption of the Hague Convention for the Suppression of Unlawful Seizure of Aircraft, Dec. 16, 1970, 22 U.S.T. 1641, T.I.A.S. No. 7192, 860 U.N.T.S. 105.

In addition to the Hague Convention, the list of anti-terrorism treaties includes (in chronological order) the OAS Convention to Prevent and Punish the Acts of Terrorism Taking the Form of Crimes Against Persons and Related Extortion that are of International Significance, Feb. 2, 1971, 27 U.S.T. 3949, T.I.A.S. No. 8413; Montreal Convention for the Suppression of Unlawful Acts Against the Safety of Civil Aviation, Sept. 23, 1971, 24 U.S.T. 564, T.I.A.S. No. 7570, 974 U.N.T.S. 177; New York Convention on the Prevention and Punishment of Crimes Against Internationally Protected Persons, Including Diplomatic Agents, Dec. 14, 1973, 28 U.S.T. 1975, T.I.A.S. No. 8532, 1035 U.N.T.S. 167; International Convention Against the Taking of Hostages, Dec. 17, 1979, T.I.A.S. No. 11081, 18 I.L.M. 1456 (1979); Convention on the Physical Protection of Nuclear Materials, Mar. 3, 1980, I.A.EA. Legal Series No. 12 (1982), 18 I.L.M. 1419 (1979); Protocol [to the 1971 Montreal Convention] for the Suppression of Unlawful Acts of Violence at Airports Serving Civil Aviation, Feb. 24, 1988, 27 I.L.M. 627 (1988); IMO Rome Convention for the Suppression of Unlawful Acts Against the Safety of Maritime Navigation, Mar. 10, 1988, 27 I.L.M. 668 (1988), together with a Protocol for the Suppression of Unlawful Acts Against the Safety of Fixed Platforms Located on the Continental Shelf, Mar. 10, 1988, 27 I.L.M. 685 (1988); Convention on the Safety of United Nations and Associated Personnel, Dec. 9, 1994, U.N. Doc. A/49/742 (1994), 34 I.L.M. 482 (1995); and International Convention for the Suppression of Terrorist Bombings, Jan. 9, 1998, 37 I.L.M. 249 (1998).

The provisions of these treaties generally are modeled on those contained in the 1970 Hague Convention. The same pattern appears in the Torture Convention [*see* chap. 9]. The principal object of the Hague Convention was to deny "safe haven" to offenders. Accordingly, the convention stipulates that certain conduct shall be considered an "offense." Each party to the convention is obligated to make the offense punishable by severe penalties. Parties also are obligated to treat the offense as one for which they will grant extradition. Any state in whose territory an alleged offender is present is bound, if it does not extradite the offender, to "submit the case to its competent authorities for the purpose of prosecution." So that states will be in a position to prosecute in default of extradition, the convention requires each party to make provision for exercising extraterritorial "jurisdiction over the offense in the case where the alleged offender is present in its territory and it does not extradite him. . ."

There has been some debate about whether the residual jurisdiction which these conventions require a state to exercise when it does not extradite an offender can properly be characterized as "universal jurisdiction." Recall the questions following *United States v. Yunis* [p. 62]. Could such jurisdiction be exercised, for instance, over nationals of a state that had not ratified the pertinent convention?

So far as U.S. law is concerned, an array of federal statutes proscribes terrorist activity. Many of these statutes implement international obligations under the relatively recent treaties mentioned above. Some are older. *United States v. Rahman*, 189 F.3d 88 (2d Cir. 1999), *cert. denied,* 120 S. Ct. 830 (2000), upheld the convictions of ten defendants charged with "offenses arising out of a wide-ranging plot to conduct a campaign of urban terrorism"; they were convicted after a nine-month trial which included evidence of the defendants "rendering assistance to those who bombed the World Trade Center, planning to bomb bridges and tunnels in New York City, murdering Rabbi Meir Kahane, and planning to murder the President of Egypt." The principal charge against them was "seditious conspiracy" under a statute (18 U.S.C. § 2384) that dates back to the Civil War.

In addition to statutes defining substantive offenses, there also are specific procedural provisions applicable when the offense involves terrorism. For example, some terrorism offenses have an extended statute of limitations. *See* 18 U.S.C. § 3286. Matters involving overseas terrorism require that prosecutors obtain authorization from the Assistant Attorney General in charge of the Criminal Division prior to starting a criminal investigation, filing an information, or seeking an indictment.

Statutes implementing the treaties mentioned above generally provide for extraterritorial jurisdiction over the specific forms of terrorism dealt with in those treaties. A fairly sweeping provision of the Omnibus Diplomatic Security and Antiterrorism Act of 1986 established federal "long-arm" jurisdiction over all terrorist attacks on U.S. nationals abroad (*see* 18 U.S.C. § 2332). An equally sweeping provision contained in the Antiterrorism and Effective Death Penalty Act of 1996 concerns acts of terrorism transcending national boundaries that affect the United States:

18 U.S.C. § 2332b. Acts of terrorism transcending national boundaries

(a) Prohibited acts.

(1) Offenses. Whoever, involving conduct transcending national boundaries and in a circumstance described in subsection (b) –

(A) kills, kidnaps, maims, commits an assault resulting in serious bodily injury, or assaults with a dangerous weapon any person within the United States; or

(B) creates a substantial risk of serious bodily injury to any other person by destroying or damaging any structure, conveyance, or other real or personal property within the United States or by attempting or conspiring to destroy or damage any structure, conveyance, or other real or personal property within the United States;

in violation of the laws of any State, or the United States, shall be punished as prescribed in subsection (c).

(2) Treatment of threats, attempts and conspiracies. Whoever threatens to commit an offense under paragraph (1), or attempts or conspires to do so, shall be punished under subsection (c).

(b) Jurisdictional bases.

(1) Circumstances. The circumstances referred to in subsection (a) are–

(A) the mail or any facility of interstate or foreign commerce is used in furtherance of the offense;

(B) the offense obstructs, delays, or affects interstate or foreign commerce, or would have so obstructed, delayed, or affected interstate or foreign commerce if the offense had been consummated;

(C) the victim, or intended victim, is the United States Government, a member of the uniformed services, or any official, officer, employee, or agent of the legislative, executive, or judicial branches, or of any department or agency, of the United States;

(D) the structure, conveyance, or other real or personal property is, in whole or in part, owned, possessed, or leased to the United States, or any department or agency of the United States;

(E) the offense is committed in the territorial sea (including the airspace above and the seabed and subsoil below, and artificial islands and fixed structures erected thereon) of the United States; or

(F) the offense is committed within the special maritime and territorial jurisdiction of the United States.

(2) Co-conspirators and accessories after the fact. Jurisdiction shall exist over all principals and co-conspirators of an offense under this section, and accessories after the fact to any offense under this section, if at least one of the circumstances described in subparagraphs (A) through (F) of paragraph (1) is applicable to at least one offender.

(c) Penalties.

(1) Penalties. Whoever violates this section shall be punished–

(A) for a killing, or if death results to any person from any other conduct prohibited by this section, by death, or by imprisonment for any term of years or for life;

(B) for kidnapping, by imprisonment for any term of years or for life;

(C) for maiming, by imprisonment for not more than 35 years;

(D) for assault with a dangerous weapon or assault resulting in serious bodily injury, by imprisonment for not more than 30 years;

(E) for destroying or damaging any structure, conveyance, or other real or personal property, by imprisonment for not more than 25 years;

(F) for attempting or conspiring to commit an offense, for any term of years up to the maximum punishment that would have applied had the offense been completed; and

(G) for threatening to commit an offense under this section, by imprisonment for not more than 10 years.

(2) Consecutive sentence. Notwithstanding any other provision of law, the court shall not place on probation any person convicted of a violation of this section; nor shall the term of imprisonment imposed under this section run concurrently with any other term of imprisonment.

(d) Proof requirements. The following shall apply to prosecutions under this section:

(1) Knowledge. The prosecution is not required to prove knowledge by any defendant of a jurisdictional base alleged in the indictment.

(2) State law. In a prosecution under this section that is based upon the adoption of State law, only the elements of the offense under State law, and not any provisions pertaining to criminal procedure or evidence, are adopted.

(e) Extraterritorial jurisdiction. There is extraterritorial Federal jurisdiction–

(1) over any offense under subsection (a), including any threat, attempt, or conspiracy to commit such offense; and

(2) over conduct which, under section 3, renders any person an accessory after the fact to an offense under subsection (a).

(f) Investigative authority. In addition to any other investigative authority with respect to violations of this title, the Attorney General shall have primary investigative responsibility for all Federal crimes of terrorism, and the Secretary of the Treasury shall assist the Attorney General at the request of the Attorney General. Nothing in this section shall be construed to interfere with the authority of the United States Secret Service under section 3056.

(g) Definitions. As used in this section –

(1) the term "conduct transcending national boundaries" means conduct occurring outside of the United States in addition to the conduct occurring in the United States;

(2) the term "facility of interstate or foreign commerce" has the meaning given that term in section 1958(b)(2);

(3) the term "serious bodily injury" has the meaning given that term in section 1365(g)(3);

(4) the term "territorial sea of the United States" means all waters extending seaward to 12 nautical miles from the baselines of the United States, determined in accordance with international law; and

(5) the term "Federal crime of terrorism" means an offense that –

(A) is calculated to influence or affect the conduct of government by intimidation or coercion, or to retaliate against government conduct; and

(B) is a violation of–

(i) section 32 (relating to destruction of aircraft or aircraft facilities), 37 (relating to violence at international airports), 81 (relating to arson within special maritime and territorial jurisdiction), 175 (relating to biological weapons), 351 (relating to congressional, cabinet, and Supreme Court assassination, kidnapping, and assault), 831 (relating to nuclear materials), 842 (m) or (n) (relating to plastic explosives), 844(e) (relating to certain bombings), 844 (f) or (i) (relating to arson and bombing of certain property), 930(c), 956 (relating to conspiracy to injure property of a foreign government), 1114 (relating to protection of officers and employees of the United States), 1116 (relating to murder or manslaughter of foreign officials, official guests, or internationally protected persons), 1203 (relating to hostage taking), 1361 (relating to injury of Government property or contracts), 1362 (relating to destruction of communication lines, stations, or systems), 1363 (relating to injury to buildings or property within special maritime and territorial jurisdiction of the United States), 1366 (relating to destruction of an energy facility), 1751 (relating to Presidential and Presidential staff assassination, kidnapping, and assault), 1992, 2152 (relating to injury of fortifications, harbor defenses, or defensive sea areas), 2155 (relating to destruction of national defense materials, premises, or utilities), 2156 (relating to production of defective national defense materials, premises, or utilities), 2280 (relating to violence against maritime navigation), 2281 (relating to violence against maritime fixed platforms), 2332 (relating to certain homicides and other violence against United States nationals occurring outside of the United States), 2332a (relating to use of weapons of mass destruction), 2332b (relating to acts of terrorism transcending national boundaries), 2332c, 2339A (relating to providing material support to terrorists), 2339B (relating to providing material support to terrorist organizations), or 2340A (relating to torture);

(ii) section 236 (relating to sabotage of nuclear facilities or fuel) of the Atomic Energy Act of 1954 (42 U.S.C. § 2284); or

(iii) section 46502 (relating to aircraft piracy) or section 60123(b) (relating to destruction of interstate gas or hazardous liquid pipeline facility) of title 49.

§ 8.02 Piracy

Crimes committed on board a ship generally come under the jurisdiction of the state whose flag the ship flies. This is regarded as an aspect of "territorial jurisdiction"; the ship is considered, in effect, a "floating part" of that state's territory. The U.S. Code catalogues jurisdiction over crimes committed on board U.S. ships as a part of the "special maritime and territorial jurisdiction of the United States." *See* 18 U.S.C. § 7(1).

The policing of attacks by pirate ships poses a special problem which has been dealt with by making piracy subject to the "universal jurisdiction" of all states (although for questions about how "universal" this jurisdiction really has been, *see* ALFRED P. RUBIN, THE LAW OF PIRACY (2d ed. 1998)). At any rate, U.S. law provides: "Whoever on the high seas, commits the crime of piracy as defined by the law of nations, and is afterwards brought into or founded in the United States, shall be imprisoned for life." 18 U.S.C. § 1651.

What are the elements of "the crime of piracy as defined by the law of nations"? These are set out in Article 15 of the Geneva Convention on the High Seas, Apr. 28, 1958, 13 U.S.T. 2312, T.I.A.S. No. 5200, 450 U.N.T.S. 82:

Piracy consists of any of the following acts:

(1) Any illegal acts of violence, detention or any act of depredation, committed for private ends by the crew or the passengers of a private ship or a private aircraft, and directed:

(a) On the high seas, against another ship or aircraft, or against persons or property on board such ship or aircraft;

(b) Against a ship, aircraft, persons or property in a place outside the jurisdiction of any State;

(2) Any act of voluntary participation in the operation of a ship or of an aircraft with knowledge of facts making it a pirate ship or aircraft;

(3) Any act of inciting or of intentionally facilitating an act described in sub-paragraph (1) or sub-paragraph (2) of this article.

Practically identical language appears in Article 101 of the 1982 Convention on the Law of the Sea, Dec. 10, 1982, 516 U.N.T.S. 205, 21 I.L.M. 1216. Other articles in the two conventions authorize all states to seize pirate ships and to arrest and try the persons on board. Article 14 of the High Seas Convention and Article 100 of the Law of the Sea Convention both provide: "All States shall co-operate to the fullest extent in the repression of piracy on the high seas or in any other place outside the jurisdiction of any State."

The definition of piracy contained in Article 15 of the 1958 Convention on the High Seas was supposed, more or less, to reflect customary international law at the time – although the inclusion of aircraft, at least, was a clear innovation. Under this definition, piracy must be committed for private ends. It cannot be committed by warships or other government vessels.

Would the hijacking of an aircraft over the high seas constitute "piracy as defined by the law of nations"? That would depend, in part, on whether the hijackers can be said to have acted for "private ends." In any event, there is the question of whether an "internal seizure" by those already on board a ship or aircraft constitutes piracy. This was a matter of controversy before 1958. The Convention on the High Seas sought to resolve the controversy by requiring that piracy must be directed "against another ship or aircraft."

The difficulties involved in applying the law of piracy to terrorism on board a ship on the high seas were vividly illustrated by the seizure of the Italian cruise ship, the *Achille Lauro,* in the Mediterranean in October 1985. The terrorists threatened to kill the passengers unless Israel released fifty Palestinian prisoners; before surrendering, they did kill Leon Klinghoffer, a Jewish passenger of U.S. nationality. This incident led to adoption of the 1988 Convention for the Suppression of Unlawful Acts Against the Safety of Maritime Navigation. *See* Malvina Halberstam, *Terrorism on the High Seas: The Achille Lauro, Piracy and the IMO Convention on Maritime Safety*, 82 AM. J. INT'L L. 269 (1988).

§ 8.03 Aircraft Hijacking and Sabotage

UNITED STATES v. REZAQ

United States Court of Appeals, District of Columbia
134 F.3d 1121 (1998)

WALD, CIRCUIT JUDGE:

Omar Mohammed Ali Rezaq appeals his conviction on one count of aircraft piracy under 49 U.S.C. app. § 1472(n) (1994). In 1985, Rezaq hijacked an Air Egypt flight shortly after takeoff from Athens, and ordered it to fly to Malta. On arrival, Rezaq shot a number of passengers, killing two of them, before he was apprehended. Rezaq pleaded guilty to murder charges in Malta, served seven years in prison, and was released in February 1993. Shortly afterwards, he was taken into custody in Nigeria by United States authorities and brought to the United States for trial. . . .

The jury did not credit Rezaq's defenses, and found him guilty of the one count with which he was charged, ... [T]he district court sentenced Rezaq to life imprisonment. (The United States had not sought the death sentence.) The district court also ordered Rezaq to pay a total of $ 254,000 in restitution, an amount which it found to represent the financial cost to the victims of his crime.

Rezaq's first group of arguments on this appeal all derive from the international nature of the crime of air piracy. He argues, first, that the international treaty barring air piracy prohibits sequential prosecutions for the same offense, and that it was therefore impermissible for the United States to try him anew for crimes for which he had already been prosecuted in Malta. Second, he asserts that the United States manufactured jurisdiction over him by bringing him into its territory, and that section 1472(n)'s statement that it applies to those "found in the United States" bars the application of section 1472(n) to those forcibly brought to the United States specifically for trial on air piracy charges. Third, Rezaq avers that it was improper for the district court to apply section 1472(n)'s "death results" provision (that is, its provision requiring the imposition of the death sentence or of life imprisonment in cases in which death results), as that provision was only intended to apply if certain jurisdictional criteria were met. Rezaq's next group of arguments relates to the conduct of his trial. . . .

We begin with Rezaq's argument that it was impermissible for the United States to try him a second time, as he had already been tried in Malta. Rezaq cannot base this argument on the Constitution's Double Jeopardy Clause, for two reasons. First, that clause does not prohibit sequential trials by different sovereigns. . . . Second, Rezaq was prosecuted in Malta for murder, attempted murder, and hostage-taking, but the United States prosecution was for air piracy. The offense of air piracy contains elements – related to the control of an airplane – that the crimes for which Rezaq was tried in Malta do not. This means, under the usual double jeopardy analysis, that the first prosecution does not bar the second.   . . .

Rezaq asserts, however, that this case is subject to a more exacting standard than the traditional double-jeopardy one. Section 1472(n), 49 U.S.C. app. § 1472(n) (1994), was enacted to implement the Convention for the Suppression of Unlawful Seizure of Aircraft (also called the "Hague Convention"), Dec. 16, 1970, 22 U.S.T. 1643, a multilateral treaty directed at preventing and punishing air piracy.   . . .   Rezaq claims that both the Hague Convention and section 1472(n) incorporate a special ban on sequential prosecution that is more restrictive than the Double Jeopardy Clause, and argues that his prosecution on air piracy charges violates that ban.

It is certainly possible that a treaty could contain a double jeopardy provision more restrictive–that is, barring more prosecutions–than the Constitution's Double Jeopardy Clause.   . . .   But Rezaq has not shown that the Hague Convention falls in this category.   . . .   Rezaq points to the provisions of the Hague Convention that require states to either extradite or prosecute offenders, and argues that they imply that a more restrictive double jeopardy rule applies. For instance, he cites Article 4(2), which provides: "Each Contracting State shall likewise take such measures as may be necessary to establish its jurisdiction over the offence in the case where the alleged offender is present in its territory and it does not extradite him pursuant to Article 8. . . ." Rezaq argues that this provision implies that extradition and prosecution are mutually exclusive options: a Contracting Party may not both extradite an offender *and* prosecute him. This rule, he asserts, in turn implies that the Hague Convention intended to bar all sequential prosecutions, whether they occur after extradition or not.

The first step in Rezaq's argument is flawed: the Hague Convention's requirement that a state either prosecute offenders or extradite them does not imply a bar on (at different times) doing both. In general, a requirement to "do A or B" does not necessarily imply a bar on doing both A *and* B; one must look at the context and the purpose of the requirement to decide whether such a bar is meant. For example, if a religious organization requires that its members either do volunteer work or make cash contributions to charity, the organization clearly does not mean to foreclose them from doing both. The purpose of this hypothetical religious mandate is to ensure that believers try to do good deeds, and this purpose is served if a believer chooses to both do volunteer work and make charitable contributions.   . . .

Here, the context makes clear that the statute's injunction to extradite or prosecute is not meant to state mutually exclusive alternatives. The extradite-or-prosecute requirement is intended to ensure that states make some effort to bring hijackers to justice, either through prosecution or extradition. There is no indication that Article 4 is intended to go beyond setting a minimum, and limit the options of states; indeed, Article 4(3) specifically provides that "this Convention does not exclude any jurisdiction exercised in accordance with national law." A reading of Article 4 that focuses on bringing hijackers to justice is also consistent with the Convention's (short) preamble, one clause of which states that "for the purpose of deterring [acts of air piracy], there is an urgent need to provide appropriate measures for punishment of offenders." Thus, the extradite-or-prosecute requirement is like the hypothetical donate-or-volunteer requirement described above; it is intended to ensure a minimum level of effort, and does not necessarily preclude the recipient of the mandate from doing more.

A reading under which the options of prosecution and extradition are mutually exclusive could also undermine the Convention's goal of ensuring "punishment of offenders." For instance, if a person is extradited from state A to state B, and B then discovers that a technical obstacle prevents it from prosecuting her, B should be able to return her to A for prosecution; any other reading of the treaty might allow a suspect to escape prosecution altogether. Or, to choose an example closer to the facts of this case, if state A tries and convicts a defendant for certain crimes associated with a hijacking (as Malta tried Rezaq for murder, attempted murder, and hostage-taking), there is no indication that A is barred from then extraditing her to B once she has served her sentence, so that B may try the defendant for different crimes associated with the same hijacking (as the United States tried Rezaq for air piracy).

The *travaux preparatoires* for the Hague Convention reinforce our conclusion that the treaty does not incorporate a special bar on sequential prosecution. They show that the treaty's negotiators considered and rejected the possibility of expressly barring sequential prosecutions through a *ne bis in idem* provision (a term for double-jeopardy provisions in international instruments; another term is *non bis in idem*). The states opposed to this idea, whose views carried the day, argued that "the principle was not applied in exactly the same manner in all States," and that "in taking a decision whether to prosecute, and, similarly, a decision whether to extradite, the State concerned will, in each case, apply its own rule on the subject of *ne bis in idem*." . . . This is, of course, exactly what the United States has done in applying its own double jeopardy rules.

Nor is there any indication that Congress, in enacting section 1472(n), read the Hague Convention differently, or intended to subject prosecutions under section 1472(n) to a heightened double jeopardy standard. The text and legislative history of section 1472(n) are both devoid of evidence pointing to such a conclusion. In the absence of any sign that either section 1472(n) or the Hague Convention undertook to impose a more stringent than usual double-jeopardy rule, we conclude that Rezaq's prosecution in Malta was not an obstacle to his subsequent prosecution, in this proceeding, on air piracy charges. . . .

Rezaq's next argument is that section 1472(n) only applies to defendants that are "afterward found in the United States," and that he was not "afterward found in the United States," but involuntarily brought here for the express purpose of prosecution.

Under a rule known as the *Ker-Frisbie* doctrine, "the power of a court to try a person for crime is not impaired by the fact that he had been brought within the court's jurisdiction by reason of a 'forcible abduction'." *Frisbie v. Collins,* 342 U.S. 519, 522, 96 L. Ed. 541, 72 S. Ct. 509 (1952) (quoting *Ker v. Illinois,* 119 U.S. 436, 30 L. Ed. 421, 7 S. Ct. 225 (1886)). This general rule does admit of some exceptions; for instance, an extradition treaty may provide that it is "the only way by which one country may gain custody of a national of the other country for the purposes of prosecution," *United States v. Alvarez-Machain,* [p. 408], and we have also suggested that there may be a "very limited" exception for certain cases of " 'torture, brutality, and similar outrageous conduct.' ". . .

Rezaq's argument is, in effect, that the phrase "afterward found in the United States" appearing in section 1472(n) creates a statutory exception to the *Ker-Frisbie* rule, and prevents the government from bringing a defendant into the United States for the express purpose of prosecution. Although we agree that Congress has the power to create statutory exceptions to the *Ker-Frisbie* doctrine, we do not think that section 1472(n) creates such an exception.

We first consider the United States's contention that *Yunis* [p.62] controls this case. . . . Rezaq, unlike Yunis, was brought to the United States for the specific purpose of prosecution on hijacking charges. . . . [T]here are no strong policies underlying section 1472(n) that render it inappropriate for the government to bring a defendant to the United States against his will for the specific purpose of prosecution. Neither the Hague Convention nor section 1472(n) appears to have been intended to establish a firm allocation of prosecutorial authority between nations. It is possible to imagine a treaty that would do so; for instance, in adopting a treaty to criminalize mislabeling of products, nations might decide that it was best for each country's consumer protection authorities to have the sole power to decide when and how mislabeling should lead to criminal charges, and draft the treaty accordingly. It might then be inappropriate for United States authorities to bring a foreign offender to the United States for trial under a criminal law enacted to implement this hypothetical treaty.

Here, however, we have already concluded that Article 4 of the Hague Convention, which addresses the assertion of national jurisdiction, is intended to establish a minimum set of circumstances in which states must assert jurisdiction, rather than to limit the circumstances in which they may do so. It follows that the Hague Convention was not intended to establish a compartmentalized scheme of national jurisdiction (like that in our hypothetical product-labeling treaty). Nor does section 1472(n) enact such a scheme. The Senate Report on the implementing legislation explained that section 1472(n) was included to implement Article 4(2) of the Convention, and therefore

includes a special provision establishing jurisdiction over the offense of hijacking wherever it occurs anywhere outside the special aircraft jurisdiction of the United States but the alleged offender is later found in the United States. This is the so-called universal jurisdiction provision which makes hijackers outlaws wherever they are found.

S. REP. NO. 93-13 at 3 - 4 (1973). This passage – particularly its statement that the provision "makes hijackers outlaws wherever they are found" – indicates that Congress saw section 1472(n) as permitting broad assertion of jurisdiction over hijackers. It shows no signs that Congress envisioned the provision as allocating jurisdiction between the United States and other nations.

The question remains, then: what does the phrase "afterward found in the United States" mean? As we observed in *Yunis,* this phrase appears to have been intended to implement the Hague Convention's requirement that the United States either extradite or prosecute all hijackers "present in" its territory. . . . Thus, the word "found" means only that the hijacker must be physically located in the United States, not that he must be first detected here. Rezaq notes that the fact that a defendant is present before a United States court necessarily implies that he is "found in the United States," so that the latter requirement will always be satisfied. But this does not mean that this language is empty of meaning; at a minimum, it confirms the rule, issuing from the Confrontation Clause of the Sixth Amendment and from the Due Process Clause, that a defendant ordinarily may not be tried in absentia. *See United States v. Gagnon,* 470 U.S. 522, 526, 84 L. Ed. 2d 486, 105 S. Ct. 1482 (1985) (per curiam).[4] . . .

Rezaq avers that it was improper for the district court to apply section 1472(n)'s "death results" provision (that is, its provision requiring the imposition

---

[4] Rezaq also points out that Congress revised section 1472(n) in 1996, and asserts that our reading of the "afterward found" language would render much of the revised statute surplusage. The revised statute, which now appears at 49 U.S.C. § 46502(b), provides in relevant part:

(2) There is jurisdiction over the offense in paragraph (1) if –

(A) a national of the United States was aboard the aircraft;

(B) an offender is a national of the United States; or

(C) an offender is afterwards found in the United States.

49 U.S.C. § 46502(b). Rezaq argues that, under our reading of "afterward found," every case will always be within section 46501(2)(C), as a defendant who is before a United States court will always be present in the United States; thus, he argues, under this reading sections (A) and (B) of the statute become unnecessary. Congress may well have had good reasons to include the three alternative bases of jurisdiction in section 46501(2). For example, some of the United States's extradition treaties require that, in order to obtain custody over a fugitive, the United States present an arrest warrant to the other state. *See, e.g.,* Agreement for the Surrender of Fugitive Offenders, Dec. 6, 1996, U.S.-Hong Kong, Art. 8, 36 I.L.M. 847, 852. Although we do not decide this question, we note that the United States might find it difficult to obtain an arrest warrant for a fugitive in Hong Kong under a statute that provides that the offender be "found in the United States"; the alternative bases of jurisdiction may thus serve as long-arm provisions.

of the death sentence or of life imprisonment in cases in which death results), as the Hague Convention only permits states to punish additional crimes associated with a hijacking if certain jurisdictional prerequisites are met. . . . But Article 4(3) expressly provides that the Convention "does not exclude any criminal jurisdiction exercised in accordance with national law." Thus, if Congress wished to reach "other acts of violence," the Hague Convention allowed it to do so. . . . It is abundantly clear that Congress intended for the "death results" provision of section 1472(n) to apply irrespective of whether the additional jurisdictional elements of Article 4(1) are present. . . .

Rezaq also argues that applying the "death results" provision to this case would violate the normal jurisdictional rules of international law. International law imposes limits on a state's "jurisdiction to prescribe," that is, its ability to render its law applicable to persons or activities outside its borders; states may only exercise jurisdiction to prescribe under a limited number of theories. *See* RESTATEMENT (THIRD) OF FOREIGN RELATIONS LAW § 401 (1987) [p. 39]. This case, however, clearly falls within at least one such theory, the so-called "passive personality principle." That principle "asserts that a state may apply law–particularly criminal law – to an act committed outside its territory by a person not its national where the victim of the act was its national." RESTATEMENT (THIRD) OF FOREIGN RELATIONS LAW § 402 cmt. g (1987). "The principle has not been generally accepted for ordinary torts or crimes, but it is increasingly accepted as applied to terrorist and other organized attacks on a state's nationals by reason of their nationality. . . ." *Id.* Scarlett Rogenkamp was a United States citizen,[*] and there was abundant evidence that she was chosen as a victim because of her nationality. . . . This suffices to support jurisdiction on the passive personality theory. . . .

[The court found all of Rezaq's arguments on to be without merit.]

NOTES AND QUESTIONS

(1) "The offense of aircraft piracy has four elements: (1) seizure or exercise of control of an aircraft; (2) by force, violence, or intimidation, or the threat thereof; (3) with wrongful intent; and (4) within the special aircraft jurisdiction of the United States." *United States v. Calloway*, 116 F.3d 1129 (6th Cir. 1997). In examining the "wrongful intent" element the court in *Calloway* stated:

In the context of an "attempt" crime, specific intent means that the defendant consciously intends the completion of acts comprising the choate offense. In other words, the completion of such acts is the defendant's purpose. Where nothing more than general criminal intent

---

[*] She was a passenger on the plane and an employee of the United States Air Force. – Eds.

is required, in contrast, the requirement may typically be satisfied by a showing that the defendant knew his actions would produce the prohibited result, or recklessly disregarded a known risk that they would do so. . . .

We shall assume for purposes of analysis that the instruction did not require the jury to find specific intent. This brings us to the question whether the statute requires such an intent.

Two of our sister circuits have held that it does not. See *United States v. Compton,* 5 F.3d 358, 360 (9th Cir. 1993); *United States v. Castaneda-Reyes,* 703 F.2d 522, 525 (11th Cir.), *cert. denied,* 464 U.S. 856, 104 S. Ct. 174, 78 L. Ed. 2d 157 (1983). Aircraft piracy is defined as "any seizure or exercise of control, by force or violence or threat of force or violence, or by any other form of intimidation, *and with wrongful intent,* of an aircraft within the special aircraft jurisdiction of the United States." 49 U.S.C. § 1472(i)(2) (now codified at 49 U.S.C. § 46502(a)(1)(A)) (emphasis supplied). The *Compton* and *Castaneda-Reyes* courts concluded that the "wrongful intent" required by this section is only a general criminal intent, and that this general criminal intent applies to the inchoate offense as well as the choate offense.

The issue is an open one in our circuit, as we believe it is in every circuit except the Ninth and the Eleventh. The general rule, however, is that attempt crimes require proof of a specific intent to complete the acts constituting the substantive offense. . . . The intent to finish the crime, coupled with affirmative acts toward that end, is a *sine qua non* of a punishable attempt. . . .

We find it difficult to see why the specific intent requirement should not apply to attempted aircraft piracy. It is true that the definition of aircraft piracy in former 49 U.S.C. § 1472(i)(2) requires only a general criminal intent, but the relevance of this datum is not immediately apparent to us – for many attempt crimes require a specific intent even though the completed offense does not. . . . If we had to decide the issue – which, for reasons to be explained shortly, we do not – we should be inclined to hold that the offense of attempted aircraft piracy requires proof of a specific intent to complete the acts constituting aircraft piracy.[*]

(2) The Aircraft Sabotage Act implements the 1971 Montreal Convention. In *United States v. Yousef,* 927 F. Supp. 673 (S.D.N.Y. 1996), Judge Kevin Thomas Duffy denied defendants' motions to dismiss a prosecution brought under this

---

[*] "The evidence of Mr. Calloway's guilt was overwhelming, and in no way did the jury instructions seriously affect the fairness or integrity of Mr. Calloway's trial. No reasonable jury could have found that Mr. Calloway did *not* have the specific intent to seize control of the plane." *Id.* at 1136. – Eds.

act, stating:

> Each Defendant has made various arguments as to why this court should not exercise extraterritorial jurisdiction over the crimes charged in the Indictment. All Defendants argue that this court does not have subject matter jurisdiction to try them for the conspiracy or the attempt to blow up United States civil aircraft in the "special aircraft jurisdiction" of the United States in violation of 18 U.S.C. §§ 32(a)(1),(2), (7) and 371 (Counts Twelve, Thirteen and Fourteen). Defendant Yousef challenges jurisdiction for the actual bombing of the Philippine aircraft in violation of 18 U.S.C. § 32(b) (Count Nineteen). All Defendants also attack the propriety of any other count which relies on these counts.
>
> Defendants' various jurisdictional arguments rely on either constitutional due process principles, statutory interpretation and other domestic law, or international law. While the form of each Defendants' argument differs, in substance each Defendant challenges the assertion of extraterritorial jurisdiction by United States courts where the offenses charged did not occur on United States soil, did not involve United States citizens as defendants, or did not result in the death or injury of a United States citizen. . . .
>
> Defendants have been charged under Section 32(a)(1),(2), and (7) in conjunction with the federal conspiracy statute, 18 U.S.C. § 371, with conspiring to bomb eleven United States airliners operating in East Asia. Defendant Yousef has also been charged in a separate count for violation of section 32(b)(3) for the actual bombing of the Philippines airliner. Had the prosecution for the Philippines airliner bombing been brought separately, the argument that "this case has far more nexus to the Philippines than it does to the United States", may have been more persuasive. However, this prosecution alleges that the Philippines airliner bombing was just one step in the overall plot to sabotage United States airliners. As such, the Philippines airliner bombing is alleged to have been part of Defendants' continuous course of conduct in relation to the overall bombing plot. Correctly construed, therefore, it becomes apparent that this court has the authority to assert extraterritorial jurisdiction over the three Defendants for the crimes charged in this indictment consistent with the statutory jurisdictional requirements of Section 32, principles of international law, and the United States Constitution. Not only does this court have the authority to exercise extraterritorial jurisdiction in this case, but, under treaty obligations of the United States, it is required to do so.
>
> Section 32, adopted as part of the Aircraft Sabotage Act, was enacted in 1984 to fulfill this country's responsibilities under the Montreal Convention for the Suppression of Unlawful Acts against the Safety of Civil Aviation, ("the Montreal Convention"), 24 U.S.T. 565, T.I.A.S. 7570, which came into effect on January 26, 1973. . . . A principal purpose of the act was to provide federal jurisdiction over individuals who were

accused of committing crimes involving aircraft sabotage and over whom the courts would not otherwise have jurisdiction under domestic law.
. . .

Murad argues that Counts Twelve through Fourteen, which charge the plot to blow up United States airliners do not satisfy the jurisdictional requirements of Section 32(a) because the indictment fails to specify a particular United States aircraft which was the subject of the alleged conspiracy, and therefore does not satisfy the statutory jurisdictional requirements. . . .

Traditional notions of jurisdiction provided that a country's jurisdiction extended internationally over vessels or aircraft flying that country's flag based on a "floating or flying territory" rationale. *See* Restatement (Third) § 402, Reporter's Note 4. This traditional concept was codified in some respects in the Aircraft Sabotage Act.

Section 32(a) proscribes destruction, bombing, and endangering the safety of any aircraft in the "special aircraft jurisdiction of the United States or any civil aircraft used, operated or employed in interstate, overseas or foreign air commerce." There are therefore two possible avenues for establishing jurisdiction under this section. The term "special aircraft jurisdiction" is defined to include "a civil aircraft of the United States" while that aircraft is in flight. 49 U.S.C. § 46501(2)(A). "Civil aircraft of the United States" is defined as "aircraft registered under chapter 441 of Title 49." 49 U.S.C. § 40102(17).

The indictment details a bombing plan by Defendants that targeted United States-flagged commercial airlines, all but one of which were bound for various cities in the United States. As part of the evidence in this case, the government will present a computer printout which it contends contains the specific flight numbers and itineraries for the aircraft involved. All the aircraft involved are from the fleets of well-known United States airline companies, which according to the government, were registered under chapter 441, making them "civil aircraft of the United States." Since the indictment alleges that the bombs were scheduled to explode while these civil aircraft were in flight, the allegations satisfy the "special aircraft jurisdiction" provision.

The indictment also satisfies the other possible avenue of jurisdiction since it alleges that the aircraft involved were "civil aircraft used, operated or employed in interstate, overseas or foreign air commerce." "Civil aircraft" is also defined as any aircraft except a "public aircraft", which is defined as an aircraft used "exclusively in the service of any government . . . . " *See* 49 U.S.C. § 40102(a)(16) & (37). "Foreign air commerce" is defined as "the transportation of passengers or property by aircraft for compensation . . . between a place in the United States and a place outside the United States when any part of the transportation or operation is by aircraft." 18 U.S.C. § 40102(22). As already stated, all the aircraft involved in this plot were civil airliners and all but one were operating in routes between a United States city and a foreign city. . . .This court, therefore, has statutory jurisdiction over the substantive crimes charged in Counts Twelve, Thirteen, and Fourteen.

(3) On December 21, 1987, the explosion of a bomb on board Pan Am Flight 103 killed 259 passengers and crew and 11 residents of Lockerbie, Scotland, where the plane crashed. On November 14, 1991, criminal charges were brought in both the U.S. and the U.K. against two Libyan nationals accused of causing the explosion. The U.N. Security Council adopted a series of resolutions imposing sanctions on Libya for not complying with requests to surrender the two defendants for trial. Libya meanwhile instituted proceedings against the U.S. and U.K. in the International Court of Justice, arguing that its obligations under the Montreal Convention were met by its own willingness to prosecute the defendants if the evidence against them were supplied to the Libyan authorities, and that the U.S. and the U.K. had breached their obligations under the convention by trying to coerce Libya into surrendering suspects whom it was entitled to try itself.

The Court's decisions regarding Provisional Measures and Preliminary Objections in the two Cases Concerning Questions of Interpretation and Application of the 1971 Montreal Convention Arising from the Aerial Incident at Lockerbie appear in 1992 I.C.J. REP. 3, 114, & 1998 I.C.J. REP. 9, 115. In 1999, arrangements were made to try the two defendants before a Scottish court sitting in the Netherlands. *See* Anthony Aust, *Lockerbie: The Other Case*, 49 INT'L & COMP. L. Q. (2000); *Special Section on Trial of Lockerbie Suspects in the Netherlands*, 38 I.L.M. 926 (1999). The trial began on May 3, 2000.

§ 8.04   Hostage - Taking

UNITED STATES v. LUE

United States Court of Appeals, Second Circuit
134 F.3d 79 (1998)

WALKER, CIRCUIT JUDGE:

Defendant, Chen De Yian, appeals from a judgment of conviction entered by the United States District Court for the Southern District of New York (Denise L. Cote, Judge), following a conditional plea of guilty arising from defendant's attempt to abduct and hold a person hostage until the hostage's relatives paid a sum of money to secure the victim's release. The defendant pled guilty to (1) violating 18 U.S.C. § 1203, the Act for the Prevention and Punishment of the Crime of Hostage-Taking ("Hostage Taking Act"), Pub. L. No. 98-473, Title II,

§ 2002(a), 98 Stat. 2186 (1984), and (2) carrying a firearm in relation to the hostage taking in violation of 18 U.S.C. § 924(c). The district court sentenced the defendant to imprisonment for 147 months followed by supervised release for five years and a special assessment of $ 100. . . .

The counts to which defendant pled guilty arose from his unsuccessful efforts to abduct Chan Fung Chung in order to force the victim's family to pay ransom to obtain his release. The indictment alleges that in or about May 1991 Chen and his co-conspirators met in New York City to discuss and plan the seizure of Chan Fung Chung. On April 24, 1992, Chen and his co-conspirators attempted to force Chan Fung Chung into an automobile on East 13th Street in Manhattan. The defendants' attempt to abduct the victim was thwarted by a firefighter and an off-duty police officer who heard the victim's cries. Although his co-conspirators escaped, Chen was arrested by New York City police officers with a .30 caliber handgun in his possession. Following the arrest, Chen pled guilty in state court to weapons-use charges and served 18 months in state prison. Subsequently, Chen was indicted on federal charges relating to the attempted abduction as well as two homicides in Virginia which were part of an alleged murder-for-hire scheme.

After the district court denied the defendant's motion to dismiss the hostage taking counts on constitutional grounds, the defendant entered into a plea agreement with the government. On November 22, 1995, Chen entered a plea of guilty to two counts of the multi-count indictment, including the only count issue in this appeal: the violation of the Hostage Taking Act, 18 U.S.C. § 1203. Under the plea agreement, Chen preserved his right to appellate review of the district court's decision that 18 U.S.C. § 1203 was constitutional. . . .

On April 26, 1984, President Reagan proposed legislation to Congress to combat international terrorism. See Message from the President of the United States Transmitting Four Drafts of Proposed Legislation to Attack the Pressing and Urgent Problem of International Terrorism, H.R. Doc. No. 98-211, 98th Cong., 2d Sess. (1984) ("Presidential Message"). This proposal included a predecessor version of the Hostage Taking Act. *Id.* at 5-9. The legislation was designed to implement the International Convention Against the Taking of Hostages, ... ratified by the Executive in 1981, ... The Convention binds the signatories to take specific steps to adopt "effective measures for the prevention, prosecution and punishment of all acts of taking of hostages as manifestations of international terrorism." In particular, the signatories agreed that

> any person who seizes or detains and threatens to kill, to injure or to continue to detain another person (hereinafter referred to as the "hostage") in order to compel a third party, namely, a State, an international intergovernmental organization, a natural or juridical person, or a group of persons, to do or abstain from doing any act as an explicit or implicit condition for the release of the hostage commits the offense of taking of hostages . . . within the meaning of this Convention.

Id. art. 1. The signatories also agreed to make hostage taking punishable in accordance with the deep gravity of the offense. Presumably to accommodate jurisdictional concerns, the terms of the Convention are inapplicable if a covered offense was committed within a single nation, the hostage and the alleged offender are nationals of that nation, and the alleged offender is found within the territory of that nation. . . . .

Pursuant to its obligation under the Convention, in late 1984, Congress passed, and the President signed, the Hostage Taking Act, which provides in pertinent part:

> (a) Except as provided in subsection (b) of this section, whoever, whether inside or outside the United States, seizes or detains and threatens to kill, to injure, or to continue to detain another person in order to compel a third person or a governmental organization to do or abstain from doing any act as an explicit or implicit condition for the release of the person detained, or attempts or conspires to do so, shall be punished by imprisonment for any term of years or for life and, if the death of any person results, shall be punished by death or life imprisonment.
>
> . . . .
>
> (b)(2) It is not an offense under this section if the conduct required for the offense occurred inside the United States, each alleged offender and each person seized or detained are nationals of the United States, and each alleged offender is found in the United States, unless the governmental organization sought to be compelled is the Government of the United States.

18 U.S.C. § 1203. This statute is the focus of defendant's constitutional challenge. . . .

Defendant first argues that the district court erred in holding that Congress has the authority to pass the Hostage Taking Act under the Necessary and Proper Clause of Article I, as an adjunct to the Executive's acknowledged authority under Article II to enter into treaties, with the advice and consent of the Senate. Chen contends that (1) the Hostage Taking Act is unconstitutional because the Hostage Taking Convention upon which it is based exceeds the Executive's authority under the Treaty Clause and (2) even if entry into the Convention is in accord with the treaty-making authority, the Hostage Taking Act is not a "plainly adapted" means of effectuating the Convention's ends and thus exceeds Congress's authority under the Necessary and Proper clause.

At the outset we note that Congress's authority under the Necessary and Proper Clause extends beyond those powers specifically enumerated in Article I, section 8. As the clause specifically states, "Congress shall have Power . . . . to make all Laws which shall be necessary and proper for carrying into Execution the foregoing powers, and all other Powers vested by this Constitution in the Government of the United States, or in any Department or Officer thereof." U.S. Const. art. I, § 8, cl. 18. Accordingly, Congress may enact laws necessary to effectuate the treaty power, enumerated in Article II of the Constitution. . . .

We need not pause long over defendant's contention that entry into the Hostage Taking Convention was beyond the Executive's authority under Article II to sign (and Congress to assent to) treaties. As defendant himself acknowledges, "to hold that the Treaty Power has been exceeded . . . . would of course be a drastic step." . . . His argument rests on the fundamental, but somewhat ambiguous, proposition in *Asakura v. City of Seattle* that the Executive's treaty power "extends to all proper subjects of negotiation between our government and other nations." . . . But, defendant argues that the Hostage Taking Convention regulates matters of purely domestic concern not touching on relations with other nations. Accordingly, he concludes that entry into the Convention was beyond the constitutional authority of the executive. Defendant is in error on two counts: (1) his overly restrictive view of the federal treaty power and (2) his evaluation of the Convention as addressing purely domestic interests. . . .

The defendant relies far too heavily on a dichotomy between matters of purely domestic concern and those of international concern, a dichotomy appropriately criticized by commentators in the field. . . .

> Contrary to what was once suggested, the Constitution does not require that an international agreement deal only with "matters of international concern." The references in the Constitution presumably incorporate the concept of treaty and of other agreements in international law. International law knows no limitations on the purpose or subject matter of international agreements, other than that they may not conflict with a peremptory norm of international law. States may enter into an agreement on any matter of concern to them, and international law does not look behind their motives or purposes in doing so. Thus, the United States may make an agreement on any subject suggested by its national interests in relations with other nations.

RESTATEMENT (THIRD) OF THE FOREIGN RELATIONS LAW OF THE UNITED STATES § 302, cmt. c (1986)(citation omitted). . . .

Whatever the potential outer limit on the treaty power of the Executive, the Hostage Taking Convention does not transgress it. At the most general level, the Convention addresses – at least in part – the treatment of foreign nationals while they are on local soil, a matter of central concern among nations. More specifically, the Convention addresses a matter of grave concern to the international community: hostage taking as a vehicle for terrorism. In fact, the preamble of the Convention explicitly so states:

> the taking of hostages is an offence of grave concern to the international community and . . . in accordance with the provisions of this Convention, any person   committing an act of hostage taking shall either be prosecuted or extradited . . .   [I]t is urgently necessary to develop

international cooperation between States in devising and adopting effective measures for the prevention, prosecution and punishment of all acts of taking of hostages as manifestations of international terrorism.

Hostage Taking Convention, preamble, T.I.A.S. No. 11,081. In short, the Hostage Taking Convention is well within the boundaries of the Constitution's treaty power. . . .

The defendant next challenges the means by which Congress effectuated the terms of the Convention: the enactment of the Hostage Taking Act. Defendant contends that the Act sweeps too broadly and, thus, exceeds Congress's authority to pass laws "necessary and proper" to the effectuation of the Convention. U.S. Const. Art. 1, § 8, cl. 18. More precisely, defendant argues that because the Hostage Taking Convention targets a specific aspect of international terrorism – hostage taking – the statute effectuating the Convention must deal narrowly with international terrorism or risk invalidity under the Necessary and Proper Clause. However, defendant's view of the congressional authority under the Necessary and Proper Clause is too cramped.

If the Hostage Taking Convention is a valid exercise of the Executive's treaty power, there is little room to dispute that the legislation passed to effectuate the treaty is valid under the Necessary and Proper Clause. . . . The Act here plainly bears a rational relationship to the Convention; indeed, it tracks the language of the Convention in all material respects. . . . The defendant contends that, even if the Hostage Taking Act passes muster under the Necessary and Proper Clause as an adjunct to the Executive's authority under the Treaty Clause, the Act nonetheless must be struck down because it impermissibly invades the authority of the states in violation of the Tenth Amendment. Specifically, defendant contends that because the Hostage Taking Act potentially criminalizes "domestic, non-political abductions," . . . . and because such abductions "are not in any meaningful way a uniquely international (or national) problem," . . . . the Act violates the principles of federalism embodied in the Tenth Amendment. We reject this argument.

The Tenth Amendment provides, in full: "The powers not delegated to the United States by the Constitution, nor prohibited by it to the States, are reserved to the States respectively, or to the people." U.S. Const. amend. X. The Constitution expressly vests the power to enter into treaties in the Executive, U.S. Const. art II, § 2, cl. 2; accordingly, the power wielded by the Executive (with the advice and consent of the Senate) is "delegated" to the federal government and not "reserved" to the states. As one distinguished commentator has noted:

Since the Treaty Power was delegated to the federal government, whatever is within its scope is not reserved to the states: the Tenth Amendment is not material. Many matters, then, may appear to be "reserved to the States" as regards domestic legislation if Congress does not have power to regulate them; but they are not reserved to the states so as to exclude their regulation by international agreement.

LOUIS HENKIN, FOREIGN AFFAIRS AND THE UNITED STATES CONSTITUTION 191 (2d ed. 1996). . . . Thus, the treaty power is not subject to meaningful limitation under the terms of the Tenth Amendment. . . .

Defendant's primary Tenth Amendment challenge to the Hostage Taking Act rests on his contention that hostage taking is a local concern and that, under *Holland,* a legislative enactment effectuating a treaty will not pass muster under the Tenth Amendment unless such an enactment addresses a uniquely national or international matter. Such a reading finds some support in the language of the Court's opinion. . . . However, we need not decide the question, because in this case there is a sufficient national (indeed, international) interest supporting Congress's passage of the Hostage Taking Act. . . .

Finally, defendant contends that the Hostage Taking Act violates the equal protection principles embodied in the Fifth Amendment's Due Process Clause. *See Bolling v. Sharpe,* 347 U.S. 497, 499, 98 L. Ed. 884, 74 S. Ct. 693 (1954). In particular, the defendant contends that the Act runs afoul of these principles because it criminalizes conduct undertaken by foreign nationals which would not be criminal if undertaken by United States' nationals and because such a classification is not supported by a substantial governmental interest.

There is little doubt, despite government protestations to the contrary, that the Hostage Taking Act discriminates against offenders on the basis of alienage. If the hostage-taking victim is a national, the Act criminalizes conduct by an alien that would not be sanctionable if undertaken by a United States citizen (except where the purpose of the crime is to compel the United States to act or refrain from acting). . . .

The principle area in dispute in defendant's equal protection challenge is, then, the appropriate level of judicial scrutiny to which the Act must be subjected. Defendant argues that the Hostage Taking Act is subject to heightened judicial scrutiny because it discriminates on the basis of alienage, an inherently suspect classification. Although defendant is correct that alienage has been treated as a suspect classification requiring heightened scrutiny, ... he fails to properly acknowledge the context in which the Court has so ruled. The Court has recognized alienage as a suspect classification only when a state or local government has sought to employ the classification to disadvantage foreign nationals. . . .

The situation is different when it is the federal government that is drawing the distinction between citizens of the United States and those of foreign countries. Generally, the federal government is not held to the same searching scrutiny when it draws lines on the basis of alienage. The Court has recognized that the federal government has national interests when dealing with aliens that are different from those of the individual states. . . . In light of the federal government's primary authority in these areas, and because "it is the business of the political branches of the Federal Government, rather than that of either the States or the Federal Judiciary, to regulate the conditions of entry and residence of aliens," . . . . state or local laws that disadvantage aliens are presumptively invalid while federal laws doing the same are accorded substantial deference.

This is not to say that foreign nationals on our soil are without any protection from federal governmental action under the equal protection component of the Fifth Amendment. They do enjoy such protection; however, it is constrained in light of the responsibility of the political branches to regulate the relationship between the United States and noncitizens. . . . [A]n array of constitutional and statutory provisions rests on the assumption that there are legitimate distinctions between citizens and aliens that "may justify attributes and benefits for one class not accorded the other." . . . In short, "the fact that an Act of Congress treats aliens differently from citizens does not in itself imply that such disparate treatment is 'invidious.'" . . .

As long as the Hostage Taking Act is rationally related to a legitimate government interest it satisfies principles of equal protection in this context. . . . In our view, the Act clears this constitutional hurdle.

The classification drawn by the Hostage Taking Act covers all aliens involved in hostage-taking incidents. The asserted purpose of the statute, along with the antecedent Convention, is to address a matter of grave concern to the international community: hostage taking as a manifestation of international terrorism. . . . We recognize that in the Hostage Taking Act Congress employs the classification of alienage to proscribe conduct which may not always bear a direct relationship to the Act's principal object of stemming acts of terrorism, and that at some point a classification of this sort may have a "relationship to [the] asserted goal [which] is so attenuated as to render the distinction arbitrary or irrational." . . . However, in this instance, Congress rationally concluded that a hostage taking within our jurisdiction involving a noncitizen is sufficiently likely to involve matters implicating foreign policy or immigration concerns as to warrant a federal criminal proscription. The connection between the act and its purpose is not so attenuated as to fail to meet the rational-basis standard. . . . For the foregoing reasons, we affirm the judgment of the district court.

Chapter 9
TORTURE

§ 9.01 The Torture Convention

CONVENTION AGAINST TORTURE AND OTHER CRUEL, INHUMAN OR DEGRADING TREATMENT OR PUNISHMENT

General Assembly Resolution 39/46, Dec. 10, 1984
39 U.N. GAOR, Supp. No. 51, at 197, U.N. Doc. A/39/51

Article 1

1. For the purposes of this Convention, the term "torture" means any act by which severe pain or suffering, whether physical or mental, is intentionally inflicted on a person for such purposes as obtaining from him or a third person information or a confession, punishing him for an act he or a third person has committed or is suspected of having committed, or intimidating or coercing him or a third person, or for any reason based on discrimination of any kind, when such pain or suffering is inflicted by or at the instigation of or with the consent or acquiescence of a public official or other person acting in an official capacity. It does not include pain or suffering arising only from, inherent in or incidental to lawful sanctions.

2. This article is without prejudice to any international instrument or national legislation which does or may contain provisions of wider application.

Article 2

1. Each State Party shall take effective legislative, administrative, judicial or other measures to prevent acts of torture in any territory under its jurisdiction.

2. No exceptional circumstances whatsoever, whether a state of war or a threat of war, internal political instability or any other public emergency, may be invoked as a justification of torture.

3. An order from a superior officer or a public authority may not be invoked as a justification of torture.

Article 3

1. No State Party shall expel, return (*"refouler"*) or extradite a person to another State where there are substantial grounds for believing that he would be in danger of being subjected to torture.

2. For the purpose of determining whether there are such grounds, the competent authorities shall take into account all relevant considerations including, where applicable, the existence in the State concerned of a consistent pattern of gross, flagrant or mass violations of human rights.

Article 4

1. Each State Party shall ensure that all acts of torture are offences under its criminal law. The same shall apply to an attempt to commit torture and to an act by any person which constitutes complicity or participation in torture.

2. Each State Party shall make these offences punishable by appropriate penalties which take into account their grave nature.

Article 5

1. Each State Party shall take such measures as may be necessary to establish its jurisdiction over the offences referred to in article 4 in the following cases:

(a) When the offences are committed in any territory under its jurisdiction or on board a ship or aircraft registered in that State;

(b) When the alleged offender is a national of that State;

(c) When the victim is a national of that State if that State considers it appropriate.

2. Each State Party shall likewise take such measures as may be necessary to establish its jurisdiction over such offences in cases where the alleged offender is present in any territory under its jurisdiction and it does not extradite him pursuant to article 8 to any of the States mentioned in paragraph 1 of this article.

3. This Convention does not exclude any criminal jurisdiction exercised in accordance with internal law.

Article 6

1. Upon being satisfied, after an examination of information available to it, that the circumstances so warrant, any State Party in whose territory a person alleged to have committed any offence referred to in article 4 is present shall take him into custody or take other legal measures to ensure

his presence. The custody and other legal measures shall be as provided in the law of that State but may be continued only for such time as is necessary to enable any criminal or extradition proceedings to be instituted.

2. Such State shall immediately make a preliminary inquiry into the facts.

3. Any person in custody pursuant to paragraph 1 of this article shall be assisted in communicating immediately with the nearest appropriate representative of the State of which he is a national, or, if he is a stateless person, with the representative of the State where he usually resides.

4. When a State, pursuant to this article, has taken a person into custody, it shall immediately notify the States referred to in article 5, paragraph 1, of the fact that such person is in custody and of the circumstances which warrant his detention. The State which makes the preliminary inquiry contemplated in paragraph 2 of this article shall promptly report its findings to the said States and shall indicate whether it intends to exercise jurisdiction.

Article 7

1. The State Party in the territory under whose jurisdiction a person alleged to have committed any offence referred to in article 4 is found shall in the cases contemplated in article 5, if it does not extradite him, submit the case to its competent authorities for the purpose of prosecution.

2. These authorities shall take their decision in the same manner as in the case of any ordinary offence of a serious nature under the law of that State. In the cases referred to in article 5, paragraph 2, the standards of evidence required for prosecution and conviction shall in no way be less stringent than those which apply in the cases referred to in article 5, paragraph 1.

3. Any person regarding whom proceedings are brought in connection with any of the offences referred to in article 4 shall be guaranteed fair treatment at all stages of the proceedings.

Article 8

1. The offences referred to in article 4 shall be deemed to be included as extraditable offences in any extradition treaty existing between States Parties. States Parties undertake to include such offences as extraditable offences in every extradition treaty to be concluded between them.

2. If a State Party which makes extradition conditional on the existence of a treaty receives a request for extradition from another State Party with which it has no extradition treaty, it may consider this Convention as the legal basis for extradition in respect of such offences. Extradition shall be subject to the other conditions provided by the law of the requested State.

3. States Parties which do not make extradition conditional on the existence of a treaty shall recognize such offences as extraditable offences between themselves subject to the conditions provided by the law of the requested State.

4. Such offences shall be treated, for the purpose of extradition between States Parties, as if they had been committed not only in the place in which they occurred but also in the territories of the States required to establish their jurisdiction in accordance with article 5, paragraph 1.

Article 9

1. States Parties shall afford one another the greatest measure of assistance in connection with criminal proceedings brought in respect of any of the offences referred to in article 4, including the supply of all evidence at their disposal necessary for the proceedings.

2. States Parties shall carry out their obligations under paragraph 1 of this article in conformity with any treaties on mutual judicial assistance that may exist between them.

Article 10

1. Each State Party shall ensure that education and information regarding the prohibition against torture are fully included in the training of law enforcement personnel, civil or military, medical personnel, public officials and other persons who may be involved in the custody, interrogation or treatment of any individual subjected to any form of arrest, detention or imprisonment.

2. Each State Party shall include this prohibition in the rules or instructions issued in regard to the duties and functions of any such person.

Article 11

Each State Party shall keep under systematic review interrogation rules, instructions, methods and practices as well as arrangements for the custody and treatment of persons subjected to any form of arrest, detention or imprisonment in any territory under its jurisdiction, with a view to preventing any cases of torture.

Article 12

Each State Party shall ensure that its competent authorities proceed to a prompt and impartial investigation, wherever there is reasonable ground to believe that an act of torture has been committed in any territory under its jurisdiction.

Article 13

Each State Party shall ensure that any individual who alleges he has been subjected to torture in any territory under its jurisdiction has the right to complain to, and to have his case promptly and impartially examined by, its competent authorities. Steps shall be taken to ensure that the complainant and witnesses are protected against all ill-treatment or intimidation as a con sequence of his complaint or any evidence given.

Article 14

1. Each State Party shall ensure in its legal system that the victim of an act of torture obtains redress and has an enforceable right to fair and adequate compensation, including the means for as full rehabilitation as possible. In the event of the death of the victim as a result of an act of torture, his dependants shall be entitled to compensation.

2. Nothing in this article shall affect any right of the victim or other persons to compensation which may exist under national law.

Article 15

Each State Party shall ensure that any statement which is established to have been made as a result of torture shall not be invoked as evidence in any proceedings, except against a person accused of torture as evidence that the statement was made.

Article 16

1. Each State Party shall undertake to prevent in any territory under its jurisdiction other acts of cruel, inhuman or degrading treatment or punishment which do not amount to torture as defined in article 1, when such acts are committed by or at the instigation of or with the consent or acquiescence of a public official or other person acting in an official capacity. In particular, the obligations contained in articles 10, 11, 12 and 13 shall apply with the substitution for references to torture of references to other forms of cruel, inhuman or degrading treatment or punishment.

2. The provisions of this Convention are without prejudice to the provisions of any other international instrument or national law which prohibits cruel, inhuman or degrading treatment or punishment or which relates to extradition or expulsion.

Notes and Questions

(1) Articles 1-16 comprise Part I of the Torture Convention. Part II (comprised of Articles 17-24) establishes a ten-member Committee Against Torture, to monitor compliance on the basis of reports submitted by the parties, its own confidential inquiries, and (if a state chooses to allow them) complaints by other states and by aggrieved individuals. Part III (comprised of Articles 25-33) contains "final clauses" pertaining to signature, ratification, amendment, etc. The Convention entered into force on June 26, 1987.

(2) The *Filartiga* case [p. 17], decided in 1980, already had concluded that torture violates customary international law. What did the Convention add to this prohibition? Consider the following observation. What are the "supportive measures" to which this statement refers?

> Many people assume that the Convention's principal aim is to *outlaw* torture and other cruel, inhuman or degrading treatment or punishment. This assumption is not correct insofar as it would imply that the prohibition of these practices is established under international law by the Convention only and that this prohibition will be binding as a rule of international law only for those States which have become parties to the Convention. On the contrary, the Convention is based upon the recognition that the above-mentioned practices are already outlawed under international law. The principal aim of the Convention is to *strengthen* the existing prohibition of such practices by a number of supportive measures.

J. Herman Burgers & Hans Danelius, The United Nations Convention against Torture: A Handbook on the Convention against Torture and Other Cruel, Inhuman or Degrading Treatment or Punishment 1 (1988).

(3) The United States ratified the Torture Convention in 1994. The Senate's advice and consent to ratification was accompanied by two reservations, five understandings, two declarations, and a proviso. *See* David P. Steward, *The Torture Convention and the Reception of International Criminal Law within the United States*, 15 Nova L. Rev. 449 (1991). These read as follows:

> I. The Senate's advice and consent is subject to the following reservations:
>
> (1) That the United States considers itself bound by the obligation under Article 16 to prevent "cruel, inhuman or degrading treatment or punishment," only insofar as the term "cruel, inhuman or degrading treatment or punishment" means the cruel, unusual and inhumane treatment or punishment prohibited by the Fifth, Eighth, and/or Fourteenth Amendments to the Constitution of the United States.
>
> (2) That pursuant to Article 30(2) the United States declares that it

does not consider itself bound by Article 30(1) [which provides that disputes between parties concerning the interpretation or application of the convention shall be settled by arbitration or else by submission to the ICJ], but reserves the right specifically to agree to follow this or any other procedure for arbitration in a particular case.

II. The Senate's advice and consent is subject to the following understandings, which shall apply to the obligations of the United States under this Convention:

(1)(a) That with reference to Article 1, the United States understands that, in order to constitute torture, an act must be specifically intended to inflict severe physical or mental pain or suffering and that mental pain or suffering refers to prolonged mental harm caused by or resulting from: (1) the intentional infliction or threatened infliction of severe physical pain or suffering; (2) the administration or application, or threatened administration or application, of mind altering substances or other procedures calculated to disrupt profoundly the senses or the personality; (3) the threat of imminent death; or (4) the threat that another person will imminently be subjected to death, severe physical pain or suffering, or the administration or application of mind altering substances or other procedures calculated to disrupt profoundly the senses or personality.

(b) That the United States understands that the definition of torture in Article 1 is intended to apply only to acts directed against persons in the offender's custody or physical control.

(c) That with reference to Article 1 of the Convention, the United States understands that "sanctions" includes judicially-imposed sanctions and other enforcement actions authorized by United States law or by judicial interpretation of such law. Nonetheless, the United States understands that a State Party could not through its domestic sanctions defeat the object and purpose of the Convention to prohibit torture.

(d) That with reference to Article 1 of the Convention, the United States understands that the term "acquiescence" requires that the public official, prior to the activity constituting torture, have awareness of such activity and thereafter breach his legal responsibility to intervene to prevent such activity.

(e) That with reference to Article 1 of the Convention, the United States understands that noncompliance with applicable legal procedural standards does not per se constitute torture.

(2) That the United States understands the phrase, "where there are substantial grounds for believing that he would be in danger of being subjected to torture," as used in Article 3 of the Convention, to mean

"if it is more likely than not that he would be tortured."

(3) That it is the understanding of the United States that Article 14 requires a State Party to provide a private right of action for damages only for acts of torture committed in territory under the jurisdiction of that State Party.

(4) That the United States understands that international law does not prohibit the death penalty, and does not consider this Convention to restrict or prohibit the United States from applying the death penalty consistent with the Fifth, Eighth and/or Fourteenth Amendments to the Constitution of the United States, including any constitutional period of confinement prior to the imposition of the death penalty.

(5) That the United States understands that this Convention shall be implemented by the United States Government to the extent that it exercises legislative and judicial jurisdiction over the matters covered by the Convention and otherwise by the state and local governments. Accordingly, in implementing Articles 10-14 and 16, the United States Government shall take measures appropriate to the Federal system to the end that the competent authorities of the constituent units of the United States of America may take appropriate measures for the fulfillment of the Convention.

III. The Senate's advice and consent is subject to the following declarations:

(1) That the United States declares that the provisions of Articles 1 through 16 of the Convention are not self-executing.

(2) That the United States declares, pursuant to Article 21, paragraph 1, of the Convention, that it recognizes the competence of the Committee against Torture to receive and consider communications to the effect that a State Party claims that another State Party is not fulfilling its obligations under the Convention. It is the understanding of the United States that, pursuant to the above mentioned article, such communications shall be accepted and processed only if they come from a State Party which has made a similar declaration.

IV. The Senate's advice and consent is subject to the following proviso, which shall not be included in the instrument of ratification to be deposited by the President:

The President of the United States shall not deposit the instrument of ratification until such time as he has notified all present and prospective ratifying parties to this Convention that nothing in this Convention requires or authorizes legislation, or other action, by the United States of America prohibited by the Constitution of the United

States as interpreted by the United States.

(4) The federal criminal statute implementing the Convention is codified at 18 U.S.C. §§ 2340-2340B. It reads as follows:

18 U.S.C. § 2340. Definitions.

As used in this chapter

(1) "torture" means an act committed by a person acting under the color of law specifically intended to inflict severe physical or mental pain or suffering (other than pain or suffering incidental to lawful sanctions) upon another person within his custody or physical control;

(2) "severe mental pain or suffering" means the prolonged mental harm caused by or resulting from—

(A) the intentional infliction or threatened infliction of severe physical pain or suffering;

(B) the administration or application, or threatened administration or application, of mind-altering substances or other procedures calculated to disrupt profoundly the senses or the personality;

(C) the threat of imminent death; or

(D) the threat that another person will imminently be subjected to death, severe physical pain or suffering, or the administration or application of mind-altering substances or other procedures calculated to disrupt profoundly the senses or personality; and

(3) "United States" includes all areas under the jurisdiction of the United States including any of the places described in sections 5 and 7 of this title and section 46501(2) of title 49.

18 U.S.C. § 2340A. Torture.

(a) Offense. Whoever outside the United States commits or attempts to commit torture shall be fined under this title or imprisoned not more than 20 years, or both, and if death results to any person from conduct prohibited by this subsection, shall be punished by death or imprisoned for any term of years or for life.

(b) Jurisdiction. There is jurisdiction over the activity prohibited in subsection (a) if—

(1) the alleged offender is a national of the United States; or

(2) the alleged offender is present in the United States, irrespective of the nationality of the victim or alleged offender.

18 U.S.C. § 2340B. Exclusive remedies.

Nothing in this chapter shall be construed as precluding the application of State or local laws on the same subject, nor shall anything in this chapter be construed as creating any substantive or procedural right enforceable by law by any party in any civil proceeding.

(5) Do the provisions in 18 U.S.C. §§ 2340-2340B fully implement the obligation to make torture, as defined in the Convention, a punishable offense? Do they do so at least with respect to torture perpetrated outside the United States by an offender who is present in the United States? What about torture perpetrated within the United States? Is that not fully covered, in any event, by other state and federal laws? Does the Torture Convention require that parties create a specific, separate offense corresponding to torture as defined in Article 1? Consider the Conclusions and Recommendations of the Committee Against Torture, May 15, 2000 (CAT/C/24/6), commenting on a report submitted by the United States:

1. The Committee considered the initial report of the United States of America . . . and adopted the following conclusions and recommendations.

A. *Introduction*

2. The Committee welcomes the submission of the comprehensive initial report of the United States of America, which, although almost five years overdue, was prepared in full accordance with the guidelines of the Committee.

3. The Committee also thanks the State party for its sincere cooperation in its dialogue with the Committee and takes note of the information supplied in the extensive oral report.

B. *Positive Aspects*

4. The Committee particularly welcomes the following:

a. The extensive legal protection against torture and other cruel, inhuman or degrading treatment or punishment that exists in the State party and the efforts pursued by the authorities to achieve transparency of its institutions and practices;

b. The broad legal recourse to compensation for victims of torture, whether or not such torture occurred in the United States of America;

c. The introduction of executive regulations preventing *refoulement* of potential torture victims;

d. The State party's contributions to the United Nations Voluntary Fund for the Victims of Torture;

e. The creation by executive order of an inter-agency working group to ensure coordination of federal efforts towards compliance with the obligations of the international human rights treaties to which the United States of America is a party;

f. The assurances given by the delegation that a universal criminal jurisdiction was assumed by the State party whenever an alleged torturer is found within its territory;

g. The obviously genuine assurances of cooperation extended to the Committee by the delegation of the State party to ensure the observance of the Convention.

C. Subjects of concern

5. The Committee expresses its concern about:

a. The failure of the State party to enact a federal crime of torture in terms consistent with article 1 of the Convention;

b. The reservation lodged to article 16 in violation of the Convention, the effect of which is to limit the application of the Convention;

c. The number of cases of police ill-treatment of civilians, and ill-treatment in prisons (including instances of inter-prisoner violence). Much of this ill-treatment by police and prison guards seems to be based upon discrimination;

d. Alleged cases of sexual assault upon female detainees and prisoners by law enforcement officers and prison personnel. Female detainees and prisoners are also very often held in humiliating and degrading circumstances;

e. The use of electro-shock devices and restraint chairs as methods of constraint that may violate the provisions of article 16 of the Convention;

f. The excessively harsh regime of the "supermaximum" prisons;

g. The use of "chain gangs," particularly in public;

h. The legal action by prisoners seeking redress, which has been significantly restricted by the requirement of physical injury as a condition to bringing a successful action under the Prison Litigation Reform Act;

i. The holding of minors (juveniles) with adults in the regular prison population.

D. Recommendations

6. The Committee recommends that the State party:

a. Although it has taken many measures to ensure compliance with the provisions of the Convention, the State party should also enact a federal crime of torture in terms consistent with article 1 of the Convention and should withdraw its reservations, interpretations and understandings relating to the Convention;

b. Take such steps as are necessary to ensure that those who violate the Convention are investigated, prosecuted and punished, especially those who are motivated by discriminatory purposes or sexual gratification;

c. Abolish electro-shock stun belts and restraint chairs as methods of restraining those in custody. Their use almost invariably leads to breaches of article 16 of the Convention;

d. Consider declaring in favour of article 22 of the Convention [which would allow the Committee to receive and consider communications from individuals claiming to be victims of a violation of the Convention by the United States];

e. Ensure that minors (juveniles) are not held in prison with the regular prison population.

f. Submit the second periodic report by 19 November 2001.

(6) The Torture Convention prohibits only practices which are officially sanctioned or in some way involve the participation of public officials. In prosecuting public officials, especially high ranking officials, there is a possible problem of official immunity under national law. Does the Convention speak to this problem? Can it be read tacitly to require that immunity not be allowed as a defense? What about the immunity of a foreign official under international law? Consider, in this connection, the decision of the House of Lords denying Augusto Pinochet immunity, as a *former* head of state, from extradition on charges of torture [*see* chap. 11].

§ 9.02 Sexual Violence as Torture

KADIC v. KARADZIC

United States Court of Appeals, Second Circuit
70 F.3d 232 (1995), cert. denied, 518 U.S. 1005 (1996)

NEWMAN, CHIEF JUDGE:

. . . . The plaintiffs-appellants are Croat and Muslim citizens of the internationally recognized nation of Bosnia-Herzegovina, formerly a republic of Yugoslavia. Their complaints, which we accept as true for purposes of this appeal, allege that they are victims, and representatives of victims, of various atrocities, including brutal acts of rape, forced prostitution, forced impregnation, torture, and summary execution, carried out by Bosnian-Serb military forces as part of a genocidal campaign conducted in the course of the Bosnian civil war. Karadzic, formerly a citizen of Yugoslavia and now a citizen of Bosnia-Herzegovina, is the President of a three-man presidency of the self-proclaimed Bosnian-Serb republic within Bosnia-Herzegovina, sometimes referred to as "Srpska," which claims to exercise lawful authority, and does in fact exercise actual control, over large parts of the territory of Bosnia-Herzegovina. In his capacity as President, Karadzic possesses ultimate command authority over the Bosnian-Serb military forces, and the injuries perpetrated upon plaintiffs were committed as part of a pattern of systematic human rights violations that was directed by Karadzic and carried out by the military forces under his command. The complaints allege that Karadzic acted in an official capacity either as the titular head of Srpska or in collaboration with the government of the recognized nation of the former Yugoslavia and its dominant constituent republic, Serbia.

The two groups of plaintiffs asserted causes of action for genocide, rape, forced prostitution and impregnation, torture and other cruel, inhuman, and degrading treatment, assault and battery, sex and ethnic inequality, summary execution, and wrongful death. They sought compensatory and punitive damages, attorney's fees, and, in one of the cases, injunctive relief. Plaintiffs grounded subject-matter jurisdiction in the Alien Tort Act, the Torture Victim Protection Act of 1991 ("Torture Victim Act"), Pub. L. No. 102-256, 106 Stat. 73 (1992), codified at 28 U.S.C. § 1350 note, the general federal-question jurisdictional statute, 28 U.S.C. § 1331, and principles of supplemental jurisdiction, 28 U.S.C. § 1367.

In early 1993, Karadzic was admitted to the United States on three separate occasions as an invitee of the United Nations. According to affidavits submitted by the plaintiffs, Karadzic was personally served with the summons and complaint in each action during two of these visits while he was physically present in Manhattan. . . . In the District Court, Karadzic moved for dismissal of both actions on the grounds of insufficient service of process, lack of personal jurisdiction, lack of subject-matter jurisdiction, and nonjusticiability of plaintiffs' claims. [The District Court dismissed for lack of subject-matter jurisdiction.]

Appellants allege three statutory bases for the subject-matter jurisdiction of the District Court – the Alien Tort Act, the Torture Victim Act, and the general federal-question jurisdictional statute.

A. The Alien Tort Act

1. General Application to Appellants' Claims. Our decision in *Filártiga* [p.17] established that [the Alien Tort Act] confers federal subject-matter jurisdiction when the following three conditions are satisfied: (1) an alien sues (2) for a tort (3) committed in violation of the law of nations (i.e., international law). . . . The first two requirements are plainly satisfied here, and the only disputed issue is whether plaintiffs have pleaded violations of international law. . . .

Karadzic contends that appellants have not alleged violations of the norms of international law because such norms bind only states and persons acting under color of a state's law, not private individuals. In making this contention, Karadzic advances the contradictory positions that he is not a state actor, even as he asserts that he is the President of the self-proclaimed Republic of Srpska. For their part, the Kadic appellants also take somewhat inconsistent positions in pleading defendant's role as President of Srpska, and also contending that "Karadzic is not an official of any government." . . .

We do not agree that the law of nations, as understood in the modern era, confines its reach to state action. Instead, we hold that certain forms of conduct violate the law of nations whether undertaken by those acting under the auspices of a state or only as private individuals. An early example of the application of the law of nations to the acts of private individuals is the prohibition against piracy. In *The Brig Malek Adhel,* 43 U.S. (2 How.) 210, 232, 11 L. Ed. 239 (1844), the Supreme Court observed that pirates were *"hostis humani generis"* (an enemy of all mankind) in part because they acted "without . . . any pretense of public authority." Later examples are prohibitions against the slave trade and certain war crimes. . . .

The liability of private persons for certain violations of customary international law and the availability of the Alien Tort Act to remedy such violations was early recognized by the Executive Branch in an opinion of Attorney General Bradford in reference to acts of American citizens aiding the French fleet to plunder British property off the coast of Sierra Leone in 1795. See Breach of Neutrality, 1 Op. Att'y Gen. 57, 59 (1795). The Executive Branch has emphatically restated in this litigation its position that private persons may be found liable under the Alien Tort Act for acts of genocide, war crimes, and other violations of international humanitarian law.

THE RESTATEMENT (THIRD) OF THE FOREIGN RELATIONS LAW OF THE UNITED STATES (1986) proclaims: "Individuals may be held liable for offenses against international law, such as piracy, war crimes, and genocide." RESTATEMENT (THIRD) pt. II, introductory note. The Restatement is careful to identify those violations that are actionable when committed by a state, *id.* § 702,[3] and a more limited category of violations of "universal concern," *id.* § 404 [reprinted in chap. 2, *supra*], partially overlapping with those listed in section 702. Though the immediate focus of section 404 is to identify those offenses for which a state has jurisdiction to punish without regard to territoriality or the nationality of the offenders, the inclusion of piracy and slave trade from an earlier era and aircraft hijacking from the modern era demonstrates that the offenses of "universal concern" include those capable of being committed by non-state actors. Although the jurisdiction authorized by section 404 is usually exercised by application of criminal law, international law also permits states to establish appropriate civil remedies, such as the tort actions authorized by the Alien Tort Act. . . .

Karadzic disputes the application of the law of nations to any violations committed by private individuals, relying on *Filartiga* and the concurring opinion of Judge Edwards in *Tel-Oren v. Libyan Arab Republic*, 726 F.2d 774, 775 (D.C. Cir. 1984), *cert. denied*, 470 U.S. 1003, 84 L. Ed. 2d 377, 105 S. Ct. 1354 (1985).[*] *Filartiga* involved an allegation of torture committed by a state

---

[3] Section 702 provides:

A state violates international law if, as a matter of state policy, it practices, encourages, or condones

(a) genocide,

(b) slavery or slave trade,

(c) the murder or causing the disappearance of individuals,

(d) torture or other cruel, inhuman, or degrading treatment or punishment,

(e) prolonged arbitrary detention,

(f) systematic racial discrimination, or

(g) a consistent pattern of gross violations of internationally recognized human rights.

[*] In *Tel-Oren*, the plaintiffs sought damages from Libya and the PLO for deaths and injuries resulting from an armed attack on a civilian bus in Israel. The district court's dismissal of the action for lack of subject-matter jurisdiction was affirmed on appeal. Libya was found to have sovereign immunity. With respect to the case against the PLO, each judge on the Court of Appeals expressed a different opinion. Judge Edwards concluded that customary international law (at least at the time) prohibited neither terrorism as such, nor murder or torture when perpetrated by non-state actors. Judge Bork took the position that the "law of nations" (as the term was understood in

official. Relying on the United Nations' Declaration on the Protection of All Persons from Being Subjected to Torture, G.A. Res. 3452 (1975), as a definitive statement of norms of customary international law prohibiting states from permitting torture, we ruled that "official torture is now prohibited by the law of nations." We had no occasion to consider whether international law violations other than torture are actionable against private individuals, and nothing in *Filartiga* purports to preclude such a result.

Nor did Judge Edwards in his scholarly opinion in *Tel-Oren* reject the application of international law to any private action. On the contrary, citing piracy and slave-trading as early examples, he observed that there exists a "handful of crimes to which the law of nations attributes individual responsibility." Reviewing authorities similar to those consulted in *Filartiga*, he merely concluded that torture – the specific violation alleged in *Tel-Oren* – was not within the limited category of violations that do not require state action.

Karadzic also contends that Congress intended the state-action requirement of the Torture Victim Act to apply to actions under the Alien Tort Act. We disagree. Congress enacted the Torture Victim Act to codify the cause of action recognized by this Circuit in *Filartiga*, and to further extend that cause of action to plaintiffs who are U.S. citizens. See H.R. Rep. No. 367, 102d Cong., 2d Sess., at 4 (1991) (explaining that codification of *Filartiga* was necessary in light of skepticism expressed by Judge Bork's concurring opinion in *Tel-Oren*). At the same time, Congress indicated that the Alien Tort Act "has other important uses and should not be replaced," because

> claims based on torture and summary executions do not exhaust the list of actions that may appropriately be covered [by the Alien Tort Act]. That statute should remain intact to permit suits based on other norms that already exist or may ripen in the future into rules of customary international law.

Id. The scope of the Alien Tort Act remains undiminished by enactment of the Torture Victim Act.

2. Specific Application of Alien Tort Act to Appellants' Claims. In order to determine whether the offenses alleged by the appellants in this litigation are violations of the law of nations that may be the subject of Alien Tort Act claims against a private individual, we must make a particularized examination of these offenses, mindful of the important precept that "evolving standards of international law govern who is within the [Alien Tort Act's] jurisdictional grant." In making that inquiry, it will be helpful to group the appellants' claims into three categories: (a) genocide, (b) war crimes, and (c) other instances of

---

1789) was fundamentally a law between states and that *Filartiga* was mistaken in reading the Alien Tort Act to provide a private cause of action for violations of new international norms which do not themselves contemplate private enforcement. Judge Robb concluded that the case presented a non-justiciable "political question." – Eds.

inflicting death, torture, and degrading treatment.

(a) Genocide. In the aftermath of the atrocities committed during the Second World War, the condemnation of genocide as contrary to international law quickly achieved broad acceptance by the community of nations. In 1946, the General Assembly of the United Nations declared that genocide is a crime under international law that is condemned by the civilized world, whether the perpetrators are "private individuals, public officials or statesmen." G.A. Res. 96(I) (1946). . . .

The Convention on the Prevention and Punishment of the Crime of Genocide, 78 U.N.T.S. 277, entered into force Jan. 12, 1951, for the United States Feb. 23, 1989, provides a more specific articulation of the prohibition of genocide in international law. The Convention, which has been ratified by more than 120 nations, including the United States, defines "genocide" to mean

> any of the following acts committed with intent to destroy, in whole or in part, a national, ethnical, racial or religious group, as such:
>
> (a) Killing members of the group;
>
> (b) Causing serious bodily or mental harm to members of the group;
>
> (c) Deliberately inflicting on the group conditions of life calculated to bring about its physical destruction in whole or in part;
>
> (d) Imposing measures intended to prevent births with the group;
>
> (e) Forcibly transferring children of the group to another group.

Convention on Genocide art. II. Especially pertinent to the pending appeal, the Convention makes clear that "persons committing genocide . . . shall be punished, whether they are constitutionally responsible rulers, public officials or private individuals." *Id.* art. IV. These authorities unambiguously reflect that, from its incorporation into international law, the proscription of genocide has applied equally to state and non-state actors.

The applicability of this norm to private individuals is also confirmed by the Genocide Convention Implementation Act of 1987, 18 U.S.C. § 1091 (1988), which criminalizes acts of genocide without regard to whether the offender is acting under color of law, *see id.* § 1091(a) ("whoever" commits genocide shall be punished), if the crime is committed within the United States or by a U.S. national, *id.* § 1091(d). Though Congress provided that the Genocide Convention Implementation Act shall not "be construed as creating any substantive or procedural right enforceable by law by any party in any proceeding," *id.* § 1092, the legislative decision not to create a new private remedy does not imply that a private remedy is not already available under the Alien Tort Act. Nothing in the Genocide Convention Implementation Act or its legislative history reveals an intent by Congress to repeal the Alien Tort Act insofar as it applies to genocide, and the two statutes are surely not repugnant to each other. Under these circumstances, it would be improper to construe the Genocide Convention Implementation Act as repealing the Alien Tort Act by implication. . . .

Appellants' allegations that Karadzic personally planned and ordered a campaign of murder, rape, forced impregnation, and other forms of torture designed to destroy the religious and ethnic groups of Bosnian Muslims and Bosnian Croats clearly state a violation of the international law norm proscribing genocide, regardless of whether Karadzic acted under color of law or as a private individual. The District Court has subject-matter jurisdiction over these claims pursuant to the Alien Tort Act.

(b) War crimes. Plaintiffs also contend that the acts of murder, rape, torture, and arbitrary detention of civilians, committed in the course of hostilities, violate the law of war. Atrocities of the types alleged here have long been recognized in international law as violations of the law of war. See *In re Yamashita,* 327 U.S. 1, 14, 90 L. Ed. 499, 66 S. Ct. 340 (1946). Moreover, international law imposes an affirmative duty on military commanders to take appropriate measures within their power to control troops under their command for the prevention of such atrocities. *Id.* at 15-16.

After the Second World War, the law of war was codified in the four Geneva Conventions, which have been ratified by more than 180 nations, including the United States. Common article 3, which is substantially identical in each of the four Conventions, applies to "armed conflicts not of an international character" and binds "each Party to the conflict . . . to apply, as a minimum, the following provisions":

Persons taking no active part in the hostilities . . . shall in all circumstances be treated humanely, without any adverse distinction founded on race, colour, religion or faith, sex, birth or wealth, or any other similar criteria.

To this end, the following acts are and shall remain prohibited at any time and in any place whatsoever with respect to the above-mentioned persons:

(a) violence to life and person, in particular murder of all kinds, mutilation, cruel treatment and torture;

(b) taking of hostages;

(c) outrages upon personal dignity, in particular humiliating and degrading treatment;

(d) the passing of sentences and carrying out of executions without previous judgment pronounced by a regularly constituted court . . . .

Geneva Convention I art. 3(1). Thus, under the law of war as codified in the Geneva Conventions, all "parties" to a conflict – which includes insurgent military groups – are obliged to adhere to these most fundamental requirements of the law of war.[8]

The offenses alleged by the appellants, if proved, would violate the most fundamental norms of the law of war embodied in common article 3, which binds parties to internal conflicts regardless of whether they are recognized nations or roving hordes of insurgents. The liability of private individuals for committing war crimes has been recognized since World War I and was confirmed at Nuremberg after World War II, and remains today an important aspect of international law. The District Court has jurisdiction pursuant to the Alien Tort Act over appellants' claims of war crimes and other violations of international humanitarian law.

(c) Torture and summary execution. In *Filartiga*, we held that official torture is prohibited by universally accepted norms of international law, and the Torture Victim Act confirms this holding and extends it to cover summary execution. However, torture and summary execution – when not perpetrated in the course of genocide or war crimes – are proscribed by international law only when committed by state officials or under color of law. . . .

In the present case, appellants allege that acts of rape, torture, and summary execution were committed during hostilities by troops under Karadzic's command and with the specific intent of destroying appellants' ethnic-religious groups. Thus, many of the alleged atrocities are already encompassed within the appellants' claims of genocide and war crimes. Of course, at this threshold stage in the proceedings it cannot be known whether appellants will be able to

---

[8] Appellants also maintain that the forces under Karadzic's command are bound by the Protocol Additional to the Geneva Conventions of 12 August 1949, Relating to the Protection of Victims of Non-International Armed Conflicts, 16 I.L.M. 1442 (1977) ("Protocol II"), which has been signed but not ratified by the United States. Protocol II supplements the fundamental requirements of common article 3 for armed conflicts that "take place in the territory of a High Contracting Party between its armed forces and dissident armed forces or other organized armed groups which, under responsible command, exercise such control over a part of its territory as to enable them to carry out sustained and concerted military operations and to implement this Protocol." Id. art. 1. In addition, plaintiffs argue that the forces under Karadzic's command are bound by the remaining provisions of the Geneva Conventions, which govern international conflicts, see Geneva Convention I art. 2, because the self-proclaimed Bosnian-Serb republic is a nation that is at war with Bosnia-Herzegovina or, alternatively, the Bosnian-Serbs are an insurgent group in a civil war who have attained the status of "belligerents," and to whom the rules governing international wars therefore apply.

At this stage in the proceedings, however, it is unnecessary for us to decide whether the requirements of Protocol II have ripened into universally accepted norms of international law, or whether the provisions of the Geneva Conventions applicable to international conflicts apply to the Bosnian-Serb forces on either theory advanced by plaintiffs.

prove the specific intent that is an element of genocide, or prove that each of the alleged torts were committed in the course of an armed conflict, as required to establish war crimes. It suffices to hold at this stage that the alleged atrocities are actionable under the Alien Tort Act, without regard to state action, to the extent that they were committed in pursuit of genocide or war crimes, and otherwise may be pursued against Karadzic to the extent that he is shown to be a state actor. . . .

3. The State Action Requirement for International Law Violations. In dismissing plaintiffs' complaints for lack of subject-matter jurisdiction, the District Court concluded that the alleged violations required state action and that the "Bosnian-Serb entity" headed by Karadzic does not meet the definition of a state. Appellants contend that they are entitled to prove that Srpska satisfies the definition of a state for purposes of international law violations and, alternatively, that Karadzic acted in concert with the recognized state of the former Yugoslavia and its constituent republic, Serbia.

(a) Definition of a state in international law. The definition of a state is well established in international law. . . . [I]t does not require recognition by other states. . . . The customary international law of human rights, such as the proscription of official torture, applies to states without distinction between recognized and unrecognized states. It would be anomalous indeed if non-recognition by the United States, which typically reflects disfavor with a foreign regime – sometimes due to human rights abuses – had the perverse effect of shielding officials of the unrecognized regime from liability for those violations of international law norms that apply only to state actors.

Appellants' allegations entitle them to prove that Karadzic's regime satisfies the criteria for a state, for purposes of those international law violations requiring state action. Srpska is alleged to control defined territory, control populations within its power, and to have entered into agreements with other governments. It has a president, a legislature, and its own currency. These circumstances readily appear to satisfy the criteria for a state in all aspects of international law. Moreover, it is likely that the state action concept, where applicable for some violations like "official" torture, requires merely the semblance of official authority. The inquiry, after all, is whether a person purporting to wield official power has exceeded internationally recognized standards of civilized conduct, not whether statehood in all its formal aspects exists.

(b) Acting in concert with a foreign state. Appellants also sufficiently alleged that Karadzic acted under color of law insofar as they claimed that he acted in concert with the former Yugoslavia, the statehood of which is not disputed. The "color of law" jurisprudence of 42 U.S.C. § 1983 is a relevant guide to whether a defendant has engaged in official action for purposes of jurisdiction under the Alien Tort Act. A private individual acts under color of law within the meaning of section 1983 when he acts together with state officials or with significant state aid. The appellants are entitled to prove their allegations that Karadzic acted under color of law of Yugoslavia by acting in concert with Yugoslav officials or with significant Yugoslavian aid.

B. The Torture Victim Protection Act

The Torture Victim Act, enacted in 1992, provides a cause of action for official torture and extrajudicial killing:

> An individual who, under actual or apparent authority, or color of law, of any foreign nation –
>
> (1) subjects an individual to torture shall, in a civil action, be liable for damages to that individual; or
>
> (2) subjects an individual to extrajudicial killing shall, in a civil action, be liable for damages to the individual's legal representative, or to any person who may be a claimant in an action for wrongful death.

Torture Victim Act § 2(a). The statute also requires that a plaintiff exhaust adequate and available local remedies, *id.* § 2(b), imposes a ten-year statute of limitations, id. § 2(c), and defines the terms "extrajudicial killing" and "torture," *id.* § 3.

By its plain language, the Torture Victim Act renders liable only those individuals who have committed torture or extrajudicial killing "under actual or apparent authority, or color of law, of any foreign nation." Legislative history confirms that this language was intended to "make clear that the plaintiff must establish some governmental involvement in the torture or killing to prove a claim," and that the statute "does not attempt to deal with torture or killing by purely private groups." H.R. Rep. No. 367, 102d Cong., 2d Sess., at 5 (1991). In construing the terms "actual or apparent authority" and "color of law," courts are instructed to look to principles of agency law and to jurisprudence under 42 U.S.C. § 1983, respectively. *Id.*

Though the Torture Victim Act creates a cause of action for official torture, this statute, unlike the Alien Tort Act, is not itself a jurisdictional statute. The Torture Victim Act permits the appellants to pursue their claims of official torture under the jurisdiction conferred by the Alien Tort Act and also under the general federal question jurisdiction of section 1331, to which we now turn.

C. Section 1331

The appellants contend that section 1331 provides an independent basis for subject-matter jurisdiction over all claims alleging violations of international law. Relying on the settled proposition that federal common law incorporates international law, they reason that causes of action for violations of international law "arise under" the laws of the United States for purposes of jurisdiction under section 1331. Whether that is so is an issue of some uncertainty that need not be decided in this case. . . . Since [the Alien Tort Act] appears to provide a remedy for the appellants' allegations of violations related to genocide, war crimes, and official torture, and the Torture Victim Act also appears to provide a remedy for their allegations of official torture, their causes of action are statutorily authorized, and . . . we need not rule definitively on whether any causes of action not specifically authorized by statute may be implied by international law standards as incorporated into United States law and grounded on section 1331 jurisdiction. . . .

The judgment of the District Court dismissing appellants' complaints for lack of subject-matter jurisdiction is reversed, and the cases are remanded for further proceedings in accordance with this opinion.

NOTES AND QUESTIONS

(1) Karadzic had no personal immunity, as a head of state, from suit in the United States because the entity of which he was president, the Republika Srpska, was not recognized as a state by the United States. Nor, although in New York an invitee of the United Nations, was he immune from service of process while not on U.N. premises. Following the Supreme Court's denial of certiorari in 1996, the two cases went back to the district court for pretrial proceedings. A year later, after he was ordered to appear in New York for his deposition, Karadzic stopped participating those proceedings. The district court ultimately entered a default judgment in plaintiffs' favor. On August 10, 2000, a jury awarded damages of $745 million. Since it is unclear how or whether any part of that amount will ever be collected, what was achieved by this judgment?

(2) The claims against Karadzic included allegations of genocide, war crimes, and torture. (He has been indicted by the International Criminal Tribunal for the former Yugoslavia for crimes against humanity as well.) Which of these claims requires proof that the conduct in question took place during an armed conflict? Does it have to be an international (as opposed to an internal) armed conflict? Which of these claims requires proof of "state action"? Does the court hold that torture, as the term is understood in international law, is capable of being committed by a non-state actor? What is the point of requiring a connection to official conduct in cases of torture? "Why should not any serious crime against human dignity, regardless of the actor or circumstances, create individual criminal accountability under international law?" Steven R. Ratner, *The Schizophrenias of International Criminal Law*, 33 TEX. INT'L L. J. 237, 253 (1998). Consider the reasons given by Judge Friendly in *IIT v. Vencap*, 519 F.2d 1001, 1015 (2d Cir. 1975), for rejecting an effort to bring an action for securities fraud under 28 U.S.C. § 1350 (the Alien Tort Claims Act), and whether these reasons adequately answer the question:

> The reference to the law of nations must be narrowly read if the section is to be kept within the confines of Article III. We cannot subscribe to plaintiffs' view that the Eighth Commandment "Thou shalt not steal" is

part of the law of nations. While every civilized nation doubtless has this as a part of its legal system, a violation of the law of nations arises only when there has been "a violation by one or more individuals of those standards, rules or customs (a) affecting the relationship between states or between an individual and a foreign state, and (b) used by those states for their common good and/or in dealings inter se."

(3) "The *Karadzic* cases were filed in the context of an international movement to force recognition of women's rights as human rights, and to include protections against violence against women within the international human rights framework." Beth Stephens & Jennifer Green, *Suing for Genocide in the United States: The Case of Jane Doe v. Radovan Karadzic, in* WAR CRIMES: THE LEGACY OF NUREMBERG 265, 268 (Belinda Cooper ed., 1999). One product of this movement has been the recognition that rape can constitute a form of torture or inhuman treatment. Since 1986, reports of the Special Rapporteur on Torture of the U.N. Commission on Human Rights have defined the rape of female prisoners while in detention or under interrogation as an act of torture. The characterization of rape and other gender-based violence as torture triggers a number of international legal consequences. These are detailed in the following case – the judgment of Trial Chamber II of the International Criminal Tribunal for the former Yugoslavia in *Prosecutor v. Furundzija.*

Another aspect of the movement to secure international recognition of women's rights has been the effort to define rape as a war crime. *See* Theodor Meron, *Rape as a Crime under International Humanitarian Law*, 87 AM. J. INT'L L. 424 (1993). Rape by soldiers has long been prohibited, at least in principle, by the laws of war. Although the Geneva Conventions of 1949 and the two Additional Protocols of 1977 prohibit rape during the course of armed conflict, it is not listed specifically as one of the "grave breaches" of those conventions over which states have "universal jurisdiction." However, "grave breaches" do include "wilful killing, torture or inhuman treatment" and "wilfully causing great suffering or serious injury to body or health." Thus, recognition of rape as a form of torture or inhuman treatment buttresses the conclusion, now widely accepted, that it also can be treated as a "grave breach" of the Geneva Conventions.

Rape figured prominently in the "ethnic cleansing" in Bosnia and in the genocide in Rwanda that led the U.N. Security Council to establish ad hoc international criminal tribunals for the former Yugoslavia and for Rwanda in 1993 and 1994 respectively. (Mass rape also figured in the campaign against supporters of President Aristide in Haiti; in 1995, the Inter-American Commission on Human Rights characterized these rapes as torture.) Rape and other forms of sexual violence have figured prominently as well in the jurisprudence of the two *ad hoc* tribunals. *See* Kelly D. Askin, *Sexual Violence in Decisions and Indictments of the Yugoslav and Rwandan Tribunals: Current Status*, 93 AM. J. INT'L L. 97 (1999). Cases decided by these tribunals hold that rape, under the requisite circumstances, may constitute a "grave breach" of the Geneva Conventions, a violation of the laws or customs of war, an act of genocide, or a "crime against humanity."

The statute establishing the International Criminal Tribunal for the former Yugoslavia (ICTY) gives it jurisdiction over genocide, crimes against humanity, and two categories of war crime: "grave breaches" of the Geneva Conventions of 1949 and "violations of the laws or customs of war." The statute establishing the International Criminal Tribunal for Rwanda (ICTR) gives it jurisdiction over genocide, crimes against humanity, and "serious violations" of either common article 3 of the Geneva Conventions or Additional Protocol II, both of which set out rules applicable in "armed conflicts not of an international character." In both statutes, rape is included among the enumerated acts that can constitute crimes against humanity. Otherwise, the ICTY statute does not mention rape. The ICTR statute, in specifying the kind of conduct that violates common article 3 of the Geneva Conventions or Additional Protocol II, includes "outrages upon personal dignity, in particular humiliating and degrading treatment, *rape, enforced prostitution and any form of indecent assault.*" (This language tracks art. 4(e) of Additional Protocol II; compare the language of common article 3 of the 1949 Conventions, quoted in *Karadzic, supra,* which does not include the words in italics.)

In *Prosecutor v. Akayesu,* Case No. ICTR-96-4-T, Judgement (Sept. 2, 1998), the Rwanda tribunal convicted the accused on various charges; these included charges of genocide and crimes against humanity stemming from sexual violence against Tutsi women who had taken refuge in the offices of the commune of which he was the chief administrator (*bourgmestre*). In concluding that, under the circumstances, rape and sexual violence constituted acts of genocide, the Trial Chamber observed (paras. 731-32):

> With regard, particularly, to . . . rape and sexual violence, the Chamber wishes to underscore the fact that in its opinion, they constitute genocide in the same way as any other act as long as they were committed with the specific intent to destroy, in whole or in part, a particular group, targeted as such. Indeed, rape and sexual violence certainly constitute infliction of serious bodily and mental harm on the victims and are even, according to the Chamber, one of the worst ways of inflict harm on the victim as he or she suffers both bodily and mental harm. In light of all the evidence before it, the Chamber is satisfied that the acts of rape and sexual violence described above, were committed solely against Tutsi women, many of whom were subjected to the worst public humiliation, mutilated, and raped several times, often in public, in the Bureau Communal premises or in other public places, and often by more than one assailant. These rapes resulted in physical and psychological destruction of Tutsi women, their families and their communities. Sexual violence was an integral part of the process of destruction, specifically targeting Tutsi women and specifically contributing to their destruction and to the destruction of the Tutsi group as a whole.

The rape of Tutsi women was systematic and was perpetrated against all Tutsi women and solely against them. . . . As part of the propaganda campaign geared to mobilizing the Hutu against the Tutsi, the Tutsi women were presented as sexual objects. . . . This sexualized representation of ethnic identity graphically illustrates that Tutsi women were subjected to sexual violence because they were Tutsi. Sexual violence was a step in the process of destruction of the Tutsi group – destruction of the spirit, of the will to live, and of life itself.

In *Prosecutor v. Delalic*, Case No. IT-96-21-T, Judgement (Nov. 16, 1998), three of the four defendants were convicted by the Yugoslav tribunal on various counts alleging the mistreatment of civilian detainees at the Celebici prison camp in central Bosnia in 1992. One defendant in particular, Hazim Delic, the deputy commander, was found to be a brutal sadist who, in addition to his other crimes, raped women in order to exert his power and instill absolute fear in them. In holding that rape could be torture and therefore a "grave breach" of the Geneva Conventions and a violation of the laws or customs of war, the Trial Chamber observed (paras. 476, 494-96):

There can be no doubt that rape and other forms of sexual assault are expressly prohibited under international humanitarian law. The terms of article 27 of the Fourth Geneva Convention specifically prohibit rape, any form of indecent assault and the enforced prostitution of women. A prohibition on rape, enforced prostitution and any form of indecent assault is further found in article 4(2) of Additional Protocol II, concerning internal armed conflicts. This Protocol also implicitly prohibits rape and sexual assault in article 4(1) which states that all persons are entitled to respect for their person and honour. Moreover, article 76(1) of Additional Protocol I expressly requires that women be protected from rape, forced prostitution and any other form of indecent assault. An implicit prohibition on rape and sexual assault can also be found in article 46 of the 1907 Hague Convention (IV) that provides for the protection of family honour and rights. Finally, rape is prohibited as a crime against humanity under article 6(c) of the Nürnberg Charter and expressed as such in Article 5 of the [ICTY] Statute. . . .

[T]he elements of torture, for the purposes of applying Articles 2 and 3 of the Statute, may be enumerated as follows: (i) There must be an act or omission that causes severe pain or suffering, whether mental or physical, (ii) which is inflicted intentionally, (iii) and for such purposes as obtaining information or a confession from the victim, or a third person, punishing the victim for an act he or she or a third person has committed or is suspected of having committed, intimidating or coercing the victim or a third person, or for any reason based on discrimination of any kind, (iv) and such act or omission being committed by, or at the instigation of, or with the consent or acquiescence of, an official or other person acting in an official capacity.

The Trial Chamber considers the rape of any person to be a despicable act which strikes at the very core of human dignity and physical integrity. The condemnation and punishment of rape becomes all the more urgent where it is committed by, or at the instigation of, a public official, or with the consent or acquiescence of such an official. Rape causes severe pain and suffering, both physical and psychological. The psychological suffering of persons upon whom rape is inflicted may be exacerbated by social and cultural conditions and can be particularly acute and long lasting. Furthermore, it is difficult to envisage circumstances in which rape, by, or at the instigation of a public official, or with the consent or acquiescence of an official, could be considered as occurring for a purpose that does not, in some way, involve punishment, coercion, discrimination or intimidation. In the view of this Trial Chamber this is inherent in situations of armed conflict.

Accordingly, whenever rape and other forms of sexual violence meet the aforementioned criteria, then they shall constitute torture, in the same manner as any other acts that meet this criteria.

The next case carries forward these conclusions.

PROSECUTOR v. FURUNDZIJA

International Criminal Tribunal for the former Yugoslavia
Case No. IT-95-17/1-T, Trial Chamber II, Judgement, Dec. 10, 1998

1. The International Tribunal is governed by its Statute, adopted by the Security Council of the United Nations on 25 May 1993, and by the Rules of Procedure and Evidence of the International Tribunal, adopted by the Judges of the International Tribunal on 11 February 1994, as amended. Under the Statute, the International Tribunal has the power to prosecute persons responsible for serious violations of international humanitarian law committed in the territory of the former Yugoslavia since 1991. Articles 2 through 5 of the Statute further confer upon the International Tribunal jurisdiction over grave breaches of the Geneva Conventions of 12 August 1949 (Article 2); violations of the laws or customs of war (Article 3); genocide (Article 4); and crimes against humanity (Article 5).

[The Trial Chamber found that the defendant, Anton Furundzija, was the commander of a special military police unit, "the Jokers," within the armed forces of the Croatian Community in Bosnia, which had declared itself an independent political entity. In May 1993, "Witness A," a Bosnian Moslem woman, was arrested by the Jokers and taken to their headquarters for interrogation. She was forced to undress and remain naked before a large number of soldiers while she was interrogated by the defendant. During the interrogation, another soldier (who was the commander of another unit) rubbed his knife against her thigh and lower stomach and threatened to put his knife inside her vagina if she did not tell the truth. The defendant then left her in the custody of this other soldier, who proceeded to rape her. Afterwards, the defendant continued to interrogate "Witness A" in another room, once more before an audience of soldiers. She was naked but covered by a small blanket. A friend of her family's, a Croatian male, was brought into the room and interrogated as well. The other soldier beat both of them on their feet with a baton. He repeatedly raped "Witness A," by the mouth, vagina, and anus, and forced her to lick his penis; the friend was made to watch in an effort to induce him to admit the allegations against her. The defendant was present or nearby throughout and did nothing to stop these acts. In fact, the tribunal found, they were performed in pursuance of the defendant's interrogation of the witnesses: as the interrogation intensified, so did the sexual assaults and rape.

The defendant was found guilty on two counts, one charging torture, the other charging "outrages on personal dignity including rape," both alleged to be in violation of the laws or customs of war referred to in Article 3 of the Tribunal's Statute. The defendant was sentenced to ten years' imprisonment – or, more precisely, to concurrent sentences of ten years on the first count and to eight years on the second count. His conviction and sentence subsequently were affirmed by the Tribunal's Appeals Chamber. *See Prosecutor v. Furundzija*, Case No. IT-95-17/1-A, Judgement (July 21, 2000).

The Trial Chamber's judgment contains the following observations on the law applicable to the charges of torture and rape.]

A. Article 3 of the Statute (Violations of the Laws or Customs of War)

131. Article 3 of the Statute of the International Tribunal provides as follows:

The International Tribunal shall have the power to prosecute persons violating the laws or customs of war. Such violations shall include, but not be limited to:

(a) employment of poisonous weapons or other weapons calculated to cause unnecessary suffering;

(b) wanton destruction of cities, towns or villages, or devastation not justified by military necessity;

(c) attack, or bombardment, by whatever means, of undefended towns, villages, dwellings, or buildings;

(d) seizure of, destruction or wilful damage done to institutions dedicated to religion, charity and education, the arts and sciences, historic monuments and works of art and science;

(e) plunder of public or private property.

132. As interpreted by the Appeals Chamber in the *Tadic Jurisdiction Decision*, Article 3 has a very broad scope. It covers any serious violation of a rule of customary international humanitarian law entailing, under international customary or conventional law, the individual criminal responsibility of the person breaching the rule. It is immaterial whether the breach occurs within the context of an international or internal armed conflict.

133. It follows that the list of offences contained in Article 3 is merely illustrative; according to the interpretation propounded by the Appeals Chamber, and as is clear from the text of Article 3, this provision also covers serious violations of international rules of humanitarian law not included in that list. In short, more than the other substantive provisions of the Statute, Article 3 constitutes an 'umbrella rule.' While the other provisions envisage classes of offences they indicate in terms, Article 3 makes an open-ended reference to all international rules of humanitarian law: pursuant to Article 3 serious violations of any international rule of humanitarian law may be regarded as crimes falling under this provision of the Statute, if the requisite conditions are met.

B. *Torture in International Law*

1. *International Humanitarian Law*

134. Torture in times of armed conflict is specifically prohibited by international treaty law, in particular by the Geneva Conventions of 1949 and the two Additional Protocols of 1977.

135. Under the Statute of the International Tribunal, as interpreted by the Appeals Chamber in the *Tadic Jurisdiction Decision*, these treaty provisions may be applied as such by the International Tribunal if it is proved that at the relevant time all the parties to the conflict were bound by them. *In casu*, Bosnia and Herzegovina ratified the Geneva Conventions of 1949 and both Additional Protocols of 1977 on 31 December 1992. Accordingly, at least common article 3 of the Geneva Conventions of 1949 and article 4 of Additional Protocol II, both of which explicitly prohibit torture, were applicable as minimum fundamental guarantees of treaty law in the territory of Bosnia and Herzegovina at the time relevant to the Indictment. In addition, in 1992, the parties to the conflict in Bosnia and Herzegovina undertook to observe the most important provisions of the Geneva Conventions, including those prohibiting torture. Thus undoubtedly the provisions concerning torture applied *qua* treaty law in the territory of Bosnia and Herzegovina as between the parties to the conflict.

136. The Trial Chamber also notes that torture was prohibited as a war crime under article 142 of the Penal Code of the Socialist Federal Republic of Yugoslavia (hereafter "SFRY"), and that the same violation has been made punishable in the Republic of Bosnia and Herzegovina by virtue of the decree-law of 11 April 1992.

137. The Trial Chamber does not need to determine whether the Geneva

Conventions and the Additional Protocols passed into customary law in their entirety, as was recently held by the Constitutional Court of Colombia, or whether, as seems more plausible, only the most important provisions of these treaties have acquired the status of general international law. In any case, the proposition is warranted that a general prohibition against torture has evolved in customary international law. . . . Torture was not specifically mentioned in the London Agreement of 8 August 1945 establishing the International Military Tribunal at Nuremberg, but it was one of the acts expressly classified as a crime against humanity under article II(1)(c) of Allied Control Council Law No. 10. As stated above, the Geneva Conventions of 1949 and the Protocols of 1977 prohibit torture in terms.

138. That these treaty provisions have ripened into customary rules is evinced by various factors. First, these treaties and in particular the Geneva Conventions have been ratified by practically all States of the world. Admittedly those treaty provisions remain as such and any contracting party is formally entitled to relieve itself of its obligations by denouncing the treaty (an occurrence that seems extremely unlikely in reality); nevertheless the practically universal participation in these treaties shows that all States accept among other things the prohibition of torture. In other words, this participation is highly indicative of the attitude of States to the prohibition of torture. Secondly, no State has ever claimed that it was authorised to practice torture in time of armed conflict, nor has any State shown or manifested opposition to the implementation of treaty provisions against torture. When a State has been taken to task because its officials allegedly resorted to torture, it has normally responded that the allegation was unfounded, thus expressly or implicitly upholding the prohibition of this odious practice. Thirdly, the International Court of Justice has authoritatively, albeit not with express reference to torture, confirmed this custom-creating process: in the *Nicaragua* case it held that common article 3 of the 1949 Geneva Conventions, which *inter alia* prohibits torture against persons taking no active part in hostilities, is now well-established as belonging to the corpus of customary international law and is applicable both to international and internal armed conflicts.

139. It therefore seems incontrovertible that torture in time of armed conflict is prohibited by a general rule of international law. In armed conflicts this rule may be applied both as part of international customary law and – if the requisite conditions are met – *qua* treaty law, the content of the prohibition being the same.

140. The treaty and customary rules referred to above impose obligations upon States and other entities in an armed conflict, but first and foremost address themselves to the acts of individuals, in particular to State officials or more generally, to officials of a party to the conflict or else to individuals acting at the instigation or with the consent or acquiescence of a party to the conflict. Both customary rules and treaty provisions applicable in times of armed conflict prohibit any act of torture. Those who engage in torture are personally accountable at the criminal level for such acts. As the International Military Tribunal at Nuremberg put it in general terms: "Crimes against international

law are committed by men, not by abstract entities, and only by punishing individuals who commit such crimes can the provisions of international law be enforced." Individuals are personally responsible, whatever their official position, even if they are heads of State or government ministers . . . .

141. It should be stressed that in international humanitarian law, depending upon the specific circumstances of each case, torture may be prosecuted as a category of such broad international crimes as serious violations of humanitarian law, grave breaches of the Geneva Conventions, crimes against humanity or genocide. . . .

2. International Human Rights Law

143. The prohibition of torture laid down in international humanitarian law with regard to situations of armed conflict is reinforced by the body of international treaty rules on human rights: these rules ban torture both in armed conflict and in time of peace. In addition, treaties as well as resolutions of international organisations set up mechanisms designed to ensure that the prohibition is implemented and to prevent resort to torture as much as possible.

144. It should be noted that the prohibition of torture laid down in human rights treaties enshrines an absolute right, which can never be derogated from, not even in time of emergency (on this ground the prohibition also applies to situations of armed conflicts). This is linked to the fact, discussed below, that the prohibition on torture is a peremptory norm or *jus cogens*. This prohibition is so extensive that States are even barred by international law from expelling, returning or extraditing a person to another State where there are substantial grounds for believing that the person would be in danger of being subjected to torture.

145. These treaty provisions impose upon States the obligation to prohibit and punish torture, as well as to refrain from engaging in torture through their officials. In international human rights law, which deals with State responsibility rather than individual criminal responsibility, torture is prohibited as a criminal offence to be punished under national law; in addition, all States parties to the relevant treaties have been granted, and are obliged to exercise, jurisdiction to investigate, prosecute and punish offenders. Thus, in human rights law too, the prohibition of torture extends to and has a direct bearing on the criminal liability of individuals.

146. The existence of this corpus of general and treaty rules proscribing torture shows that the international community, aware of the importance of outlawing this heinous phenomenon, has decided to suppress any manifestation of torture by operating both at the interstate level and at the level of individuals. No legal loopholes have been left.

3. Main Features of the Prohibition Against Torture in International Law

147. There exists today universal revulsion against torture: as a USA Court

put it in *Filartiga v. Pena-Irala*, "the torturer has become, like the pirate and the slave trader before him, *hostis humani generis*, an enemy of all mankind." This revulsion, as well as the importance States attach to the eradication of torture, has led to the cluster of treaty and customary rules on torture acquiring a particularly high status in the international normative system, a status similar to that of principles such as those prohibiting genocide, slavery, racial discrimination, aggression, the acquisition of territory by force and the forcible suppression of the right of peoples to self-determination. The prohibition against torture exhibits three important features, which are probably held in common with the other general principles protecting fundamental human rights.

(a) The Prohibition Even Covers Potential Breaches

148. Firstly, given the importance that the international community attaches to the protection of individuals from torture, the prohibition against torture is particularly stringent and sweeping. . . . As was authoritatively held by the European Court of Human Rights in *Soering* [*see* chap. 16], international law intends to bar not only actual breaches but also potential breaches of the prohibition against torture (as well as any inhuman and degrading treatment). It follows that international rules prohibit not only torture but also (i) the failure to adopt the national measures necessary for implementing the prohibition and (ii) the maintenance in force or passage of laws which are contrary to the prohibition. . . .

(b) The Prohibition Imposes Obligations Erga Omnes

151. Furthermore, the prohibition of torture imposes upon States obligations *erga omnes*, that is, obligations owed towards all the other members of the international community, each of which then has a correlative right. In addition, the violation of such an obligation simultaneously constitutes a breach of the correlative right of all members of the international community and gives rise to a claim for compliance accruing to each and every member, which then has the right to insist on fulfilment of the obligation or in any case to call for the breach to be discontinued.

152. Where there exist international bodies charged with impartially monitoring compliance with treaty provisions on torture, these bodies enjoy priority over individual States in establishing whether a certain State has taken all the necessary measures to prevent and punish torture and, if they have not, in calling upon that State to fulfil its international obligations. The existence of such international mechanisms makes it possible for compliance with international law to be ensured in a neutral and impartial manner.

(c) The Prohibition Has Acquired the Status of Jus Cogens

153. While the *erga omnes* nature just mentioned appertains to the area of international enforcement (*lato sensu*), the other major feature of the principle proscribing torture relates to the hierarchy of rules in the international

normative order. Because of the importance of the values it protects, this principle has evolved into a peremptory norm or *jus cogens*, that is, a norm that enjoys a higher rank in the international hierarchy than treaty law and even "ordinary" customary rules. The most conspicuous consequence of this higher rank is that the principle at issue cannot be derogated from by States through international treaties or local or special customs or even general customary rules not endowed with the same normative force.

154. Clearly, the *jus cogens* nature of the prohibition against torture articulates the notion that the prohibition has now become one of the most fundamental standards of the international community. Furthermore, this prohibition is designed to produce a deterrent effect, in that it signals to all members of the international community and the individuals over whom they wield authority that the prohibition of torture is an absolute value from which nobody must deviate.

155. The fact that torture is prohibited by a peremptory norm of international law has other effects at the inter-state and individual levels. At the inter-state level, it serves to internationally de-legitimise any legislative, administrative or judicial act authorising torture. It would be senseless to argue, on the one hand, that on account of the *jus cogens* value of the prohibition against torture, treaties or customary rules providing for torture would be null and void *ab initio*, and then be unmindful of a State say, taking national measures authorising or condoning torture or absolving its perpetrators through an amnesty law. If such a situation were to arise, the national measures, violating the general principle and any relevant treaty provision, would produce the legal effects discussed above and in addition would not be accorded international legal recognition. Proceedings could be instituted by potential victims if they had *locus standi* before a competent international or national judicial body with a view to asking it to hold the national measure to be internationally unlawful; or the victim could bring a civil suit for damage in a foreign court, which would therefore be asked *inter alia* to disregard the legal value of the national authorising act. What is even more important is that perpetrators of torture acting upon or benefiting from those national measures may nevertheless be held criminally responsible for torture, whether in a foreign State, or in their own State under a subsequent regime. In short, in spite of possible national authorisation by legislative or judicial bodies to violate the principle banning torture, individuals remain bound to comply with that principle. As the International Military Tribunal at Nuremberg put it: "individuals have international duties which transcend the national obligations of obedience imposed by the individual State."

156. Furthermore, at the individual level, that is, that of criminal liability, it would seem that one of the consequences of the *jus cogens* character bestowed by the international community upon the prohibition of torture is that every State is entitled to investigate, prosecute and punish or extradite individuals accused of torture, who are present in a territory under its jurisdiction. Indeed, it would be inconsistent on the one hand to prohibit torture to such an extent as to restrict the normally unfettered treaty-making power of sovereign States,

and on the other hand bar States from prosecuting and punishing those torturers who have engaged in this odious practice abroad. This legal basis for States' universal jurisdiction over torture bears out and strengthens the legal foundation for such jurisdiction found by other courts in the inherently universal character of the crime. It has been held that international crimes being universally condemned wherever they occur, every State has the right to prosecute and punish the authors of such crimes. As stated in general terms by the Supreme Court of Israel in *Eichmann*, and echoed by a USA court in *Demjanjuk* [*see* chap. 18], "it is the universal character of the crimes in question *i.e.* international crimes which vests in every State the authority to try and punish those who participated in their commission."

157. It would seem that other consequences include the fact that torture may not be covered by a statute of limitations, and must not be excluded from extradition under any political offence exemption.

4. *Torture Under Article 3 of the Statute*

158. Torture is not specifically prohibited under Article 3 of the Statute. As noted in paragraph 133 of this Judgement, Article 3 constitutes an 'umbrella rule,' which makes an open-ended reference to all international rules of humanitarian law. In its "Decision On The Defendant's Motion To Dismiss Counts 13 and 14 of The Indictment (Lack Of Subject Matter Jurisdiction)" issued on 29 May 1998, the Trial Chamber held that Article 3 of the Statute covers torture and outrages upon personal dignity including rape, and that the Trial Chamber has jurisdiction over alleged violations of Article 3 of the Statute.

5. *The Definition of Torture*

159. International humanitarian law, while outlawing torture in armed conflict, does not provide a definition of the prohibition. Such a definition can instead be found in article 1(1) of the 1984 Torture Convention [*supra*] . . . .

160. This definition was regarded by Trial Chamber I of ICTR, in *Prosecutor v. Jean-Paul Akayesu*, as *sic et simpliciter* applying to any rule of international law on torture, including the relevant provisions of the ICTR Statute. However, attention should be drawn to the fact that article 1 of the Convention explicitly provides that the definition contained therein is "for the purposes of this Convention." It thus seems to limit the purport and contents of that definition to the Convention solely. An extra-conventional effect may however be produced to the extent that the definition at issue codifies, or contributes to developing or crystallising customary international law. Trial Chamber II of the International Tribunal has rightly noted in *Delalic* that indeed the definition of torture contained in the 1984 Torture Convention is broader than, and includes, that laid down in the 1975 Declaration of the United Nations General Assembly and in the 1985 Inter-American Convention, and has hence concluded that that definition "thus reflects a consensus which the Trial Chamber considers to be representative of customary international law." This Trial Chamber shares such conclusion, although on legal grounds that it shall briefly set out. First of

all, there is no gainsaying that the definition laid down in the Torture Convention, although deliberately limited to the Convention, must be regarded as authoritative, *inter alia*, because it spells out all the necessary elements implicit in international rules on the matter. Secondly, this definition to a very large extent coincides with that contained in the United Nations Declaration on Torture of 9 December 1975. It should be noted that this Declaration was adopted by the General Assembly by consensus. This fact shows that no member State of the United Nations had any objection to such definition. In other words, all the members of the United Nations concurred in and supported that definition. Thirdly, a substantially similar definition can be found in the Inter-American Convention. Fourthly, the same definition has been applied by the United Nations Special Rapporteur and is in line with the definition suggested or acted upon by such international bodies as the European Court of Human Rights and the Human Rights Committee.

161. The broad convergence of the aforementioned international instruments and international jurisprudence demonstrates that there is now general acceptance of the main elements contained in the definition set out in article 1 of the Torture Convention.

162. The Trial Chamber considers however that while the definition referred to above applies to any instance of torture, whether in time of peace or of armed conflict, it is appropriate to identify or spell out some specific elements that pertain to torture as considered from the specific viewpoint of international criminal law relating to armed conflicts. The Trial Chamber considers that the elements of torture in an armed conflict require that torture:

(i) consists of the infliction, by act or omission, of severe pain or suffering, whether physical or mental; in addition

(ii) this act or omission must be intentional;

(iii) it must aim at obtaining information or a confession, or at punishing, intimidating, humiliating or coercing the victim or a third person, or at discriminating, on any ground, against the victim or a third person;

(iv) it must be linked to an armed conflict;

(v) at least one of the persons involved in the torture process must be a public official or must at any rate act in a non-private capacity, *e.g.* as a de facto organ of a State or any other authority- wielding entity.

As is apparent from this enumeration of criteria, the Trial Chamber considers that among the possible purposes of torture one must also include that of humiliating the victim. This proposition is warranted by the general spirit of international humanitarian law: the primary purpose of this body of law is to safeguard human dignity. The proposition is also supported by some general provisions of such important international treaties as the Geneva Conventions and Additional Protocols, which consistently aim at protecting persons not taking part, or no longer taking part, in the hostilities from "outrages upon personal dignity." The notion of humiliation is, in any event close to the notion of intimidation, which is explicitly referred to in the Torture Convention's definition of torture.

163. As evidenced by international case law, the reports of the United Nations Human Rights Committee and the United Nations Committee Against Torture, those of the Special Rapporteur, and the public statements of the European Committee for the Prevention of Torture, this vicious and ignominious practice can take on various forms. International case law, and the reports of the United Nations Special Rapporteur evince a momentum towards addressing, through legal process, the use of rape in the course of detention and interrogation as a means of torture and, therefore, as a violation of international law. Rape is resorted to either by the interrogator himself or by other persons associated with the interrogation of a detainee, as a means of punishing, intimidating, coercing or humiliating the victim, or obtaining information, or a confession, from the victim or a third person. In human rights law, in such situations the rape may amount to torture, as demonstrated by the finding of the European Court of Human Rights in *Aydin* and the Inter-American Court of Human Rights in *Meijia*.

164. Depending upon the circumstances, under international criminal law rape may acquire the status of a crime distinct from torture; this will be covered in the following section of the Judgement.

C. Rape and Other Serious Sexual Assaults in International Law

1. International Humanitarian Law

165. Rape in time of war is specifically prohibited by treaty law: the Geneva Conventions of 1949, Additional Protocol I of 1977 and Additional Protocol II of 1977. Other serious sexual assaults are expressly or implicitly prohibited in various provisions of the same treaties.

166. At least common article 3 to the Geneva Conventions of 1949, which implicitly refers to rape, and article 4 of Additional Protocol II, which explicitly mentions rape, apply *qua* treaty law in the case in hand because Bosnia and Herzegovina ratified the Geneva Conventions and both Additional Protocols on 31 December 1992. Furthermore, as stated in paragraph 135 above, on 22 May 1992, the parties to the conflict undertook to observe the most important provisions of the Geneva Conventions and to grant the protections afforded therein.

167. In addition, the Trial Chamber notes that rape and inhuman treatment were prohibited as war crimes by article 142 of the Penal Code of the SFRY and that Bosnia and Herzegovina, as a former Republic of that federal State, continues to apply an analogous provision.

168. The prohibition of rape and serious sexual assault in armed conflict has also evolved in customary international law. . . . While rape and sexual assaults were not specifically prosecuted by the Nuremberg Tribunal, rape was expressly classified as a crime against humanity under article II(1)(c) of Control Council Law No. 10. The Tokyo International Military Tribunal convicted Generals Toyoda and Matsui of command responsibility for violations of the laws or customs of war committed by their soldiers in Nanking, which included widespread rapes and sexual assaults. The former Foreign Minister of Japan, Hirota, was also convicted for these atrocities. This decision and that of the United States Military Commission in *Yamashita*, along with the ripening of the fundamental prohibition of "outrages upon personal dignity" laid down in common article 3 into customary international law, has contributed to the evolution of universally accepted norms of international law prohibiting rape as well as serious sexual assault. These norms are applicable in any armed conflict.

169. It is indisputable that rape and other serious sexual assaults in armed conflict entail the criminal liability of the perpetrators.

2. *International Human Rights Law*

170. No international human rights instrument specifically prohibits rape or other serious sexual assaults. Nevertheless, these offences are implicitly prohibited by the provisions safeguarding physical integrity, which are contained in all of the relevant international treaties. The right to physical integrity is a fundamental one, and is undeniably part of customary international law.

171. In certain circumstances, however, rape can amount to torture and has been found by international judicial bodies to constitute a violation of the norm prohibiting torture, as stated above in paragraph 163.

3. *Rape Under the Statute*

172. The prosecution of rape is explicitly provided for in Article 5 of the Statute of the International Tribunal as a crime against humanity. Rape may also amount to a grave breach of the Geneva Conventions, a violation of the laws or customs of war or an act of genocide, if the requisite elements are met, and may be prosecuted accordingly.

173. The all-embracing nature of Article 3 of the Statute has already been discussed in paragraph 133 of this Judgement. In its "Decision on the Defendant's Motion to Dismiss Counts 13 and 14 of the Indictment (Lack of Subject- Matter Jurisdiction)" of 29 May 1998, the Trial Chamber held that Article 3 of the Statute covers outrages upon personal dignity including rape.

4. *The Definition of Rape*

174. The Trial Chamber notes the unchallenged submission of the

Prosecution in its Pre-trial Brief that rape is a forcible act: this means that the act is "accomplished by force or threats of force against the victim or a third person, such threats being express or implied and must place the victim in reasonable fear that he, she or a third person will be subjected to violence, detention, duress or psychological oppression." This act is the penetration of the vagina, the anus or mouth by the penis, or of the vagina or anus by other object. In this context, it includes penetration, however slight, of the vulva, anus or oral cavity, by the penis and sexual penetration of the vulva or anus is not limited to the penis.

175. No definition of rape can be found in international law. However, some general indications can be discerned from the provisions of international treaties. In particular, attention must be drawn to the fact that there is prohibition of both rape and "any form of indecent assault" on women in article 27 of Geneva Convention IV, article 76(1) of Additional Protocol I and article 4(2)(e) of Additional Protocol II. The inference is warranted that international law, by specifically prohibiting rape as well as, in general terms, other forms of sexual abuse, regards rape as the most serious manifestation of sexual assault. This is, *inter alia*, confirmed by Article 5 of the International Tribunal's Statute, which explicitly provides for the prosecution of rape while it implicitly covers other less grave forms of serious sexual assault through Article 5(i) as "other inhuman acts."

176. Trial Chamber I of the ICTR has held in *Akayesu* that to formulate a definition of rape in international law one should start from the assumption that "the central elements of the crime of rape cannot be captured in a mechanical description of objects or body parts." According to that Trial Chamber, in international law it is more useful to focus "on the conceptual framework of State sanctioned violence." It then went on to state the following:

Like torture, rape is used for such purposes as intimidation, degradation, humiliation, discrimination, punishment, control or destruction of a person. Like torture, rape is a violation of personal dignity, and rape in fact constitutes torture when inflicted by or at the instigation of or with the consent or acquiescence of a public official or others person acting in an official capacity. The Chamber defines rape as a physical invasion of a sexual nature, committed on a person under circumstances which are coercive.

This definition has been upheld by Trial Chamber II *quater* of the International Tribunal in *Delalic*.

177. This Trial Chamber notes that no elements other than those emphasised may be drawn from international treaty or customary law, nor is resort to general principles of international criminal law or to general principles of international law of any avail. The Trial Chamber therefore considers that, to arrive at an accurate definition of rape based on the criminal law principle of specificity (*Bestimmtheitgrundsatz*, also referred to by the maxim *nullum crimen sine lege stricta*), it is necessary to look for principles of criminal law common to the major legal systems of the world. These principles may be

derived, with all due caution, from national laws.

178. Whenever international criminal rules do not define a notion of criminal law, reliance upon national legislation is justified, subject to the following conditions: (i) unless indicated by an international rule, reference should not be made to one national legal system only, say that of common-law or that of civil-law States. Rather, international courts must draw upon the general concepts and legal institutions common to all the major legal systems of the world. This presupposes a process of identification of the common denominators in these legal systems so as to pinpoint the basic notions they share; (ii) since "international trials exhibit a number of features that differentiate them from national criminal proceedings," account must be taken of the specificity of international criminal proceedings when utilising national law notions. In this way a mechanical importation or transposition from national law into international criminal proceedings is avoided, as well as the attendant distortions of the unique traits of such proceedings.

179. The Trial Chamber would emphasise at the outset, that a trend can be discerned in the national legislation of a number of States of broadening the definition of rape so that it now embraces acts that were previously classified as comparatively less serious offences, that is sexual or indecent assault. This trend shows that at the national level States tend to take a stricter attitude towards serious forms of sexual assault: the stigma of rape now attaches to a growing category of sexual offences, provided of course they meet certain requirements, chiefly that of forced physical penetration.

180. In its examination of national laws on rape, the Trial Chamber has found that although the laws of many countries specify that rape can only be committed against a woman, others provide that rape can be committed against a victim of either sex. The laws of several jurisdictions state that the actus reus of rape consists of the penetration, however slight, of the female sexual organ by the male sexual organ. There are also jurisdictions which interpret the *actus reus* of rape broadly. The provisions of civil law jurisdictions often use wording open for interpretation by the courts. Furthermore, all jurisdictions surveyed by the Trial Chamber require an element of force, coercion, threat, or acting without the consent of the victim: force is given a broad interpretation and includes rendering the victim helpless. Some jurisdictions indicate that the force or intimidation can be directed at a third person. Aggravating factors commonly include causing the death of the victim, the fact that there were multiple perpetrators, the young age of the victim, and the fact that the victim suffers a condition, which renders him/her especially vulnerable such as mental illness. Rape is almost always punishable with a maximum of life imprisonment, but the terms that are imposed by various jurisdictions vary widely.

181. It is apparent from our survey of national legislation that, in spite of inevitable discrepancies, most legal systems in the common and civil law worlds consider rape to be the forcible sexual penetration of the human body by the penis or the forcible insertion of any other object into either the vagina or the

anus.

182. A major discrepancy may, however, be discerned in the criminalisation of forced oral penetration: some States treat it as sexual assault, while it is categorised as rape in other States. Faced with this lack of uniformity, it falls to the Trial Chamber to establish whether an appropriate solution can be reached by resorting to the general principles of international criminal law or, if such principles are of no avail, to the general principles of international law.

183. The Trial Chamber holds that the forced penetration of the mouth by the male sexual organ constitutes a most humiliating and degrading attack upon human dignity. The essence of the whole corpus of international humanitarian law as well as human rights law lies in the protection of the human dignity of every person, whatever his or her gender. The general principle of respect for human dignity is the basic underpinning and indeed the very *raison d'être* of international humanitarian law and human rights law; indeed in modern times it has become of such paramount importance as to permeate the whole body of international law. This principle is intended to shield human beings from outrages upon their personal dignity, whether such outrages are carried out by unlawfully attacking the body or by humiliating and debasing the honour, the self-respect or the mental well being of a person. It is consonant with this principle that such an extremely serious sexual outrage as forced oral penetration should be classified as rape.

184. Moreover, the Trial Chamber is of the opinion that it is not contrary to the general principle of *nullum crimen sine lege* to charge an accused with forcible oral sex as rape when in some national jurisdictions, including his own, he could only be charged with sexual assault in respect of the same acts. It is not a question of criminalising acts which were not criminal when they were committed by the accused, since forcible oral sex is in any event a crime, and indeed an extremely serious crime. Indeed, due to the nature of the International Tribunal's subject-matter jurisdiction, in prosecutions before the Tribunal forced oral sex is invariably an aggravated sexual assault as it is committed in time of armed conflict on defenceless civilians; hence it is not simple sexual assault but sexual assault as a war crime or crime against humanity. Therefore so long as an accused, who is convicted of rape for acts of forcible oral penetration, is sentenced on the factual basis of coercive oral sex – and sentenced in accordance with the sentencing practice in the former Yugoslavia for such crimes, pursuant to Article 24 of the Statute and Rule 101 of the Rules – then he is not adversely affected by the categorisation of forced oral sex as rape rather than as sexual assault. His only complaint can be that a greater stigma attaches to being a convicted rapist rather than a convicted sexual assailant. However, one should bear in mind the remarks above to the effect that forced oral sex can be just as humiliating and traumatic for a victim as vaginal or anal penetration. Thus the notion that a greater stigma attaches to a conviction for forcible vaginal or anal penetration than to a conviction for forcible oral penetration is a product of questionable attitudes. Moreover any such concern is amply outweighed by the fundamental principle of protecting human dignity, a principle which favours broadening the definition of rape.

185. Thus, the Trial Chamber finds that the following may be accepted as the objective elements of rape:

(i) the sexual penetration, however slight:

(a) of the vagina or anus of the victim by the penis of the perpetrator or any other object used by the perpetrator; or

(b) of the mouth of the victim by the penis of the perpetrator;

(ii) by coercion or force or threat of force against the victim or a third person.

186. As pointed out above, international criminal rules punish not only rape but also any serious sexual assault falling short of actual penetration. It would seem that the prohibition embraces all serious abuses of a sexual nature inflicted upon the physical and moral integrity of a person by means of coercion, threat of force or intimidation in a way that is degrading and humiliating for the victim's dignity.　As both these categories of acts are criminalised in international law, the distinction between them is one that is primarily material for the purposes of sentencing.

Part 3
PROCEDURE

Chapter 10
EXTRATERRITORIAL APPLICATION OF U.S. CONSTITUTION

§ 10.01 Introduction

With increased globalization, questions arise as to whether the U.S. Constitution applies extraterritorially. Does it apply to criminal investigations being conducted outside the United States? Does it apply when other countries seek United States assistance with their investigations? Does the U.S. Constitution only afford rights to citizens of the United States? What happens when the laws of another country conflict with U.S. law? These, and other questions, serve as the focus of this chapter.

In years past, the United States maintained consular courts in certain countries that were thought to have sub-standard legal systems. *See* Geoffrey R. Watson, *Offenders Abroad: The Case for Nationality-Based Criminal Jurisdiction*, 17 YALE J. INT'L L. 41, 49-52 (1992). These courts exercised criminal jurisdiction over U.S. citizens accused of committing crimes in those countries. These courts did not provide a right to a grand jury indictment or jury trial, but did offer the right to confrontation and right to counsel. *See* Michael Abbell & Mark Andrew Sherman, *The Bill of Rights In Transnational Criminal Litigation*, 41 THE CHAMPION 22 (Sept./Oct. 1992). Consular courts do not exist today. Often considered to be "a form of legal imperialism," "consular jurisdiction died slowly." *See* Watson, *supra* at 50, 52.

Following World War II, with large numbers of U.S. military personnel stationed abroad, the question of jurisdiction over their criminal activities became acute. A series of U.S. Supreme Court decisions held that U.S. military courts could not constitutionally try civilian dependants accompanying the armed forces overseas because those courts do not offer trial by jury and other procedures guaranteed by the Bill of Rights. *See, e.g., Reid v. Covert*, 354 U.S. 1 (1957). Since the U.S. has not established general nationality-based jurisdiction, this left civilians to be tried by foreign courts for crimes committed abroad.[*]

---

[*] It has been argued that a jurisdictional gap exists regarding the ability of the United States to try civilians who accompany the military overseas and commit crimes on a U.S. military installation. *See* United States v. Gatlin, 216 F.3d 207 (2d Cir. 2000).

Status of Forces Agreements negotiated with NATO and other countries where U.S. troops are stationed allocate criminal jurisdiction as between the United States and the host country. *See* JOSEPH M. SNEE & KENNETH A, PYE, STATUS OF FORCES AGREEMENT: CRIMINAL JURISDICTION (1957). Article 7(9) of the NATO Status of Forces Agreement provides:

> Whenever a member of a force or civilian component of a dependent is prosecuted under the jurisdiction of a receiving State he shall be entitled:
>
> a. to a prompt and speedy trial;
>
> b. to be informed, in advance of trial, of the specific charge or charges made against him;
>
> c. to be confronted with the witnesses against him;
>
> d. to have compulsory process for obtaining witnesses in his favour, if they are within the jurisdiction of the receiving State;
>
> e. to have legal representation of his own choice for his defence or to have free or assisted legal representation under the conditions prevailing for the time being in the receiving State;
>
> f. if he considers it necessary, to have the services of a competent interpreter; and
>
> g. to communicate with a representative of the Government of the sending State and when the rules of the court permit, to have such a representative present at his trial.

NATO Status of Forces Agreement, June 19, 1951, 4 U.S.T. 1792, T.I.A.S. No. 2846, 199 U.N.T.S. 67. There is an obvious effort here to assure certain minimal procedural guarantees when individuals face charges in foreign courts.*

H.R. 3380 proposes a Military Extraterritorial Jurisdiction Act that would provide federal jurisdiction "over offenses committed outside the United States by persons employed by or accompanying the Armed Forces, or by members of the Armed Forces who are released or separated from active duty prior to being identified and prosecuted for the commission of such offenses." – Eds.

* The U.S. Senate's consent to ratification of the Status of Forces Agreement was coupled with a resolution expressing "the sense of the Senate" that (1) where a commanding officer finds there is danger that an accused who is to be tried in a foreign court "will not be protected because of the absence or denial of constitutional rights he would enjoy in the United States, the commanding officer shall request the authorities of the receiving state to waive jurisdiction . . ."; and that (2) a U.S. military observer should attend any trial held in a receiving state under the agreement and report "any

Compare this provision with Article 14 of the International Covenant on Civil and Political Rights [*see* chap. 16].

Questions regarding the extraterritorial application of the Bill of Rights have been presented in several different contexts. *See generally* Bruce Zagaris, *U.S. International Cooperation Against Transnational Organized Crime*, 44 WAYNE L. REV. 1401, 1447-63 (1998). Questions about whether the U.S. government could agree to trial of U.S. citizens before an international court that does not provide all the procedural protections guaranteed by the Bill of Rights have been offered as an objection to U.S. participation in the International Criminal Court [*see* chap. 20].

§ 10.02 Fourth Amendment

UNITED STATES v. VERDUGO-URQUIDEZ

Supreme Court of the United States
494 U.S. 259, 110 S. Ct. 1056, 108 L. Ed. 2d 222 (1990)

CHIEF JUSTICE REHNQUIST delivered the opinion of the Court.

The question presented by this case is whether the Fourth Amendment applies to the search and seizure by United States agents of property that is owned by a nonresident alien and located in a foreign country. We hold that it does not.

Respondent Rene Martin Verdugo-Urquidez is a citizen and resident of Mexico. He is believed by the United States Drug Enforcement Agency (DEA) to be one of the leaders of a large and violent organization in Mexico that smuggles narcotics into the United States. Based on a complaint charging respondent with various narcotics-related offenses, the Government obtained a warrant for his arrest on August 3, 1985. In January 1986, Mexican police officers, after discussions with United States marshals, apprehended Verdugo-Urquidez in Mexico and transported him to the United States Border Patrol station in Calexico, California. There, United States marshals arrested

---

failure to comply with the provisions" of Article 7(9), 4 U.S.T. at 1828-29. To be on the safe side, the armed forces have adopted a policy of seeking waivers of foreign jurisdiction whenever possible. At least in capital cases, however, this policy has run up against European reluctance on human rights grounds to cede jurisdiction in cases in which defendants face charges punishable by death under U.S. law. *See* Steven J. Lepper, *Short v. The Kingdom of the Netherlands: Is it Time to Renegotiate the NATO Status of Forces Agreement?*, 24 VAND. J. TRANSNAT'L L. 867 (1991). [*See also* chap. 16, *infra.*] – Eds.

respondent and eventually moved him to a correctional center in San Diego, California, where he remains incarcerated pending trial.

Following respondent's arrest, Terry Bowen, a DEA agent assigned to the Calexico DEA office, decided to arrange for searches of Verdugo-Urquidez's Mexican residences located in Mexicali and San Felipe. Bowen believed that the searches would reveal evidence related to respondent's alleged narcotics trafficking activities and his involvement in the kidnaping and torture-murder of DEA Special Agent Enrique Camarena Salazar (for which respondent subsequently has been convicted in a separate prosecution) . . . . Bowen telephoned Walter White, the Assistant Special Agent in charge of the DEA office in Mexico City, and asked him to seek authorization for the search from the Director General of the Mexican Federal Judicial Police (MFJP). After several attempts to reach high ranking Mexican officials, White eventually contacted the Director General, who authorized the searches and promised the cooperation of Mexican authorities. Thereafter, DEA agents working in concert with officers of the MFJP searched respondent's properties in Mexicali and San Felipe and seized certain documents. In particular, the search of the Mexicali residence uncovered a tally sheet, which the Government believes reflects the quantities of marijuana smuggled by Verdugo-Urquidez into the United States.

The District Court granted respondent's motion to suppress evidence seized during the searches, concluding that the Fourth Amendment applied to the searches and that the DEA agents had failed to justify searching respondent's premises without a warrant. A divided panel of the Court of Appeals for the Ninth Circuit affirmed. 856 F.2d 1214 (1988). It cited this Court's decision in *Reid v. Covert,* 354 U.S. 1 (1957), which held that American citizens tried by United States military authorities in a foreign country were entitled to the protections of the Fifth and Sixth Amendments, and concluded that "The Constitution imposes substantive constraints on the federal government, even when it operates abroad.". . . Relying on our decision in *INS v. Lopez-Mendoza,* 468 U.S. 1032 (1984), where a majority of Justices assumed that illegal aliens in the United States have Fourth Amendment rights, the Ninth Circuit majority found it "difficult to conclude that Verdugo-Urquidez lacks these same protections.". . . It also observed that persons in respondent's position enjoy certain trial-related rights, and reasoned that "it would be odd indeed to acknowledge that Verdugo-Urquidez is entitled to due process under the fifth amendment, and to a fair trial under the sixth amendment, . . . and deny him the protection from unreasonable searches and seizures afforded under the fourth amendment.". . . Having concluded that the Fourth Amendment applied to the searches of respondent's properties, the court went on to decide that the searches violated the Constitution because the DEA agents failed to procure a search warrant. Although recognizing that "an American search warrant would be of no legal validity in Mexico," the majority deemed it sufficient that a warrant would have "substantial constitutional value in this country," because it would reflect a magistrate's determination that there existed probable cause to search and would define the scope of the search. . .

The dissenting judge argued that this Court's statement in *United States v. Curtiss-Wright Export Corp.,* 299 U.S. 304, 318 (1936), that "neither the Constitution nor the laws passed in pursuance of it have any force in foreign territory unless in respect of our own citizens," foreclosed any claim by respondent to Fourth Amendment rights. More broadly, he viewed the Constitution as a "compact" among the people of the United States, and the protections of the Fourth Amendment were expressly limited to "the people." We granted certiorari. . . .

Before analyzing the scope of the Fourth Amendment, we think it significant to note that it operates in a different manner than the Fifth Amendment, which is not at issue in this case. The privilege against self-incrimination guaranteed by the Fifth Amendment is a fundamental trial right of criminal defendants. . . . Although conduct by law enforcement officials prior to trial may ultimately impair that right, a constitutional violation occurs only at trial. . . . The Fourth Amendment functions differently. It prohibits "unreasonable searches and seizures" whether or not the evidence is sought to be used in a criminal trial, and a violation of the Amendment is "fully accomplished" at the time of an unreasonable governmental intrusion. . . . For purposes of this case, therefore, if there were a constitutional violation, it occurred solely in Mexico. Whether evidence obtained from respondent's Mexican residences should be excluded at trial in the United States is a remedial question separate from the existence *vel non* of the constitutional violation. . . .

The Fourth Amendment provides:

"The right of the people to be secure in their persons, houses, papers, and effects, against unreasonable searches and seizures, shall not be violated, and no Warrants shall issue, but upon probable cause, supported by Oath or affirmation, and particularly describing the place to be searched, and the persons or things to be seized."

That text, by contrast with the Fifth and Sixth Amendments, extends its reach only to "the people." Contrary to the suggestion of *amici curiae* that the Framers used this phrase "simply to avoid [an] awkward rhetorical redundancy, ... "the people" seems to have been a term of art employed in select parts of the Constitution. The Preamble declares that the Constitution is ordained and established by "the People of the United States." The Second Amendment protects "the right of the people to keep and bear Arms," and the Ninth and Tenth Amendments provide that certain rights and powers are retained by and reserved to "the people." *See also* U.S. Const., Amdt. 1 ("Congress shall make no law . . . abridging . . . *the right of the people* peaceably to assemble") (emphasis added); Art. I, § 2, cl. 1 ("The House of Representatives shall be composed of Members chosen every second Year *by the People of the several States*") (emphasis added). While this textual exegesis is by no means conclusive, it suggests that "the people" protected by the Fourth Amendment, and by the First and Second Amendments, and to whom rights and powers are reserved in the Ninth and Tenth Amendments, refers to a class of persons who are part of a national community or who have otherwise developed sufficient connection with this country to be considered part of that community. . . . The language of these Amendments contrasts with the words "person" and "accused" used in the Fifth and Sixth Amendments regulating procedure in criminal cases.

What we know of the history of the drafting of the Fourth Amendment also suggests that its purpose was to restrict searches and seizures which might be conducted by the United States in domestic matters. The Framers originally decided not to include a provision like the Fourth Amendment, because they believed the National Government lacked power to conduct searches and seizures. . . . Many disputed the original view that the Federal Government possessed only narrow delegated powers over domestic affairs, however, and ultimately felt an Amendment prohibiting unreasonable searches and seizures was necessary. Madison, for example, argued that "there is a clause granting to Congress the power to make all laws which shall be necessary and proper for carrying into execution all of the powers vested in the Government of the United States," and that general warrants might be considered "necessary" for the purpose of collecting revenue. . . . The driving force behind the adoption of the Amendment, as suggested by Madison's advocacy, was widespread hostility among the former colonists to the issuance of writs of assistance empowering revenue officers to search suspected places for smuggled goods, and general search warrants permitting the search of private houses, often to uncover papers that might be used to convict persons of libel. . . . The available historical data show, therefore, that the purpose of the Fourth Amendment was to protect the people of the United States against arbitrary action by their own Government; it was never suggested that the provision was intended to restrain the actions of the Federal Government against aliens outside of the United States territory.

There is likewise no indication that the Fourth Amendment was understood by contemporaries of the Framers to apply to activities of the United States directed against aliens in foreign territory or in international waters. . . . The global view taken by the Court of Appeals of the application of the Constitution is also contrary to this Court's decisions in the *Insular Cases*, which held that not every constitutional provision applies to governmental activity even where the United States has sovereign power. . . . Indeed, we have rejected the claim that aliens are entitled to Fifth Amendment rights outside the sovereign territory of the United States. . . .

To support his all-encompassing view of the Fourth Amendment, respondent points to language from the plurality opinion in *Reid v. Covert*, 354 U.S. 1 (1957). *Reid* involved an attempt by Congress to subject the wives of American servicemen to trial by military tribunals without the protection of the Fifth and Sixth Amendments. The Court held that it was unconstitutional to apply the Uniform Code of Military Justice to the trials of the American women for capital crimes. Four Justices "rejected the idea that when the United States acts *against citizens* abroad it can do so free of the Bill of Rights." . . . (emphasis added). The plurality went on to say:

"The United States is entirely a creature of the Constitution. Its power and authority have no other source. It can only act in accordance with all the limitations imposed by the Constitution. When the Government reaches out to punish *a citizen* who is abroad, the shield which the Bill of Rights and other parts of the Constitution provide to protect his life and liberty should not be stripped away just because he happens to be in another land." . . .

Respondent urges that we interpret this discussion to mean that federal officials are constrained by the Fourth Amendment wherever and against whomever they act. But the holding of *Reid* stands for no such sweeping proposition: it decided that United States citizens stationed abroad could invoke the protection of the Fifth and Sixth Amendments. The concurring opinions by Justices Frankfurter and Harlan in *Reid* resolved the case on much narrower grounds than the plurality and declined even to hold that United States citizens were entitled to the full range of constitutional protections in all overseas criminal prosecutions. . . . Since respondent is not a United States citizen, he can derive no comfort from the *Reid* holding.

Verdugo-Urquidez also relies on a series of cases in which we have held that aliens enjoy certain constitutional rights. . . . These cases, however, establish only that aliens receive constitutional protections when they have come within the territory of the United States and developed substantial connections with the country. . . . Respondent is an alien who has had no previous significant voluntary connection with the United States, so these cases avail him not.

Justice Stevens' concurrence in the judgment takes the view that even though the search took place in Mexico, it is nonetheless governed by the requirements of the Fourth Amendment because respondent was "lawfully present in the United States . . . even though he was brought and held here against his will." . . . But this sort of presence – lawful but involuntary – is not of the sort to indicate any substantial connection with our country. The extent to which respondent might claim the protection of the Fourth Amendment if the duration of his stay in the United States were to be prolonged – by a prison sentence, for example – we need not decide. When the search of his house in Mexico took place, he had been present in the United States for only a matter of days. We do not think the applicability of the Fourth Amendment to the search of premises in Mexico should turn on the fortuitous circumstance of whether the custodian of its nonresident alien owner had or had not transported him to the United States at the time the search was made.

The Court of Appeals found some support for its holding in our decision in *INS v. Lopez-Mendoza,* 468 U.S. 1032 (1984), where a majority of Justices assumed that the Fourth Amendment applied to illegal aliens in the United States. We cannot fault the Court of Appeals for placing some reliance on the case, but our decision did not expressly address the proposition gleaned by the court below. The question presented for decision in *Lopez-Mendoza* was limited to whether the Fourth Amendment's exclusionary rule should be extended to civil deportation proceedings; it did not encompass whether the protections of the Fourth Amendment extend to illegal aliens in this country. . . .

Respondent also contends that to treat aliens differently from citizens with respect to the Fourth Amendment somehow violates the equal protection component of the Fifth Amendment to the United States Constitution. . . . Not only are history and case law against respondent, but as pointed out in *Johnson v. Eisentrager,* 393 U.S. 763 (1950), the result of accepting his claim would have significant and deleterious consequences for the United States in conducting activities beyond its boundaries. The rule adopted by the Court of Appeals would apply not only to law enforcement operations abroad, but also to other foreign policy operations which might result in "searches or seizures." The United States frequently employs armed forces outside this country – over 200 times in our history – for the protection of American citizens or national security. . . . Application of the Fourth Amendment to those circumstances could significantly disrupt the ability of the political branches to respond to foreign situations involving our national interest. Were respondent to prevail, aliens with no attachment to this country might well bring actions for damages to remedy claimed violations of the Fourth Amendment in foreign countries or in international waters. . . .

We think that the text of the Fourth Amendment, its history, and our cases discussing the application of the Constitution to aliens and extraterritorially require rejection of respondent's claim. At the time of the search, he was a citizen and resident of Mexico with no voluntary attachment to the United States, and the place searched was located in Mexico. Under these circumstances, the Fourth Amendment has no application.

For better or for worse, we live in a world of nation-states in which our Government must be able to "function effectively in the company of sovereign nations." . . . Some who violate our laws may live outside our borders under a regime quite different from that which obtains in this country. Situations threatening to important American interests may arise halfway around the globe, situations which in the view of the political branches of our Government require an American response with armed force. If there are to be restrictions on searches and seizures which occur incident to such American action, they must be imposed by the political branches through diplomatic understanding, treaty, or legislation.

The judgment of the Court of Appeals is accordingly Reversed.

JUSTICE KENNEDY, concurring.

I agree that no violation of the Fourth Amendment has occurred and that we must reverse the judgment of the Court of Appeals. Although some explanation of my views is appropriate given the difficulties of this case, I do not believe they depart in fundamental respects from the opinion of the Court, which I join.

In cases involving the extraterritorial application of the Constitution, we have taken care to state whether the person claiming its protection is a citizen, ... or an alien. . . . The distinction between citizens and aliens follows from the undoubted proposition that the Constitution does not create, nor do general principles of law create, any juridical relation between our country and some undefined, limitless class of noncitizens who are beyond our territory. We should note, however, that the absence of this relation does not depend on the idea that only a limited class of persons ratified the instrument that formed our Government. Though it must be beyond dispute that persons outside the United States did not and could not assent to the Constitution, that is quite irrelevant to any construction of the powers conferred or the limitations imposed by it. . . .

For somewhat similar reasons, I cannot place any weight on the reference to "the people" in the Fourth Amendment as a source of restricting its protections. With respect, I submit these words do not detract from its force or its reach. Given the history of our Nation's concern over warrantless and unreasonable searches, explicit recognition of "the right of the people" to Fourth Amendment protection may be interpreted to underscore the importance of the right, rather than to restrict the category of persons who may assert it. The restrictions that the United States must observe with reference to aliens beyond its territory or jurisdiction depend, as a consequence, on general principles of interpretation, not on an inquiry as to who formed the Constitution or a construction that some rights are mentioned as being those of "the people."

I take it to be correct, as the plurality opinion in *Reid* v. *Covert* sets forth, that the Government may act only as the Constitution authorizes, whether the actions in question are foreign or domestic. . . . But this principle is only a first step in resolving this case. The question before us then becomes what constitutional standards apply when the Government acts, in reference to an alien, within its sphere of foreign operations. . . .

The conditions and considerations of this case would make adherence to the Fourth Amendment's warrant requirement impracticable and anomalous. Just as the Constitution in the *Insular Cases* did not require Congress to implement all constitutional guarantees in its territories because of their "wholly dissimilar traditions and institutions," the Constitution does not require United States agents to obtain a warrant when searching the foreign home of a nonresident alien. If the search had occurred in a residence within the United States, I have little doubt that the full protections of the Fourth Amendment would apply. But that is not this case. The absence of local judges or magistrates available to issue warrants, the differing and perhaps unascertainable conceptions of reasonableness and privacy that prevail abroad, and the need to cooperate with foreign officials all indicate that the Fourth Amendment's warrant requirement should not apply in Mexico as it does in this country. For this reason, in addition to the other persuasive justifications stated by the Court, I agree that no violation of the Fourth Amendment has occurred in the case before us. The rights of a citizen, as to whom the United States has continuing obligations, are not presented by this case.

I do not mean to imply, and the Court has not decided, that persons in the position of the respondent have no constitutional protection. The United States is prosecuting a foreign national in a court established under Article III, and all of the trial proceedings are governed by the Constitution. All would agree, for instance, that the dictates of the Due Process Clause of the Fifth Amendment protect the defendant. . . . Nothing approaching a violation of due process has occurred in this case.

JUSTICE STEVENS, concurring in the judgment.

In my opinion aliens who are lawfully present in the United States are among those "people" who are entitled to the protection of the Bill of Rights, including the Fourth Amendment. Respondent is surely such a person even though he was brought and held here against his will. I therefore cannot join the Court's sweeping opinion. I do agree, however, with the Government's submission that the search conducted by the United States agents with the approval and cooperation of the Mexican authorities was not "unreasonable" as that term is used in the first Clause of the Amendment. I do not believe the Warrant Clause has any application to searches of noncitizens' homes in foreign jurisdictions because American magistrates have no power to authorize such searches. I therefore concur in the Court's judgment. . . .

JUSTICE BRENNAN, with whom JUSTICE MARSHALL, dissenting.

Today the Court holds that although foreign nationals must abide by our laws even when in their own countries, our Government need not abide by the Fourth Amendment when it investigates them for violations of our laws. I respectfully dissent. . . .

Particularly in the past decade, our Government has sought, successfully, to hold foreign nationals criminally liable under federal laws for conduct committed entirely beyond the territorial limits of the United States that nevertheless has effects in this country. Foreign nationals must now take care not to violate our drug laws, our antitrust laws, our securities laws, and a host of other federal criminal statutes. The enormous expansion of federal criminal jurisdiction outside our Nation's boundaries has led one commentator to suggest that our country's three largest exports are now "rock music, blue jeans, and United States law." . . .

The Constitution is the source of Congress' authority to criminalize conduct, whether here or abroad, and of the Executive's authority to investigate and prosecute such conduct. But the same Constitution also prescribes limits on our Government's authority to investigate, prosecute, and punish criminal conduct, whether foreign or domestic. . . .

What the majority ignores, however, is the most obvious connection between Verdugo-Urquidez and the United States: he was investigated and is being prosecuted for violations of United States law and may well spend the rest of his life in a United States prison. The "sufficient connection" is supplied not by Verdugo-Urquidez, but by the Government. Respondent is entitled to the protections of the Fourth Amendment because our Government, by investigating him and attempting to hold him accountable under United States criminal laws, has treated him as a member of our community for purposes of enforcing our laws. He has become, quite literally, one of the governed. Fundamental fairness and the ideals underlying our Bill of Rights compel the conclusion that when we impose "societal obligations," . . . such as the obligation to comply with our criminal laws, on foreign nationals, we in turn are obliged to respect certain correlative rights, among them the Fourth Amendment.

By concluding that respondent is not one of "the people" protected by the Fourth Amendment, the majority disregards basic notions of mutuality. If we expect aliens to obey our laws, aliens should be able to expect that we will obey our Constitution when we investigate, prosecute, and punish them. We have recognized this fundamental principle of mutuality since the time of the Framers. . . .

Mutuality is essential to ensure the fundamental fairness that underlies our Bill of Rights. Foreign nationals investigated and prosecuted for alleged violations of United States criminal laws are just as vulnerable to oppressive Government behavior as are United States citizens investigated and prosecuted for the same alleged violations. Indeed, in a case such as this where the Government claims the existence of an international criminal conspiracy, citizens and foreign nationals may be codefendants, charged under the same statutes for the same conduct and facing the same penalties if convicted. They may have been investigated by the same agents pursuant to the same enforcement authority. When our Government holds these codefendants to the same standards of conduct, the Fourth Amendment, which protects the citizen from unreasonable searches and seizures, should protect the foreign national as well.

Mutuality also serves to inculcate the values of law and order. By respecting the rights of foreign nationals, we encourage other nations to respect the rights of our citizens. Moreover, as our Nation becomes increasingly concerned about the domestic effects of international crime, we cannot forget that the behavior of our law enforcement agents abroad sends a powerful message about the rule of law to individuals everywhere. . . . This principle is no different when the United States applies its rules of conduct to foreign nationals. If we seek respect for law and order, we must observe these principles ourselves. Lawlessness breeds lawlessness.

Finally, when United States agents conduct unreasonable searches, whether at home or abroad, they disregard our Nation's values. For over 200 years, our country has considered itself the world's foremost protector of liberties. The privacy and sanctity of the home have been primary tenets of our moral, philosophical, and judicial beliefs. Our national interest is defined by those values and by the need to preserve our own just institutions. We take pride in our commitment to a Government that cannot, on mere whim, break down doors and invade the most personal of places. We exhort other nations to follow our example. How can we explain to others – and to ourselves – that these long cherished ideals are suddenly of no consequence when the door being broken belongs to a foreigner?

The majority today brushes aside the principles of mutuality and fundamental fairness that are central to our Nation's constitutional conscience. The Court articulates a "sufficient connection" test but then refuses to discuss the underlying principles upon which any interpretation of that test must rest. I believe that by placing respondent among those governed by federal criminal laws and investigating him for violations of those laws, the Government has made him a part of our community for purposes of the Fourth Amendment. . .

In its effort to establish that respondent does not have sufficient connection to the United States to be considered one of "the people" protected by the Fourth Amendment, the Court relies on the text of the Amendment, historical evidence, and cases refusing to apply certain constitutional provisions outside the United States. None of these, however, justifies the majority's cramped interpretation of the Fourth Amendment's applicability.

The majority looks to various constitutional provisions and suggests that " 'the people' seems to have been a term of art." But the majority admits that its "textual exegesis is by no means conclusive." One member of the majority even states that he "cannot place any weight on the reference to 'the people' in the Fourth Amendment as a source of restricting its protections." The majority suggests a restrictive interpretation of those with "sufficient connection" to this country to be considered among "the people," but the term "the people" is better understood as a rhetorical counterpoint to "the Government," such that rights that were reserved to the "the people" were to protect all those subject to "the Government." . . .

In drafting both the Constitution and the Bill of Rights, the Framers strove to create a form of Government decidely different from their British heritage. Whereas the British Parliament was uncontrained, the Framers intended to create a Government of limited powers. . . .

The majority's rejection of respondent's claim to Fourth Amendment protection is apparently motivated by its fear that application of the Amendment to law enforcement searches against foreign nationals overseas "could significantly disrupt the ability of the political branches to respond to foreign situations involving our national interest." . . . The majority's doomsday scenario – that American Armed Forces conducting a mission to protect our national security with no law enforcement objective "would have to articulate specific facts giving them probable cause to undertake a search or seizure" . . . – is fanciful. Verdugo-Urquidez is protected by the Fourth Amendment because our Government, by investigating and prosecuting him, has made him one of "the governed." . . . Accepting respondent as one of "the governed," however, hardly requires the Court to accept enemy aliens in wartime as among "the governed" entitled to invoke the protection of the Fourth Amendment. . . .

Moreover, with respect to non-law-enforcement activities not directed against enemy aliens in wartime but nevertheless implicating national security, doctrinal exceptions to the general requirements of a warrant and probable cause likely would be applicable more frequently abroad, thus lessening the purported tension between the Fourth Amendment's strictures and the Executive's foreign affairs power. Many situations involving sensitive operations abroad likely would involve exigent circumstances such that the warrant requirement would be excused. . . . Therefore, the Government's conduct would be assessed only under the reasonableness standard, the application of which depends on context. . . .

Because the Fourth Amendment governs the search of respondent's Mexican residences, the District Court suppressed the evidence found in that search because the officers conducting the search did not obtain a warrant. . . . The Warrant Clause would serve the same primary functions abroad as it does domestically, and I see no reason to distinguish between foreign and domestic searches. . . .

The Warrant Clause cannot be ignored simply because Congress has not given any United States magistrate authority to issue search warrants for foreign searches. . . . Congress cannot define the contours of the Constitution. If the Warrant Clause applies, Congress cannot excise the Clause from the Constitution by failing to provide a means for United States agents to obtain a warrant. . . .

Nor is the Warrant Clause inapplicable merely because a warrant from a United States magistrate could not "authorize" a search in a foreign country. Although this may be true as a matter of international law, it is irrelevant to our interpretation of the Fourth Amendment. As a matter of United States constitutional law, a warrant serves the same primary function overseas as it does domestically; it assures that a neutral magistrate has authorized the search and limited its scope. The need to protect those suspected of criminal activity from the unbridled discretion of investigation offciers is no less important abroad than at home. . . .

When we tell the world that we expect all people, wherever they may be, to abide by our laws, we cannot in the same breath tell the world that our law enforcement officers need not do the same. Because we cannot expect others to respect our laws until we respect our Constitution, I respectfully dissent.

JUSTICE BLACKMUN, dissenting.

I cannot accept the Court of Appeals' conclusion, echoed in some portions of JUSTICE BRENNAN'S dissent, the Fourth Amendment governs every action by an

American official that can be characterized as a search or seizure. American agents acting abroad generally do not purport to exercise sovereign authority over the foreign nationals with whom they come in contact. The relationship between these agents and foreign nationals is therefore fundamentally different from the relationship between United States officials and individuals residing within this country.

I am inclined to agree with JUSTICE BRENNAN, however, that when a foreign national is held accountable for purported violations of United States criminal laws, he has effectively been treated as one of "the governed" and therefore is entitled to Fourth Amendment protections. Although the Government's exercise of power abroad does not ordinarily implicate the Fourth Amendment, the enforcement of domestic criminal law seems to me to be the paradigmatic exercise of sovereignty over those who are compelled to obey. . . . Under these circumstances I believe that respondent is entitled to invoke protections of the Fourth Amendment. I agree with the Government, however, that an American magistrate's lack of power to authorize a search abroad renders the Warrant Clause inapplicable to the search of a noncitizen's residence outside this country. . . . The Fourth Amendment nevertheless requires that the search be "reasonable." And when the purpose of a search is the procurement of evidence for a criminal prosecution, we have consistently held that the search, to be reasonable, must be based upon probable cause. Neither the District Court not the Court of Appeals addressed the issue of probable cause, and I do not believe that a reliable determination could be made on the basis of the record before us. I therefore would vacate the judgment of the Court of Appeals and remand the case for further proceedings.

NOTES AND QUESTIONS

(1) What does *Verdugo-Urquidez* imply about Fourth Amendment rights of U.S. citizens abroad? Does the case apply to aliens within the United States? To what extent do excludable aliens in the United States have Fourth Amendment rights? Consider the court's ruling in *Theck v. Warden, Immigration and Naturalization Service*, 22 F. Supp.2d 1117 (C.D. Cal. 1998):

On August 19, 1997, petitioner Park Theck filed the instant habeas corpus petition challenging his ongoing detention by the Immigration and Naturalization Service ("INS"). The plaintiff claims that INS has violated (1) international law, (2) the Constitution and (3) its own rules by detaining him for over six months after a final deportation order was entered. Furthermore, petitioner claims that the INS has violated his civil rights by preventing him from marrying his girlfriend, Susana Gonzalez, a Spanish citizen, Petition, at 5, and his property rights by repeatedly searching his suitcase, which has now disappeared. . . .

The immigration laws create two types of proceedings in which aliens can be denied the hospitality of the United States: deportation and exclusion hearings. . . . Deportation refers to the removal from the country of aliens who already are physically in the United States, and exclusion refers to keeping undesirable aliens from entering the United States. Since petitioner was detained while seeking admission into the United States, he is considered an   excludable alien. . . .

Petitioner claims, inter alia, that the INS has violated his constitutional rights by refusing to allow him to marry his girlfriend Susana Gonzalez, a Spanish citizen. Petitioner also claims that, by violating his constitutional right to marry, the INS also has violated his Fourth Amendment right to be free from unreasonable seizures. Here, it appears that petitioner's current detention is justified only because the INS has yet to find another country who will take him. Petitioner argues that if he is allowed to marry Ms. Gonzalez, as is his constitutional right, he would be deportable to Spain. Petitioner's continuing detention becomes an unreasonable seizure, therefore, when he is unconstitutionally denied the ability to change his status in such a way that would free him from detention.

It is undisputed that the petitioner is an excludable alien who, by virtue of the "entry fiction," is not considered to have been admitted into the United States. This legal fiction, however, generally is applied only in connection with immigration and deportation proceedings and "does not limit the right of excludable aliens detained within United States territory to humane treatment." . . . Although it is "clear that excludable aliens have no procedural due process rights in the admission process, the law is not settled with regard to nonprocedural rights." . . The courts have recognized that excludable aliens are entitled to some constitutional protections. *See Plyler v. Doe,* 457 U.S. 202, 211-12, 102 S. Ct. 2382, 2391-92, 72 L. Ed. 2d 786 (1982) (the Fifth, Sixth, and Fourteenth Amendments apply to all persons within the United States, including excludable aliens); *Wong Wing v. United States,* 163 U.S. 228, 238, 16 S. Ct. 977, 41 L. Ed. 140 (1896) (Fifth, Sixth and Fourteenth Amendments apply to all within the boundaries of a state, including aliens); *Lynch v. Cannatella,* 810 F.2d 1363, 1370 (5th Cir. 1987) (excludable aliens are entitled to certain Fifth and Fourteenth Amendment protections); *Jean v. Nelson,* 727 F.2d 957, 972 (11th Cir. 1984) (en banc) (although excludable aliens cannot challenge either admission or parole decisions under a claim of constitutional right, certain substantive constitutional rights may exist and have been recognized in other contexts); *United States v. Henry,* 604 F.2d 908, 914 (5th Cir. 1979) (excludable aliens entitled to Fifth Amendment protections). As a general matter, persons within the jurisdiction of the United States should be considered to be protected by the Constitution, unless it has been expressly held otherwise. Here, petitioner is not challenging either admission or parole decisions, but rather is asserting his fundamental right to marry and his right to be free from unreasonable seizures. Given the lack of case law holding otherwise, the court finds that plaintiff does enjoy these constitutional rights. . . . The INS has offered no legitimate penological reason why petitioner should not be allowed to exercise his constitutional right to marry. Absent such a showing, the INS cannot refuse to allow petitioner to marry. . . .

Petitioner has been in custody intermittently since he attempted to enter this country on November 19, 1994 and continuously since October 13, 1995, when he returned from South Korea after being refused entry there. The INS has attempted to obtain permission to deport petitioner either to China or South Korea, but neither of these countries, nor presumably any other country, will admit him. Petitioner, therefore, remains in custody and could end up serving what amounts to a life term if he is never determined to be deportable to another country.

Petitioner's continuing incarceration is justified only because he is not admissible to the United States and because there is nowhere else to send him. It is only when there is a lack of other alternatives that such incarceration could be reasonable. If, however, the petitioner was deportable, the INS would have to deport him, absent some other overriding interest.

Petitioner alleges that if he is permitted to marry Ms. Gonzalez, a Spanish citizen, he will be deportable to Spain and the INS would have no continuing right to detain him. If these allegations are true, when petitioner is denied the right to marry, he is also denied the ability to be freed from his present detention. Denying petitioner the right to marry, in these circumstances, results in an unreasonable seizure under the Fourth Amendment.

The courts generally have assumed, without explicitly holding, that illegal aliens possess Fourth Amendment rights. . . . In *United States v. Verdugo-Urquidez,* . . . the Supreme Court held that the Fourth Amendment did not apply to a search by United States agents in Mexico of a Mexican citizen's property. The holding in *Verdugo* is limited to extraterritorial searches and seizures. . . . *Verdugo* does not apply here, where the extraterritorial application of the Fourth Amendment is not at issue.

If the court does not grant relief to petitioner, he faces what could amount to a life prison sentence. Although such detention of an excludable alien has been held to be reasonable when there are no other alternatives, it becomes unreasonable when, as here, there is another alternative. If, as petitioner alleges, marriage to Ms. Gonzalez would enable him to be deported to Spain and, therefore, to be freed from detention, then the refusal to allow petitioner to marry results in an unreasonable seizure under the Fourth Amendment. . . . Absent a legitimate penological interest to the contrary, the petitioner has a right to make himself deportable, in order to prevent him from being incarcerated indefinitely. A fortiori, petitioner must be allowed to exercise his constitutional right to marry. . . .

(2) Do United States citizens, who happen to be outside the country, have Fourth Amendment rights? "[T]he Fourth Amendment does not restrict actions of foreign law enforcement officers acting outside the United States." Thus, "evidence secured by a foreign officer, if turned over to an American court, may be admitted against the victim of the search." JOSHUA DRESSLER, UNDERSTANDING CRIMINAL PROCEDURE 2d § 5.04(E) (1996). Two exceptions have developed to this general premise. In *United States v. Barona*, 56 F.3d 1087 (9th Cir. 1995), the court stated:

> . . . . When determining the validity of a foreign wiretap, we start with two general and undisputed propositions. The first is that Title III of the Omnibus Crime Control and Safe Streets Act of 1968, 18 U.S.C. §§ 2510-21, "has no extraterritorial force." . . . Our analysis, then, is guided only by the applicable principles of constitutional law. The second proposition is that "neither our Fourth Amendment nor the judicially created exclusionary rule applies to acts of foreign officials."
> . . .
>
> Two "very limited exceptions" apply. . . . One exception, clearly inapplicable here, occurs "if the circumstances of the foreign search and seizure are so extreme that they 'shock the [judicial] conscience,' [so that] a federal appellate court in the exercise of its supervisory powers can require exclusion of the evidence." . . . This type of exclusion is not based on our Fourth Amendment jurisprudence, but rather on the recognition that we may employ our supervisory powers when absolutely necessary to preserve the integrity of the criminal justice system. . . .
>
> The second exception to the inapplicability of the exclusionary rule applies when "United States agents' participation in the investigation is so substantial that the action is a joint venture between United States and foreign officials." . . . If a joint venture is found to have existed, "the law of the foreign country must be consulted at the outset as part of the determination whether or not the search was reasonable." If foreign law was not complied with, "the good faith exception to the exclusionary rule becomes part of the analysis." "The good faith exception is grounded in the realization that the exclusionary rule does not function as a deterrent in cases in which the law enforcement officers acted on a reasonable belief that their conduct was legal." . . .

Id. at 1090-93. In *United States v. Maturo*, 982 F.2d 57, 61 (2d Cir. 1992), the court noted that,

> [w]ithin the second category for excluding evidence, constitutional requirements may attach in two situations: (1) where the conduct of foreign law enforcement officials' rendered them agents, or virtual

agents, of United States law enforcement officials. . . ; or (2) where the cooperation between the United States and foreign law enforcement agencies is designed to evade constitutional requirements applicable to American officials.

(3) The court in *Verdugo* stated "that aliens receive constitutional protections when they have come within the territory of the United States and developed substantial connections with this country" When has one "developed substantial connections with this country"?   Should courts interpret "substantial connections" as it "has been used in the minimum-contacts test in personal jurisdiction questions"? *See* David Haug, Recent Developments, *United States: Extraterritorial Application of the Fourth Amendment* – United States v. Verdugo-Urquidez, 110 S.Ct. 1056 (1990), 32 HARV. INT'L L.J. 295, 301n.39 (1991).

(4) In *Wang v. Reno*, 81 F.3d 808 (9th Cir. 1996), the court distinguished the *Verdugo* decision when placed in the context of the Fifth Amendment.   In addition to noting that the Fifth Amendment "provides protection to the 'person' rather than 'the people,'" the court stated that "unlike *Verdugo-Urquidez*, this case does not concern an isolated, extraterritorial violation of the Constitution. . . . Rather, the two-year American prosecutorial effort violated Wang's due process rights on American soil, where he as forced in an American courtroom, to choose between committing the crime of perjury or telling the truth and facing torture and possible execution. Thus, we conclude that Wang is guaranteed due process under the Fifth Amendment."

(5)What role does the Fourth Amendment have with regard to searches at U.S. borders? Does it make a difference if a person is exiting or entering the United States? In *United States v. Beras*, 183 F.3d 22 (1st Cir. 1999), the court stated:

> It is well established that "the Fourth Amendment's balance of reasonableness is qualitatively different at the international border than in the interior." . . .   Under the border search exception, "routine searches of the persons and effects of entrants are not subject to any requirement of reasonable suspicion, probable cause, or warrant." . . . The Supreme Court, however, has not yet addressed the issue of whether the border search exception applies to outgoing as well as incoming travelers. Nor has this circuit ruled on the issue. . . . Every other circuit to consider the issue, to our knowledge, has held that the border search exception applies to outgoing as well as incoming travelers. *See United States v. Ezeiruaku*, 936 F.2d 136, 143 (3d Cir. 1991); *United States v. Berisha*, 925 F.2d 791, 795 (5th Cir. 1991); *United States v. Udofot*, 711 F.2d 831, 839-40 (8th Cir. 1983); *United States v. Ajlouny*, 629 F.2d 830, 834-35 (2d Cir. 1980); *United States v. Stanley*, 545 F.2d 661, 667 (9th Cir. 1976); *cf. United States v. Hernandez-Salazar*, 813 F.2d 1126, 1138 (11th Cir. 1987) (without deciding whether the border search exception "applies equally in all respects to incoming and outgoing searches," holding that the Fourth

Amendment "permits warrantless searches of persons and property departing the United States on the basis of reasonable suspicion that a currency reporting violation is occurring"). These cases have drawn support from dicta in *California Bankers Ass'n v. Shultz,* 416 U.S. 21, 63, 39 L. Ed. 2d 812, 94 S. Ct. 1494 (1974), where the Supreme Court stated: "Those entering and leaving the country may be examined as to their belongings and effects, all without violating the Fourth Amendment."

We join our sister circuits and conclude that the border search exception to the Fourth Amendment applies to outgoing travelers. In our view, there is a convincing policy justification for extending the exception. The border search exception arises from the "longstanding concern for the protection of the integrity of the border[, . . . a] concern [that] is, if anything, heightened by the veritable national crisis in law enforcement caused by smuggling of illicit narcotics." . . . As the Third Circuit has recognized, this concern also arises with respect to outgoing travelers:

> National interests in the flow of currency justify the diminished recognition of privacy inherent in crossing into and out of the borders of the United States . . . . Although there is not the slightest suggestion that the appellee here was implicated in drug trafficking, in an environment that sees a massive importation of drugs across our borders, we are cognizant that there must be a concomitant outflow of cash to pay for this nefarious traffic.

Ezeiruaku, 936 F.2d at 143.

(6) When travel is via airplane, is there an extension of where the search may be conducted? Can international agreements foreclose Forth Amendment arguments? In *United States v. Walczak* [p. 51], the Ninth Circuit Court of Appeals held:

> . . . . Walczak argues that the search violated the fourth amendment's proscription against unreasonable searches. Searches at the border are reasonable as an essential prerogative of a sovereign to protect its border. Therefore persons and vehicles crossing the border into this country may be searched without probable cause or a warrant. . . . The Supreme Court has held that searches may take place at the border or at its "functional equivalent." *Almeida-Sanchez v. United States,* 413 U.S. 266, 272, 37 L. Ed. 2d 596, 93 S. Ct. 2535 (1973). This is because modern air travel renders it "unreasonable to expect that persons can [always] be searched at the exact moment they cross an international border." . . .

Modern advances in air transportation call for even more responsive protective procedures. Accordingly, in 1974, the United States and Canada entered into an executive agreement authorizing United States

Customs "preclearance" operations at various Canadian airports, including Vancouver Airport. . . .

International agreements other than treaties may fall into any of three categories: congressional-executive agreements, executed by the President upon specific authorizing legislation from Congress; executive agreements pursuant to treaty, executed by the President in accord with specific instructions in a prior, formal treaty; and executive agreements executed pursuant to the President's own constitutional authority. . . . Congress has not specifically authorized the President to conclude executive agreements such as this in the realm of civil aviation, but clearly did contemplate that the executive branch would negotiate "agreement[s] with foreign governments for the establishment or development of air navigation, including air routes and services." . . . The agreement is not specifically of the second category, because while there is some relationship to the Convention on International Civil Aviation, Dec. 7, 1944, . . . the Convention does not literally authorize the President to enter into agreements implementing it.

The Supreme Court has recognized that of necessity the President may enter into certain binding agreements with foreign nations not strictly congruent with the formalities required by the Constitution's Treaty Clause [Art. II, § 2]. . . . The authority to enter into executive agreements derives from the power over foreign relations accorded to the President by the Constitution. . . .

If an agreement is within the President's power over foreign concords and relations, there seem to be no formal requirements as to how it must be made. It can be signed by the President or by his authority; it may be by delegation by him to his Secretaries of State, Ambassadors, or lesser authorized government officials. . . . The Supreme Court has never held an executive agreement *ultra vires* for lack of Senate consent. . . . Since the 1974 Agreement was designed to implement the goals of the Convention, which itself is an Article II treaty, and since Congress contemplated that agreements having to do with civil aviation would be negotiated by the executive branch, the agreement in question is among those which the President may conclude on his own authority.

Because constitutionally valid executive agreements are to be applied by the courts as the law of the land, . . . the Agreement on Air Transport Preclearance has the full force of law, and it governs in this case.

The agreement provides that

the inspecting party may extend the application of any of its customs, immigration, agriculture and public health laws and regulations to aircraft, passengers, aircraft crew, baggage, cargo and aircraft stores in the territory of the other Party which are subject to preclearance to the extent consistent with the law of the country in which the inspection takes place.

Art. VII, at 767.

Various regulations define the activities which are to take place at preclearance facilities. "Preclearance is the tentative examination and inspection of air travelers and their baggage at foreign places where U.S. Customs personnel are stationed for that purpose." . . . "Articles in baggage . . . shall be considered as accompanying a passenger if examined at an established preclearance station and the baggage is hand-carried   . . ." 19 C.F.R. § 148.4(c) (1985). By allowing preclearance at Vancouver, the agreement authorizes U.S. Customs officials stationed at a preclearance facility to search persons bound for the United States as thoroughly as though the search were taking place at the border. Therefore the search of Walczak at the preclearance station did not violate the fourth amendment. . . .

(7) What is the role Fourth Amendment when outside the United States, but on the high seas? In *United States v. Hayes*, 653 F.2d 8 (5th Cir. 1981) the court stated:

We address next appellants' claim that the CHARLES M was seized and boarded in violation of the fourth amendment and, therefore, the district court erred in not suppressing the fruits of the search. In *United States v. Hilton*, 619 F.2d 127 (1st Cir.), *cert. denied*, 449 U.S. 887, 101 S. Ct. 243, 66 L. Ed. 2d 113 (1980), this court sustained the Coast Guard's authority pursuant to 14 U.S.C. § 89(a)[3] to conduct safety and document

---

[3] 14 U.S.C. § 89(a) provides:

(a) The Coast Guard may make inquiries, examinations, inspections, searches, seizures, and arrests upon the high seas and waters over which the United States has jurisdiction, for the prevention, detection, and suppression of violations of laws of the United States. For such purposes, commissioned, warrant, and petty officers may at any time go on board of any vessel subject to the jurisdiction, or to the operation of any law, of the United States, address inquiries to those on board, examine the ship's documents and papers, and examine, inspect, and search the vessel and use all necessary force to compel compliance. When from such inquires, examination, inspection or search it appears that a breach of the laws of the United States rendering a person liable to arrest is being, or had been committed, by any person, such person shall be arrested or, if escaping to shore, shall be immediately pursued and arrested on shore, or other lawful and appropriate action shall be taken; or if it shall appear that a breach of the laws of the United States has been committed so as to render such vessel, or the merchandise, or any part thereof, on board of, or brought into the United States by, such vessel, liable to forfeiture, or so as to render such vessel liable to a fine or penalty and if necessary to secure such fine or penalty, such vessel or such merchandise, or both, shall be seized.

investigations on American flag vessels located in international waters. We conclude that "the limited intrusion presented by a document and safety inspection on the high seas even in the absence of a warrant or suspicion of wrongdoing, is reasonable under the fourth amendment." . . . The search here was within the scope of Coast Guard authority. Once on board and in the routine course of inspection, a member of the boarding party found marijuana in plain view. The Coast Guard did not proceed beyond the bounds of its inspection authority. . . .

See also Note, Megan Jaye Kight, *Constitutional Barriers to Smooth Sailing:14 U.S.C. § 89(a) and the Fourth Amendment,* 72 IND. L.J. 571 (1997). Additionally consider 19 U.S.C.A. § 1581 which provides:

(a) Customs officers. Any officer of the customs may at any time go on board of any vessel or vehicle at any place in the United States or within the customs waters or, as he may be authorized, within a customs-enforcement area established under the Anti-Smuggling Act, or at any other authorized place without as well as within his district, and examine the manifest and other documents and papers and examine, inspect, and search the vessel or vehicle and every part thereof and any person, trunk, package, or cargo on board, and to this end may hail and stop such vessel or vehicle, and use all necessary force to compel compliance

. . . .

(h) Application of section to treaties of United States. The provisions of this section shall not be construed to authorize or require any officer of the United States to enforce any law of the United States upon the high seas upon a foreign vessel in contravention of any treaty with a foreign government enabling or permitting the authorities of the United States to board, examine, search, seize, or otherwise to enforce upon said vessel upon the high seas the laws of the United States except as such authorities are or may otherwise be enabled or permitted under special arrangement with such foreign government.

§ 10.03 Fifth Amendment

UNITED STATES v. BALSYS

Supreme Court of the United States
524 U.S. 666, 118 S. Ct. 2218, 141 L. Ed. 2d 575 (1998)

JUSTICE SOUTER delivered the opinion of the Court.[*]

. . . .

I

Respondent Aloyzas Balsys is a resident alien living in Woodhaven, New York, having obtained admission to this country in 1961 under the Immigration and Nationality Act, 8 U.S.C. § 1201, on an immigrant visa and alien registration issued at the American Consulate in Liverpool. In his application, he said that he had served in the Lithuanian army between 1934 and 1940, and had lived in hiding in Plateliai, Lithuania, between 1940 and 1944. Balsys swore that the information was true, and signed a statement of understanding that if his application contained any false information or materially misleading statements, or concealed any material fact, he would be subject to criminal prosecution and deportation.

OSI [Office of Special Investigations of the Criminal Division of the United States Department of Justice], which was created to institute denaturalization and deportation proceedings against suspected Nazi war criminals, is now investigating whether, contrary to his representations, Balsys participated in Nazi persecution during World War II. Such activity would subject him to deportation for persecuting persons because of their race, religion, national origin, or political opinion under §§ 1182(a)(3)(E), 1251(a)(4)(D) as well as for lying on his visa application under §§ 1182(a)(6)(C)(i), 1251(a)(1)(A).

When OSI issued a subpoena requiring Balsys to testify at a deposition, he appeared and gave his name and address, but he refused to answer any other questions, such as those directed to his wartime activities in Europe between 1940-1945 and his immigration to the United States in 1961. In response to all such questions, Balsys invoked the Fifth Amendment privilege against compelled self-incrimination, claiming that his answers could subject him to criminal prosecution. He did not contend that he would incriminate himself under domestic law, but claimed the privilege because his responses could subject him to criminal prosecution by Lithuania, Israel, and Germany.

OSI responded with a petition in Federal District Court to enforce the subpoena under § 1225(a). Although the District Court found that if Balsys were

---

[*]JUSTICE SCALIA and JUSTICE THOMAS join only Parts I, II, and III of this opinion.

to provide the information requested, he would face a real and substantial danger of prosecution by Lithuania and Israel (but not by Germany), it granted OSI's enforcement petition and ordered Balsys to testify, treating the Fifth Amendment as inapplicable to a claim of incrimination solely under foreign law. 918 F. Supp. 588 (E.D.N.Y. 1996). Balsys appealed, and the Court of Appeals for the Second Circuit vacated the District Court's order, holding that a witness with a real and substantial fear of prosecution by a foreign country may assert the Fifth Amendment privilege to avoid giving testimony in a domestic proceeding, even if the witness has no valid fear of a criminal prosecution in this country. 119 F.3d 122 (1997). We granted certiorari to resolve a conflict among the Circuits on this issue and now reverse. . . .

II

. . . . The Self-Incrimination Clause of the Fifth Amendment provides that "no person . . . shall be compelled in any criminal case to be a witness against himself." U.S. Const., Amdt. 5. Resident aliens such as Balsys are considered "persons" for purposes of the Fifth Amendment and are entitled to the same protections under the Clause as citizens. . . . The parties do not dispute that the Government seeks to "compel" testimony from Balsys that would make him "a witness against himself." The question is whether there is a risk that Balsys's testimony will be used in a proceeding that is a "criminal case."

Balsys agrees that the risk that his testimony might subject him to deportation is not a sufficient ground for asserting the privilege, given the civil character of a deportation proceeding. *See INS v. Lopez-Mendoza,* 468 U.S. 1032, 1038-1039, 82 L. Ed. 2d 778, 104 S. Ct. 3479 (1984). If, however, Balsys could demonstrate that any testimony he might give in the deportation investigation could be used in a criminal proceeding against him brought by the Government of either the United States or one of the States, he would be entitled to invoke the privilege. It "can be asserted in any proceeding, civil or criminal, administrative or judicial, investigatory or adjudicatory," in which the witness reasonably believes that the information sought, or discoverable as a result of his testimony, could be used in a subsequent state or federal criminal proceeding. . . . But Balsys makes no such claim, contending rather that his entitlement to invoke the privilege arises because of a real and substantial fear that his testimony could be used against him by Lithuania or Israel in a criminal prosecution. The reasonableness of his fear is not challenged by the Government, and we thus squarely face the question whether a criminal prosecution by a foreign government not subject to our constitutional guarantees presents a "criminal case" for purposes of the privilege against self-incrimination.

III

Balsys relies in the first instance on the textual contrast between the Sixth Amendment, which clearly applies only to domestic criminal proceedings, and the compelled self-incrimination Clause, with its facially broader reference to "any criminal case." The same point is developed by Balsys's *amici,* who argue that "any criminal case" means exactly that, regardless of the prosecuting authority. According to the argument, the Framers' use of the adjective "any" precludes recognition of the distinction raised by the Government, between prosecution by a jurisdiction that is itself bound to recognize the privilege and prosecution by a foreign jurisdiction that is not. . . . In the Fifth Amendment context, the Clause in question occurs in the company of guarantees of grand jury proceedings, defense against double jeopardy, due process, and compensation for property taking. Because none of these provisions is implicated except by action of the government that it binds, it would have been strange to choose such associates for a Clause meant to take a broader view, and it would be strange to find such a sweep in the Clause now. . . . The oddity of such a reading would be especially stark if the expansive language in question is open to another reasonable interpretation, as we think it is. Because the Fifth Amendment opens by requiring a grand jury indictment or presentment "for a capital, or otherwise infamous crime," the phrase beginning with "any" in the subsequent Self-Incrimination Clause may sensibly be read as making it clear that the privilege it provides is not so categorically limited. It is plausible to suppose the adjective was inserted only for that purpose, not as taking the further step of defining the relevant prosecutorial jurisdiction internationally. We therefore take this to be the fair reading of the adjective "any," and we read the Clause contextually as apparently providing a witness with the right against compelled self-incrimination when reasonably fearing prosecution by the government whose power the Clause limits, but not otherwise. Since there is no helpful legislative history, and because there was no different common law practice at the time of the Framing, . . . there is no reason to disregard the contextual reading. This Court's precedent has indeed adopted that so-called same-sovereign interpretation.

In 1964 our precedent took a turn away from the unqualified proposition that fear of prosecution outside the jurisdiction seeking to compel testimony did not implicate a Fifth or Fourteenth Amendment privilege, as the case might be. In *Murphy v. Waterfront Comm'n of N. Y. Harbor,* 378 U.S. 52, 12 L. Ed. 2d 678, 84 S. Ct. 1594 (1964), we reconsidered the converse of the situation in *Murdock,* whether a witness in a state proceeding who had been granted immunity from state prosecution could invoke the privilege based on fear of prosecution on federal charges. In the course of enquiring into a work stoppage at several New Jersey piers, the Waterfront Commission of New York Harbor subpoenaed the defendants, who were given immunity from prosecution under the laws of New Jersey and New York. . . . This Court held the defendants could be forced to testify not because fear of federal prosecution was irrelevant but because the Self-Incrimination Clause barred the National Government from using their state testimony or its fruits to obtain a federal conviction. We explained "that the constitutional privilege against self-incrimination protects a state witness against incrimination under federal as well as state law and a federal witness against incrimination under state as well as federal law." . . .

Murphy is a case invested with two alternative rationales. Under the first, the result reached in *Murphy* was undoubtedly correct, given the decision rendered that very same day in *Malloy v. Hogan,* 378 U.S. 1, 12 L. Ed. 2d 653,

84 S. Ct. 1489 (1964), which applied the doctrine of Fourteenth Amendment due process incorporation to the Self-Incrimination Clause, so as to bind the States as well as the National Government to recognize the privilege. . . . Prior to *Malloy*, the Court had refused to impose the privilege against self-incrimination against the States through the Fourteenth Amendment, . . . thus leaving state-court witnesses seeking exemption from compulsion to testify to their rights under state law, as supplemented by the Fourteenth Amendment's limitations on coerced confessions. *Malloy*, however, established that "the Fourteenth Amendment secures against state invasion the same privilege that the Fifth Amendment guarantees against federal infringement – the right of a person to remain silent unless he chooses to speak in the unfettered exercise of his own will, and to suffer no penalty . . . for such silence." . . .

As the Court immediately thereafter said in *Murphy*, *Malloy* "necessitated a reconsideration" of the unqualified *Murdock* rule that a witness subject to testimonial compulsion in one jurisdiction, state or federal, could not plead fear of prosecution in the other. . . . After *Malloy*, the Fifth Amendment limitation could no longer be seen as framed for one jurisdiction alone, each jurisdiction having instead become subject to the same claim of privilege flowing from the one limitation. Since fear of prosecution in the one jurisdiction bound by the Clause now implicated the very privilege binding upon the other, the *Murphy* opinion sensibly recognized that if a witness could not assert the privilege in such circumstances, the witness could be "whipsawed into incriminating himself under both state and federal law even though the constitutional privilege against self-incrimination is applicable to each." . . . *Murphy* accordingly held that a federal court could not receive testimony compelled by a State in the absence of a statute effectively providing for federal immunity, and it did this by imposing an exclusionary rule prohibiting the National Government "from making any such use of compelled testimony and its fruits" . . . After *Murphy*, the immunity option open to the Executive Branch could only be exercised on the understanding that the state and federal jurisdictions were as one, with a federally mandated exclusionary rule filling the space between the limits of state immunity statutes and the scope of the privilege. As so understood, *Murphy* stands at odds with Balsys's claim.

There is, however, a competing rationale in *Murphy*, investing the Clause with a more expansive promise. The *Murphy* majority opened the door to this view by rejecting this Court's previous understanding of the English common-law evidentiary privilege against compelled self-incrimination, which could have informed the Framers' understanding of the Fifth Amendment privilege. . . . In sum, to the extent that the *Murphy* majority went beyond its response to *Malloy* and undercut *Murdock*'s rationale on historical grounds, its reasoning cannot be accepted now. Long before today, indeed, *Murphy*'s history was shown to be fatally flawed. . . .

Murphy's policy catalog would provide support, at a rather more concrete level, for Balsys's argument that application of the privilege in situations like his would promote the purpose of preventing government overreaching, which on anyone's view lies at the core of the Clause's purposes. This argument begins with the premise that "cooperative internationalism" creates new incentives for the Government to facilitate foreign criminal prosecutions. Because crime, like legitimate trade, is increasingly international, a corresponding degree of international cooperation is coming to characterize the enterprise of criminal prosecution. The mission of the OSI as shown in this case exemplifies the international cooperation that is said to undermine the legitimacy of treating separate governmental authorities as separate for purposes of liberty protection in domestic courts. Because the Government now has a significant interest in seeing individuals convicted abroad for their crimes, it is subject to the same incentive to overreach that has required application of the privilege in the domestic context. Balsys says that this argument is nothing more than the reasoning of the *Murphy* Court when it justified its recognition of a fear of state prosecution by looking to the significance of "cooperative federalism," the teamwork of state and national officials to fight interstate crime.

But Balsys invests *Murphy*'s "cooperative federalism" with a significance unsupported by that opinion. . . . Since in this case there is no analog of *Malloy,* imposing the Fifth Amendment beyond the National Government, there is no premise in *Murphy* for appealing to "cooperative internationalism" by analogy to "cooperative federalism." Any analogy must, instead, be to the pre-*Murphy* era when the States were not bound by the privilege. Then, testimony compelled in a federal proceeding was admissible in a state prosecution, despite the fact that shared values and similar criminal statutes of the state and national jurisdictions presumably furnished incentive for overreaching by the Government to facilitate criminal prosecutions in the States.

But even if *Murphy* were authority for considering "cooperative federalism" and "cooperative internationalism" as reasons supporting expansion of the scope of the privilege, any extension would depend ultimately on an analysis of the likely costs and benefits of extending the privilege as Balsys requests. If such analysis were dispositive for us, we would conclude that Balsys has not shown that extension of the protection would produce a benefit justifying the rule he seeks.

The Court of Appeals directed careful attention to an evaluation of what would be gained and lost on Balsys's view. It concluded, for example, that few domestic cases would be adversely affected by recognizing the privilege based upon fear of foreign prosecution, . . . that American contempt sanctions for refusal to testify are so lenient in comparison to the likely consequences of foreign prosecution that a witness would probably refuse to testify even if the privilege were unavailable to him, that by statute and treaty the United States could limit the occasions on which a reasonable fear of foreign prosecution could be shown, as by modifying extradition and deportation standards in cases involving the privilege, and that because a witness's refusal to testify may be used as evidence in a civil proceeding, deportation of people in Balsys's position would not necessarily be thwarted by recognizing the privilege as he claims it.

The Court of Appeals accordingly thought the net burden of the expanded privilege too negligible to justify denying its expansion. We remain skeptical, however. While we will not attempt to comment on every element of the Court of Appeals's calculation, two of the points just noted would present difficulty. First, there is a question about the standard that should govern any decision to justify a truly discretionary ruling by making the assumption that it will induce the Government to adopt legislation with international implications or to seek international agreements, in order to mitigate the burdens that the ruling would otherwise impose. Because foreign relations are specifically committed by the Constitution to the political branches, U.S. Const., Art II, § 2, cl. 2, we would not make a discretionary judgment premised on inducing them to adopt policies in relation to other nations without squarely confronting the propriety of grounding judicial action on such a premise.

Second, the very assumption that a witness's silence may be used against him in a deportation or extradition proceeding due to its civil nature, . . . raises serious questions about the likely gain from recognizing fear of foreign prosecution. For if a witness claiming the privilege ended up in a foreign jurisdiction that, for whatever reason, recognized no privilege under its criminal law, the recognition of the privilege in the American courts would have gained nothing for the witness. This possibility, of course, presents a sharp contrast with the consequences of recognizing the privilege based on fear of domestic prosecution. If testimony is compelled, *Murphy* itself illustrates that domestic courts are not even wholly dependent on immunity statutes to see that no use will be made against the witness; the exclusionary principle will guarantee that. . . . Whatever the cost to the Government may be, the benefit to the individual is not in doubt in a domestic proceeding.

Since the likely gain to the witness fearing foreign prosecution is thus uncertain, the countervailing uncertainty about the loss of testimony to the United States cannot be dismissed as comparatively unimportant. That some testimony will be lost is highly probable, since the United States will not be able to guarantee immunity if testimony is compelled (absent some sort of cooperative international arrangement that we cannot assume will occur). While the Court of Appeals is doubtless correct that the expected consequences of some foreign prosecutions may be so severe that a witness will refuse to testify no matter what, not every foreign prosecution may measure up so harshly as against the expectable domestic consequences of contempt for refusing to testify. We therefore must suppose that on Balsys's view some evidence will in fact be lost to the domestic courts, and we are accordingly unable to dismiss the position of the United States in this case, that domestic law enforcement would suffer serious consequences if fear of foreign prosecution were recognized as sufficient to invoke the privilege.

In sum, the most we would feel able to conclude about the net result of the benefits and burdens that would follow from Balsys's view would be a Scotch verdict. If, then, precedent for the traditional view of the scope of the Clause were not dispositive of the issue before us, if extending the scope of the privilege were open to consideration, we still would not find that Balsys had shown that recognizing his claim would be a sound resolution of the competing interests involved.

V

This is not to say that cooperative conduct between the United States and foreign nations could not develop to a point at which a claim could be made for recognizing fear of foreign prosecution under the Self-Incrimination Clause as traditionally understood. If it could be said that the United States and its allies had enacted substantially similar criminal codes aimed at prosecuting offenses of international character, and if it could be shown that the United States was granting immunity from domestic prosecution for the purpose of obtaining evidence to be delivered to other nations as prosecutors of a crime common to both countries, then an argument could be made that the Fifth Amendment should apply based on fear of foreign prosecution simply because that prosecution was not fairly characterized as distinctly "foreign." The point would be that the prosecution was as much on behalf of the United States as of the prosecuting nation, so that the division of labor between evidence-gatherer and prosecutor made one nation the agent of the other, rendering fear of foreign prosecution tantamount to fear of a criminal case brought by the Government itself.

Whether such an argument should be sustained may be left at the least for another day, since its premises do not fit this case. It is true that Balsys has shown that the United States has assumed an interest in foreign prosecution, as demonstrated by OSI's mandate and American treaty agreements requiring the Government to give to Lithuania and Israel any evidence provided by Balsys. But this interest does not rise to the level of cooperative prosecution. There is no system of complementary substantive offenses at issue here, and the mere support of one nation for the prosecutorial efforts of another does not transform the prosecution of the one into the prosecution of the other. . . . In this case there is no basis for concluding that the privilege will lose its meaning without a rule precluding compelled testimony when there is a real and substantial risk that such testimony will be used in a criminal prosecution abroad. . . . Accordingly, the judgment of the Court of Appeals is reversed, and the case is remanded for further proceedings consistent with this opinion. . . . It is so ordered.

JUSTICE STEVENS, concurring.

While I join the Court's opinion without reservation, I write separately to emphasize these points.

The clause that protects every person from being "compelled in any criminal case to be a witness against himself" is a part of the broader protection afforded by the Fifth Amendment to the Constitution. That Amendment constrains the power of the Federal Government to deprive any person "of life, liberty, or property, without due process of law," just as the Fourteenth Amendment imposes comparable constraints on the power of the States. The primary office of the clause at issue in this case is to afford protection to persons whose liberty has been placed in jeopardy in an American tribunal. The Court's holding today will not have any adverse impact on the fairness of American criminal trials.

The fact that the issue in this case has been undecided for such a long period of time suggests that our ruling will have little, if any, impact on the fairness of trials conducted in other countries. Whether or not that suggestion is accurate, I do not believe our Bill of Rights was intended to have any effect on the conduct of foreign proceedings. If, however, we were to accept respondent's interpretation of the clause, we would confer power on foreign governments to impair the administration of justice in this country. . . . A law enacted by a foreign power making it a crime for one of its citizens to testify in an American proceeding against another citizen of that country would immunize those citizens from being compelled to testify in our courts. Variants of such a hypothetical law are already in existence. Of course, the Court might craft exceptions for such foreign criminal laws, but it seems far wiser to adhere to a clear limitation on the coverage of the Fifth Amendment, including its privilege against self-incrimination. That Amendment prescribes rules of conduct that must attend any deprivation of life, liberty, or property in our Nation's courts.

JUSTICE GINSBERG, dissenting.

The privilege against self-incrimination, "closely linked historically with the abolition of torture," is properly regarded as a "landmark in man's struggle to make himself civilized." E. GRISWOLD, THE FIFTH AMENDMENT TODAY 7 (1955) . . . . In my view, the Fifth Amendment privilege against self-incrimination prescribes a rule of conduct generally to be followed by our Nation's officialdom. It counsels officers of the United States (and of any State of the United States) against extracting testimony when the person examined reasonably fears that his words would be used against him in a later criminal prosecution. As a restraint on compelling a person to bear witness against himself, the Amendment ordinarily should command the respect of United States interrogators, whether the prosecution reasonably feared by the examinee is domestic or foreign. . . . On this understanding of the "fundamental decency" the Fifth Amendment embodies, "its expression of our view of civilized governmental conduct," . . . I join JUSTICE BREYER's dissenting opinion.

JUSTICE BREYER, with whom JUSTICE GINSBERG joins, dissenting.

Were Aloyzas Balsys to face even a theoretical possibility that his testimony could lead a State to prosecute him for murder, the Fifth Amendment would prohibit the Federal Government from compelling that testimony. The Court concludes, however, that the Fifth Amendment does not prohibit compulsion here because Balsys faces a real and substantial danger of prosecution not, say, by California, but by a foreign nation. The Fifth Amendment, however, provides that "no person . . . shall be compelled in *any* criminal case to be a witness against himself." . . . That precedent, as well as the basic principles underlying the privilege, convince me that the Fifth Amendment's privilege against self-incrimination should encompass, not only feared domestic prosecutions, but also feared foreign prosecutions where the danger of an actual foreign prosecution is substantial.. . . .

In sum, I see no reason why the Court should resurrect the pale shadow of *Murdock's* "same sovereign" rule, a rule that *Murphy* demonstrated was without strong historical foundation and that would serve no more valid a purpose in today's world than it did during *Murphy's* time. *Murphy* supports recognizing the privilege where there is a real and substantial threat of prosecution by a foreign government. Balsys is among the few to have satisfied this threshold. The basic values which this Court has said underlie the Fifth Amendment's protections are each diminished if the privilege may not be claimed here. And surmountable practical concerns should not stand in the way of constitutional principle.

For these and related reasons elaborated by the Second Circuit, I respectfully dissent.

NOTES AND QUESTIONS

(1) As a result of the Court's ruling in this case, Balsys, left the United States "rather than testify about his World War II activities in Lithuania." As part of a settlement with the Department of Justice, Balsys, agreed to leave the United States permanently and "conceded that he misrepresented and concealed his true wartime activities when he entered the United States." William C. Mann, *War Criminal Suspect Won't Testify, Quits U.S.*, ATL. J. CONST., May 31, 1999, at B9.

(2) Can a court order a defendant or witness to sign a directive authorizing a foreign financial institution to release documents? Does such an order violate the defendant or witnesses' rights against self-incrimination? In *In re Grand Jury Subpoena (Two Grand Jury Contemnors v. United States)*, 826 F.2d 1166 (2d Cir. 1987), Circuit Judge Altimari stated:

Appellants, two witnesses before the grand jury, appeal from orders of the United States District Court for the Southern District of New York (Vincent L. Broderick, Judge), which held them in civil contempt for refusing to sign directives authorizing foreign financial institutions to release documents and information to the government, and ordered them confined until they signed the directives. 28 U.S.C. § 1826(a). Appellants contend *inter alia* that compelled execution of the directives, as written, would violate their fifth amendment privilege against self-incrimination and right to due process of law. . . .

To establish a fifth amendment violation, appellants must therefore demonstrate the existence of three elements: 1) compulsion, 2) a testimonial communication, and 3) the incriminating nature of that

communication. . . . The compulsion element is clearly present here.
. . . More troublesome, though, is the question of whether ordering
appellants to sign the directives – and thus requiring them to authorize
disclosure of records and information if any exist – constitutes
testimonial self-incrimination. We conclude, however, that it does not.

At the outset, we emphasize that appellants do not contend, nor could
they argue, that their fifth amendment privilege extends to preclude the
financial institutions from producing records or information regarding
appellants' transactions. . . . Thus, since the directives are the only
communications which appellants were compelled to make, they are the
only possible source of a fifth amendment violation. . . .

In this regard, we have twice approved of the compelled execution of a
directive in the face of fifth amendment self-incrimination challenges.
. . . [W]e adopted the Eleventh Circuit's approach toward resolving
these questions as set forth in *United States v. Ghidoni* [732 F.2d 814
(11th Cir. 1984)]. In *Ghidoni*, the Eleventh Circuit was confronted with
the same question presented in the instant appeal. The directive at issue
there differed from the ones here in only minor respects. For example,
it was entitled "consent directive," rather than "directive," and, in
addition to using language indicating that it was directed to any bank
where appellant had an account, it also named a specific bank, whereas
the directives at issue here do not name any specific bank or financial
institution.

After first setting out general fifth amendment principles, the *Ghidoni*
court then reviewed the directive in light of those Supreme Court
decisions addressing the testimonial and incriminating aspects of the
compelled production of documents, *i.e.*, *United States v. Doe*, 465 U.S.
605, 79 L. Ed. 2d 552, 104 S. Ct. 1237 (1984), and *Fisher v. United
States*, 425 U.S. 391, 48 L. Ed. 2d 39, 96 S. Ct. 1569 (1976). Thus, the
Ghidoni court likened the situation before it – where an individual was
being compelled to authorize and direct a third party, *i.e.*, the banks, to
produce documents – to the situations presented in *Doe* and *Fisher*,
where an individual was compelled to produce the documents himself.

The *Ghidoni* court, accordingly, examined the directive to determine
whether it contained any testimonial assertion regarding the documents
sought from the banks. The court concluded that the directive was
"devoid of any testimonial aspects," . . . . after it found that "nothing
in the directive implie[d] that [bank] accounts exist," that it contained
no statements regarding possession or control over such accounts, and
that it could not be used to authenticate any records obtained. . . .
The court thus concluded that compelled execution of the directive
would not violate the privilege against self-incrimination because the
directive itself was not testimonial in nature. . . . In upholding the
compelled execution of the directive, the court further observed that the
defendant was only being compelled to "waive a barrier [i.e., foreign

states' confidentiality laws] to permit the bank to produce documents" – an *act* which it concluded provided no testimonial assertions. . . .

The *Ghidoni* decision is not without criticism. Its approach to these questions was recently rejected by the First Circuit in *In Re Grand Jury Proceedings (Ranauro),* 814 F.2d 791 (1st Cir. 1987). *In Ranauro,* the First Circuit agreed with the *Ghidoni* court's conclusion that the directive itself does not assert that any records exist, that the appellant has control over such accounts, or that any records obtained would be authentic. . . . The court observed, however, that the directive did "admit and assert [the appellant's] consent," . . . and thus it concluded that his assertion of consent could be potentially incriminating, because it might later be used "to prove the ultimate facts that accounts in [appellant's] name existed or that [appellant] controlled those accounts." . . . The court, accordingly, concluded that compelled execution of the directive would violate the fifth amendment. . . .

While we see some merit in the First Circuit's approach, we are constrained here to apply our precedent in *N.D.N.Y. Grand Jury Subpoena,* and follow the analysis set forth in *Ghidoni.* We therefore hold that because the directives here contain no testimonial assertions, the district court orders compelling appellants to sign the directives provide no basis for a fifth amendment violation. The directives here, as in *Ghidoni,* do not contain any assertions by appellant regarding the existence of, or control over, foreign bank accounts. They authorize disclosure of records and information only if such accounts exist. We also agree with the *Ghidoni* court's conclusion that the directives could not be used to authenticate any bank records obtained.

. . . . In light of our holding today, it is clear that the fifth amendment would not stand as a bar to admission of the directives into evidence at trial because the directives contain no testimonial assertions that are incriminating, and thus do not implicate fifth amendment questions. . . . We also note, however, that since the directives contain no statements regarding existence of, or control over, any accounts, they should be excluded from evidence because they lack any probative value. . . .

Appellants argue that when the district court entered its order excluding the directives from evidence, it accordingly created a de facto use immunity for statements made in the directives. We disagree. When the district court entered its orders precluding admission of the directives into evidence, it was merely ruling on evidentiary questions relating to materiality, relevance, prejudice, etc., all of which could be and were resolved in the sound discretion of the district court. We conclude here that, because the directives lack any probative testimonial value on the issue of existence or control, . . . the district court properly excluded them from evidence. . . .

(3) Will a grand jury subpoena duces tecum be enforced, where producing the records will subject a bank to a violation of another country's criminal laws? In *In re Grand Jury Proceedings (United States v. Bank of Nova Scotia)*, 691 F.2d 1384, 1391 (11th Cir. 1982), the court stated:

> Absent direction from the Legislative and Executive branches of our federal government, we are not willing to emasculate the grand jury process whenever a foreign nation attempts to block our criminal justice process. It is unfortunate the Bank of Nova Scotia suffers from differing legal commands of separate sovereigns, but as we stated in *Field*:

> In a world where commercial transactions are international in scope, conflicts are inevitable. Courts and legislatures should take every reasonable precaution to avoid placing individuals in the situation [the Bank] finds itself. Yet, this court simply cannot acquiesce in the proposition that United States criminal investigations must be thwarted whenever there is conflict with the interest of other states.

In re Grand Jury Proceedings. United States v. Field, 535 F.2d at 410.

Some courts use a balancing test to determine whether an Internal Revenue summons, that would subject individuals to criminal liability in another country, should be enforced. *See United States v. First National Bank of Chicago*, 699 F.2d 341 (7th Cir. 1983) (using a balancing test, court said compelling disclosure would be improper); *United States v. Chase Manhattan Bank*, 584 F. Supp. 1080 (S.D. N.Y. 1984) (balancing of national interests required order enforcing the summons). Will the *Balsys* decision affect how future courts resolve these issues?

§ 10.04 Sixth Amendment

UNITED STATES v. KOLE

United States Court of Appeals for the Third Circuit
164 F.3d 164 (1998)

MCKEE, CIRCUIT JUDGE:

. . . . In the instant case, Kole and a coconspirator were apprehended in New Jersey and charged with attempting to import heroin. Kole subsequently pled guilty to one count of conspiring to import 3.5 kilograms of heroin into the United States in violation of 21 U.S.C. § 942(a). Following the change of plea proceeding, the government filed an information under 21 U.S.C. § 851(a) in an effort to enhance Kole's sentence to a term of imprisonment of at least 20 years based upon her drug conviction in the Philippines.

Kole argued that 21 U.S.C. § 851(c)(2) precluded the court from using the Philippine conviction to enhance her sentence because she had been denied a jury trial in the Philippines, and because her defense counsel there labored under a conflict of interest that caused her to be denied effective assistance of counsel. Since § 851(c)(2) expressly bars consideration of any prior conviction that "was obtained in violation of the Constitution of the United States," Kole asserted that the sentencing court could not apply the mandatory minimum for repeat felony drug offenders contained in 21 U.S.C. § 960(b)(1)(A). . . . . [T]he court ruled that the Philippine conviction was a prior drug felony for purposes of sentencing, and sentenced Kole to the mandatory minimum period of incarceration (20 years) under 21 U.S.C. § 960(b)(1). This appeal followed.

. . . . The district court ruled that, although Kole was not entitled to a jury trial, her Philippine conviction could still be used to enhance her sentence under § 960 because the conviction was obtained in a manner that was consistent with notions of fundamental fairness embodied in the Constitution, and was therefore "not obtained in violation of the Constitution" as that phrase is used in § 851. The court also ruled that Kole had not met her burden of showing that her defense attorney's joint representation of herself and Ike deprived her of effective assistance of counsel.

Here, we must decide whether the Constitution applies Ex Proprio vigore to the Philippines. . . . We conclude that Congress did not intend a contrary result when it enacted 21 U.S.C. § 851. Rather, as the district court concluded, Congress intended only to ensure fundamental fairness by excluding any conviction that was obtained in a manner inconsistent with concepts of fundamental fairness and liberty endemic in the Due Process Clause of the Fifth Amendment of the United States Constitution. . . .

Kole's argument is bottomed upon an assumption that Congress could not have intended to allow a conviction that was obtained in violation of such a fundamental right to enhance a subsequent sentence in a court of the United States. However, this position overlooks the purpose behind § 960 as well as the fact that jury trials, though fundamental to the system of justice established under the United States Constitution, are nevertheless relatively unique to that system. . . . Although the Court answered that question in the affirmative as applied to the American legal system, it left no doubt that other societies may well be able to fashion a system with no juries that is fundamentally fair to the accused, thus comporting with our concept of due process. . . .

Judge Felix's opinion reflects the kind of careful, searching analysis of evidence that one would expect from a trial judge in the United States. The fact that Kole was denied a jury trial under the jurisdiction where she obtained her "prior conviction for a felony drug offense" in no way undermines her conviction there.

The text of 21 U.S.C. § 960 reflects a congressional intent to significantly increase sentences for drug offenders with prior convictions for felony drug offenses. Repeat drug offenders are clearly more culpable than first time offenders, and the enhanced sentences required under § 960 serve to incapacitate and punish those who have continued their involvement with drug trafficking despite prior prosecution. Given Congress' concern, it would not be logical to limit the enhancement to those persons who had been convicted of a prior drug felony (or its equivalent) only in the United States. . . . We do not think that Congress enacted a law that was intended to reach persons involved in international drug trafficking and then limited enhanced penalties to those persons who had previously been convicted in a court in the United States. That is inconsistent with Congress' attempt to reach those involved in importing or exporting controlled substances. Yet, since the United States Constitution does not apply to any foreign sovereign, that would be the result of adopting Ms. Kole's argument. . . .

Kole also argues that use of the Philippine conviction violated her Sixth Amendment right to counsel because her trial attorney labored under an irreconcilable conflict of interest that prevented him from effectively representing her. In *Strickland v. Washington,* 466 U.S. 668, 687, 80 L. Ed. 2d 674, 104 S. Ct. 2052 (1984), the Court established a two-part test for evaluating a claim of ineffective assistance of counsel and we apply it here. Under *Strickland,* a defendant must show that "counsel's representation fell below an objective standard of reasonableness." . . . If defendant is able to make that showing, he or she must then establish that counsel's dereliction prejudiced the defendant. Where the claim rests upon an alleged conflict of interest, defendant "must identify something that counsel chose to do or not do, as to which he had conflicting duties, and must show that the course taken was influenced by that conflict." In other words, the defendant must "show some actual conflict of interest that adversely affected his counsel's performance in order to prevail." . . .

Here, Kole alleges that the joint representation created a simultaneous duty to represent Ike that prevented her defense attorney from distinguishing between her involvement and his. . . . Her argument suggests that her attorney could have attempted to equate Kole's role with that of the codefendants who were acquitted rather than being lumped with her fiance. However, "hindsight rationalization alone cannot support a claim of ineffective assistance of counsel." . . . Kole's attorney mounted a vigorous attack on the credibility of the police, and informant Williams. As noted above, he was able to raise serious questions as to the credibility of the prosecutor's witnesses. In fact, the trial judge did not credit substantial portions of the prosecution's case.

Moreover, the appendix filed in this court contains a "Demurrer to Evidence" that defense counsel filed following trial, and prior to Judge Felix issuing his opinion. . . . In that demurrer Kole's attorney argues that all of the physical evidence must be suppressed based upon the warrantless search, the lack of credibility of the prosecution witnesses including the police, the chemist's expertise and bias, Jacqueline Williams' open case with the police, and the likelihood of her bias based upon asserted promises that the case would be dismissed if she cooperated against Kole. . . .

There is no irreconcilable tension in defense counsel's strategy. Indeed, Kole's attorney would have been hard pressed to draw distinctions between her involvement and Ike's while arguing that the police and Williams were lying about finding evidence inside of their apartment. As noted above, "an actual conflict of interest occurs when counsel cannot use his best efforts to exonerate one defendant for fear of implicating the other." . . .

Although Kole asserts her Philippine attorney could have used a different strategy had he not also represented Ike, she has not met her burden of proving that she was prejudiced by the joint representation. Moreover, we do not think that the strategy actually adopted compromised her defense. Since Kole and Ike occupied the apartment and had equal access to the suitcase with the heroin, a coordinated attack on the prosecution's cooperating witness, and upon the police was strategically sound. . . . It is the particular circumstances of a joint prosecution of husband and wife, rather than the fact of the relationship, that creates any conflict of interest between spouses in a joint prosecution. Although the circumstances could be such that a conflict of interest would flow from the relationship of husband and wife, this is not such a case. Kole has not established such circumstances existed when she was convicted in the Philippines. Judge Felix did conclude that Kole and Ike had joint control over the apartment, and joint access to the heroin inside of it, but the conflict of interest Kole complains of is more a creature of hindsight than of record. . . .
For the reasons set forth above, we affirm the district court's imposition on Kole of an enhanced sentence of twenty years under 21 U.S.C. § 960(b)(1)(A).[*]

NOTES AND QUESTIONS

(1)   Defendants are accorded compulsory process under the Sixth Amendment. May the government deport a person from the United States that may be a witness the defendant may wish to call at his or her trial in the United States? Consider the following statements from Justice Rehnquist's majority opinion in *United States v. Valenzuela-Bernal*, 458 U.S. 858, 102 S.Ct. 3440, 73 L.Ed.2d 1193 (1982):

> The power to regulate immigration – an attribute of sovereignty essential to the preservation of any nation – has been entrusted by the Constitution to the political branches of the Federal Government. . . In exercising this power, Congress has adopted a policy of apprehending illegal aliens at or near the border and deporting them promptly. . . .

---

[*]   For further discussion of the use of foreign convictions, *see* chap. 15. – Eds.

The only recent decision of this Court dealing with the right to compulsory process guaranteed by the Sixth Amendment suggests that more than the mere absence of testimony is necessary to establish a violation of the right. *See Washington v. Texas,* 388 U.S. 14 (1967). Indeed, the Sixth Amendment does not by its terms grant to a criminal defendant the right to secure the attendance and testimony of any and all witnesses: it guarantees him "compulsory process for obtaining *witnesses in his favor.*" U.S. Const., Amdt. 6 (emphasis added). . . . Such an absence of fairness is not made out by the Government's deportation of the witnesses in this case unless there is some explanation of how their testimony would have been favorable and material. . . .

JUSTICE BRENNAN, with whom JUSTICE MARSHALL joins, dissenting.

Today's holding flaunts a transparent contradiction. On the one hand, the Court recognizes respondent's constitutional right, under the Compulsory Process Clause of the Sixth Amendment, to the production of all witnesses whose testimony would be relevant and material to his defense. . . . But on the other hand, the Court holds that the Government may deport illegal-alien eyewitnesses to respondent's alleged crime immediately upon their apprehension, before respondent or his attorney have had any opportunity to interview them – thus depriving respondent of the surest and most obvious means by which he could establish the materiality and relevance of such witnesses' testimony. . . . Truly, the Court giveth, and the Court taketh away. But surely a criminal defendant has a constitutional right to interview eyewitnesses to his alleged crime before they are whisked out of the country by his prosecutor. The Court's decision today makes a mockery of that right. . . .

(2) The Sixth Amendment also provides defendants with the right "to be confronted with the witnesses against him." In *United States v. Davis,* 767 F.2d 1025, 1032 (2d Cir. 1985), the court admitted Swiss bank records despite defendant not being present at the hearing at which the records were authenticated. Finding no violation of the confrontation clause, the court noted that "the Swiss bank records bore the best possible indication of reliability – Davis' admission of their authenticity." The court stated, "[i]n light of the rigorous procedures used to authenticate the documents and Davis' concession, it is highly unlikely that Davis' presence at the hearing (or the authenticating witnesses' presence at the trial) would have weakened the reliability of the records."

(3) Do defendant's have Confrontation Rights when witnesses are outside the jurisdiction of the United States? Consider the propriety of using the deposition of a key witness, as presented in the following case.

UNITED STATES v. MCKEEVE

United States Court of Appeals for the First Circuit
131 F.3d 1 (1997)

SELYA, CIRCUIT JUDGE:

. . . . The appellant objects in this court, as he did below, to admission at trial of the deposition testimony of the British shipping agent, Alex Redpath. His cardinal contention is that the admission of this evidence abrogated his rights under the Confrontation Clause. . . .

The parties – who agree on little else – share the view that Redpath was a key witness. Initially, the prosecution gained Redpath's assurances that he would travel to the United States and testify at the trial. As the day of reckoning approached, Redpath experienced a change of heart. Because the district court lacked subpoena power over Redpath (who lived and worked in Great Britain), the government moved for leave to depose him abroad. The motion invoked a procedural rule that provides in pertinent part:

> Whenever due to exceptional circumstances of the case it is in the interest of justice that the testimony of a prospective witness of a party be taken and preserved for use at trial, the court may upon motion of such party and notice to the parties order that testimony of such witness be taken by deposition . . . .

Fed. R. Crim. P. 15(a).

The government proposed to mitigate any Confrontation Clause issues by transporting the appellant and his counsel to the site of the deposition and videotaping the proceedings. This proposal proved problematic for two reasons. First, the U.S. Marshals Service lacks jurisdiction to retain custody of federal detainees on foreign soil and the Central Authority of the United Kingdom would not agree to assume temporary custody of McKeeve so that he could attend the deposition. Second, British magistrates typically prohibit the videotaping and audiotaping of depositions, and made no exception in this instance. The district court nonetheless found that Redpath was an unavailable witness and that the interest of justice warranted the deposition. Working within the spare confines of the British scheme, the court directed the government to transport the appellant's attorney to the deposition and to install two telephone lines – one that would allow the appellant to monitor the deposition from his prison cell and another that would allow him to consult privately with counsel during the deposition. The court reserved a ruling on the Confrontation Clause objections until the time of trial.

Redpath's deposition was taken before a British magistrate in the Solihull Magistrates' Court, Birmingham, England. Lawyers for the government and for both defendants attended and questioned the deponent. A solicitor (who doubled in brass as the clerk of the Magistrates' Court) contemporaneously prepared a transcript. The appellant monitored the proceedings by means of a live telephone link. At the conclusion of the session, the solicitor certified the transcript as accurate and forwarded it to the district court. When the prosecution subsequently offered the deposition at trial, Judge Keeton overruled the appellant's objections and allowed the government to read it into evidence. . . .

The use of deposition testimony in criminal trials is disfavored, largely because such evidence tends to diminish a defendant's Sixth Amendment confrontation rights. . . . But the shrinking size of the globe means that certain criminal activities increasingly manifest an international cachet and, because federal courts frequently lack the power to compel a foreign national's attendance at trial, Rule 15 may offer the only practicable means of procuring critical evidence. The resultant tension between the defendant's Confrontation Clause rights and the prosecution's need to obtain evidence from persons domiciled abroad, while new to this circuit, threatens to become a recurring theme.

The various subsections of Rule 15 govern the method and manner by which depositions in criminal cases are to be taken. The appellant tacitly concedes that the taking of Redpath's deposition did not contravene the rule's formal requirements. Nevertheless, compliance with Rule 15 is a necessary, but not sufficient, condition to the use of a deposition at trial. The admissibility of the testimony is quite another matter. *See* Fed. R. Crim. P. 15(e). The appellant cloaks himself in the mantle of the Confrontation Clause and makes his stand at this juncture.

The Confrontation Clause's "central concern . . . is to ensure the reliability of the evidence against a criminal defendant by subjecting it to rigorous testing in the context of an adversary proceeding before the trier of fact." . . . The Clause addresses that concern principally by affording a criminal defendant the right to confront appearing witnesses face to face and the right to conduct rigorous cross-examination of those witnesses. . . . Ordinarily, then, when the government purposes to introduce a deposition at trial in lieu of live testimony, a defendant has the right to be present during the deposition so that he may confront the deponent. . . .

Withal, we know on the best of authority that the Confrontation Clause cannot be applied mechanically, but, rather, must be interpreted "in the context of the necessities of trial and the adversary process." . . . In other words, the right of confrontation is not absolute. Yet, filtering constitutional concerns through a seine woven of practical necessity is a tricky business, and different situations likely will yield different accommodations.

When the government conducts a Rule 15 deposition in a foreign land with a view toward introducing it at trial, the Confrontation Clause requires, at a minimum, that the government undertake diligent efforts to facilitate the defendant's presence. . . . We caution, however, that although such efforts must be undertaken in good faith, they need not be heroic, and the possibility of using a deposition does not evaporate even if those efforts prove fruitless. In that event the district court must determine, on a case-specific basis, whether reasonable alternative measures can preserve adequately the values that underpin the defendant's confrontation rights. In cases where actions by, or the laws of, a foreign nation effectively preclude the defendant's presence, furnishing the defendant with the capability for live monitoring of the deposition, as well as a separate (private) telephone line for consultation with counsel, usually will satisfy the demands of the Confrontation Clause. . . .

In this case, the record reveals that the prosecution made reasonable and diligent efforts to secure the appellant's attendance at Redpath's deposition: it offered to defray the cost of transporting the appellant and his counsel to the deposition and requested that British authorities accept temporary custody of him to ensure his presence. Only a lack of cooperation by the host nation stymied the appellant's appearance, and the Justice Department was powerless to coerce British assistance. The appellant points to nothing more that the prosecution plausibly could have done to facilitate a face-to-face confrontation. What is more, when the British authorities balked, Judge Keeton fashioned a reasonable alternative, and the prosecution provided the requisite telephonic links between the appellant's prison cell and the Solihull Magistrates' Court. Under the prevailing circumstances, the government's efforts to secure (or, alternatively, to approximate) a face-to-face confrontation were constitutionally adequate.

This finding, in itself, does not defeat the appellant's constitutional challenge. Face-to-face confrontation in a courtroom setting has yet another virtue; it permits the trier of fact better to observe a witness's demeanor. . . . Like the right of confrontation itself, however, this value is not absolute. Thus, even when a witness is unavailable to testify at trial, the Clause countenances the admission of certain extrajudicial statements as long as they possess sufficient indicia of reliability. . . .

For this purpose, "reliability can be inferred without more in a case where the evidence falls within a firmly rooted hearsay exception." . . . So it is here: Fed. R. Evid. 804(b)(1) limns a hearsay exception for former testimony of an unavailable witness. This exception's roots are deeply embedded in American jurisprudence. . . . Consistent with this tradition, courts seem disinclined to find any Confrontation Clause transgression when the prosecution offers deposition testimony under this rule. . . . We join these courts and hold that evidence properly within the former testimony hearsay exception is, by definition, not vulnerable to a challenge based upon the Confrontation Clause.

To bring Redpath's testimony within the protective embrace of this holding, the government had to make a threshold showing (1) that the witness was unavailable, and (2) that the deposition constituted former testimony. The appellant contests both points.

The standard test for unavailability is whether the witness's attendance could be procured "by process or other reasonable means." Fed. R. Evid. 804(a)(5). In a criminal context, however, Confrontation Clause concerns color the Rule 804 availability inquiry and heighten the government's burden. . . . Thus, the prosecution must actively attempt to secure the witness's presence at trial. . . . Here, as we noted above, the government made an assiduous effort to convince Redpath to attend the trial. We fail to discern any further action that the prosecutor reasonably could have taken to bring the witness before the jury.

. . . . To be sure, the deposition did not comport in all respects with American practice, but that circumstance alone does not render the testimony not "in compliance with law" and therefore beyond the reach of Rule 804(b)(1). . . .

The appellant's final plaint is that the Redpath deposition was not videotaped. History undermines this plaint. The former testimony exception to the Confrontation Clause predates the development of videotaping technology by nearly a century. . . . Thus, the exception obviously does not envision the need to present the trier of fact with a video recording of the declarant's testimony. In a case like this one – where the host nation prohibits videotaping – the district court's refusal to condition its authorization of the deposition on the use of such a technique did not offend the Constitution.

We hasten to add, however, that our opinion should not be read to discourage the use of videotaped depositions in this type of situation. Having the trier of fact observe the testimonial demeanor of the witness enhances important Confrontation Clause values, including the perception of fairness in criminal trials. . . . For these reasons, although videotaping is not constitutionally required, we urge the district courts, if videotaping is feasible, to give serious consideration to granting defendants' requests to employ the technique.

To sum up, the Redpath deposition satisfies the Rule 804(b)(1) standard. Moreover, the very characteristics which contribute to that conclusion – e.g., administration of an oath; unlimited direct and cross-examination; ability to lodge objections; oversight by a judicial officer; compilation of the transcript by a trained solicitor; and linguistic compatibility – also provide sufficient indicia of reliability to assuage any reasonable Confrontation Clause concerns. . . . The district court did not err in admitting the deposition testimony into evidence.

Chapter 11
IMMUNITIES FROM JURISDICTION

§ 11.01 Diplomatic and Consular Immunities

SALAZAR v. BURRESCH

United States District Court for the Central District of California
47 F. Supp. 2d 1105 (1999)

MATZ, DISTRICT JUDGE:

In 1997, Plaintiff Rafael Salazar was the Consul General of the Republic of Guatemala in Los Angeles, California. On April 4, 1997, at approximately 1:00 p.m., Plaintiff was involved in a car accident on the Pomona Freeway. Defendant California Highway Patrol ("CHP") Officer J. Burresch arrived on the scene shortly after the accident. According to Burresch, Plaintiff appeared intoxicated. Plaintiff informed Burresch that he was consul general and entitled to immunity. After Plaintiff allegedly became unruly, Burresch handcuffed Plaintiff and caused him to be transported to the police station. At the station, Plaintiff's handcuffs were removed and Burresch completed his investigation by issuing Plaintiff a citation. Plaintiff then submitted to a breath test which showed a blood alcohol level of .20%, well above the .08% level of presumed intoxication under California law. He is currently awaiting trial in Los Angeles Municipal Court on drunk driving charges.

[Salazar filed a civil rights action against various defendants, including Officer Burresch and Officer Myhre who had administered the breath test. Among other claims, the complaint alleged] "violation of federal treaty rights," i.e., Article 41 of the 1963 Vienna Convention on Consular Relations ("VCCR") . . . . This matter is currently before the Court on these Defendants' motion for summary judgment. . . .

For purposes of this order, it is unnecessary for the Court to resolve the question of whether there is a private right of action under the VCCR. The Court will assume (without in any way finding) that there is such a cause of action. . . . As set forth in detail below, the Court concludes that even if a private right of action under the VCCR does exist, no material issue of fact exists on the question of whether the CHP Officer Defendants violated Plaintiff's rights under the VCCR; they did not. . . .

Article 41 of the 1963 Vienna Convention on Consular Relations ("VCCR") provides that "Consular officers shall not be liable to arrest or detention pending trial, except in the case of a grave crime and pursuant to a decision by a competent judicial authority." "A 'grave crime' has been interpreted by the Department of State to mean a felony." *U.S. v. Cole*, 717 F. Supp. 309, 323 n. 5 (E.D. Pa. 1989) (holding that Yugoslavian consul-general was not entitled to consular immunity from money laundering charges because money-laundering constituted a "grave offense"). "Article 41 does not provide consular officers with immunity for non-grave crimes; rather, it has been interpreted as requiring only that consular officers not be imprisoned until convicted." *Id.* at 323 n. 5. . . .

The United States Department of State has published guidelines interpreting the VCCR and thereby providing guidance to law enforcement officers on how the VCCR applies to their duties. That publication, titled "Guidance for Law Enforcement Officers – Personal Rights and Immunities of Foreign Diplomatic and Consular Personnel," provides in pertinent part as follows:

General
The vast majority of the persons entitled to privileges and immunities in the United States are judicious in their actions and keenly aware of the significance attached to their actions as representatives of their sending country. On rare occasions, however, a member of this class or of his or her family may be involved in a criminal law violation. The more common violations involve traffic offenses, such as . . . driving while intoxicated. . . .

When, in the course of responding to or investigating an apparent violation of criminal law, a police officer is confronted with a person claiming immunity, official Department of State identification should immediately be requested in order to verify the person's status and immunity. . . .

When proper identification is available, the individual's immunity should be fully respected to the degree to which the particular individual is entitled. If it is established that the individual is entitled to the full inviolability and immunity of a diplomatic agent, he or she may not be arrested and should not, except in extraordinary circumstances (see Personal Inviolability vs. Public Safety below), be handcuffed or detained in any way. . . .

Personal Inviolability vs. Public Safety
. . . All such personal inviolability is, however, qualified by the understanding, well established in international law, that the host country does not give up its right to protect the safety and welfare of its populace and retains the right, in extraordinary circumstances, to prevent the commission of a crime. Thus, in circumstances where public safety is in imminent danger or it is apparent that a serious crime may otherwise be committed, police authorities may intervene to the extent necessary to halt such activity. This naturally includes the power of the

police to defend themselves from personal harm.

Traffic Enforcement

. . . [A] police officer should never hesitate to follow normal procedures to intervene in a traffic violation which he or she has observed – even if immunity ultimately bars any further action at the scene, the officer should always stop persons committing moving violations, issue a citation if appropriate, and report the incident in accordance with usual procedures. Sobriety tests may be offered in accordance with local procedures but may not be required or compelled. If the police officer judges the individual to be intoxicated, the officer should not (even in the case of diplomatic agents) permit the individual to continue to drive. The officer's primary concern in this connection should be the safety of the community and of the intoxicated individual. Depending on the circumstances, the following options are available. The officer may, with the individual's permission, take the individual to the police station or other location where he or she may recover sufficiently to drive. The officer may summon, or allow the individual to summon, a friend or relative to drive; or the police officer may call a taxi for the individual. If appropriate, the police may choose to provide the individual with transportation.

Plaintiff contends that Burresch violated his rights under the VCCR by handcuffing Plaintiff and by taking him to the station (essentially "arresting" him). Plaintiff contends Defendant Myhre violated his rights under the VCCR by administering the breath test. The Court deals with each of these allegations separately.

A. Handcuffing Plaintiff.

The undisputed facts demonstrate that only after Plaintiff became "extremely agitated and began shouting and flailing his arms about wildly . . . [and] due to plaintiff's obvious intoxication and combative behavior," did Burresch handcuff Plaintiff. Moreover, Burresch did so out of concern for his own safety. . . . Although Plaintiff disputes Burresch's description of Plaintiff's behavior as "combative" and denies that he was ever a threat to Burresch's safety, Plaintiff does not dispute that he was shouting or flailing his arms about wildly. . . .

The provision in the Department of State manual that permits officers to "intervene to the extent necessary" to halt activity that places public safety in "imminent danger" includes (but is not limited to) defending themselves from personal harm. Under these facts, this Court concludes that there is no triable issue on whether Burresch's initial handcuffing of Plaintiff violated the VCCR; it did not. . . .

Moreover, even assuming that Plaintiff remained handcuffed for an hour and a half, this Court concludes that, under the circumstances, that length of time was permissible under the VCCR. Burresch originally placed the handcuffs on Plaintiff at the accident site, because of his concern about safety. It took at least 60 minutes to bring Plaintiff to the station. According to Gutierrez [the Acting Officer in Charge], at the station Plaintiff was still "in an agitated state." But after Plaintiff "calmed down," the handcuffs were removed. When a person is obviously drunk, has been shouting and flailing his arms and appears "agitated," it is reasonable to believe that he still presents a safety threat. Thus, this Court concludes that there is also no triable issue on the question of whether leaving Plaintiff in handcuffs for an hour and a half violated the VCCR; as interpreted by the Department of State, it did not.

B. Taking Plaintiff to the Station.

Plaintiff argues that rather than taking him to the station, Burresch should have taken Plaintiff home. . . . Plaintiff argues that by taking him to the station, Burresch effectively put him under arrest, in violation of the VCCR. Burresch argues that he was justified in taking Plaintiff to the station. He explains: "Due to plaintiff's level of intoxication and extensive damage to his vehicle, I decided, pursuant to CHP policy, to have plaintiff transported to the CHP area office in order to complete my investigation of the accident, verify plaintiff's diplomatic status and arrange transportation of plaintiff to his residence." At the station, Burresch "completed my investigation and contacted the United States State Department to verify plaintiff's diplomatic status."

The Department of State manual does not expressly allow an officer to take an individual to the station to conduct an investigation. (Nor does it forbid it.) Burresch has not introduced any evidence that he would not have been able to verify Plaintiff's diplomatic status at the accident scene (e.g., by radioing in to the station and having someone there contact the State Department). However, the cars of Burresch and Salazar were stopped in a freeway lane near the median of the Pomona Freeway, and Plaintiff and Burresch were standing there. It would not have been reasonable or prudent for Burresch to remain on the freeway to complete his investigation. Although Burresch could have placed Plaintiff in his car, exited the freeway, and continued his investigation on the off-ramp, having placed Plaintiff in a patrol car it was equally reasonable for him to continue to the station to complete the processing.

Moreover, for Burresch to cause Plaintiff to be taken to the station . . . was entirely consistent with the Department of State guidelines, which authorized Burresch to "protect the safety and welfare of [the] populace . . . to prevent the commission of a crime and . . . where public safety is in imminent danger . . . to intervene to the extent necessary to halt such activity." The VCCR provides that even for mere traffic violations (much less criminal offenses, such as "DUI"), an officer may, with the official's permission, take the official to the police station or other location where he may recover sufficiently to drive. Here, Burresch states in his declaration that, after explaining to Plaintiff that he was going to arrange transportation for Plaintiff to the station and then to Plaintiff's home, Plaintiff "appeared to agree." Plaintiff has introduced no evidence that he did not agree.

Even if Plaintiff had introduced evidence that he did not agree with Burresch's decision to take him to the station in order to arrange transportation, this Court would have to grant Burresch's motion. Intoxication by its very nature creates not only a safety hazard but an impediment to making a reasoned decision. Therefore, when the official is drunk an officer may reasonably disregard the "permission" element of the option authorized by the VCCR to transport the official to the station.

C. Breath Test.

Plaintiff's next argument is that the CHP Officer Defendants violated his rights by giving him a breath test. Plaintiff has submitted no evidence, however, that Burresch had anything to do with a breath test. Instead, the undisputed evidence is that Officer Gutierrez offered Plaintiff the test and that Defendant Myhre administered it.

As to Myhre, moreover, the Court must grant the motion because the evidence is undisputed that Gutierrez asked Plaintiff whether he would agree to take the test and that he agreed to do so. . . . To be sure, his counsel claimed at the hearing that Salazar had no choice, but there is no evidence that Salazar was threatened, beaten, tricked or coerced. He was asked and he agreed.

The undisputed evidence demonstrates that the conduct of Burresch and Myhre was in compliance with the VCCR, as interpreted by the Department of State Guidelines. Accordingly, this Court grants these Defendants' motion for summary judgment as to Plaintiff's claim under the VCCR.

<hr/>

NOTES AND QUESTIONS

(1) Consuls, like diplomats, represent their country abroad, but ordinarily are concerned with commercial rather than with political relations. The multilateral Vienna Convention on Consular Relations, April 24, 1963, 21 U.S.T. 77, T.I.A.S. No. 6820, 596 U.N.T.S. 261, brought the status of career consuls (as opposed to honorary consuls) closer to that of diplomats. Nonetheless, even under the Convention, as the foregoing case indicates, consuls, unlike diplomats, have no immunity from criminal prosecution, and have immunity from arrest only for non-grave crimes.

(2) The modern law on diplomatic immunity is codified in the Vienna Convention on Diplomatic Relations, April 18, 1961, 23 U.S.T. 3227, T.I.A.S. No. 7502, 500 U.N.T.S. 95. Article 29 of that Convention provides: "The person of a diplomatic agent shall be inviolable. He shall not be liable to any form of

arrest or detention. . ." Article 31(1) provides without qualification: "A diplomatic agent shall enjoy immunity from the criminal jurisdiction of the receiving State." The United States became a party to the Convention in 1972. The Diplomatic Relations Act of 1978 (codified at 22 U.S.C. §§ 254a-254e) provides: "Any action or proceeding brought against an individual who is entitled to immunity with respect to such action or proceeding under the Vienna Convention on Diplomatic Relations . . . shall be dismissed" (22 U.S.C. § 254d).

(3) Suppose Salazar, the plaintiff in the foregoing case, had been a diplomat rather than a consul. Would the case have come out differently? Note that, with respect to traffic violations, the State Department guidelines, on which the court relies, do not distinguish between diplomats and consuls.

(4) Does immunity from arrest and prosecution exempt the diplomat from observance of local law? On the contrary, diplomats are said to be immune from the receiving state's efforts to *enforce* its rules, but not (except perhaps with respect to official acts) from its jurisdiction to *prescribe* rules of proper conduct for all persons within its territory. Article 41(1) of the 1961 Vienna Convention expressly stipulates that "it is the duty of all persons enjoying [diplomatic] privileges and immunities to respect the laws and regulations of the receiving State." In principle, then, the diplomat can commit a crime and is exempt only from prosecution. Thus, a person who conspires with a diplomat to engage in criminal activity can be found guilty of conspiracy or complicity, even though the diplomat is immune from prosecution. *See Farnsworth v. Zerbst*, 98 F.2d 541, 544 (5th Cir. 1938). And, if the sending state waives this immunity, the diplomat can be prosecuted as well. Likewise, since the immunity is only from prosecution, not from observing substantive law, a diplomat who remains in the receiving state after diplomatic status terminates can be arrested and tried for crimes committed, at least in a private capacity, while still a diplomat. *See* RESTATEMENT (THIRD) OF FOREIGN RELATIONS LAW § 464, Reporters' Note 10 (1986).

(5) Are there any circumstances in which the receiving state is justified in refusing to accord a diplomat absolute immunity from criminal jurisdiction? The State Department guidelines indicate that, in emergency situations, the police may restrain a diplomat if it is necessary to do so in order to protect public safety or to prevent a serious crime. It is generally agreed that nothing in the law of diplomatic immunity precludes their doing so, despite the silence of the Vienna Convention on this point. But the restraint must be temporary, only so long as the danger persists.

(6) Are there any circumstances in which diplomats who abuse their position for criminal purposes can be said to have forfeited their immunity? Is the nature and seriousness of a crime relevant to whether immunity should be recognized or denied? It has been suggested from time to time that a state may be justified in refusing to allow diplomatic immunity in cases of serious crimes, such as espionage, directed against the receiving state itself. In 1916, Secretary

of State Lansing indicated that, in part because of the seriousness of the offense, the United States would not recognize the immunity of a German military attaché accused of conspiracy to violate the neutrality laws. *See* 4 GREEN HACKWORTH, DIGEST OF INTERNATIONAL LAW 517 (1942). Most commentators, however, have criticized this statement as a departure from generally accepted principles of international law.

(7) Does diplomatic immunity necessarily bar prosecution for war crimes or other international offenses? Former diplomats were convicted in war crimes trials held after World War II [*see* chap. 18]. But they did not enjoy diplomatic status at the time of trial. They therefore had no immunity from prosecution, only immunity from having their official acts questioned in foreign courts, and the latter is trumped by the rule that, in prosecutions for crimes under international law, the fact that the defendant acted as a head of state or responsible government official cannot exempt the defendant from criminal responsibility. (How far this rule applies to crimes other than war crimes, and in national as well as in international criminal courts, was a central issue in the *Pinochet* case, which we will consider in the next section.)

It has been suggested in the wake of the *Pinochet* decision that, for the sake of "normative coherence," *active* as well as *former* heads of state should be denied immunity from prosecution in other countries for crimes under international law. *See* Andrea Bianchi, *Immunity versus Human Rights: The Pinochet Case*, 10 EUR. J. INT'L L. 237 (1999). On the same grounds, one might argue, so should *active* diplomats. Consider, however, the following episode, as more indicative, perhaps, of actual state practice:

> In early April 1997, a Peruvian army-intelligence officer, Leonor La Rosa, stated publicly that fellow intelligence officers had committed acts of torture against her in early 1997. On April 8, Peruvian authorities acted on those accusations by relieving Major Tomás Ricardo Anderson Kohatsu and three other officer of their duties, and by arresting and charging them, under Peru's military code, with abuse of authority. On May 9, a Peruvian military court convicted the four officers of negligence and abuse of authority. In addition to imposing fines, the court sentenced them to eight years in prison. In February 1998, however, Major Anderson and another officer were quietly released from prison.

> In March 2000, Major Anderson traveled to Washington, D.C., to take part in a hearing on wiretapping before the Inter-American Commission on Human Rights. On March 9, the Federal Bureau of Investigation (FBI) detained Major Anderson at an airport in Houston, Texas, for possible arrest and prosecution for acts of torture. When the Justice Department consulted the U.S. Department of State, however, Under Secretary of State Thomas R. Pickering decided that Major Anderson was entitled to immunity from prosecution as a diplomatic representative of his government present in the United States for an official appearance before an international organization. The FBI

therefore allowed Major Anderson to depart the United States on March 10.

Sean D. Murphy, *Contemporary Practice of the United States Relating to International Law*, 94 AM. J. INT'L L. 516, 535-36 (2000).

How did Major Anderson's position differ from that of the defendant in *Kadic v. Karadzic* [*see* chap. 9], who was found not to have immunity from service of process while in New York for an official appearance before an international organization?

§ 11.02   Head of State and Act of State Immunities

REGINA v. BOW STREET METROPOLITAN STIPENDIARY MAGISTRATE AND OTHERS, EX PARTE PINOCHET UGARTE (NO. 3)

House of Lords
[2000] 1 App. Cas. 147, [1999] 2 All E.R. 97

[Augusto Pinochet Ugarte was the former president of Chile. While he was visiting England for medical treatment, the Spanish authorities requested his extradition. On October 16, 1998, he was served with a provisional arrest warrant, issued by a metropolitan stipendiary magistrate in London, alleging that, during the decade between September 1973 and December 1983, he participated in the murder of Spanish citizens living in Chile. A second provisional arrest warrant, issued on October 22, 1998, alleged his participation in torture, conspiracy to torture, detention of hostages, conspiracy to detain hostages, and in a conspiracy to commit murder which extended to Spain and other European countries. Pinochet applied for judicial review and habeas corpus. On October 28, 1998, both warrants were quashed by the Queen's Bench Divisional Court. The first warrant was found not to allege an extraditable offense because it involved the assertion of extraterritorial jurisdiction by Spain under circumstances where a British court would not have extraterritorial jurisdiction in the analogous situation of British citizens murdered abroad. Both warrants were found to be invalid, in any event, because Pinochet, as a former head of state, was held to have immunity from arrest and extradition proceedings in the United Kingdom for acts committed when he was head of state. [1998] All E.R. 509.

The Crown Prosecution Service, representing the Spanish government, was granted leave to appeal to the House of Lords on the ground that a point of law of general public importance was involved, "namely, the proper interpretation and scope of the immunity enjoyed by a former head of state from arrest and extradition proceedings in the United Kingdom in respect of acts committed while head of state." Before the appeal was heard, the list of charges against Pinochet was expanded to include numerous other acts perpetrated between 1972 and 1989. On November 25, 1998, by a 3-2 decision, the appeal was allowed and Pinochet was held not to enjoy immunity with respect to international crimes such as torture and hostage-taking committed when he was head of state. [1998] 4 All E.R. 897. However, on January 15, 1999, the House of Lords set aside this decision and ordered the matter reheard because Lord Hoffman, one of the Law Lords participating in the decision, had undisclosed ties to Amnesty International, an intervenor in the proceedings. [1999] 1 All E.R. 577. The panel that reheard the case was composed of seven members: Lord Browne-Wilkinson, Lord Goff of Chieveley, Lord Hope of Craighead, Lord Hutton, Lord Saville of Newgidate, Lord Millett, and Lord Phillips of Worth Matravers. Each delivered a separate opinion.]

LORD BROWNE-WILKINSON:

My Lords, as is well known, this case concerns an attempt by the government of Spain to extradite Senator Pinochet from this country to stand trial in Spain for crimes committed (primarily in Chile) during the period when Senator Pinochet was head of state in Chile. . . . The power to extradite from the United Kingdom for an 'extradition crime' is now contained in the Extradition Act 1989. That Act defines what constitutes an 'extradition crime.' For the purposes of the present case, the most important requirement is that the conduct complained of must constitute a crime under the law both of Spain and of the United Kingdom. This is known as the double criminality rule.

Since the Nazi atrocities and the Nuremberg trials, international law has recognised a number of offences as being international crimes. Individual states have taken jurisdiction to try some international crimes even in cases where such crimes were not committed within the geographical boundaries of such states. The most important of such international crimes for present purposes is torture which is regulated by the Convention against Torture and Other Cruel, Inhuman or Degrading Treatment or Punishment, 1984 [see chap. 9]. The obligations placed on the United Kingdom by that convention (and on the other 110 or more signatory states who have adopted the Convention) were incorporated into the law of the United Kingdom by section 134 of the Criminal Justice Act 1988. That Act came into force on 29 September 1988. Section 134 created a new crime under United Kingdom law, the crime of torture. As required by the Torture Convention 'all' torture wherever committed worldwide was made criminal under United Kingdom law and triable in the United Kingdom. No one has suggested that before section 134 came into effect torture committed outside the United Kingdom was a crime under United Kingdom law. Nor is it suggested that section 134 was retrospective so as to make torture committed outside the United Kingdom before 29 September 1988 a United Kingdom crime. Since torture outside the United Kingdom was not a crime under U.K. law until 29 September 1988, the principle of double criminality which requires an act to be a crime under both the law of Spain and of the

United Kingdom cannot be satisfied in relation to conduct before that date if the principle of double criminality requires the conduct to be criminal under United Kingdom law *at the date it was committed*. If, on the other hand, the double criminality rule only requires the conduct to be criminal under UK law *at the date of extradition* the rule was satisfied in relation to all torture alleged against Senator Pinochet whether it took place before or after 1988. . . .

On 11 September 1973 a right-wing coup evicted the left-wing regime of President Allende. The coup was led by a military junta, of whom Senator (then General) Pinochet was the leader. At some stage he became head of state. The Pinochet regime remained in power until 11 March 1990 when Senator Pinochet resigned.

There is no real dispute that during the period of the Senator Pinochet regime appalling acts of barbarism were committed in Chile and elsewhere in the world: torture, murder and the unexplained disappearance of individuals, all on a large scale. Although it is not alleged that Senator Pinochet himself committed any of those acts, it is alleged that they were done in pursuance of a conspiracy to which he was a party, at his instigation and with his knowledge. He denies these allegations. None of the conduct alleged was committed by or against citizens of the United Kingdom or in the United Kingdom.

In 1998 Senator Pinochet came to the United Kingdom for medical treatment. The judicial authorities in Spain sought to extradite him in order to stand trial in Spain on a large number of charges. Some of those charges had links with Spain. But most of the charges had no connection with Spain. . . .

[Because the expanded list of charges included conduct occurring before Pinochet became head of state, counsel for Pinochet argued at the second hearing before the House of Lords] that certain of the charges, in particular those relating to torture and conspiracy to torture, were not 'extradition crimes' because *at the time the acts were done* the acts were not criminal under the law of the United Kingdom. Once raised, this point could not be confined simply to the period (if any) before Senator Pinochet became head of state. If the double criminality rule requires it to be shown that at the date of the conduct such conduct would have been criminal under the law of the United Kingdom, any charge based on torture or conspiracy to torture occurring before 29 September 1988 (when section 134 of the 1988 Act came into force) could not be an 'extradition crime' and therefore could not in any event found an extradition order against Senator Pinochet. . . .

[Lord Browne-Wilkinson found that the wording and history of the definition of an "extradition crime" in section 2 of the Extradition Act 1989 indicated that] the conduct must be criminal under the law of the United Kingdom at the conduct date and not only at the request date. . . . The consequences of requiring torture to be a crime under U.K. law at the date the torture was committed are considered in Lord Hope's speech. As he demonstrates, the charges of torture and conspiracy to torture relating to conduct before 29

September 1988 (the date on which section 134 came into effect) are not extraditable, i.e. only those parts . . . which relate to the period after that date . . . are extradition crimes relating to torture. . . .

Lord Hope also considers, and I agree, that the only charge relating to hostage-taking does not disclose any offence under the Taking of Hostages Act, 1982 [since there was no allegation that hostages were taken in order to compel a third party to do or abstain from doing some action]. I must therefore consider whether, in relation to the two surviving categories of charge, Senator Pinochet enjoys sovereign immunity. But first it is necessary to consider the modern law of torture.

Apart from the law of piracy, the concept of personal liability under international law for international crimes is of comparatively modern growth. The traditional subjects of international law are states not human beings. But consequent upon the war crime trials after the 1939-45 World War, the international community came to recognise that there could be criminal liability under international law for a class of crimes such as war crimes and crimes against humanity. Although there may be legitimate doubts as to the legality of the Charter of the [Nuremberg Tribunal], in my judgment those doubts were stilled by the Affirmation of the Principles of International Law recognised by the Charter of Nuremberg Tribunal adopted by the United Nations General Assembly on 11 December 1946 [see chap. 18]. . . . At least from that date onwards the concept of personal liability for a crime in international law must have been part of international law. In the early years state torture was one of the elements of a war crime. In consequence torture, and various other crimes against humanity, were linked to war or at least to hostilities of some kind. But in the course of time this linkage with war fell away and torture, divorced from war or hostilities, became an international crime on its own. *See Prosecutor v. Furundzija* [chap. 9, *supra*]. Ever since 1945, torture on a large scale has featured as one of the crimes against humanity.

Moreover, the Republic of Chile accepted before your Lordships that the international law prohibiting torture has the character of *jus cogens* or a peremptory norm, i.e. one of those rules of international law which have a peculiar status. . . . The *jus cogens* nature of the international crime of torture justifies states in taking universal jurisdiction over torture wherever committed. International law provides that offences *jus cogens* may be punished by any state because the offenders are 'common enemies of all mankind and all nations have an equal interest in their apprehension and prosecution': *Demjanjuk v Petrovsky,* 776 F.2d 571 (6th Cir. 1985) [see chap. 18].

It was suggested by Miss Montgomery Q.C., for Senator Pinochet, that although torture was contrary to international law it was not strictly an international crime in the highest sense. In the light of the authorities . . . I have no doubt that long before the Torture Convention state torture was an international crime in the highest sense. The Torture Convention was agreed not in order to create an international crime which had not previously existed but to provide an international system under which the international criminal – the torturer – could find no safe haven. . . .

The first question on the Convention is to decide whether acts done by a head of state are done by 'a public official or a person acting in an official capacity' within the meaning of Article 1. The same question arises under section 134 of the 1988 Act. The answer to both questions must be the same. . . . It became clear during the argument that both the Republic of Chile and Senator Pinochet accepted that the acts alleged against Senator Pinochet, if proved, were acts done by a public official or person acting in an official capacity within the meaning of Article 1. In my judgment these concessions were correctly made. Unless a head of state authorising or promoting torture is an official or acting in an official capacity within Article 1, then he would not be guilty of the international crime of torture even within his own state. That plainly cannot have been the intention. In my judgment it would run completely contrary to the intention of the Convention if there was anybody who could be exempt from guilt. The crucial question is not whether Senator Pinochet falls within the definition in Article 1: he plainly does. The question is whether, even so, he is procedurally immune from process. To my mind the fact that a head of state can be guilty of the crime casts little, if any, light on the question whether he is immune from prosecution for that crime in a foreign state. . . .

[I]f Senator Pinochet is not entitled to immunity in relation to the acts of torture alleged to have occurred after 29 September 1988 it will be the first time, so far as counsel have discovered, when a local domestic court has refused to afford immunity to a head of state or former head of state on the grounds that there can be no immunity against prosecution for certain international crimes. . . . Given the importance of the point, it is surprising how narrow is the area of dispute. . . The issue is whether international law grants state immunity in relation to the international crime of torture and, if so, whether the Republic of Chile is entitled to claim such immunity even though Chile, Spain and the United Kingdom are all parties to the Torture Convention and therefore 'contractually' bound to give effect to its provisions from 8 December 1988 at the latest.*

It is a basic principle of international law that one sovereign state (the forum state) does not adjudicate on the conduct of a foreign state. The foreign state is entitled to procedural immunity from the processes of the forum state. This immunity extends to both criminal and civil liability. State immunity probably grew from the historical immunity of the person of the monarch. In any event, such personal immunity of the head of state persists to the present day: the head of state is entitled to the same immunity as the state itself. The diplomatic representative of the foreign state in the forum state is also afforded the same immunity in recognition of the dignity of the state which he represents. This

---

*   Spain had ratified the Convention on October 21, 1987. Chile ratified effective October 30, 1988; the United Kingdom effective December 8, 1988. – Eds.

immunity enjoyed by a head of state in power and an ambassador in post is a complete immunity attaching to the person of the head of state or ambassador and rendering him immune from all actions or prosecutions whether or not they relate to matters done for the benefit of the state. Such immunity is said to be granted *ratione personae*.

What then when the ambassador leaves his post or the head of state is deposed? The position of the ambassador is covered by the Vienna Convention on Diplomatic Relations, 1961. After providing for immunity from arrest (art. 29) and from criminal and civil jurisdiction (art. 31), Article 39(1) provides that the ambassador's privileges shall be enjoyed from the moment he takes up post; and subsection 2(2) provides:

> When the functions of a person enjoying privileges and immunities have come to an end, such privileges and immunities shall normally cease at the moment when he leaves the country, or on expiry of a reasonable period in which to do so, but shall subsist until that time, even in case of armed conflict. However, with respect to acts performed by such a person in the exercise of his functions as a member of the mission immunity shall continue to subsist.

The continuing partial immunity of the ambassador after leaving post is of a different kind from that enjoyed *ratione personae* while he was in post. Since he is no longer the representative of the foreign state he merits no particular privileges or immunities as a person. However in order to preserve the integrity of the activities of the foreign state during the period when he was ambassador, it is necessary to provide that immunity is afforded to his *official* acts during his tenure in post. If this were not done the sovereign immunity of the state could be evaded by calling in question acts done during the previous ambassador's time. Accordingly under Article 39(2) the ambassador, like any other official of the state, enjoys immunity in relation to his official acts done while he was an official. This limited immunity, *ratione materiae*, is to be contrasted with the former immunity *ratione personae* which gave complete immunity to all activities whether public or private.

In my judgment at common law a former head of state enjoys similar immunities, *ratione materiae*, once he ceases to be head of state. He too loses immunity *ratione personae* on ceasing to be head of state. As ex-head of state he cannot be sued in respect of acts performed whilst head of state in his public capacity. Thus, at common law, the position of the former ambassador and the former head of state appears to be much the same: both enjoy immunity for acts done in   performance of their respective functions whilst in office. . . . Accordingly, in my judgment, Senator Pinochet as former head of state enjoys immunity *ratione materiae* in relation to acts done by him as head of state as part of his official functions as head of state.

The question then which has to be answered is whether the alleged organisation of state torture by Senator Pinochet (if proved) would constitute an act committed by Senator Pinochet as part of his official functions as head of state. It is not enough to say that it cannot be part of the functions of the head of state to commit a crime. Actions which are criminal under the local law can still have been done officially and therefore give rise to immunity *ratione materiae*. The case needs to be analysed more closely.

Can it be said that the commission of a crime which is an international crime against humanity and *jus cogens* is an act done in an official capacity on behalf of the state? I believe there to be strong ground for saying that the implementation of torture as defined by the Torture Convention cannot be a state function. . . .

I have doubts whether, before the coming into force of the Torture Convention, the existence of the international crime of torture as *jus cogens* was enough to justify the conclusion that the organisation of state torture could not rank for immunity purposes as performance of an official function. At that stage there was no international tribunal to punish torture and no general jurisdiction to permit or require its punishment in domestic courts. Not until there was some form of universal jurisdiction for the punishment of the crime of torture could it really be talked about as a fully constituted international crime. But in my judgment the Torture Convention did provide what was missing: a worldwide universal jurisdiction. Further, it required all member states to ban and outlaw torture. How can it be for international law purposes an official function to do something which international law itself prohibits and criminalises? Thirdly, an essential feature of the international crime of torture is that it must be committed 'by or with the acquiescence of a public official or other person acting in an official capacity.' As a result all defendants in torture cases will be state officials. Yet, if the former head of state has immunity, the man most responsible will escape liability while his inferiors (the chiefs of police, junior army officers) who carried out his orders will be liable. I find it impossible to accept that this was the intention.

Finally, and to my mind decisively, if the implementation of a torture regime is a public function giving rise to immunity *ratione materiae*, this produces bizarre results. Immunity *ratione materiae* applies not only to ex-heads of state and ex-ambassadors but to all state officials who have been involved in carrying out the functions of the state. . . . [I]f the implementation of the torture regime is to be treated as official business sufficient to found an immunity for the former head of state, it must also be official business sufficient to justify immunity for his inferiors who actually did the torturing. . . . Therefore the whole elaborate structure of universal jurisdiction over torture committed by officials is rendered abortive and one of the main objectives of the Torture Convention – to provide a system under which there is no safe haven for torturers – will have been frustrated. In my judgment all these factors together demonstrate that the notion of continued immunity for ex-heads of state is inconsistent with the provisions of the Torture Convention.

For these reasons in my judgment if, as alleged, Senator Pinochet organised and authorised torture after 8 December 1988 he was not acting in any capacity which gives rise to immunity *ratione materiae* because such actions were contrary to international law, Chile had agreed to outlaw such conduct and Chile had agreed with the other parties to the Torture Convention that all signatory states should have jurisdiction to try official torture (as defined in the Convention) even if such torture were committed in Chile. . . .

As to the charges of murder and conspiracy to murder, no one has advanced any reason why the ordinary rules of immunity should not apply and Senator Pinochet is entitled to such immunity.

For these reasons, I would allow the appeal so as to permit the extradition proceedings to proceed on the allegation that torture in pursuance of a conspiracy to commit torture . . . was being committed by Senator Pinochet after 8 December 1988 when he lost his immunity. . . .

LORD GOFF OF CHIEVELEY:

The central question in the appeal is whether Senator Pinochet is entitled as former head of state to the benefit of state immunity *ratione materiae* in respect of the charges advanced against him. . . . Before the Divisional Court, and again before the first Appellate Committee, it was argued on behalf of the government of Spain that Senator Pinochet was not entitled to the benefit of state immunity basically on two grounds, *viz.* first, that the crimes alleged against Senator Pinochet are so horrific that an exception must be made to the international law principle of state immunity; and second, that the crimes with which he is charged are crimes against international law, in respect of which state immunity is not available. Both arguments were rejected by the Divisional Court, but a majority of the first Appellate Committee accepted the second argument. . . . Lord Slynn of Hadley and Lord Lloyd of Berwick, however, delivered substantial dissenting opinions. In particular, Lord Slynn considered in detail 'the developments in international law relating to what are called international crimes.' On the basis of the material so reviewed by him, he concluded:

It does not seem to me that it has been shown that there is any state practice or general consensus let alone a widely supported convention that all crimes against international law should be justiciable in national courts on the basis of the universality of jurisdiction. Nor is there any *jus cogens* in respect of such breaches of international law which require that a claim of state or head of state immunity, itself a well-established principle of international law, should be overridden.

He went on to consider whether international law now recognises that some crimes, and in particular crimes against humanity, are outwith the protection of head of state immunity. He referred to the relevant material, and observed:

. . . except in regard to crimes in particular situations before international tribunals these measures did not in general deal with the question as to whether otherwise existing immunities were taken away. Nor did they always specifically recognise the jurisdiction of, or confer jurisdiction on, national courts to try such crimes.

He then proceeded to examine the Torture Convention (1984), the Genocide Convention (1948), and the Taking of Hostages Convention (1983), and concluded that none of them had removed the long established immunity of former heads of state. . . . I wish to record my respectful agreement with the analysis, and conclusions, of Lord Slynn set out in the passages from his opinion to which I have referred. . . .

The principle of state immunity is expressed in the Latin maxim *par in parem non habet imperium*, the effect of which is that one sovereign state does not adjudicate on the conduct of another. This principle applies as between states, and the head of a state is entitled to the same immunity as the state itself, as are the diplomatic representatives of the state. That. . . principle applies in criminal proceedings. . . [T]he mere fact that the conduct is criminal does not of itself exclude the immunity, otherwise there would be little point in the immunity from criminal process; and this is so even where the crime is of a serious character. It follows, in my opinion, that the mere fact that the crime in question is torture does not exclude state immunity. It has however been stated by Sir Arthur Watts [*The Legal Position in International Law of Heads of States, Heads of Government and Foreign Ministers*, 247 HAGUE RECUEIL DES COURS (1994-III)] that a head of state may be personally responsible 'for acts of such seriousness that they constitute not merely international wrongs (in the broad sense of a civil wrong) but rather international crimes which offend against the public order of the international community.' . . .

So far as torture is concerned, however, there are two points to be made. The first is that it is evident . . . that Sir Arthur is referring not just to a specific crime as such, but to a crime which offends against the public order of the international community, for which a head of state may be *internationally* (his emphasis) accountable. The instruments cited by him show that he is concerned here with crimes against peace, war crimes and crimes against humanity. Originally these were limited to crimes committed in the context of armed conflict, as in the case of the Nuremberg and Tokyo Charters, and still in the case of the Statute of the Tribunal for the Former Yugoslavia, though there it is provided that the conflict can be international or internal in character. Subsequently, the context has been widened to include (*inter alia*) torture 'when committed as part of a widespread or systematic attack against a civilian population' on specified grounds. A provision to this effect appeared in the International Law Commission's Draft Code of Crimes of 1996 (which was, I understand, provisionally adopted in 1988), and also appeared in the Statute of the Tribunal for Rwanda (1994), and in the Rome Statute of the International Criminal Court (1998). . . . I should add that these developments were foreshadowed in the International Law Commission's Draft Code of Crimes of 1954; but this was not adopted, and there followed a long gap of about 35 years before the developments in the 1990s to which I have referred. It follows that these provisions are not capable of evidencing any settled practice in respect of torture outside the context of armed conflict until well after 1989 which is the latest date with which we are concerned in the present case. The second point is that these instruments are all concerned with international responsibility before international tribunals, and not with the exclusion of state immunity in criminal proceedings before national courts. This supports the conclusion of Lord Slynn that 'except in regard to crimes in particular situations before international tribunals these measures did not in general deal with the question whether otherwise existing immunities were taken away,' with which I have already expressed my respectful agreement.

It follows that, if state immunity in respect of crimes of torture has been excluded at all in the present case, this can only have been done by the Torture Convention itself. . . . It is to be observed that no mention is made of state immunity in the Convention. Had it been intended to exclude state immunity, it is reasonable to assume that this would have been the subject either of a separate article, or of a separate paragraph in Article 7. . . . Since therefore exclusion of immunity is said to result from the Torture Convention and there is no express term of the Convention to this effect, the argument has, in my opinion, to be formulated as dependent upon an implied term in the Convention. . . .

On behalf of the government of Chile Dr Collins [submitted] that a state's waiver of its immunity by treaty must always be express. With that submission, I agree. . . . [I]t appears to me to be clear that, in accordance both with international law, and with the law of this country which on this point reflects international law, a state's waiver of its immunity by treaty must, as Dr Collins submitted, always be express. Indeed, if this was not so, there could well be international chaos as the courts of different state parties to a treaty reach different conclusions on the question whether a waiver of immunity was to be implied.

However it is, as I understand it, suggested that this well-established principle can be circumvented in the present case on the basis that it is not proposed that state parties to the Torture Convention have agreed to waive their state immunity in proceedings brought in the states of other parties in respect of allegations of torture within the Convention. It is rather that, for the purposes of the Convention, such torture does not form part of the functions of public officials or others acting in an official capacity including, in particular, a head of state. Moreover since state immunity *ratione materiae* can only be claimed in respect of acts done by an official in the exercise of his functions as such, it would follow, for example, that the effect is that a former head of state does not enjoy the benefit of immunity *ratione materiae* in respect of such torture after he has ceased to hold office.

In my opinion, the principle which I have described cannot be circumvented in this way. I observe first that the meaning of the word 'functions' as used in this context is well established. The functions of, for example, a head of state are governmental functions, as opposed to private acts; and the fact that the head of state performs an act, other than a private act, which is criminal does not deprive it of its governmental character. This is as true of a serious crime, such as murder or torture, as it is of a lesser crime. As Lord Bingham of Cornhill C.J. said in the Divisional Court:

> . . . a former head of state is clearly entitled to immunity in relation to criminal acts performed in the course of exercising public functions. One cannot therefore hold that any deviation from good democratic practice is outside the pale of immunity. If the former sovereign is immune from process in respect of some crimes, where does one draw the line?

It was in answer to that question that the appellants advanced the theory that one draws the line at crimes which may be called 'international crimes.' If, however, a limit is to be placed on governmental functions so as to exclude from them acts of torture within the Torture Convention, this can only be done by means of an implication arising from the Convention itself. Moreover, as I understand it, the only purpose of the proposed implied limitation upon the functions of public officials is to deprive them, or as in the present case a former head of state, of the benefit of state immunity; and in my opinion the policy which requires that such a result can only be achieved in a treaty by express agreement, with the effect that it cannot be so achieved by implication, renders it equally unacceptable that it should be achieved indirectly by means of an implication such as that now proposed. . . .

[T]he assumption underlying the argument that the continued availability of state immunity is inconsistent with the obligations of state parties to the Convention is in my opinion not justified. . . . First of all, in the majority of cases which may arise under the Convention, no question of state immunity will arise at all, because the public official concerned is likely to be present in his own country. Even when such a question does arise, there is no reason to assume that state immunity will be asserted by the state of which the alleged torturer is a public official; on the contrary, it is only in unusual cases, such as the present, that this is likely to be done. In any event, however, not only is there no mention of state immunity in the Convention, but in my opinion it is not inconsistent with its express provisions that, if steps are taken to extradite him or to submit his case to the authorities for the purpose of prosecution, the appropriate state should be entitled to assert state immunity. In this connection, I comment that it is not suggested that it is inconsistent with the Convention that immunity *ratione personae* should be asserted; if so, I find it difficult to see why it should be inconsistent to assert immunity *ratione materiae*.

. . . . [N]othing in the negotiating history of the Torture Convention throws any light on the proposed implied term. Certainly the *travaux preparatoires* shown to your Lordships reveal no trace of any consideration being given to waiver of state immunity. . . . It is surely most unlikely that during the years in which the draft was under consideration no thought was given to the possibility of the state parties to the Convention waiving state immunity. Furthermore, if agreement had been reached that there should be such a waiver, express provision would inevitably have been made in the Convention to that effect. Plainly, however, no such agreement was reached. . . . In this connection it must not be overlooked that there are many reasons why states, although recognising that in certain circumstances jurisdiction should be vested in another national court in respect of acts of torture committed by public officials within their own jurisdiction, may nevertheless have considered it imperative that they should be able, if necessary, to assert state immunity. The Torture Convention applies not only to a series of acts of systematic torture, but to the commission of, even acquiescence in, a single act of physical or mental torture. Extradition can nowadays be sought, in some parts of the world, on the basis of a simple allegation unsupported by prima facie evidence. In certain circumstances torture may, for compelling political reasons, be the subject of an amnesty, or some other form of settlement, in the state where it has been, or is alleged to have been, committed.

Furthermore, if immunity *ratione materiae* was excluded, former heads of state and senior public officials would have to think twice about travelling abroad, for fear of being the subject of unfounded allegations emanating from states of a different political persuasion. In this connection, it is a mistake to assume that state parties to the Convention would only wish to preserve state immunity in cases of torture in order to shield public officials guilty of torture from prosecution elsewhere in the world. Such an assumption is based on a misunderstanding of the nature and function of state immunity, which is a rule of international law restraining one sovereign state from sitting in judgment on the sovereign behaviour of another. . . . State immunity *ratione materiae* operates therefore to protect former heads of state, and (where immunity is asserted) public officials, even minor public officials, from legal process in foreign countries in respect of acts done in the exercise of their functions as such, including accusation and arrest in respect of alleged crimes. It can therefore be effective to preclude any such process in respect of alleged crimes, including allegations which are misguided or even malicious – a matter which can be of great significance where, for example, a former head of state is concerned and political passions are aroused. Preservation of state immunity is therefore a matter of particular importance to powerful countries whose heads of state perform an executive role, and who may therefore be regarded as possible targets by governments of states which, for deeply felt political reasons, deplore their actions while in office. But, to bring the matter nearer home, we must not overlook the fact that it is not only in the United States of America that a substantial body of opinion supports the campaign of the IRA to overthrow the democratic government of Northern Ireland. It is not beyond the bounds of possibility that a state whose government is imbued with this opinion might seek to extradite from a third country, where he or she happens to be, a responsible Minister of the Crown, or even a more humble public official such as a police inspector, on the ground that he or she has acquiesced in a single act of physical or mental torture in Northern Ireland. . . .

For the above reasons, I am of the opinion that by far the greater part of the charges against Senator Pinochet must be excluded as offending against the double criminality rule; and that, in respect of the surviving charges . . . Senator Pinochet is entitled to the benefit of state immunity *ratione materiae* as a former head of state. I would therefore dismiss the appeal of the government of Spain from the decision of the Divisional Court.

LORD HOPE OF CRAIGHEAD:

[Lord Hope subjected the expanded list of charges against Pinochet to close analysis on the premise that conduct constituted an extradition crime only if punishable in the U.K. at the time it took place, and that the operative date, with respect to the charges of torture, was September 28, 1998, when section 134 of the Criminal Justice Act 1988 came into effect. The result of this analysis was to restrict the number of charges which alleged extradition crimes to a small handful: those alleging murder or conspiracy to murder in Spain, two alleging conspiracies to commit torture which extended beyond September 28, 1998, and one alleging a single act of torture on June 24,1989. These were the only charges as to which the question of immunity for governmental acts was relevant.]

. . . . [T]he sovereign or governmental acts of one state are not matters upon which the courts of other states will adjudicate. The fact that acts done for the state have involved conduct which is criminal does not remove the immunity. Indeed the whole purpose of the residual immunity *ratione materiae* is to protect the former head of state against allegations of such conduct after he has left office. A head of state needs to be free to promote his own state's interests during the entire period when he is in office without being subjected to the prospect of detention, arrest or embarrassment in the foreign legal system of the receiving state. The conduct does not have to be lawful to attract the immunity.

It may be said that it is not one of the functions of a head of state to commit acts which are criminal according to the laws and constitution of his own state or which customary international law regards as criminal. But I consider that this approach to the question is unsound in principle. The principle of immunity *ratione materiae* protects all acts which the head of state has performed in the exercise of the functions of government. The purpose for which they were performed protects these acts from any further analysis. There are only two exceptions to this approach which customary international law has recognised. The first relates to criminal acts which the head of state did under the colour of his authority as head of state but which were in reality for his own pleasure or benefit. . . . The second relates to acts the prohibition of which has acquired the status under international law of *jus cogens*. This compels all states to refrain from such conduct under any circumstances and imposes an obligation *erga omnes* to punish such conduct. . . .

But even in the field of such high crimes as have achieved the status of *jus cogens* under customary international law there is as yet no general agreement that they are outside the immunity to which former heads of state are entitled from the jurisdiction of foreign national courts. There is plenty of source material to show that war crimes and crimes against humanity have been separated out from the generality of conduct which customary international law has come to regard as criminal. . . . [But] except in regard to crimes in particular situations where international tribunals have been set up to deal with them and it is part of the arrangement that heads of state should not have any immunity, there is no general recognition that there has been a loss of immunity from the jurisdiction of foreign national courts. . . .

That is the background against which I now turn to the Torture Convention. . . . [I]t would be wrong to regard the Torture Convention as having by necessary implication removed the immunity *ratione materiae* from former heads of state in regard to every act of torture of any kind which might be alleged against him falling within the scope of Article 1. . . . [T]he definition in Article 1 is so wide that any act of official torture, so long as it involved 'severe' pain or suffering, would be covered by it. . . . There is no requirement that it should have been perpetrated on such a scale as to constitute an international crime in the sense described by Sir Arthur Watts, that is to say a crime which offends against the public order of the international community. A single act of torture by an official against a national of his state within that state's borders will do. The risks to which former heads of state would be exposed on leaving office of being detained in foreign states upon an allegation that they had acquiesced in an act of official torture would have been so obvious to governments that it is hard to believe that they would ever have agreed to this. . . .

Nevertheless there remains the question whether the immunity can survive Chile's agreement to the Torture Convention if the torture which is alleged was of such a kind or on such a scale as to amount to an international crime. . . . The allegations which the Spanish judicial authorities have made against Senator Pinochet fall into that category. . . . [W] are not dealing in this case – even upon the restricted basis of those charges on which Senator Pinochet could lawfully be extradited if he has no immunity – with isolated acts of official torture. We are dealing with the remnants of an allegation that he is guilty of what would now, without doubt, be regarded by customary international law as an international crime. This is because he is said to have been involved in acts of torture which were committed in pursuance of a policy to commit systematic torture within Chile and elsewhere as an instrument of government. . . .

I think that there are sufficient signs that the necessary developments in international law were in place by [1988]. The careful discussion of the *jus cogens* and *erga omnes* rules in regard to allegations of official torture in

Siderman de Blake v. Argentina,[*] which I regard as persuasive on this point, shows that there was already widespread agreement that the prohibition against official torture had achieved the status of a *jus cogens* norm. . . . Then there is the Torture Convention of 10 December 1984. Having secured a sufficient number of signatories, it entered into force on 26 June 1987. In my opinion, once the machinery which it provides was put in place to enable jurisdiction over such crimes to be exercised in the courts of a foreign state, it was no longer open to any state which was a signatory to the Convention to invoke the immunity *ratione materiae* in the event of allegations of systematic or widespread torture committed after that date being made in the courts of that state against its officials or any other person acting in an official capacity. . . .

I would not regard this as a case of waiver. Nor would I accept that it was an implied term of the Torture Convention that former heads of state were to be deprived of their immunity *ratione materiae* with respect to all acts of official torture as defined in Article 1. It is just that the obligations which were recognised by customary international law in the case of such serious international crimes by the date when Chile ratified the Convention are so strong as to override any objection by it on the ground of immunity *ratione materiae* to the exercise of the jurisdiction over crimes committed after that date which the United Kingdom had made available.

I consider that the date as from which the immunity *ratione materiae* was lost was 30 October 1988, which was the date when Chile's ratification of the Torture Convention on 30 September 1988 took effect . . . . Chile, having ratified the Convention, . . . was deprived of the right to object to the extraterritorial jurisdiction which the United Kingdom was able to assert over these offences when [section 134 of the Criminal Justice Act 1988] came into force. But I am content to accept the view of my noble and learned friend Lord Saville of Newdigate that Senator Pinochet continued to have immunity until 8 December 1988 when the United Kingdom ratified the Convention.

It follows that . . . I too would allow the appeal [only] to the extent necessary to permit the extradition to proceed on the charges of torture and conspiracy to torture relating to the period after 8 December 1988.

LORD HUTTON:

I am in agreement with [Lord Browne-Wilkinson's] reasoning and conclusion

---

[*] In *Siderman de Blake v. Argentina*, 965 F.2d 699 (9th Cir. 1992) *cert. denied*, 507 U.S. 1017 (1993), the court found that (1) torture by Argentine officials in 1976 constituted the violation of a *jus cogens* norm; (2) the fact that there had been a violation of *jus cogens* was insufficient to trump sovereign immunity, which is completely controlled by the Foreign Sovereign Immunities Act of 1976; but (3) Argentina implicitly waived its sovereign immunity by previously having involved the U.S. courts in its efforts to persecute the plaintiff. – Eds.

that the definition of an 'extradition crime' in the Extradition Act 1989 requires the conduct to be criminal under United Kingdom law at the date of commission. I am also in agreement with the analysis and conclusions of my noble and learned friend Lord Hope of Craighead as to the alleged crimes in respect of which Senator Pinochet could be extradited apart from any issue of immunity. I further agree with the view of Lord Browne-Wilkinson that Senator Pinochet is entitled to immunity in respect of charges of murder and conspiracy to murder, but I wish to make some observations on the issue of immunity claimed by Senator Pinochet in respect of charges of torture and conspiracy to torture. . . .

[T]he crucial question for decision is whether, if committed, the acts of torture (in which term I include acts of torture and conspiracy to commit torture) alleged against Senator Pinochet were carried out by him in the performance of his functions as head of state. . . . It is clear that the acts of torture which Senator Pinochet is alleged to have committed were not acts carried out in his private capacity for his personal gratification. If that had been the case they would have been private acts and it is not disputed that Senator Pinochet, once he had ceased to be head of state, would not be entitled to claim immunity in respect of them. It was submitted on his behalf that the acts of torture were carried out for the purposes of protecting the state and advancing its interests, as Senator Pinochet saw them, and were therefore governmental functions and were accordingly performed as functions of the head of state. It was further submitted that the immunity which Senator Pinochet claimed was the immunity of the State of Chile itself. . . .

[S]ince the end of the Second World War there has been a clear recognition by the international community that certain crimes are so grave and so inhuman that they constitute crimes against international law and that the international community is under a duty to bring to justice a person who commits such crimes. Torture has been recognised as such a crime. . . . As your Lordships hold that there is no jurisdiction to extradite Senator Pinochet for acts of torture prior to 29 September 1988, which was the date on which section 134 of the Criminal Justice Act 1988 came into operation, it is unnecessary to decide when torture became a crime against international law prior to that date, but I am of opinion that acts of torture were clearly crimes against international law and that the prohibition of torture had required the status of *ius cogens* by that date.

[T]he issue in the present case is whether Senator Pinochet, as a former head of state, can claim immunity (*ratione materiae*) on the grounds that acts of torture committed by him when he was head of state were done by him in exercise of his functions as head of state. In my opinion he is not entitled to claim such immunity. The Torture Convention 1984 makes it clear that no state is to tolerate torture by its public officials or by persons acting in an official capacity . . . . Therefore, having regard to the provisions of the Torture Convention, I do not consider that Senator Pinochet or Chile can claim that the commission of acts of torture after 29 September 1988 were functions of the head of state. The alleged acts of torture by Senator Pinochet were carried out under colour of his position as head of state, but they cannot be regarded as functions of a head of state under international law when international law expressly prohibits torture as a measure which a state can employ in any circumstances whatsoever and has made it an international crime. . . .

A number of international instruments define a crime against humanity as one which is committed on a large scale. . . . However, Article 4 of the Torture Convention provides that: 'Each state party shall ensure that *all* acts of torture are offences under its criminal law.' (emphasis added). Therefore I consider that a single act of torture carried out, or instigated by, a public official, or other person acting in a official capacity constitutes a crime against international law, and that torture does not become an international crime only when it is committed or instigated on a large scale. Accordingly, I am of the opinion that Senator Pinochet cannot claim that a single act of torture, or a small number of acts of torture carried out by him did not constitute international crimes and did not constitute acts committed outside the ambit of his functions as head of state. . . .

For the reasons which I have given, I am of opinion that Senator Pinochet is not entitled to claim immunity in the extradition proceedings in respect of conspiracy to torture and acts of torture alleged to have been committed by him after 29 September 1988 and, to that extent, I would allow the appeal. . . .

LORD SAVILLE OF NEWDIGATE:

On this appeal two questions of law arise. . . [T]he first question of law is whether any of the crimes of which [Senator Pinochet]stands accused in Spain is an extradition crime within the meaning of the 1989 Act. As to this, I am in agreement with the reasoning and conclusions in the speech of my noble and learned friend Lord Browne-Wilkinson. I am also in agreement with the reasons given by my noble and learned friend Lord Hope of Craighead in his speech for concluding that only those few allegations that he identifies amount to extradition crimes. . . .

The second question of law is whether, in respect of these extradition crimes, Senator Pinochet can resist the extradition proceedings brought against him on the grounds that he enjoys immunity from these proceedings. . . . [I]n general under customary international law a former head of state enjoy[s] immunity from criminal proceedings in other countries in respect of what he did in his official capacity as head of state. . . . The only possible relevant qualification or exception in the circumstances of this case relates to torture.

I am not persuaded that before the Torture Convention there was any such qualification or exception. Although the systematic or widespread use of torture became universally condemned as an international crime, it does not follow that a former head of state, who as head of state used torture for state purposes, could under international law be prosecuted for torture in other countries where

previously under that law he would have enjoyed immunity *ratione materiae*.
. . .

[T]he Convention . . . covers what can be described as official torture and
must therefore include torture carried out for state purposes. . . . To my mind,
it must follow that a head of state, who for state purposes resorts to torture,
would be a person acting in an official capacity within the meaning of this
convention. He would indeed, to my mind, be a prime example of an official
torturer.

It does not follow from this that the immunity enjoyed by a serving head of
state, which is entirely unrelated to whether or not he was acting in an official
capacity, is thereby removed in cases of torture. In my view it is not, since
immunity *ratione personae* attaches to the office and not to any particular
conduct of the office holder. On the other hand, the immunity of a former head
of state does attach to his conduct whilst in office and is wholly related to what
he did in his official capacity.

So far as the states that are parties to the Convention are concerned, I cannot
see how, so far as torture is concerned, this immunity can exist consistently
with the terms of that Convention. Each state party has agreed that the other
state parties can exercise jurisdiction over alleged official torturers found within
their territories, by extraditing them or referring them to their own appropriate
authorities for prosecution; and thus, to my mind, can hardly simultaneously
claim an immunity from extradition or prosecution that is necessarily based on
the official nature of the alleged torture.

Since 8 December 1988 Chile, Spain and this country have all been parties
to the Torture Convention. So far as these countries at least are concerned it
seems to me that from that date these state parties are in agreement with each
other that the immunity *ratione materiae* of their former heads of state cannot
be claimed in cases of alleged official torture. . . .

I do not reach this conclusion by implying terms into the Torture Convention,
but simply by applying its express terms. A former head of state who it is
alleged resorted to torture for state purposes falls, in my view, fairly and
squarely within those terms and, on the face of it, should be dealt with in
accordance with them. . . . It is said that any waiver by states of immunities
must be express, or at least unequivocal. I would not dissent from this as a
general proposition, but it seems to me that the express and unequivocal terms
of the Torture Convention fulfil any such requirement. To my mind these terms
demonstrate that the states who have become parties have clearly and
unambiguously agreed that official torture should now be dealt with in a way
which would otherwise amount to an interference in their sovereignty.

I would accordingly allow this appeal to the extent necessary to permit the
extradition proceedings to continue in respect of the crimes of torture and
(where it is alleged that torture resulted) of conspiracy to torture, allegedly

committed by Senator Pinochet after 8 December 1988. . . .

LORD PHILLIPS OF WORTH MATRAVERS:

What is the precise nature of the double criminality rule that governs whether conduct amounts to an extradition crime and what parts of Senator Pinochet's alleged conduct satisfy that rule? On the first issue I agree with the conclusion reached by Lord Browne-Wilkinson and on the second I agree with the analysis of my noble and learned friend, Lord Hope of Craighead. . . . It is on the issue of immunity that I would wish to add some comments of my own. . . .

If Senator Pinochet were still the head of state of Chile, he and Chile would be in a position to complain that the entire extradition process was a violation of the duties owed under international law to a person of his status. A head of state on a visit to another country is inviolable. He cannot be arrested or detained, let alone removed against his will to another country, and he is not subject to the judicial processes, whether civil or criminal, of the courts of the state that he is visiting. But Senator Pinochet is no longer head of state of Chile. While, as a matter of courtesy, a state may accord a visitor of Senator Pinochet's distinction certain privileges, it is under no legal obligation to do so. He accepts, and Chile accepts, that this country no longer owes him any duty under international law by reason of his status *ratione personae*. Immunity is claimed, *ratione materiae*, on the ground that the subject matter of the extradition process is the conduct by Senator Pinochet of his official functions when he was head of state. . . .

There would seem to be two explanations for immunity *ratione materiae*. The first is that to sue an individual in respect of the conduct of the state's business is, indirectly, to sue the state. The state would be obliged to meet any award of damage made against the individual. This reasoning has no application to criminal proceedings. The second explanation for the immunity is the principle that it is contrary to international law for one state to adjudicate upon the internal affairs of another state. Where a state or a state official is impleaded, this principle applies as part of the explanation for immunity. Where a state is not directly or indirectly impleaded in the litigation, so that no issue of state immunity as such arises, the English and American courts have nonetheless, as a matter of judicial restraint, held themselves not competent to entertain litigation that turns on the validity of the public acts of a foreign state, applying what has become known as the act of state doctrine. . . .

In the latter part of this century there has been developing a recognition among states that some types of criminal conduct cannot be treated as a matter for the exclusive competence of the state in which they occur. . . Since the Second World War states have recognised that not all criminal conduct can be left to be dealt with as a domestic matter by the laws and the courts of the territories in which such conduct occurs. There are some categories of crime of such gravity that they shock the consciousness of mankind and cannot be tolerated by the international community. Any individual who commits such a crime offends against international law. The nature of these crimes is such that they are likely to involve the concerted conduct of many and liable to involve the complicity of the officials of the state in which they occur, if not of the state itself. In these circumstances it is desirable that jurisdiction should exist to prosecute individuals for such conduct outside the territory in which such conduct occurs.

I believe that it is still an open question whether international law recognises universal jurisdiction in respect of international crimes – that is the right, under international law, of the courts of any state to prosecute for such crimes wherever they occur. In relation to war crimes, such a jurisdiction has been asserted by the State of Israel, notably in the prosecution of Adolf Eichmann, but this assertion of jurisdiction does not reflect any general state practice in relation to international crimes. Rather, states have tended to agree, or to attempt to agree, on the creation of international tribunals to try international crimes. They have however, on occasion, agreed by conventions, that their national courts should enjoy jurisdiction to prosecute for a particular category of international crime wherever occurring.

[N]o established rule of international law requires state immunity *ratione materiae* to be accorded in respect of prosecution for an international crime. International crimes and extraterritorial jurisdiction in relation to them are both new arrivals in the field of public international law. I do not believe that state immunity *ratione materiae* can coexist with them. The exercise of extraterritorial jurisdiction overrides the principle that one state will not intervene in the internal affairs of another. It does so because, where international crime is concerned, that principle cannot prevail. An international crime is as offensive, if not more offensive, to the international community when committed under colour of office. Once extraterritorial jurisdiction is established, it makes no sense to exclude from it acts done in an official capacity.

There can be no doubt that the conduct of which Senator Pinochet stands accused by Spain is criminal under international law. The Republic of Chile has accepted that torture is prohibited by international law and that the prohibition of torture has the character of *jus cogens* and or obligation *erga omnes*. It is further accepted that officially sanctioned torture is forbidden by international law. The information provided by Spain accuses Senator Pinochet not merely of having abused his powers as head of state by committing torture, but of subduing political opposition by a campaign of abduction, torture and murder that extended beyond the boundaries of Chile. When considering what is alleged, I do not believe that it is correct to attempt to analyse individual elements of this campaign and to identify some as being criminal under international law and others as not constituting international crimes. If Senator Pinochet behaved as Spain alleged, then the entirety of his conduct was a violation of the norms of international law. He can have no immunity against prosecution for any crime that formed part of that campaign. . . .

For these reasons, I would allow the appeal in respect of so much of the conduct alleged against Senator Pinochet as constitutes extradition crimes.

LORD MILLETT:

The doctrine of state immunity is the product of the classical theory of international law. This taught that states were the only actors on the international plane; the rights of individuals were not the subject of international law. States were sovereign and equal: it followed that one state could not be impleaded in the national courts of another; *par in parem non habet imperium*. States were obliged to abstain from interfering in the internal affairs of one another. International law was not concerned with the way in which a sovereign state treated its own nationals in its own territory. It is a cliche of modern international law that the classical theory no longer prevails in its unadulterated form. The idea that individuals who commit crimes, recognised as such by international law, may be held internationally accountable for their actions, is now an accepted doctrine of international law.
. . .

Two overlapping immunities are recognised by international law: immunity *ratione personae* and immunity *ratione materiae*. They are quite different and have different rationales.

Immunity *ratione personae* is a status immunity. An individual who enjoys its protection does so because of his official status. It enures for his benefit only so long as he holds office. While he does so he enjoys absolute immunity from the civil and criminal jurisdiction of the national courts of foreign states. But it is only narrowly available. It is confined to serving heads of state and heads of diplomatic missions, their families and servants. It is not available to serving heads of government who are not also heads of state, military commanders and those in charge of the security forces, or their subordinates. It would have been available to Hitler but not to Mussolini or Tojo. . . .

The immunity of a serving head of state is enjoyed by reason of his special status as the holder of his state's highest office. He is regarded as the personal embodiment of the state itself. It would be an affront to the dignity and sovereignty of the state which he personifies and a denial of the equality of sovereign states to subject him to the jurisdiction of the municipal courts of another state, whether in respect of his public acts or private affairs. His person is inviolable; he is not liable to be arrested or detained on any ground whatever. The head of a diplomatic mission represents his head of state and thus embodies the sending state in the territory of the receiving state. While he remains in office he is entitled to the same absolute immunity as his head of state, in relation both to his public and private acts.

This immunity is not in issue in the present case. Senator Pinochet is not a serving head of state. If he were, he could not be extradited. It would be an intolerable affront to the Republic of Chile to arrest him or detain him.

Immunity *ratione materiae* is very different. This is a subject matter immunity. It operates to prevent the official and governmental acts of one state from being called into question in proceedings before the courts of another, and only incidentally confers immunity on the individual. It is therefore a narrower immunity but it is more widely available. It is available to former heads of state and heads of diplomatic missions, and any one whose conduct in the exercise of the authority of the state is afterwards called into question, whether he acted as head of government, government minister, military commander or chief of police, or subordinate public official. The immunity is the same whatever the rank of the office holder. This too is common ground. It is an immunity from the civil and criminal jurisdiction of foreign national courts, but only in respect of governmental or official acts. The exercise of authority by the military and security forces of the state is the paradigm example of such conduct. The immunity finds its rationale in the equality of sovereign states and the doctrine of non-interference in the internal affairs of other states . . . . The immunity is sometimes also justified by the need to prevent the serving head of state, or diplomat, from being inhibited in the performance of his official duties by fear of the consequences after he has ceased to hold office. This last basis can hardly be prayed in aid to support the availability of the immunity in respect of criminal activities prohibited by international law.

Given its scope and rationale, it is closely similar to, and may be indistinguishable from, aspects of the Anglo-American 'act of state' doctrine. As I understand the difference between them, state immunity is a creature of international law and operates as a plea in bar to the jurisdiction of the national court, whereas the act of state doctrine is a rule of domestic law which holds the national court incompetent to adjudicate upon the lawfulness of the sovereign acts of a foreign state. . . .

The charges brought against Senator Pinochet are concerned with his public and official acts, first as commander in chief of the Chilean army and later as head of state. He is accused of having embarked on a widespread and systematic reign of terror in order to obtain power and then to maintain it. If the allegations against him are true, he deliberately employed torture as an instrument of state policy. As international law stood on the eve of the Second World War, his conduct as head of state after he seized power would probably have attracted immunity *ratione materiae*. If so, I am of opinion that it would have been equally true of his conduct during the period before the coup was successful. He was not then, of course, head of state. But he took advantage of his position as commander in chief of the army and made use of the existing military chain of command to deploy the armed forces of the state against its constitutional government. These were not private acts. They were official and governmental or sovereign acts by any standard.

The immunity is available whether the acts in question are illegal or unconstitutional or otherwise unauthorised under the internal law of the state, since the whole purpose of state immunity is to prevent the legality of such acts from being adjudicated upon in the municipal courts of a foreign state. A sovereign state has the exclusive right to determine what is and is not illegal or unconstitutional under its own domestic law. Even before the end of the Second World War, however, it was questionable whether the doctrine of state immunity accorded protection in respect of conduct which was prohibited by international law. . . .

By the time Senator Pinochet seized power, the international community had renounced the use of torture as an instrument of state policy. The Republic of Chile accepts that, by 1973, the use of torture by state authorities was prohibited by international law and that the prohibition had the character of *jus cogens* or obligation *erga omnes*. But it insists that this does not confer universal jurisdiction or affect the immunity of a former head of state *ratione materiae* from the jurisdiction of foreign national courts.

In my opinion, crimes prohibited by international law attract universal jurisdiction under customary international law if two criteria are satisfied. First, they must be contrary to a peremptory norm of international law so as to infringe a *jus cogens*. Secondly, they must be so serious and on such a scale that they can justly be regarded as an attack on the international legal order. Isolated offences, even if committed by public officials, would not satisfy these criteria. . . . Every state has jurisdiction under customary international law to exercise extraterritorial jurisdiction in respect of international crimes which satisfy the relevant criteria. Whether its courts have extraterritorial jurisdiction under its internal domestic law depends, of course, on its constitutional arrangements and the relationship between customary international law and the jurisdiction of its criminal courts. The jurisdiction of the English criminal courts is usually statutory, but it is supplemented by the common law. Customary international law is part of the common law, and accordingly I consider that the English courts have and always have had extraterritorial criminal jurisdiction in respect of crimes of universal jurisdiction under customary international law.

In my opinion, the systematic use of torture on a large scale and as an instrument of state policy had joined piracy, war crimes and crimes against peace as an international crime of universal jurisdiction well before 1984. I consider that it had done so by 1973. For my own part, therefore, I would hold that the courts of this country already possessed extraterritorial jurisdiction in respect of torture and conspiracy to torture on the scale of the charges in the present case and did not require the authority of statute to exercise it. . . .

I turn finally to the plea of immunity *ratione materiae* in relation to the . . . allegations of torture, conspiracy to torture and conspiracy to murder. I can deal with the charges of conspiracy to murder quite shortly. The offences are alleged to have taken place in the requesting state. The plea of immunity *ratione materiae* is not available in respect of an offence committed in the forum state, whether this be England or Spain.

The definition of torture, both in the Convention and section 134 of the 1988

Act, is in my opinion entirely inconsistent with the existence of a plea of immunity *ratione materiae*. The offence can be committed *only* by or at the instigation of, or with the consent or acquiescence of, a public official or other person acting in an official capacity. The official or governmental nature of the act, which forms the basis of the immunity, is an essential ingredient of the offence. No rational system of criminal justice can allow an immunity which is coextensive with the offence.

In my view a serving head of state or diplomat could still claim immunity *ratione personae* if charged with an offence under section 134. He does not have to rely on the character of the conduct of which he is accused. The nature of the charge is irrelevant; his immunity is personal and absolute. But the former head of state and the former diplomat are in no different position from anyone else claiming to have acted in the exercise of state authority. If the respondent's arguments were accepted, section 134 would be a dead letter. Either the accused was acting in a private capacity, in which case he cannot be charged with an offence under the section; or he was acting in an official capacity, in which case he would enjoy immunity from prosecution. . . .

My Lords, the Republic of Chile was a party to the Torture Convention, and must be taken to have assented to the imposition of an obligation on foreign national courts to take and exercise criminal jurisdiction in respect of the official use of torture. I do not regard it as having thereby waived its immunity. In my opinion there was no immunity to be waived. The offence is one which could only be committed in circumstances which would normally give rise to the immunity. The international community had created an offence for which immunity *ratione materiae* could not possible be available. International law cannot be supposed to have established a crime having the character of a *jus cogens* and at the same time to have provided an immunity which is coextensive with the obligation it seeks to impose. . .

For my own part, I would allow the appeal in respect of the charges relating to the offences in Spain and to torture and conspiracy to torture, wherever and whenever carried out. . . .

NOTES AND QUESTIONS

(1) Given the seven separate opinions expressed, what exactly did the House of Lords hold on rehearing of the *Pinochet* case? In presenting the Report of the Appellate Committee to the House on March 24, 1999, Lord Browne-Wilkinson provided the following summary:

> In today's judgment, six members of the Committee hold that, under the ordinary law of extradition, Senator Pinochet cannot be extradited to face charges in relation to torture occurring before 29th September 1988

because until that date the double criminality principle was not satisfied. The result of this decision is to eliminate the majority of the charges levelled against Senator Pinochet. . . Most of the allegations against Senator Pinochet relate to the period of the coup in Chile in 1973 and the years immediately thereafter. The only charges left which are extradition crimes comprise one isolated charge of torture after 29th September 1988, certain conspiracies to torture relating to the period from 29th September 1988 to January 1990 and certain charges of conspiracy in Spain to commit murder in Spain. As to these very limited charges the question of immunity remains relevant. . . .

Although six members of the Appellate Committee hold that he is not entitled to immunity on torture charges, our reasons vary somewhat. Three of us (my noble and learned friends Lord Hope of Craighead, Lord Saville of Newdigate and myself) consider that Senator Pinochet only lost his immunity when the Torture Convention became binding on Spain, United Kingdom and Chile. This occurred on 8th December 1988 when the United Kingdom ratified the Convention. Lord Hutton holds that Senator Pinochet's immunity ended on 29th September 1988 (when the Criminal Justice Act 1988, section 134, came into force). Lord Millett and Lord Phillips of Worth Matravers hold that Senator Pinochet was never at any stage entitled to immunity. Although the reasoning varies in detail, the basic proposition common to all, save Lord Goff of Chieveley, is that torture is an international crime over which international law and the parties to the Torture Convention have given universal jurisdiction to all courts wherever the torture occurs. A former head of state cannot show that to commit an international crime is to perform a function which international law protects by giving immunity. Lord Goff is of the view that neither in international law nor by virtue of the Torture Convention has Senator Pinochet been deprived of the benefit of immunity as a former head of state.

The majority therefore considers that Senator Pinochet can be extradited only for the extradition crimes of torture and conspiracy to torture alleged to have been committed after 8th December 1988.

(2) Which of the several opinions is more persuasive? Why should the date on which the Torture Convention was ratified be treated as a decisive consideration? What does it mean to say (in Lord Browne-Wilkinson's words) that torture was an "international crime in the highest sense" before 1984, but not a "fully constituted international crime"? If official torture already violated a norm of *jus cogens*, why should a treaty be required to confer universal jurisdiction?

Assuming that universal jurisdiction over a particular crime is permitted by international law, can it be exercised as a matter of national law in the absence of statute? In any event, does universal jurisdiction necessarily license the courts of one state to pronounce unilaterally on the conduct of officials of another state? Is there a possible difference, in this regard, between torture, which by definition requires "state action," and other international crimes? What are the implications of the various opinions for immunity with respect to international crimes other than torture?

Is universal jurisdiction over torture necessarily incompatible with retention of immunity for former heads of state? What do the various opinions imply, moreover, with respect to the immunity of *current* heads of state? Would a current head of state be immune from prosecution before an international tribunal? If not, why should there be immunity before a national tribunal? Does the majority in *Pinochet* "weaken the moral force of its ruling" on immunity by limiting it to former heads of state? *See* Hazel Fox, *The Pinochet Case No. 3*, 48 INT'L & COMP. L. Q. 687, 702 (1999). Or does the immunity of a current head of state, like that of the state itself, at least for official acts, have to be taken as a given in the present international system?

In a part of his opinion not quoted above, Lord Hope refers to "[t]he *jus cogens* character of the immunity enjoyed by serving heads of state *ratione personae*." However, Article 27 of the Rome Statute for an International Criminal Court [*see* chap. 20] provides that no immunities under either national or international law "shall bar the court from exercising its jurisdiction." Insofar as Article 27 seems to subject current heads of state to the court's jurisdiction, does it impermissibly derogate from a rule of *jus cogens*?

(3) The *Pinochet* proceedings are said to have "posed, in the most direct terms, a choice between two competing visions of international legal order." Michael Byers, *The Law and Politics of the Pinochet Case,* 10 DUKE J. COMP. & INT'L L. 415, 421 (2000). One is the "classical theory" which in the past obligated states to abstain from interfering in the internal affairs of other states. The other is the picture of an emerging world order in which protection of human rights against egregious violations, if need be by imposing criminal sanctions on the responsible officials, is regarded as a universal imperative. *See also* William J. Aceves, *Liberalism and International Legal Scholarship: The Pinochet Case and the Move Toward a Universal System of Transnational Law Litigation*, 41 HARV. INT'L L. J. 129 (2000). Which of these "visions" more nearly describes present-day international law? Do they have to be treated as mutually exclusive? In thinking about this question, consider the relevance of Faulkner's dictum: "The past is never dead. It's not even past." WILLIAM FAULKNER, REQUIEM FOR A NUN 92 (1951).

(4) According to some observers, "the second panel of judges, with the exception of Lord Millett – and possibly Lord Hutton – clearly desired that Pinochet be allowed to leave for Chile." Michael Byers, *supra* Note (3), at 436. But "[t]o overrule the decision of the initial panel would have been to suggest that justice was only luck of the draw," which was "the last thing the Law Lords wanted to suggest." *Id.* at 434. Eliminating all but a few relatively insignificant charges offered a way out of this dilemma, since it would give the Home Secretary (whose "authority to proceed" is required for extradition proceedings

to continue) grounds for reconsidering his earlier decision to authorize proceedings against Pinochet, and so might serve to release Pinochet without explicitly overruling the first panel. *See also* THE ECONOMIST, Mar. 27, 1999, at 57, 58.

The Home Secretary reconsidered his decision, but on April 15, 1999, again gave authority for extradition to proceed. Meanwhile, the Spanish added further allegations of torture taking place after 1988 to the extradition request. Extradition between Spain and Britain is governed by the European Convention on Extradition, Dec. 13, 1957, E.T.S. No. 24, 359 U.N.T.S. 273, which does not require a requesting state to produce even *prima facie* evidence of the charges against the accused. The only question is whether the offense for which extradition is requested is one for which the accused properly can be extradited. Thus, on the basis of the Spanish allegations, the magistrate's court committed Pinochet for extradition on thirty-four charges of torture and one of conspiracy to commit torture. *Kingdom of Spain v. Augusto Pinochet Ugarte, Judgment* (Bow Street Magistrates' Court, Oct. 8, 1999), *available at* <http://www.open.gov.uk/lcd/magist/pinochet.htm>.

Normally, in extradition law, the principle of specialty precludes trying a defendant for any offenses other than those for which he was extradited [*see* chap. 13]. Had Pinochet ultimately been extradited, would the trial in Spain have been limited to proof of incidents of torture after 1988, with evidence of the worst part of the repression in Chile in the 1970s excluded? Not necessarily. *See* Edward M. Wise, *Pinochet, Speciality, and Jus Cogens, in* PROCEEDINGS OF THE AMERICAN BRANCH OF THE INTERNATIONAL LAW ASSOCIATION 1999-2000, at 359 (2000). Crimes committed before December 8, 1988, could still be used as evidence of participation in a conspiracy which extended beyond that date. For a U.S. case in point, *see United States v. Flores*, 538 F.2d 939 (2d Cir. 1976).

In the end, the Home Secretary announced on January 11, 2000, that he was "minded" to deny extradition on the ground that Pinochet was medically unfit to stand trial. Despite efforts to challenge this finding, the Home Secretary affirmed his decision on March 2, 2000. Pinochet left for Chile the same day. *See* PARL. DEB., H.C. (HANSARD), Mar. 2, 2000, cols. 571-75.

Since the United Kingdom declined to extradite Pinochet, was it obligated under Article 7 of the Torture Convention [chap. 9, *supra*] to "submit the case to its competent authorities for the purpose of prosecution"? Look carefully at the language of Article 7 and of Article 5 to which it refers. Is this one of the "cases contemplated in article 5"? In fact, before releasing Pinochet, the British government did submit the case to the Director of Public Prosecutions, who decided that there was no realistic prospect of trying him in England. *See* PARL. DEB., H.C. (HANSARD), Mar. 2, 2000, cols. 589-92.

(5) In Chile, an amnesty decreed by the Pinochet regime on March 10, 1978, covered official crimes committed between the 1973 coup and the date of the amnesty. (At the insistence of the United States, an exception was made for the

assassins of former foreign minister Orlando Letelier, who was killed by Chilean agents in Washington, D.C., in 1976.) The amnesty was upheld by the Chilean Supreme Court in 1990. However, after Pinochet's arrest in London, criminal proceedings were initiated in Chile involving crimes committed by his regime both before and after 1978. *See* N.Y. TIMES, Oct. 3, 1999, § 1, at 1, 6. In July 1999, the Supreme Court endorsed the doctrine that the amnesty does not cover cases involving the disappearances of victims whose bodies have never been accounted for: in such cases, the crime is ongoing and extends beyond the amnesty. As a senator-for-life, Pinochet himself had personal immunity from prosecution. But, on August 8, 2000, the Supreme Court upheld a ruling stripping him of this immunity. *See* N.Y. TIMES, Aug. 9, 2000, at A3.

(6) When Pinochet was detained in England, the argument was made that outsiders had no business upsetting the delicate compromise by which democracy in Chile had been restored. If anything, the proceedings against him seem to have strengthened democracy in Chile. Even so, the questions of how far a successor regime is obligated to punish human rights violations committed by a despotic predecessor, how far it is bound to respect an amnesty insisted on by the prior regime as a condition of relinquishing power, how far "truth commissions" represent an acceptable substitute for criminal prosecution in the effort to come to terms with the past, and similar questions of "transitional justice," remain controversial. Amnesty laws, such as the Chilean decree-law of March 10, 1978, have been found to be incompatible with international obligations to respect human rights by both the Inter-American Commission on Human Rights and the U.N. Human Rights Committee. *See Chanfeau Orayce v. Chile*, Case 11.505 et al., Report No. 25/98, Inter-Am. C.H.R. 512, OEA/ser. L/V/II.98, doc. 7 rev. (1997); *Rodriguez v. Uruguay*, U.N. Doc. CCPR/C/51/D/322/1988 (1994).

(7) Would U.S. law allow criminal proceedings against a current or former foreign head of state? *See United States v. Noriega*, 117 F.3d 1206 (11th Cir. 1997) [chap. 14, *infra*]. As the *Noriega* case indicates, head-of-state immunity is not clearly covered by the Foreign Sovereign Immunities Act of 1976; and U.S. courts are apt to defer to the executive branch in deciding this question. For other cases, *see* Philip M. Moremen, *National Court Decisions as State Practice, in* PROCEEDINGS OF THE AMERICAN BRANCH OF THE INTERNATIONAL LAW ASSOCIATION 1999-2000, at 102, 146-48 (2000). The question is most likely to come up in litigation under the Alien Tort Statute. For an argument in favor of judicial deference to executive resistance to such litigation, *see* Curtis A. Bradley & Jack L. Goldsmith, *Pinochet and International Human Rights Litigation*, 97 MICH. L. REV. 2129 (1999).

(8) The case against Pinochet inspired proceedings in Senegal on charges of torture against the former president of Chad, Hissène Habré, who had been living in Senegal since he was toppled from power in 1990. *See* N.Y. TIMES, Feb. 4, 2000, at A3. However, the charges were dismissed five months later after the new president of Senegal removed the judge presiding over the case. *See* N.Y. TIMES, July 21, 2000, at A18.

Chapter 12
MUTUAL ASSISTANCE AND OBTAINING EVIDENCE FROM ABROAD

§ 12.01 Letters Rogatory

28 U.S.C. § 1781. Transmittal of letter rogatory or request

(a) The Department of State has power, directly, or through suitable channels–

(1) to receive a letter rogatory issued, or request made, by a foreign or international tribunal, to transmit it to the tribunal, officer, or agency in the United States to whom it is addressed, and to receive and return it after execution; and

(2) to receive a letter rogatory issued, or request made, by a tribunal in the United States, to transmit it to the foreign or international tribunal, officer, or agency to whom it is addressed, and to receive and return it after execution.

(b) This section does not preclude –

(1) the transmittal of a letter rogatory or request directly from a foreign or international tribunal to the tribunal, officer, or agency in the United States to whom it is addressed and its return in the same manner; or

(2) the transmittal of a letter rogatory or request directly from a tribunal in the United States to the foreign or international tribunal, officer, or agency to whom it is addressed and its return in the same manner.

---

28 U.S.C. § 1782. Assistance to foreign and international tribunals and to litigants before such tribunals

(a) The district court of the district in which a person resides or is found may order him to give his testimony or statement or to produce a document or other thing for use in a proceeding in a foreign or international tribunal, including criminal investigations conducted before formal accusation. The order may be made pursuant to a letter rogatory issued, or request made, by a foreign or international tribunal or upon the application of any interested person and may direct that the testimony or statement be given, or the document or other thing be produced, before a person appointed by the court. By virtue of his appointment, the person appointed has power to administer any necessary oath and take the testimony or statement. The order may prescribe the practice and procedure, which may be in whole or part the practice and procedure of the foreign country or the international tribunal, for taking the testimony or statement or producing the document or other thing. To the extent that the order does not prescribe otherwise, the testimony or statement shall be taken, and the document or other thing produced, in accordance with the Federal Rules of Civil Procedure.

A person may not be compelled to give his testimony or statement or to produce a document or other thing in violation of any legally applicable privilege.

(b) This chapter [28 U.S.C. §§ 1781 et seq.] does not preclude a person within the United States from voluntarily giving his testimony or statement, or producing a document or other thing, for use in a proceeding in a foreign or international tribunal before any person and in any manner acceptable to him.

IN RE: LETTER ROGATORY FROM THE JUSTICE COURT, DISTRICT OF MONTREAL, CANADA – JOHN FECAROTTA

United States Court of Appeals for the Sixth Circuit
523 F.2d 562 (1975)

MILLER, CIRCUIT JUDGE:

Appellant, John Fecarotta, a resident of Detroit, challenges the district court's refusal to quash a subpoena duces tecum it had directed to the appellant's bank in Detroit. The subpoena was in response to a request by a Canadian tribunal for judicial assistance in a pending criminal prosecution against appellant.

On August 19, 1974, the Justice Court of Sessions of the Peace, District of Montreal, Canada, ordered that a letter rogatory[1] be sent to the appropriate

---

[1] Letters rogatory are defined in *The Signe,* 37 F. Supp. 819, 820 (E.D. La. 1941):

Letters rogatory are the medium, in effect, whereby one country, speaking through one of its courts, requests another country, acting through its own courts and by methods of court procedure peculiar thereto and entirely within the latter's control, to assist the administration of justice in the former country; such request being made, and being usually granted, by reason of the comity existing between nations in ordinary peaceful times.

United States authorities requesting the production of all bank account records listed in the names of John Fecarotta and/or Juanita Fecarotta held by the Detroit Bank and Trust Company. John Fecarotta had been charged with a violation of the Narcotic Control Act of Canada, and the prosecution sought access to his bank records in connection with the prosecution of the alleged offense. The Justice Court requested the assistance of our country's federal courts only after it had been satisfied that the bank account information was necessary to the prosecution's case. Upon receipt of the letter rogatory, the Department of Justice made application to the District Court for the Eastern District of Michigan for an order to compel the bank to produce the documents sought by the foreign tribunal. On September 5, 1974, the district court accepted the letter rogatory and, under the authority of 28 U.S.C. § 1782, issued a subpoena duces tecum to officers of the Detroit Bank and Trust Company. The subpoena commanded the bank's officials to appear with the records in question to be deposed concerning their contents. Fecarotta was notified of the date of the taking of the deposition and he immediately sought to quash the subpoena on the grounds that § 1782 is not applicable to criminal prosecutions, or in the alternative,* that the court in its discretion could and should refuse to grant the subpoena because of the danger that the information might be used improperly in the Canadian trial. This motion was overruled and the subpoena was ordered to be issued. Pending appeal to this Court, the production order has been stayed.

. . . . While it has been held that federal courts have inherent power to issue and respond to letters rogatory, ... such jurisdiction has largely been regulated by congressional legislation. Where Congress has intervened, the scope of the congressional authorization necessarily limits and defines the judicial power to render and seek such assistance. Thus a party against whom the requested information is to be used has standing to challenge the validity of such a subpoena on the ground that it is in excess of the terms of the applicable statute, here 28 U.S.C. § 1782. We hold that Fecarotta has standing to challenge the validity of the subpoena on the theory that it is not authorized by § 1782, the governing statute.

We turn to the appellant's contention that § 1782 does not authorize or permit the compulsory production of evidence for use in a foreign *criminal* proceeding. Traditionally, the United States has enacted statutes to provide judicial assistance for courts in other countries. . . . The original enactment authorizing federal courts to assist foreign tribunals was the Act of March 2, 1855. This statute granted broad powers to the United States courts to compel the testimony of witnesses to assist foreign courts. . . . Primarily because of misindexing, the Act passed into obscurity and later was crippled by a subsequent statute. . . .

---

*In 1996 Congress amended 28 U.S.C. § 1782 inserting "including criminal investigations conducted before formal accusations," after "proceedings in a foreign or international tribunal. Pub.L. 104-106 § 1342(b). – Eds.

This country's early begrudging attitude in granting assistance to foreign courts was evidenced by the Act of March 3, 1863, a law that largely undercut the 1855 legislation. The 1863 Act permitted the federal courts to take testimony [only in suits] "for the recovery of money or property depending in any court in any foreign country with which the United States are at peace, and in which the government of such foreign country shall be a party or shall have an interest. . . . " It was not until 1948 that the requirement that the foreign government be a party or have an interest was deleted. The 1948 amendment also expanded the statute to encompass "*any civil action* pending in any court in a foreign country." [emphasis added]. One year later the restrictive phrase "civil action" was changed to read "*any judicial proceeding* pending in any court in a foreign country." [emphasis added].

The narrow scope of these statutes was underscored and reinforced by the decisions of federal courts. For instance, in *Janssen v. Belding - Corticelli, Ltd.,* 84 F.2d 577 (3d Cir. 1936), the court declared that the only power it had regarding letters rogatory was that granted to it by the Constitution or by statute. Under the statutes then in force, the district court could neither issue a subpoena duces tecum to secure documentary evidence nor could it conduct a "roving oral examination" of the witnesses in the absence of interrogatories. . . . Additionally, the courts have not favored the use of letters rogatory to secure evidence for introduction in criminal cases or investigations. . . .

The 1964 amendments, however, were a significant departure by Congress from its cautious approach to international judicial assistance over the past century. The revisions were the result of proposals submitted by the Commission on International Rules of Judicial Procedure. Congress created the Commission in 1958 and authorized it to study and evaluate all the federal code provisions and rules, both civil and criminal, relating to international judicial assistance. The goal of the Commission was to revise the law in order to provide "wide judicial assistance . . . on a wholly unilateral basis." . . . As the legislative history reveals, the purpose behind the proposals was to prod other nations into following the lead of the United States in expanding procedures for the assistance of foreign litigants. . . . The current § 1782 represents in part the changes made by the 1964 amendments.

The crucial issue on this appeal is whether § 1782 applies to documentary evidence sought for use in a foreign *criminal* proceeding. Noting that the statute's predecessors were not thought to cover criminal cases, the appellant argues that § 1782 neither expressly nor impliedly applies to the instant situation. We are convinced, however, that Congress clearly intended for the provision to extend this nation's assistance to the *criminal* processes of a foreign country. . . .

In his remaining argument, Fecarotta maintains that any testimony taken under § 1782 and later introduced against him at trial would contravene his right of confrontation under the sixth amendment. The letter rogatory from the Canadian court specifically provides that Fecarotta is to be represented by his counsel at the deposition. . . . Since the appellant's claim is based upon nothing more than the bald assertion of potential harm, we find his argument to be without merit. . . .

Under § 1782 "the grant of power is unrestricted, but entirely within the discretion of the Court." . . . There is no showing that the district court abused its discretion either in applying the provision to a pending criminal case or in permitting the evidence to be taken in compliance with Canadian practice and procedure.

AFFIRMED. . . .

UNITED STATES v. REAGAN

United States Court of Appeals for the Sixth Circuit
453 F.2d 165 (1971)

WILLIAM E. MILLER, CIRCUIT JUDGE:

This is an appeal from a conviction for voluntary manslaughter. 18 U.S.C. § 1111 provides that murder in the first degree is the unlawful killing of a human being with malice aforethought or if committed in perpetration of any robbery or burglary within "the special maritime * * * jurisdiction of the United States."

. . . . The appellant was charged with three counts under 18 U.S.C. § 1111: first, with intentional and premeditated murder of Joseph Speidell, a fellow seaman; second, with murder in perpetration of a robbery; and third, with murder in perpetration of burglary. After a five week trial beginning in October 1970, the district court dismissed the third count of the indictment and submitted the case to the jury on the first two counts, also charging the jury that it could consider whether the appellant was guilty of the lesser included offense of voluntary manslaughter made a federal offense by 18 U.S.C. § 1112 if committed within the special maritime jurisdiction of the United States. The jury found the appellant guilty of the lesser included offense of voluntary manslaughter and not guilty of all other charges. Following denial of his motion for a new trial appellant perfected his appeal to this Court.

The events out of which the charges against appellant arose occurred on an American vessel, the *SS Thunderbird*, in the harbor of Bremerhaven, Germany, close to the noon hour on December 16, 1966. The harbor is located on the east bank of the Weser River which flows north past Bremen and Bremerhaven into the North Sea. Bremerhaven is approximately sixty kilometers inland from the boundary which separates German inland waters and the international waters of the North Sea. As a result of extreme tides, the harbor is separated from the Weser River by locks. These are opened to permit vessels to enter and depart the harbor only at certain stages of the tide. . . .

The German authorities were called and Reagan was taken into custody. On December 17, 1966, the day after the slaying, he was judicially committed to a State mental institution in Bremen. The *SS Thunderbird* departed Bremerhaven about 1:00 p.m. on this date. Reagan remained in the German institution till after the ship returned to Bremerhaven about April 1, 1967. On April 5, 1967, a Judge of the appropriate German County Court refused to issue a Warrant of Arrest for the crime of murder sought by the German Prosecutor, finding no probable cause for an arrest.

After his release in Bremen, Reagan returned to the Kennedy Airport where, though no charges were pending against him, he was met by agents of the Coast Guard and F.B.I. and told to return to his home in Cleveland and not to sail on foreign voyages. Thereafter, the U.S. Coast Guard in Bremen, acting for the F.B.I., requested the appropriate German authorities to release to them the records pertaining to the Reagan matter. This request was denied on the ground that under German law such records may not be released without the consent of the accused, a consent which Reagan refused to give. On November 3, 1967 Judge James C. Connell of the United States District Court for the Northern District of Ohio, Eastern Division, requested from the "appropriate judicial authorities in Land Bremen, Federal Republic of Germany" the records sought by the F.B.I. and the Coast Guard. The request in the form but not in the words of a "letter rogatory" is set forth below.[1] Pursuant to this request, the

---

[1]

IN THE UNITED STATES DISTRICT COURT FOR THE NORTHERN DISTRICT OF OHIO EASTERN DIVISION

REQUEST FOR INTERNATIONAL JUDICIAL ASSISTANCE

To the appropriate judicial authorities in the Land Bremen, Federal Republic of Germany:

There is currently pending within the jurisdiction of this Court an investigation into an alleged homicide committed on December 16, 1966, by Howard Reagan, an American National, on Joseph J. Speidell, at Bremerhaven, Germany. It is this Court's understanding that the Prosecutor in Bremerhaven, Federal Republic of Germany conducted an investigation of the alleged offense beginning in the month of December, 1966.

The United States authorities in this district are currently conducting an investigation of the same incident. It would be most helpful, and in the furtherance of justice, if the investigative files of the German authorities in Bremerhaven, including, but not limited to, oral or written statements of all witnesses, reports of investigative officers, reports of any autopsy or post-mortem medical examination of the deceased, medical or psychiatric reports

German file was sent to the district court and made available to the office of the U. S. Attorney in early 1968.

On September 12, 1969 a grand jury indictment was returned. On September 15, 1969 it was opened, docketed and a warrant for the appellant's arrest was issued. He was then taken into custody. The trial and appellant's conviction followed. From this conviction appellant perfected his appeal.

Appellant makes numerous contentions. He asserts: the district court was without subject matter jurisdiction; the indictment was deficient in that it failed to allege an essential element of jurisdiction; the delay in prosecuting him constituted a denial of his due process rights . . . ; the request for international judicial assistance was without the jurisdiction of the district court at the time issued and constituted an abuse of discretion; the failure of the district court to suppress evidence which was the fruit of the request was reversible error; the admission of the testimony of a German police official who was brought to this country by the government was reversible error in light of the court's failure to provide for the bringing of defense witnesses to this country from Germany; he was placed in double jeopardy because of the German proceeding; the failure to declare a mistrial upon his emotional outburst at trial constituted a reversible error; and finally appellant says that the evidence was insufficient to support a conviction for voluntary manslaughter. We have carefully considered each of these contentions on the basis of the record and pertinent authorities. We find it necessary to discuss only the issues concerning jurisdiction and the issuance of a letter rogatory.

---

from any examination of the suspect (Reagan), any photographs, and any oral or written statements of the suspect (Reagan), could be made available to the United States investigative authorities. To that end, a request is hereby made that the pertinent files and exhibits, currently in the possession or in the custody of the German authorities in Bremerhaven, be made available to this Court.

The Courts of the United States are authorized by statute, 28 U.S.C. 1781, et seq., to extend similar assistance to the tribunals of the Federal Republic of Germany. Such assistance has been, and is being, rendered; thus, reciprocity is assured.

The Court assures the judicial authorities in the Land Bremen that any records or exhibits which may be made available, pursuant to this request, will be promptly returned, after they have served their purpose.

The Court takes this opportunity to extend to the Judicial authorities of the Land Bremen the assurance of its highest consideration.

Nov. 3, 1967
s/ James C. Connell

JUDGE, UNITED STATES DISTRICT COURT

. . . . It is our view that there was no "assertion of jurisdiction" by Germany and, therefore, that the district court was not without jurisdiction. . . . A different case would be presented if Reagan had been brought to trial in Germany or perhaps even if he had been indicted in Germany. We hold that the district court did have proper subject matter jurisdiction.

LETTERS ROGATORY

The appellant argues that the district court exceeded its jurisdiction in requesting international judicial assistance through the medium of a "letter rogatory" since there was no "case or controversy" before it, and that it therefore erred in not suppressing the fruits of this request. We must disagree although concededly the contention is not without some support.

28 U.S.C. § 1781 recognizes, impliedly at least, the power of federal courts to transmit letters rogatory to foreign tribunals. . . . In *United States v. Staples,* 256 F.2d 290 (1958), the Ninth Circuit pointed correctly to the source of a court's power to issue letters rogatory:

This Court, like all courts of the United States, has *inherent* power to issue Letters Rogatory. The manner of taking proof is left to our discretion. . . . (Emphasis added.)

We find no definitive authority, however, as to precisely when this power attaches in a given case.

The opinion of the Court of Appeals in *In re Pacific Ry. Comm'n,* 12 Sawy. 559, 32 F. 241 (Cir. Ct. N.D.Cal., 1887), is suggestive though not squarely in point. There the Court held that the Pacific Railway Commission created by Act of Congress did not have the power to issue letters rogatory. Speaking of this instrument, the Court stated:

There are certain powers inherent in all courts. The power to preserve order in their proceedings, and to punish for contempt of their authority, are instances of this kind. And by jurists and text writers the power of the courts of record of one country, as a matter of comity, to furnish assistance, so far as is consistent with their own jurisdiction, to the courts of another country, by taking the testimony of witnesses to be used in the foreign country, or by ordering it to be taken before a magistrate or commissioner, has also been classed among their inherent powers. "For by the law of nations," says Greenleaf, "courts of justice of different countries are bound mutually to aid and assist each other, for the furtherance of justice; and hence, when the testimony of a foreign witness is necessary, the court before which the action is pending may send to the court within whose jurisdiction the witness resides a writ, either patent or close, usually termed a letter rogatory, or a commission *sub mutuae vicissitudinis obtentu ac in juris subsidium,* from those words contained in it. By this instrument the court abroad is informed of the pendency of the cause, and the names of the foreign witnesses, and is requested to cause their depositions to be taken in due course of law, for the furtherance of justice, *with an offer on the part of the tribunal making the request to do the like for the other in a similar case.*" Treatise on Evidence, vol. 1, § 320. The comity in behalf of which this power is exercised cannot, of course, be invoked by any mere investigating commission . . . . (Emphasis added.)

. . . . Proceedings to perpetuate testimony, where litigation is expected or apprehended, are within the ordinary jurisdiction of courts of equity, and come under the designation of "cases in equity" in the constitution. . . .

Similarly, it would seem that preliminary steps taken by a federal court to obtain evidence from a foreign power, in aid of its jurisdiction in criminal cases, would be within its Article III power over cases and controversies.

Absent substantial and controlling authority, we are unwilling to hold here that a court may only issue a letter rogatory after an indictment is returned in a criminal case. We are not persuaded that the issuance of such an ex parte instrument is incompatible with the fair operation of our system of justice.

It should be pointed out that the German record was used not as the principal part of the prosecution's case, but for purposes which appear to have been limited in nature. . . . Ample testimony was presented to the jury, apart from the foreign record, concerning Reagan's appearance and actions immediately following the stabbing and his own incriminating statements made in the presence of shipmates. Such evidence appears to us to have been decisive in linking the appellant with the murder on shipboard. . . .

Appellant's further contentions enumerated above have been carefully considered and we find them to be without merit.

The judgment of the district court is therefore Affirmed.

NOTES AND QUESTIONS

(1) There are some serious drawbacks to using the letters rogatory process. Consider the comments of Lisa Cacheris, a member of the Office of International Affairs, Criminal Division of the U.S. Department of Justice:

The obvious pitfall of the letter rogatory process is that it can be extremely time consuming, and when a prosecutor wants a particular piece of evidence for use at a trial that is set for a date certain chances are the prosecutor may not get it in time. It is also a mechanism that is often available only postindictment. To the extent that a prosecutor is seeking evidence to use in a grand jury investigation, or even prior to that point, such evidence usually cannot be obtained through letters rogatory. With all of its drawbacks, we are still relegated to asking for judicial assistance via letters rogatory with the majority of jurisdictions from which we seek evidence.

Remarks of Lisa Cacheris, Proceedings of the Eighty-Fifth Annual Meeting of the American Society of International Law, *in* 85 AM. SOC'Y INT'L L. PROC. 383, 392 (1991).

(2) The government, however, can have the statute of limitations suspended when requesting information from a foreign country. Will this suspension apply to letters rogatory? How long can the statute of limitations be extended. Consider this issue as presented in *Bischel v. United States*, 61 F.3d 1429 (9th Cir. 1995):

> This appeal requires us to decide when there has been "final action" on an official request for evidence in a foreign country, where the court has suspended the running of the statute of limitations pursuant to 18 U.S.C. § 3292.[1]

> Stephen Bischel was convicted of numerous offenses arising out of "broker's crosses" on investments sold by La Jolla Trading Group, which

---

[1] 18 U.S.C. § 3292 provides:

(a)(1) Upon application of the United States, filed before return of an indictment, indicating that evidence of an offense is in a foreign country, the district court before which a grand jury is impaneled to investigate the offense shall suspend the running of the statute of limitations for the offense if the court finds by a preponderance of the evidence that an official request has been made for such evidence and that it reasonably appears, or reasonably appeared at the time the request was made, that such evidence is, or was, in such foreign country.

. . .

(b) Except as provided in subsection (c) of this section, a period of suspension under this section shall begin on the date on which the official request is made and end on the date on which the foreign court or authority takes final action on the request.

(c) The total of all periods of suspension under this section with respect to an offense –

(1) shall not exceed three years; and

(2) shall not extend a period within which a criminal case must be initiated for more than six months if all foreign authorities take final action before such period would expire without regard to this section.

he owned. Because these transactions involved British commodity brokers, the government requested assistance of United Kingdom authorities through letters rogatory and obtained a court order under § 3292(a)(1) to suspend the running of the statute of limitations pending "final action" on the request.

Records were received pursuant to the official request at a time when the statute of limitations would normally have run on many of the offenses charged in the indictment; a Certificate of Authenticity that was also requested had not yet been received when the indictment was returned. We hold that "final action on the request" for purposes of § 3292 includes all of the items requested in the letters rogatory. Since the certification had been requested but had not yet been received, the district court did not clearly err in finding that "final action" had not been taken. The statute of limitations, therefore, continued to be suspended so that none of the counts now at issue was time barred. We also conclude that a § 3292 order suspending the running of the statute of limitations speaks as of the date the official request is made, not when the order suspending the statute is entered, and that to begin the period of suspension when the letters rogatory are issued does not run afoul either of the Ex Post Facto Clause or of Bischel's rights to due process. . . .

"Final action" is not defined in the text of the statute. However, construing the concept of "final action" to include a dispositive response to each item set out in the official request, including a request for certification, is consistent with the statutory structure and legislative history. It also makes practical sense.

Section 3292(b) hinges the end of the period of suspension on final action by foreign authorities on "the request." The "request" referred to is the official request for "evidence of an offense" that is in a foreign country. 18 U.S.C. § 3292(a)(1). "Evidence of an offense" is essentially worthless unless admissible. Admissibility turns in part on authenticity. Fed. R. Evid. 902(3). Thus, certifying that primary evidence is what it purports to be is inevitably part of the "evidence of an offense" within the meaning of § 3292(a)(1). We also look at legislative history here because the statutory words "final action" do not unambiguously resolve the interpretational task we face. Our construction comports with the legislative history indicating that § 3292, which was passed as part of the Comprehensive Crime Control Act of 1984, P.L. 98-473, was prompted by concern both for the difficulty of obtaining records in other countries, and of admitting them into evidence. . . . Finally, the interests of certainty counsel against the construction Bischel suggests. He would have us hold that "final action" takes place when the last of the records requested has been received. However, there is no ready way of knowing when the last of anything has happened. Instead, pegging "final action" to disposition, up or down, of each of the items in the official request provides a more certain benchmark by which to measure whether the action that has been taken is "final" or not.

We therefore conclude that "final action" for purposes of § 3292 means a dispositive response by the foreign sovereign to both the request for records and for a certificate of authenticity of those records, as both were identified in the "official request." . . .

Bischel maintains that § 3292 violates the Due Process Clause as applied to him because it takes away his right to a fixed statute of limitations and removes the predictability of a specific time limit beyond which he could not be prosecuted. Yet Bischel fails to locate the source of any right to a fixed period of limitations. In any event, § 3292(c) sets a clear point beyond which the limitations period may not be extended: either three years if there is no "final action" at all, or no more than six months if there is "final action" within the period.

Bischel also argues that § 3292 is constitutionally infirm because it lacks any requirement that the government diligently seek evidence located in a foreign country. . . . [W]e decline to read a diligence requirement into § 3292. . . . AFFIRMED.

See also United States v. Meador, 138 F.3d 986 (5th Cir. 1998) ("[W]hen the foreign government believes it has completed its engagement and communicates that belief to our government, that foreign government has taken a 'final action' for the purposes of § 3292(b).").

(3) When will a defendant be permitted to use letters rogatory to obtain evidence from a foreign country? Consider District Judge Scheindlin's "Opinion and Order" concerning a defense request for letters rogatory in the case of *United States v. Korogodsky*, 4 F. Supp.2d 262 (S.D. N.Y. 1998):

On March 16, 1998, Defendant Alex Korogodsky ("Korogodsky") requested the issuance of a letter rogatory to Russian authorities. Korogodsky also moves to dismiss the Indictment, arguing that his inability to subpoena foreign witnesses will (1) deprive him of his Sixth Amendment right to compulsory process, and (2) violate the confrontation clause of the Sixth Amendment. . . .

Korogodsky is charged, inter alia, with conspiracy to commit wire fraud and wire fraud, in violation of 18 U.S.C. §§ 371 and 1343. The charges arise out of an alleged scheme by Korogodsky and others ("the conspirators") to defraud 30 Russian firms (the "victim firms") of over $ 10 million and to transport the funds to the United States. . . .

The Government has represented that it expects to call witnesses from only five of the 30 victim firms. The Government will apparently prove that the conspirators attempted to defraud the remaining 25 victim firms by offering (1) accomplice testimony, (2) the purported contracts between the conspirators and the victim firms, and (3) bank documents allegedly reflecting money transfers from the victim firms to Newtel. These contracts and bank records will be offered pursuant to 18 U.S.C. § 3505.[3]

. . . . Korogodsky's letter rogatory seeks sworn statements from 32 persons who fall into three categories: (1) representatives of victim firms; (2) representatives of banks and other businesses that provided the victim firms with financing to make payments to Newtel; and (3) representatives of companies that agreed to insure the victim firms' performance under the contracts. The Government does not intend to call any of these individuals at trial.

Korogodsky's letter rogatory would require these persons to provide written information about the following: their educational background and employment history; background information about the formation, ownership, capitalization and bank accounts of their firm; their dealings, if any, with Newtel, Korogodsky or (regarding the banks and insurers) Newtel's contract partners; any criminal record of the witness, his company, or their status as a target or subject of a criminal or civil investigation; any physical or mental disability or emotional disturbance or drug or alcohol addiction of the witness; and any payments, leniency promises or immunity grants from law enforcement officials.

---

[3]Section 3505 provides, in pertinent part, that:

(a)(1) In a criminal proceeding in a court of the United States, a foreign record of regularly conducted activity, or a copy of such record, shall not be excluded by the hearsay rule if a foreign certification attests that –

(A) such record was made at, or near the time of the occurrence of the matters set forth, by (or from information transmitted by) a person with knowledge of those matters;

(B) such record was kept in the course of a regularly conducted business activity;

(C) the business activity made such a record as a regular practice; and

(D) if such record is not the original, such record is a duplicate of the original;

unless the source of the information or the method or circumstances of its preparation indicate lack of trustworthiness.

(2) A foreign certification under this section shall authenticate such record or duplicate.

Korogodsky contends that he should be permitted to pursue the letter rogatory because it: (1) might generate evidence of the victim firms' own misconduct; and (2) would allow him to test the reliability of the § 3505 foreign certifications. The Government opposes the letter rogatory request, in part, because it believes that obtaining responses to the request may take months or even years. . . .

The use of depositions in criminal cases is governed by Fed. R. Crim. P. 15, which permits a party in "exceptional circumstances" to depose its own witness in order to preserve the witness' testimony. Rule 15(d) directs that depositions are to be taken in the manner provided in civil actions, and Fed. R. Civ. P. 28(b)(3) authorizes the taking of depositions in foreign countries "pursuant to a letter rogatory." Thus, a court has discretion to issue letters rogatory on behalf of a party in a criminal action pursuant to Rule 15. . . .

Courts have interpreted the "exceptional circumstances" standard of Rule 15 to require (1) that the witness will be unavailable at trial; and (2) that the information sought is material to the party's case. . . . The burden is on the party seeking the foreign deposition to prove such exceptional circumstances. Thus, to obtain a letter rogatory, the moving party must prove both the materiality of the information sought and the witness' unavailability.

. . . . Korogodsky's first asserted purpose for questioning the officers of the victim firms is to establish that these firms were themselves engaged in criminal misconduct when they allegedly contracted with Newtel. Thus, as an initial matter, Korogodsky must show that evidence of the victim firms' alleged wrongdoing would be material to his defense.

To convict Korogodsky of the wire fraud charges, the Government must prove that the conspirators contracted to sell goods to the victim firms with the intent to defraud them. It is no defense that the victims of the fraud may have been engaged in some misconduct. Moreover, the Government does not intend to call any of the individuals whom Korogodsky seeks to depose. Thus, the credibility of the victim firms' officers will not be an issue at trial. Accordingly, Korogodsky's letter rogatory questions concerning the possible misconduct of the victim firms are not relevant, much less material, to the wire fraud counts with which he is charged. . . .

Korogodsky has also failed to show that the prospective deponents would be unavailable at trial. . . . Here, the defendant has made no representation whatsoever that the potential deponents would be unavailable at trial. In fact, at oral argument defense counsel suggested that the deponents could well be available to testify at trial. . . .

Korogodsky argues that under the confrontation clause of the Sixth Amendment, he has a right to the letter rogatory as a means of determining the reliability of the Government's § 3505 certifications. The confrontation clause does not bar the statement of a hearsay declarant who is unavailable to testify at trial, so long as his statement "bears sufficient indicia of reliability to assure an adequate basis for evaluating the truth of the declaration." . . . Several courts have addressed the question whether the admissibility of evidence pursuant to § 3505 violates the confrontation clause because the records custodian is unavailable for cross-examination. These courts have uniformly held that so long as the documents bear sufficient indicia of reliability, the confrontation clause is not violated. . . .

However, none of these decisions directly addresses the issue presented here: Under what circumstances should a court grant a defendant's pretrial request to depose a company's officers, via letter rogatory, in order to determine the reliability of the company's records. . . . A defendant is entitled to a letter rogatory which questions a foreign witness who has submitted a § 3505 certification, but only with respect to the reliability of the relevant document. This approach affords a defendant the opportunity to challenge the testimony that the government intends to use against him at trial. The question, then, is whether the questions propounded by Korogodsky concern the reliability of either the Newtel contracts obtained from the files of the victim firms or money transfer records obtained from the Russian banks. . . . Finally, because it appears that the Government does not intend to introduce documents obtained from Russian insurance companies, there is no basis for questioning officers of these companies. . . .

With respect to the questions directed at the officers of the alleged victim firms, the Defendant has failed to show either (1) that any misconduct on the part of the victim firms is material to his defense; or (2) that his questions relate to the reliability of the Newtel contracts obtained from their files. Nor do the questions directed at the banks challenge the reliability of the banks' money transfer records. Finally, Korogodsky's questions for the insurance companies have no apparent bearing on his defense in general or on the Government's § 3505 evidence in particular. Accordingly, Korogodsky's letter rogatory request is denied in its entirety.

. . . . Defendant contends that because the Court cannot subpoena Russian citizens to testify at his trial, the Indictment should be dismissed as violative of his Sixth Amendment right to compulsory process. This argument fails for two reasons. First, the right to compulsory process exists only where a defendant "make[s] some plausible showing of how [the desired witness'] testimony would have been both material and favorable to his defense." . . .

Second, the Sixth Amendment provides a right to compulsory process only if the desired witness is within the court's subpoena power. . . . A court's inability to subpoena a foreign witness does not implicate the compulsory process clause, even if that witness could provide testimony that is material and favorable to the defendant.   .   .   .   Thus, Korogodsky's right to compulsory process is not violated though the court cannot compel the testimony of the Russian citizens whom Korogodsky may wish to call at trial.

. . . . Defendant has cited to no authority in support of his assertion that the confrontation clause of the Sixth Amendment requires the dismissal of the Indictment. If the admission of any of the Government's proposed evidence would violate Korogodsky's rights under the confrontation clause, then the Court will exclude the proposed evidence, not dismiss the Indictment.

It appears that the Government's § 3505 certifications contain the only testimony that Korogodsky will not have an opportunity to challenge through cross-examination. The admissibility of this evidence will be determined at a hearing to be held. . . .

For the reasons stated above, Defendant's letter rogatory request and his motion to dismiss the Indictment based on the confrontation clause and the right to compulsory process and are denied. A hearing to determine the admissibility of the Government's § 3505 evidence will be held. . . .

§ 12.02 Mutual Legal Assistance Treaties & Executive Agreements

"[T]he United States has more than 20 mutual legal assistance treaties (MLATs) worldwide." Michael Abbell, *DOJ Renews Assault on Defendants' Right to use Treaties to Obtain Evidence from Abroad,* 21 CHAMPION 21 (1997). "While the contents of an MLAT request is basically the same as that of a letters rogatory request, MLATs do not require a court order to request the assistance and the prosecutor can write up the request stating specifically what he or she is seeking." Remarks of Lisa Cacheris, Proceedings of the Eighty-Fifth Annual Meeting of the American Society of International Law, 85 AM. SOC'Y INT'L L. PROC. 383, 393 (1991). MLATs, however, may prove ineffective in that "[t]hey do not contain all the offenses the United States would prefer." C. Todd Jones, *Compulsion Over Comity: The United States' Assault on Foreign Bank Secrecy,* 12 NW. J. INT'L L. & BUS. 454 (1992). In some cases, the treaties are specialized. For example, "[t]he United States presently has forty tax treaties in force and several others in various stages of negotiation." *Id.* at 477.

The Department of Justice has opposed the use of MLATs by criminal defendants. *See* Michael Abbell, *DOJ Renews Assault on Defendants' Right to use Treaties to Obtain Evidence from Abroad,* 21 CHAMPION 21 (1997). Defendants have also failed in raising issues regarding purported treaty violations. In *United States v. Davis,* 767 F.2d 1025 (2d Cir. 1985), Senior District Judge Palmieri stated:

> That Davis has no standing to raise a purported violation of Article 18, Paragraph 5 of the Treaty in this context is made absolutely clear by both the interpretative letters signed by the United States and Switzerland and by the Technical Analysis of the Treaty. The interpretative letters signed on May 25, 1973, provide that it is the understanding of the United States and Swiss governments that a person alleging a violation of Article 5 of the Treaty (which deals with limitations on the use of information obtained pursuant to the Treaty) "has no standing to have such allegations considered in any proceeding in the United States . . . His recourse would be for him to inform the Central Authority of Switzerland for consideration only as a matter between governments." . . . The Technical Analysis provides that "restrictions in the Treaty shall not give rise to a right of any person to take action to suppress or exclude evidence or to obtain judicial relief." *Technical Analysis of the Treaty between the United States and Switzerland on Mutual Assistance in Criminal Matters* (reprinted in *Message from the President Transmitting the Treaty with the Swiss Confederation on Mutual Assistance in Criminal Matters,* 94th Cong., 2d Sess. at 63-64 (1976)). *See Cardenas v. Smith,* 733 F.2d 909, 918 (D.C. Cir. 1984). More generally, this Court has written that "even where a treaty provides certain benefits for nationals of a particular state – such as fishing rights – it is traditionally held that 'any rights arising from such provisions are, under international law, those of states and . . . individual rights are only derivative through the states.'" *United States Ex Rel. Lujan v. Gengler,* 510 F.2d 62, 67 (2d Cir.), *cert. denied,* 421 U.S. 1001, 44 L. Ed. 2d 668, 95 S. Ct. 2400 (1975), quoting *Restatement (Second) of the Foreign Relations Law of the United States* § 115, comment e (1965) (criminal defendant abducted in Bolivia and brought to the United States for trial had no standing to raise violation of the charters of the United Nations and the Organization of American States in the absence of protest by a signatory state). *See also United States v. Reed,* 639 F.2d 896, 902 (2d Cir. 1981) (criminal defendant abducted in Bahamas in violation of extradition treaty had no standing to raise its violation in absence of protest by the Bahamas).

Id. at 1029-30. There, however, may be standing to raise a deprivation of a constitutional right when there is a violation of a mutual assistance treaty. *See United States v. Sturman,* 951 F.2d 1466 (6th Cir. 1992) (court found that since defendants had not been deprived of their constitutional rights, there was no need to consider whether they had standing to raise these claims.)

In addition to MLATs, one also finds executive agreements. In discussing executive agreements, Lisa Cacheris remarked:

> The executive agreements that I alluded to earlier are not treaties. They are similar to MLATs in terms of procedures and content but are limited in scope. One example is the 1988 U.S.-U.K. Drug Trafficking Agreement, which provides for assistance only with respect to drug crimes. Executive agreements have served as an intermediate step and are being replaced by the much broader Mutual Legal Assistance Treaties as they are negotiated and brought into force.

Remarks of Lisa Cacheris, Proceedings of the Eighty-Fifth Annual Meeting of the American Society of International Law, 85 AM. SOC'Y INT'L L. PROC. 383, 393 (1991).

§ 12.03 Depositions and Grand Jury Subpoenas

UNITED STATES v. DROGOUL

United States Court of Appeals for the Eleventh Circuit
1 F.3d 1546 (1993)

KRAVITCH, CIRCUIT JUDGE:

This interlocutory appeal stems from a pretrial dispute in the government's prosecution of appellee Christopher Drogoul. The sole question before us is whether the district court abused its discretion in denying the government's motion to take the depositions of several foreign nationals in Italy. We hold that it did and, accordingly, reverse. . . .

Drogoul was manager of the Atlanta branch of Banca Nazionale del Lavoro (BNL), a bank headquartered in Rome, Italy and owned largely by the Italian government. He is charged in a multicount indictment with, inter alia, wire fraud, conspiracy, and making false statements to government agencies. The crux of the government's allegations is that Drogoul defrauded BNL by making and concealing unauthorized loans and credit extensions totalling several billion dollars to agencies and instrumentalities of the Republic of Iraq.

Drogoul pled guilty in June 1992 to sixty counts of a 347-count original indictment. . . . In April 1993, the government moved the district court for an order authorizing it to take the video and audiotaped depositions of thirteen Italian nationals before an Italian judicial officer in Rome, for potential use at trial in the United States. The government averred that the prospective deponents' testimony is material to the prosecution, that the deponents are unwilling to testify in the United States, and that they cannot be compelled to do so. In a written order entered on April 30, 1993, the district court denied the government's request. The court found that the government had shown neither that the witnesses are unavailable to testify in the United States nor that the procedures for taking the depositions would comport with due process. The court noted in particular that "the government has failed to procure the affidavits of any of the witnesses themselves indicating that they are unwilling to travel to the United States for Drogoul's trial." Accordingly, the court concluded that the government failed to demonstrate exceptional circumstances justifying the taking of foreign depositions. In addition, the court expressed concern that the government had approached Italian authorities as early as February 1993 to arrange for the possible taking of the depositions, but did not inform either the court or the defendant about its intentions until April 1993 when it filed its original motion to take the depositions.

In response to the district court's concerns regarding the prospective deponents' availability, the government enlisted the assistance of the Government of Italy to ascertain more conclusively the witnesses' willingness to testify in the United States. Pursuant to a treaty request lodged with the Italian government, an Italian judicial officer interviewed the thirteen potential witnesses as to whether they would travel to the United States to testify at Drogoul's trial. Six of the witnesses declared they would be willing to testify in the United States; seven declared they would not.

Based on the witnesses' declarations – particularly those of the seven who indicated they would not testify in this country – the government moved for reconsideration of the order denying its motion to take foreign depositions. Supporting this motion was a letter from the Italian magistrate who had interviewed the thirteen witnesses. The letter certified that the seven witnesses had announced they would not testify at Drogoul's trial. Despite this new information, in an oral ruling rendered June 10, 1993, the district court refused to reconsider its earlier decision, apparently because the government's request was untimely under local court rules. . . .

The government appealed, and we reversed. Because the government's "Motion for Reconsideration" was based in part on significant new information not contained in its original motion – the letter from the Italian magistrate reporting the witnesses' in-court declarations – we held that the district court should have construed the motion as a timely renewed motion to take foreign depositions. . . . Accordingly, we remanded the case to the district court to consider the merits of the government's motion.

On remand, the district court denied the government's motion once more. This time the court did not focus on the availability of the witnesses or the materiality of their testimony: It "assumed that the government has finally shown unavailability and materiality as required by Rule 15 [of the Federal Rules of Criminal Procedure]." Rather the court held that the government "has not shown that the procedures surrounding the taking of the deposition testimony will meet constitutional standards." In particular, the court had misgivings about the potential accuracy of the translation of the Italian testimony and about the provisions for Drogoul to engage in meaningful cross-examination. The court also reiterated its earlier displeasure with the government's delay in notifying both the court and Drogoul of its intention to take the foreign depositions.

The government's appeal from this order of the district court is what is at issue. . . . We now reverse.

Depositions generally are disfavored in criminal cases. . . . Their "only authorized purpose is to preserve evidence, not to afford discovery." . . . In particular, because of the absence of procedural protections afforded parties in the United States, foreign depositions are suspect and, consequently, not favored. . . . Nevertheless, the Federal Rules of Criminal Procedure expressly authorize parties to take depositions and use them at trial, when doing so is necessary to achieve justice and may be done consistent with the defendant's constitutional rights.

Whenever due to exceptional circumstances of the case it is in the interest of justice that the testimony of a prospective witness of a party be taken and preserved for use at trial, the court may upon motion of such party and notice to the parties order that testimony of such witness be taken by deposition . . . . Fed. R. Crim. P. 15(a). . . .

The burden is on the moving party to establish exceptional circumstances justifying the taking of depositions. . . . Whether to authorize depositions is a decision committed to the discretion of the district court which will be disturbed only for an abuse of discretion. . . . For purposes of analysis, we divide the prospective deponents into two groups: the seven who have declared they will not testify at Drogoul's trial and the six who have declared they would. . . .

The primary reasons for the law's normal antipathy toward depositions in criminal cases are the factfinder's usual inability to observe the demeanor of deposition witnesses, and the threat that poses to the defendant's Sixth Amendment confrontation rights. . . . On the other hand, it is well established that when a witness is unavailable to testify at trial, former testimony given by that witness may be introduced consistent with the defendant's constitutional rights. . . . Thus, ordinarily, exceptional circumstances exist within the meaning of Rule 15(a) when the prospective deponent is unavailable for trial and the absence of his or her testimony would result in an injustice. . . . The principal consideration guiding whether the absence of a particular witness's testimony would produce injustice is the materiality of that testimony to the case. . . . When a prospective witness is unlikely to appear at trial and his or her testimony is critical to the case, simple fairness requires permitting the moving party to preserve that testimony – by deposing the witness – absent significant countervailing factors which would render the taking of the deposition unjust.

In denying the government's motion to take foreign depositions the district court assumed that the government established the unavailability of the prospective deponents and the materiality of their expected testimony. The court held nonetheless that those factors were outweighed by countervailing considerations: the lack of guaranteed procedures protecting the defendant's due process rights and the government's supposed dilatory conduct in providing notice of its intent to seek the depositions. To determine whether these factors offset the unavailability of the witnesses and the materiality of their testimony, we must review the evidence regarding the prospective deponents' willingness to testify at trial and the importance of the deponents' testimony to the case. Accordingly, notwithstanding the district court's assumption that they were minimally satisfied, we elaborate on these two paramount considerations. . .

The moving party may demonstrate the probable unavailability of a prospective deponent "through affidavits or otherwise." . . . Significantly, that showing need not be conclusive before a deposition can be taken. . . . "It would be unreasonable and undesirable to require the government to assert with certainty that a witness will be unavailable for trial months ahead of time, simply to obtain authorization to take his deposition." . . . A more concrete showing of unavailability, of course, may be required at the time of trial before a deposition will be admitted in evidence. . . . A potential witness is unavailable for purposes of Rule 15(a), however, whenever a substantial likelihood exists that the proposed deponent will not testify at trial. In that situation, justice usually will be served by allowing the moving party to take the deposition, thereby preserving the party's ability to utilize the testimony at trial, if necessary. . . .

The government has made a strong showing that seven of the thirteen potential deponents are substantially unlikely to be available to testify at Drogoul's trial. Because the witnesses are foreign nationals located outside the United States, they are beyond the subpoena power of the district court. . . . Under a treaty between the United States and Italy, potential witnesses may be ordered by the Italian government to testify in the United States, but one who refuses to do so may not be removed to this country. Treaty on Mutual Assistance in Criminal Matters, Nov. 9, 1985, U.S.-Italy, art. 15, 24 I.L.M. 1539, 1541.[18] Thus, the prospective deponents cannot be compelled to testify at

---

[18] The treaty provides, in pertinent part:

1. The Requested State, upon request that a person in that State appear and testify in connection with a criminal investigation or proceeding in the Requesting State, shall compel that person to appear and testify in the Requesting State by means of the procedures for compelling the appearance and testimony of witnesses in the Requested State if:

Drogoul's trial. The government has proffered a letter from an Italian judicial officer (the authenticity of which Drogoul has not challenged) certifying that the seven witnesses have declared in open court their unwillingness to testify in the United States. This evidence is potent proof of unavailability for purposes of Rule 15(a). . . .

The government also has made a strong showing of materiality. Indeed, the expected testimony of all thirteen prospective deponents is highly material to this case. . . . Perhaps Drogoul expressed it best when he acknowledged in his brief to this court: "The testimony of these thirteen witnesses lies at the very core of the charges in the indictment, and its refutation the heart of the defense." . . . We can hardly imagine testimony more critical to this case.

Because the government established the key factors of probable unavailability and materiality (in this case, substantial materiality), the question becomes whether the district court acted within its discretion when it held that these considerations were, in this case, outweighed by certain countervailing factors. . . .

Of "primary concern" to the district court were the potential accuracy of the translation from Italian of the deposition testimony and the availability (or unavailability) to Drogoul of meaningful cross-examination. We believe these concerns to be largely premature and speculative. To the extent they are valid, they are insufficient to counterbalance the government's need to preserve for possible use at trial testimony which Drogoul concedes goes to the very core of this case.

Nothing in the record suggests that a correct translation cannot be obtained in this case, or that Drogoul even will object to the translation. Translations are an established part of practice in the federal courts. . . . Moreover, the depositions in this case are to be both audio and videotaped. If any question does arise with respect to the translation, an appropriate translator may be appointed to review the tapes and help resolve the dispute. Until the depositions

---

a. the Requested State has no reasonable basis to deny the request;

b. the person could be compelled to appear and testify in similar circumstances in the Requested State; and

c. the Central Authority of the Requesting State certifies that the person's testimony is relevant and material.

2. A person who fails to appear as directed shall be subject to sanctions under the laws of the Requested State as if that person had failed to appear in similar circumstances in that State. Such sanctions shall not include removal of the person to the Requesting State.

Treaty on Mutual Assistance in Criminal Matters, art. 15., 24 I.L.M. at 1541. . . .

are taken and translated, and an objection lodged, it is sheer speculation that the translation will pose a problem in this case.

Similarly, the district court's concerns regarding Drogoul's right of cross-examination are premature. To be sure, the defendant's right to confront witnesses is "the most important factor to be taken into account in determining whether to allow the use of a deposition at a criminal trial." . . . We fail to see, however, how the mere taking of depositions threatens that right. Only when deposition testimony is sought to be introduced in evidence are the defendant's confrontation rights truly implicated. Before then the process is simply one of preserving testimony for possible subsequent use. At trial, if admission of the deposition would violate the Sixth Amendment, the court could – indeed should – exclude the deposition. . . . At the time, the district court will be in a superior position to analyze the confrontation issue, because it will be able to review the actual deposition transcripts, audiotapes, and/or videotapes to determine whether in fact introducing the depositions would be inconsistent with the defendant's constitutional rights. . . .

It might have been within the district court's discretion to deny the government's deposition request – notwithstanding the unavailability of the prospective deponents and the crucial nature of their testimony – were it abundantly clear that the depositions could not possibly be admitted at trial. The court need not, at the cost of time and money, engage in an act of futility by authorizing depositions that clearly will be inadmissible at trial. But such is not the case here. Although oral questioning by counsel generally is not permitted in Italian courts, the government apparently has received assurances that oral examination will be allowed. Even if it is not, defense counsel will be able to submit questions for the Italian court to ask. In addition, the depositions will be videotaped, enabling a jury to observe the demeanor of the witnesses. . . . Both Drogoul and his counsel may travel to the depositions at the government's expense. Fed. R. Crim. P. 15(c). Several courts of appeals have affirmed the use at trial of deposition testimony obtained pursuant to procedures akin to those proposed in this case. . . . Thus, the likelihood that the Confrontation Clause would preclude admission of the highly material deposition testimony in this case is not so absolute as to warrant forbidding the government from at least preserving that testimony.

Likewise, the possibility that irremediable problems will develop with respect to translation of the depositions is too remote for one to conclude that taking the depositions would be a mere exercise in futility. If irreconcilable differences arise after the depositions have been taken and the translations made, then the depositions might properly be excluded from evidence at that time. . . .

In refusing to allow the government to depose the Italian witnesses, the district court failed to recognize the crucial distinction that exists between the propriety of taking depositions versus the propriety of using the depositions at trial. . . . The court's concerns about the procedures surrounding the depositions are best addressed if and when the government seeks to introduce the depositions in evidence. . . .

The district court's second main reason for denying the request for foreign depositions was the government's purported delay in seeking the depositions and in notifying both Drogoul and the court as to its intentions. . . . We hold that the district court erred to the extent that it denied the request for depositions solely on the ground that taking the depositions would delay the trial. As Drogoul has conceded, the expected deposition testimony goes to the heart of the issues in this case. Setting forth a per se rule against delay in the face of this crucial testimony is an abuse of discretion. . . .

Furthermore, the district court grossly overweighed the government's dilatoriness in informing both it and Drogoul regarding the plan to depose the Italian witnesses. Rule 15(b) provides merely that the party taking the deposition "shall give to every party reasonable written notice of the time and place for taking the deposition." The reasonableness of the notice is a function of the time necessary for the opposing party to prepare for the deposition and thereby protect his rights. Here, the government filed its original motion on April 21, 1993. The motion requested that the depositions be taken May 25-28, 1993, more than a month later. This would have afforded Drogoul ample time to prepare. Rule 15 does not require a moving party to consult with the opposing party in advance regarding the scheduling of a deposition.

We do have some concerns about the fact that the government, which apparently was in contact with the Italian authorities as early as February 1993, did not move to take the depositions until late April 1993. We are also aware that allowing the depositions at this point might necessitate delaying the trial,and that Drogoul already has been in jail for sixteen months. Nevertheless, when the government filed its original motion the rescheduled trial was almost five months away. The government then acted diligently in responding to the district court's original concerns regarding the unavailability of the witnesses, working with the Italian judiciary to obtain the in-court declarations of the prospective deponents regarding their willingness to testify in the United States. Immediately upon receiving the letter from the Italian magistrate, on June 4, 1993 – still more than three months before trial – the government filed its renewed request to take depositions. The district court erred in holding that the government's lack of due diligence outweighed the strong showing of unavailability and materiality in this case. Accordingly, the district court should have allowed the government to depose the seven prospective witnesses who declared they would not testify in the United States.

 . . . . Exceptional circumstances and the interests of justice also warrant allowing the government to take the depositions of the six prospective witnesses who announced they would be willing to testify at Drogoul's trial. Whether to allow the depositions of these witnesses is, admittedly, a more difficult question than whether to allow the depositions of the other seven, because the government's showing as to the unavailability of these witnesses is obviously not as strong. We must remember, however, that unavailability is not the focus per se of Rule 15(a). Unavailability is required for use of the depositions at trial. Fed. R. Crim. P. 15(e). All that is necessary to take depositions is a showing that "exceptional circumstances" exist and that justice would be served by preserving the deposition testimony. . . .

. . . . Far from being a substantial waste of time and resources, therefore, allowing the depositions of the six additional witnesses would involve the expenditure of only marginally more time, money, and effort. Furthermore, although the six prospective deponents stated in May 1993 that they were willing to come to the United States, they too are beyond the subpoena power of the United States courts. The possibility remains that they could change their minds, in which case it would be impossible for the government to present their testimony. . . .

Of course, before the depositions of the six could be used at trial the government would have to establish the deponents' unavailability. . . . This might be a difficult task in view of the witnesses' previous declarations. Nevertheless, we believe that three factors together – the significance to the case of the deponents' expected testimony; the fact that the deponents are beyond the reach of any American subpoena; and, critically, the fact that the parties already must take depositions in Italy – provide sufficiently exceptional circumstances to satisfy Rule 15(a). . . . The district court should have allowed the depositions of these prospective witnesses as well. . . . The August 4, 1993 order of the district court denying the government's renewed motion to take the depositions of thirteen Italian witnesses in Italy is REVERSED. The case is REMANDED to the district court for further proceedings consistent with this opinion.

MARC RICH & CO. v. UNITED STATES

United States Court of Appeals for the Second Circuit
707 F.2d 663 (1983)

VAN GRAAFEILAND, CIRCUIT JUDGE:

Marc Rich & Co., A.G. appeals from an order of the United States District Court for the Southern District of New York (Sand, J.), which held it in civil contempt for failing to comply with the court's order directing it to produce certain records pursuant to a grand jury subpoena duces tecum* and which imposed a coercive fine to take effect upon the disposition of this expedited appeal. We affirm.

Appellant is a Swiss commodities trading corporation dealing in the international market in bulk raw materials such as petroleum, metals, and minerals. Its principal office is in Zug, Switzerland. Although it has forty branch offices in thirty countries around the world, it has no office in the United States. However, Marc Rich & Co. International Limited (International), a wholly-owned subsidiary of appellant, does business in the State of New York. The same five persons serve as the directors of the two companies. Three board members are Swiss residents, and two, Marc Rich and Pincus Green, reside in the United States and are employed by International as traders.

In March, 1982, a federal grand jury in the Southern District of New York was investigating an alleged tax evasion scheme, involving appellant, International, and the principals of each company, whereby, during 1980, International diverted a minimum of $20 million of its taxable income to appellant. On March 9, 1982, a grand jury subpoena duces tecum was served on International for the production of business records relating to crude oil transactions during 1980 and 1981. International complied with the subpoena. On April 15, 1982, a grand jury subpoena duces tecum, addressed to appellant and served on International, called for production by appellant of similar records.

On June 9, 1982, appellant moved to quash the subpoena on the grounds that appellant was not subject to the in personam jurisdiction of the court and that Swiss law prohibited the production of the materials demanded. In an opinion dated August 25, 1982, Judge Sand denied the motion to quash, finding that personal jurisdiction existed and that the operation of Swiss law was no bar to the production of the documents. When appellant persisted in its refusal, Judge Sand adjudged it to be in civil contempt. Appellant's arguments on appeal center principally on the issue of jurisdiction. . . .

Congress has made clear its intent that this nation's income tax laws are applicable to foreign corporations. . . . Under well-settled rules of international law, the authority of Congress to impose punishment for violation of these laws is equally clear. Of the five generally recognized principles of international criminal jurisdiction – territorial, nationality, protective, universality, and passive personality . . . . the territorial and protective principles justify the enforcement of penal revenue statutes such as 26 U.S.C. §§ 7201 and 7206. The territorial principle is applicable when acts outside a jurisdiction are intended to produce and do produce detrimental effects within it. *United States v. Pizzarusso,* [p. 33]. Under the protective principle, a state "has jurisdiction to prescribe a rule of law attaching legal consequences to

---

* *See also* chap. 10 for a discussion of grand jury subpoenas. – Eds.

conduct outside its territory that threatens . . . the operation of its governmental functions, provided the conduct is generally recognized as a crime under the law of states that have reasonably developed legal systems." . . .

Where, as here, the territorial principle is applicable, the Government may punish a defendant in the same manner as if it were present in the jurisdiction when the detrimental effects occurred. "The principle that a man who outside of a country wilfully puts in motion a force to take effect in it is answerable at the place where the evil is done, is recognized in the criminal jurisprudence of all countries." . . .

It would be strange, indeed, if the United States could punish a foreign corporation for violating its criminal laws upon a theory that the corporation was constructively present in the country at the time the violation occurred, . . . but a federal grand jury could not investigate to ascertain the probability that a crime had taken place. . . . The grand jury is an appendage or agency of the court. . . . It may investigate any crime that is within the jurisdiction of the court. . . . Its duty to inquire cannot be limited to conduct occurring in the district in which it sits. . . .

In performing its duty of inquiry, the grand jury must have the right to summon witnesses and to require the production of documentary evidence. "The grand jury's authority to subpoena witnesses is not only historic, . . . but essential to its task." . . . So long as the court which must enforce the grand jury process can obtain personal jurisdiction of the summoned witness, the witness may not resist the summons on the sole ground that he is a non-resident alien. . . . Neither may the witness resist the production of documents on the ground that the documents are located abroad. . . . The test for the production of documents is control, not location. . . .

The question, then, in the instant case is whether the district court had such personal jurisdiction over appellant that it could enforce obedience to the grand jury subpoena. We agree with counsel for both sides that Judge Sand should not have looked to New York State's long-arm statutes in answering this question. . . . The subject of the grand jury's investigation is the possible violation of federal revenue statutes, and its right to inquire of appellant depends upon appellant's contacts with the entire United States, not simply the state of New York. . . . Nonetheless, we are satisfied that the district judge arrived at the correct result.

With *McGee v. International Life Ins. Co.*, 355 U.S. 220, 2 L. Ed. 2d 223, 78 S. Ct. 199 (1957) as our lodestar, we have subscribed to the "modern notion" that where a person has sufficiently caused adverse consequences within a state, he may be subjected to its judicial jurisdiction so long as he is given adequate notice and an opportunity to be heard. . . . Section 50 of the American Law Institute's Restatement (Second) of Conflict of Laws (1971), similarly provides:

A state has power to exercise judicial jurisdiction over a foreign corporation which causes effects in the state by an act done elsewhere with respect to any cause of action arising from these effects unless the nature of these effects and of the corporation's relationship to the state makes the exercise of such jurisdiction unreasonable.

While this principle must be applied with caution in matters which have international complications, . . . we think it clearly applicable in the instant case. That the United States is injuriously affected by the wrongful evasion of its revenue laws is beyond dispute. Under such circumstances, it well may be that the occurrence of the offense itself is sufficient to support a claim of jurisdiction, provided adequate notice and an opportunity to be heard has been given. . . . However, appellant's contacts with the United States were not limited to appellant's alleged extraterritorial violation of United States revenue laws.

If appellant did violate the United States tax laws, a question whose answer must await the possible return of an indictment, that violation occurred in cooperation with appellant's wholly-owned subsidiary, Marc Rich & Co. International, Ltd., which is authorized to do business in New York State and does so. Moreover, two of the five members of appellant's board of directors, who are also on the board of Marc Rich & Co. International, are residents of the United States. At least one of these directors is alleged to have been directly involved in the scheme to divert the taxable income of International. If, in fact, there was a conspiracy among all of these parties to evade the tax laws, both the conspiracy and at least some of the conspiratorial acts occurred in the United States. . . . Under such circumstances, service of a subpoena upon appellant's officers within the territorial boundaries of the United States would be sufficient to warrant judicial enforcement of the grand jury's subpoena. . . .

We find no merit in appellant's argument that ratification of the service upon it of the subpoena would be tantamount to creating a novel federal long-arm rule without congressional authorization. . . .

Briefly summarized, appellant's argument puts the cart before the horse. A federal court's jurisdiction is not determined by its power to issue a subpoena; its power to issue a subpoena is determined by its jurisdiction. . . .

The crucial issue on this appeal is how much of a jurisdictional showing the Government had to make in order to warrant the issuance of the subpoena directed to appellant. Appellant contends that the district court committed reversible error in holding that, although the Government had to show in the first instance that it had a good faith basis for asserting jurisdiction, once it did so, the burden of proving lack of jurisdiction shifted to appellant. We agree with appellant's argument concerning burden of proof but disagree with appellant's contention that reversal is required. Based upon our own review of the affidavits submitted in the district court, . . . we are satisfied that the Government made a sufficient showing of personal jurisdiction to justify the district court's order.

In the seminal case of *Blair v. United States,* 250 U.S. 273, 63 L. Ed. 979, 39 S. Ct. 468 (1919), Justice Pitney, writing for the Court, said that grand jury witnesses "are not entitled to take exception to the jurisdiction of the grand jury or the court over the particular subject-matter that is under investigation." . . . He continued, "At least, the court and grand jury have authority and jurisdiction to investigate the facts in order to determine the question whether the facts show a case within their jurisdiction." . . .

Although Justice Pitney was discussing subject matter rather than personal jurisdiction, the same reasoning may be applied in cases such as the instant one, where the appellant is not challenging enforcement of the grand jury subpoena on the due process grounds of notice and an opportunity to be heard, . . . Requiring the Government to prove by a preponderance of evidence the facts upon which it bases its claim of personal jurisdiction "might well invert the grand jury function, requiring that body to furnish answers to its questions before it could ask them." . . . "[A] sufficient basis for an indictment may only emerge at the end of the investigation when all the evidence has been received." . . .

Such a showing has been made in the instant case. For example, affidavits submitted by the Government disclose that, in 1980, approximately 40% of International's crude oil purchases, worth $345 million, were from appellant. International then realized a gross loss of over $110 million in selling to its domestic customers. There is sufficient likelihood that unlawful tax manipulation was taking place between appellant and its wholly-owned subsidiary to make it "reasonable and just, according to our traditional conception of fair play and substantial justice" to require appellant to respond to the grand jury's inquiries. . . .

Affirmed.

Chapter 13
EXTRADITION

§ 13.01 Extradition to the United States

UNITED STATES v. VAN CAUWENBERGHE

United States Court of Appeals for the Ninth Circuit
827 F.2d 424 (1987)

NELSON, CIRCUIT JUDGE:

Wilfried Van Cauwenberghe, a citizen of Belgium, appeals from a criminal conviction on one count of wire fraud under 18 U.S.C. § 1343 (1982) and one count of interstate transportation of a victim of fraud under 18 U.S.C. § 2314 (1982). Following a jury trial, Van Cauwenberghe was convicted of participating with two Americans in a scheme to defraud a Belgian investment broker and a family-owned Belgian corporation of 3.6 million dollars relating to the purchase and development of a condominium tract near Kansas City. Van Cauwenberghe argues that numerous errors were made requiring reversal of his extradition from Switzerland, his indictment, and his trial. In addition, Van Cauwenberghe argues that the district court should have returned certain property to him because it was seized illegally, and that his sentence was improper. . . .

Between 1979 and 1981, Van Cauwenberghe participated with two Americans, Alan H. Blair and Gerald L. Bilton, in a scheme to defraud Roger Biard, a Belgian investment broker, and a Belgian corporation owned by members of the Vanden Stock family, of 3.6 million dollars relating to the purchase and development of Concorde Bridge Townhouses, an apartment complex near Kansas City, Missouri. Van Cauwenberghe, Blair, and Bilton were indicted on seven counts, including three counts of wire fraud (18 U.S.C. § 1343), three counts of interstate transportation of a victim of fraud (18 U.S.C. § 2314), and one count of conspiracy to commit fraud (18 U.S.C. § 371), in October 1984. The government learned that Van Cauwenberghe, a Belgian citizen, would be traveling from Brussels to Geneva on a brief business trip and, on November 20, 1984, filed a provisional arrest request with Swiss authorities pursuant to Article VI of the Treaty on Extradition, May 14, 1900, United States-Switzerland, 31 Stat. 1928, T.S. No. 354 ("Treaty").[1] Van Cauwenberghe

---

[1] The government could not proceed against Van Cauwenberghe in Belgium because Belgium does not extradite its nationals.

was arrested by Swiss authorities as he stepped off his plane in Geneva on January 14, 1985. . . . The government subsequently filed a formal extradition request on March 12, 1985.

Van Cauwenberghe challenged his extradition before the Swiss courts including the Swiss Federal Tribunal, Switzerland's highest court, which, on September 25, 1985, held that Van Cauwenberghe was extraditable under the Treaty for all of the offenses charged except conspiracy. Accordingly, Van Cauwenberghe was extradited to the United States on September 26, 1985.

. . . . The theory of Van Cauwenberghe's defense at trial was that he was merely an innocent pawn in the fraudulent scheme, not a culpable participant. . . . The jury found all three defendants guilty on both counts. . . .

The right "to demand and obtain extradition of an accused criminal is created by treaty." . . . The offense complained of must ordinarily, therefore, be listed as an extraditable crime in the treaty. . . . In addition, "under the doctrine of 'dual criminality,' an accused person can be extradited only if the conduct complained of is considered criminal by the jurisprudence or under the laws of both the requesting and requested nations." . . . This dual criminality requirement has been expressly incorporated into the Treaty. . . . To satisfy this "dual criminality" requirement,

> "the law does not require that the name by which the crime is described in the two countries shall be the same; nor that the scope of liability shall be coextensive, or, in other respects, the same in the two countries. It is enough if the particular act charged is criminal in both jurisdictions."

. . . . As a matter of international comity, "the doctrine of 'specialty' prohibits the requesting nation from prosecuting the extradited individual for any offense other than that for which the surrendering state agreed to extradite." . . . However, since the doctrine is based on comity, its "protection exists only to the extent that the surrendering country wishes." . . . Therefore, the "'extradited party may be tried for a crime other than that for which he was surrendered *if the asylum country consents*." . . .

Van Cauwenberghe argues that his extradition was improper because the Treaty does not identify wire fraud and interstate transportation of a victim of fraud as extraditable offenses. The Treaty does not expressly name these specific offenses but includes "obtaining money or other property by false pretenses [and] receiving money . . . knowing the same to have been . . . fraudulently obtained." . . . Moreover, the government insists that Van Cauwenberghe's argument is foreclosed by the Swiss Federal Tribunal's decision because "determination of whether a crime is within the provisions of an extradition treaty is within the sole purview of the requested state. . . . " We agree.

Johnson [*v. Browne*, 205 U.S. 309 (1907)] involved an extradition request by the United States to Canada. The Canadian government determined that one of the offenses for which extradition was sought, conspiring to defraud the government, was not a form of fraud provided for in the subdivision of the article of the treaty listing extraditable fraud offenses. . . . The Supreme Court held that "whether the crime came within the provision of the treaty was a matter for the decision of the Dominion authorities, and such decision was final by the express terms of the treaty itself." . . . Article II of the treaty in *Johnson* dealt only with offenses of a political character and expressly stated that "if any question shall arise as to whether a case comes within the provisions of this article, the decision of the authorities of the government in whose jurisdiction the fugitive shall be at the time shall be final." . . .

Because of this language in the *Johnson* treaty, Van Cauwenberghe argues that the holding in *Johnson* should be read narrowly. We believe, however, that the *Johnson* holding need not be read narrowly and that the first half of the sentence makes a broader statement regarding the proper deference to be accorded a surrendering country's decision on extraditability. The Canadian government's decision was not that the offense was non-extraditable because it was of a political character, a position that might have justified a narrower reading of *Johnson*. Instead, it maintained that the offense did not fall within the treaty's category of extraditable fraud offenses. . . . Thus, we believe that the first half of the sentence addressed the proper deference to be accorded a surrendering country's decision as to whether a particular offense comes within a treaty's extradition provision.

In *McGann* [*v. U.S. Bd. of Parole*, 488 F.2d 39 (3rd Cir. 1973)], the Third Circuit also construed *Johnson* broadly. *McGann* involved the propriety of an extradition from Jamaica in which the Jamaican court held a parole violator extraditable under its treaty with the United States. The *McGann* court found the *Johnson* language controlling: "The holding of *Johnson v. Browne* . . . precludes any review of the Jamaican court's decision as to the extraditable nature of the offense. . . ." We agree with the Third Circuit's reading of *Johnson*. According deference to the surrendering country's decision as to extraditability already underlies the related "doctrine of specialty." It would render that doctrine practically meaningless to hold that courts cannot try an extradited party for offenses other than those for which the surrendering government agreed to extradite, but need not defer to the surrendering government's threshold decision as to whether an offense is extraditable.

We therefore defer to the Swiss Federal Tribunal's decision as to Van Cauwenberghe's extraditability under the Treaty and hold that Van Cauwenberghe was properly extradited. . . .

NOTES AND QUESTIONS

(1) Do the underlying policies behind the principle of dual criminality and the rule of specialty suggest that these two principles are closely aligned? Consider the discussion of these concepts as presented in *United States v. Saccoccia*, 58 F.3d 754 (1st Cir. 1995):

> Although the principles of dual criminality and specialty are closely allied, they are not coterminous. . . .
>
> The principle of dual criminality dictates that, as a general rule, an extraditable offense must be a serious crime (rather than a mere peccadillo) punishable under the criminal laws of both the surrendering and the requesting state. . . . The current extradition treaty between the United States and Switzerland embodies this concept. *See* Treaty of Extradition, May 14, 1900, U.S.-Switz., Art. II, 31 Stat. 1928, 1929-30 (Treaty).
>
> The principle of dual criminality does not demand that the laws of the surrendering and requesting states be carbon copies of one another. Thus, dual criminality will not be defeated by differences in the instrumentalities or in the stated purposes of the two nations' laws. . . . By the same token, the counterpart crimes need not have identical elements. *See Matter of Extradition of Russell*, 789 F.2d 801, 803 (9th Cir. 1986). Instead, dual criminality is deemed to be satisfied when the two countries' laws are substantially analogous. . . . Moreover, in mulling dual criminality concerns, courts are duty bound to defer to a surrendering sovereign's reasonable determination that the offense in question is extraditable. . . .
>
> Mechanically, then, the inquiry into dual criminality requires courts to compare the law of the surrendering state that purports to criminalize the charged conduct with the law of the requesting state that purports to accomplish the same result. If the same conduct is subject to criminal sanctions in both jurisdictions, no more is exigible. . . .
>
> The principle of specialty – a corollary to the principle of dual criminality – . . . . generally requires that an extradited defendant be tried for the crimes on which extradition has been granted, and none other. . . . The extradition treaty in force between the United States and Switzerland embodies this concept, providing that an individual may not be "prosecuted or punished for any offense committed before the demand for extradition, other than that for which the extradition is granted . . . ." Treaty, Art. IX.
>
> Enforcement of the principle of specialty is founded primarily on international comity. . . . The requesting state must "live up to whatever promises it made in order to obtain extradition" because

preservation of the institution of extradition requires the continuing cooperation of the surrendering state. . . . Since the doctrine is grounded in international comity rather than in some right of the defendant, the principle of specialty may be waived by the asylum state. . . .

Specialty, like dual criminality, is not a hidebound dogma, but must be applied in a practical, commonsense fashion. Thus, obeisance to the principle of specialty does not require that a defendant be prosecuted only under the precise indictment that prompted his extradition . . . or that the prosecution always be limited to specific offenses enumerated in the surrendering state's extradition order. . . . In the same vein, the principle of specialty does not impose any limitation on the particulars of the charges lodged by the requesting nation, nor does it demand departure from the forum's existing rules of practice.

In the last analysis, then, the inquiry into specialty boils down to whether, under the totality of the circumstances, the court in the requesting state reasonably believes that prosecuting the defendant on particular charges contradicts the surrendering state's manifested intentions, or, phrased another way, whether the surrendering state would deem the conduct for which the requesting state actually prosecutes the defendant as interconnected with (as opposed to independent from) the acts for which he was extradited. . . .

(2) What is the procedure to be followed by a United States Attorney in trying to extradite someone to the United States? What documents are necessary to process the extradition? Consider the following procedure outlined in the United States Attorney's Manual.

§ 9-15.240 Documents Required in Support of Request for Extradition

The request for extradition is made by diplomatic note prepared by the Department of State and transmitted to the foreign government through diplomatic channels. It must be accompanied by the documents specified in the treaty. The Office of International Affairs (OIA) will advise the prosecutor of the documentary requirements, but it is the responsibility of the prosecutor to prepare and assemble them and forward the original and four copies to OIA in time to be reviewed, authenticated, translated, and sent through the Department of State to the foreign government by the deadline.

OIA will provide samples of the documents required in support of the request for extradition. Although every treaty varies, all generally require:

– An affidavit from the prosecutor explaining the facts of the case. *See* Criminal Resource Manual at 605.

– Copies of the statutes alleged to have been violated and the statute of limitations. *See* Criminal Resource Manual at 607.

– If the fugitive has not been convicted, certified copies of the arrest warrant and complaint or indictment. *See* Criminal Resource Manual at 606.

– Evidence, in the form of affidavits or grand jury transcripts, establishing that the crime was committed, including sufficient evidence (i.e., photograph, fingerprints, and affidavit of identifying witness) to establish the defendant's identity (CAVEAT: The use of grand jury transcripts or trial transcripts should, if at all possible, be avoided). *See* Criminal Resource Manual at 608.

– If the fugitive has been convicted, a certified copy of the order of judgment and committal establishing the conviction, an affidavit stating the sentence was not or was only partially served and the amount of time remaining to be served, and evidence concerning identity. *See* Criminal Resource Manual at 609.

Prosecutors should be aware that there are few workable defenses to extradition, although appeals and delays are common. Fugitives, however, may be able to contest extradition on the basis of minor inconsistencies resulting from clerical or typographical errors. Although these can be remedied eventually, they take time to untangle. Therefore, pay careful attention to detail in preparing the documents.

18 U.S.C. § 3187 sets out the procedure for obtaining provisional arrest and detention pending formal documentation.

(3) What steps should be taken by a United States Attorney when he or she is unable to extradite an individual to the United States? Consider the U.S. Attorney's Manual 9-15.225:

§ 9-15.225 Procedure When Fugitive is Non-Extraditable

If the fugitive is not extraditable, other steps may be available to return him or her to the United States or to restrict his or her ability to live and travel overseas. *See* USAM 9-15.600 et seq. These steps, if taken, should likewise be documented.

Courts may require the government to request the extradition of a fugitive as soon as his or her location becomes known, unless the effort would be useless. If the decision is made to not seek extradition in a particular case, the prosecutor and the Office of International Affairs (OIA) will make a record to document why extradition was not possible in the event of a subsequent Speedy Trial challenge.

(4) Where extradition is not possible from one country, can the government lure the individual into another country in order to proceed with an extradition?* Consider the following two sections of the U.S. Attorneys Manual:

§ 9-15.620 Extradition From a Third Country

If the fugitive travels outside the country from which he or she is not extraditable, it may be possible to request his or her extradition from another country. This method is often used for fugitives who are citizens in their country of refuge. Some countries, however, will not permit extradition if the defendant has been lured into their territory. Such ruses may also cause foreign relations problems with both the countries from which and to which the lure takes place. Prosecutors must notify the Office of International Affairs before pursuing any scenario involving an undercover or other operation to lure a fugitive into a country for law enforcement purposes (extradition, deportation, prosecution).

§ 9-15.630 Lures

A lure involves using a subterfuge to entice a criminal defendant to leave a foreign country so that he or she can be arrested in the United States, in international waters or airspace, or in a third country for subsequent extradition, expulsion, or deportation to the United States. Lures can be complicated schemes or they can be as simple as inviting a fugitive by telephone to a party in the United States.

A noted above, some countries will not extradite a person to the United States if the person's presence in that country was obtained through the use of a lure or other ruse [see also chap. 14]. In addition, some countries may view a lure of a person from its territory as an infringement on its sovereignty. Consequently, a prosecutor must consult with the Office of International Affairs before undertaking a lure to the United States or a third country.

(5) The U.S. Attorney's Manual provides the government policy on rule of specialty:

§ 9-15.500 Post Extradition Considerations: Limitations on Further Prosecution

Every extradition treaty limits extradition to certain offenses. As a corollary, all extradition treaties restrict prosecution or punishment of the fugitive to the offense for which extradition was granted unless (1)

---

* Another possibility is abduction which is discussed in chap. 14. – Eds.

the offense was committed after the fugitive's extradition or (2) the fugitive remains in the jurisdiction after expiration of a "reasonable time" (generally specified in the extradition treaty itself) following completion of his punishment. This limitation is referred to as the Rule of Specialty. Prosecutors who wish to proceed against an extradited person on charges other than those for which extradition was granted must contact the Office of International Affairs (OIA) for guidance regarding the availability of a waiver of the Rule by the sending State.

Frequently, defendants who have been extradited to the United States attempt to dismiss or limit the government's case against them by invoking the Rule of Specialty. There is a split in the courts on whether the defendant has standing to raise specialty: some courts hold that only a party to the Treaty (i.e., the sending State) may complain about an alleged violation of the specialty provision, other courts allow the defendant to raise the issue on his own behalf, and other courts take a middle position and allow the defendant to raise the issue if it is likely that the sending State would complain as well. Whenever a defendant raises a specialty claim, the prosecutor should contact OIA for assistance in responding.

Defendants also occasionally make other substantive or procedural challenges to their extradition. It is impossible to anticipate all the creative challenges that may be devised; if a returned defendant challenges his extradition, you should contact OIA.

(6) Do prosecutors have to strictly adhere to the rule of specialty? Although many courts in the U.S. allow prosecutors leeway in adding charges following an extradition, there are some courts that adhere to a strict application of the doctrine of specialty. *See generally* Hugh Chadwick Thatcher, Note, *The Doctrine of Specialty: An Argument for a More Restrictive Rauscher Interpretation After State v. Pang*, 31 VAND. J. TRANSNAT'L L. 1321 (1998).

Does it make a difference in applying the doctrine of specialty how many counts are charged against the defendant? In *United States v. LeBaron*, 156 F.3d 621(5th Cir. 1998), Circuit Judge Emilio M. Garza stated:

[T]he doctrine of specialty is concerned primarily with prosecution for different substantive offenses than those for which consent has been given, and not prosecution for additional or separate counts of the same offense. The appropriate test for a violation of specialty "is 'whether the extraditing country would consider the acts for which the defendant was prosecuted as independent from those for which he was extradited.' "

See also United States v. Saccoccia, 58 F.3d 757, 784 (1st Cir. 1995) ("forfeiture is neither a free-standing criminal offense nor an element of a racketeering offense under RICO, but is simply an incremental punishment for that prescribed conduct. Consequently, a defendant may be subjected to a forfeiture order even if extradition was not specifically granted in respect to the forfeiture allegations.").

(7) Do many countries refuse to extradite their nationals? Are countries following a recognized principle of international law when they refuse to extradite their nationals? *See generally* Michael Plachta, *(Non-) Extradition of Nationals: A Neverending Story?*, 13 EMORY INT'L L. REV. 77 (1999); Joshua H. Warmund, Comment, *Removing Drug Lords and Street Pushers: The Extradition of Nationals in Columbia and the Dominican Republic*, 22 FORDHAM INT'L L.J. 2372 (1999). Consider the case of Samuel Sheinbein, who was born in the United States, fled to Israel, and resisted extradition on the basis of his claim to Israeli citizenship under Israel's nationality law. His conviction in Israel for having committed a homicide in the United States was criticized when he received a sentence that was considered to be too lenient as compared to what he might have received in the United States. *See Teen's Plea Deal in Israel Angers U.S. Prosecutor,* ATL. J. CONST., Aug. 26, 1999, at A8; Jack Katzenell, *Israel Convicts U.S. Teen of Murder*, ATL. J. CONST, Sept. 3, 1999, at C4. *See also* Abraham Abramovsky & Jonathan I. Edelstein, *The Sheinbein Case and the Israeli-American Extradition Experience: A Need for Compromise*, 32 VAND. J. TRANSAT'L L. 305 (1999).

(8) Do some countries face internal repercussions if they extradite individuals to the United States? *See* Barry Meier, *Pledges of Extradition Accompany Columbian Drug Arrests*, N.Y. TIMES, Oct. 14, 1999, at A3 (In the past Colombia refused to extradite Colombian nationals sought by the United States on narcotics charges. It was said that the Colombian courts faced "terrorists acts by drug traffickers opposed to facing trial in the United States"). In 1997 Colombia changed its Constitution to permit the extradition of nationals. *Id.*

(9) Do countries refuse to extradite individuals to the United States because they regard U.S. criminal procedure unfair? France initially refused to extradite Ira Einhorn to the United States because a Philadelphia court had convicted him in absentia (when he absented himself during his trial for murder), and sentenced him to life imprisonment, with no opportunity for a retrial. French law permits trials in absentia but insists on the possibility of a retrial once the accused returns to the jurisdiction. After Pennsylvania passed a law that would provide a possible retrial for Einhorn, a French court ruled that he could be extradited to the United States. *See French Prime Minister Finds Einhorn Extraditable to the U.S.*, 16 INT'L ENFORCEMENT L. REP. 900 (2000).

Can extradition be contingent upon the extradited individual being exempt from receiving a death sentence? *See* chap. 16 for further discussion.

§ 13.02 Extradition from the United States

UNITED STATES v. LUI KIN-HONG

United States Court of Appeals for the First Circuit
110 F.3d 103 (1997), reh. en banc denied ,1997 U.S. App. LEXIS 7587

LYNCH, CIRCUIT JUDGE:

The United States District Court granted a writ of habeas corpus to Lui Kin-Hong ("Lui"), who sought the writ after a magistrate judge certified to the Secretary of State that she may, in her discretion, surrender Lui for extradition to the Crown Colony of Hong Kong. The United Kingdom, on behalf of Hong Kong, had sought Lui's extradition on a warrant for his arrest for the crime of bribery. Lui's petition for habeas corpus was premised on the fact that the reversion of Hong Kong to the People's Republic of China will take place on July 1, 1997, and it will be impossible for the Crown Colony to try and to punish Lui before that date. The United States appeals. We reverse the order of the district court granting the writ of habeas corpus.

The United States argues that Lui is within the literal terms of the extradition treaties between the United States and the United Kingdom, that the courts may not vary from the language of the treaties, and that the certification must issue. Lui argues that the language of the treaties does not permit extradition, an argument which is surely wrong. Lui's more serious argument is that the Senate, in approving the treaties, did not mean to permit extradition of someone to be tried and punished by a government different from the government which has given its assurances in the treaties.

Lui does not claim that he faces prosecution in Hong Kong on account of his race, religion, nationality, or political opinion. He does not claim to be charged with a political offense.** The treaties give the courts a greater role when such considerations are present. Here, Lui's posture is that of one charged with an ordinary crime. His claim is that to surrender him now to Hong Kong is, in effect, to send him to trial and punishment in the People's Republic of China. The Senate, in approving the treaties, could not have intended such a result, he argues, and so the court should interpret the treaties as being inapplicable to

---

* Although the en banc vote was to deny a rehearing, Circuit Judge Stahl wrote a dissenting opinion stating that, "the district court correctly concluded that Lui cannot be certified for extradition because the United Kingdom fails to 'live up to the terms of its extradition agreement with the United States.'" – Eds.

** *See infra* § 13.03 for a discussion regarding the political offense exception. – Eds.

his case. Absent a treaty permitting extradition, he argues, he may not be extradited.

While Lui's argument is not frivolous, neither is it persuasive. The Senate was well aware of the reversion when it approved a supplementary treaty with the United Kingdom in 1986. The Senate could easily have sought language to address the reversion of Hong Kong if it were concerned, but did not do so. The President has recently executed a new treaty with the incoming government of Hong Kong, containing the same guarantees that Lui points to in the earlier treaties, and that treaty has been submitted to the Senate. In addition, governments of our treaty partners often change, sometimes by ballot, sometimes by revolution or other means, and the possibility or even certainty of such change does not itself excuse compliance with the terms of the agreement embodied in the treaties between the countries. Treaties contain reciprocal benefits and obligations. The United States benefits from the treaties at issue and, under their terms, may seek extradition to the date of reversion of those it wants for criminal offenses.

Fundamental principles in our American democracy limit the role of courts in certain matters, out of deference to the powers allocated by the Constitution to the President and to the Senate, particularly in the conduct of foreign relations. Those separation of powers principles, well rehearsed in extradition law, preclude us from rewriting the treaties which the President and the Senate have approved. The plain language of the treaties does not support Lui. Under the treaties as written, the courts may not, on the basis of the reversion, avoid certifying to the Secretary of State that Lui may be extradited. The decision whether to surrender Lui, in light of his arguments, is for the Secretary of State to make.

This is not to say American courts acting under the writ of habeas corpus, itself guaranteed in the Constitution, have no independent role. There is the ultimate safeguard that extradition proceedings before United States courts comport with the Due Process Clause of the Constitution. On the facts of this case, there is nothing presenting a serious constitutional issue of denial of due process. Some future case may, on facts amounting to a violation of constitutional guarantees, warrant judicial intervention. This case does not.

. . . . Lui is charged in Hong Kong with conspiring to receive and receiving over US $ 3 million in bribes from Giant Island Ltd. ("GIL") or GIL's subsidiary, Wing Wah Company ("WWC"). Lui, formerly a senior officer of the Brown & Williamson Co., was "seconded" in 1990 to its affiliated company, the British American Tobacco Co. (Hong Kong) Ltd. ("BAT-HK"), where he became Director of Exports in 1992. The charges result from an investigation by the Hong Kong Independent Commission Against Corruption ("ICAC"). The Hong Kong authorities charge that GIL and WWC, to which BAT-HK distributed cigarettes, paid bribes in excess of HK $ 100 million (approximately US $ 14 to $ 15 million) to a series of BAT-HK executives, including Lui. The bribes were allegedly given in exchange for a virtual monopoly on the export of certain brands of cigarettes to the People's Republic of China ("PRC") and to Taiwan. Among the cigarettes distributed were the popular Brown & Williamson brands of Kent, Viceroy, and Lucky Strike. GIL purchased three-quarters of a billion dollars in cigarettes from 1991 to 1994, mostly from BAT-HK.

A former GIL shareholder, Chui To-Yan ("Chui"), cooperated with the authorities and, it is said, would have provided evidence of Lui's acceptance of bribes. Some of Lui's alleged co-conspirators attempted to dissuade Chui from cooperating. Chui was later abducted, tortured, and murdered. The ICAC claims that the murder was committed to stop Chui from testifying. Lui is not charged in the murder conspiracy. Lui was in the Philippines (which has no extradition treaty with Hong Kong) on a business trip when the Hong Kong authorities unsuccessfully sought to question him in April 1994. Lui has not returned to Hong Kong since then.

At the request of the United Kingdom ("UK"), acting on behalf of Hong Kong, United States marshals arrested Lui as he got off a plane at Boston's Logan Airport on December 20, 1995. The arrest was for the purpose of extraditing Lui to Hong Kong. . . . The magistrate judge commenced extradition hearings on May 28, 1996. . . . The magistrate judge found that there was probable cause to believe that Lui had violated Hong Kong law on all but one of the charges in the warrant. Magistrate Judge Karol, pursuant to 18 U.S.C. § 3184,* issued a

---

* 18 U.S.C. § 3184 provides:

Whenever there is a treaty or convention for extradition between the United States and any foreign government, or in cases arising under section 3181(b), any justice or judge of the United States, or any magistrate [United States magistrate judge] authorized so to do by a court of the United States, or any judge of a court of record of general jurisdiction of any State, may, upon complaint made under oath, charging any person found within his jurisdiction, with having committed within the jurisdiction of any such foreign government any of the crimes provided for by such treaty or convention, or provided for under sectin 3181(b), issue his warrant for the apprehension of the person so charged, that he may be brought before such justice, judge, or magistrate [United States magistrate judge], to the end that the evidence of criminality may be heard and considered. Such complaint may be filed before and such warrant may be issued by a judge or magistrate [United States magistrate judge] of the United States District Court for the District of Columbia if the whereabouts within the United States of the person charged are not known or, if there is reason to believe the person will shortly enter the United States. If, on such hearing, he deems the evidence sufficient to sustain the charge under the provisions of the proper treaty or convention, or under section 3181(b), he shall certify the same, together with a copy of all the testimony taken before him, to the Secretary of State, that a warrant may issue upon the requisition of the proper authorities of such foreign government, for the surrender of such person, according to the stipulations of the treaty or convention; and he shall issue his warrant for the commitment of the person so charged to the proper jail, there to remain until such surrender shall be made.

careful decision certifying Lui's extraditability on August 29, 1996. *In re Extradition of Lui Kin-Hong (" Lui Extradition"),* 939 F. Supp. 934 (D. Mass. 1996). On September 3, 1996, Lui filed an amended petition for a writ of habeas corpus, the only avenue by which a fugitive sought for extradition (a "relator") may attack the magistrate judge's decision, with the district court.

After a hearing, the district court issued a memorandum and order granting the writ on January 7, 1997. *Lui Kin-Hong v. United States ("Lui Habeas"),* 957 F. Supp. 1280 (D. Mass. Jan. 7, 1997). The district court reasoned that, because the Crown Colony could not try Lui and punish him before the reversion date, the extradition treaty between the United States and the UK, which is applicable to Hong Kong, prohibited extradition. . . . Because no extradition treaty between the United States and the new government of Hong Kong has been confirmed by the United States Senate, the district court reasoned, the magistrate judge lacked jurisdiction to certify extraditability. . . . The district court denied the government's motion for reconsideration on January 13, 1997. This court then stayed the district court's order and expedited the present appeal.

At the time Lui was arrested in Boston in December 1995, more than eighteen months remained before the reversion of Hong Kong to the PRC on July 1, 1997. . . .

The extradition request was made pursuant to the Extradition Treaty Between the Government of the United States of America and the Government of the United Kingdom of Great Britain and Northern Ireland, June 8, 1972, 28 U.S.T. 227 (the "Treaty"), as amended by the Supplementary Treaty Between the Government of the United States of America and the Government of the United Kingdom of Great Britain and Northern Ireland, June 25, 1985, T.I.A.S. No. 12050 (the "Supplementary Treaty"). The original Treaty was made applicable to Hong Kong, among other British territories, . . . The Supplementary Treaty is applicable to Hong Kong by its terms. . . .

Hong Kong's status as a Crown Colony is coming to an end on July 1, 1997, when Hong Kong is to be restored to the PRC. The impending reversion, at the expiration of the UK's ninety-nine year leasehold, was formally agreed upon by the UK and the PRC in 1984; the United States was not a party to this agreement. . . . United States Senate ratification of the Supplementary Treaty occurred on July 17, 1986, well after the widely publicized signing of the Joint Declaration. . . . Clearly, the Senate was aware of the planned reversion when it approved the applicability to Hong Kong of the Supplementary Treaty. The Supplementary Treaty does not contain an exception for relators who can show that their trial or punishment will occur after the date of reversion. Indeed, the Supplementary Treaty is entirely silent on the question of reversion.

Id. – Eds.

The United States does not have an extradition treaty with the PRC. However, on December 20, 1996, the United States signed an extradition treaty with the government of the nascent HKSAR, which provides for reciprocal post-reversion extradition. . . . The New Treaty will not enter into force until the Senate gives its advice and consent. . . .

In the United States, the procedures for extradition are governed by statute. . . . The statute establishes a two-step procedure which divides responsibility for extradition between a judicial officer and the Secretary of State. The judicial officer's duties are set out in 18 U.S.C. § 3184. In brief, the judicial officer, upon complaint, issues an arrest warrant for an individual sought for extradition, provided that there is an extradition treaty between the United States and the relevant foreign government and that the crime charged is covered by the treaty. . . . If a warrant issues, the judicial officer then conducts a hearing to determine if "he deems the evidence sufficient to sustain the charge under the provisions of the proper treaty." . . . If the judicial officer makes such a determination, he "shall certify" to the Secretary of State that a warrant for the surrender of the relator "may issue." . . . The judicial officer is also directed to provide the Secretary of State with a copy of the testimony and evidence from the extradition hearing. . . .

It is then within the Secretary of State's sole discretion to determine whether or not the relator should actually be extradited. . . . Additionally, the Secretary may attach conditions to the surrender of the relator. . . . The State Department alone, and not the judiciary, has the power to attach conditions to an order of extradition. . . . Of course, the Secretary may also elect to use diplomatic methods to obtain fair treatment for the relator. . . .

Thus, under 18 U.S.C. § 3184, the judicial officer's inquiry is limited to a narrow set of issues concerning the existence of a treaty, the offense charged, and the quantum of evidence offered. The larger assessment of extradition and its consequences is committed to the Secretary of State. This bifurcated procedure reflects the fact that extradition proceedings contain legal issues peculiarly suited for judicial resolution, such as questions of the standard of proof, competence of evidence, and treaty construction, yet simultaneously implicate questions of foreign policy, which are better answered by the executive branch. Both institutional competence rationales and our constitutional structure, which places primary responsibility for foreign affairs in the executive branch, ... support this division of labor.

In implementing this system of split responsibilities for extradition, courts have developed principles which ensure, among other things, that the judicial inquiry does not unnecessarily impinge upon executive prerogative and expertise. . . . These principles of construction require courts to:

interpret extradition treaties to produce reciprocity between, and expanded rights on behalf of, the signatories: "[Treaties] should be liberally construed so as to effect the apparent intention of the parties to secure equality and reciprocity between them. For that reason, if a treaty fairly admits of two constructions, one restricting the rights which may be claimed under it, and the other enlarging it, the more liberal construction is to be preferred."

. . . . Another principle that guides courts in matters concerning extradition is the rule of non-inquiry. More than just a principle of treaty construction, the rule of non-inquiry tightly limits the appropriate scope of judicial analysis in an extradition proceeding. Under the rule of non-inquiry, courts refrain from "investigating the fairness of a requesting nation's justice system," . . . and from inquiring "into the procedures or treatment which await a surrendered fugitive in the requesting country." . . . The rule of non-inquiry, like extradition procedures generally, is shaped by concerns about institutional competence and by notions of separation of powers. . . . It is not that questions about what awaits the relator in the requesting country are irrelevant to extradition; it is that there is another branch of government, which has both final say and greater discretion in these proceedings, to whom these questions are more properly addressed.

Lui contends that, on July 1, 1997, the reversion of Hong Kong to the PRC will result in his being subjected to trial and punishment by a regime with which the United States has no extradition treaty. This future event, Lui argues, operates retroactively to render his extradition illegal, as of today, because, he says, extradition is only legitimate where trial and punishment will be administered by the regime with which the United States has a treaty.

Although Lui is correct that the government has conceded that he will not be tried before reversion, it is also quite possible that the scenario he depicts will not arise. The new extradition treaty with the HKSAR may be approved by the United States Senate, establishing a continuity of treaties through and beyond July 1, 1997. The United States government may choose to extend the current Treaty by executive agreement. To the extent that Lui's argument depends on the fairness of the procedures he will be subjected to, he asks this court to decide that the PRC will not adhere to the Joint Declaration with the UK, in which it declared its intention to maintain Hong Kong's legal system for fifty years.

All of these questions involve an evaluation of contingent political events. The Supreme Court has said that the indicia of a non-justiciable political question include:

a textually demonstrable constitutional commitment of the issue to a coordinate political department; or a lack of judicially discoverable and manageable standards for resolving it; or the impossibility of deciding without an initial policy determination of a kind clearly for nonjudicial discretion; or the impossibility of a court's undertaking independent resolution without expressing lack of respect due coordinate branches of government; or an unusual need for unquestioning adherence to a political decision already made; or the potentiality of embarrassment from multifarious pronouncements by various departments on one question.

Baker v. Carr, 369 U.S. 186, 217, 7 L. Ed. 2d 663, 82 S. Ct. 691 (1962). While not all of these ingredients are present here, several are. Moreover, unlike many "political questions," whose resolution, absent judicial determination, must await the vagaries of the political process, here there is a statutory scheme which provides for the resolution of these questions by an identified member of the executive branch. The case for judicial resolution is thus weaker than with many such questions.

The principles of reciprocity and liberal construction also counsel against construing the Treaties so as to prohibit Lui's extradition. Hong Kong, through the United Kingdom, has entered bilateral treaties with the United States. The United States has sought extradition of criminals from Hong Kong in the past, and may wish to continue to do so up until July 1, 1997. If the executive chooses to modify or abrogate the terms of the Treaties that it negotiated, it has ample discretion to do so. However, if this court were to read a cut-off date vis-a-vis extraditions to Hong Kong into the Treaties, it would risk depriving both parties of the benefit of their bargain.

None of these principles, including non-inquiry, may be regarded as an absolute. We, like the Second Circuit, "can imagine situations where the relator, upon extradition, would be subject to procedures or punishment so antipathetic to a federal court's sense of decency as to require reexamination of the principles" discussed above. . . . This is not such a case. Lui is wanted for economic, not political, activities whose criminality is fully recognized in the United States. His extradition is sought by the current Hong Kong regime, a colony of Great Britain, which, as Lui himself points out, is one of this country's most trusted treaty partners. Moreover, Lui has been a fugitive from Hong Kong since 1994. He has been subject to extradition since entering the United States in December 1995. That now only a few months remain before the reversion of Hong Kong is partly attributable to strategic choices made by Lui himself. There is nothing here which shocks the conscience of this court. . . .

There is no dispute that the Treaty, as supplemented by the Supplementary Treaty, is currently in effect and is applicable to Hong Kong. The district court, in granting Lui's habeas petition, reasoned that "the Treaty, by its own terms, does not allow the extradition of a person to Hong Kong if the Crown Colony of Hong Kong is unable to try and to punish that person." . . . The government counters that the terms of the Treaty clearly allow Lui's extradition. There is nothing in the plain language of the Treaties that would permit the construction made by the district court. The principles discussed above argue persuasively against reading judicially created limitations into the Treaties' unambiguous text. . . .

We begin our analysis of the Treaties with a brief overview of the Treaties' operative provisions. Article I of the Treaty states the basic reciprocal compact, providing that:

> Each Contracting Party undertakes to extradite to the other, in the circumstances and subject to the conditions specified in this Treaty, any person found in its territory who has been accused or convicted of any offense within Article III, committed within the jurisdiction of the other Party.

Treaty, art. I.

Article III contains the "dual criminality" requirement, a requirement that is "central to extradition law and [one that] has been embodied either explicitly or implicitly in all prior extradition treaties between the United States and Great Britain." . . . Article III, in relevant part, provides that:

> Extradition shall be granted for an act or omission the facts of which disclose an offense within any of the descriptions listed in the Schedule annexed to this Treaty . . . or any other offense, if: (a) the offense is punishable under the laws of both Parties by imprisonment or other form of detention for more than one year or by the death penalty . . . .

Treaty, art. III(1). The annexed Schedule lists twenty-nine general crimes, including bribery, the crime of which Lui is accused. . . .

Article V contains various affirmative defenses, including the "political offense" exception. As a general matter, the political offense exception "is now a standard clause in almost all extradition treaties of the world." . . . The political offense exception in the Treaty prohibits extradition where "(i) the offense for which extradition is requested is regarded by the requested Party as one of a political character; or (ii) the person sought proves that the request for his extradition has in fact been made with a view to try or punish him for an offense of a political character." . . .

The Supplementary Treaty narrows the availability of this political offense exception. It lists a range of crimes – all crimes of violence – that may not be regarded as political offenses for the purpose of raising the political offense exception. . . . The Supplementary Treaty also offers an affirmative defense to fugitives sought for crimes of violence who, by virtue of its article 1, are unable to raise the political offense exception. . . . Such a fugitive may block extradition by establishing:

> by a preponderance of the evidence that the request for extradition has in fact been made with a view to try or punish him on account of his race, religion, nationality, or political opinions, or that he would, if surrendered, be prejudiced at his trial or punished, detained or restricted in his personal liberty by reason of his race, religion, nationality or political opinions.

Id. art. 3(a).

The procedural requisites of an extradition request are specified in article VII of the Treaty. The request must be accompanied by, inter alia, a description of the fugitive, a statement of facts of the offense, and the text of the law under which he is charged. . . . For accused (as opposed to already convicted) fugitives, the request must also include a valid arrest warrant and "such evidence as, according to the law of the requested Party, would justify his committal for trial if the offense had been committed in the territory of the requested Party, including evidence that the person requested is the person to whom the warrant of arrest refers." . . .

Article XII contains the "specialty" requirement, a common feature of extradition treaties. Specialty has two basic components. First, the requesting state may not try the fugitive for any crimes other than the specific crime for which extradition was sought and granted. Second, the requesting state may not re-extradite the fugitive to a third state. . . .

Both the district court and Lui focus on four Treaty provisions in concluding that the Treaty is inapplicable to Lui. . . . We address these provisions in turn, concluding that the obligation of the United States to extradite Lui, specified in article I of the Treaty, is not undermined by any of these provisions. . . .

The district court understood the warrant requirement of article VII(3) to serve the purpose of permitting "the requested sovereign to know that the relator has been accused . . . pursuant to the laws of the requesting sovereign, and that he will be tried and punished in accordance with that sovereign's laws." . . . In this case, the district court reasoned, since Lui would not be tried in accordance with the present Hong Kong regime's laws, the warrant requirement was not met. . . .

There is nothing in the language of article VII(3), or the rest of article VII, which indicates that the warrant requirement serves the greater function attributed to it by the district court. Indeed, the warrant requirement appears to do nothing more than to help the judicial officer in the requested country to confirm that there are in fact charges properly pending against the relator in the requested country, and that the relator is actually the person sought. It does not authorize the investigation which the district court envisioned, and indeed such an investigation is foreclosed by the rule of non-inquiry. A warrant was provided by the Hong Kong authorities here, and Lui does not attack its validity or authenticity. The warrant requirement was plainly satisfied. . . .

The district court understood the purpose of the dual criminality requirement, as stated in article III of the Treaty, to be "to provide the requested sovereign with the opportunity to examine the substantive law of the requesting sovereign in the context of the Treaty." . . . The court stated that the requirement serves to "underscore[] the expectation running through the Treaty that [Lui] is to be tried, judged, and punished in accordance with the laws of the requesting sovereign." . . .

There is nothing in the text of article III of the Treaty that supports this sweeping conclusion. The dual criminality requirement, by its plain terms, is satisfied if the crime of which the relator is accused appears on the annexed Schedule or is punishable in both countries by at least one year's imprisonment. Bribery, as noted above, appears on the annexed Schedule.

The purpose of the dual criminality requirement is simply to ensure that extradition is granted only for crimes that are regarded as serious in both countries. . . . The dual criminality requirement is satisfied here. . . .

The district court also relied on article 3(a) of the Supplementary Treaty, which, it stated, requires the judicial officer "to examine the reasons for the requesting sovereign's desire to try and to punish the relator." . . . In this case, stated the district court, article 3(a) "underscores again the Treaty's requirement and expectation that extradition . . . may not take place if the requesting sovereign . . . is unable to try and punish Lui in the relatively few days left before its reversion to China." . . .

The Supplementary Treaty article 3(a) defense is simply inapplicable here. Supplementary Treaty article 3(a) describes a defense which is available only to fugitives charged with one of the crimes specified in article 1 of the Supplementary Treaty, all of which are crimes of violence. Lui's alleged crime – bribery – is not among the crimes enumerated in the Supplementary Treaty's article 1.

Indeed, the very purpose of the Supplementary Treaty was to cabin the political offense exception so that perpetrators of certain violent offenses would be precluded from avoiding extradition simply because their criminal activity was inspired by political motivation. . . . Lui properly does not claim that he is entitled to the article V(1)(c) political offense exception. . . . Moreover, article 3(a) allows the judicial officer to make only a narrowly circumscribed inquiry. "An extradition target must establish by a preponderance of the evidence that, if he were surrendered, the legal system of the requesting country would treat him differently from other similarly situated individuals because of his race, religion, nationality, or political opinions." . . . Lui made no such showing of discrimination, and the district court, in making its own predictions about the post-reversion justice system in Hong Kong, exceeded the narrow inquiry permitted by article 3(a). . . .

The district court understood the Treaty's specialty provision to signify that "the Treaty allows only for extradition for offenses that can be tried and punished by the requesting sovereign." . . . Because the specialty obligation cannot be enforced by the United States after reversion, reasoned the district court, article XII is violated ab initio, and Lui cannot be extradited. . . . The rule of specialty literally has no application here. The rule has two basic requirements: that the relator be tried for the crimes charged in the extradition warrant and that the relator not be re-extradited to another country. There is no claim that either of these is violated. . . .

If Lui's position were correct, the enforceability of many extradition treaties to which the United States is a party would be thrown into grave doubt. Regimes come and go, as, indeed, do states. Moreover, 18 U.S.C. § 3184, which defines the role of the courts in the extradition process, gives no discretion to the judicial officer to refuse to certify extraditability on the ground that a treaty partner cannot assure the requested country that rights under a treaty will be enforced or protected. . . .

Of course, Lui may express his concerns about the post-reversion enforceability of specialty to the Secretary of State, who, in her discretion, may choose not to surrender him. We note that the newly signed, as yet unratified, extradition treaty between the United States and the HKSAR provides that specialty protection "shall apply to fugitive offenders who have been surrendered between the parties prior to the entry into force" of the new treaty. . . . It is not the role of the judiciary to speculate about the future ability of the United States to enforce treaty obligations. . . .

Lui also challenges the determination of the magistrate judge that there was probable cause to believe that Lui had violated Hong Kong law on eight of the nine charges in the warrant. . . . Lui argued that the government's evidence was insufficient to support an inference of bribery and that there was, in any event, an innocent explanation. The government argued that the undisputed facts were sufficient to establish probable cause, and that the explanation was inherently implausible. In addition, the government argued, it had two "smoking gun" statements directly saying the payments were bribes. [The court found the statements reliable.]

For these reasons we reverse the grant of habeas corpus by the district court. . . .

NOTES AND QUESTIONS

(1) Does extradition from the U.S. require a treaty? In *Ntakirutimana v. Reno*, 184 F.3d 419 (5th Cir. 1999), *cert. denied* 120 S.Ct. 977 (2000), Circuit Judge Garza stated:

. . . . Ntakirutimana alleges that Article II of the Constitution of the United States requires that an extradition occur pursuant to a treaty. It is unconstitutional, he claims, to extradite him to the ICTR

[International Criminal Tribunal for Rwanda]* pursuant to a statute in the absence of a treaty. Accordingly, he claims it is unconstitutional to extradite him on the basis of the Agreement and Pub. Law 104-106 (the "Congressional-Executive Agreement").The district court concluded that it is constitutional to surrender Ntakirutimana in the absence of an "extradition treaty," because a statute authorized extradition. . . .

To determine whether a treaty is required to extradite Ntakirutimana, we turn to the text of the Constitution. Ntakirutimana contends that Article II, Section 2, Clause 2 of the Constitution requires a treaty to extradite. This Clause, which enumerates the President's foreign relations power, provides in part that "[the President] shall have Power, by and with the Advice and Consent of the Senate, to make Treaties, provided two thirds of the Senators present concur; and he shall nominate, and by and with the Advice and Consent of the Senate, shall appoint Ambassadors, other public Ministers and Consuls . . . ." U.S. CONST. art. II, § 2, cl. 2. This provision does not refer either to extradition or to the necessity of a treaty to extradite. The Supreme Court has explained, however, that "the power to surrender is clearly included within the treaty-making power and the corresponding power of appointing and receiving ambassadors and other public ministers." *Terlinden v. Ames,* 184 U.S. 270, 289, 22 S. Ct. 484, 492, 46 L. Ed. 534 (1902) (citation omitted).

Yet, the Court has found that the Executive's power to surrender fugitives is not unlimited. In *Valentine v. United States,* 299 U.S. 5, 57 S. Ct. 100, 81 L. Ed. 5 (1936), the Supreme Court considered whether an exception clause in the United States's extradition treaty with France implicitly granted to the Executive the discretionary power to surrender citizens. The Court first stated that the power to provide for extradition is a national power that "is not confided to the Executive in the absence of treaty or legislative provision." . . .

The Court then considered whether any statute authorized the Executive's discretion to extradite. The Court commented that:

> Whatever may be the power of the Congress to provide for extradition independent of treaty, that power has not been exercised save in relation to a foreign country or territory "occupied by or under the control of the United States." Aside from that limited provision, the Act of Congress relating to extradition simply defines the procedure to carry out an existing extradition treaty or convention.

Id. at 9, 57 S. Ct. at 102-03 (citations omitted). The Court concluded that

---

* *See* chap. 19 for additional discussion of International Criminal Tribunal For Rwanda. – Eds.

no statutory basis conferred the power on the Executive to surrender a citizen to the foreign government. . . . The Court subsequently addressed whether the treaty conferred the power to surrender, and found that it did not. . . . The Court concluded that, "we are constrained to hold that [the President's] power, in the absence of statute conferring an independent power, must be found in the terms of the treaty and that, as the treaty with France fails to grant the necessary authority, the President is without the power to surrender the respondents." . . . The Court added that the remedy for this lack of power "lies with the Congress, or with the treaty-making power wherever the parties are willing to provide for the surrender of citizens." . . .

Valentine indicates that a court should look to whether a treaty *or statute* grants executive discretion to extradite. Hence, *Valentine* supports the constitutionality of using the Congressional-Executive Agreement to extradite Ntakirutimana. Ntakirutimana attempts to distinguish *Valentine* on the ground that the case dealt with a *treaty* between France and the United States. Yet, *Valentine* indicates that a statute suffices to confer authority on the President to surrender a fugitive. . . . Ntakirutimana suggests also that *Valentine* expressly challenged the power of Congress, independent of treaty, to provide for extradition. *Valentine,* however, did not place a limit on Congress's power to provide for extradition. . . . Thus, although some authorization by law is necessary for the Executive to extradite, neither the Constitution's text nor *Valentine* require that the authorization come in the form of a treaty.

Notwithstanding the Constitution's text or *Valentine,* Ntakirutimana argues that the intent of the drafters of the Constitution supports his interpretation. He alleges that the delegates to the Constitutional Convention intentionally placed the Treaty power exclusively in the President and the Senate. The delegates designed this arrangement because they wanted a single executive agent to negotiate agreements with foreign powers, and they wanted the senior House of Congress – the Senate – to review the agreements to serve as a check on the executive branch. Ntakirutimana also claims that the rejection of alternative proposals suggests that the framers believed that a treaty is the only means by which the United States can enter into a binding agreement with a foreign nation.

We are unpersuaded by Ntakirutimana's extended discussion of the Constitution's history. Ntakirutimana does not cite to any provision in the Constitution or any aspect of its history that requires a treaty to extradite. Ntakirutimana's argument, which is not specific to extradition, is premised on the assumption that a treaty is required for an international agreement. To the contrary, "the Constitution, while expounding procedural requirements for treaties alone, apparently contemplates alternate modes of international agreements." . . .

Ntakirutimana next argues that historical practice establishes that a treaty is required to extradite. According to Ntakirutimana, the United States has never surrendered a person except pursuant to an Article II treaty, and the only involuntary transfers without an extradition treaty have been to "a foreign country or territory 'occupied by or under the control of the United States.' ". . . . This argument fails for numerous reasons. First,*Valentine* did not suggest that this "historical practice" limited Congress's power. . . . Second, the Supreme Court's statements that a statute may confer the power to extradite also reflect a historical understanding of the Constitution. . . . Even if Congress has rarely exercised the power to extradite by statute, a historical understanding exists nonetheless that it may do so. Third, in some instances in which a fugitive would not have been extraditable under a treaty, a fugitive has been extradited pursuant to a statute that "filled the gap" in the treaty. . . . Thus, we are unconvinced that the President's practice of usually submitting a negotiated treaty to the Senate reflects a historical understanding that a treaty is required to extradite. . . .

CIRCUIT JUDGE DEMOSS, dissenting in this case, stated:

The executive and legislative branches of government erroneously disregarded their obligation to respect the structure provided by the Constitution when they purported to enter this extradition agreement. We should issue a writ of habeas corpus, and Ntakirutimana should not be surrendered. The extradition agreement in place between the United States and the Tribunal is unenforceable, as it has not been properly ratified. The agreement's implementing legislation is unconstitutional insofar as it purports to ratify the Surrender Agreement by a means other than that prescribed by the Treaty Clause. The two acts seek impermissibly to evade the mandatory constitutional route for implementing such an agreement. I therefore respectfully dissent.

(2) What constitutional rights will be afforded individuals that the United States government is considering for extradition? In the absence of probable cause, does a provisional arrest in anticipation of an extradition meet constitutional standards? If this individual flees the United States prior to a resolution of whether the government can extradite, will the unauthorized departure foreclose raising constitutional issues? Consider the majority and dissenting opinion in the case of *Parretti v. United States*, 143 F.3d 508 (9th Cir. 1998):

PREGERSON, CIRCUIT JUDGE:

. . . . We took this case en banc to consider whether the arrest of Giancarlo Parretti pursuant to an Extradition Treaty with France violated the Fourth Amendment and whether his detention without bail prior to France's decision to request his extradition violated the Due Process Clause of the Fifth Amendment, or, whether this appeal should be dismissed under the fugitive disentitlement doctrine because Parretti fled the United States while his appeal was pending before a panel of this court. Because Parretti is a fugitive from justice, we exercise our discretion under the disentitlement doctrine and dismiss his appeal. Therefore, we find it unnecessary to address his constitutional claims. . . . The Supreme Court has "consistently and unequivocally approved dismissal as an appropriate sanction when a prisoner is a fugitive during the ongoing appellate process." . . . The fugitive disentitlement doctrine empowers us to dismiss the appeal of a defendant who flees the jurisdiction of the United States after timely appealing. An appellate court's power to disentitle a fugitive from access to the appellate process is grounded in equity. . . . Our court has exercised its discretion and dismissed the appeal of a criminal defendant who became a fugitive from justice while his appeal was pending. . . .

Several rationales that underlie the fugitive disentitlement doctrine apply to this appeal. First, although Parretti's status as a fugitive does not "strip the case of its character as an adjudicable case or controversy," it does disentitle him from calling upon the resources of the court to resolve his claims. . . . By fleeing the jurisdiction of the United States, Parretti forfeited his right to appellate review under the fugitive disentitlement doctrine. . . .

Second, Parretti has fled the United States. He remains a fugitive beyond the reach of this court's jurisdiction. If we were to reach the merits of Parretti's constitutional claims and affirm the district court, such a decision could not secure Parretti's presence before the district court, nor could it assure that any "judgment . . . issued would prove enforceable." . . .

Third, "dismissal by an appellate court after a defendant has fled its jurisdiction serves an important deterrent function and advances an interest in efficient, dignified appellate practice." . . .

Fourth, the adversary character of criminal litigation may be compromised when the defendant is a fugitive. . . . A defendant's flight threatens the effective operation of the appellate process because the fugitive's counsel may have little or no incentive to represent his client should further proceedings be necessary. . . . APPEAL DISMISSED

REINHARDT, J., DISSENTING:

In this case, the court faces two extremely important issues that warrant our most thorough consideration. The positions advanced by the government on both constitutional questions are remarkable and should be examined with the greatest of care. In doing so, we should bear in mind that what the government tells us it can do to a foreign citizen in

this case, it can just as easily do to a United States citizen in the next.
. . .

First, the government maintains that when a foreign country simply suggests that it is considering requesting extradition, the United States government can arrest the person without a showing of probable cause and keep him locked up for months without bail. This position is at odds with one of our most basic constitutional principles – that the government cannot seize a person off the streets (or from a lawyer's office) and deny him his liberty without first showing probable cause to believe he has engaged in criminal activity. The government's contention that probable cause in the context of a provisional arrest is merely probable cause to believe that a foreign country has issued an arrest warrant is plainly incorrect. Such a showing would never, in any other circumstances, suffice to support the arrest of a person in this country, and there is no reason why it should suffice in the case of provisional arrests.

As to the bail issue, the government relies on cryptic language in an ambiguous case written by the Supreme Court almost 100 years ago for its argument that an almost irrebuttable presumption against bail exists in extradition cases. . . . By failing to address the government's argument, we leave this circuit's law on the bail issue exactly where it was before this case – in total disarray. . . .

The fallacy in the government's positions is amply demonstrated in the panel's majority opinions, which I adopt in full; they still accurately set forth the law. Notwithstanding the compelling nature of the constitutional issues, however, the majority has avoided deciding them by invoking the fugitive disentitlement doctrine under the most unusual of circumstances. Because the doctrine is inapplicable to the circumstances presented here, it is this court's duty to reach the merits of the case. Accordingly, I dissent.

I briefly review the procedural history of this case in order to demonstrate why applying the fugitive disentitlement doctrine in this case is unusual and serves no purpose. On October 18, 1995, Giancarlo Parretti was arrested by federal agents, pursuant to a warrant issued by a United States Magistrate Judge on the basis of allegations that an international warrant had been issued against him in France. On the basis of a letter from the government of France indicating that it would seek Parretti's extradition, the magistrate judge denied bail and ordered that he be detained pending the extradition hearing. Parretti filed a petition for habeas corpus in the district court, arguing that his prolonged detention was unconstitutional. On November 9, the district court denied the petition.

Soon thereafter, Parretti filed an emergency motion with this court. On November 21, after Parretti had been incarcerated for 33 days, a panel of this court heard oral argument and ordered his immediate release on two independent grounds. First, the panel found that Parretti's arrest violated the Fourth Amendment because it was effected without a showing of probable cause to believe that he had committed an extraditable offense. Second, the panel concluded that Parretti's continued detention violated his Fifth Amendment right to due process because the district court specifically found that he presented neither a risk of flight nor a danger to the community. In a published opinion issued subsequently, the panel elaborated fully on its reasons for granting Parretti's emergency motion.

After the panel issued its order, but prior to the time the panel issued its full opinion, the district court implemented the order and Parretti was released on bail. Eight days after his release, the government, at the behest of France, filed a formal request for Parretti's extradition, at which time the district court made the requisite probable cause finding. The government did not, however, seek to have Parretti taken into federal custody again. Instead, sometime afterwards, jurisdiction over Parretti was assumed by the state of Delaware. He was then tried and convicted on criminal charges in a Delaware state court. Pending sentencing on these offenses, Parretti fled the Delaware court's jurisdiction. Thereafter, the panel's full opinion was released, and the government sought and we granted, at its suggestion, rehearing en banc because of the government's objections to the content of the panel's decision on the constitutional questions. Parretti has, of course, obtained all the relief he ever desired from the court and seeks nothing further.

In light of these procedural and factual circumstances, it is clear that the fugitive disentitlement doctrine has no applicability. Indeed, neither party has urged the court to invoke the doctrine and both parties agree that the doctrine has no relevance to the case. The purpose of the doctrine is to deny to those who have fled the court's jurisdiction any benefits of the court system. Here, Parretti received all the relief he could possibly obtain prior to fleeing and he seeks no further benefit from the court. Our dismissal of the case will deny Parretti nothing – it is only the government that seeks relief now, and it seeks relief not from the order we issued, but from the precedential effect of our opinion on the serious constitutional questions that arise in many extradition cases. The fugitive disentitlement doctrine makes sense *only* when we deny the *fugitive* some form of relief from the court, not when we frustrate our own ability to resolve critical constitutional questions. In the words of the Supreme Court, as quoted by the majority, . . . the doctrine makes sense only as a "sanction" against the defendant.

As the majority's opinion amply demonstrates, the fugitive disentitlement doctrine is properly invoked only in cases in which the defendant seeks to benefit from the use of our limited judicial resources. That is not the case here. I therefore dissent.

(3) In 1985, a District of Columbia District Court held federal extradition statute, 18 U.S.C. § 3184, unconstitutional. The court agreed with plaintiffs "that the extradition statute purports to confer upon the Secretary of State the power to review and set aside the legal conclusions of federal extradition judges and is therefore unconstitutional." *Lobue v. Christopher*, 893 F. Supp. 65, 67 (D. D.C. 1995). Although the plaintiffs were provided relief, the Circuit Court vacated the order. *Lobue v. Christopher*, 82 F.3d 1081 (D.C. Cir. 1996). Other courts have, likewise, found that the statute is constitutional. *See, e.g., Manrique Carreno v. Johnson*, 899 F. Supp. 624 (S.D. Fla. 1995), *Extradition of Sutton*, 905 F. Supp. 631 (E.D. Mo. 1995). Does the extradition statute raise concerns with regard to separation of powers? *See generally* Allison Marston, Comment, *Innocents Abroad: An Analysis of the Constitutionality of the International Extradition Statute,* 33 STAN. J. INT'L L. 343 (1997) (suggesting reforms to extradition statute).

(4) If an extradition treaty includes a statute of limitations, can an individual be extradited after the applicable time period? Consider this issue as raised in the case below.

ROSS v. UNITED STATES MARSHAL FOR THE EASTERN DISTRICT OF OKLAHOMA

United States Court of Appeals for the Tenth Circuit
168 F.3d 1190 (1999)

BRORBY, CIRCUIT JUDGE:

The Government of Northern Ireland, United Kingdom issued warrants for the arrest of Appellant, George Finbar Ross, for forty-one charged offenses stemming from Mr. Ross' alleged involvement in a fraudulent investment scheme. The United States subsequently arrested Mr. Ross pursuant to an extradition treaty existing between the United States and the United Kingdom. After a magistrate judge certified his extradition, Mr. Ross filed a petition for writ of habeas corpus pursuant to 28 U.S.C. § 2241 challenging his extradition. The district court denied the petition and Mr. Ross filed this appeal. We exercise jurisdiction pursuant to 28 U.S.C. § 2253 and we affirm. . . .

The scope of review of a magistrate judge's extradition order under a treaty with a foreign country is limited to "determining whether the magistrate had jurisdiction, whether the offense charged is within the treaty and, by a somewhat liberal construction, whether there was any evidence warranting the finding that there was reasonable ground to believe the accused guilty." . . .

In this case, Mr. Ross does not contest the magistrate's jurisdiction nor challenge the evidence of his guilt. Rather, he argues the offenses charged are not within the treaty because: (1) the charges are time-barred under the relevant statute of limitations, and (2) the warrants charging Mr. Ross with "false accounting" do not meet the dual criminality requirement. . . .

Article V of the Extradition Treaty provides extradition shall not be granted if the prosecution has become time-barred according to the law of either the requesting or requested country. . . . No Northern Ireland statute of limitations applies to Mr. Ross' charges. The applicable United States law provides for a five-year statute of limitations. 18 U.S.C. § 3282. The statute may be tolled, however, if the accused is a fugitive "fleeing from justice." 18 U.S.C. § 3290.

In this case, Northern Ireland seeks extradition based on charges brought approximately twelve years after Mr. Ross committed the alleged offenses – well beyond the statutory limit. However, the district court concluded the statute tolled because Mr. Ross was fleeing from justice when he moved to the United States in October 1983. . . .

As a preliminary matter, we must first determine what constitutes "fleeing from justice" under the statute. The circuit courts are currently split on the issue. A small minority of circuits have held mere absence from the jurisdiction in which the crime was committed is enough to toll the statute. *In re Assarsson,* 687 F.2d 1157, 1162 (8th Cir. 1982); *McGowen v. United States,* 70 App. D.C. 268, 105 F.2d 791, 792 (D.C. Cir. 1939). The district court, on the other hand, adopted the majority view, which requires the prosecution to prove the accused had an intent to avoid arrest or prosecution. *See Greever,* 134 F.3d at 780; *United States v. Rivera-Ventura,* 72 F.3d 277, 283 (2d Cir. 1995); *United States v. Fonseca-Machado,* 53 F.3d 1242, 1244 (11th Cir.), *cert. denied,* 516 U.S. 925 (1995); *United States v. Marshall,* 856 F.2d 896, 900 (7th Cir. 1988); *United States v. Gonsalves,* 675 F.2d 1050, 1052 (9th Cir.), *cert. denied,* 459 U.S. 837, 74 L. Ed. 2d 78, 103 S. Ct. 83 (1982); *Donnell v. United States,* 229 F.2d 560, 565 (5th Cir. 1956); *Brouse v. United States,* 68 F.2d 294, 295 (1st Cir. 1933). The Supreme Court has not squarely addressed the issue. However, in considering the predecessor to 18 U.S.C. § 3290, the Court in *Streep v. United States,* 160 U.S. 128, 40 L. Ed. 365, 16 S. Ct. 244 (1895) implicitly recognized intent as an element of fleeing from justice, ... Consistent with *Streep,* we conclude "fleeing from justice" requires the government to prove, by a preponderance of the evidence, the accused acted with the intent to avoid arrest or prosecution.

Having thus determined the appropriate standard of proof, we must decide whether the district court committed clear error in finding Mr. Ross had the requisite intent to flee arrest or prosecution when he moved to the United States. We believe the record supports the district court's conclusion. By October 1983, the investigatory record indicates Mr. Ross was aware of the International Investment's ongoing fraudulent scheme – he knew International Investment used investors' money to make multiple unsecured loans for his benefit and to pay interest to previous investors. Mr. Ross also likely knew International Investment was insolvent or rapidly approaching insolvency, and that International Investment would soon have to submit to a full audit to maintain its Gibraltar banking license, thereby revealing the fraudulent scheme. Based on this evidence, it was not clearly erroneous for the district court to infer Mr. Ross' intent to flee arrest or prosecution.

The fact that Northern Ireland had not yet initiated its investigation does not change this conclusion. An accused may form the requisite intent even though prosecution has not actually begun. . . . In other words, an intent to avoid an *anticipated* arrest or prosecution is sufficient to toll the statute.

We likewise reject Mr. Ross' argument that he did not have the intent to avoid prosecution because the charged conduct occurred after he moved. A prosecutor's decision as to which charges to file is a matter of discretion and involves consideration of many factors. . . . We fail to see how this decision-making process limited or restricted Mr. Ross' intent to flee prosecution in October 1983. More important, the record indicates Mr. Ross was aware of the potential criminality of his conduct and its imminent discovery in October 1983. Because this evidence forms a sufficient basis from which to infer Mr. Ross' intent to avoid an anticipated prosecution, we conclude the district court's determination was not clearly erroneous. . . .

Under Article III of the Extradition Treaty, an offense must meet the dual criminality requirement in order to be extraditable. . . . The doctrine of dual criminality requires the offense with which the accused is charged to be "punishable as a serious crime in both the requesting and requested states." . . . To satisfy the dual criminality requirement, the requesting and requested countries' statutes must be substantially analogous or "punish conduct falling within the broad scope of the same generally recognized crime." . . .

The magistrate concluded the offenses listed in Mr. Ross' extradition request met the dual criminality requirement. Specifically, the magistrate determined Mr. Ross' alleged conduct is criminal under the United States statutes prohibiting mail and wire fraud, 18 U.S.C. §§ 1341 and 1343, and the Oklahoma false pretenses statute; Okla. Stat. tit. 21, § 1541.2. Mr. Ross argues the warrants charging him with "false accounting" do not meet the duality requirement. . . .

Warrants six through forty-one charge Mr. Ross with violating § 17(1)(b) of the Theft Act (Northern Ireland) of 1969 which makes it a crime for one to produce or make use of a misleading, false or deceptive account or other document made for accounting purposes, "with a view to gain for himself or another or with intent to cause loss to another." Mr. Ross argues this section of the Theft Act is not substantially analogous to the federal mail and wire fraud statutes because those statutes, unlike the Theft Act, require proof the defendant carried out a fraudulent scheme through use of the mails or wire transmissions. We disagree. The Theft Act and the mail and wire fraud statutes proscribe the same basic conduct-use of false representations to defraud or obtain property. . . . The element requiring use of the mails or interstate wire transmission is merely a jurisdictional requirement which makes the underlying crime federal in nature. . . . The criminal conduct each statute proscribes remains substantially analogous, thus satisfying the dual criminality requirement. . . .

The judgment of the district court is AFFIRMED.

---

§ 13.03 Political Offense Exception

QUINN v. ROBINSON

United States Court of Appeals for the Ninth Circuit
783 F.2d 776 (1986)

REINHARDT, CIRCUIT JUDGE:

Pursuant to 18 U.S.C. § 3184 (1982) and the governing treaty between the United States and the United Kingdom of Great Britain and Northern Ireland ("United Kingdom"), Extradition Treaty of June 8, 1972, United States – United Kingdom, 28 U.S.T. 227, T.I.A.S. No. 8468 [hereinafter cited as Treaty], the United Kingdom seeks the extradition of William Joseph Quinn, a member of the Irish Republican Army ("IRA"), in order to try him for the commission of a murder in 1975 and for conspiring to cause explosions in London in 1974 and 1975. After a United States magistrate found Quinn extraditable, Quinn filed a petition for a writ of habeas corpus. The district court determined that Quinn cannot be extradited because a long-standing principle of international law which has been incorporated in the extradition treaty at issue – the political offense exception – bars extradition for the charged offenses. The United States government, on behalf of the United Kingdom, appeals.

This case requires us to examine the parameters of a foreign sovereign's right to bring about the extradition of an accused who maintains that the offense with which he is charged are of a political character. Ultimately we must determine whether the political offense exception is applicable to the type of violent offenses Quinn is alleged to have committed. We undertake this task with the aid of very little helpful precedent. The United States Supreme Court has discussed the political offense exception only once, and then during the nineteenth century. *See Ornelas v. Ruiz,* 161 U.S. 502, 40 L. Ed. 787, 16 S. Ct. 689 (1896). . . . The only time we considered the subject, *see Karadzole v.*

Artukovic, 247 F.2d 198 (9th Cir. 1957), the Supreme Court vacated our opinion, *see Karadzole v. Artukovic,* 355 U.S. 393, 78 S. Ct. 381, 2 L. Ed. 2d 356 (1958) (mem.), an opinion which, in any event, has subsequently been roundly and uniformly criticized. . . . Only one circuit has previously considered in any detail how or whether the exception applies when the accused person or persons have engaged in conduct involving the use of some of the more violent techniques or tactics that have come to mark the activities of contemporary insurgent or revolutionary movements. *Eain v. Wilkes,* 641 F.2d 504 (7th Cir.), *cert. denied,* 454 U.S. 894, 70 L. Ed. 2d 208, 102 S. Ct. 390 (1981). The few opinions of other circuits that have considered the exception shed no light on the difficult questions we must resolve here. Therefore, we must carefully examine the historic origins of the political offense exception, analyze the various underpinnings of the doctrine, trace its development in the lower courts and elsewhere, and seek to apply whatever principles emerge to the realities of today's political struggles. . . .

A. The Extradition Treaty

The right of a foreign sovereign to demand and obtain extradition of an accused criminal is created by treaty. . . . In the absence of a treaty there is no duty to extradite, . . . and no branch of the United States government has any authority to surrender an accused to a foreign government except as provided for by statute or treaty. . . .

The extradition treaty between the United States and the United Kingdom provides for the reciprocal extradition of persons found within the territory of one of the nations who have been accused or convicted of certain criminal offenses committed within the jurisdiction of the other nation. . . . Murder and conspiracy to cause explosions, the offense with which Quinn has been charged, are extraditable offense under the Treaty. . . . United States citizenship does not bar extradition by the United States. . . . However, under the doctrine of "dual criminality," an accused person can be extradited only if the conduct complained of is considered criminal by the jurisprudence or under the laws of both the requesting and requested nations. . . . In addition, there must be evidence that would justify committing the accused for trial under the law of the nation from whom extradition is requested if the offense had been committed within the territory of that nation. . . . The doctrine of "specialty" prohibits the requesting nation from prosecuting the extradited individual for any offense other than that for which the surrendering state agreed to extradite. . . .

The treaty between the United States and the United Kingdom provides certain exceptions to extradition, notwithstanding the existence of probable cause to believe that the accused has committed the charged offense. In particular, the treaty specifies that "extradition shall not be granted if . . . the offense for which extradition is requested is regarded by the requested party as one of a political character . . . ."

As it has in other recent extradition cases, . . . the government contends that both the magistrate and the district court lacked jurisdiction to determine whether the political offense exception bars extradition. According to the government, the language of both the jurisdictional statute and the treaty precludes a judicial determination of whether the exception applies. Moreover, the government contends, such a determination involves political questions that only the executive branch of the government can resolve. Like every court before us that has considered these arguments, . . . and like those that have not explicitly considered them but have proceeded to determine whether the exception applies, . . . we believe the government's contentions to be meritless.
. . .

The government next argues that because three of the factors enumerated in *Baker v. Carr,* 369 U.S. 186, 217, 7 L. Ed. 2d 663, 82 S. Ct. 691 (1962), are present in this case, the judiciary should abstain, under the political question doctrine, from determining whether the political offense exception applies. The government contends that determining whether the exception applies requires a policy determination of a kind clearly inappropriate for the exercise of judicial discretion, that different pronouncements from the executive and judiciary on matters necessary to a determination of the applicability of the exception could embarrass the government, and that the issue does not lend itself to resolution through judicially discoverable manageable standards. . . . In identifying the specific *Baker v. Carr* factors that it claims are present in this case, the government begins by noting that in order to consider whether the political offense exception applies, a court must determine whether a political uprising was in progress in the foreign land when the offense occurred. . . . The government contends that such a factual finding requires a policy determination. We disagree. We need not determine whether the uprising was "justified" or was motivated by political forces of which we approve. Rather, we must determine simply whether an uprising was in progress. . . .

The government also contends that the presence of a second factor enumerated in *Baker v. Carr* counsels judicial abstention. The government argues that a judicial determination that Quinn's extradition is precluded by the political offense exception would "recognize" political terrorists and would thus constitute a potentially embarrassing pronouncement different than the pronouncements of the executive branch. . . . [W]e do not believe the executive branch has refused to recognize the existence of terrorists. Rather, in some cases, it may have refused to recognize the *legitimacy* of these groups. We fail to see why a judicial acknowledgment that terrorist groups exist would constitute a "recognition" of those groups in the sense of legitimizing their actions. . . .

Far from embarrassing the executive branch, assigning to the judiciary the responsibility for determining when the exception applies actually affords a degree of protection to the executive branch. As a political branch, the executive could face undue pressure when public and international opposition to the activities of an unpopular group create conflicts with the treaty obligation created by the political offense exception. . . . By assigning the initial determination of when the exception applies to the impartial judiciary – particularly life-tenured Article III judges – Congress has substantially lessened the risk that majoritarian consensus of favor due or not due to the country seeking extradition will interfere with individual liberty. . . . The treaty's assignment to the judiciary of the task of determining the applicability of the political offense exception "reflects a congressional judgment that that decision not be made on the basis of what may be the current view of any one political administration." *In re Doherty,* 599 F. Supp. 270, 277 n.6 (S.D.N.Y. 1984).

Nor does the assignment to the judiciary of the initial determination of the applicability of the political offense exception deprive the executive branch of all discretion to determine that a person claiming the protection of that exception should not be extradited. The executive branch has the ultimate authority to decide whether to extradite the accused after a judicial determination that the individual is, in fact, extraditable. . . . Although the Secretary of State's authority to refuse extradition is presumably constrained by our treaty obligations, the contours of executive branch discretion in this area have never been expressly delineated. . . .

Finally, the government points out the difficulty of defining which offenses are of a political character. It suggests that this difficulty demonstrates an absence of judicially discoverable manageable standards, another factor that, according to *Baker v. Carr,* counsels for judicial abstention. As in many areas of the law, and as we discuss further in the remainder of this opinion, there has always been debate about the precise contours of the political offense exception. But the absence of perfect predictive ability in discerning whether a given act falls within the exception is not synonymous with an absence of manageable standards. Rather, as with other complex legal problems, the basic standards that guide us in deciding whether the exception applies are refined on a case-by-case basis as new situations arise. The determination whether there was a violent political disturbance in the requesting country at the time of the alleged acts and whether the acts were incidental to the disturbance, ... are mixed questions of law and fact, that do not require a political judgment. . . . We fail to see how the judicial construction of 18 U.S.C. § 3184 and the applicable treaty, and the application of these laws to the facts of a given case, differs from all other judicial decisionmaking. . . .

The scope of the district court's review of a magistrate's extradition order on a petition for writ of habeas corpus is limited to "whether the magistrate had jurisdiction, whether the offense [sic] charged is within the treaty and, by a somewhat liberal extension, whether there was any evidence warranting the finding that there was reasonable ground to believe the accused guilty." . . .

It would make little sense for us to ignore the factual findings of the judicial tribunal that made the initial factual determinations and defer, instead, to the differing factual findings made by a similar tribunal that merely reviewed the record of the earlier proceedings and held no evidentiary hearing of its own.

Rather, we must determine whether the habeas court erred, as a matter of law, in overruling the magistrate's factual findings. Accordingly, we will defer to the extradition tribunal's factual findings unless we agree with the district court that they are clearly erroneous. . . .

IV. THE DEVELOPMENT OF THE POLITICAL OFFENSE EXCEPTION

A. *Origin of the Exception*

The first-known extradition treaty was negotiated between an Egyptian Pharaoh and a Hittite King in the Thirteenth Century B.C. . . . However, the concept of political offenses as an exception to extradition is a rather recent development. In the centuries after the first known extradition treaty, and throughout the Middle Ages, extradition treaties were used primarily to return political offenders, rather than the perpetrators of common crimes, to the nations seeking to try them for criminal acts. . . . It was not until the early nineteenth century that the political offense exception, now almost universally accepted in extradition law, was incorporated into treaties. . . .

The political offense exception is premised on a number of justifications. First, its historical development suggests that it is grounded in a brief that individuals have a "right to resort to political activism to foster political change." . . . Second, the exception reflects a concern that individuals – particularly unsuccessful rebels – should not be returned to countries where they may be subjected to unfair trials and punishments because of their political opinions. . . . Third, the exception comports with the notion that governments – and certainly their nonpolitical branches – should not intervene in the internal political struggles of other nations. . . .

B. *Comparative Legal Standards*

None of the political offense provisions in treaties includes a definition of the word "political." . . . Thus, the term "political offense" has received various interpretations by courts since the mid-nineteenth century. . . . Not every offense that is politically motivated falls within the exception. Instead, courts have devised various tests to identify those offenses that comport with the justifications for the exception and that, accordingly, are not extraditable.

Within the confusion about definitions it is fairly well accepted that there are two distinct categories of political offenses: "pure political offenses" and "relative political offenses." . . . Pure political offenses are acts aimed directly at the government, . . . and have none of the elements of ordinary crimes, . . . These offenses, which include treason, sedition, and espionage, . . . do not violate the private rights of individuals. . . . Because they are frequently specifically excluded from the list of extraditable crimes given in a treaty, ... courts seldom deal with whether these offenses are extraditable, ... and it is generally agreed that they are not. . . .

The definitional problems focus around the second category of political offenses – the relative political offenses. These include "otherwise common crimes committed in connection with a political act," . . . or "common crimes . . . committed for political motives or in a political context." . . . Courts have developed various tests for ascertaining whether "the nexus between the crime and the political act is sufficiently close . . . [for the crime to be deemed] not extraditable." . . . The judicial approaches can be grouped into three distinct categories: (1) the French "objective" test; (2) the Swiss "proportionality" or "predominance" test; and (3) the Anglo-American "incidence" test. . . . More recent developments allow for further distinctions between the British test and the test employed in the United States. . . .

The early French test, most clearly represented in *In re Giovanni Gatti*, [1947] Ann. Dig. 145 (No. 70) (France, Ct. App. of Grenoble), considered an offense non-extraditable only if it directly injured the rights of the state. . . . Applying this rigid formula, French courts refused to consider the motives of the accused. . . . The test primarily protects only pure political offenses, . . . and is useless in attempts to define whether an otherwise common crime should not be extraditable because it is connected with a political act, motive, or context. . . . Because politically motivated and directed acts may injure private as well as state rights, the objective test fails to satisfy the various purposes of the political offense exception. . . . Nevertheless, this test has one benefit: because it is so limited, it is not subject to abuse; perpetrators of common crimes will not be protected because of alleged political motivations. . . .

In contrast to the traditional French test, Swiss courts apply a test that protects both pure and relative political offenses. The Swiss test examines political motivation of the offender, ... but also requires (a) a consideration of the circumstances surrounding the commission of the crime, . . . and (b) either a proportionality between the means and the political ends, or a predominance of the political elements, over the common criminal elements. . . .

At least one commentator has suggested that the first condition of the Swiss test is a requirement of a direct connection between the crime and the political goal – a condition that essentially requires the presence of a political movement. . . . Others point out that the early Swiss requirement that a crime be incident to a political movement has been explicitly rejected in later cases. . . . More recent Swiss cases concentrate less on the accused's motive, relying instead almost entirely on an ends-means test under which potentially motivated conduct is protected by the exception only if the danger created by the conduct is proportionate to the objectives, *i.e.*, if the means employed are the only means of accomplishing the end and the interests at stake are sufficiently important to justify the danger and harm to others. . . .

The comprehensiveness and flexibility of the "predominance" or "proportionality" test allows it to be conformed to changing realities of a modern world. . . . But because the relative value of the ends and the necessity of using the chosen means must be considered, the criteria applied by Swiss courts incorporate highly subjective and partisan political considerations within the balancing test. . . . The test explicitly requires an evaluation of the importance of the interests at stake, the desirability of political change, and the acceptability of the means used to achieve the ends. The infusion of ideological factors in the determination which offenses are non-extraditable threatens both the humanitarian objectives underlying the exception and the concern about foreign non-intervention in domestic political struggles. Moreover, it severely undermines the notion that such determinations can be made by an apolitical, unbiased judiciary concerned primarily with individual liberty. . . .

The "incidence" test that is used to define a non-extraditable political offense in the United States and Great Britain was first set forth by the Divisional Court in *In re Castioni,* [1891] 1 Q.B. 149 (1890). In that case, the Swiss government requested that Great Britain extradite a Swiss citizen who, with a group of other angry citizens, had stormed the palace gates and killed a government official in the process. . . . The court denied extradition, finding that Castioni's actions were "incidental to and formed a part of political disturbances," . . . . and holding that common crimes committed "in the course" and "in the furtherance" of a political disturbance would be treated as political offenses. . . .

Although both the United States and Great Britain rely explicitly on *Castioni,* each has developed its own version of the incidence test. . . .

C. Original Formulation of the United States Incidence Test

The United States, in contrast to Great Britain, has adhered more closely to the *Castioni* test in determining whether conduct is protected by the political offense exception. The seminal United States case in this area is *In re Ezeta,* 62 F. 972 (N.D. Cal. 1894), in which the Salvadoran government requested the extradition of a number of individuals accused of murder and robbery. The fugitives maintained that the crimes had been committed while they unsuccessfully attempted to thwart a revolution. . . . Extradition was denied because the acts were "committed during the progress of actual hostilities between contending forces," . . . and were "closely identified" with the uprising "in an unsuccessful effort to suppress it." . . . However, an alleged act that occurred four months prior to the start of armed violence was held not to be protected by the incidence test despite the accused's contention that El Salvador's extradition request was politically motivated. . . .

As we noted at the outset, the Supreme Court has addressed the political offense issue only once. In *Ornelas v. Ruiz,* [161 U.S. 502 (1896)], . . . Mexico sought the extradition of an individual for murder, arson, robbery and kidnapping committed in a Mexican border town, at or about the time revolutionary activity was in progress. The Court allowed extradition on the basis that the habeas court had applied an improper, non-deferential standard of review to the extradition court's findings. . . . It continued by listing four factors pertinent to the political offense inquiry in the case: (1) the character of the foray; (2) the mode of attack; (3) the persons killed or captured; and (4) the kind of property taken or destroyed. . . . It found that although the raid (in December 1892) may have been contemporaneous with a revolutionary movement (in 1891), it was not of a political character because it was essentially unrelated to the uprising. The Court noted that the purported political aspects of the crimes were negated "by the fact that immediately after this occurrence, though no superior armed force of the Mexican government was in the vicinity to hinder their advance into the country, the bandits withdrew with their booty across the river into Texas." . . .

Since *Ornelas*, lower American courts have continued to apply the incidence test set forth in *Castioni* and *Ezeta* with its two-fold requirement: (1) the occurrence of an uprising or other violent political disturbance at the time of the charged offense, . . . and (2) a charged offense that is "incidental to," "in the course of," or "in furtherance of" the uprising. . . . While the American view that an uprising must exist is more restrictive than the modern British view and while we, unlike the British, remain hesitant to consider the motives of the accused or the requesting state. . . . American courts have been rather liberal in their construction of the requirement that the act be "incidental to" an uprising. . . .

The American approach has been criticized as being "both underinclusive and overinclusive," . . . and as "yield[ing] anomalous . . . results." . . . Although these criticisms have some merit, neither flaw in the American incidence test is serious. Some commentators have suggested that the test is underinclusive because it exempts from judicially guaranteed protection all offenses that are not contemporaneous with an uprising even though the acts may represent legitimate political resistance. . . .

A number of commentators suggest, on the other hand, that the American test is overbroad because it makes non-extraditable some offenses that are not of a political character merely because the crimes took place contemporaneously with an uprising. . . .

[W]e do not consider the "underinclusiveness" and "overinclusiveness" problems of the incidence test to have been as severe as has been suggested by some of the commentators. Rather, we believe that the incidence test, when properly applied, has served the purposes and objectives of the political offense exception well. More recently, a number of courts have begun to question whether, in light of changing political practices and realities, properly applied, has served the purposes and objectives of the political offense exception well. More recently, a number of courts have begun to question whether, in light of changing political practices and realities, we should continue to use the traditional American version of that test. They have suggested that basic modifications may be required and, specifically, that certain types of conduct engaged in by some contemporary insurgent groups, conduct that we in our society find unacceptable, should be excluded from coverage. For the reasons we explain below, we believe that the American test in its present form remains not only workable but desirable; that the most significant problems that concern those advocating changes in the test can be dealt with without making the changes they propose; and that efforts to modify the test along the lines suggested would plunge our judiciary into a political morass and require the type of subjective judgments we have so wisely avoided until now.

D. *The Recent Political Offense Cases*

Recently, the American judiciary has split almost evenly over whether the traditional American incidence test should be applied to new methods of political violence in two categories – domestic revolutionary violence and international terrorism – or whether fundamental new restrictions should be imposed on the use of the political offense exception. . . .

V. THE POLITICAL OFFENSE EXCEPTION AND THE REALITIES OF CONTEMPORARY POLITICAL STRUGGLES

A. *The Political Reality: The Contours of Contemporary Revolutionary Activity*

The recent lack of consensus among United States courts confronted with requests for the extradition of those accused of violent political acts committed outside the context of an organized military conflict reflects some confusion about the purposes underlying the political offense exception. . . . The premise of the analysis performed by modern courts favoring the adoption of new restrictions on the use of the exception is either that the objectives of revolutionary violence undertaken by dispersed forces and directed at civilians are by definition, not political, ... or that, regardless of the actors' objectives, the conduct is not politically legitimate because it "is inconsistent with intentional standards of civilized conduct." . . .

A number of courts appear tacitly to accept a suggestion by some commentators that begins with the observation that the political offense exception can be traced to the rise of democratic governments. . . . Because of this origin, these commentators argue, the exception was only designed to protect the right to rebel against tyrannical governments, ... and should not be applied in an ideologically neutral fashion. . . . These courts then proceed to apply the exception in a non-neutral fashion but, in doing so, focus on and explicitly reject only the *tactics*, rather than the true object of their concern, the political *objectives*. . . . The courts that are narrowing the applicability of the exception in this manner appear to be moving beyond the role of an impartial judiciary by determining tacitly that particular political objectives are not "legitimate."

We strongly believe that courts should not undertake such a task. The political offense test traditionally articulated by American courts, as well as the text of the treaty provisions, ... is ideologically neutral. We do not believe it appropriate to make qualitative judgments regarding a foreign government or a struggle designed to alter that government. . . .

A second premise may underlie the analyses of courts that appear to favor narrowing the exception, namely, that modern revolutionary *tactics* which include violence directed at civilians are not politically "legitimate." This assumption, which may well constitute an understandable response to the recent rise of international terrorism, skews any political offense analysis because of an inherent conceptual shortcoming. In deciding what tactics are acceptable, we seek to impose on other nations and cultures our own traditional notions of how internal political struggles should be conducted.

The structure of societies and governments, the relationships between nations and their citizens, and the modes of altering political structures have changed dramatically since our courts first adopted the *Castioni* test. Neither wars nor revolutions are conducted in as clear-cut or mannerly a fashion as they once were. Both the nature of the acts committed in struggles for self-determination. . . . and the geographic location of those struggles have changed considerably since the time of the French and American revolutions. Now challenges by insurgent movements to the existing order take place most frequently in Third World countries rather than in Europe or North America. In contrast to the organized, clearly identifiable, armed forces of past revolutions, today's struggles are often carried out by networks of individuals joined only by a common interest in opposing those in power.

It is understandable that Americans are offended by the tactics used by many of those seeking to change their governments. Often these tactics are employed by persons who do not share our cultural and social values or mores. Sometimes they are employed by those whose views of the nature, importance, or relevance of individual human life differ radically from ours. Nevertheless, it is not our place to impose our notions of civilized strife on people who are seeking to overthrow the regimes in control of their countries in contexts and circumstances that we have not experienced, and with which we can identify only with the greatest difficulty. It is the fact that the insurgents are seeking to change their governments that makes the political offense exception applicable, not their reasons for wishing to do so or the nature of the acts by which they hope to accomplish that goal.

Politically motivated violence, carried out by dispersed forces and directed at private sector institutions, structures, or civilians, is often undertaken – like the more organized, better disciplined violence of preceding revolutions – as part of an effort to gain the right to self-government. . . . We believe the tactics that are used in such internal political struggles are simply irrelevant to the question whether the political offense exception is applicable.

B. *Relationship Between the Justifications for the Exception, the Incidence Test, and Contemporary Political Realities*

One of the principal reasons our courts have had difficulty with the concept of affording certain contemporary revolutionary tactics the protection of the political offense exception is our fear and loathing of international terrorism. . . . The desire to exclude international terrorists from the coverage of the political offense exception is a legitimate one; the United States unequivocally condemns all international terrorism. However, the restrictions that some courts have adopted in order to remove terrorist activities from coverage under the political offense exception are overbroad. As we have noted, not all politically-motivated violence undertaken by dispersed forces and directed at civilians is international terrorism and not all such activity should be exempted from the protection afforded by the exception. . . .

There is no need to create a new mechanism for defining "political offenses" in order to ensure that the two important objectives we have been considering are met: (a) that international terrorists will be subject to extradition, and (b) that the exception will continue to cover the type of domestic revolutionary conduct that inspired its creation in the first place. While the precedent that guides us is limited, the applicable principles of law are clear. The incidence test has served us well and requires no significant modification. The growing problem of international terrorism, serious as it is, does not compel us to reconsider or redefine that test. The test we have used since the 1800's simply does not cover acts of international terrorism.

1. *The "Incidence" Test*

As all of the various tests for determining whether an offense is extraditable make clear, not every offense of a political character is non-extraditable. In the United States, an offense must meet the incidence test which is intended, like the tests designed by other nations, to comport with the justifications for the exception. We now explain the reasons for our conclusion that the traditional United States incidence test by its terms (a) protects acts of domestic violence in connection with a struggle for political self-determination, but (b) was not intended to and does not protect acts of international terrorism.

2. *The "Uprising" Component*

The incidence test has two components – the "uprising" requirement and the "incidental to" requirement. The first component, the requirement that there be an "uprising," "rebellion," or "revolution," has not been the subject of much discussion in the literature, although it is firmly established in the case law. . . . Most analyses of whether the exception applies have focused on whether the act in question was in furtherance of or incidental to a given uprising. Nevertheless, it is the "uprising" component that plays the key role in ensuring that the incidence test protects only those activities that the political offense doctrine was designed to protect. . . .

The uprising component serves to limit the exception to its historic purposes. It makes the exception applicable only when a certain level of violence exists and when those engaged in that violence are seeking to accomplish a particular objective. The exception does not apply to political acts that involve less fundamental efforts to accomplish change or that do not attract sufficient adherents to create the requisite amount of turmoil. . . . Equally important, the uprising component serves to exclude from coverage under the exception criminal conduct that occurs outside the country or territory in which the uprising is taking place. The term "uprising" refers to a revolt by indigenous people against their own government or an occupying power. That revolt can occur only within the country or territory in which those rising up reside. By definition acts occurring in other lands are not part of the uprising. The political offense exception was designed to protect those engaged in internal or domestic struggles over the form or composition of their own government, including, of course, struggles to displace an occupying power. It was not designed to protect international political coercion or blackmail, or the exportation of violence and strife to other locations – even to the homeland of an oppressor nation. Thus, an uprising is not only limited temporally, it is limited spatially. . . .

While determining the proper geographic boundaries of an "uprising" involves a legal issue that ordinarily will be fairly simple to resolve, there may be some circumstances under which it will be more difficult to do so. We need not formulate a general rule that will be applicable to all situations. It is sufficient in this case to state that for purposes of the political offense exception an "uprising" cannot extend beyond the borders of the country or territory in which a group of citizens or residents is seeking to change their particular government or governmental structure.

It follows from what we have said that an "uprising" can exist only when the turmoil that warrants that characterization is created by nationals of the land in which the disturbances are occurring. . . .

3. *The "Incidental to" Component*

When describing the second requirement of the incidence test, the "incidental to" component, American courts have used the phrases "in the course of," "connected to," and "in furtherance of" interchangeably. We have applied a rather liberal standard when determining whether this part of the test has been met and have been willing to examine all of the circumstances surrounding the commission of the crime. . . . We believe the traditional liberal construction of the requirement that there be a nexus between the act and the uprising, ... is appropriate. There are various types of acts that, when committed in the course of an uprising, are likely to have been politically motivated. There is little reason, under such circumstances, to impose a strict nexus standard. Moreover, the application of a strict test would in some instances jeopardize the rights of the accused. . . .

VI. THE INCIDENCE TEST APPLIED TO THE CHARGED OFFENSES

. . . . Quinn is accused of having been a member of a conspiracy involving the Balcombe Street Four and he does not challenge the probable cause finding on this charge; his fingerprints were found on the bombs and within the flats where bombs were constructed. Quinn has already been convicted of and has served a prison sentence for his membership in the IRA. There is no evidence that he was involved in the conspiracy for other than political reasons, and his alleged co-conspirators, the Balcombe Street Four, were convicted of politically motivated bombings. Moreover, the PIRA's use of bombing campaigns as a political tactic is well-documented. Accepting the magistrate's factual findings, which are not clearly erroneous, and applying the legal standards we have explained above, we think it quite clear that if an uprising, as that term is defined for purposes of the political offense exception, existed at the time the offenses were committed, the bombings were incidental to that uprising.

Furthermore, because various disparate acts may be incidental to an uprising, we agree with the district court's conclusion that the Tibble murder would be incidental to the uprising, although we believe the analysis performed by both the magistrate and the district court is in error with respect to this incident. It does not matter if the killer's motivation in killing Officer Tibble was to conceal a bomb factory or to avoid capture. A murder of a police officer is related to an uprising whether the reason for the act is to avoid discovery of munitions or to avoid reduction of "forces" by capture. Regardless which of these goals motivated the killer, if an uprising existed at the time, this offense as well was incidental to it. . . .

With regard to the uprising prong of the incidence test, we must again review the magistrate's factual findings under the clearly erroneous standard and his legal conclusions *de novo*. The district court failed to do this, construing the magistrate's conclusion that there was an uprising throughout the United Kingdom solely as a finding of fact. The district court summarized the magistrate's factual findings as to the levels of violence that existed in Northern Ireland and elsewhere in the United Kingdom at the time Quinn allegedly committed the charged offenses, and properly adopted them. However, the district court failed to analyze the magistrate's legal conclusion that because the requisite level of violence existed in Northern Ireland and because Northern Ireland is "in a constitutional sense" a part of the United Kingdom, an uprising existed in the United Kingdom as a whole. . . . It is clear from the record that the magistrate correctly concluded that the level of violence outside Northern Ireland was insufficient in itself to constitute an "uprising."

There is a second and even more significant reason why the "uprising" prong is not met in this case. As the magistrate found, what violence there was not being generated by citizens or residents of England. In fact, the magistrate determined that a large percentage of the bombing incidents in England were attributable to the Balcombe Street Four. The critical factor is that nationals of Northern Ireland, seeking to alter the government in that territorial entity, exported their struggle for political change across the seas to a separate geographical entity – and conducted that struggle in a country in which the nationals and residents were not attempting to alter their own political structure.

. . . . We do not question whether the PIRA sought to coerce the appropriate sovereign. Nor do we pass judgment on the use of violence as a form of political coercion or the efficacy of the violent attacks in England. But, as we have already said, ... the word "uprising" means exactly that: it refers to a people *rising up*, in their own land, against the government of that land. It does not cover terrorism or other criminal conduct exported to other locations. Nor can the existence of an uprising be based on violence committed by persons who do not reside in the country or territory in which the violence occurs.

In light of the justifications for the political offense exception, the formulation of the incidence test as it has traditionally been articulated, and the cases in which the exception has historically been applied, we do not believe it would be proper to stretch the term "uprising" to include acts that took place in England as a part of a struggle by nationals of Northern Ireland to change the form of government in their own land. Accordingly, we need not decide whether had an uprising occurred, the protection afforded by the exception would have been extended to one who, like Quinn, is a citizen of a different and uninvolved nation. . . . Because the incidence test is not met, neither the bombing conspiracy nor the murder of Police Constable Tibble is a non-extraditable offense under the political offense exception to the extradition treaty between the United States and the United Kingdom. . . .

VIII. CONCLUSION

For extradition to be denied for an otherwise extraditable crime on the basis that it falls within the protective ambit of the political offense exception, the incidence test must ordinarily be met. (We reserve the question whether offenses committed by government officials or in connection with wars between nations are covered by the exception and, if so, whether a different test would be appropriate.) The incidence test has two components, designed so that the exception comports with its original justifications and protects acts of the kind that inspired its inclusion in extradition treaties. First, there must be an uprising – a political disturbance related to the struggle of individuals to alter or abolish the existing government in their country. An uprising is both temporarily and spatially limited. Second, the charged offense must have been committed in furtherance of the uprising; it must be related to the political struggle or be consequent to the uprising activity. Neither the objectives of the uprising nor the means employed to achieve those objectives are subject to judicial scrutiny. And while the nature of the uprising group and any evidence of the accused's motivations may be relevant, proof on these elements is not required or necessarily determinative. Acts of international terrorism do not meet the incidence test and are thus not covered by the political offense exception. Crimes against humanity also are beyond the scope of the exception.

The conspiracy to cause explosions and the murder with which Quinn is charged do not fall within the political offense exception. Although an uprising existed in Northern Ireland at the time the charged offenses were committed, there was no uprising in England. The crimes did not take place within a territorial entity in which a group of nationals were seeking to change the form of the government under which they live; rather the offenses took place in a different geographical location. We do not decide whether Quinn's status as a citizen of an uninvolved nation would also preclude him from receiving the protection of the exception. . . . We vacate the writ of habeas corpus and remand to the district court. We hold that Quinn may be extradited on the murder charge but that the district court must consider whether the conspiracy charge is time-barred before extradition is permitted for that offense.

VACATED AND REMANDED

DUNIWAY, CIRCUIT JUDGE . . . . :

I concur in the judgment, but I cannot concur in the lengthy opinion of Judge Reinhardt and the very extensive dicta that it expounds.

I agree that the magistrate had jurisdiction, including jurisdiction to determine whether the offenses with which Quinn is charged were of a political character. I agree that the district court had jurisdiction on habeas corpus to decide that question and that we have jurisdiction on appeal to consider it. I have no doubt that the evidence is sufficient to enable, indeed, to require, the magistrate, the district court, and this court to say that the offenses charged against Quinn are extraditable offenses, and that the only basis upon which extradition could be denied is the treaty provision that "extradition shall not be granted if . . . the offense . . . is regarded by the requested party, [the United States], as one of a political character."

My principal difficulty is with part V of Judge Reinhardt's thoughtful and careful opinion, and especially with part V, B, 2, and the geographical limitation announced there. . . . The limitation may be useful to us in this case, but I doubt that it is a valid one. . . . Particularly today, with the airplane, the helicopter the high speed motor vehicle, the railroad, the speedboat and submarine genuinely revolutionary activities can take place outside the geographic boundaries of the requesting state. I fear that if we adopt the geographic limitation propounded in the opinion today, we will find ourselves trying to work our way around it tomorrow. . . .

FLETCHER, CIRCUIT JUDGE, concurring and dissenting:

I respectfully dissent from my colleagues' conclusion that Quinn may now be extradited on the murder charge. The decision facing this court is excruciatingly difficult. Quinn is accused of hideous crimes – violent and cruel and some of them cowardly. Innocent victims were targeted for receipt of letter bombs mailed anonymously. A decision that the full force of the law should not be invoked to punish persons found guilty of such acts seems inconceivable. However, the political offense exception to the treaty of extradition has a long history of protecting persons rebelling against their governments.

This longstanding tradition among western nations is an acknowledgment of the right of the governed to oppose unjust governments. Although the nations, ours included, have acknowledged the heinous nature of violent political crimes, they have nonetheless, under treaties and statutes, denied extradition when an individual's conduct falls within the narrow exception for the "political offense." . . . Judge Reinhardt is rightly concerned that "uprising" not encompass "terrorism or other criminal conduct exported to other locations." I share his concern. But in my view, the acts of Irish nationalists against the British in London are not international "terrorism or other criminal conduct exported to other locations." The longstanding ties between England and Northern Ireland, which Judge Reinhardt acknowledges are "well established," cannot be avoided or ignored. Although Northern Ireland may have been "separated" from Great Britain by treaty when the Irish Free State was created, it remained a part of the United Kingdom with representation in the British Parliament and it has been occupied by British troops lo these many years. The acts of terrorism in England by members of the PIRA can hardly be termed acts of international terrorism. . . .

Given my conclusion that the offenses of which Quinn is accused are protected under the political offense exception, I must address whether this protection extends to one who, like Quinn, is a citizen of a different nation from that in which the uprising is occurring. I do not believe that mercenaries or volunteers in a foreign conflict can claim protection under the political offense exception. I deduce from Judge Reinhardt's views on international terrorism that he would agree. To be entitled to protection, an individual would have to demonstrate tangible and substantial connections with the country in which an uprising occurs. It could be short of citizenship, but there must be a showing of substantial connection – for example, that he or she had lived in the country or territory and planned to continue to live there under a changed regime.

In Quinn's case, we lack sufficient information with which to make any such evaluation. We know that Quinn is a United States citizen, and that he resided in San Francisco during the years immediately preceding his arrest. . . . Because we do not know the extent of Quinn's ties to Northern Ireland, I would remand the case for an initial determination by the district court as to whether Quinn should be treated as an Irish national and afforded the protection of the political offense exception. Accordingly, I dissent from the holding that Quinn may now be extradited on the murder charge.

I agree with my colleagues that Quinn may not be extradited on the conspiracy charge at least until after the district court considers the question of the statute of limitations. However, I believe that the district court should not be required to reach that question unless it first concludes that Quinn's ties to Northern Ireland were insufficient to invoke the protection of the political offense exception. For the reasons I have explained, I concur in the holding remanding the conspiracy count.

NOTES AND QUESTIONS

(1) How much evidence needs to be produced to support a refusal to extradite under the political offense exception? In *The Matter of the Extradition of Smyth*, 61 F.3d 711 (9th Cir. 1995), the Ninth Circuit Court of Appeals examined a district court denial of certification of extradition. In reversing the lower court decision, Circuit Judge Schroeder stated:

> This is a proceeding brought by the United States on behalf of the United Kingdom to extradite James J. Smyth to Northern Ireland. Smyth was convicted of the attempted murder of a prison officer in Belfast, Northern Ireland in 1978 and sentenced to 20 years' imprisonment. He escaped from the Maze Prison in Northern Ireland in September of 1983 and arrived in San Francisco several months later. The United States, at the request of the United Kingdom, seeks Smyth's extradition to Northern Ireland to serve the remainder of his prison term. Extradition is sought pursuant to the United States - United Kingdom Extradition Treaty, June 8, 1972, U.S. - U.K., 28 U.S.T. 227, and the Supplementary Extradition Treaty, June 25, 1985, U.S. - U.K., art. 3(a), *reprinted in* S. Exec. Rep. No. 17, 99th Cong., 2nd Sess. 15-17 (1986)(Supplementary Treaty). . . . The Supplementary Treaty followed in the wake of a series of decisions by United States courts refusing to extradite to Northern Ireland individuals who had been charged with or convicted of acts of political violence. The treaty provisions, negotiated by President Reagan and Prime Minister Thatcher, and modified by the United States Senate, represent a difficult compromise between outrage and compassion: the outrage of the British government over the refusal of the United States to extradite persons whom the United Kingdom considered terrorists, and the compassion of the United States for individuals who, if extradited, might suffer unfair treatment and incarceration on account of their religious or political associations, not because of their criminal acts.

> The Supplementary Treaty's key substantive provision, Article 3(a), creates a defense to extradition. It provides:

>> Notwithstanding any other provision of this Supplementary Treaty, extradition shall not occur if the person sought establishes to the satisfaction of the competent judicial authority by a preponderance of the evidence that the request for extradition has in fact been made with a view to try or punish him on account of his race, religion, nationality or political opinions, or that he would, if surrendered, be prejudiced at his trial or punished, detained or restricted in his personal liberty by reason of his race, religion, nationality or political opinions.

> Supplementary Treaty, art. 3(a). . . .

Beginning in 1979, a series of United States court decisions denied extradition of IRA members because the underlying offenses constituted "political acts." . . . These decisions angered the British Government, which viewed them as condoning violent terrorist conduct. . . . The Reagan Administration in 1981 proposed legislation for a new treaty that would have entirely eliminated judicial application of the political offense exception to extraditions to the United Kingdom. The Departments of Justice and State, both of whom assisted in drafting the original bill, expressed concern that continued judicial application of the political offense exception to extradition would turn the United States into a haven for terrorists and adversely affect foreign relations. *See* Barbara Ann Banoff & Christopher H. Pyle, *"To Surrender Political Offenders": The Political Offense Exception to Extradition in United States Law,* 16 N.Y.U. J. INT'L L. & POL. 169, 170 (1984).

The Senate, however, was not comfortable with the wholesale elimination of the political offense exception from U.S.-U.K. extradition proceedings. It therefore limited the abrogation of the political offense exception in Article 1 of the Supplementary Treaty to enumerated violent offenses and added Article 3(a) as a means by which fugitives sought for extradition on such offenses could nonetheless challenge their extradition.

The Senate Report described the Supplementary Treaty as "one of the most divisive and contentious issues the Committee [on Foreign Relations] has faced this Congress. The Committee has worked long and hard to develop a compromise that can win broad, bipartisan support." . . . The Report further characterized the compromise as "an effort to balance anti-terrorism concerns and the right of due process for individuals." . . . As such, Article 3(a) is not a mere reformulation of the political offense exception; the provision invites an altogether new inquiry in the extradition context. Rather than focusing on the motivations of the accused (which the political offense exception encourages), the Article 3(a) defense to extradition focuses on the treatment the accused will likely receive at the hands of the requesting country's criminal justice system. . . .

Article 3(a) clearly places the burden upon the person sought for extradition to establish "by a preponderance of the evidence" that the exception applies. Supplementary Treaty, art. 3(a). To establish a defense under the second clause of Article 3(a), the extraditee must establish that if surrendered, he would be "prejudiced at his trial or punished, detained or restricted in his personal liberty by reason of his race, religion, nationality, or political opinions." *Id.* . . .

This is the first case in which a person challenging extradition to Northern Ireland has raised a defense under Article 3(a) of the Supplementary Treaty. Because of the lack of precedent, the district court held several preliminary hearings to decide the scope of the evidence that would be discoverable and admissible to support the Article 3(a) defense. On May 6, 1993, the district court issued its first written order in the case, *In re Extradition of Smyth, 820 F. Supp. 498 (N.D. Cal. 1993)*. The court ruled that Article 3(a) created an exception to, but did not nullify, the traditional rule of noninquiry in extradition matters and that it permitted an individual asserting the defense to establish that the individual would be prejudiced as a result of discriminatory treatment within the requesting country's criminal justice system. . . . The court went on to define the scope of permissible inquiry along lines which set the course of the litigation and shaped the nature of its ultimate findings. The court held that Article 3(a) authorized inquiry regarding three categories of evidence:

> (1) evidence of Smyth's treatment by security forces prior to his 1977 arrest, admissible as "background [that could] tend to show a pattern of discriminatory treatment aimed specifically at . . ."

> (2) evidence of the conditions of confinement in Northern Ireland that Smyth would face, provided the evidence showed "that any poor treatment suffered is a result of discrimination on the basis of race, religion, nationality or political view," . . . . and

> (3) evidence related to likely post-incarceration "restraints on . . . liberty" motivated by the grounds listed in Article 3(a), admissible only if such evidence showed that the government "explicitly tolerated or has been materially involved in any plots to restrain [Smyth's] liberty or assassinate him" or if it showed a "pattern of [such] conduct involving a government entity," . . .

We believe that had Smyth demonstrated by a preponderance of the evidence that, after he served the approximately two to five years of his remaining prison time, he likely would be a target of similar conduct by persons within Northern Ireland's justice system, then he would have qualified for the defense to extradition contained in Article 3(a). There was, however, little such evidence. Nearly all of the testimony of harassment of Republican ex-prisoners concerned conduct that occurred in the past. Some of it related to conduct of security forces in the Republic of Ireland rather than in Northern Ireland. There was conflicting evidence as to whether in the future Smyth would be barred from travel outside Northern Ireland after his release. . . .

Here, we conclude the district court erred in at least two respects. In the first place, resort to the withholding of deportation regulation that presumes a *present* danger of persecution from past experience of persecution cannot validate the district court's presumption of a risk of persecution two to five years in the *future*. Second, the district court erred in relying extensively upon evidence of the general discriminatory effects of the Diplock system upon Catholics and suspected Republican sympathizers. That evidence does not relate to the treatment Smyth is likely to receive as a consequence of extradition, as required under Article 3(a). . . .

Considered in this context, the language of Article 3(a) must mean that a federal court in an extradition proceeding may look to the treatment that likely will be accorded the extraditee upon the charge for which extradition is sought. This inquiry need not necessarily be limited to the prosecution and formal term of imprisonment, but Article 3(a) does not permit denial of extradition on the basis of an inquiry into the general political conditions extant in Northern Ireland. The history of the provision shows that it requires an individualized inquiry.

Accordingly, in order to defeat extradition on the basis of his prospective treatment at the hands of the justice system extending beyond the duration of his formal imprisonment term, Smyth would have to demonstrate by a preponderance of the evidence that the criminal justice system in Northern Ireland likely would exact additional retribution for his crime beyond the remaining term of imprisonment, and that such additional punishment would be inflicted on account of Smyth's political or religious beliefs, and not on account of his having attempted to murder a prison guard. This is a difficult burden and one which Smyth did not shoulder successfully. The evidence did not establish, independent of the presumptions discussed below, that Smyth would suffer religiously or politically motivated punishment after serving his prison term. . . .

(2) Does an extradition ruling, under the political offense exception, have any effect on the "serious nonpolitical crime" assessment in a deportation determination? In *Barapind v. Reno*, 2000 U.S. App. Lexis 21760 (9th Cir. 2000), the court stated:

In a parallel, but converse, provision to the "political offense" exception to extradition, the INA excludes from withholding of deportation aliens for whom "there are serious reasons for considering that the alien has committed a serious nonpolitical crime." 8 U.S.C. § 1253(h)(2)(C); *see also* 8 U.S.C. §§ 1101(a)(42)(A) and 1253(h)(2)(A). However, the "political offense" determination in extradition proceedings and the "serious nonpolitical crime" assessment in immigration proceedings are separate and distinct inquiries. . . . A determination that an alien's acts are "political offenses" for purposes of denying extradition should have no effect on the BIA's determination of whether an asylum applicant has committed a serious nonpolitical offense because "extradition determinations have no *res judicata* effect in subsequent judicial proceedings." . . .

Can the Board of Immigration Appeals (BIA) hold in abeyance an asylum application, pending a resolution of an extradition proceeding? *See id.* (holding that BIA may hold asylum adjudication in abeyance pending extradition proceeding) (*see also* chap. 14).

Chapter 14
ABDUCTION AND OTHER ALTERNATIVES TO EXTRADITION

Depending on the circumstances, various devices apart from extradition may be used to obtain the return of a fugitive for trial. *See* ETHAN A. NADELMANN, COPS ACROSS BORDERS: THE INTERNATIONALIZATION OF U.S. CRIMINAL LAW ENFORCEMENT 436-57 (1993). These alternative methods sometimes are referred to as "disguised," "informal," or "irregular" extradition or rendition. Not all of them are unlawful. Three kinds of alternatives to extradition can be distinguished. *See* Alona E. Evans, *Acquisition of Custody over the International Fugitive Offender – Alternatives to Extradition: A Survey of United States Practice*, 40 BRIT. Y.B. INT'L L. 77 (1964).

First, in certain situations, a treaty may provide for the expedited rendition of fugitives outside the ordinary framework of extradition. Thus, allied soldiers (under Status of Forces Agreements), deserting seamen, and those who commit crimes on board aircraft may be handed over to another country for trial through a sort of *"brevi manu* extradition." *Id.* at 80. Recent provisions for the surrender of fugitives to international criminal tribunals also fall within this category.

Second, exclusion or deportation under the immigration laws can be used to achieve the same results as extradition and even to circumvent deliberately the requirements of the law of extradition. The use of deportation when extradition fails is considered in the first section of the present chapter.

Third, there are cases in which rendition is achieved through unlawful means. Whether particular means for acquiring custody of an offender are unlawful may itself be a controversial question. Luring fugitives, for instance, out of countries where they are safe from extradition, to places where they can be arrested by U.S. law enforcement authorities, or by foreign authorities prepared to surrender them to the U.S., is regarded as a permissible tactic for bringing offenders before the U.S. courts [*see, e.g., United States v. Yunis*, chap. 2, *supra*]. In other countries, it may be regarded as a form of kidnapping, by fraud instead of force, and therefore a violation of the territorial sovereignty of the state of refuge, as well as a violation of the rights of the fugitive under applicable human rights instruments. *See Report of the Committee on Extradition and Human Rights, in* INTERNATIONAL LAW ASSOCIATION, REPORT OF THE SIXTY-SIXTH CONGRESS 142, 162 (1994). Where the means used to obtain custody are determined to be unlawful, there is the further question of whether that determination should operate as a bar to exercising jurisdiction over the fugitive. This question is considered in the second section of the present chapter.

§ 14.01 Deportation

RUIZ MASSIEU v. RENO

United States District Court for the District of New Jersey
915 F. Supp. 681 (1996)

MARYANNE TRUMP BARRY, DISTRICT JUDGE:

Plaintiff, Mario Ruiz Massieu, seeks a permanent injunction enjoining the deportation proceeding instituted against him pursuant to 8 U.S.C. § 1251(a)(4)(C)(i) and a declaration that the statute, which has not previously been construed in any reported judicial opinion, is unconstitutional. That statute, by its express terms, confers upon a single individual, the Secretary of State, the unfettered and unreviewable discretion to deport any alien lawfully within the United States, not for identified reasons relating to his or conduct in the United States or elsewhere but, rather, because that person's mere presence here would impact in some unexplained way on the foreign policy interests of the United States. Thus, the statute represents a breathtaking departure both from well established legislative precedent which commands deportation based on adjudications of defined impermissible conduct by the alien in the United States, and from well established precedent with respect to extradition which commands extradition based on adjudications of probable cause to believe that the alien has engaged in defined impermissible conduct elsewhere. . . .

Mr. Ruiz Massieu entered this country legally and is not alleged to have committed any act within this country which requires his deportation. Nor, on the state of this record, can it be said that there exists probable cause to believe that Mr. Ruiz Massieu has committed any act outside of this country which warrants his extradition, for the government has failed in four separate proceedings before two Magistrate Judges to establish probable cause. Deportation of Mr. Ruiz Massieu is sought merely because he is here and the Secretary of State and Mexico have decided that he should go back. . . .

The facts of this case read more like a best-selling novel than a typical deportation proceeding. Mario Ruiz Massieu, a citizen of Mexico, is a member of one of Mexico's most influential and politically active families, and, in recent years, has occupied several positions at the upper-most echelons of the Mexican government. For much of the past twenty years, Mr. Ruiz Massieu lived an academic life both as a professor and director of the National University of Mexico. During that time, he authored a number of books on topics such as education, history, law and politics. In 1993, however, Mr. Ruiz Massieu was thrust into the vanguard of Mexican politics as a member of the Institutional

Revolutionary Party ("the PRI"), Mexico's only established ruling party. He was appointed Deputy Attorney General in 1993, Under Secretary for the Department of Government in 1994, and Deputy Attorney General, again, in May of 1994.

On September 28, 1994, Mr. Ruiz Massieu's brother, Jose Francisco Ruiz Massieu – Secretary General of the PRI and an outspoken critic of the Mexican political system – was assassinated. Within hours, Mario Ruiz Massieu, as Deputy Attorney General, began an investigation into his brother's murder. In the ensuing weeks, fourteen people were apprehended and indicted as part of a conspiracy uncovered through Mr. Ruiz Massieu's investigatory efforts. Many of the arrested conspirators named Manuel Munoz Rocha, a PRI official, as the architect of the conspiracy. Mr. Munoz Rocha, however, was shielded by official immunity, and could not be interviewed by the Attorney General's office in connection with the case. Mr. Ruiz Massieu requested that President Carlos Salinas de Gortari waive Rocha's immunity, a request that the PRI vigorously opposed. Eventually, the immunity was waived, but not before Mr. Munoz Rocha had disappeared. He was never interviewed or arrested, and remains unaccounted for to this day.

Fifty-seven days after his brother's assassination, Mr. Ruiz Massieu resigned as Deputy Attorney General and withdrew his membership in the PRI. In a dramatic and widely publicized speech on November 23, 1994, Mr. Ruiz Massieu announced that he was resigning from both his office and his party because of the PRI's continuous efforts to frustrate his investigation into his brother's murder. Specifically, he alleged that the PRI was obstructing his search for the persons who might have ordered former Deputy Munoz Rocha to act – persons whom Mr. Ruiz Massieu alleged to be very high-ranking members of the PRI.

In February of 1995, Mr. Ruiz Massieu published a book elaborating on the themes of his resignation address. . . Immediately, Mexican authorities alleged that Mr. Ruiz Massieu committed the crimes of intimidation, concealment and "against the administration of justice" (a crime analogous to obstruction of justice in this country) in connection with the investigation of his brother's assassination. Contemporaneously, Mr. Ruiz Massieu claimed that he and his family began to receive both death and kidnapping threats. On March 2, 1995, he appeared for an official interrogation before Mexican authorities concerning the allegations of his criminal activity committed while in office.

Later that same day, Mr. Ruiz Massieu and his family lawfully entered the United States as non-immigrant visitors at Houston, Texas, where they have owned a home since October of 1994. After remaining at their Houston home for the night, the family boarded a plane en route to Spain. When the plane touched down at Newark Airport on March 3, 1995, Mr. Ruiz Massieu was arrested by United States Customs officials, pursuant to 31 U.S.C. § 5316, on a charge of reporting only approximately $18,000 of the $44,322 in his possession. The charge was never pursued and was subsequently dismissed at the government's request.

On March 5, 1995, two days after his arrest in Newark, a Mexican court issued an arrest warrant for Mr. Ruiz Massieu charging him with intimidation, concealment, and "against the administration of justice." The following day, at Mexico's request, the United States presented a complaint for Mr. Ruiz Massieu's provisional arrest and sought his extradition to face the charges set forth in the Mexican arrest warrant. On June 9, 1995, a Mexican court consolidated the allegations into a single charge of "against the administration of justice."[3]

On June 13, 1995, the first extradition proceeding began before Magistrate Judge Ronald J. Hedges. After lengthy hearings . . . Magistrate Judge Hedges declined to issue a certificate of extraditability. In so doing, he determined that the government had failed to demonstrate even probable cause to believe that Mr. Ruiz Massieu committed the crimes charged. Significantly, Magistrate Judge Hedges also found that many of the statements submitted by the government were "incredible and unreliable," and might have been altered to remove certain recantations and exculpatory statements. In addition, he found, and the government did not deny, that multiple statements were procured by torture inflicted by the Mexican authorities, including the inculpatory testimony of one of the government's primary affiants.

On June 20, 1995, two days before Magistrate Judge Hedges issued his initial opinion, Mexico filed its second request for extradition based on newly filed charges of embezzlement. The charges focused on the $9,000,000 in the Houston bank account and 2,500,000 pesos allegedly disbursed without adequate documentation while Mr. Ruiz Massieu was in office. In an opinion filed September 25, 1995, Magistrate Judge Hedges again declined to issue a certificate of extraditability on the ground that the government had failed to demonstrate probable cause, or present any evidence whatsoever, that the funds had been illegally obtained or disbursed.

Undeterred, on August 31, 1995, the government refiled its initial request for extradition based on the charge of "against the administration of justice." Although the government produced nine new statements allegedly incriminating Mr. Ruiz Massieu, Magistrate Judge Hedges remained unpersuaded. By letter opinion dated November 13, 1995, the court again ruled that there was no probable cause to believe that Mr. Ruiz Massieu committed

---

[3] In the interim, the United States froze and seized, under seal and without notice or explanation, Mr. Ruiz Massieu's Houston bank account containing approximately nine million dollars. On June 15, 1995, the government instituted a civil forfeiture action against the account. [See United States v. Nine Million Forty One Thousand, Five Hundred Ninety Eight Dollars and Sixty Eight Cents, 976 F. Supp. 642 (S.D. Tex. 1997), aff'd, 163 F.3d 238 (5th Cir. 1998), cert. denied, 527 U.S. 1023 (1999).]

the acts alleged, and dismissed the complaint.

On October 10, 1995, the government instituted yet a fourth extradition proceeding by refiling its prior application based on the previously rejected embezzlement charges. This time, the application was heard before Magistrate Judge Stanley R. Chesler. . . . Like Magistrate Judge Hedges before him, Magistrate Judge Chesler issued a lengthy opinion denying the certification of extraditability. Focusing on the government's paucity of evidence, Magistrate Judge Chesler stated that "the bottom line is that the government's efforts to establish an inference of criminality on the basis of unexplained wealth fails because it does not rise to the level where any nexus between those funds and the funds which Mr. Massieu is alleged to have embezzled has been established." On January 11, 1996, a Mexican court dismissed the embezzlement charges.

With that, the government seemingly accepted defeat as to Mr. Ruiz Massieu's extraditability. It was then, however, that this case took a turn toward the truly Kafkaesque. On December 22, 1995, immediately after Magistrate Judge Chesler issued his opinion, Mr. Ruiz Massieu was taken into custody by the Immigration and Naturalization Service ("the INS") pursuant to a previously unserved and unannounced detainer dated September 29, 1995. In addition, he was served with an INS Order to Show Cause and Notice of Hearing. The notice advised Mr. Ruiz Massieu that he was ordered to show cause as to why he should not be deported because, the Secretary of State has made a determination that, pursuant to Section 241(a)(4)(C) of the Immigration and Nationality Act, 8 U.S.C. § 1251(a)(4)(C), there is reasonable ground to believe your presence or activities in the United States would have potentially serious adverse foreign policy consequences for the United States. No further explanation of the ground for Mr. Ruiz Massieu's alleged deportability was tendered.

Sometime after notice was served on Mr. Ruiz Massieu, the INS produced an October 2, 1995, letter addressed to Attorney General Janet Reno from Secretary of State Warren Christopher. The letter urged the Attorney General to effect Mr. Ruiz Massieu's "expeditious deportation" "to Mexico" based on the Secretary's conclusion that Mr. Ruiz Massieu's presence in the United States will have potentially serious adverse foreign policy consequences for the United States. The letter referenced the "serious allegations" that are pending in Mexico against Mr. Ruiz Massieu and the recent strides that both governments have taken in "our ability to cooperate and confront criminality on both sides of the border." At bottom, the Secretary's request was premised on the proposition that "our inability to return to Mexico Mr. Ruiz Massieu – a case the Mexican Presidency has told us is of the highest importance – would jeopardize our ability to work with Mexico on law enforcement matters. It might also cast a potentially chilling effect on other issues our two governments are addressing."

The relevant deportation statute, § 241(a)(4)(C)(i) of the Immigration and Naturalization Act ("INA"), provides simply that "an alien whose presence or activities in the United States the Secretary of State has reasonable ground to believe would have potentially serious adverse foreign policy consequences for the United States is deportable." Because an indication of the Secretary of State's belief is all that the statute by its terms requires, the October 2, 1995 letter, alone, comprised (and remains) the universe of evidence that the INS has offered to support its charge of Mr. Ruiz Massieu's deportability. A master calendar proceeding, the first stage of deportation hearings, was scheduled to begin on January 19, 1996. On January 17, 1996, however, Mr. Ruiz Massieu filed a complaint in this court requesting that the deportation proceedings be preliminarily and permanently enjoined, and that section 241(a)(4)(C) of the INA be declared unconstitutional.

The complaint contains three core constitutional claims: (1) the deportation proceeding evidences selective enforcement in retaliation for Mr. Ruiz Massieu's exercise of his First Amendment right to criticize the Mexican political system; (2) the deportation proceeding represents a "de facto" extradition and is an attempt to overrule, albeit indirectly, four federal court decisions, in violation of the separation of powers; and (3) section 241(a)(4)(C)(i) is unconstitutionally vague, in violation of the due process clause of the Fifth Amendment. . . .

In terms of due process, plaintiff attacks § 241(a)(4)(C)(i) on two distinct, though related, grounds. The first contention is that the statute is void for vagueness. The second is that, by its terms, the statute denies plaintiff, and any alien deported thereunder, a meaningful opportunity to be heard before being subjected to the severe deprivation of liberty that is deportation. Additionally, the court has sua sponte raised the issue of whether the statute is so devoid of standards that it represents an unconstitutional delegation of legislative power to the executive. . . .

A. Void-for-Vagueness

. . . . [T]he void-for-vagueness doctrine. . . requires that prohibitory statutes define the conduct proscribed with "sufficient definiteness that ordinary people can understand what conduct is prohibited and in a manner that does not encourage arbitrary and discriminatory enforcement." . . . . It simply cannot be disputed, and indeed the government does not, that [§ 241(a)(4)(C)(i)] provides absolutely no notice to aliens as to what is required of them under the statute. Simply stated, it "contains no standard for determining what a suspect has to do in order to satisfy" its requirements. . . . While there may be a common understanding, in a definitional sense, of what "foreign policy" is, no one outside the Department of State and, perhaps, the President ever knows what our nation's frequently covert foreign policy is at any given time. Thus, there is no conceivable way that an alien could know, *ex-ante*, how to conform his or her activities to the requirements of the law. Of course, it is even less likely that an alien could know that his or her mere presence here would or could cause adverse foreign policy consequences when our foreign policy is unpublished, ever-changing, and often highly confidential. . . .

Related to the void-for-vagueness doctrine's notice requirement is "the requirement that the legislature establish minimal guidelines to govern law enforcement," so as not to permit "arbitrary and erratic" applications of the law. Here, again, the statute fails to pass constitutional muster. Rather than providing the Secretary of State with a definite standard, [it] grants the Secretary unfettered discretion. . . .

"Foreign policy" cannot serve as the talisman behind which Congress may abdicate its responsibility to pass only sufficiently clear and definite laws when those laws may be enforced against the individual. Although the executive's discretionary authority over foreign affairs is well established, Congress cannot empower the executive to employ that authority against the individual except through constitutional means. See *Valentine v. United States ex rel. Neidecker,* 299 U.S. 5, 9, 81 L. Ed. 5, 57 S. Ct. 100 ("the Constitution creates no executive prerogative to dispose of the liberty of the individual. Proceedings against him must be authorized by law. There is no executive discretion to surrender him to a foreign government, unless that discretion is governed by law"). If the Constitution was adopted to protect individuals against anything, it was the abuses made possible through just this type of unbounded executive authority.

There can be no more graphic illustration of the exercise of unbounded executive authority than that seen in this case. In this case, the Secretary has determined that plaintiff is expendable – for "foreign policy" reasons which the Secretary need neither explicate nor defend – merely because Mexico wants plaintiff back. Had plaintiff overstayed his welcome, had he entered this country illegally, or had he committed a crime while here – all clearly defined grounds for deportation – he would be entitled to a host of protections, not the least of which would be notice of the prohibited conduct and a meaningful opportunity to be heard. Similarly, if it were believed that plaintiff had committed a crime in Mexico, his extradition would, presumably, have again been sought and, again, there would be no problem of vagueness and he would be entitled to substantial protections. Extradition, after all, is the time-tested mechanism used by this country and other civilized countries to send a criminal back, a mechanism that the government has unsuccessfully utilized vis-a-vis plaintiff in four separate court proceedings. Section 241(a)(4)(C)(i) does an end run around and, indeed, subverts the extradition framework, which would never permit the return of an alien merely because he is considered undesirable by his government. . . . [It] authorizes a heretofore unknown scope of executive enforcement power *vis-a-vis* the individual with utterly no standards provided to the Secretary of State or to the legal aliens subject to its provisions. Section 241(a)(4)(C)(i) is void for vagueness.

B. Opportunity to be Heard

For many of the same reasons that § 241(a)(4)(C)(i) is void for vagueness, the statute also deprives aliens such as plaintiff of due process of law by denying them a meaningful opportunity to be heard. . . . [I]n order to determine whether the opportunity afforded to plaintiff under the INA is constitutionally sufficient, this court must apply the now familiar three-part balancing test enunciated by the Supreme Court in *Mathews v. Eldridge,* 424 U.S. 319, 335, 47 L. Ed. 2d 18, 96 S. Ct. 893 (1976). Phrased in terms relevant to the case at bar, this court must consider: (1) the importance to all aliens of not being imprisoned, forced to leave the United States, and sent to the country of our government's choosing; (2) the adequacy of the hearing afforded and the likelihood that increased procedures would diminish the risk of an erroneous deprivation of liberty; and (3) the governmental interest, as well as that of the public, in allowing the Secretary of State to declare an alien deportable in the interests of our foreign policy as well as the increased cost of requiring additional procedures. . . . [Applying this test, the court found that (1) the interest of plaintiff and other aliens in] avoiding the complete deprivation of liberty that results from executive confinement and deportation. . . . is unquantifiably grave. . . . [(2)] In light of the "grave nature of deportation,"due process requires, at a minimum, that plaintiff be afforded a meaningful opportunity to be heard. . . . [And (3)] as important as the nation's foreign policy is, this court is aware of no rationale that would justify this extraordinary grant of discretion given the Secretary of State when other equally lofty interests do not warrant a comparable suspension of an alien's constitutional rights. . . . [Thus] a balancing of the appropriate factors tips well in plaintiff's favor. Absent a meaningful opportunity to be heard, the Secretary of State's unreviewable and concededly "unfettered discretion" to deprive an alien, who lawfully entered this country, of his or her liberty to the extent exemplified by this case is, in this court's view, unconstitutional.

C. Unconstitutional Delegation of Legislative Powers

For many of the same reasons that § 241(a)(4)(C)(i) of the INA is violative of the due process clause, it also is an unconstitutional delegation of legislative power to the executive. . . . The Constitution grants the power to make laws exclusively to the people's representatives in Congress. . . . It has long been recognized, however, that some level of legislative delegation is necessary to the efficient administration of the ever-broadening regulatory course charted by Congress. Accordingly, "the most that may be asked under the separation-of-powers doctrine is that Congress lay down the general policy and standards that animate the law, leaving the agency to refine those standards, 'fill in the blanks,' or apply the standards to particular cases." The delegation doctrine, then, functions to ensure that Congress will remain the nation's primary policy maker by requiring it to articulate intelligible standards to guide (1) the exercise of the delegatee's authority, and (2) the judiciary's ability to review the exercise of that authority against a congressionally mandated policy. Section 241(a)(4)(C)(i) fails on both counts. . . . Here, the government has offered no means of limiting the Secretary's authority under § 241(a)(4)(C)(i) by reference to the text, related statutes, legislative history, or common understandings. Neither can this court conceive of a way to judicially circumscribe the discretion afforded to the Secretary so as to impose a "recognized standard" upon the Secretary's otherwise "totally unrestricted freedom of choice." . . . More importantly, the Supreme Court's recent nondelegation jurisprudence has emphasized that the adequacy of the standards provided to a delegatee cannot be evaluated in a vacuum, but must be measured in light of the procedures and standards available to ensure meaningful judicial review. . . . In this way, the Court has brought the focus of the nondelegation doctrine back to its functional core – to safeguard the separation of powers by ensuring that the members of Congress, as the elected lawmaking representatives of the people, remain directly accountable both to their constituents and to the Constitution through the process of judicial review. . . .

With § 241(a)(4)(C)(i), Congress has delegated discretionary authority to the executive that not only is virtually standardless, but is utterly unreviewable by Article I and Article III courts alike. As discussed in Sections A and B, above, the statute completely deprives plaintiff of a meaningful opportunity to be heard and to rebut the allegations of deportability against him. The other side of that same coin, then, is that the judiciary will be prevented from performing its duty to meaningfully review the Secretary's exercise of his discretion . . . . Section 241(a)(4)(C)(i) . . provides no standards or procedures to allow for judicial review of an agency's discretionary deprivation of an alien's liberty. Accordingly, this court concludes that by leaving deportability determinations to the wholly unguided and unreviewable discretion of the Secretary of State, § 241(a)(4)(C)(i) represents an unconstitutional delegation of legislative power by which Congress eliminated the judiciary's constitutionally required function of review while abdicating its lawmaking responsibilities in favor of standardless executive discretion.

For the reasons stated above, this court now finds that § 241(a)(4)(C)(i) of the INA is unconstitutional. Accordingly, the deportation proceedings instituted against plaintiff, pursuant thereto, will be permanently enjoined.

NOTES AND QUESTIONS

(1) The district court's decision in *Ruiz Massieu* was reversed on appeal on the ground that the plaintiff had failed to exhaust his administrative remedies. *See Massieu v. Reno*, 91 F.3d 416 (3d Cir. 1996), *cert. denied*, 527 U.S. 1023 (1999). On May 30, 1997, an immigration judge ruled that Ruiz Massieu was not deportable because the government had produced insufficient evidence to show that his presence in the United States would have potentially serious adverse foreign policy consequences. The INS appealed to the Board of Immigration Appeals. In a 12-2 decision, the board found that the Secretary of State's determination was conclusive and vacated the immigration judge's ruling. *See*

In re Ruiz-Massieu, Interim Decision No. 3400 (B.I.A, June 10, 1999). In August 1999, Ruiz Massieu was indicted by a federal grand jury in Houston; the indictment charged that the $9 million he had deposited in Texas banks represented payoffs from narcotics traffickers. On September 15, 1999, two days before he was to appear in Houston for arraignment, Ruiz Massieu committed suicide, by taking an overdose of antidepressants, at the Palisades Park, New Jersey, apartment where he had been living under house arrest for four years. *See* N.Y. TIMES, Sept. 16, 1999, at A3.

(2) One of the plaintiff's claims in *Ruiz Massieu* was that it is impermissible to use deportation to circumvent the safeguards provided by the law of extradition. The district court did not pass on this claim, since it found the statutory basis for deportation to be unconstitutional. Suppose deportation had been based on a section of the Immigration and Nationality Act whose constitutionality was not in doubt. Would the fact that it was being used to bypass extradition procedures be a valid reason for enjoining deportation? Consider the following statement by the Board of Immigration Appeals in its Interim Decision in the *Ruiz Massieu* case:

> The respondent argues that the Attorney General should not be allowed to deport him, having failed in her attempt to comply with the Mexican government's attempt to extradite him to Mexico. Extradition proceedings are separate and apart from any immigration proceeding. The standards of proof are different. As the Service has pointed out, not all of the charges brought in Mexico were cited as a basis for extradition. Also, the existence of criminal charges is not the only possible basis for a determination that the respondent's presence may have adverse foreign policy consequences. We note that other aliens have been deported after extradition requests were denied by the courts. In *Matter of McMullen*, 17 I. & N. Dec. 542 (B.I.A. 1980), the government petition for extradition was denied. The respondent was, nevertheless, found deportable. The board stated:
>
>> Decisions resulting from extradition proceedings are not entitled to res judicata effect in later proceedings. Moreover, the res judicata bar goes into effect only where a valid, final judgment has been rendered on the merits, and it is well established that decisions and orders regarding extraditability "embody no judgment on the guilt or innocence of the accused. . . . " The issues involved in a deportation hearing differ from those involved in an extradition case, and resolution of even a common issue in one proceeding is not binding in the other.

In *Matter of Doherty*, 599 F.Supp. 270 (S.D.N.Y. 1984), the respondent was not extradited because the judge, sitting as a magistrate, found that the crimes he committed were political; nevertheless, Doherty was found deportable based on his own concession of deportability. The Attorney General rejected his designation of a country of deportation under section 243(a) of the Act as prejudicial to the interests of the United States. The United States Court of Appeals for the Second Circuit found that section 243(a) gives the Attorney General broad discretion to determine what constitutes prejudice to national interests. *Doherty v. United States Dep't of Justice,* 908 F.2d 1108 (2d Cir. 1990), *rev'd on other grounds, INS v. Doherty,* 502 U.S. 314 (1992).

(3) According to the *Report of the Committee on Extradition and Human Rights, in* INTERNATIONAL LAW ASSOCIATION, REPORT OF THE SIXTY-SIXTH CONFERENCE 142, 164 (1994):

[T]here is no rule which prohibits a state from deporting a suspected criminal to another state, particularly his state of nationality, to stand trial there. This practice is widely condemned as it deprives the deportee of the rights to which he would be entitled if he were extradited. In particular it deprives him of the right to raise the political offence exception. Despite such objections the practice occurs in many countries.

The cases in which the use of deportation to bypass extradition procedures has been judicially condemned typically have involved some kind of further misconduct on the part of the authorities either of the forum state or of the state from which the fugitive was deported or both. In *Regina v. Horseferry Road Magistrates' Court, Ex parte Bennett,* [1994] 1 App. Cas. 42 (H.L.), the House of Lords held that if, as alleged, the South African and British police had colluded in using deportation as a substitute for extradition, a British court should, in the exercise of its supervisory power, stay the prosecution and order the release of the accused. This holding is limited, however, to cases in which there has been collusion in the decision to deport, and possibly requires some additional illegality, abuse of power, violation of international law, or the domestic law of the foreign state involved. *See Regina v. Staines Magistrates' Court, Ex parte Westfallen,* [1998] 4 All E. R. 210, [1998] 1 W.L.R. 652 (Q.B.). In *Bozano v. France,* Eur. Ct. Hum. Rts. (Dec. 18, 1986), where the French courts had refused to extradite a fugitive to Italy, and the French police deported him to Switzerland, which in turn extradited him to Italy, the European Court of Human Rights found a violation of the right to personal liberty guaranteed by Article 5(1) of the European Convention on Human Rights. But, again, the decision turned on the conclusion that the French police probably had violated French law and, in any event, had acted in an arbitrary manner which went beyond what is usual in cases of deportation. The question of whether Italy could conceivably be obligated to reopen the prosecution was not before the court.

§ 14.02 Abduction

UNITED STATES v. ALVAREZ-MACHAIN

Supreme Court of the United States
504 U.S. 655, 112 S. Ct. 2188, 119 L. Ed. 2d 441 (1992)

CHIEF JUSTICE REHNQUIST delivered the opinion of the Court:

The issue in this case is whether a criminal defendant, abducted to the United States from a nation with which it has an extradition treaty, thereby acquires a defense to the jurisdiction of this country's courts. We hold that he does not, and that he may be tried in federal district court for violations of the criminal law of the United States.

Respondent, Humberto Alvarez-Machain, is a citizen and resident of Mexico. He was indicted for participating in the kidnap and murder of United States Drug Enforcement Administration (DEA) special agent Enrique Camarena-Salazar and a Mexican pilot working with Camarena, Alfredo Zavala-Avelar. The DEA believes that respondent, a medical doctor, participated in the murder by prolonging Agent Camarena's life so that others could further torture and interrogate him. On April 2, 1990, respondent was forcibly kidnaped from his medical office in Guadalajara, Mexico, to be flown by private plane to El Paso, Texas, where he was arrested by DEA officials. The District Court concluded that DEA agents were responsible for respondent's abduction, although they were not personally involved in it. . . .

Respondent moved to dismiss the indictment, claiming that his abduction constituted outrageous governmental conduct, and that the District Court lacked jurisdiction to try him because he was abducted in violation of the extradition treaty between the United States and Mexico. Extradition Treaty, May 4, 1978, [1979] United States-United Mexican States, 31 U.S.T. 5059, T.I.A.S. No. 9656 (Extradition Treaty or Treaty). The District Court rejected the outrageous governmental conduct claim, but held that it lacked jurisdiction to try respondent because his abduction violated the Extradition Treaty. . . . The Court of Appeals affirmed the dismissal of the indictment and the repatriation of respondent. . . . We granted certiorari, . . . and now reverse.

Although we have never before addressed the precise issue raised in the present case, we have previously considered proceedings in claimed violation of an extradition treaty and proceedings against a defendant brought before a court by means of a forcible abduction. We addressed the former issue in *United States v. Rauscher,* 119 U.S. 407, 30 L. Ed. 425, 7 S. Ct. 234 (1886); more precisely, the issue whether the Webster-Ashburton Treaty of 1842, 8 Stat. 576, which governed extraditions between England and the United States, prohibited the prosecution of defendant Rauscher for a crime other than the crime for which he had been extradited. Whether this prohibition, known as the doctrine of specialty, was an intended part of the treaty had been disputed between the two nations for some time. . . . Justice Miller delivered the opinion of the Court, which carefully examined the terms and history of the treaty; the practice of nations in regards to extradition treaties; the case law from the States; and the writings of commentators, and reached the following conclusion:

> "[A] person who has been brought within the jurisdiction of the court *by virtue of proceedings under an extradition treaty*, can only be tried for one of the offences described in that treaty, and for the offence with which he is charged in the proceedings for his extradition, until a reasonable time and opportunity have been given him, after his release or trial upon such charge, to return to the country from whose asylum he had been forcibly taken under those proceedings." . . . (emphasis added).

In addition, Justice Miller's opinion noted that any doubt as to this interpretation was put to rest by two federal statutes which imposed the doctrine of specialty upon extradition treaties to which the United States was a party. . . . Unlike the case before us today, the defendant in *Rauscher* had been brought to the United States by way of an extradition treaty; there was no issue of a forcible abduction.

In *Ker v. Illinois,* 119 U.S. 436, 30 L. Ed. 421, 7 S. Ct. 225 (1886), also written by Justice Miller and decided the same day as *Rauscher*, we addressed the issue of a defendant brought before the court by way of a forcible abduction. Frederick Ker had been tried and convicted in an Illinois court for larceny; his presence before the court was procured by means of forcible abduction from Peru. A messenger was sent to Lima with the proper warrant to demand Ker by virtue of the extradition treaty between Peru and the United States. The messenger, however, disdained reliance on the treaty processes, and instead forcibly kidnaped Ker and brought him to the United States. We distinguished Ker's case from *Rauscher*, on the basis that Ker was not brought into the United States by virtue of the extradition treaty between the United States and Peru, and rejected Ker's argument that he had a right under the extradition treaty to be returned to this country only in accordance with its terms. We rejected Ker's due process argument more broadly, holding in line with "the highest authorities" that "such forcible abduction is no sufficient reason why the party should not answer when brought within the jurisdiction of the court which has the right to try him for such an offence, and presents no valid objection to his trial in such court." . . .

In *Frisbie v. Collins,* 342 U.S. 519, 96 L. Ed. 541, 72 S. Ct. 509, *rehearing denied,* 343 U.S. 937, 96 L. Ed. 1344, 72 S. Ct. 768 (1952), we applied the rule in *Ker* to a case in which the defendant had been kidnaped in Chicago by Michigan officers and brought to trial in Michigan. We upheld the conviction over objections based on the Due Process Clause and the federal Kidnaping Act and stated:

> "This Court has never departed from the rule announced in *[Ker]* that the power of a court to try a person for crime is not impaired by the fact that he had been brought within the court's jurisdiction by reason of a 'forcible abduction.' No persuasive reasons are now presented to justify overruling this line of cases. They rest on the sound basis that due process of law is satisfied when one present in court is convicted of crime after having been fairly apprized of the charges against him and after a fair trial in accordance with constitutional procedural safeguards. There is nothing in the Constitution that requires a court to permit a guilty person rightfully convicted to escape justice because he was brought to trial against his will." . . .

The only differences between *Ker* and the present case are that *Ker* was decided on the premise that there was no governmental involvement in the abduction, ... and Peru, from which Ker was abducted, did not object to his prosecution. . . . Respondent finds these differences to be dispositive, ... contending that they show that respondent's prosecution, like the prosecution of *Rauscher,* violates the implied terms of a valid extradition treaty. The Government, on the other hand, argues that *Rauscher* stands as an "exception" to the rule in *Ker* only when an extradition treaty is invoked, and the terms of the treaty provide that its breach will limit the jurisdiction of a court. Therefore, our first inquiry must be whether the abduction of respondent from Mexico violated the Extradition Treaty between the United States and Mexico. If we conclude that the Treaty does not prohibit respondent's abduction, the rule in *Ker* applies, and the court need not inquire as to how respondent came before it.

In construing a treaty, as in construing a statute, we first look to its terms to determine its meaning. . . . The Treaty says nothing about the obligations of the United States and Mexico to refrain from forcible abductions of people from the territory of the other nation, or the consequences under the Treaty if such an abduction occurs. . . . According to respondent, Article 9 embodies the terms of the bargain which the United States struck: If the United States wishes to prosecute a Mexican national, it may request that individual's extradition. Upon a request from the United States, Mexico may either extradite the individual or submit the case to the proper authorities for prosecution in Mexico. In this way, respondent reasons, each nation preserved its right to choose whether its nationals would be tried in its own courts or by the courts of the other nation. This preservation of rights would be frustrated if either nation were free to abduct nationals of the other nation for the purposes of prosecution. More broadly, respondent reasons, as did the Court of Appeals, that all the processes and restrictions on the obligation to extradite established by the Treaty would make no sense if either nation were free to resort to forcible kidnaping to gain the presence of an individual for prosecution in a manner not contemplated by the Treaty. . . .

Article 9 does not purport to specify the only way in which one country may gain custody of a national of the other country for the purposes of prosecution. In the absence of an extradition treaty, nations are under no obligation to surrender those in their country to foreign authorities for prosecution. . . . Extradition treaties exist so as to impose mutual obligations to surrender individuals in certain defined sets of circumstances, following established procedures. . . . The Treaty thus provides a mechanism which would not otherwise exist, requiring, under certain circumstances, the United States and Mexico to extradite individuals to the other country, and establishing the procedures to be followed when the Treaty is invoked.

The history of negotiation and practice under the Treaty also fails to show that abductions outside of the Treaty constitute a violation of the Treaty. As the Solicitor General notes, the Mexican Government was made aware, as early as 1906, of the *Ker* doctrine, and the United States' position that it applied to forcible abductions made outside of the terms of the United States-Mexico Extradition Treaty. Nonetheless, the current version of the Treaty, signed in 1978, does not attempt to establish a rule that would in any way curtail the effect of *Ker*. Moreover, although language which would grant individuals exactly the right sought by respondent had been considered and drafted as early as 1935 by a prominent group of legal scholars sponsored by the faculty of Harvard Law School, no such clause appears in the current Treaty.

Thus, the language of the Treaty, in the context of its history, does not support the proposition that the Treaty prohibits abductions outside of its terms. The remaining question, therefore, is whether the Treaty should be interpreted so as to include an implied term prohibiting prosecution where the defendant's presence is obtained by means other than those established by the Treaty. . . .

Respondent contends that the Treaty must be interpreted against the backdrop of customary international law, and that international abductions are "so clearly prohibited in international law" that there was no reason to include such a clause in the Treaty itself. The international censure of international abductions is further evidenced, according to respondent, by the United Nations Charter and the Charter of the Organization of American States. Respondent does not argue that these sources of international law provide an independent basis for the right respondent asserts not to be tried in the United States, but rather that they should inform the interpretation of the Treaty terms.

The Court of Appeals deemed it essential, in order for the individual defendant to assert a right under the Treaty, that the affected foreign government had registered a protest. . . . Respondent agrees that the right exercised by the individual is derivative of the nation's right under the Treaty, since nations are authorized, notwithstanding the terms of an extradition treaty, to voluntarily render an individual to the other country on terms completely outside of those provided in the treaty. The formal protest, therefore, ensures that the "offended" nation actually objects to the abduction and has not in some way voluntarily rendered the individual for prosecution. Thus the Extradition Treaty only prohibits gaining the defendant's presence by means other than those set forth in the Treaty when the nation from which the defendant was abducted objects.

This argument seems to us inconsistent with the remainder of respondent's argument. The Extradition Treaty has the force of law, and if, as respondent asserts, it is self-executing, it would appear that a court must enforce it on behalf of an individual regardless of the offensiveness of the practice of one nation to the other nation. In *Rauscher*, the Court noted that Great Britain had taken the position in other cases that the Webster-Ashburton Treaty included the doctrine of specialty, but no importance was attached to whether or not Great Britain had protested the prosecution of Rauscher for the crime of cruel and unusual punishment as opposed to murder.

More fundamentally, the difficulty with the support respondent garners from international law is that none of it relates to the practice of nations in relation to extradition treaties. In *Rauscher*, we implied a term in the Webster-Ashburton Treaty because of the practice of nations with regard to extradition treaties. In the instant case, respondent would imply terms in the Extradition Treaty from the practice of nations with regards to international law more generally. Respondent would have us find that the Treaty acts as a prohibition against a violation of the general principle of international law that one government may not "exercise its police power in the territory of another state." . . . . There are many actions which could be taken by a nation that would violate this principle, including waging war, but it cannot seriously be contended that an invasion of the United States by Mexico would violate the terms of the Extradition Treaty between the two nations. . . .

Respondent and his *amici* may be correct that respondent's abduction was "shocking," . . . and that it may be in violation of general international law principles. Mexico has protested the abduction of respondent through diplomatic notes, ... and the decision of whether respondent should be returned to Mexico, as a matter outside of the Treaty, is a matter for the Executive Branch. We conclude, however, that respondent's abduction was not in violation of the Extradition Treaty between the United States and Mexico, and therefore the rule of *Ker* v. *Illinois* is fully applicable to this case. The fact of respondent's forcible abduction does not therefore prohibit his trial in a court in the United States for violations of the criminal laws of the United States. . . .

The judgment of the Court of Appeals is therefore reversed, and the case is remanded for further proceedings consistent with this opinion. . . .

JUSTICE STEVENS, with whom JUSTICE BLACKMUN and JUSTICE O'CONNOR join, dissenting.

The Court correctly observes that this case raises a question of first impression. . . . The case is unique for several reasons. It does not involve an ordinary abduction by a private kidnaper, or bounty hunter, as in *Ker* nor does it involve the apprehension of an American fugitive who committed a crime in one State and sought asylum in another, as in *Frisbie*. Rather, it involves this country's abduction of another country's citizen; it also involves a violation of the territorial integrity of that other country, with which this country has signed an extradition treaty.

A Mexican citizen was kidnaped in Mexico and charged with a crime committed in Mexico; his offense allegedly violated both Mexican and American law. Mexico has formally demanded on at least two separate occasions that he be returned to Mexico and has represented that he will be prosecuted and, if convicted, punished for his offense. It is clear that Mexico's demand must be honored if this official abduction violated the 1978 Extradition Treaty between the United States and Mexico. In my opinion, a fair reading of the treaty in light of our decision in *Rauscher* and applicable principles of international law, leads inexorably to the conclusion that the District Court, . . . and the Court of Appeals for the Ninth Circuit, ... correctly construed that instrument.

The extradition treaty with Mexico is a comprehensive document containing 23 articles and an appendix listing the extraditable offenses covered by the agreement. The parties announced their purpose in the preamble: The two governments desire "to cooperate more closely in the fight against crime and, to this end, to mutually render better assistance in matters of extradition." From the preamble, through the description of the parties' obligations with respect to offenses committed within as well as beyond the territory of a requesting party, the delineation of the procedures and evidentiary requirements for extradition, the special provisions for political offenses and capital punishment, and other details, the Treaty appears to have been designed to cover the entire subject of extradition. Thus, Article 22, entitled "Scope of Application," states that the "Treaty shall apply to offenses specified in Article 2 committed before and after this Treaty enters into force," and Article 2 directs that "extradition shall take place, subject to this Treaty, for willful acts which fall within any of [the extraditable offenses listed in] the clauses of the Appendix." Moreover, as noted by the Court, Article 9 expressly provides that neither contracting party is bound to deliver up its own nationals, although it may do so in its discretion, but if it does not do so, it "shall submit the case to its competent authorities for purposes of prosecution."

The Government's claim that the Treaty is not exclusive, but permits forcible governmental kidnaping, would transform these, and other, provisions into little more than verbiage. For example, provisions requiring "sufficient" evidence to grant extradition (Art. 3), withholding extradition for political or military offenses (Art. 5), withholding extradition when the person sought has already been tried (Art. 6), withholding extradition when the statute of limitations for the crime has lapsed (Art. 7), and granting the requested country discretion to refuse to extradite an individual who would face the death penalty in the requesting country (Art. 8), would serve little purpose if the requesting country could simply kidnap the person. As the Court of Appeals for the Ninth Circuit recognized in a related case, "each of these provisions would be utterly frustrated if a kidnapping were held to be a permissible course of governmental conduct." . . . In addition, all of these provisions "only make sense if they are understood as *requiring* each treaty signatory to comply with those procedures whenever it wishes to obtain jurisdiction over an individual who is located in another treaty nation." . . .

It is true, as the Court notes, that there is no express promise by either party to refrain from forcible abductions in the territory of the other nation. . . . Relying on that omission, the Court, in effect, concludes that the Treaty merely creates an optional method of obtaining jurisdiction over alleged offenders, and that the parties silently reserved the right to resort to self-help whenever they deem force more expeditious than legal process. If the United States, for example, thought it more expedient to torture or simply to execute a person rather than to attempt extradition, these options would be equally available because they, too, were not explicitly prohibited by the Treaty. That, however, is a highly improbable interpretation of a consensual agreement, which on its face appears to have been intended to set forth comprehensive and exclusive rules concerning the subject of extradition. In my opinion, "the manifest scope and object of the treaty itself," plainly imply a mutual undertaking to respect the territorial integrity of the other contracting party. That opinion is confirmed by a consideration of the "legal context" in which the Treaty was negotiated. . . .

In *Rauscher*, the Court construed an extradition treaty that was far less comprehensive than the 1978 Treaty with Mexico. . . . After Rauscher had been extradited for murder, he was charged with the lesser offense of inflicting cruel and unusual punishment on a member of the crew of a vessel on the high seas. Although the treaty did not purport to place any limit on the jurisdiction of the demanding state after acquiring custody of the fugitive, this Court held that he could not be tried for any offense other than murder. Thus, the treaty constituted the exclusive means by which the United States could obtain jurisdiction over a defendant within the territorial jurisdiction of Great Britain.

The Court noted that the treaty included several specific provisions, such as the crimes for which one could be extradited, the process by which the extradition was to be carried out, and even the evidence that was to be produced, and concluded that "the fair purpose of the treaty is, that the person shall be delivered up to be tried for that offence and for no other." . . . The Court reasoned that it did not make sense for the treaty to provide such specifics only to have the person "pas[s] into the hands of the country which charges him with the offence, free from all the positive requirements and just implications of the treaty under which the transfer of his person takes place." . . . . To interpret the treaty in a contrary way would mean that a country could request extradition of a person for one of the seven crimes covered by the treaty, and then try the person for another crime, such as a political crime, which was clearly not covered by the treaty; this result, the Court concluded, was clearly contrary to the intent of the parties and the purpose of the treaty. . . .

Thus, the Extradition Treaty, as understood in the context of cases that have addressed similar issues, suffices to protect the defendant from prosecution despite the absence of any express language in the Treaty itself purporting to limit this Nation's power to prosecute a defendant over whom it had lawfully acquired jurisdiction.

Although the Court's conclusion in *Rauscher* was supported by a number of judicial precedents, the holdings in these cases were not nearly as uniform as the consensus of international opinion that condemns one nation's violation of the territorial integrity of a friendly neighbor. It is shocking that a party to an extradition treaty might believe that it has secretly reserved the right to make seizures of citizens in the other party's territory. . . . Thus, a leading treatise explains:

"A State must not perform acts of sovereignty in the territory of another State. . . .

"It is . . . a breach of International Law for a State to send its agents to the territory of another State to apprehend persons accused of having committed a crime. Apart from other satisfaction, the first duty of the offending State is to hand over the person in question to the State in whose territory he was apprehended." 1 OPPENHEIM'S INTERNATIONAL LAW 295, and n.1 (H. Lauterpacht 8th ed. 1955).

Commenting on the precise issue raised by this case, the chief reporter for the American Law Institute's Restatement of Foreign Relations used language reminiscent of Justice Story's characterization of an official seizure in a foreign jurisdiction as "monstrous":

"When done without consent of the foreign government, abducting a person from a foreign country is a gross violation of international law and gross disrespect for a norm high in the opinion of mankind. It is a blatant violation of the territorial integrity of another state; it eviscerates the extradition system (established by a comprehensive network of treaties involving virtually all states)."

In the *Rauscher* case, the legal background that supported the decision to imply a covenant not to prosecute for an offense different from that for which extradition had been granted was far less clear than the rule against invading the territorial integrity of a treaty partner that supports Mexico's position in this case. If *Rauscher* was correctly decided – and I am convinced that it was – its rationale clearly dictates a comparable result in this case. . . .

A critical flaw pervades the Court's entire opinion. It fails to differentiate between the conduct of private citizens, which does not violate any treaty obligation, and conduct expressly authorized by the Executive Branch of the Government, which unquestionably constitutes a flagrant violation of international law, and in my opinion, also constitutes a breach of our treaty obligations. Thus, at the outset of its opinion, the Court states the issue as "whether a criminal defendant, abducted to the United States from a nation with which it has an extradition treaty, thereby acquires a defense to the jurisdiction of this country's courts." . . . That, of course, is the question decided in *Ker* it is not, however, the question presented for decision today.

The importance of the distinction between a court's exercise of jurisdiction over either a person or property that has been wrongfully seized by a private citizen, or even by a state law enforcement agent, on the one hand, and the attempted exercise of jurisdiction predicated on a seizure by federal officers acting beyond the authority conferred by treaty, on the other hand, is explained by Justice Brandeis in his opinion for the Court in *Cook v. United States,* 288 U.S. 102, 77 L. Ed. 641, 53 S. Ct. 305 (1933). That case involved a construction of a Prohibition Era treaty with Great Britain that authorized American agents to board certain British vessels to ascertain whether they were engaged in importing alcoholic beverages. A British vessel was boarded 11 1/2 miles off the coast of Massachusetts, found to be carrying unmanifested alcoholic beverages, and taken into port. The Collector of Customs assessed a penalty which he attempted to collect by means of libels against both the cargo and the seized vessel.

The Court held that the seizure was not authorized by the treaty because it occurred more than 10 miles off shore. The Government argued that the illegality of the seizure was immaterial because, as in *Ker*, the court's jurisdiction was supported by possession even if the seizure was wrongful. Justice Brandeis acknowledged that the argument would succeed if the seizure had been made by a private party without authority to act for the Government, but that a different rule prevails when the Government itself lacks the power to seize. . . .

The Court's failure to differentiate between private abductions and official invasions of another sovereign's territory also accounts for its misplaced reliance on the 1935 proposal made by the Advisory Committee on Research in International Law. . . . As the text of that proposal plainly states, it would have rejected the rule of the *Ker* case. The failure to adopt that recommendation does not speak to the issue the Court decides today. The Court's admittedly "shocking" disdain for customary and conventional international law principles,. . . . is thus entirely unsupported by case law and commentary. . . .

As the Court observes at the outset of its opinion, there is reason to believe that respondent participated in an especially brutal murder of an American law enforcement agent. That fact, if true, may explain the Executive's intense interest in punishing respondent in our courts. Such an explanation, however, provides no justification for disregarding the Rule of Law that this Court has a duty to uphold. That the Executive may wish to reinterpret the Treaty to allow for an action that the Treaty in no way authorizes should not influence this Court's interpretation. Indeed, the desire for revenge exerts "a kind of hydraulic pressure . . . before which even well settled principles of law will bend," . . . . but it is precisely at such moments that we should remember and be guided by our duty "to render judgment evenly and dispassionately according to law, as each is given understanding to ascertain and apply it." . . . The way that we perform that duty in a case of this kind sets an example that other tribunals in other countries are sure to emulate.

The significance of this Court's precedents is illustrated by a recent decision of the Court of Appeal of the Republic of South Africa. Based largely on its understanding of the import of this Court's cases – including our decision in *Ker* – that court held that the prosecution of a defendant kidnaped by agents of South Africa in another country must be dismissed. . . . The Court of Appeal of South Africa – indeed, I suspect most courts throughout the civilized world – will be deeply disturbed by the "monstrous" decision the Court announces today. For every nation that has an interest in preserving the Rule of Law is affected, directly or indirectly, by a decision of this character. As Thomas Paine warned, an "avidity to punish is always dangerous to liberty" because it leads a nation "to stretch, to misinterpret, and to misapply even the best of laws." To counter that tendency, he reminds us:

> "He that would make his own liberty secure must guard even his enemy from oppression; for if he violates this duty he establishes a precedent that will reach to himself."

I respectfully dissent.

NOTES AND QUESTIONS

(1) In December 1992, Alverez-Machain was tried and acquitted of the murder. He returned to Mexico. On July 9, 1993, he filed a civil action, under 42 U.S.C. § 1983 and various other federal statutes, against both the U.S. agents and two Mexican nationals who participated in his abduction. The complaint was amended in January 1994 to include a claim against the U.S. government in lieu of its individual agents. The district court dismissed plaintiff's constitutional claims arising out of harms suffered in Mexico (as opposed to harms suffered while being detained in the United States), denied for the most part the government's motions to dismiss based on the statute of limitations and on qualified immunity, and denied motions to dismiss by the Mexican defendants. On interlocutory appeal, the Ninth Circuit upheld most of the trial court's rulings, but reversed its decision that the Torture Victim Protection Act of 1992 did not apply to events taking place before it was enacted. *See Alvarez Machain v. United States*, 107 F.3d 696 (9th Cir.), *cert. denied*, 522 U.S. 814 (1997).

On March 18, 1999, the district court granted summary judgment for the United States on the ground that the actions taken by its agents were privileged, since a warrant had been issued for the plaintiff's arrest. But it granted summary judgment against one of the Mexican defendants, Sosa, on the ground that state-sponsored transborder kidnapping is a violation of international law redressible under the Alien Tort Claims Act. A bench trial on damages was held on May 19, 1999. The trial court entered a judgment of $25,000, discounting the plaintiff's claims of ill-treatment in Mexico and excluding from consideration harms suffered once the plaintiff was arrested by federal agents in the United States. The case is on appeal, by both sides, to the Ninth Circuit. *See* <http:// www.aclu-sc.org/litigation/international.htm>.

(2) In *United States v. Matta-Ballesteros*, 71 F.3d 754 (9th Cir. 1995) *amended* 98 F.3d 1100 (9th Cir. 1996), the court found jurisdiction over the defendant despite the fact that he was abducted from Honduras and taken to the United States for trial. The court found that "[t]he treaties between the United States and Honduras contain preservations of rights similar to those which *Alvarez-Machain* held did not sufficiently specify extradition as the only way in which one country may gain custody of a foreign national for purposes of prosecution." In ruling on Matta-Ballesteros' argument that the circumstances of his abduction warranted dismissal, the court stated:

> The Supreme Court has long held that the manner by which a defendant is brought to trial does not affect the government's ability to try him. . . . Though we may be deeply concerned by the actions of our government, it is clear in light of recent Supreme Court precedent that the circumstances surrounding Matta-Ballesteros's abduction do not divest this court of jurisdiction in this case. . . . In the shadow cast by *Alvarez-Machain,* attempts to expand due process rights into the realm of foreign abductions, as the Second Circuit did

in *United States v. Toscanino,* 500 F.2d 267 (2d Cir. 1974), have been cut short.

In *Toscanino,* the defendant alleged that United States agents abducted him from Uruguay, pistol-whipped, bound, blindfolded, brutally tortured, and interrogated him for seventeen days, and finally drugged and brought him to the United States by airplane, all with the knowledge of an Assistant United States Attorney. . . . That court held that if Toscanino's allegations were true, his indictment was subject to dismissal based on the federal court's supervisory powers over the administration of criminal justice first outlined by the Supreme Court in *McNabb v. United States,* 318 U.S. 332, 340-41, 87 L. Ed. 819, 63 S. Ct. 608 (1943). In holding that the supervisory powers of the court could require dismissal, *Toscanino* relied in part on Supreme Court decisions addressing other types of outrageous governmental conduct, ...

This court has held, however, that we have inherent supervisory powers to order dismissal of prosecutions for only three legitimate reasons: (1) to implement a remedy for the violation of a recognized statutory or constitutional right; (2) to preserve judicial integrity by ensuring that a conviction rests on appropriate considerations validly before a jury; and (3) to deter future illegal conduct. . . .

The circumstances surrounding Matta-Ballesteros's abduction, while disturbing to us and conduct we seek in no way to condone, meet none of these criteria. It is particularly troublesome to us that the alleged acts were conducted by United States Marshals, officials who purportedly act in our best interest. . . . While it may seem unconscionable to some that officials serving the interests of justice themselves become agents of criminal intimidation, like the DEA agents in *Alvarez-Machain,* their purported actions have violated no recognized constitutional or statutory rights. They have likewise engaged in no illegal conduct which this court could attempt to deter in the future by invoking its supervisory powers.

The *only* way we could exercise our supervisory powers in this particular case is if the defendant could demonstrate governmental misconduct "of the most shocking and outrageous kind," so as to warrant dismissal. . . . Matta-Ballesteros has not. His alleged treatment, even if taken as true, does not meet this rigorous standard, and the acts alleged were not nearly as egregious as those committed in *Toscanino.*

The district court conducted a limited evidentiary hearing, concluding that Matta-Ballesteros failed to make " 'a strong showing of grossly cruel and unusual barbarities inflicted upon him by persons who can be characterized as paid agents of the United States.' . . .

Defendant's allegations of mistreatment, even if taken as true, do not constitute such barbarism as to warrant dismissal of the indictment under the caselaw." . . .

During the evidentiary hearing, the court heard testimony from Matta-Ballesteros about the purported torture, and he submitted pictures taken upon his arrival at the federal prison as well as a report on stun guns and the declarations of several eyewitnesses who declared he was shocked with the stun guns. The court also considered testimony or declarations from a psychologist and two physicians who examined Matta-Ballesteros, Dr. Donald Valles and Dr. John Van der Decker, who indicated that the cause of his injuries was inconclusive. Additionally, the court considered the declarations and testimony of Juan Morales and Roberto Escobar, United States Marshals who were present at Matta-Ballesteros's capture in Honduras, and who transported him from the Dominican Republic to Marion. They contradicted his testimony, and alleged that he was not tortured and that no stun gun was used on him.

While we may have a suspicion of Matta-Ballesteros's inhumane treatment, and the evidence reasonably could support a finding that he was tortured, it could also support the conclusion of the district court. Because the district court's account of the evidence is plausible in light of the record viewed in its entirety, we may not reverse it even though we may be convinced that, sitting as the trier of fact, we would have weighed the evidence differently. . . . We are therefore bound by the district court's findings, and hold that its determination regarding the alleged torture was not clearly erroneous.

Thus, much as we may want to dismiss this case through an exercise of our supervisory powers, to do so would be unwarranted. The district court did not abuse its discretion in refusing to exercise such powers.

(3) What exactly is the argument in favor of dismissing the charges against a defendant who has been brought within a court's jurisdiction through the use of unlawful force? Is it a matter of a court's supervisory power over law enforcement authorities? Is it a matter of the court keeping its hands clean by refusing to become an accomplice to illegal activities? Is it a matter of vindicating the basic rights of the accused, or of finding an appropriate remedy for a violation of international law involving a breach of the territorial sovereignty of another country? Consider the somewhat similar debate with respect to different possible bases for the rule excluding evidence obtained through an illegal search and seizure in violation of the Fourth Amendment. How would a rule requiring courts to decline jurisdiction in cases of kidnapping differ in its precise application depending on which of the several possible arguments in support of such a rule were adopted?

UNITED STATES v. NORIEGA

United States Court of Appeals for the Eleventh Circuit
117 F.3d 1206 (1997)

KRAVITCH, SENIOR CIRCUIT JUDGE:

Manuel Antonio Noriega appeals: (1) his multiple convictions stemming from his involvement in cocaine trafficking; and (2) the district court's denial of his motion for a new trial based on newly discovered evidence. In attacking his convictions, Noriega asserts that the district court should have dismissed the indictment against him due to his status as a head of state and the manner in which the United States brought him to justice. Noriega also contends that the district court committed two reversible evidentiary errors. Alternatively, he seeks a new trial based on his discovery of: (1) the government's suppression of its pact with a non-witness; and/or (2) certain allegations, lodged after his conviction, that a group associated with the undisclosed, cooperating non-witness bribed a prosecution witness. We affirm Noriega's convictions and the district court's order denying his new trial motion.

. . . . On February 4, 1988, a federal grand jury for the Southern District of Florida indicted Manuel Antonio Noriega on drug-related charges. At that time, Noriega served as commander of the Panamanian Defense Forces in the Republic of Panama. Shortly thereafter, Panama's president, Eric Arturo Delvalle, formally discharged Noriega from his military post, but Noriega refused to accept the dismissal. Panama's legislature then ousted Delvalle from power. The United States, however, continued to acknowledge Delvalle as the constitutional leader of Panama. Later, after a disputed presidential election in Panama, the United States recognized Guillermo Endara as Panama's legitimate head of state.

On December 15, 1989, Noriega publicly declared that a state of war existed between Panama and the United States. Within days of this announcement by Noriega, President George Bush directed United States armed forces into combat in Panama for the stated purposes of "safeguarding American lives, restoring democracy, preserving the Panama Canal treaties, and seizing Noriega to face federal drug charges in the United States." *United States v. Noriega,* 746 F. Supp. 1506, 1511 (S.D. Fla. 1990). The ensuing military conflagration resulted in significant casualties and property loss among Panamanian civilians. Noriega lost his effective control over Panama during this armed conflict, and he surrendered to United States military officials on January 3, 1990. Noriega then was brought to Miami to face the pending federal charges.

Following extensive pre-trial proceedings and a lengthy trial, a jury found Noriega guilty of eight counts in the indictment and not guilty of the remaining two counts. The district court entered judgments of conviction against Noriega upon the jury's verdict and sentenced him to consecutive imprisonment terms of 20, 15 and five years, respectively. . . . .

At trial, the government presented the testimony of numerous witnesses as well as documentary evidence to prove Noriega's guilt. Noriega, through both cross-examination and defense witness testimony, fervently contested the veracity of the witnesses and the significance of the documents offered by the government. Under the defense theory of the case, Noriega's subordinates used his name in their drug-trafficking schemes, but Noriega had no personal connection to the alleged offenses. . . . .

From the early 1970s to 1989, Noriega secured progressively greater dominion over state military and civilian institutions in Panama, first as his nation's chief of military intelligence and later as commander of the Panamanian Defense Forces. In the early 1980s, Noriega's position of authority brought him into contact with a group of drug traffickers from the Medellin area of Colombia (the "Medellin Cartel"). Various Medellin Cartel operatives met with Noriega's associates and, later, with Noriega personally, regarding the Medellin Cartel's desire to ship cocaine through Panama to the United States. Eventually, Noriega and the Medellin Cartel reached the first of a series of illicit agreements. Thereafter, from 1982 through 1985, with Noriega's assistance, the Medellin Cartel transported significant quantities of cocaine through Panama to the United States. It also utilized its relationship with Noriega to move ether for cocaine processing and substantial cash proceeds from drug sales from the United States to or through Panama.

Noriega and his associates personally met with Medellin Cartel leaders in Colombia, Panama and Cuba regarding the transhipping arrangement, unofficial asylum for Medellin Cartel members fleeing prosecution and a botched plan to operate a cocaine processing laboratory in the Darien region of Panama. The Medellin Cartel directed large cash payments to Noriega in connection with its drug, ether and cash shipments through Panama. During this period, Noriega opened secret accounts in his name and the names of his family members with the Bank of Credit and Commerce International ("BCCI") in Panama. Noriega's associates made large, unexplained cash deposits into these accounts for him. In 1988, Noriega transferred approximately $ 20,000,000 of his amassed fortune to banks in Europe. The government ultimately located more than $ 23,000,000 of funds traceable to Noriega in financial institutions outside of Panama.

Noriega challenges his convictions on five distinct grounds: the first three relate to the district court's decision to exercise jurisdiction over this case and the final two concern evidentiary rulings by the district court. . . . . .

Noriega first argues that the district court should have dismissed the indictment against him based on head-of-state immunity. He insists that he was entitled to such immunity because he served as the de facto, if not the de jure, leader of Panama. The district court rejected Noriega's head-of-state immunity claim because the United States government never recognized Noriega as Panama's legitimate, constitutional ruler.

The Supreme Court long ago held that "the jurisdiction of courts is a branch of that which is possessed by the nation as an independent sovereign power. The jurisdiction of the nation within its own territory is necessarily exclusive and absolute. It is susceptible of no limitation not imposed by itself." *The Schooner Exchange v. M'Faddon,* 11 U.S. (7 Cranch) 116, 136, 3 L. Ed. 287 (1812). The Court, however, ruled that nations, including the United States, had agreed implicitly to accept certain limitations on their individual territorial jurisdiction based on the "common interest impelling [sovereign nations] to mutual intercourse, and an interchange of good offices with each other . . . ." *Id.* at 137. Chief among the exceptions to jurisdiction was "the exemption of the person of the sovereign from arrest or detention within a foreign territory." . . .

The principles of international comity outlined by the Court in *The Schooner Exchange* led to the development of a general doctrine of foreign sovereign immunity which courts applied most often to protect foreign nations in their corporate form from civil process in the United States. . . . To enforce this foreign sovereign immunity, nations concerned about their exposure to judicial proceedings in the United States:

> followed the accepted course of procedure [and] by appropriate representations, sought recognition by the State Department of [their] claim of immunity, and asked that the [State] Department advise the Attorney General of the claim of immunity and that the Attorney General instruct the United States Attorney for the [relevant district] to file in the district court the appropriate suggestion of immunity . . . .

Ex Parte Republic of Peru, 318 U.S. 578, 581, 87 L. Ed. 1014, 63 S. Ct. 793 (1943) (citations omitted). As this doctrine emerged, the "Court consistently [] deferred to the decisions of the political branches – in particular, those of the Executive Branch – on whether to take jurisdiction over actions against foreign sovereigns and their instrumentalities." . . .

In 1976, Congress passed the Foreign Sovereign Immunities Act ("FSIA"), 28 U.S.C. §§ 1602-1611. The FSIA "contains a comprehensive set of legal standards governing claims of immunity in every civil action against a foreign state or its political subdivisions, agencies, or instrumentalities." . . . It codified the State Department's general criteria for making suggestions of immunity, and transferred the responsibility for case-by-case application of these principles from the Executive Branch to the Judicial Branch. . . . Because the FSIA addresses neither head-of-state immunity, nor foreign sovereign immunity in the criminal context, head-of-state immunity could attach in cases, such as this one, only pursuant to the principles and procedures outlined in *The Schooner Exchange* and its progeny. As a result, this court must look to the Executive Branch for direction on the propriety of Noriega's immunity claim. . . .

Generally, the Executive Branch's position on head-of-state immunity falls into one of three categories: the Executive Branch (1) explicitly suggests immunity; (2) expressly declines to suggest immunity; or (3) offers no guidance. Some courts have held that absent a formal suggestion of immunity, a putative head of state should receive no immunity. . . . In the analogous pre-FSIA, foreign sovereign immunity context, the former Fifth Circuit accepted a slightly broader judicial role. It ruled that, where the Executive Branch either expressly grants or denies a request to suggest immunity, courts must follow that direction, but that courts should make an independent determination regarding immunity when the Executive Branch neglects to convey clearly its position on a particular immunity request. . . .

. . . . The Executive Branch has not merely refrained from taking a position on this matter; to the contrary, by pursuing Noriega's capture and this prosecution, the Executive Branch has manifested its clear sentiment that Noriega should be denied head-of-state immunity. Noriega has cited no authority that would empower a court to grant head-of-state immunity under these circumstances. Moreover, given that the record indicates that Noriega never served as the constitutional leader of Panama, that Panama has not sought immunity for Noriega and that the charged acts relate to Noriega's private pursuit of personal enrichment, Noriega likely would not prevail even if this court had to make an independent determination regarding the propriety of immunity in this case. . . . Accordingly, we find no error by the district court on this point.

Noriega next contends his conviction should be reversed because he alleges he was brought to the United States in violation of the Treaty Providing for the Extradition of Criminals, May 25, 1904, United States of America-Republic of Panama, 34 Stat. 2851 ("U.S.-Panama Extradition Treaty"). The Supreme Court's decision in *United States v. Alvarez-Machain* [*supra*], forecloses this argument. In *Alvarez-Machain*, the Court considered the issue of "whether a criminal defendant, abducted to the United States from a nation with which it has an extradition treaty, thereby acquires a defense to the jurisdiction of this country's courts." . . . In answer, the Court stated: "We hold that he does not, and that he may be tried in federal district court for violations of the criminal law of the United States." . . .

In reaching this decision, the Court considered whether the treaty at issue expressly barred abductions. It determined that the treaty's provision that "'neither Contracting Party shall be bound to deliver up its own nationals . . .' [fails] to specify the only way in which one country may gain custody of a national of the other country for purposes of prosecution." . . . The Court also rejected the argument that, by entering into an extradition treaty with Mexico, the United States impliedly agreed to seek custody of persons in Mexico only via extradition. . . .

The article of the U.S.- Panama Extradition Treaty upon which Noriega relies for his extradition treaty claim contains almost the same language as the provision of the U.S.- Mexico Extradition Treaty at issue in *Alvarez-Machain*. . . . Noriega contends that Alvarez-Machain is distinguishable despite the near identity of the relevant clauses because, at the time the United States entered into the U.S.-Panama Extradition Treaty, it knew or should have known that Panama's constitution prohibited the extradition of its nationals. This bald assertion, even if accepted, does not save Noriega's claim. A clause in Panama's constitution regarding the extradition of Panamanians, at most, informs the United States of the hurdles it will face when pursuing such extraditions in Panama; such a provision says nothing about the treaty signatories' rights to opt for self-help (i.e., abduction) over legal process (i.e., extradition).

Under *Alvarez-Machain*, to prevail on an extradition treaty claim, a defendant must demonstrate, by reference to the express language of a treaty and/or the established practice thereunder, that the United States affirmatively agreed not to seize foreign nationals from the territory of its treaty partner. Noriega has not carried this burden, and therefore, his claim fails. . . .

In his pre-trial motion, Noriega also sought the dismissal of the indictment against him on the ground that the manner in which he was brought before the district court (i.e., through a military invasion) was so unconscionable as to constitute a violation of substantive due process. Noriega also argued that to the extent the government's actions did not shock the judicial conscience sufficiently to trigger due process sanctions, the district court should exercise its supervisory power to decline jurisdiction. The district court rejected Noriega's due process argument, and it declared Noriega's alternative supervisory power rationale non-justiciable. On appeal, Noriega offers no substantive argument regarding the due process prong of this claim, but rather discusses only his alternative supervisory power theory. Because, however, the due process and supervisory power issues are intertwined, we discuss them both.

Noriega's due process claim "falls squarely within the [Supreme Court's] *Ker-Frisbie* doctrine, which holds that a defendant cannot defeat personal jurisdiction by asserting the illegality of the procurement of his presence." . . . Noriega has not alleged that the government mistreated him personally, and thus, he cannot come within the purview of the caveat to *Ker-Frisbie* recognized by the Second Circuit in *United States v. Toscanino*, 500 F.2d 267 (2d Cir. 1974), were this court inclined to adopt such an exception. . . . Further, whatever harm Panamanian civilians suffered during the armed conflict that preceded Noriega's arrest cannot support a due process claim in this case. . . .

Noriega's attempt to evade the implications of the *Ker-Frisbie* doctrine by appealing to the judiciary's supervisory power is equally unavailing. Although, "in the exercise of supervisory powers, federal courts may, within limits, formulate procedural rules not specifically required by the Constitution or the Congress," . . . we are aware of no authority that would allow a court to exercise its supervisory power to dismiss an indictment based on harm done by the government to third parties. To the contrary, the Supreme Court has held that "the supervisory power merely permits federal courts to supervise 'the administration of criminal justice' among the parties before the bar." . . . For all the foregoing reasons, Noriega's convictions are AFFIRMED, and the district court's order denying Noriega's motion for a new trial is AFFIRMED.

Chapter 15
PRISONER TRANSFER AND OTHER POST-CONVICTION PROBLEMS

§ 15.01 Prisoner Transfer Treaties

ROSADO v. CIVILETTI

United States Court of Appeals for the Second Circuit
621 F.2d 1179 (1980)

KAUFMAN, CHIEF JUDGE:

. . . . In the case before us, petitioners are held in custody under federal authority. They have urged the district court to discharge its constitutional obligation to hear their claims and release them from custody. They have demonstrated that their convictions, under the laws of the sovereign state of Mexico, manifested a shocking insensitivity to their dignity as human beings and were obtained under a criminal process devoid of even a scintilla of rudimentary fairness and decency. Accordingly, we reaffirm the authority of the federal courts to hear due process claims raised, as they are here, by citizens held prisoner within the territorial jurisdiction of the United States. Nevertheless, we also recognize the laudable efforts of the executive and legislative branches, by both treaty and statute, to ameliorate, to their utmost power, the immense suffering of United States citizens held in Mexican jails. Indeed, because the statutory procedures governing transfers of these prisoners to United States custody are carefully structured to ensure that each of them voluntarily and intelligently agreed to forego his right to challenge the validity of his Mexican conviction, and because we must not ignore the interests of those citizens still imprisoned abroad, we hold that the present petitioners are estopped from receiving the relief they now seek.

I

In 1978, Efran Caban, Raymond Velez, Pedro Rosado, and Felix Melendez filed petitions in the District of Connecticut seeking release from federal incarceration in the Danbury Correctional Facility. The petitioners, all United States citizens, had been arrested in Mexico in November 1975 for narcotics offenses. They were subsequently convicted and sentenced to nine years' imprisonment by the Mexican courts. In December 1977, the petitioners were transferred to United States custody pursuant to a treaty between the United States and Mexico providing for the execution of penal sentences imposed by the

427

courts of one nation in the prisons of the other. Under the terms of the treaty, each transferring prisoner is required to consent to his transfer, and is permitted to contest the legality of any change of custody in the courts of the receiving nation. Thus, the petitioners in this case argued that their consents to transfer had been unlawfully coerced and that their continued detention by United States authorities based upon the convictions in Mexico violated their right to due process of law guaranteed by the Fifth Amendment. . . .

On July 31, 1979, Judge Daly granted the petitions of Caban, Velez, and Rosado, holding, in a thoughtful opinion, that the prisoners' consents to transfer had been unlawfully coerced by the brutal conditions of their confinement in Mexico. Emphasizing what he deemed to be circumstances unique to these petitioners, the district judge observed that the men lived in daily fear of bodily harm, and believed with justification that they would be killed if they remained incarcerated in Mexico. Consequently, he concluded, "petitioners would have signed anything, regardless of the consequences, to get out of Mexico." In view of our duty to make an independent determination of the voluntariness of petitioners' consents to transfer, we shall first explore the history of petitioners' confinement in Mexico and the United States, then proceed to consider the legal principles raised by the Government's appeal in this difficult and perplexing case.

A

. . . . In substance, the petitioners' testimony establishes that Caban and Freddie DePalm, also a United States citizen, departed New York's Kennedy Airport on November 18, 1975 for a vacation in Acapulco, Mexico. At the airport, the two men had become acquainted with Velez and the three sat together and conversed during the flight to Mexico. When their Aero Mexico airliner made its first scheduled landing in Mexico City, the passengers were informed there would be a one hour delay before proceeding to Acapulco. During the layover, Caban, DePalm, and Velez decided to leave the airport terminal and go to a Holiday Inn nearby. While browsing in the hotel's gift shop, the Americans were approached by six Mexicans in civilian dress, guns drawn, who stated that the Americans were under arrest. No arrest warrants were produced, nor did the Mexicans identify themselves as police officials. Nonetheless, Caban, DePalm, and Velez were each handcuffed and taken to an isolated area of the airport terminal.

In the terminal, Caban watched his captors drag Velez into a room, then heard Velez cry out in pain for close to an hour. Caban himself was taken into a separate room where he was searched, stripped and his legs bound. A watch, jewelry, and $400 in cash were taken from his person, but no drugs or contraband were found in his possession. Caban was then shown a photograph of a man represented to be Ramon Rodriguez and asked whether he knew him. When he denied any knowledge of Rodriguez, water was poured over his naked body and an electric cattle prod applied, first to his mouth, then to his testicles and buttocks. His persistent denial of any acquaintance with the man in the photograph led to repeated torture with the electric prod. Thereafter, Caban's interrogators suspended him from the ceiling by clamping a handcuff to his wrist and attaching it to a hook, causing him to lose consciousness from time to time. He remained in this position throughout the day while his captors continued to beat him, threatening to kill him if he refused to admit an acquaintance with Rodriguez. By the end of the day, the weight of Caban's suspended body against the handcuff caused a bone in his arm to break and tear through his wrist.

That night, Caban, DePalm, and Velez were taken to Los Separos detention center in Mexico City. Caban noticed that Velez was swollen and bruised, and that he was unable to walk unassisted. At Los Separos, the men were placed in small separate cells containing cement slabs for beds and no plumbing. They were held incommunicado for eight days. The food was inedible and the entire cellblock reeked of human excrement. Throughout their stay at Los Separos, interrogators continued to beat and torture the men with an electric prod in an attempt to elicit confessions.

Two days after Caban's arrest in Mexico City, Rosado was arrested in Acapulco upon his arrival on a flight from New York. Though unemployed, Rosado had planned to take a two-day vacation in Acapulco. After passing through customs at the airport, he was confronted by five plainclothes Mexicans bearing pistols and a submachine gun, who asked him to accompany them to a room in the airport. In the room, Rosado saw Melendez, who also had been detained upon his arrival in Acapulco. Rosado was held in the room for two hours while his luggage and personal effects were searched. His ticket, visa, jewelry, and $900 in cash were seized, and he was then driven to a nearby police station along with Melendez.

The following morning, the two Americans were flown to Mexico City along with several other prisoners arrested that day and, like Caban, DePalm, and Velez, ended their journeys at Los Separos. When they arrived, Rosado saw the badly beaten body of a man he later learned to be Caban. Melendez was taken into an interrogation room, and Rosado listened from an adjacent holding area as Melendez screamed in apparent agony. After Melendez was returned to the holding area, Rosado was asked by one Mexican officer whether he was ready to tell the truth. When Rosado's responses failed to satisfy his inquisitor, his hands were handcuffed behind his back, his pants lowered, and an electric prod was applied for several minutes at a time to his testicles and penis. Rosado then watched as Melendez was similarly questioned, with the interrogators alternating between beatings and electric torture.

After seven or eight days of unceasing brutality, each of the prisoners was finally taken to the prosecutor's office at Los Separos. Caban was told to sign a statement acknowledging his acquaintance with Rodriguez, but refused. Instead, he signed a paper disclaiming any knowledge of Rodriguez or his activities. Rosado was given a statement confessing participation in a gang seeking to import cocaine into Mexico, but he too refused to sign, stating that his sole purpose in coming to Mexico was for a vacation. At no time during the prisoners' initial detention and interrogation were they apprised of the charges against them, or permitted to consult with counsel.

Following their visits to the prosecutor, Caban, DePalm, Velez, Rosado, and Melendez were all transferred to Lecumberri Prison, the so-called "Black Castle," where they were crowded into tiny, unheated cells with only two or three beds for ten or twelve prisoners. . . . Shortly after their transfer to Lecumberri, the prisoners were brought to *los hugados*, a courtroom within the prison. There, they were crowded into a small pen separated from the courtroom by a chain link fence. A judge's law secretary briefly informed the men that they had been charged with illegal importation of cocaine, and then sent them back to their cells. Approximately one month later, the prisoners returned to *los hugados* and were formally advised by the law secretary that they had been indicted for illegal importation of cocaine. The men were shown copies of the statements that had previously been read to them by the prosecutor at Los Separos, and asked whether they were true. Both Caban and Rosado disclaimed the reports, insisting that they were false. The law secretary offered to help the prisoners for a fee but was told that they did not have enough money. The entire proceeding lasted no longer than ten minutes.

Two weeks after this "arraignment," the prisoners were brought back to *los hugados*, ostensibly for a *correo constitutional*, that is, an opportunity to confront the witnesses against them. Inside the courtroom, Caban saw the officers who had detained and questioned him at the Mexico City Airport, but none of the officers who had arrested Rosado in Acapulco was present. Once again, the law secretary presided over the proceeding, asking each officer whether he ratified his earlier statement against the defendants. At no time were the prisoners permitted to cross-examine the arresting officers, to read the officers' statements, or to speak to the charges against them. The entire proceeding was over in less than fifteen minutes.

Seven months later, on August 10, 1976, the men returned to *los hugados* and were informed by the law secretary that a judge had considered their cases and had sentenced each man to nine years' imprisonment. At no time did they see the judge who sentenced them, obtain the assistance of counsel, or confront the witnesses against them.

In October 1976, Lecumberri was closed by the Mexican authorities and the appellees were transferred to Oriente Prison, a more modern and sanitary facility. . . . The prisoners remained at Oriente until July 1977, when they were moved to Santa Marta Penitentiary. Initially, the men were placed in "the hole," a windowless, unheated cell in which there was one bed and no toilet. There, the men were held incommunicado for approximately ten days until the prison director informed them that they would be moved to more habitable cells in the dormitory if they promised to pay him $2,000. Although the men knew they did not have sufficient money to pay the director, they promised to pay and were moved to better quarters in the dormitory. Soon, however, the men learned that Santa Marta differed little from Lecumberri. In addition to the dormitory fee, prisoners regularly paid for the basic necessities of life. Those who disobeyed the guards, or were slow in making payments, were subject to brutal beatings by a favored group of inmates known as the "Fourth Guard." At night, those who had angered the Fourth Guard would be taken from their cells, beaten, stabbed, and frequently left for dead. As a result, both Caban and Rosado feared for their lives, since they were certain the Fourth Guard would kill them if they did not soon raise the $2,000 dormitory fee promised to the director.

B

In 1974, public attention was drawn to the outrageous conditions of confinement in Mexico's jails when Congressmen and journalists in the United States began to investigate complaints of American prisoners and their families. . . . Following a case-by-case review of some 514 Americans incarcerated in Mexico, the State Department's Bureau of Security and Consular Affairs reported in January 1976 that the alleged deprivations of basic rights formed a "credible pattern." . . . Finally, in June 1976, Mexico's Foreign Minister proposed a treaty between the two countries permitting the citizens of either nation who had been convicted in the courts of the other country to serve their sentences in the penal institutions of their native land. Negotiations progressed rapidly and a treaty was signed by representatives of both nations in Mexico City on November 25, 1976. Following extensive hearings in the Senate Foreign Relations and Judiciary Committees, the full Senate unanimously approved the treaty by a vote of 90 to 0 on July 21, 1977. (A similar treaty between the United States and Canada was ratified by the Senate two days earlier by a vote of 95 to 0.) Enabling legislation was approved by Congress and signed into law on October 28, 1977, and the treaty became effective on November 30, 1977.

Under the Treaty, a United States citizen convicted of a criminal offense in Mexico may transfer from Mexican to American custody for the balance of his sentence provided certain conditions are met. The offense for which he has been convicted must also be generally punishable in the United States, and can be neither a political nor immigration offense. Moreover, the transferring offender must be both a national of the United States and not a domiciliary of Mexico. Only prisoners with a minimum of six months remaining on their sentence, and for whom no appeal or collateral attack is currently pending in the Mexican courts, are eligible for transfer. Finally, Mexico, the United States, and the transferring prisoner must all give their consent to the change in custody. (To ensure that a prisoner's consent to transfer is given voluntarily and with full knowledge of its conditions, the implementing legislation enacted by Congress provides for a United States magistrate or citizen specifically designated by a judge of the United States to travel to Mexico and to make all necessary inquiries of the offender to determine whether his consent is given voluntarily and knowingly. 18 U.S.C. § 4108. In addition, the offender may receive the advice of counsel prior to the consent verification proceeding, and those who cannot afford counsel must have counsel appointed for them by the verifying officer. *Id.* § 4109.)

The potential benefits to a prisoner transferring under the Treaty are considerable. Not only will he be repatriated to his homeland where the culture and language will be familiar and his family closer at hand, but the Treaty specifically provides that the law of the Receiving State will govern his eligibility for parole, the conditions of his confinement, and any attack he may bring upon the validity of his transfer or the constitutionality of the Treaty and its implementing legislation. In addition, a transferred offender is protected against double jeopardy in the United States on account of the crime for which he was convicted in Mexico, and any prejudice to his civil rights in the United States other than the collateral consequences normally accorded a Mexican conviction by American law. Both the Treaty and implementing legislation specifically provide, however, that the courts of the transferring nation shall have exclusive jurisdiction over proceedings brought by a transferring offender to challenge, modify, or set aside convictions or sentences handed down by its courts. An American citizen seeking transfer to United States custody is required to understand and agree that any action challenging his conviction or sentence must be brought in Mexican, not United States, courts, and any transferred offender who succeeds in establishing the invalidity of his transfer in a United States court may be returned to Mexico to serve the balance of his sentence.

C

Two months after Caban, Velez, and Rosado promised but failed to pay $2,000 to the director of Santa Marta, representatives from the United States Embassy visited the men at the prison and informed them of the possibility of transfer to United States custody pursuant to the Treaty. They were each given booklets prepared by the United States Department of Justice explaining the terms of the Treaty and the consequences of an election to transfer. . . . After the prisoners expressed an interest in transferring to United States custody, an attorney from the Federal Public Defender's Office in Texas met with each individually and explained in detail the consequences of a transfer under the Treaty. On December 5, 1977, the men appeared separately before a United States magistrate at the prison to verify their consents to transfer. The magistrate questioned each petitioner about his knowledge of the Treaty's provisions, specifically asking each man whether he understood and agreed to abide by the condition requiring challenges to his conviction or sentence to be brought by proceedings instituted in Mexican courts. . . . In each case, once the magistrate satisfied himself that the applicant's consent to transfer was given knowingly and voluntarily, without threat or coercion, he permitted the petitioner to sign a standard form of consent.

II

In appraising the voluntariness of the petitioners' consents to transfer, Judge Daly relied primarily upon *Schneckloth v. Bustamonte*, 412 U.S. 218, 93 S. Ct.

2041, 36 L. Ed. 2d 854 (1973), in which the Supreme Court upheld the validity of a citizen's consent to a police search of his automobile under the Fourth Amendment. In *Schneckloth*, the Court eschewed any "talismanic definition" of voluntariness, stressing instead that the issue presented a "question of fact to be determined from all the circumstances." In the context of searches and seizures, the Court noted that a balance must be struck between our collective interest in effective law enforcement, and our constitutional insistence upon personal freedom from unwarranted governmental intrusions. Striking that balance in *Schneckloth*, the Court implicitly recognized that its rule would serve to define the degree to which overzealous law enforcement would be deterred, and individual rights vindicated.

In the case at bar, however, we are in no position to deter by our decision the acts complained of by petitioners. The sources of torture, abuse, and coercion to which they point as invalidating their consents emanate not from United States authorities, but Mexican officers, acting within the territorial sovereignty of Mexico, without American direction or involvement. Although the Bill of Rights does apply extraterritorially to protect American citizens against the illegal conduct of United States agents, *Reid v. Covert*, 354 U.S. 1, 77 S. Ct. 1222, 1 L. Ed. 2d 1148 (1957); *United States v. Toscanino*, 500 F.2d 267 (2d Cir. 1974), it does not and cannot protect our citizens from the acts of a foreign sovereign committed within its territory. *Neely v. Henkel*, 180 U.S. 109, 21 S. Ct. 302, 45 L. Ed. 448 (1901); *United States v. Lira*, 515 F.2d 68 (2d Cir.), *cert. denied*, 423 U.S. 847, 96 S. Ct. 87, 46 L. Ed. 2d 69 (1975). For example, in *Lira*, a Chilean national was abducted from his home by Chilean police, beaten, tortured with electric shocks, and then placed on a plane for New York, where he was arrested by federal narcotics agents. In upholding the jurisdiction of the district court to try Lira, we expressly held that relief from acts of torture by foreign agents could be granted only upon a showing of direct United States governmental involvement. Otherwise, we reasoned, the court's holding would serve no deterrent function, and vindicate no constitutionally recognized right. . . .

It is noted that a contrary holding in *Lira* would not only have failed to vindicate any constitutional right of the defendant, but also would have obstructed our national interest in effective law enforcement. Since the United States makes no claim to a valid law enforcement interest with respect to these petitioners, it may be argued that a court should not deny a remedy to one tortured abroad when to do so would serve no countervailing interest.

But the United States does assert two other interests in upholding the validity of these petitioners' consents, both comparably significant. First is the Government's substantial interest in promoting good relations with Mexico by honoring its criminal convictions and recognizing the integrity of its criminal justice system. Since Mexico is a sovereign nation in no sense subject to the judgments of this Court, we could neither deter its officials from committing similar cruelties in the future, nor vindicate the individual interests of those still incarcerated in Mexican prisons, by invalidating these petitioners' consents.

At most, we would simply complicate our delicate relations with Mexico. More important, however, is the interest of those Americans who are currently, or may soon find themselves, caught up in Mexico's criminal justice system. If, here, the conduct of Mexican officials on Mexican soil were held to be determinative of the voluntariness of an American prisoner's consent to transfer, those prisoners most desperately in need of transfer to escape torture and extortion, including the petitioners at bar, would never be able to satisfy a magistrate that their consents were voluntarily given.

This anomalous result stems in part from the district court's adoption of a standard of voluntariness designed to govern consensual searches and seizures within the United States. Though we can find no case presenting facts on point to guide us in these extraordinary circumstances, it is readily apparent that a decision whether to permit a police officer to search one's car does not remotely resemble the choice presented to these petitioners under the Treaty. In our view the choice that faces an American imprisoned in Mexico in deciding whether to transfer more closely resembles a decision confronted by nearly every criminal defendant today: whether to plead guilty and accept a set of specified sanctions ranging from probation to a possibly long prison sentence, or to stand trial and face unknown dispositions ranging from possible acquittal to a severe maximum sentence or even death. In the plea bargaining context, as in the case at bar, the choice involves liberty and incarceration on both sides of the equation.

Accordingly, we turn for guidance to the line of cases construing the voluntariness of guilty pleas, beginning with *United States v. Jackson*, 390 U.S. 570, 88 S. Ct. 1209, 20 L. Ed. 2d 138 (1968). In *Jackson*, the Court invalidated a provision of the Federal Kidnapping Act permitting imposition of the death penalty only upon the jury's recommendation, because it concluded the provision unnecessarily induced defendants to waive their constitutional right to a trial by jury. The holding promptly spawned a number of challenges to guilty pleas in general, asserting that the defendant's plea had been involuntarily induced by the risk of receiving a death sentence if he insisted upon his right to a jury trial. In response, the Court quickly made clear that not all guilty pleas were invalid simply because the death penalty could be imposed only after trial by jury. In *Brady v. United States*, 397 U.S. 742, 90 S. Ct. 1463, 25 L. Ed. 2d 747 (1970), the Court explained that the question centers on whether the provision "needlessly penalize[d] the assertion of a constitutional right." If not, the voluntariness of a given plea is to be judged by whether it was a knowing, intelligent act "done with sufficient awareness of the relevant circumstances and likely consequences."

Subsequently, in *North Carolina v. Alford*, 400 U.S. 25, 91 S. Ct. 160, 27 L. Ed. 2d 162 (1970), the Court emphasized that the "voluntariness" of a guilty plea is determined by considering, not whether the defendant's decision reflected a wholly unrestrained will, but rather whether it constituted a deliberate, intelligent choice between available alternatives. . . . Focusing upon the alternatives open to the defendant when he entered his plea, the Court concluded that the decision to forego a jury trial and thus avoid the risk of a death sentence represented a voluntary and intelligent choice among the available alternatives. "When his plea is viewed in light of the evidence against him, which substantially negated his claim of innocence and which further provided a means by which the judge could test whether the plea was being intelligently entered . . . its validity cannot be seriously questioned." Since the evidence of guilt was, for practical purposes, conclusive, the choice between trial by jury and potential death on the one hand, or pleading guilty and certain imprisonment on the other, was not unjustifiably coercive.

Similarly, if the instant petitioners' consents to transfer are viewed in light of the alternatives legitimately available to them, it cannot be seriously doubted that their decisions were voluntarily and intelligently made. . . . Their choice was . . . between continued incarceration under the brutal regime that prevailed in Mexican prisons, or repatriation. In either event, they would retain their right to seek redress from the Mexican courts, but could not challenge their convictions or sentences in United States courts. Though it may well be, as Judge Daly concluded, that anyone in similar circumstances would choose to transfer, the same may also be said for the defendant in *Alford*. In view of the alternatives legitimately available to petitioners, we conclude that their consents to transfer were voluntarily and intelligently made.

III

Regardless of the validity of the petitioners' consents to transfer, it is also claimed that the Treaty and enabling legislation deprive petitioners of their liberty without due process of law in violation of the Fifth Amendment. Though a transferring prisoner's arrest, interrogation, trial, and ultimate conviction all occur in Mexico, at the hands of Mexican authorities, his liberty is restricted by United States authorities once he is placed in American custody. Accordingly, we must determine whether the United States Government may imprison a citizen in execution of a criminal sentence imposed by a foreign tribunal acting within its jurisdiction and, at the same time, deny him access to a United States court to challenge the fundamental fairness of the criminal process that led to his conviction abroad.

A

In dictum too old to question, Chief Justice Marshall declared that "[t]he courts of no country execute the penal laws of another." *The Antelope*, 23 U.S. (10 Wheat.) 66, 123, 6 L. Ed. 268 (1825). . . . [However,] nothing in the doctrine enunciated by Marshall precludes a sovereign power from extending recognition to another's penal laws where it chooses to do so. Nor does Marshall's dictum suggest any principle limiting the power of sovereign nations to enter into mutual compacts or treaties obligating the signatories to honor and enforce the penal decrees of one another. In the United States, the constitutionality of such measures was decided long ago when the Supreme Court upheld an extradition agreement with foreign nations as a valid exercise of the treaty-making power.

Even where the treaty fails to secure to those who are extradited to another country the same constitutional safeguards they would enjoy in an American criminal trial, it does not run afoul of the Constitution. Moreover, criminal convictions imposed by foreign tribunals have served as predicates for enhanced sentencing under state multi-offender statutes.

The instant Treaty does not call upon the United States to enforce Mexico's penal laws or procedures, but only to execute criminal convictions entered in its courts against American citizens who elect to transfer to United States custody. Thus, once a prisoner has consented to transfer, the United States is bound simply to take custody of the offender and, with a few significant exceptions (the principal exception being the reservation to Mexico of jurisdiction over challenges to the prisoners' conviction or sentence) detain him as if he had been convicted in a United States court. The Treaty serves to ameliorate the condition of Americans imprisoned in Mexico by offering them an opportunity for repatriation and, hopefully, better prison conditions and more positive means for rehabilitation. In lessening the number of United States citizens incarcerated in Mexico, the Treaty additionally serves to relieve a worrisome source of tension in Mexican-American relations. In view of these benevolent purposes, we believe the Treaty is a valid exercise of the treaty-making power conferred by Art. II, § 2, cl. 2 of the Constitution.

B

Although we can discern no constitutional impediment to a judgment by the President and Congress that the transfer of convicted criminal defendants is a worthy object of international accord, the execution of foreign penal decrees may not serve as an artifice to circumvent the procedural and substantive guaranties of the Bill of Rights. . . . It is undisputed that these petitioners have received none of the process constitutionally required for the trial and conviction of criminals in United States courts. Nonetheless, they are incarcerated under federal authority. . . . Accordingly, we must determine whether Congress can provide for the deprivation of a citizen's liberty through incarceration, while withholding all right of access to United States courts to test the basis for his confinement.

It is an unassailable tenet of our constitutional system that the Government's power to punish citizens may be exercised only in accordance with the due process of law prescribed by the Bill of Rights. Whether the constitutional guarantee of due process further requires that any imposition of punishment carry with it a right of access to a United States court to test the basis for the sanctions imposed is a question never fully resolved. In the case at bar, the Government seeks to deprive the petitioners of their liberty in recognition of a conviction returned by a court beyond the jurisdiction of the United States. Though our research has disclosed no case directly in point, the nature and extent of process to be accorded those committing crimes abroad has been considered in a variety of related contexts.

In *In re Ross*, 140 U.S. 453, 11 S. Ct. 897, 35 L. Ed. 581 (1891), the Supreme Court denied habeas relief to a seaman imprisoned in the United States following his conviction for murder by an American consular court sitting in Japan. Under a treaty with that country, the United States was given jurisdiction over criminal offenses committed by Americans in Japan. The implementing legislation enacted by Congress vested jurisdiction to try all such offenses in consular tribunals. In challenging his conviction in the consular court, Ross argued that he had been denied due process since he had not been indicted or tried by a jury. The court rejected these claims out of hand, holding that the "Constitution can have no operation in another country. When . . . the representatives or officers of our government are permitted to exercise authority of any kind in another country, it must be on such conditions as the two countries may agree, the laws of neither one being obligatory upon the other."

The Court had occasion to reconsider *Ross* in *Reid v. Covert, supra*. Covert, the wife of an American serviceman stationed in England, was charged with her husband's killing. Pursuant to a provision of the Uniform Code of Military Justice, all persons accompanying the armed forces abroad were subject to court-martial by a military tribunal for any criminal offense related to the military. Mrs. Covert was tried, convicted, and sentenced to life imprisonment by a military court-martial, then incarcerated in the United States. A district court order granting her release on a writ of habeas corpus was first reversed by the Supreme Court, then affirmed on reconsideration. In withdrawing its earlier decision, a plurality of the Court expressly rejected the reasoning of *Ross*: "[w]hen the Government reaches out to punish a citizen who is abroad, the shield which the Bill of Rights and other parts of the Constitution provide to protect his life and liberty should not be stripped away just because he happens to be in another land." Two concurring justices attempted to distinguish *Ross* by limiting its applicability to instances where historical or political necessities dictate a flexible approach. But a majority agreed that insofar as *Ross* disclaimed any extraterritorial force to the Constitution, it was no longer good law.

Covert was tried and convicted in an American tribunal under a treaty that conferred jurisdiction on United States authorities over crimes committed by American citizens. In the instant case, however, petitioners were convicted in Mexican courts for crimes committed within that country. A somewhat analogous situation was presented in *Hirota v. MacArthur*, 338 U.S. 197, 69 S. Ct. 197, 93 L. Ed. 1902 (1948), where two Japanese citizens held in United States custody in Japan following their conviction for war crimes by an international tribunal sought leave to file original petitions for writs of habeas corpus in the Supreme Court. The Court denied leave, holding that it lacked power or authority to review the convictions.

The following term, the Court again considered petitions filed on behalf of enemy aliens held in custody abroad by United States authorities. *Johnson v. Eisentrager*, 339 U.S. 763, 70 S. Ct. 936, 94 L. Ed. 1255 (1950). While stressing the historic right of access to American courts enjoyed by citizens, the Court found no constitutional right to sue for habeas relief in United States courts where the petitioner was an alien enemy who never resided in the United States, was captured beyond American territory, and was tried, convicted, and imprisoned abroad for offenses committed outside the United States.   In contrast to *Eisentrager*, however, the petitioners at bar are United States citizens incarcerated within the territory of the United States.

Another useful point of reference is found in cases where a foreign sovereign seeks to extradite an American citizen for trial abroad. Where extradition is sought pursuant to a valid treaty, the Supreme Court has held that the relator cannot prevent his extradition simply by alleging that the criminal process he will receive fails to accord with constitutional guaranties.   Since the Constitution bears no relation to crimes committed beyond the jurisdiction of the United States against the laws of a foreign sovereign, a citizen who "commits a crime in a foreign country cannot complain if required to submit to such modes of trial and to such punishment as the laws of that country may prescribe for its own people, unless a different mode be provided for by treaty stipulations." *Neely v. Henkel, supra.* Thus, where a relator challenges the fairness of foreign process, courts "are bound by the existence of an extradition treaty to assume that the trial will be fair."

In *Neely*, however, minimal safeguards to ensure a fair trial in the foreign tribunal were provided. Moreover, this court has previously indicated that the presumption of fairness routinely accorded the criminal process of a foreign sovereign may require closer scrutiny if a relator persuasively demonstrates that extradition would expose him to procedures or punishment "antipathetic to a federal court's sense of decency." *Gallina v. Fraser*, 278 F.2d 77, 79 (2d Cir.), *cert. denied*, 364 U.S. 851, 81 S. Ct. 97, 5 L. Ed. 2d 74 (1960); *United States ex rel. Bloomfield v. Gengler*, 507 F.2d 925 (2d Cir. 1974). Finally, to the extent that the United States itself acts to detain a relator pending extradition, it is bound to accord him due process. Thus, although the Constitution cannot limit the power of a foreign sovereign to prescribe procedures for the trial and punishment of crimes committed within its territory, it does govern the manner in which the United States may join the effort.

In our view, however, the cases that provide the closest analogy to the instant petitions are those stemming from congressional efforts to limit the immigration of Chinese and Japanese aliens to the United States. . . . In *The Chinese Exclusion Case*, 130 U.S. 581, 9 S. Ct. 623, 32 L. Ed. 1068 (1889), the Supreme Court upheld the power of Congress to provide for the exclusion of Asian aliens solely by means of executive action. Subsequently, the Court held that the power to exclude aliens at the border necessarily included the power to expel those found within the United States without creating any right to judicial review of the administrative action. . . . [However,] in *The Japanese Immigrant Case*, 189 U.S. 86, 23 S. Ct. 611, 47 L. Ed. 721 (1903), the Court . . . . decided that the final authority conferred upon executive officers to pass upon the status of Asian immigrants did not permit arbitrary disregard of the fundamental principles inherent in due process of law. "One of these principles," the Court stated, "is that no person shall be deprived of his liberty without opportunity, at some time, to be heard, before such officers, in respect of the matters upon which that liberty depends.". . . [I]n *Chin Yow v. United States*, 208 U.S. 8, 28 S. Ct. 201, 52 L. Ed. 369 (1908), [the petitioner] claimed that he was a native-born American citizen. . . [H]is petition for a writ of habeas corpus sought relief from the administrative order denying his entry on the ground that he had been denied a fair opportunity to present his case for citizenship to the executive authorities. . . [W]riting for the majority, [Justice] Holmes stressed the constitutional requirement of a hearing reasonably calculated to produce a correct result. . . . . Finally, in *Ng Fung Ho v. White*, 259 U.S. 276, 42 S. Ct. 492, 66 L. Ed. 938 (1922), the Court [decided that] the threat to liberty posed by the exclusion of one claiming to be a citizen was so grave that the determination of citizenship could not be entrusted to executive officers. "Against the danger of such deprivation without the sanction afforded by judicial proceedings, the Fifth Amendment affords protection in its guarantee of due process of law."

The right to a fair procedure reasonably calculated to produce a correct determination of the basis for the imposition of penal sanctions lies at the heart of the due process of law protected by the Fifth Amendment. As *Chin Yow* and *Ng Fung Ho* teach, the United States may not deprive an individual of his liberty unless such a procedure is first accorded. Where one has been denied his right to a fair hearing prior to the imposition of penal sanctions restraining his liberty, habeas corpus provides the appropriate remedy.

In the case at bar, petitioners face not the danger of deprivation, but the reality of liberty already lost. Nonetheless, it is undisputed that at no time did they receive even the barest rudiments of a process calculated to arrive at the truth of the accusations against them. They did not receive the assistance of counsel during the Mexican criminal proceedings against them, nor were they ever accorded an opportunity to appear before the judge who allegedly decided their case. They were not permitted to address the charges against them, or present any evidence at all. No opportunity was given Rosado to confront the witnesses against him, and neither Caban nor Velez was allowed to cross-examine their accusers. Most egregious of all, the law secretary who presided over the proceedings against the petitioners offered the influence of his position to help petitioners for a fee.

Under such circumstances, we believe these petitioners have a right to test the basis for their continued confinement in a United States court. In reaching this conclusion, we by no means imply that each element of due process as known to American criminal law must be present in a foreign criminal proceeding before Congress may give a conviction rendered by a foreign tribunal binding effect. Indeed, we are keenly sensitive to the historical and cultural limitations of our own constitutional heritage, and respect the similarly indigenous underpinnings of the process accorded criminal defendants abroad. We simply hold that a petitioner incarcerated under federal authority pursuant to a foreign conviction cannot be denied all access to a United States court when he presents a persuasive showing that his conviction was obtained without the benefit of any process whatsoever. Having thus determined that petitioners possess a right to challenge the basis for their continued confinement under United States custody, we must proceed to consider the merits of their claim, unless there appears some further reason to withhold relief.

IV

During the petitioners' consent verification proceedings in Mexico, each was specifically asked whether he understood and agreed to abide by the Treaty provision granting Mexico exclusive jurisdiction over all proceedings seeking to challenge, modify, or set aside sentences imposed by its courts. Each indicated that he understood the provision and agreed to abide by the condition. Accordingly, we must decide whether the petitioners are now estopped from challenging their Mexican convictions in United States courts.

In enacting the enabling legislation, Congress went to great lengths to ensure that a transferring prisoner would not only be informed of the Treaty's provisions, but agree to abide by them as well. Section 4108(b)(1) of Title 18 expressly provides that the verifying officer "shall inquire of the offender whether he understands and agrees" that Mexico is given exclusive jurisdiction to hear challenges to his conviction and sentence.

As originally introduced in the Senate, the bill that ultimately became § 4108 simply required that a transferring offender be informed that "by his consent (to transfer) he waives all rights he might have had to institute proceedings in the courts of the United States seeking to challenge . . . his conviction or sentence." A memorandum prepared for the State Department and submitted to the House subcommittee considering the bill noted, however, that a transferring offender did not possess a right of access to United States courts at the time he executed his consent in Mexico. Accordingly, it cautioned, a consent which purported to waive a right the offender did not possess at the time it was executed might not withstand judicial scrutiny upon the prisoner's transfer to the United States. Instead, it suggested, Congress should employ the doctrine of estoppel and require transferring prisoners to agree not to challenge their Mexican convictions in United States courts.

After witnesses at both House and Senate hearings emphasized the crucial importance of securing a binding, voluntary consent to transfer that would preclude returning prisoners from challenging their Mexican convictions in United States courts, the bill was amended in the Senate Judiciary Committee to require an express agreement by the prisoner to bring any attacks upon his conviction or sentence solely in the Mexican courts. . .

As we have mentioned, Mexico, the United States, and each offender requesting transfer must give their consent to the change in custody before a prisoner may be transferred. The consents contemplated by the Treaty entail much more than simple expressions of the desire to transfer, and the permission to do so. They also include reciprocal representations by each of the parties upon which the others rely in deciding to give their consent. For example, the United States promises Mexico that it will execute the prisoner's Mexican conviction and provide biannual reports on the status of the offenders who have transferred to the United States. It also promises the prisoner that he will enjoy the benefit of parole in accordance with United States law. Mexico agrees to relinquish custody of an individual found to have committed a criminal offense within its jurisdiction, while promising to hear subsequent challenges to the sentences rendered by its courts. For his part, the transferring prisoner agrees to his change in custody, and further promises to abide by the terms of the Treaty, including the reservation of jurisdiction to Mexico over all challenges to convictions and sentences imposed by its courts.

It requires little imagination to conclude, in light of this background, that if petitioners had refused to agree to abide by the Treaty's conditions, neither Mexico nor the United States would have consented to their transfers. Accordingly, petitioners would have continued to be imprisoned in Mexico, without right of access to American courts. But that fact alone does not persuade us their bargain should be enforced. If, in holding these petitioners to their agreement, we would serve no substantial and legitimate governmental interest which the United States put in jeopardy in reliance upon their promises not to attack their convictions in American courts, we would have difficulty in concluding that their custody should be continued. Unless the Government can satisfy us that it relied to its detriment upon the petitioners' agreement, we see no purpose served in closing our doors to their due process claims. Moreover, in view of our holding that petitioners acquired a right of access to a United States court once they were transferred to American custody, we believe their acceptance of the jurisdictional condition can be sustained only if voluntary and intelligent. We shall consider, therefore, whether the petitioners voluntarily and intelligently agreed to challenge their convictions solely in Mexican courts, and whether the United States advances a sufficiently important interest in holding these prisoners to their bargain.

As with petitioners' consents, we believe *Jackson, supra,* and *Alford, supra,* state the governing principles for determining the voluntariness and intelligence of their agreements. Viewed in the light of the alternatives available to them, we find petitioners' decisions to promise to abide by the Treaty's limitation upon their right to seek relief to have been both informed and intelligent. If, as we have said, they had insisted upon their right, once held in federal custody, to seek review of their Mexican convictions in a United States court, neither the United States nor Mexico would have consented to their transfers. If, however, they agreed to abide by the limitations of the Treaty, petitioners could escape the brutal conditions of Mexican confinement, acquire a hitherto unenjoyed right to parole, and have virtually the same opportunity to challenge their Mexican convictions in Mexico's courts as they previously enjoyed. In addition, petitioners would gain access to United States courts for all claims unrelated to their convictions or sentences.

Although petitioners' decisions to accept the jurisdictional condition to their transfer thus appear to be intelligent choices among the available alternatives, it is less certain that their decisions may be termed "voluntary" within the meaning of *Jackson, supra*. Arguably, the choice between sacrifice of a right to seek judicial redress from a United States court once repatriated, and continued imprisonment in Mexico, "needlessly penalize[d]" the prisoners' constitutional right to a federal forum once they were placed in United States custody. We are satisfied, however, that the congressional decision to require offenders transferring to American custody to agree to abide by the jurisdictional provision was neither needless nor arbitrary. Moreover, we believe the conditional requirement that prisoners agree to challenge their convictions solely in the courts of the transferring nation legitimately serves two important interests that can be vindicated only by holding these prisoners to their agreements.

In assessing the interacting interests of the United States and foreign nations, "we must move with the circumspection appropriate when [a court] is adjudicating issues inevitably entangled in the conduct of our international relations." Since Mexico was unwilling to enter a treaty that provided for review of its criminal judgments by United States courts, American negotiators did not have a completely free hand in structuring the Treaty's terms. Guided throughout by their humane concern to ameliorate the plight of hundreds of United States citizens imprisoned in Mexico, the negotiators obviously extracted a significant number of important concessions. At the same time, however, our negotiators were anxious to improve relations with Mexico and hopefully eliminate what had become an important source of tension between the two nations.

Of paramount importance, however, is the interest of those Americans currently incarcerated in Mexico. Whatever hope the Treaty extends of escaping the harsh realities of confinement abroad will be dashed for hundreds of Americans if we permit these three petitioners to rescind their agreement to limit their attacks upon their convictions to Mexico's courts. We refuse to scuttle the one certain opportunity open to Americans incarcerated abroad to return home, an opportunity, we note, the benefit of which Caban, Velez, and Rosado have already received. In holding these petitioners to their bargain, we by no means condone the shockingly brutal treatment to which they fell prey. Rather, we hold open the door for others similarly victimized to escape their torment.

The judgment of the district court is reversed.

NOTES AND QUESTIONS

(1) In addition to the treaties with Mexico and Canada, the United States has entered into prisoner exchange agreements with Bolivia, Panama, Turkey, Peru, Thailand, and France, and has become a party to the multilateral European Convention on the Transfer of Sentenced Persons. *See* M. Cherif Bassiouni & Grace M. W. Gallagher, *Transfer of Prisoners: Policies and Practices of the United States, in* 2 INTERNATIONAL CRIMINAL LAW 505, 505 n. 5 (M. Cherif Bassiouni ed., 2d ed. 1999).

(2) Other cases upholding the constitutionality of prisoner transfer treaties include *Pfeifer v. U.S. Bureau of Prisons*, 615 F.2d 873 (9th Cir. 1980); *Mitchell v. United States*, 483 F. Supp. 291 (E.D. Wis. 1980). The question of constitutionality was much debated at the time the treaties with Mexico and Canada were concluded. One of the witnesses before the Senate Foreign Relations Committee was Herbert Wechsler, who argued in favor of constitutionality. Compare Judge Kaufman's reasoning in *Rosado* with Professor Wechsler's somewhat less tortured argument:

First: The purpose and effect of the two treaties is not to impose afflictive sanctions on the offenders who may be transferred with their consent from a foreign country to their home country for service of their sentences but rather to alleviate the special hardship incident to confinement or restraint away from home. The assurance of such reciprocal benefits for citizens or nationals of the contracting countries is plainly an appropriate object of the treaty power. . . .

Second: The treaties envisage the use of national power and authority to imprison or restrain as criminals American citizens or nationals who have been convicted abroad of crimes committed abroad within the jurisdiction of a foreign country. . . . It has been suggested that the due process clause of the Fifth Amendment prohibits such imprisonment if the foreign conviction was obtained by procedures lacking those safeguards of the Bill of Rights that the Fourteenth Amendment has been held to impose on state procedures. This seems to me a wholly insupportable conclusion. . . . The Fifth Amendment was no more designed than was the Fourteenth to limit Mexican or Canadian procedures. . . . [N]othing said by Mr. Justice Black in the plurality opinion in *Reid v. Covert* as to the application of the Bill of Rights to trial abroad in American courts or the subjection of the treaty power to the limitations of the Bill of Rights has any application to this problem. The treaty takes away no right that these offenders otherwise would have. Absent the transfer, their convictions and their sentences remain in force and they must serve the sentence in a foreign land. The question that is posed reduces simply, in my view, to this: is it a reasonable exercise of governmental power to imprison or restrain at their election individuals who otherwise would be imprisoned or restrained abroad, and to do so subject to the mitigations that the treaties articulate by making applicable our release procedures and subject also to the safeguards with respect to an informed consent that the legislation would provide. I see no room for argument upon that issue.

Third: If I am right in the analysis I have suggested, no additional complexity is introduced by the provision limiting collateral attack on the conviction or the sentence to the courts of the transferring state. This is not a suspension of the privilege of the writ of habeas corpus. The writ remains available; it is simply a good return that the offender is imprisoned in accordance with the treaty and its implementing legislation. If the treaty and the statute are valid, as I believe they are, the detention does not violate the Constitution, laws or treaties of the United States. The application for the writ must, therefore, be denied.

Penal Treaties with Mexico and Canada: Hearings Before the Senate Comm. on Foreign Relations, 95th Cong. 90, 93-94 (1977).

(3) Article IV(4) of the Treaty with Mexico sets out broad criteria for determining the appropriateness of a transfer: "In deciding upon the transfer of an offender . . . each Party shall bear in mind all factors bearing upon the probability that the transfer will contribute to the social rehabilitation of the offender, including the nature and severity of his offense and his previous criminal record, if any, his medical condition, the strength of his connections by residence, presence in the territory, family relations and otherwise to the social life of the Transferring State and the Receiving State." Otherwise, no officially published federal regulations set out the guidelines to be used in deciding whether or not to allow a transfer. In *Scalise v. Meese*, 687 F. Supp. 1239 (N.D. Ill. 1988), the district court held that the U.S. implementing legislation imposed a duty on the Attorney General to issue such regulations, which could be enforced through a writ of mandamus; but this decision was reversed by the Seventh Circuit in *Scalise v. Thornburgh*, 891 F.2d 640 (7th Cir. 1989). Similarly, in *Marquez-Ramos v. Reno*, 69 F.3d 477 (10th Cir. 1995), the Tenth Circuit held that the Attorney General's decision to deny a transfer was entirely discretionary and not subject to review through mandamus. In fact, within the Department of Justice, decisions involving prisoner transfers have been delegated to the Criminal Division's Office of Enforcement Operations, which has drawn up non-binding guidelines for use in such cases. *See* Maureen T. Walsh & Bruce Zagaris, *The United States-Mexico Treaty on the Execution of Penal Sanctions: The Case for Reevaluating the Treaty and Its Politics in View of the NAFTA and Other Developments*, 2 SW. J. OF L. & TRADE AM. 385, 410-12 (1995).

(4) Under Article V(2) of the Treaty with Mexico, provided the prisoner is not subjected to a longer sentence than that imposed by the transferring state, "the completion of a transferred offender's sentence shall be carried out according to the laws and procedures of the Receiving State, including the application of any provisions for reduction of the term of confinement by parole, conditional

release, or otherwise." How has this been affected by adoption of the Federal Sentencing Guidelines? In *Kleeman v. U. S. Parole Commission*, 125 F.3d 725 (9th Cir. 1987), the Ninth Circuit observed:

> In transfer cases, the [U.S. Parole] Commission "is charged with the task of translating a foreign sentence into terms appropriate to domestic penal enforcement." Specifically, the Commission must apply the federal sentencing guidelines to the investigative reports and recommendations of the United States Probation Service to determine a combined term of imprisonment and supervised release for the transferred offender "as though the offender were convicted in the United States district court of a similar offense." 18 U.S.C. § 4106A(b)(1)(A). Regulations provide: "The Commission shall take into account the offense definition under foreign law, the length of the sentence permitted by that law, and the underlying circumstances of the offense behavior, to establish a guideline range that fairly reflects the seriousness of the offense behavior committed in the foreign country." 28 C.F.R. § 2.62(g).

In the *Kleeman* case, the prisoner had been convicted of "simple homicide" (*homicidio simple*) in Baja California, Mexico, and sentenced to ten years' imprisonment. She was granted a transfer to complete service of her sentence in the United States and placed at the Federal Correctional Institution in Dublin, California. The U.S. Probation Office prepared a post-sentence report in anticipation of the transfer hearing which concluded that the most analogous United States offense to the offense of conviction in Mexico was voluntary manslaughter. Accordingly, it listed the applicable guideline range for sentencing as 41 to 51 months. The U.S. Parole Commission's final transfer determination concluded that Kleeman's offense was most similar to second degree murder and set her sentence at 72 months, with 48 months of supervised release. The Ninth Circuit held that

> the crime of "homicidio simple" of which Kleeman was convicted in Mexico covers certain types of conduct that would be classified as voluntary manslaughter under our law. One convicted of "homicidio simple" may have committed an act that we would treat as murder in the second degree or only as voluntary manslaughter. Because we agree, as a matter of law, that the facts do not establish Kleeman acted with malice, we conclude that the comparable United States offense is voluntary manslaughter. . . . Therefore, we reverse and remand to the Commission to reclassify Kleeman's offense as voluntary manslaughter and to determine her term of imprisonment and supervised release accordingly.

(5) "If a Mexican national, who has been convicted of a crime under state law in the United States and has been transferred to Mexico to serve his sentence, escapes from the custody of Mexican authorities and returns to this country, may the Attorney General apprehend him without a warrant and return him

to Mexican authorities without extradition proceedings?" *Tavarez v. U.S. Attorney General*, 668 F.2d 805, 806 (5th Cir. 1982). In *Tavarez*, the Fifth Circuit held that formal extradition proceedings are not required, provided the person who is apprehended as an escapee from a foreign prison is given the opportunity to consult with counsel and to raise any issue concerning the legality of his return in a petition for federal habeas corpus.

§ 15.02 Recognition of Foreign Criminal Judgments

In *Rosado v. Civiletti*, in the preceding section, Judge Kaufman quotes John Marshall's famous dictum in *The Antelope*, 23 U.S. (10 Wheat.) 66, 123 (1825): "The courts of no country execute the penal laws of another." Contrast the situation obtaining in civil cases, where the U.S. courts, as a matter of comity, routinely enforce foreign judgments.

Although not precisely a matter of "executing" foreign penal laws, several modes of international cooperation can result in U.S. courts aiding the efforts of other countries to enforce their own penal laws. These modes of cooperation include mutual assistance [*see* chap. 12] and extradition [*see* chap 13]. European nations have developed the further possibility of transferring criminal proceedings from one country to another. *See* Julian Schutte, *Transfer of Criminal Proceedings: The European System*, *in* 2 INTERNATIONAL CRIMINAL LAW 643 (M. Cherif Bassiouni ed., 2d ed. 1999).

Apart from prisoner transfers, which appear to represent a genuine exception to Marshall's dictum, there are various other ways in which U.S. law may indirectly give effect to a foreign criminal conviction. *See generally* A. Kenneth Pye, *The Effect of Foreign Criminal Judgments Within the United States*, 32 U.M.K.C. L. REV. 114 (1964), *reprinted in* INTERNATIONAL CRIMINAL LAW 479 (Gerhard O. W. Mueller & Edward M. Wise eds., 1965). The cases in which questions about the effect of foreign convictions arise can be grouped largely into five categories.

First, the foreign conviction may be pleaded as a bar to a second trial for the same offense in the United States. Since a different sovereign was involved, a second trial would not be barred by the constitutional ban on double jeopardy. But a statute may require that the previous trial or conviction be treated as a bar to reprosecution. *See* id. at 485-86.

Second, a foreign criminal conviction may provide a basis under the Immigration and Nationality Act for excluding an alien from the United States.

Third, a criminal conviction may be a ground of disqualification, for instance, for a driver's license, or for a license to practice a certain profession or trade, for government employment, for jury service, for public office, or for voting. Insofar as a foreign conviction counts for these purposes, domestic effect is given to the foreign conviction.

Fourth, a witness's record of criminal convictions may be used to attack the competency or credibility of the witness. Insofar as a foreign conviction can be used for this purpose, effect again is given to foreign penal law.

Finally, a foreign conviction may be taken into account for purposes of sentencing – to make the defendant an habitual or multiple offender, or as a factor to be scored under sentencing guidelines. Some repeat offender statutes explicitly authorize, some explicitly prohibit, the use of foreign convictions for these purposes. Others are ambiguous or silent about the use of foreign convictions. *See* Martha Kimes, Note, *The Effect of Foreign Criminal Convictions Under American Repeat Offender Statutes: A Case Against the Use of Foreign Crimes in Determining Habitual Criminal Status*, 35 COLUM. J. TRANSNAT'L L. 503, 506-10 (1997). The cases interpreting ambiguous statutes have come out on both sides of the question: some allow and some refuse to allow consideration of a foreign conviction for purposes of sentence enhancement. *See id.* 510-14.

In *United States v. Kole* [chap. 10, *supra*], a prior conviction in the Philippines served as a predicate for treating the defendant as a repeat felony drug offender subject to the 20 year mandatory minimum prescribed in 21 U.S.C. § 960. The federal statute itself barred consideration for this purpose of a prior conviction "obtained in violation of the Constitution of the United States." With respect to foreign convictions, the court declined to interpret the statute as requiring that the prior conviction must have been obtained in full conformity with the Bill of Rights, but rather read it as designed only to exclude a "conviction that was obtained in a manner inconsistent with concepts of fundamental fairness and liberty. . . " What if the statute had not made a specific exception for convictions "obtained in violation of the Constitution"? Would a U.S. court be entitled to rely, for purposes of sentence enhancement, on a conviction obtained in a manner that contravened "fundamental fairness"? Is this a general limitation on the use of foreign convictions by or in the U.S. courts that applies whether or not it is expressly stipulated by statute? Insofar as this limitation applies, how closely should a court in the United States scrutinize the "fairness" of a foreign system of criminal procedure? What are the criteria to be used in assessing the "fairness" of an alien system? Consider the following case.

UNITED STATES v. MOSKOVITS

United States District Court for the Eastern District of Pennsylvania
784 F. Supp. 183 (1991)

POLLAK, DISTRICT JUDGE:

BENCH OPINION

In September of 1988, I sentenced Mr. Moskovits to a period of incarceration of seventeen years. Ten years of that sentence was on Count 8 of the indictment, which alleged possession with intent to distribute a cocaine-containing substance which was over 500 grams. Under the statutory scheme, conviction on that count called for a mandatory sentence of five years as a minimum. The mandatory minimum under that statute is increased to ten years, where the person convicted has had a previous felony drug conviction under federal or state or foreign law. . . . The defense was apprised that the government would ask for enhancement on the basis of Mr. Moskovits' conviction in Mexico, in 1983, of the offense of importing narcotic drugs into Mexico. . . .

The central contention made on Mr. Moskovits' behalf, is that the Mexican conviction, which was the basis for enhancement – that is to say my decision that a mandatory minimum sentence of ten years was called for on Count 8 – was an invalid conviction because it was the result of procedures which are not consonant with American constitutional requirements, and hence would not form the basis of sentence enhancement in this United States court. The core of defendant's contention is that the Mexican proceedings were invalid because Mr. Moskovits did not have counsel at crucial phases of the proceeding. . . .

I will not undertake to rehearse the full chronology of what happened . . . Suffice it to say, Mr. Moskovits was apprehended at the airport on June 29, 1983, was found by arresting officers to have drugs with him, and was interrogated, made an inculpatory statement, which was signed by Mr. Moskovits. The statement was in Spanish. Mr. Moskovits appended to the margin of the statement on the first page thereof in English the legend, "Under great emotional stress, I admit that this document contains truth."

There were certain preliminary proceedings in July, pursuant to which Mr. Moskovits was held in custody. An attorney, who apparently was not retained, made an appearance on Mr. Moskovits' behalf, but withdrew from the ambiguous representation on August 8. At that time, Mr. Moskovits was advised by the judge that he, Mr. Moskovits, had three days to retain a new attorney, and failing that, a government attorney would be appointed to represent him. The record does not disclose that any such appointment was in fact made.

The record further discloses that Mr. Moskovits next had legal representation on August 22, when Mr. Moskovits' father and Mr. Gilberto Rojo Herrera entered into a retainer agreement.   There is disagreement between the government and the defendant as to the nature of that retainer agreement. The position taken by Mr. Moskovits is that the purpose of the retainer was solely to secure a fixed sentence which would enable Mr. Moskovits then to be transferred to United States custody under the Prisoner Exchange Treaty. . . . It is the government's view that the contract of retainer impose[d] on Mr. Herrera a broader mission. . . [going] beyond a petition for a fixed minimum sentence. . . . I don't find it necessary to resolve the dispute with respect to what the purpose of the retainer agreement was, whether the limited one perceived by the defense, or the broader one perceived by the government.

Suffice it to note that, before Mr. Herrera was retained on August 22, there was the first of the two so-called Careo hearings.   At those hearings, Mr. Moskovits appeared without counsel present, and confronted his accusers. The understanding is that the Careo proceeding, which has no clear analogue in American jurisprudence, is an opportunity for such a face-to-face presentation. At the Careo proceeding on August 10, there appears to have been an extended presentation by the arresting officers. Attendant on that [was] the reception of Mr. Moskovits' statement, the one to which I had referred, which was inculpatory and to which he appended the English notation, that it was signed under emotional stress. Mr. Moskovits had the opportunity, which he evidently exercised, to give testimony himself and to explain the inadequacies and inconsistencies of the arresting officer's testimony, and to represent the inappropriateness of their behavior.   There was a further Careo hearing on August 29, one week after the retention of Mr. Herrera. Mr. Herrera was not present at the August 29 proceeding either. That proceeding was thought to supplement the August 10 proceeding, and to relate to a so-called missing witness. Again, Mr. Moskovits was there, and clearly represented himself with vigor, but he did not have counsel at his side.

With respect to the nature of Careo hearings, the only evidence supplied to this court is contained in affirmation of one Jose Cruz, a Mexican attorney who has status in New York, not as a member of the bar, but as one admitted to advise on foreign law, that is to say Mexican law. In Mr. Cruz' affirmation, he says:

> I am fully familiar with the Mexican law relating to the so-called "Careo" hearings, and I hereby certify that, in accordance with Article 266 of the "Federal Criminal Procedures Code" of Mexico, the only persons who may appear at such hearings are the parties involved, a judge, and an interpreter, if necessary. The attorney for the defense is not allowed to be present since his or her appearance could influence the demeanor of the parties.

> "Careo" hearings are not, in themselves, a trial under Mexican law, but only a phase of the procedure which aids the judge in finding the truth.

. . .

After the "Careo" hearing, the judge's impression of the said hearing will be just another piece of evidence but this, by itself, may not direct a resolution of the case in one direction or another, since the "Careo" is not a piece of evidence determinative of the resolution of the case.

The discussion by Mr. Cruz is a very modest one. Perhaps it poses more questions than it answers. It is, however, the only information which has been presented either by the government or by the defense. This was a defense submission. There has been earnest argument about how central the Careo hearings are in Mexican criminal procedure.

With respect to the particulars of the process as it affected Mr. Moskovits – that, of course, is the focus of our interest here today – it appears that after the second Careo hearing, on September 6, there was a ruling by the court – and it does not appear whether this was done in a courtroom proceeding or was simply an order – that recited that the parties were free to submit such further evidence as they thought appropriate, but that no such submissions were made.

On September 15, the first proceeding in which it appears as a matter of record that Mr. Herrera participated in some formal sense, was Mr. Herrera's submission to the court, responsive to a motion for judgment that was filed by the Office of the Attorney General on September 13. . . [O]n September 20, the court made an extended review of the prior proceedings, and, in particular, considered the material brought forward at the Careo proceedings with respect to Mr. Moskovits' apprehension, statements which Mr. Moskovits had reportedly made, and the contention made by Mr. Herrera on Mr. Moskovits' behalf that Mr. Moskovits should be "absolved," a contention which the court rejected in favor of finding Mr. Moskovits guilty. With respect to sentence, the court concluded that for this defendant, who had no prior criminal record, a seven-year sentence would suffice. And so sentence was imposed. . . [N]ine days later, a court determined that appeal time had run. Neither the government nor the defense had appealed, and so the seven-year sentence was final and was to be executed.

The record in the Mexican court, as described, calls on us, in my judgment, to return once again to the question already adumbrated, what is the role of the Careo proceeding in Mexican law. As noted, the proceeding was bifurcated. Most of it took place on August 10, a supplementary phase on August 29. Mr. Moskovits did not have an attorney, at either phase, present at the proceeding. . . . What we have then is two days of Careo proceedings, which appear to be the only proceedings at which live testimony was offered, at which there was an opportunity for cross-examination, and on neither of those days was Mr. Moskovits attended by counsel. Evidently, the government also was not represented by counsel in these proceedings.

The government of the United States contends that. . . it would be a mistake to equate the Careo proceedings with those crucial phases of an American criminal proceeding at which evidence is adduced.   The better analogy, it is argued, is that these are in the nature of preliminary proceedings akin to a probable cause hearing. Defense, for its part, contends that certain preliminary hearings, having taken place in July in Mr. Moskovits' case, would better carry the legend of probable cause proceedings.

I find more than a little difficulty accepting the view that the Careo proceedings are to be regarded as preliminary proceedings analogous to the probable cause phase in our jurisprudence. If one takes that nomenclature, one then asks, preliminary to what? Where is the central evidentiary proceeding that in our terms would be a trial? The government's view is that such an opportunity for presentation of the defense case, if there would be one, was, at least in this instance, made judicially available on September 6, when the court ruled that the parties had the opportunity to offer evidence as they respectably felt appropriate, and then when no such submissions were made, determined that the record was closed. . . . [But] the fact is that no submission was made, and so the evidentiary record, on the basis of which the court found guilt and imposed sentence on September 20, was the evidentiary record made at the Careo hearings.

The first question then to be considered is whether, if we take that the proceedings in Mr. Moskovits' case were in accord with standard Mexican criminal procedure, that makes the resultant conviction and sentence secure as a basis for sentence enhancement in our court.

There is nothing before this court to suggest that the procedures utilized in Mr. Moskovits' case departed from Mexican requirements. So I will assume for purposes of discussion that they were in conformity with – at least then – prevailing Mexican requirements. It is the position, of course, of the defense that Mexican requirements are irrelevant because they fail to guarantee the American constitutional norms; irrelevant, that is to say, insofar as the Mexican conviction is relied on in the United States court for sentence enhancement purposes. The government's position is that so long as there was conformity with Mexican requirements and with norms of fundamental fairness, the Mexican conviction and sentence can be relied upon by this court for its sentence enhancement purposes.

Accepting the government's position means that we should test a foreign conviction not by its conformity with every ingredient of what in American terms is fundamental criminal procedure, but we should test a foreign conviction by its conformity with those particular norms of American criminal procedures, jurisprudence constitutionalized, that are the particular domain of absolute rock bottom fundamental fairness.

How does one draw distinctions? In *United States v. Wilson*, 556 F.2d 1177, 1178 (4th Cir.), *cert. denied*, 434 U.S. 986, 54 L. Ed. 2d 481, 98 S. Ct. 614 (1977), the Court of Appeals noted that a German criminal conviction could be relied upon by an American court, notwithstanding the absence of a jury in German criminal procedure. A jury is part of the American constitutional armament. It is guaranteed in federal prosecution by the Bill of Rights, and has been judicially found, via the Fourteenth Amendment, to be an ingredient of the due process which states are required to observe in state criminal proceedings. It would, however, be a form of cultural imperialism for the United States to insist that it would not countenance, for U.S. purposes, recognition of a foreign criminal judgment which came from a legal culture which did not employ the jury. I don't doubt Congress' authority to say that the jury is so important that it wouldn't permit, in looking at foreign criminal judgments for sentence enhancement purposes, reliance on a criminal conviction emanating from Germany or France. But it would seem to me an improbable way to accomplish legitimate American goals of insisting on fairness in American courts. In contradistinction to the jury ingredient, I would find the presence or absence of counsel.

The Supreme Court of the United States found that counsel are required in state criminal proceedings, by virtue of the Constitution of the United States, long before the Supreme Court found that juries were required in state criminal proceedings by the Constitution of the United States. The distinction is not merely a chronological one in the development of the American jurisprudence. The distinction has to do with the basis on which the right to counsel cases lie. The distinction is that without an attorney at one's side, most lay persons are essentially helpless to meet criminal charges. So that what is in form a hearing, is in fact not a hearing when an accused does not have a lawyer. That observation about how the criminal process works is an observation that would not have geographical boundaries, if the Supreme Court were right in its perception about the criminal process in the United States. The determination is one that would seem to me to apply equally well to Mexico or to the United Kingdom or to South Africa or to the Soviet Union or to Zimbabwe.

Accordingly, I think we cannot countenance reliance on a foreign criminal conviction where it can be said, on the basis of the record made, that there was a failure to provide for counsel at crucial stages of the process. That is a conclusion which, in the first instance, I would determine as a matter of statutory implication. I read the statute that Congress passed, which imposes a ten-year minimum via sentence enhancement in reliance on foreign drug convictions, as a statute which implies that the foreign conviction shall be one which meets norms of fundamental fairness as perceived by United States courts. The participation of counsel at crucial stages of the criminal proceeding is one such fundamental norm.

I say I come to that conclusion as a matter of statutory construction because I would attribute to Congress no lower standard. But I would add that if one could suppose the possibility that Congress had not imported such a requirement into the statute, there would be very grave questions as to the constitutionality of that aspect of the sentencing enhancement provision.

In Mr. Moskovits' case, it is plain that he did not have counsel at the August 10 phase of the Careo proceeding. That is to say, he did not have counsel with him, nor was there an attorney either appointed or retained to represent him. The August 10 proceeding was the one at which the bulk of the evidence was reviewed and relied on by the judge on September 20, as adduced. By August 29, the supplementary Careo proceeding, Mr. Moskovits had an attorney representing him, but the attorney was not present at the supplementary Careo proceeding.

If we are to follow Mr. Cruz' analysis of Mexican law – and this record gives me no basis for reliance on anything else – Mr. Herrera could not have been present at the August 29 proceeding, even had he wished to do so. It is the case that Mr. Herrera took no steps that are shown by the record to offer supplementary testimony, that is to say, to pursue the opportunity afforded on September 6th. It is also the case that Mr. Herrera did make a written submission on September 15, and was present in person when judgment was announced on September 20.

I cannot find those belated and marginal activities of counsel sufficient to cure the absence of counsel of August 10, or again on August 29. The requirement which the Supreme Court of our country has found to be a central dimension of American criminal procedure is the presence of counsel at all significant stages of the criminal proceeding. And certainly the Careo proceedings, as they related to Mr. Moskovits' prosecution, can only be characterized as crucial. My understanding is that the Supreme Court calls for the presence of counsel at all significant stages in the American criminal proceeding, and what analysis we can make of the Mexican procedures, as they affected Mr. Moskovits, would show the Careo hearings to have been crucial.

Accordingly, I conclude that the Mexican procedures, resulting in a conviction and sentence of Mr. Moskovits, cannot be regarded as a valid conviction and sentence from the perspective of a United States court.

What is the legal implication of that for this case? The Supreme Court of the United States determined in *United States v. Tucker*, 404 U.S. 443, 30 L. Ed. 2d 592, 92 S. Ct. 589 (1972), that where it was shown that a sentencing judge had relied on criminal convictions, prior criminal convictions, when he was engaged in the sentencing process, and that two of the criminal convictions relied on were invalid for lack of counsel, it was appropriate to remand the case for resentencing. The Supreme Court did not say that the sentencing judge was precluded from considering the tainted criminal proceedings. What the Supreme Court appeared to be saying, through Justice Stewart, and the dissent of Justice Blackmun and Chief Justice Burger, was that if there was ground for supposing that the sentencing judge was operating on the understanding that these were valid convictions, and that had he known they were not valid convictions, he might have arrived at a different sentence, then a remand for resentencing was appropriate.

The *Tucker* case was followed by *United States v. Fleishman*, 684 F.2d 1329, 1346 (9th Cir.), *cert. denied*, 459 U.S. 1044, 74 L. Ed. 2d 614, 103 S. Ct. 464 (1982), in which the Court of Appeals declined to remand for resentencing. In *Fleishman*, the court . . . concluded that resentencing was not called for because the sentencing judge had relied on the uncounseled convictions, not because he thought the convictions *per se* were necessarily valid – the representation that they were uncounseled were made to the judge – but because he thought they reflected prior criminal behavior which he could properly take into account.

That means, in effect, that the question of whether the invalid prior conviction taints the sentence depends on what light the sentencing judge gained from the prior convictions. If it was the conviction *qua* conviction that the sentencing judge looked to, and in that sense relied upon the validity of the conviction under U.S. constitutional norm, then a post-sentence determination that the relied on convictions were invalid would call for resentencing. If, however, the relied on convictions were simply evidentiary of a pattern of antisocial behavior, which to the sentencing judge was relevant to present sentence, then resentencing would not be called for. And so one must look to what the sentencing judge had in mind.

In this case, that inquiry is not a difficult one to make. In this case, the sentencing judge explained on the record that the prior conviction of September 20, 1983, required the sentencing judge to impose a minimum sentence of ten years on Count 8. The sentencing judge, when presented with no reason not to accept that judgment, sentenced accordingly. The sentencing judge was operating under a statutory mandate. He was not exercising his discretion one way or another with respect to whether the Mexican proceedings showed Mr. Moskovits to have been a miscreant a number of years before. Accordingly, since in this case the sentencing judge was relying on the legal verity, the constitutional integrity in American fundamental fairness terms, of the Mexican conviction, the determination made in this 2255 proceeding that the Mexican conviction cannot properly be relied on because it does not comport with fundamental fairness, would appear to require that the sentence imposed be reconsidered. . . .

Accordingly, I will direct that Mr. Moskovits' sentence will be vacated, and we will schedule a new sentencing date.

NOTES AND QUESTIONS

(1) Moskovits was resentenced to fifteen years' imprisonment. Subsequently, however, Judge Pollak ordered a new trial on the ground that the defendant also had been denied the effective assistance of counsel at his trial in the U.S. because counsel had not inquired into the validity of the Mexican conviction before advising the defendant that it was likely to be used for impeachment

purposes if the defendant testified. *See United States v. Moskovits*, 844 F.
Supp. 202 (E.D. Pa. 1993). Moskovits was retried before a different judge. On
appeal, his conviction was affirmed, but a sentence to twenty years'
imprisonment was vacated on the ground that it impermissibly exceeded the
fifteen years imposed by Judge Pollak. *See United States v. Moskovits*, 86 F.3d
1303 (3d Cir. 1996), *cert. denied*, 519 U.S. 1120 (1997).

(2) Who bears the burden of proof as to the fairness of a foreign conviction?
Does it depend on the purpose for which the conviction is to be used? Consider
the following statement in *People v. Wallach*, 110 Mich. App. 37, 312 N.W.2d
387 (1981), where the Michigan Court of Appeals found it to be error, although
harmless error, for the trial court to have ruled that the prosecution could use
the defendant's prior Canadian convictions for purposes of impeachment:

> While no previous Michigan case has ruled on whether evidence of
> foreign convictions can be used for impeachment purposes, a similar
> problem was considered in *People v Braithwaite*, 67 Mich. App. 121, 240
> N.W.2d 293 (1976). In *Braithwaite*, this Court flatly held that evidence
> of a conviction under Canadian law would never be a permissible
> consideration in determining what sentence to impose. The prosecution
> contends that *Braithwaite* is distinguishable since it deals with
> sentencing. However, we are not prepared to say that it is more
> egregious to consider evidence of a foreign conviction for purposes of
> sentencing than it is to use the same conviction in the trial process. If
> anything, the latter is more offensive. To the extent that one is
> concerned about the fundamental fairness of the conviction rendered in
> the other country, it is certainly preferable to have evidence of that
> conviction considered in sentencing as opposed to admitting it during
> the trial where it can affect the very integrity of any guilty verdict
> rendered.

> We agree with the prosecution, however, that the blanket prohibition of
> *Braithwaite* should not be followed. The question in any given case
> should be whether the foreign legal system lacks procedural protections
> necessary for fundamental fairness. While few, if any, of the other legal
> systems in the world are as conscientiously dedicated to ensuring that
> the rights of the accused are as scrupulously honored as the various
> legal systems in the United States, many of these systems do provide
> substantial safeguards for the accused, making it inherently unlikely
> that innocent persons will be convicted of offenses which they did not
> commit. The problem of the use of evidence of foreign convictions
> involves a balancing of competing policy interests. On the one hand, we
> do not want to make use of evidence of convictions obtained in a system
> which is not fundamentally fair. On the other hand, we do not want
> miscreants to look upon Michigan as a sanctuary where their criminal
> activity in foreign countries can have no bearing on issues raised by new
> illegalities. If evidence of past convictions is relevant to impeach, as
> similar acts evidence, in sentencing, or otherwise, and the system in

which they were rendered sufficiently safeguards the rights of the accused, there exists no compelling reason not to make use of evidence of these convictions, where appropriate.

The prosecution cites us to two federal cases which place the burden on the defendant of establishing that the foreign legal system lacks the procedural protections necessary to guarantee fundamental fairness for the accused. *United States v Wilson*, 556 F. 2d 1177 (4th Cir.), *cert denied*, 434 U.S. 986 (1977), *United States v Manafzadeh*, 592 F.2d 81 (2d Cir. 1979). We are urged to follow this same procedure. At this point our views depart from those of the prosecution. In Michigan, the prosecution must sustain the burden of proof on the issue of whether evidence of a prior conviction can be used for impeachment purposes. We see no reason to depart from this standard where admissibility of evidence of a prior conviction also hinges on the fundamental fairness of the foreign legal system. In the case sub judice, no showing was made by the prosecution that the specific legal system in which defendant was convicted is fundamentally fair. Therefore, it was error to allow the use of evidence of the Canadian convictions for impeachment purposes.

(3) Can a court rely on the evidence supporting a questionable foreign conviction without relying on the conviction itself? Consider *United States v. Delmarle*, 99 F.3d 80 (2d Cir. 1996), in which the defendant challenged his sentence for transmitting child pornography, in part on the ground that the district court erroneously had departed upward under the Federal Sentencing Guidelines by taking into account, as part of his criminal history, an *in absentia* Italian conviction for sexual misconduct with minors. In passing on this claim, Judge Kearse observed:

The Guidelines require the sentencing court to calculate a defendant's criminal history principally with reference to his prior sentences as categorized in Guidelines §§ 4A1.1 and 4A1.2. . . . . Under Guidelines § 4A1.2(h), a sentence for a foreign conviction is not to be counted.

The Guidelines encourage the sentencing court, however, to consider departing from the criminal history category computed strictly pursuant to §§ 4A1.1 and 4A1.2 "if reliable information indicates that the criminal history category does not adequately reflect the seriousness of the defendant's past criminal conduct or the likelihood that the defendant will commit other crimes." Indeed, § 4A1.2(h) itself notes that a sentence resulting from a foreign conviction "may be considered under § 4A1.3".
. . . .

In the present case, Delmarle's criminal history category was calculated under §§ 4A1.1 and 4A1.2 without regard to . . . his conviction in Italy for sexual misconduct with three young boys. The resulting criminal history category was I, the lowest category. The district court departed upward by two criminal history category steps pursuant to § 4A1.3 on the ground that category I did not adequately reflect Delmarle's past criminal conduct or the likelihood that he would commit further crimes. Delmarle challenges the departure, contending that . . . the Italian conviction was not entered in accordance with due process. We see no. . . . error in the district court's treatment of the Italian conviction. When the sentencing judge has been apprised of possible constitutional infirmities surrounding a foreign conviction – or even is informed of a conviction that has been vacated for constitutional infirmity – he may nonetheless consider any reliable information concerning the conduct that led to that conviction in order, in an exercise of informed discretion, to determine whether the conduct warrants a departure.

In the present case, Delmarle maintains that the Italian conviction was obtained without due process, having been entered *in absentia* after Delmarle was expelled from Italy by order of the Italian court, and should have been disregarded for that reason. The district court did not rely on the fact of the Italian conviction, however. The events, which occurred while Delmarle was working in Italy as a civilian employee with the United States military, had been investigated by both an Italian agency and the United States Military Police. The court considered the investigative report of the United States Military Police, which was accompanied by extensive documentation. The court found that the investigative records showed that on several occasions, Delmarle had "used his own children as bait to encourage [neighbors'] children to be overnight guests at his home," and that "while they slept in their sleeping bags he molested them." The court found that the information in the report was "reliable and relevant." Delmarle did not point to any specific part of the report or the records that he contended was unreliable; he made only the most conclusory challenge to the reliability of "the information on which the [Italian] conviction was based," and argued without elaboration that the underlying evidence was "insufficient." His conclusory argument is insufficient to warrant questioning the district court's assessment that the information was reliable.

(4) How closely should a sentencing judge inquire into the fairness of foreign proceedings? Consider the district court's response to the defendant's challenge to use of a prior German conviction in *United States v. Makki*, 47 F. Supp.2d 25 (D.D.C. 1999). In *Makki*, the defendant pleaded guilty to charges of possessing and using an altered U.S. passport. The government, on sentencing, requested the court to depart upward under the Federal Sentencing Guidelines and change the defendant's criminal history category from I to IV, in part on the basis of his 1989 German conviction for "attempting to participate in a felony causing an explosion." In ruling on this request, Judge Friedman stated:

The defendant has no criminal convictions in the United States and therefore has zero criminal history points under the Guidelines. Under a traditional analysis, the defendant therefore would have a Criminal

History of I. The government, however, requests that the Court depart from the otherwise applicable Guideline sentencing range to a Criminal History Category of IV pursuant to Section 4A1.3 of the Sentencing Guidelines. Section 4A1.3 allows the Court to depart upward "if reliable information indicates that the criminal history category does not adequately reflect the seriousness of the defendant's past criminal conduct or the likelihood that the defendant will commit other crimes." "Reliable information" includes, among other things, (1) "prior sentence[s] not used in computing the criminal history category (e.g., sentences for foreign or tribal offenses)," and (2) "prior similar adult criminal conduct not resulting in a criminal conviction." The government has the burden of justifying any upward departure by a preponderance of the evidence. . . .

Regarding the "seriousness of the defendant's past criminal conduct," the government asserts that an upward departure is justified because a Criminal History Category of I does not reflect (1) defendant's 1989 conviction in Germany, (2) defendant's false statements on his 1993 visa applications, and (3) defendant's other alleged terrorist activities. . . The Court concludes that defendant's criminal conviction in Germany and the misrepresentations made in connection with his 1993 visa applications should be considered as reliable information justifying a departure under Section 4A1.3, but that his alleged membership in the Hizballah and his alleged terrorist activities should not.

A foreign sentence is explicitly contemplated as a grounds for an upward departure under Section 4A1.3. The German Judgment provides a summary of the court proceedings and testimony which led to defendant's conviction for "attempting to participate in a felony of causing an explosion." Among the factual findings the German court made were that defendant was conspiring with others to conduct surveillance of American and Israeli sites in Germany in order to identify potential targets for terrorist bombing attacks and that defendant was personally involved in such surveillance. The German court also found that defendant had attempted to send a message to a person in Lebanon stating in code that he had located United States and Israeli targets in Germany and that he would carry out attacks on them if he was provided with weapons and dynamite. The German court rejected his defense that he acted under duress. While defendant argues that the Court should not give full credence to the fairness of criminal proceedings and judgments in all foreign countries, the Court has no reason to view German courts with any skepticism. Defendant was represented by counsel in the German proceedings, was confronted with the witnesses against him and was permitted to testify in his own behalf. The Court will consider defendant's German conviction.

Chapter 16
INTERNATIONAL HUMAN RIGHTS AND CRIMINAL PROCEDURE

§ 16.01 General Principles

The Second World War was the great catalyst for international concern with human rights. Before the war, how a state treated its own citizens generally was thought to be beyond the reach of international law. International law was the law governing relations between states. It did not protect individuals as such. After the war, the whole axis of international law began to shift, from an almost exclusive emphasis on states to concern with the rights and welfare of individuals. The Nuremberg Trial [see chap. 18] contributed to this shift in perceptions about the nature of international law. The imposition of criminal liability on individuals for breaches of international law confirmed that international law was no longer a body of rules concerned only with states; it dramatized the possibility of an international legal universe in which individual human beings as well as states figure as participants.

There were circumstances in which the law of the pre-war era did protect individuals indirectly. Under international law, as it developed in the nineteenth and early twentieth centuries, a state was bound to accord a certain minimum standard of justice to foreigners whom it had admitted to its territory – although compensation for failure to observe this standard belonged not to the injured individual but to the state of which that individual was a national. There was no guarantee that the home state would push for redress. Only strong states were in a position to do so. But, at least in principle, it was recognized that aliens were protected by an international standard of fair treatment. The international standard of justice was taken, in numerous arbitral decisions, to require the following guarantees for the defendant in a criminal case:

> There must be some grounds for his arrest. An arrested person must be given an opportunity to communicate with the consul of his state if he requests it. He is entitled to be brought before a judge within a reasonable period following his arrest. Otherwise, there is an illegal detention. He must also be fairly treated during such detention. He is entitled to be informed of all the charges against him. He must be enabled to defend himself with the aid of counsel. Possibly, the right is simply to retain counsel and not to have counsel provided for at the expense of the state of trial. He is entitled not to be exposed to undue delay in the proceedings. He should be brought to trial within a reasonable time. He is entitled to a fair trial before an impartial

tribunal. He is entitled to seriousness on the part of the court. The provisions of local law must not be disregarded; the same is true with respect to relevant treaty provisions. He must be given the opportunity to summon witnesses in his own behalf and to interrogate them. He must not be exposed to cruel and inhuman treatment during the proceedings nor by way of punishment after the proceedings.

Lester Orfield, *What Constitutes Fair Criminal Procedure under Municipal and International Law*, 12 U. PITT. L. REV. 35, 42-43 (1950).

These rules applied, however, only to foreigners. Governments generally were free to treat their own citizens as they liked. What a state did to its own citizens was its own business – a matter of "domestic jurisdiction" – and nothing about which other states were entitled to complain.

Again, there were exceptions. There were efforts through international action to accord certain protections against their own states to distinct classes of people: "humanitarian intervention" to protect religious minorities from atrocious persecution; nineteenth century treaties aimed at the abolition of the slave trade and slavery; the earlier Geneva Conventions affording protections to sick and wounded soldiers and prisoners of war; the early labor treaties, concluded toward the beginning of the twentieth century, on the rights of workers in industrial employment; the system developed under the League of Nations for protecting ethnic minorities in central Europe. These exceptions, however, remained on the margin of traditional international law which, by and large, was not concerned with protecting human rights.

A revolutionary change occurred at the end of the Second World War. The crucial event was the founding of the United Nations in 1945. The Second World War had been a war to vindicate human rights (in a way that made it different from previous wars, except perhaps the U.S. Civil War – which was a catalyst for similarly significant changes in U.S. constitutional law). References to human rights recur in the U.N. Charter. Article 68 provides for the creation of the U.N. Commission on Human Rights – the only commission specifically named in the Charter. It was understood that the first task of the Commission, once it came into being, would be to draft an international bill of rights.

At the Commission's first session in February 1947, Eleanor Roosevelt was elected chair, and there was much discussion of the form that the international bill of rights should take. Several possibilities were considered: a resolution of the General Assembly, a multilateral treaty, an amendment to the U.N. Charter. A consensus emerged that the bill should be a declaration of rights to be adopted by a resolution of the General Assembly. At its second session a year later, the Commission decided that the international bill of rights should have three components: first, the declaration of rights; second, a convention setting out the rights contained in the declaration in more precise language, together with specification of the limitations to which each right was subject; and, third, measures of implementation – machinery for enforcement to be contained in a document apart from the declaration and the convention. Later this scheme was revised again so as to incorporate measures of implementation in the convention, which was both to describe human rights in precise enforceable language and to establish machinery for enforcement. Ultimately, it was decided to have two separate conventions or "covenants": one on civil and political rights, the other on social, economic, and cultural rights, each with its own measures of implementation. The two covenants were adopted by the General Assembly in 1966.

The first component of the international bill of rights, the Universal Declaration of Human Rights, was adopted by the General Assembly in Paris at 3 a.m. on the night of December 10, 1948. The previous day the General Assembly had adopted the Genocide Convention [see chap. 21]. The Universal Declaration of Human Rights contains thirty articles. Article 1 enunciates the basic principle of the Declaration: "All human beings are born free and equal in dignity and rights. They are endowed with reason and conscience and should act towards one another in a spirit of brotherhood." Article 2 sets out the principle of non-discrimination in the enjoyment of human rights. Articles 3-21 are devoted to civil and political rights such as the rights to life, liberty, and property, to freedom from torture or inhumane and degrading treatment, to freedom from arbitrary arrest, detention or exile, to a fair and public hearing by an independent and impartial tribunal, to freedom of thought and religion, to freedom of expression, to peaceful assembly and association, and to take part in the government of one's country. Articles 22-27 deal with economic and social rights: rights to social security, to work, to fair pay and fair conditions of work, to rest and leisure, to an adequate standard of living, to education, and to participate in the cultural life of the community. Articles 29-30 set out certain general limitations on the exercise of human rights requiring, for instance, that they be exercised with respect for the rights and freedoms of others.

In form, the Universal Declaration of Human Rights is simply a General Assembly resolution. Under the U.N. Charter, the General Assembly can only make recommendations. It has no power to make law or to impose binding obligations on states. Eleanor Roosevelt's closing speech in Paris emphasized that the Declaration was not a treaty and imposed no legal obligations, but was rather a statement of principles setting up (as its Preamble says) "a common standard of achievement for all peoples and all nations."

It was recognized at the time that, to be effective, international enforcement of human rights required acceptance of three further principles not stated in the Universal Declaration of Human Rights: (1) that states are under an obligation to respect the rights set out in the Declaration; (2) that observance of human rights being a matter of international obligation, it is within the province of the U.N. to respond to violations of human rights as violations of international law; and (3) that not only governments – which often are reluctant to do so – but also individuals should have a right to complain about human rights violations to the U.N. or to some other agency empowered to do something about them. Since 1948, these principles have been partly but not completely realized.

First, in the fifty-two years since 1948, practically every state in the world has voted for subsequent U.N. resolutions that speak of an obligation to observe the provisions of the Universal Declaration. These resolutions treat the declaration as if it had acquired binding force, as if it were a law which nations are bound to obey. Thus, at least on paper, there appears to be general agreement that the Declaration, contrary to what was thought in 1948, actually does commit states to respect human rights.

How this can be so is a matter of controversy. According to one view, the U.N. Charter itself imposes an obligation to respect human rights, and the Declaration represents an authoritative statement of the particular rights that are included within that obligation. According to another view, the Declaration of Human Rights has acquired the force of customary international law through constant acquiescence by governments in the proposition that it is law. There are problems with both these views. It is also difficult to see how certain provisions of the Declaration – for instance, the statement in Article 24 that "[e]veryone has a right to . . . periodic holidays with pay" – could possibly represent binding legal rules. More plausible, perhaps, is the view that some, but not all, of the provisions of the Declaration have acquired the force of customary international law – or rather that customary norms have developed whose content is the same as that of particular provisions in the Declaration. In any event, a state which has avowed that it is bound to respect human rights – as practically all states have – is rather more likely, when accused of a human rights violation, to deny that a violation occurred than to deny that it is obligated to respect human rights.

The project that began with the Universal Declaration was completed with adoption of the two covenants on human rights – the International Covenant on Civil and Political Rights and the International Covenant on Economic, Social and Cultural Rights – in 1966. Both came into effect in 1976. The two covenants have legal force as treaties for the states which are parties to them.

The Covenant on Economic, Social and Cultural Rights requires states to submit periodic reports on measures adopted in order to comply with the covenant. The Covenant on Civil and Political Rights establishes a Human Rights Committee (not to be confused with the Commission on Human Rights established under the U.N. Charter). Parties are required to submit reports every five years to this Committee. There also is an optional complaint procedure under which parties to the Covenant may complain to the Committee about non-compliance by another party. In addition, an Optional Protocol to the Covenant permits aggrieved individuals to submit complaints to the Committee: after receiving a response from the state which has been charged with a violation, the Committee is to "forward its views to the State Party concerned and to the individual." No sanctions are provided for non-compliance with the Committee's expression of its view that the Covenant has been violated.

In addition to the two covenants, numerous other human rights treaties have been adopted under the auspices of the United Nations. Each imposes obligations with respect to a particular subset of human rights. These additional human rights treaties include four of special importance: the 1965 International Convention on the Elimination of All Forms of Racial Discrimination, the 1979 Convention on the Elimination of All Forms of Discrimination Against Women, the 1984 Torture Convention [*see* chap. 9], and the 1989 Convention on the Rights of the Child. Like the Covenant on Civil and Political Rights, each of these four conventions establishes a committee to monitor compliance. Although the International Covenant on Economic, Social and Cultural Rights contemplates that reports about compliance will be transmitted to the U.N. Economic and Social Council (ECOSOC), the Council itself, in 1985, established a special committee to supervise implementation of the Covenant. These six committees (the Human Rights Committee, the Committee on Economic, Social and Cultural Rights, the Committee on the Elimination of Racial Discrimination; the Committee on the Elimination of Discrimination against Women, the Committee against Torture, and the Committee on the Rights of the Child) are referred to as "treaty bodies" (as opposed to "Charter bodies" like the U.N. Commission on Human Rights).

The Commission on Human Rights has been authorized as well to consider individual complaints when they reflect a consistent pattern of violations of human rights. For the first twenty years of its existence, the Commission was thought to be without any power at all to deal with the numerous complaints regarding human rights violations that, from the beginning, have flooded into the United Nations. Since 1967, several different procedures have evolved by which the Commission may respond, at least in part, to such complaints. These include annual public debate focusing on countries in which gross violations of human rights are alleged to have occurred (a procedure that derives from ECOSOC Resolution 1235 (XLII), adopted in 1967); confidential investigation of individual communications that reveal "a consistent pattern of gross and reliably attested violations of human rights" (a procedure that derives from ECOSOC Resolution 1503 (XLVIII), adopted in 1970); and the appointment of "thematic" rapporteurs or working groups to consider violations relating to a specific theme such as disappearances, arbitrary executions, arbitrary detention, violence against women, etc.

Apart from human rights treaties and from declarations about the obligations of states, such as the General Assembly's 1975 Declaration on Torture relied on in the *Filartiga* case [chap. 1, *supra*], the United Nations has produced various standard-setting instruments that purport only to provide guidelines for international action and for national legislation. The U.N. "crime prevention and criminal justice program" has generated a whole compendium of such "standards" in the field of criminal justice. *See* ROGER S. CLARK, THE UNITED NATIONS CRIME PREVENTION AND CRIMINAL JUSTICE PROGRAM: FORMULATION OF STANDARDS AND EFFORTS AT THEIR IMPLEMENTATION (1994). The U.N. Standard Minimum Rules for the Treatment of Prisoners are, perhaps, the best known example. *See also* INTERNATIONAL HUMAN RIGHTS: PROBLEMS OF LAW, POLICY, & PRACTICE 276-322 (Richard B. Lillich & Hurst Hannum eds., 3d ed. 1995).

Besides the activities of the United Nations in the field of human rights, there are three regional arrangements for human rights protection.

In 1950, the Council of Europe adopted the European Convention on Human Rights. The Council of Europe (a much larger entity than the fifteen-member European Union) originally was founded to promote the unity of western European democracies; it now includes forty-one member states from both western and eastern Europe. The European Convention on Human Rights is a comprehensive statement of fundamental rights implemented by the possibility of complaint to the European Court of Human Rights. In the original scheme of the Convention, complaints were screened first by a European Commission on Human Rights. Since 1998, they have gone directly to the Court.

The Organization of American States has two overlapping mechanisms for enforcement of human rights. First, the Inter-American Commission on Human Rights, established in 1960, has competence to hear complaints regarding violations of the American Convention on Human Rights of 1969, which entered into force in 1978. It may decide to refer a complaint to the Inter-American Court of Human Rights if the state involved has accepted the Court's jurisdiction. Second, the Commission is competent to examine complaints regarding a violation of the American Declaration of the Rights and Duties of Man of 1948 by any OAS member, including states which are not parties to the American Convention on Human Rights. Thus, complaints against the United States, which is not a party to the Convention, have nonetheless been entertained by the Commission.

There also is an African Commission of Human and Peoples' Rights established under the African [Banjul] Charter on Human and Peoples' Rights, June 27, 1981, 21 I.L.M. 59 (1981), which entered into force in 1986.

§ 16.02   Specific Provisions

INTERNATIONAL COVENANT ON CIVIL AND POLITICAL RIGHTS

General Assembly Resolution 2200A (XXI), Dec. 19, 1966
21 U.N. GAOR Supp. No. 16, at 52, U.N. Doc. A/6316 (1966)

PART I

Article I

1. All peoples have the right of self-determination. By virtue of that right they freely determine their political status and freely pursue their economic, social

and cultural development.

2. All peoples may, for their own ends, freely dispose of their natural wealth and resources without prejudice to any obligations arising out of international economic co-operation, based upon the principle of mutual benefit, and international law. In no case may a people be deprived of its own means of subsistence.

3. The States Parties to the present Covenant, including those having responsibility for the administration of Non-Self-Governing and Trust Territories, shall promote the realization of the right of self-determination, and shall respect that right, in conformity with the provisions of the Charter of the United Nations.

PART II

Article 2

1. Each State Party to the present Covenant undertakes to respect and to ensure to all individuals within its territory and subject to its jurisdiction the rights recognized in the present Covenant, without distinction of any kind, such as race, colour, sex, language, religion, political or other opinion, national or social origin, property, birth or other status.

2. Where not already provided for by existing legislative or other measures, each State Party to the present Covenant undertakes to take the necessary steps, in accordance with its constitutional processes and with the provisions of the present Covenant, to adopt such legislative or other measures as may be necessary to give effect to the rights recognized in the present Covenant.

3. Each State Party to the present Covenant undertakes:

(a) To ensure that any person whose rights or freedoms as herein recognized are violated shall have an effective remedy, notwithstanding that the violation has been committed by persons acting in an official capacity;

(b) To ensure that any person claiming such a remedy shall have his right thereto determined by competent judicial, administrative or legislative authorities, or by any other competent authority provided for by the legal system of the State, and to develop the possibilities of judicial remedy;

(c) To ensure that the competent authorities shall enforce such remedies when granted.

Article 3

The States Parties to the present Covenant undertake to ensure the equal right of men and women to the enjoyment of all civil and political rights set forth in the present Covenant.

Article 4

1. In time of public emergency which threatens the life of the nation and the existence of which is officially proclaimed, the States Parties to the present Covenant may take measures derogating from their obligations under the present Covenant to the extent strictly required by the exigencies of the situation, provided that such measures are not inconsistent with their other obligations under international law and do not involve discrimination solely on the ground of race, colour, sex, language, religion or social origin.

2. No derogation from articles 6, 7, 8 (paragraphs 1 and 2), 11, 15, 16 and 18 may be made under this provision.

3. Any State Party to the present Covenant availing itself of the right of derogation shall immediately inform the other States Parties to the present Covenant, through the intermediary of the Secretary-General of the United Nations, of the provisions from which it has derogated and of the reasons by which it was actuated. A further communication shall be made, through the same intermediary, on the date on which it terminates such derogation.

Article 5

1. Nothing in the present Covenant may be interpreted as implying for any State, group or person any right to engage in any activity or perform any act aimed at the destruction of any of the rights and freedoms recognized herein or at their limitation to a greater extent than is provided for in the present Covenant.

2. There shall be no restriction upon or derogation from any of the fundamental human rights recognized or existing in any State Party to the present Covenant pursuant to law, conventions, regulations or custom on the pretext that the present Covenant does not recognize such rights or that it recognizes them to a lesser extent.

PART III

Article 6

1. Every human being has the inherent right to life. This right shall be protected by law. No one shall be arbitrarily deprived of his life.

2. In countries which have not abolished the death penalty, sentence of death may be imposed only for the most serious crimes in accordance with the law in force at the time of the commission of the crime and not contrary to the provisions of the present Covenant and to the Convention on the Prevention and Punishment of the Crime of Genocide. This penalty can only be carried out pursuant to a final judgement rendered by a competent court.

3. When deprivation of life constitutes the crime of genocide, it is understood

that nothing in this article shall authorize any State Party to the present Covenant to derogate in any way from any obligation assumed under the provisions of the Convention on the Prevention and Punishment of the Crime of Genocide.

4. Anyone sentenced to death shall have the right to seek pardon or commutation of the sentence. Amnesty, pardon or commutation of the sentence of death may be granted in all cases.

5. Sentence of death shall not be imposed for crimes committed by persons below eighteen years of age and shall not be carried out on pregnant women.

6. Nothing in this article shall be invoked to delay or to prevent the abolition of capital punishment by any State Party to the present Covenant.

Article 7

No one shall be subjected to torture or to cruel, inhuman or degrading treatment or punishment. In particular, no one shall be subjected without his free consent to medical or scientific experimentation.

Article 8

1. No one shall be held in slavery; slavery and the slave-trade in all their forms shall be prohibited.

2. No one shall be held in servitude.

1. (a) No one shall be required to perform forced or compulsory labour;

(b) Paragraph 3 (a) shall not be held to preclude, in countries where imprisonment with hard labour may be imposed as a punishment for a crime, the performance of hard labour in pursuance of a sentence to such punishment by a competent court;

(c) For the purpose of this paragraph the term "forced or compulsory labour" shall not include:

(i) Any work or service, not referred to in subparagraph (b), normally required of a person who is under detention in consequence of a lawful order of a court, or of a person during conditional release from such detention;

(ii) Any service of a military character and, in countries where conscientious objection is recognized, any national service required by law of conscientious objectors;

(iii) Any service exacted in cases of emergency or calamity threatening the life or well-being of the community;

(iv) Any work or service which forms part of normal civil obligations.

Article 9

1. Everyone has the right to liberty and security of person. No one shall be subjected to arbitrary arrest or detention. No one shall be deprived of his liberty except on such grounds and in accordance with such procedure as are established by law.

2. Anyone who is arrested shall be informed, at the time of arrest, of the reasons for his arrest and shall be promptly informed of any charges against him.

3. Anyone arrested or detained on a criminal charge shall be brought promptly before a judge or other officer authorized by law to exercise judicial power and shall be entitled to trial within a reasonable time or to release. It shall not be the general rule that persons awaiting trial shall be detained in custody, but release may be subject to guarantees to appear for trial, at any other stage of the judicial proceedings, and, should occasion arise, for execution of the judgement.

4. Anyone who is deprived of his liberty by arrest or detention shall be entitled to take proceedings before a court, in order that court may decide without delay on the lawfulness of his detention and order his release if the detention is not lawful.

5. Anyone who has been the victim of unlawful arrest or detention shall have an enforceable right to compensation.

Article 10

1. All persons deprived of their liberty shall be treated with humanity and with respect for the inherent dignity of the human person.

2.   (a) Accused persons shall, save in exceptional circumstances, be segregated from convicted persons and shall be subject to separate treatment appropriate to their status as unconvicted persons;

    (b) Accused juvenile persons shall be separated from adults and brought as speedily as possible for adjudication.

3. The penitentiary system shall comprise treatment of prisoners the essential aim of which shall be their reformation and social rehabilitation. Juvenile offenders shall be segregated from adults and be accorded treatment appropriate to their age and legal status.

Article 11

No one shall be imprisoned merely on the ground of inability to fulfil a contractual obligation.

Article 12

1. Everyone lawfully within the territory of a State shall, within that territory, have the right to liberty of movement and freedom to choose his residence.

2. Everyone shall be free to leave any country, including his own.

3. The above-mentioned rights shall not be subject to any restrictions except those which are provided by law, are necessary to protect national security, public order (*ordre public*), public health or morals or the rights and freedoms of others, and are consistent with the other rights recognized in the present Covenant.

4. No one shall be arbitrarily deprived of the right to enter his own country.

Article 13

An alien lawfully in the territory of a State Party to the present Covenant may be expelled therefrom only in pursuance of a decision reached in accordance with law and shall, except where compelling reasons of national security otherwise require, be allowed to submit the reasons against his expulsion and to have his case reviewed by, and be represented for the purpose before, the competent authority or a person or persons especially designated by the competent authority.

Article 14

1. All persons shall be equal before the courts and tribunals. In the determination of any criminal charge against him, or of his rights and obligations in a suit at law, everyone shall be entitled to a fair and public hearing by a competent, independent and impartial tribunal established by law. The press and the public may be excluded from all or part of a trial for reasons of morals, public order (*ordre public*) or national security in a democratic society, or when the interest of the private lives of the parties so requires, or to the extent strictly necessary in the opinion of the court in special circumstances where publicity would prejudice the interests of justice; but any judgement rendered in a criminal case or in a suit at law shall be made public except where the interest of juvenile persons otherwise requires or the proceedings concern matrimonial disputes or the guardianship of children.

2. Everyone charged with a criminal offence shall have the right to be presumed innocent until proved guilty according to law.

3. In the determination of any criminal charge against him, everyone shall be entitled to the following minimum guarantees, in full equality:

(a) To be informed promptly and in detail in a language which he understands of the nature and cause of the charge against him;

(b) To have adequate time and facilities for the preparation of his defence and to communicate with counsel of his own choosing;

(c) To be tried without undue delay;

(d) To be tried in his presence, and to defend himself in person or through legal assistance of his own choosing; to be informed, if he does not have legal assistance, of this right; and to have legal assistance assigned to him, in any case where the interests of justice so require, and without payment by him in any such case if he does not have sufficient means to pay for it;

(e) To examine, or have examined, the witnesses against him and to obtain the attendance and examination of witnesses on his behalf under the same conditions as witnesses against him;

(f) To have the free assistance of an interpreter if he cannot understand or speak the language used in court;

(g) Not to be compelled to testify against himself or to confess guilt.

4. In the case of juvenile persons, the procedure shall be such as will take account of their age and the desirability of promoting their rehabilitation.

5. Everyone convicted of a crime shall have the right to his conviction and sentence being reviewed by a higher tribunal according to law.

6. When a person has by a final decision been convicted of a criminal offence and when subsequently his conviction has been reversed or he has been pardoned on the ground that a new or newly discovered fact shows conclusively that there has been a miscarriage of justice, the person who has suffered punishment as a result of such conviction shall be compensated according to law, unless it is proved that the non-disclosure of the unknown fact in time is wholly or partly attributable to him.

7. No one shall be liable to be tried or punished again for an offence for which he has already been finally convicted or acquitted in accordance with the law and penal procedure of each country.

Article 15

1. No one shall be held guilty of any criminal offence on account of any act or omission which did not constitute a criminal offence, under national or international law, at the time when it was committed. Nor shall a heavier penalty be imposed than the one that was applicable at the time when the criminal offence was committed. If, subsequent to the commission of the offence, provision is made by law for the imposition of the lighter penalty, the offender shall benefit thereby.

2. Nothing in this article shall prejudice the trial and punishment of any person for any act or omission which, at the time when it was committed, was criminal according to the general principles of law recognized by the community of nations.

Article 16

Everyone shall have the right to recognition everywhere as a person before the law.

Article 17

1. No one shall be subjected to arbitrary or unlawful interference with his privacy, family, home or correspondence, nor to unlawful attacks on his honour and reputation.

2. Everyone has the right to the protection of the law against such interference or attacks.

Article 18

1. Everyone shall have the right to freedom of thought, conscience and religion. This right shall include freedom to have or to adopt a religion or belief of his choice, and freedom, either individually or in community with others and in public or private, to manifest his religion or belief in worship, observance, practice and teaching.

2. No one shall be subject to coercion which would impair his freedom to have or to adopt a religion or belief of his choice.

3. Freedom to manifest one's religion or beliefs may be subject only to such limitations as are prescribed by law and are necessary to protect public safety, order, health, or morals or the fundamental rights and freedoms of others.

4. The States Parties to the present Covenant undertake to have respect for the liberty of parents and, when applicable, legal guardians to ensure the religious and moral education of their children in conformity with their own convictions.

Article 19

1. Everyone shall have the right to hold opinions without interference.

2. Everyone shall have the right to freedom of expression; this right shall include freedom to seek, receive and impart information and ideas of all kinds, regardless of frontiers, either orally, in writing or in print, in the form of art, or through any other media of his choice.

3. The exercise of the rights provided for in paragraph 2 of this article carries with it special duties and responsibilities. It may therefore be subject to certain

restrictions, but these shall only be such as are provided by law and are necessary:

(a) For respect of the rights or reputations of others;

(b) For the protection of national security or of public order (*ordre public*), or of public health or morals.

Article 20

1. Any propaganda for war shall be prohibited by law.

2. Any advocacy of national, racial or religious hatred that constitutes incitement to discrimination, hostility or violence shall be prohibited by law.

Article 21

The right of peaceful assembly shall be recognized. No restrictions may be placed on the exercise of this right other than those imposed in conformity with the law and which are necessary in a democratic society in the interests of national security or public safety, public order (*ordre public*), the protection of public health or morals or the protection of the rights and freedoms of others.

Article 22

1. Everyone shall have the right to freedom of association with others, including the right to form and join trade unions for the protection of his interests.

2. No restrictions may be placed on the exercise of this right other than those which are prescribed by law and which are necessary in a democratic society in the interests of national security or public safety, public order (*ordre public*), the protection of public health or morals or the protection of the rights and freedoms of others. This article shall not prevent the imposition of lawful restrictions on members of the armed forces and of the police in their exercise of this right.

3. Nothing in this article shall authorize States Parties to the International Labour Organisation Convention of 1948 concerning Freedom of Association and Protection of the Right to Organize to take legislative measures which would prejudice, or to apply the law in such a manner as to prejudice, the guarantees provided for in that Convention.

Article 23

1. The family is the natural and fundamental group unit of society and is entitled to protection by society and the State.

2. The right of men and women of marriageable age to marry and to found a family shall be recognized.

3. No marriage shall be entered into without the free and full consent of the intending spouses.

4. States Parties to the present Covenant shall take appropriate steps to ensure equality of rights and responsibilities of spouses as to marriage, during marriage and at its dissolution. In the case of dissolution, provision shall be made for the necessary protection of any children.

Article 24

1. Every child shall have, without any discrimination as to race, colour, sex, language, religion, national or social origin, property or birth, the right to such measures of protection as are required by his status as a minor, on the part of his family, society and the State.

2. Every child shall be registered immediately after birth and shall have a name.

3. Every child has the right to acquire a nationality.

Article 25

Every citizen shall have the right and the opportunity, without any of the distinctions mentioned in article 2 and without unreasonable restrictions:

(a) To take part in the conduct of public affairs, directly or through freely chosen representatives;

(b) To vote and to be elected at genuine periodic elections which shall be by universal and equal suffrage and shall be held by secret ballot, guaranteeing the free expression of the will of the electors;

(c) To have access, on general terms of equality, to public service in his country.

Article 26

All persons are equal before the law and are entitled without any discrimination to the equal protection of the law. In this respect, the law shall prohibit any discrimination and guarantee to all persons equal and effective protection against discrimination on any ground such as race, colour, sex, language, religion, political or other opinion, national or social origin, property, birth or other status.

Article 27

In those States in which ethnic, religious or linguistic minorities exist, persons belonging to such minorities shall not be denied the right, in community with the other members of their group, to enjoy their own culture, to profess and practise their own religion, or to use their own language.

NOTES AND QUESTIONS

(1) Part IV of the Covenant (comprising Articles 28-45) establishes the Human Rights Committee. Part V comprises two articles (Articles 46-47) which provide that nothing in the Covenant shall impair either existing powers of U.N. agencies with respect to human rights violations or "the inherent right of all peoples to enjoy and utilize fully and freely their natural wealth and resources." Part VI (comprising Articles 48-53) contains the final clauses dealing with signature, ratification, entry into force, amendment, etc. The Covenant came into force on March 23, 1976.

(2) What are the differences between the procedural guarantees for a criminal defendant contained in the International Covenant on Civil and Political Rights and those contained in the U.S. Bill of Rights and made applicable to the states through the Fourteenth Amendment? Which set of guarantees appears to afford stronger protection to the defendant? To what extent do the differences stem from the fact that, as an instrument meant to apply internationally, the Covenant has to allow for differences in criminal procedure as between common law and in civil law countries? To what extent are international human rights instruments like the Covenant apt to contribute to a convergence of systems of criminal procedure in countries belonging to these two traditions? For an account of the convergence in criminal procedure in Europe that has come about as a result of the European Convention on Human Rights, *see* Bert Swart & James Young, *The European Convention on Human Rights and Criminal Justice in the Netherlands and the United Kingdom*, in CRIMINAL JUSTICE IN EUROPE: A COMPARATIVE STUDY 57 (Christopher Harding, et al., eds., 1995).

(3) The United States became a party to the International Covenant on Civil and Political Rights belatedly in 1992. Ratification was subject to five reservations, five understandings, and three declarations. The extent to which the United States qualified its obligations under the Covenant has prompted questions about whether the United States really is a party at all. *See, e.g.,* William A. Schabas, *Invalid Reservations to the ICCPR: Is the United States Still a Party?*, 21 BROOKLYN J. INT'L L. 227 (1995). The U.S. reservations, understandings, and declarations read as follows:

Reservations:

(1) That article 20 does not authorize or require legislation or other action by the United States that would restrict the right of free speech and association protected by the Constitution and laws of the United States.

(2) That the United States reserves the right, subject to its Constitutional constraints, to impose capital punishment on any person (other than a pregnant woman) duly convicted under existing or future

laws permitting the imposition of capital punishment, including such punishment for crimes committed by persons below eighteen years of age.

(3) That the United States considers itself bound by article 7 to the extent that "cruel, inhuman or degrading treatment or punishment" means the cruel and unusual treatment or punishment prohibited by the Fifth, Eighth, and-or Fourteenth Amendments to the Constitution of the United States.

(4) That because U.S. law generally applies to an offender the penalty in force at the time the offence was committed, the United States does not adhere to the third clause of paragraph 1 of article 15.

(5) That the policy and practice of the United States are generally in compliance with and supportive of the Covenant's provisions regarding treatment of juveniles in the criminal justice system. Nevertheless, the United States reserves the right, in exceptional circumstances, to treat juveniles as adults, notwithstanding paragraphs 2 (b) and 3 of article 10 and paragraph 4 of article 14. The United States further reserves to these provisions with respect to States with respect to individuals who volunteer for military service prior to age 18.

Understandings:

(1) That the Constitution and laws of the United States guarantee all persons equal protection of the law and provide extensive protections against discrimination. The United States understands distinctions based upon race, color, sex, language, religion, political or other opinion, national or social origin, property, birth or any other status – as those terms are used in article 2, paragraph 1 and article 26 – to be permitted when such distinctions are, at minimum, rationally related to a legitimate governmental objective. The United States further understands the prohibition in paragraph 1 of article 4 upon discrimination, in time of public emergency, based "solely" on the status of race, color, sex, language, religion or social origin, not to bar distinctions that may have a disproportionate effect upon persons of a particular status.

(2) That the United States understands the right to compensation referred to in articles 9 (5) and 14 (6) to require the provision of effective and enforceable mechanisms by which a victim of an unlawful arrest or detention or a miscarriage of justice may seek and, where justified, obtain compensation from either the responsible individual or the appropriate governmental entity. Entitlement to compensation may be subject to the reasonable requirements of domestic law.

(3) That the United States understands the reference to "exceptional

circumstances" in paragraph 2 (a) of article 10 to permit the imprisonment of an accused person with convicted persons where appropriate in light of an individual's overall dangerousness, and to permit accused persons to waive their right to segregation from convicted persons. The United States further understands that paragraph 3 of article 10 does not diminish the goals of punishment, deterrence, and incapacitation as additional legitimate purposes for a penitentiary system.

(4) That the United States understands that subparagraphs 3 (b) and (d) of article 14 do not require the provision of a criminal defendant's counsel of choice when the defendant is provided with court-appointed counsel on grounds of indigence, when the defendant is financially able to retain alternative counsel, or when imprisonment is not imposed. The United States further understands that paragraph 3 (e) does not prohibit a requirement that the defendant make a showing that any witness whose attendance he seeks to compel is necessary for his defense. The United States understands the prohibition upon double jeopardy in paragraph 7 to apply only when the judgment of acquittal has been rendered by a court of the same governmental unit, whether the Federal Government or a constituent unit, as is seeking a new trial for the same cause.

(5) That the United States understands that this Covenant shall be implemented by the Federal Government to the extent that it exercises legislative and judicial jurisdiction over the matters covered therein, and otherwise by the state and local governments; to the extent that state and local governments exercise jurisdiction over such matters, the Federal Government shall take measures appropriate to the Federal system to the end that the competent authorities of the state or local governments may take appropriate measures for the fulfillment of the Covenant.

Declarations:

(1) That the United States declares that the provisions of articles 1 through 27 of the Covenant are not self-executing.

(2) That it is the view of the United States that States Party to the Covenant should wherever possible refrain from imposing any restrictions or limitations on the exercise of the rights recognized and protected by the Covenant, even when such restrictions and limitations are permissible under the terms of the Covenant. For the United States, article 5, paragraph 2, which provides that fundamental human rights existing in any State Party may not be diminished on the pretext that the Covenant recognizes them to a lesser extent, has particular relevance to article 19, paragraph 3 which would permit certain restrictions on the freedom of expression. The United States declares

that it will continue to adhere to the requirements and constraints of its Constitution in respect to all such restrictions and limitations.

(3) That the United States declares that the right referred to in article 47 ["the inherent right of all peoples to enjoy and utilize fully and freely their natural wealth and resources"] may be exercised only in accordance with international law.

§16.03   The Death Penalty

SOERING v. UNITED KINGDOM

European Court of Human Rights
161 Eur. Ct. H. R.. (ser. A) (1989)

As to the Facts

I. Particular circumstances of the case

11. The applicant, Mr Jens Soering, was born on 1 August 1966 and is a German national. He is currently detained in prison in England pending extradition to the United States of America to face charges of murder in the Commonwealth of Virginia.

12. The homicides in question were committed in Bedford County, Virginia, in March 1985. The victims, William Reginald Haysom (aged 72) and Nancy Astor Haysom (aged 53), were the parents of the applicant's girlfriend, Elizabeth Haysom, who is a Canadian national. Death in each case was the result of multiple and massive stab and slash wounds to the neck, throat and body. At the time the applicant and Elizabeth Haysom, aged 18 and 20 respectively, were students at the University of Virginia. They disappeared together from Virginia in October 1985, but were arrested in England in April 1986 in connection with cheque fraud.

13. The applicant was interviewed in England between 5 and 8 June 1986 by a police investigator from the Sheriff's Department of Bedford County. . . [T]he investigator recorded the applicant as having admitted the killings. . . The applicant had stated that he was in love with Miss Haysom but that her parents were opposed to the relationship. He and Miss Haysom had therefore planned to kill them. They rented a car in Charlottesville and travelled to Washington where they set up an alibi. The applicant then went to the parents' house, discussed the relationship with them and, when they told him that they would do anything to prevent it, a row developed during which he killed them with a knife. On 13 June 1986 a grand jury of the Circuit Court of Bedford County

indicted him on charges of murdering the Haysom parents. The charges alleged capital murder of both of them and the separate non-capital murders of each.

14. On 11 August 1986 the Government of the United States of America requested the applicant's and Miss Haysom's extradition under the terms of the Extradition Treaty of 1972 between the United States and the United Kingdom . . . .

15. On 29 October 1986 the British Embassy in Washington addressed a request to the United States authorities in the following terms:

> Because the death penalty has been abolished in Great Britain, the Embassy has been instructed to seek an assurance, in accordance with the terms of . . . the Extradition Treaty, that, in the event of Mr Soering being surrendered and being convicted of the crimes for which he has been indicted . . . , the death penalty, if imposed, will not be carried out.

> Should it not be possible on constitutional grounds for the United States Government to give such an assurance, the United Kingdom authorities ask that the United States Government undertake to recommend to the appropriate authorities that the death penalty should not be imposed or, if imposed, should not be executed.

16. On 30 December 1986 the applicant was interviewed in prison by a German prosecutor (*Staatsanwalt*) from Bonn. . . . On 11 February 1987 the local court in Bonn issued a warrant for the applicant's arrest in respect of the alleged murders. On 11 March the Government of the Federal Republic of Germany requested his extradition to the Federal Republic under the Extradition Treaty of 1872 between the Federal Republic and the United Kingdom. . . .

18. On 8 May 1987 Elizabeth Haysom was surrendered for extradition to the United States. After pleading guilty on 22 August as an accessory to the murder of her parents, she was sentenced on 6 October to 90 years' imprisonment (45 years on each count of murder).

19. On 20 May 1987 the United Kingdom Government informed the Federal Republic of Germany that the United States had earlier "submitted a request, supported by prima facie evidence, for the extradition of Mr Soering." The United Kingdom Government notified the Federal Republic that they had "concluded that, having regard to all the circumstances of the case, the court should continue to consider in the normal way the United States request." They further indicated that they had sought an assurance from the United States authorities on the question of the death penalty and that "in the event that the court commits Mr Soering, his surrender to the United States authorities would be subject to the receipt of satisfactory assurances on this matter."

20. On 1 June 1987 Mr Updike swore an affidavit in his capacity as Attorney for Bedford County, in which he certified as follows:

I hereby certify that should Jens Soering be convicted of the offence of capital murder as charged in Bedford County, Virginia . . . a representation will be made in the name of the United Kingdom to the judge at the time of sentencing that it is the wish of the United Kingdom that the death penalty should not be imposed or carried out.

This assurance was transmitted to the United Kingdom Government under cover of a diplomatic note on 8 June. It was repeated in the same terms in a further affidavit from Mr Updike sworn on 16 February 1988 and forwarded to the United Kingdom by diplomatic note on 17 May 1988. In the same note the Federal Government of the United States undertook to ensure that the commitment of the appropriate authorities of the Commonwealth of Virginia to make representations on behalf of the United Kingdom would be honoured.

During the course of the present proceedings the Virginia authorities informed the United Kingdom Government that Mr Updike was not planning to provide any further assurances and intended to seek the death penalty in Mr Soering's case because the evidence, in his determination, supported such action.

21. On 16 June 1987 at the Bow Street Magistrates' Court committal proceedings took place before the Chief Stipendiary Magistrate. The Government of the United States adduced evidence that on the night of 30 March 1985 the applicant killed William and Nancy Haysom at their home in Bedford County, Virginia. In particular, evidence was given of the applicant's own admissions as recorded in the affidavit of the Bedford County police investigator.

On behalf of the applicant psychiatric evidence was adduced from a consultant forensic psychiatrist . . . that he was immature and inexperienced and had lost his personal identity in a symbiotic relationship with his girlfriend – a powerful, persuasive and disturbed young woman. . . . The Chief Magistrate found that the evidence . . . was not relevant to any issue that he had to decide and committed the applicant to await the Secretary of State's order for his return to the United States.

24 . . . . [O]n 3 August 1988 the Secretary of State signed a warrant ordering the applicant's surrender to the United States authorities. However, the applicant has not been transferred to the United States by virtue of the interim measures indicated in the present proceedings firstly by the European Commission and then by the European Court

25. On 5 August 1988 the applicant was transferred to a prison hospital where he remained until early November 1988 under the special regime applied to suicide-risk prisoners. According to psychiatric evidence adduced on behalf of the applicant . . . the applicant's dread of extreme physical violence and homosexual abuse from other inmates in death row in Virginia is in particular

having a profound psychological effect on him. The psychiatrist's report records a mounting desperation in the applicant, together with objective fears that he may seek to take his own life.

II. Relevant domestic law and practice in the United Kingdom

36. There is no provision in the Extradition Acts relating to the death penalty, but Article IV of the United Kingdom-United States Treaty provides:

> If the offence for which extradition is requested is punishable by death under the relevant law of the requesting Party, but the relevant law of the requested Party does not provide for the death penalty in a similar case, extradition may be refused unless the requesting Party gives assurances satisfactory to the requested Party that the death penalty will not be carried out.

37. In the case of a fugitive requested by the United States who faces a charge carrying the death penalty, it is the Secretary of State's practice, pursuant to Article IV of the United Kingdom-United States Extradition Treaty, to accept an assurance from the prosecuting authorities of the relevant State that a representation will be made to the judge at the time of sentencing that it is the wish of the United Kingdom that the death penalty should be neither imposed no carried out. This practice has been described by Mr David Mellor, then Minister of State at the Home Office, in the following terms:

> The written undertakings about the death penalty that the Secretary of State obtains from the Federal authorities amount to an undertaking that the views of the United Kingdom will be represented to the judge. At the time of sentencing he will be informed that the United Kingdom does not wish the death penalty to be imposed or carried out. That means that the United Kingdom authorities render up a fugitive or are prepared to send a citizen to face an American court on the clear understanding that the death penalty will not be carried out – it has never been carried out in such cases. It would be a fundamental blow to the extradition arrangements between our two countries if the death penalty were carried out on an individual who had been returned under those circumstances. (Hansard, 10 March 1987, col. 955)

There has, however, never been a case in which the effectiveness of such an undertaking has been tested.

III. Relevant domestic law in the Commonwealth of Virginia

42. The sentencing procedure in a capital murder case in Virginia is a separate proceeding from the determination of guilt. Following a determination of guilt of capital murder, the same jury, or judge sitting without a jury, will forthwith proceed to hear evidence regarding punishment. All relevant evidence concerning the offence and the defendant is admissible. Evidence in mitigation

is subject to almost no limitation, while evidence of aggravation is restricted by statute. . .

44. The imposition of the death penalty on a young person who has reached the age of majority – which is 18 years – is not precluded under Virginia law. Age is a fact to be weighed by the jury. . . .

48. Following a moratorium consequent upon a decision of the United States Supreme Court (*Furman v. Georgia*, 92 S. Ct. 2726 (1972)), imposition of the death penalty was resumed in Virginia in 1977, since which date seven persons have been executed. The means of execution used is electrocution.

The Virginia death penalty statutory scheme . . . has been judicially determined to be constitutional. It was considered to prevent the arbitrary or capricious imposition of the death penalty and narrowly to channel the sentencer's discretion. . . The death penalty under the Virginia capital murder statute has also been held not to constitute cruel and unusual punishment or to deny a defendant due process or equal protection. . . The Supreme Court of Virginia rejected the submission that death by electrocution would cause "the needless imposition of pain before death and emotional suffering while awaiting execution of sentence."

56. The average time between trial and execution in Virginia, calculated on the basis of the seven executions which have taken place since 1977, is six to eight years. The delays are primarily due to a strategy by convicted prisoners to prolong the appeal proceedings as much as possible. The United States Supreme Court has not as yet considered or ruled on the "death row phenomenon" and in particular whether it falls foul of the prohibition of "cruel and unusual punishment" under the Eighth Amendment to the Constitution of the United States.

61. There are currently 40 people under sentence of death in Virginia. The majority are detained in Mecklenburg Correctional Center, which is a modern maximum-security institution with a total capacity of 335 inmates. . . .

63. The size of a death row inmate's cell is 3m by 2.2m. Prisoners have an opportunity for approximately 7 hours' recreation per week in summer and approximately 6 hours' per week, weather permitting, in winter. The death row area has two recreation yards, both of which are equipped with basketball courts and one of which is equipped with weights and weight benches. Inmates are also permitted to leave their cells on other occasions, such as to receive visits, to visit the law library or to attend the prison infirmary. In addition, death row inmates are given one hour out-of-cell time in the morning in a common area. Each death row inmate is eligible for work assignments, such as cleaning duties. When prisoners move around the prison they are handcuffed, with special shackles around the waist.

When not in their cells, death row inmates are housed in a common area called "the pod." The guards are not within this area and remain in a box outside. In the event of disturbance or inter-inmate assault, the guards are not allowed to intervene until instructed to do so by the ranking officer present.

64. The applicant adduced much evidence of extreme stress, psychological deterioration and risk of homosexual abuse and physical attack undergone by prisoners on death row, including Mecklenburg Correctional Center. This evidence was strongly contested by the United Kingdom Government on the basis of affidavits sworn by administrators from the Virginia Department of Corrections.

68. A death row prisoner is moved to the death house 15 days before he is due to be executed. The death house is next to the death chamber where the electric chair is situated. Whilst a prisoner is in the death house he is watched 24 hours a day. He is isolated and has no light in his cell. The lights outside are permanently lit. A prisoner who utilises the appeals process can be placed in the death house several times.

69. Relations between the United Kingdom and the United States of America on matters concerning extradition are conducted by and with the Federal and not the State authorities. However, in respect of offences against State laws the Federal authorities have no legally binding power to provide, in an appropriate extradition case, an assurance that the death penalty will not be imposed or carried out. In such cases the power rests with the State. If a State does decide to give a promise in relation to the death penalty, the United States Government has the power to give an assurance to the extraditing Government that the State's promise will be honoured.

According to evidence from the Virginia authorities, Virginia's capital sentencing procedure and notably the provision on post-sentencing reports would allow the sentencing judge to consider the representation to be made on behalf of the United Kingdom Government pursuant to the assurance given by the Attorney for Bedford County. In addition, it would be open to the Governor to take into account the wishes of the United Kingdom Government in any application for clemency.

IV. Relevant law and practice of the Federal Republic of Germany

71. German criminal law applies to acts committed abroad by a German national if the act is liable to punishment at the place where the offence is committed.

72. Murder is . . . . punishable with life imprisonment, the death penalty having been abolished under the Constitution (Article 102 of the Basic Law, 1949).

73. Under the terms of the Juvenile Court Act (1953) as amended, if a young adult – defined as a person who is 18 but not yet 21 years of age at the time of the criminal act – commits an offence, the judge will apply the provisions applicable to a juvenile – defined as a person who is at least 14 but not yet 18

years of age – if, inter alia, "the overall assessment of the offender's personality, having regard also to the circumstances of his environment, reveals that, according to his moral and mental development, he was still equal to a juvenile at the time of committing the offence." The sentence for young adults who come within this section is youth imprisonment of 6 months to 10 years or, under certain conditions, of indeterminate duration. Where, on the other hand, the young adult offender's personal development corresponds to his age, the general criminal law applies but the judge may pass a sentence of 10 to 15 years' imprisonment instead of a life sentence.

As to the Law

80. The applicant alleged that the decision by the Secretary of State for the Home Department to surrender him to the authorities of the United States of America would, if implemented, give rise to a breach by the United Kingdom of Article 3 of the [European] Convention [on Human Rights], which provides: "No one shall be subjected to torture or to inhuman or degrading treatment or punishment."

A. Applicability of Article 3 in cases of extradition

81. The alleged breach derives from the applicant's exposure to the so-called "death row phenomenon." This phenomenon may be described as consisting in a combination of circumstances to which the applicant would be exposed if, after having been extradited to Virginia to face a capital murder charge, he were sentenced to death.

82 . . . . The applicant . . . submitted that Article 3 not only prohibits the Contracting States from causing inhuman or degrading treatment or punishment to occur within their jurisdiction but also embodies an associated obligation not to put a person in a position where he will or may suffer such treatment or punishment at the hands of other States. For the applicant, at least as far as Article 3 is concerned, an individual may not be surrendered out of the protective zone of the Convention without the certainty that the safeguards which he would enjoy are as effective as the Convention standard.

83. The United Kingdom Government, on the other hand, contended that Article 3 should not be interpreted so as to impose responsibility on a Contracting State for acts which occur outside its jurisdiction. . . . To begin with, they maintained, it would be straining the language of Article 3 intolerably to hold that by surrendering a fugitive criminal the extraditing State has "subjected" him to any treatment or punishment that he will receive following conviction and sentence in the receiving State. Further arguments advanced . . . were that it interferes with international treaty rights; it leads to a conflict with the norms of international judicial process, in that it in effect involves adjudication on the internal affairs of foreign States not Parties to the Convention or to the proceedings before the Convention institutions; it entails grave difficulties of evaluation and proof in requiring the examination of alien systems of law and of conditions in foreign States; the practice of national courts

and the international community cannot reasonably be invoked to support it; it causes a serious risk of harm in the Contracting State which is obliged to harbour the protected person, and leaves criminals untried, at large and unpunished.

In the alternative, the United Kingdom Government submitted that the application of Article 3 in extradition cases should be limited to those occasions in which the treatment or punishment abroad is certain, imminent and serious. In their view, the fact that by definition the matters complained of are only anticipated, together with the common and legitimate interest of all States in bringing fugitive criminals to justice, requires a very high degree of risk, proved beyond reasonable doubt, that ill-treatment will actually occur.

85 . . . . [N]o right not to be extradited is as such protected by the Convention. Nevertheless, in so far as a measure of extradition has consequences adversely affecting the enjoyment of a Convention right, it may, assuming that the consequences are not too remote, attract the obligations of a Contracting State under the relevant Convention guarantee. . . .

86. Article 1 of the Convention, which provides that "the High Contracting Parties shall secure to everyone within their jurisdiction the rights and freedoms defined in Section I," sets a limit, notably territorial, on the reach of the Convention. . . . Further, the Convention does not govern the actions of States not Parties to it, nor does it purport to be a means of requiring the Contracting States to impose Convention standards on other States. Article 1 cannot be read as justifying a general principle to the effect that, notwithstanding its extradition obligations, a Contracting State may not surrender an individual unless satisfied that the conditions awaiting him in the country of destination are in full accord with each of the safeguards of the Convention. . . . in particular. . . .

These considerations cannot, however, absolve the Contracting Parties from responsibility under Article 3 for all and any foreseeable consequences of extradition suffered outside their jurisdiction.

87. In interpreting the Convention regard must be had to its special character as a treaty for the collective enforcement of human rights and fundamental freedoms. Thus, the object and purpose of the Convention as an instrument for the protection of individual human beings require that its provisions be interpreted and applied so as to make its safeguards practical and effective. . . .

88 . . . . The question remains whether the extradition of a fugitive to another State where he would be subjected or be likely to be subjected to torture or to inhuman or degrading treatment or punishment would itself engage the responsibility of a Contracting State under Article 3. That the abhorrence of torture has such implications is recognised in Article 3 of the United Nations Convention Against Torture and Other Cruel, Inhuman or Degrading Treatment or Punishment, which provides that "no State Party shall . . .

extradite a person where there are substantial grounds for believing that he would be in danger of being subjected to torture." The fact that a specialised treaty should spell out in detail a specific obligation attaching to the prohibition of torture does not mean that an essentially similar obligation is not already inherent in the general terms of Article 3 of the European Convention. It would hardly be compatible with the underlying values of the Convention, that "common heritage of political traditions, ideals, freedom and the rule of law" to which the Preamble refers, were a Contracting State knowingly to surrender a fugitive to another State where there were substantial grounds for believing that he would be in danger of being subjected to torture, however heinous the crime allegedly committed.

Extradition in such circumstances, while not explicitly referred to in the brief and general wording of Article 3, would plainly be contrary to the spirit and intendment of the Article, and in the Court's view this inherent obligation not to extradite also extends to cases in which the fugitive would be faced in the receiving State by a real risk of exposure to inhuman or degrading treatment or punishment proscribed by that Article.

89. What amounts to "inhuman or degrading treatment or punishment" depends on all the circumstances of the case. Furthermore, inherent in the whole of the Convention is a search for a fair balance between the demands of the general interest of the community and the requirements of the protection of the individual's fundamental rights. As movement about the world becomes easier and crime takes on a larger international dimension, it is increasingly in the interest of all nations that suspected offenders who flee abroad should be brought to justice. Conversely, the establishment of safe havens for fugitives would not only result in danger for the State obliged to habour the protected person but also tend to undermine the foundation of extradition. These considerations must also be included among the factors to be taken into account in the interpretation and application of the notions of inhuman and degrading treatment or punishment in extradition cases.

91. In sum, the decision by a Contracting State to extradite a fugitive may give rise to an issue under Article 3 and hence engage the responsibility of that State under the Convention, where substantial grounds have been shown for believing that the person concerned, if extradited, faces a real risk of being subjected to torture or to inhuman or degrading treatment or punishment in the requesting country. The establishment of such responsibility inevitably involves an assessment of conditions in the requesting country against the standards of Article 3 of the Convention. Nonetheless, there is no question of adjudicating on or establishing the responsibility of the receiving country, whether under general international law, under the Convention or otherwise. In so far as any liability under the Convention is or may be incurred, it is liability incurred by the extraditing Contracting State by reason of its having taken action which has as a direct consequence the exposure of an individual to proscribed ill-treatment.

B. Application of Article 3 in the particular circumstances of the present case

92 . . . . It therefore has to be determined on the above principles whether the foreseeable consequences of Mr Soering's return to the United States are such as to attract the application of Article 3. This inquiry must concentrate firstly on whether Mr Soering runs a real risk of being sentenced to death in Virginia, since the source of the alleged inhuman and degrading treatment or punishment, namely the "death row phenomenon," lies in the imposition of the death penalty. Only in the event of an affirmative answer to this question need the Court examine whether exposure to the "death row phenomenon" in the circumstances of the applicant's case would involve treatment or punishment incompatible with Article 3.

1. Whether the applicant runs a real risk of a death sentence and hence of exposure to the "death row phenomenon"

98. . . . [O]bjectively it cannot be said that the undertaking to inform the judge at the sentencing stage of the wishes of the United Kingdom eliminates the risk of the death penalty being imposed. In the independent exercise of his discretion the Commonwealth's Attorney has himself decided to seek and to persist in seeking the death penalty because the evidence, in his determination, supports such action. If the national authority with responsibility for prosecuting the offence takes such a firm stance, it is hardly open to the Court to hold that there are no substantial grounds for believing that the applicant faces a real risk of being sentenced to death and hence experiencing the "death row phenomenon."

99. The Court's conclusion is therefore that the likelihood of the feared exposure of the applicant to the "death row phenomenon" has been shown to be such as to bring Article 3 into play.

2. Whether in the circumstances the risk of exposure to the "death row phenomenon" would make extradition a breach of Article 3.

(a) *General considerations*

100. As is established in the Court's case-law, ill-treatment, including punishment, must attain a minimum level of severity if it is to fall within the scope of Article 3. The assessment of this minimum is, in the nature of things, relative; it depends on all the circumstances of the case, such as the nature and context of the treatment or punishment, the manner and method of its execution, its duration, its physical or mental effects and, in some instances, the sex, age and state of health of the victim.

Treatment has been held by the Court to be both "inhuman" because it was premeditated, was applied for hours at a stretch and "caused, if not actual bodily injury, at least intense physical and mental suffering", and also "degrading" because it was "such as to arouse in [its] victims feelings of fear, anguish and inferiority capable of humiliating and debasing them and possibly breaking their physical or moral resistance." In order for a punishment or treatment associated with it to be "inhuman" or "degrading." the suffering or humiliation involved must in any event go beyond that inevitable element of suffering or humiliation connected with a given form of legitimate punishment. In this connection, account is to be taken not only of the physical pain experienced but also, where there is a considerable delay before execution of the punishment, of the sentenced person's mental anguish of anticipating the violence he is to have inflicted on him.

101. Capital punishment is permitted under certain conditions by Article 2(1) of the Convention, which reads: "Everyone's right to life shall be protected by law. No one shall be deprived of his life intentionally save in the execution of a sentence of a court following his conviction of a crime for which this penalty is provided by law." In view of this wording, the applicant did not suggest that the death penalty per se violated Article 3. He, like the two Government Parties, agreed with the Commission that the extradition of a person to a country where he risks the death penalty does not in itself raise an issue under either Article 2 or Article 3. On the other hand, Amnesty International in their written comments argued that the evolving standards in Western Europe regarding the existence and use of the death penalty required that the death penalty should now be considered as an inhuman and degrading punishment within the meaning of Article 3.

102. Certainly, "the Convention is a living instrument which . . . must be interpreted in the light of present-day conditions"; and, in assessing whether a given treatment or punishment is to be regarded as inhuman or degrading for the purposes of Article 3, "the Court cannot but be influenced by the developments and commonly accepted standards in the penal policy of the member States of the Council of Europe in this field." De facto the death penalty no longer exists in time of peace in the Contracting States to the Convention. In the few Contracting States which retain the death penalty in law for some peacetime offences, death sentences, if ever imposed, are nowadays not carried out. This "virtual consensus in Western European legal systems that the death penalty is, under current circumstances, no longer consistent with regional standards of justice," to use the words of Amnesty International, is reflected in Protocol No. 6 to the Convention, which provides for the abolition of the death penalty in time of peace. Protocol No. 6 was opened for signature in April 1983, which in the practice of the Council of Europe indicates the absence of objection on the part of any of the Member States of the Organisation; it came into force in March 1985 and to date has been ratified by thirteen Contracting States to the Convention, not however including the United Kingdom.

Whether these marked changes have the effect of bringing the death penalty per se within the prohibition of ill-treatment under Article 3 must be determined on the principles governing the interpretation of the Convention.

103. The Convention is to be read as a whole and Article 3 should therefore be construed in harmony with the provisions of Article 2. On this basis Article 3 evidently cannot have been intended by the drafters of the Convention to include a general prohibition of the death penalty since that would nullify the clear wording of Article 2(1).

Subsequent practice in national penal policy, in the form of a generalised abolition of capital punishment, could be taken as establishing the agreement of the Contracting States to abrogate the exception provided for under Article 2(1) and hence to remove a textual limit on the scope for evolutive interpretation of Article. However, Protocol No. 6, as a subsequent written agreement, shows that the intention of the Contracting Parties as recently as 1983 was to adopt the normal method of amendment of the text in order to introduce a new obligation to abolish capital punishment in time of peace and, what is more, to do so by an optional instrument allowing each State to choose the moment when to undertake such an engagement. In these conditions, notwithstanding the special character of the Convention, Article 3 cannot be interpreted as generally prohibiting the death penalty.

104. That does not mean however that circumstances relating to a death sentence can never give rise to an issue under Article 3. The manner in which it is imposed or executed, the personal circumstances of the condemned person and a disproportionality to the gravity of the crime committed, as well as the conditions of detention awaiting execution, are examples of factors capable of bringing the treatment or punishment received by the condemned person within the proscription under Article 3. Present-day attitudes in the Contracting States to capital punishment are relevant for the assessment whether the acceptable threshold of suffering or degradation has been exceeded.

(b) *The particular circumstances*

i. *Length of detention prior to execution*

106. The period that a condemned prisoner can expect to spend on death row in Virginia before being executed is on average six to eight years. This length of time awaiting death is, as the Commission and the United Kingdom Government noted, in a sense largely of the prisoner's own making in that he takes advantage of all avenues of appeal which are offered to him by Virginia law. . . . Nevertheless, just as some lapse of time between sentence and execution is inevitable if appeal safeguards are to be provided to the condemned person, so it is equally part of human nature that the person will cling to life by exploiting those safeguards to the full. However well-intentioned and even potentially beneficial is the provision of the complex of post-sentence procedures in Virginia, the consequence is that the condemned prisoner has to endure for many years the conditions on death row and the anguish and mounting tension of living in the ever-present shadow of death.

ii. *Conditions on death row*

107. As to conditions in Mecklenburg Correctional Center, where the applicant could expect to be held if sentenced to death, the Court bases itself on the facts which were uncontested by the United Kingdom Government, without finding it necessary to determine the reliability of the additional evidence adduced by the applicant, notably as to the risk of homosexual abuse and physical attack undergone by prisoners on death row. The stringency of the custodial regime in Mecklenburg [is] . . . described in some detail above. In this connection, the United Kingdom Government drew attention to the necessary requirement of extra security for the safe custody of prisoners condemned to death for murder. Whilst it might thus well be justifiable in principle, the severity of a special regime such as that operated on death row in Mecklenburg is compounded by the fact of inmates being subject to it for a protracted period lasting on average six to eight years.

iii. *The applicant's age and mental state*

108. At the time of the killings, the applicant was only 18 years old and there is some psychiatric evidence, which was not contested as such, that he "was suffering from [such] an abnormality of mind . . . as substantially impaired his mental responsibility for his acts."

Unlike Article 2 of the Convention, Article 6 of the 1966 International Covenant on Civil and Political Rights and Article 4 of the 1969 American Convention on Human Rights expressly prohibit the death penalty from being imposed on persons aged less than 18 at the time of commission of the offence. Whether or not such a prohibition be inherent in the brief and general language of Article 2 of the European Convention, its explicit enunciation in other, later international instruments, the former of which has been ratified by a large number of States Parties to the European Convention, at the very least indicates that as a general principle the youth of the person concerned is a circumstance which is liable, with others, to put in question the compatibility with Article 3 of measures connected with a death sentence.

It is in line with the Court's case-law . . . to treat disturbed mental health as having the same effect for the application of Article 3.

109. . . . [T]he applicant's youth at the time of the offence and his then mental state, on the psychiatric evidence as it stands, are therefore to be taken into consideration as contributory factors tending, in his case, to bring the treatment on death row within the terms of Article 3.

iv. *Possibility of extradition to the Federal Republic of Germany*

110. For the United Kingdom Government . . . , the possibility of extraditing or deporting the applicant to face trial in the Federal Republic of Germany, where the death penalty has been abolished under the Constitution,

is not material for the present purposes. Any other approach, the United Kingdom Government submitted, would lead to a "dual standard" affording the protection of the Convention to extraditable persons fortunate enough to have such an alternative destination available but refusing it to others not so fortunate.

This argument is not without weight. Furthermore, the Court cannot overlook either the horrible nature of the murders with which Mr Soering is charged or the legitimate and beneficial role of extradition arrangements in combating crime. . . . However, sending Mr Soering to be tried in his own country would remove the danger of a fugitive criminal going unpunished as well as the risk of intense and protracted suffering on death row. It is therefore a circumstance of relevance for the overall assessment under Article 3 in that it goes to the search for the requisite fair balance of interests and to the proportionality of the contested extradition decision in the particular case.

(c) *Conclusion*

111. For any prisoner condemned to death, some element of delay between imposition and execution of the sentence and the experience of severe stress in conditions necessary for strict incarceration are inevitable. The democratic character of the Virginia legal system in general and the positive features of Virginia trial, sentencing and appeal procedures in particular are beyond doubt. The Court agrees . . . that the machinery of justice to which the applicant would be subject in the United States is in itself neither arbitrary nor unreasonable, but, rather, respects the rule of law and affords not inconsiderable procedural safeguards to the defendant in a capital trial. Facilities are available on death row for the assistance of inmates, notably through provision of psychological and psychiatric services.

However, in the Court's view, having regard to the very long period of time spent on death row in such extreme conditions, with the ever present and mounting anguish of awaiting execution of the death penalty, and to the personal circumstances of the applicant, especially his age and mental state at the time of the offence, the applicant's extradition to the United States would expose him to a real risk of treatment going beyond the threshold set by Article 3. A further consideration of relevance is that in the particular instance the legitimate purpose of extradition could be achieved by another means which would not involve suffering of such exceptional intensity or duration. Accordingly, the Secretary of State's decision to extradite the applicant to the United States would, if implemented, give rise to a breach of Article 3. . . .

NOTES AND QUESTIONS

(1) Soering ultimately was extradited to the United States after the United Kingdom received assurances that he would not be tried in Virginia for a crime carrying the death penalty. He was tried and convicted on June 22, 1990, on two

counts of first-degree murder and sentenced to two terms of life imprisonment. *See* INTERNATIONAL HUMAN RIGHTS: PROBLEMS OF LAW, POLICY, & PRACTICE 768 (Richard B. Lillich & Hurst Hannum eds., 3d ed. 1995); *Soering v. Deeds*, 255 Va. 457, 499 S.E.2d 514 (1998) (denial of habeas corpus).

(2) What precisely does *Soering* hold? Is it that *any* provision of a human rights treaty will "trump" a state's obligations under an extradition treaty? Will the obligation under Article 3 of the European Convention not to subject an individual to "torture or inhuman or degrading treatment or punishment" *always* do so? When a state's obligations under two treaties conflict, why should its obligation under a human rights treaty be accorded priority? Insofar as the ban on torture and inhuman or degrading treatment or punishment is supposed to be a norm of customary international law, would a state be obligated to refuse extradition in circumstances like those in *Soering* even if it were not a party to the European Convention on Human Rights? Could the customary norm be invoked in an extradition hearing in a domestic court as a defense against extradition? *See Report of the Committee on Extradition and Human Rights, in* INTERNATIONAL LAW ASSOCIATION, REPORT OF THE SIXTY-SIXTH CONFERENCE 151-52 (1994). On the relationship between extradition and human rights obligations generally, *see also* John Dugard & Christine Van den Wyngaert, *Reconciling Extradition with Human Rights*, 92 AM. J. INT'L L. 187 (1998).

(3) Does the death penalty itself violate internationally-guaranteed human rights? On the death penalty in international law generally, *see* William A. Schabas, THE ABOLITION OF THE DEATH PENALTY IN INTERNATIONAL LAW (2d ed. 1997).

In *State v. Makwanyane*, 1995 (3) SALR 391 (CC), the South African Constitutional Court concluded that the death penalty violated the South African constitutional prohibition of cruel, inhuman, or degrading punishment. However, in paragraph 103 of the *Soering* judgment, the European Court concluded that the death penalty *per se* does not violate the European Convention on Human Rights (although it is prohibited by the Protocol No. 6 to that Convention).

Is a party to Protocol No. 6 bound, apart from the "death row phenomenon," to refuse extradition on a capital charge? In a Dutch case, *The Netherlands v. Short*, 29 I.L.M. 1375 (1990), U.S. military authorities had asked the Netherlands to surrender, under the NATO Status of Forces Agreement, an American solider accused of having murdered his wife, but refused to give assurances that the death penalty would not be imposed. The Netherlands was a party to Protocol No. 6, so there was a direct conflict between the obligation not to subject individuals to the death penalty and the obligations imposed by the Status of Forces Agreement. The Dutch Supreme Court was not prepared to find find that Protocol No. 6 necessarily prevailed over the obligation to surrender the accused, but, balancing the competing interests, did hold that Short's interest in not being surrendered was entitled to priority. In the end, he was surrendered when the U.S. authorities agreed not to charge him with a capital crime.

In a 1996 Italian case discussed in Andrea Bianchi, *International Decision: Venezia v. Ministero di Grazia e Giustizia*, 91 AM. J. INT'L L. 727 (1997), the Italian Constitutional Court held that it violated the Italian Constitution to vest Italian officials in extradition cases with discretion to rule on the sufficiency of the assurances given by the United States that capital punishment would not be imposed.

(4) Does *Soering* hold that the "death row phenomenon" in itself violates Article 3? Or was more, having to do with Soering's age and mental state, required? In *Kindler v. Canada*, U.N.Doc. CCPR/C/48/D/470/1991 (1993), the U.N. Human Rights Committee took the view, in a case involving extradition from Canada to the United States, that "prolonged periods of detention under a severe custodial regime on death row cannot generally be considered to constitute cruel, inhuman or degrading treatment if the convicted person is merely availing himself of appellate remedies." Is this necessarily inconsistent with the European Court's decision in *Soering*? Consider, however, the decision in *Pratt v. Attorney General for Jamaica*, [1994] 2 App. Cas. 1 (P.C. 1993), in which the Judicial Committee of the Privy Council stated that a delay of five years after imposition of a death sentence would amount to inhuman and degrading punishment in violation of an article of the Jamaican Constitution modeled on Article 3 of the European Convention. Responding to the argument that the delay was largely a result of the appellants' deliberate resort to appellate remedies, the Judicial Committee observed:

> It is part of the human condition that a condemned man will take every opportunity to save his life through use of the appellate procebdure. If the appellate procedure enables the prisoner to prolong the appellate hearings over a period of years, the fault is to be attributed to the appellate system that permits such delay and not to the prisoner who takes advantage of it.

Other foreign cases on point are reviewed in Justice Breyer's dissent from the denial of certiorari in *Knight v. Florida*, 120 S. Ct. 459 (1999). *See also Lackey v. Texas*, 514 U.S. 1045 (1995) (Stevens, J., memorandum respecting denial of certiorari).

In *Knight v. Florida, supra*, the Supreme Court again declined to rule on "death row phenomenon." The lower courts almost invariably have found that it does not present a reason for reversing capital sentences. *See, e.g., White v. Johnson*, 79 F.3d 432 (5th Cir. 1996); *Chambers v. Bowersox*, 157 F.3d 560 (8th Cir. 1998); *McKenzie v. Day*, 57 F.3d 1461 (9th Cir. 1995), *cert. denied*, 514 U.S. 1104 (1995); *Stafford v. Ward*, 59 F.3d 1025 (10th Cir. 1995), *cert. denied*, 515 U.S. 1173 (1995).

(5) Might the mode of execution used in the requesting state amount to a reason for refusing extradition. In *Ng v. Canada*, U.N. Doc.

CCPR/C/49/D/469/1991 (1994), the Human Rights Committee concluded that use of the gas chamber in California had been shown to involve prolonged agony and suffering and therefore violated Article 7 of the International Covenant on Civil and Political Rights. *See also Fierro v. Gomez*, 77 F.3d 301 (9th Cir.), *vacated*, 519 U.S. 918 (1996).

(6) The so-called "juvenile death penalty" raises a separate issue. In paragraph 108 of the *Soering* judgment, in making the point that the defendant's youth is a factor to be considered in determining the acceptability of the death penalty, the Court refers to other treaties that expressly prohibit imposition of capital punishment on persons under eighteen at the time of the commission of the offense. Should this be relevant to a decision about whether the "juvenile death penalty" constitutes "cruel and unusual punishment" for purposes of the Eighth Amendment to the U.S. Constitution? In *Thompson v. Oklahoma*, 487 U.S. 815 (1988), a plurality of the U.S. Supreme Court found that capital punishment for a murder committed when the defendant was fifteen years old was unconstitutional. In *Stanford v. Kentucky*, 492 U.S. 361 (1989), a majority of the Court found that capital punishment for a murder committed when the defendant was sixteen or seventeen was not unconstitutional. Justice Scalia, dissenting in *Thompson* and writing for the majority in *Stanford*, rejected the relevance, when it comes to interpreting the U.S. Constitution, of international comparisons and of international instruments banning the imposition of the death penalty for crimes committed by persons below eighteen.

In *Roach & Pinkerton v. United States*, Case 9647, Report No. 3/87, Inter-Am. C.H.R. 148, OEA/ser.L/V/II.71, doc. 9 rev. 1 (1987), the Inter-American Commission on Human Rights agreed with the United States "that there does not now exist a norm of customary international law establishing 18 to be the minimum age for imposition of the death penalty." It went on to say:

> 60. The Commission, however, does not find the age question dispositive of the issue before it, which is whether the absence of a federal prohibition within U.S. domestic law on the execution of juveniles, who committed serious crimes under the age of 18, is in violation of the American Declaration.

> 61. The Commission finds that the diversity of state practice in the U.S. – reflected in the fact that some states have abolished the death penalty, while others allow a potential threshold limit of applicability as low as 10 years of age – results in very different sentences for the commission of the same crime. The deprivation by the State of an offender's life should not be made subject to the fortuitous element of where the crime took place. Under the present system of laws in the United States, a hypothetical sixteen year old who commits a capital offense in Virginia may potentially be subject to the death penalty, whereas if the same individual commits the same offense on the other side of the Memorial

Bridge, in Washington, D.C., where the death penalty has been abolished for adults as well as for juveniles, the sentence will not be death.

62. For the federal Government of the United States to leave the issue of the application of the death penalty to juveniles to the discretion of state officials results in a patchwork scheme of legislation which makes the severity of the punishment dependent, not, primarily, on the nature of the crime committed, but on the location where it was committed. . . . The failure of the federal government to preempt the states as regards this most fundamental right – the right to life – results in a pattern of legislative arbitrariness throughout the United States which results in the arbitrary deprivation of life and inequality before the law, contrary to Articles I and II of the American Declaration of the Rights and Duties of Man, respectively.

(7) Article 36(1)(b) of the 1963 Vienna Convention on Consular Relations [*see* chap. 11, *supra*] gives foreign nationals the right to request that consular officials of their home state be notified, without delay, whenever they are arrested or detained, so that those officials can interview and arrange appropriate legal representation for them; it also provides that, upon arrest, a foreign national must be informed of these rights, also "without delay." Does failure to observe these rules constitute a reason for suppressing a confession or for reversing the conviction of the foreign national? The question can arise, of course, in cases that do not involve the death penalty. *See, e.g., United States v. Lombera-Camorlinga*, 170 F.3d 1241 (9th Cir. 1999), *rev'd en banc*, 206 F.3d 882 (9th Cir. 2000); *United States v. Alvarado-Torres*, 45 F.Supp.2d 986 (S.D. Calif. 1999). But it has figured most prominently in cases that do.

In *Breard v. Greene*, 523 U.S. 371 (1998), the petitioner was a Paraguayan national sentenced to death in Virginia. Both he and the government of Paraguay had unsuccessfully challenged his conviction on the ground that he had not been informed of his right to consular access. *See Breard v. Netherland*, 949 F. Supp. 1255 (E.D. Va. 1996), *aff'd sub nom. Breard v. Pruett*, 134 F.3d 615 (4th Cir. 1998); *Republic of Paraguay v. Allen*, 949 F. Supp. 1269 (E.D.Va. 1996), *aff.'d*, 134 F.3d 622 (4th Cir. 1998). Paraguay then instituted proceedings against the United States in the International Court of Justice (ICJ). On April 9, 1998, the ICJ issued an order indicating that the United States should try to ensure that Breard was not executed pending a decision on the merits. *Case Concerning the Vienna Convention on Consular Relations (Paraguay v. United States)*, Provisional Measures, 1988 I.C.J. 248 (Order of Apr. 9, 1998). Nonetheless, on April 14, 1998, the U.S. Supreme Court denied certiorari and refused to stay Breard's execution. He was put to death later that evening. Ultimately, the United States issued a formal apology to Paraguay and promised to take steps to ensure that the rights of foreign nationals in the U.S. are respected; and, at Paraguay's request, the proceedings in the ICJ were discontinued. 1998 I.C.J. 426 (Order of Nov. 10, 1998). *See Agora: Breard*, 92 AM. J. INT'L L. 666 (1998).

In a similar case, Karl and Walter LaGrand were German nationals sentenced to death in Arizona. The German government issued several diplomatic requests for clemency on the ground that they never had been informed of their right to consular access. Nevertheless, Karl LaGrand was executed on February 24, 1999. Walter LaGrand's execution was scheduled for March 3. On March 2, 1999, Germany instituted proceedings against the United States before the ICJ, and on March 3, the ICJ issued an order asking the U.S. to ensure that Walter LaGrand was not executed pending a decision on the merits. *Case Concerning the Vienna Convention on Consular Relations (Germany v. United States)*, Provisional Measures, 1999 I.C.J. 9 (Order of Mar. 3, 1999). The same day the U.S. Supreme Court declined to exercise its original jurisdiction in a suit filed by Germany against both the United States and the governor of Arizona. *Federal Republic of Germany v. United States*, 526 U.S. 111 (1999). Walter LaGrand was executed later that evening. Germany's case against the U.S. in the ICJ is still pending. *See* William J. Aceves, *International Decisions: Vienna Convention on Consular Relations*, 93 AM. J. INT'L L. 924 (1999).

Part 4
THE PROSECUTION OF INTERNATIONAL CRIMES

Chapter 17
WHAT CRIMES ARE INTERNATIONAL CRIMES?

§ 17.01 The Concept of an International Crime

In an early essay on "International Criminal Law," Sir John Fischer Williams noted that the expression "international crime" appeared "to have at least two meanings: one, a crime against international law, and the other, a crime which brings or may bring the offender into conflict with the laws of more than one country. It is this second sense which is the more popular use of the phrase, and which is associated with the 'international criminal' who is known to the authorities of more than one police force." SIR JOHN FISCHER WILLIAMS, CHAPTERS ON CURRENT INTERNATIONAL LAW AND THE LEAGUE OF NATIONS 232, 243 (1929). But only "international crime" in the first sense, he thought, had "an interest for the international lawyer." *Id.* at 244.

In what way might the act of an individual be considered "a crime against international law" and so constitute, in the first sense, an "international crime"? In this connection, a distinction is sometimes drawn, as indicated in chapter 1, between (a) "offenses of international concern," *i.e.*, offenses which international law authorizes or requires states to prosecute and punish under their own municipal law, and (b) "crimes under international law," *i.e.* crimes for which international law imposes criminal liability directly on individuals. So long as international law was thought to be concerned only with relations between states, and not with the rights or duties of individuals, it was questionable whether it could impose liability directly on individual offenders. Insofar as the law addressed itself only to states, it could repress individual conduct only by authorizing or requiring states to do so through their domestic legal systems. Since the end of the Second World War, however, with the recognition that individuals can have both international rights and duties [*see* chap. 16], "there has been an increasing trend towards the expansion of individual responsibility directly established under international law." 1 OPPENHEIM'S INTERNATIONAL LAW 506 (Sir Robert Jennings & Sir Arthur Watts eds., 9th ed. 1992).

Under customary international law as it had developed before 1945, states were supposed to be responsible for treating foreigners admitted to their territory in accordance with international standards of justice. As a result, a state might incur international liability not only for failing to accord an alien criminal defendant the minimal procedural guarantees discussed in chapter 16, but also for failing to use due diligence to prevent the commission of crimes of violence against aliens or for failing to take adequate steps to detect, prosecute, and punish the perpetrators of such crimes. Other customary international rules required states to repress crimes committed on their territory against foreign diplomats, and to suppress, by threatening criminal sanctions for, hostile expeditions launched from their territory against foreign governments with which they were not at war. Neutrality laws, for instance, represented an effort to implement these obligations. *See* Edward M. Wise, *Note on International Standards of Criminal Law and Administration*, in INTERNATIONAL CRIMINAL LAW 135, 152-59 (Gerhard O. W. Mueller & Edward M. Wise eds., 1965).

Since 1945, partly in response to controversies concerning the content and validity of older customary rules, "[t]he general trend . . . has been to enhance the role of treaties in international law-making." PETER MALANCZUK, AKEHURST'S MODERN INTRODUCTION TO INTERNATIONAL LAW 37 (7th ed. 1997). In line with this trend, discussions of the circumstances under which states are obligated to enact municipal laws proscribing "offenses of international concern" have come to focus almost exclusively on obligations to criminalize that have their source in multilateral treaties. By one count, there are at least 274 multilateral treaties that require states to treat certain conduct as criminal. The categories of crime covered by these treaties include aggression, genocide, crimes against humanity, war crimes, crimes against U.N. and associated personnel, unlawful use of weapons, theft of nuclear materials, mercenarism, apartheid, slavery, torture, unlawful human experimentation, piracy, aircraft hijacking, unlawful acts against maritime navigation, unlawful acts against internationally protected persons, taking of civilian hostages, unlawful use of the mails, unlawful traffic in drugs, destruction or theft of national treasures, unlawful acts against the environment, international traffic in obscene materials, falsification and counterfeiting, unlawful interference with submarine cables, and bribery of foreign public officials. *See* M. Cherif Bassiouni, *The Sources and Content of International Criminal Law: A Theoretical Framework*, in 1 INTERNATIONAL CRIMINAL LAW 3 (M. Cherif Bassiouni ed., 2d ed. 1999).

The crimes that states are thereby obligated to repress can be classified in different ways. The most generally useful scheme may be one that distinguishes between various types of international crime on the basis of the degree of official involvement in the conduct constituting the crime. Accordingly, international crime can be divided roughly into three general heads.

The first general heading includes violations of international norms directed toward restraining the conduct of state officials acting under color of law. (Offenses within this group are the ones that usually are singled out as well as constituting "crimes under international law" for which the individuals who commit them bear direct international responsibility.) The prototypical offenses under this heading are conventional war crimes such as violations of the Hague and Geneva Conventions. Also included are the two other categories of crime that were prosecuted at Nuremberg: crimes against peace and crimes against humanity. These offenses comprise the "classical domain" of international criminal law. By extension, this heading also includes genocide, apartheid, and torture. These crimes do not invariably require state action, nor do they always have to be connected to an armed conflict. But the underlying reason for international concern might be said to be that they all involve a misuse of power, of the monopoly of violence commanded by state or quasi-state officials.

The second heading includes the crimes associated with terrorist activities that have been the subject of the relatively recent conventions discussed in chapter 8. Unlike the first class of international crimes, the acts in question need not be committed directly by state or quasi-state officials. Nonetheless, a paramount reason for international concern has been, in fact, the lax attitude, sometimes seeming to amount to complicity, taken toward such offenses by states in which offenders have found refuge. The object of these conventions is to deny offenders "safe haven," to close bolt holes. The offense of piracy, commonly termed an "international crime," although usually for the wrong reason, is, in some respects, the prototypical offense under this heading.

The third heading covers other acts of private individuals that have been subjected to treaty prohibition because they involve either transnational traffic in illicit commodities (such as narcotics, endangered species, and, at one time, obscene publications), or harm to a common or mutual interest of states requiring international cooperation for its effective suppression (for instance, overfishing, marine pollution, interference with submarine cables, unlawful use of the mails, or counterfeiting of currency). For a list of U.S. statutes implementing such treaties, see Edward M. Wise, *International Crimes and Domestic Criminal Law*, 38 DEPAUL L. REV. 923, 956-66 (1989).

There is considerable variation in the language used in such treaties to impose an obligation to repress particular kinds of conduct. It can range from a statement by which the parties simply agree to cooperate in suppressing the conduct in question, to a more definite obligation to subject it to criminal sanctions and to prosecute and punish offenders. The preferred form of words during the past thirty years has been the language introduced in the 1970 Hague Convention on Unlawful Seizure of Aircraft, which requires states to make the offense defined in the convention a crime punishable by severe penalties under their own municipal law, to take steps to establish their jurisdiction over the offense, whether or not it was committed in their territory, and either to extradite an offender or else submit the case to the competent authorities for the purpose of prosecution. See M. CHERIF BASSIOUNI & EDWARD M. WISE, AUT DEDERE AUT JUDICARE: THE DUTY TO EXTRADITE OR PROSECUTE IN INTERNATIONAL LAW 8-9 (1995).

It is impossible to determine *a priori*, on the basis of its intrinsic characteristics, whether particular conduct constitutes an "international crime"

– just as it is not possible in domestic law to distinguish criminal from non-criminal conduct on the basic of the intrinsic qualities of the conduct in question. In a domestic context, the only satisfactory definition of a crime, at least for legal purposes, is a formal definition to the effect that a crime is an act which the law prohibits and provides shall give rise to certain consequences. Those consequences are roughly of two types. First, a criminal act triggers criminal proceedings, usually initiated and controlled by the state rather than by a private individual. Second, those proceedings involve punishment, as opposed to civil liability, as a possible outcome. In an international context as well, the only satisfactory definition of an "international crime," at least for legal purposes, is one that focuses on whether the law as revealed in state practice prescribes that the conduct in question can or should give rise to criminal proceedings (whether national or international) and to penal consequences. "The practice of States is the conclusive determinant in the creation of international law (including international criminal law), and not the desirability of stamping out obnoxious patterns of human behaviour." Yoram Dinstein, *International Criminal Law*, 20 ISRAEL L. REV. 206, 221 (1985).

The treaty rules requiring states to repress particular crimes are addressed to states themselves, not to the individuals whose conduct they seek to influence. Yet rules of domestic criminal law can also be represented in the same way as a set of directions to state officials about how to proceed in criminal cases rather than as commands issued to the public at large. *See* Meir Dan-Cohen, *Decision Rules and Conduct Rules: On Acoustic Separation in Criminal Law*, 87 HARV. L. REV. 625 (1984). This compounds the difficulty, so long as trial takes place in a municipal court, of saying whether, above and beyond the obligation imposed on states, there also is an international obligation imposed on individuals, of discerning practical differences between "real" international crimes or "crimes under international law" (which involve the infraction of international law directly by individuals) and offenses which states punish under their municipal law in consequence of an international obligation to do so. *See* Dinstein, *supra*, at 227-28. The situation has started to change, with the establishment of two *ad hoc* international tribunals [*see* chap. 19] and a permanent international criminal court about to come into being [*see* chap. 20]. These tribunals have been set up to deal with "classical" international crimes committed by official or quasi-official offenders: genocide, crimes against humanity, war crimes, and possibly aggression. For the moment, at least, these would seem to be the international crimes for which it is generally agreed that individuals can incur direct responsibility under international law. (They are also the crimes to which the International Law Commission's 1996 Draft Code of Crimes Against the Peace and Security of Mankind is for the most part limited.)

§ 17.02 Related Concepts

[A] Universal Jurisdiction

"Universal jurisdiction," as indicated in chapter 1, refers to the competence of any state which obtains custody of the offender to proscribe and punish an offense with which it has no connection based on territoriality or nationality and by which it has not been particularly affected. THE RESTATEMENT (THIRD) OF FOREIGN RELATIONS LAW § 404 (1986) indicates that the list of offenses subject to universal jurisdiction includes "piracy, slave trade, attacks on or hijacking of aircraft, genocide, war crimes, and perhaps certain acts of terrorism." *See also* Kenneth C. Randall, *Universal Jurisdiction under International Law*, 66 TEX. L. REV.785 (1988). In the wake of the *Pinochet* case [*see* chap. 11], the offense of torture would no doubt occupy a prominent place on any such list today. Universal jurisdiction authorizes states to apply their law to certain offenses. Whether they are obligated to do so as well is, in principle, a separate question.

The standard example of a crime over which universal jurisdiction exists is piracy. Perpetrators of piracy often are described as *hostes humani generis* – enemies of all mankind. This is said to be the basis for the authority given to all states to capture and try pirates. In one view, the reason for universal jurisdiction over piracy is that pirates directly violate international law. In another view, international law simply authorizes states to subject piracy to their own municipal laws on the basis of universal jurisdiction. The prosecution takes place under municipal law. Universal jurisdiction serves to permit states with powerful navies to take action against pirate vessels without violating the principle that normally prohibits interference with foreign ships on the high seas.

The same difference of opinion has sometimes been expressed with regard to war crimes. In one view, the international rules regarding war crimes do no more than to create a basis for the exercise of an extraordinary jurisdiction on the part of belligerents to prosecute in their own courts enemy soldiers who commit violations of the laws of war. Insofar as criminal responsibility attaches for the commission of a war crime, it attaches only under national law. In another view, the punishment of war crimes always has proceeded on the assumption that the laws of war are binding not only on states but also on their individual nationals. In prosecuting violations of the laws of war, a state acts not merely to enforce its own law, but to enforce international law: "what is punished is the breach of international law; and the case is thus different from the punishment, under national law, of acts in respect of which international law gives a liberty to all states to punish, but does not itself declare criminal." IAN BROWNLIE, PRINCIPLES OF PUBLIC INTERNATIONAL LAW 308 (5th ed. 1998). Since the Nuremberg Trial, this has become the prevailing view with respect to crimes against humanity and genocide as well as violations of the laws of war. (Slavery and torture may be regarded, for this purpose, as specific instances of such offenses.)

The tendency in treaties modeled on 1970 Hague Convention on Unlawful Seizure of Aircraft is to require a state to assert jurisdiction over an offender present in its territory who has not been extradited to another state having closer jurisdictional ties to the offense. Although it is sometimes claimed that they do, these treaties are not generally regarded as creating direct individual criminal responsibility under international law.

[B] Offenses Against the Law of Nations

"The term 'crimes against the law of nations' . . . originated in the criminal law of States to designate acts of individuals directed against foreign States and their representatives. However, it subsequently came to be applied to other crimes in so far as conventional or customary international law binds or entitles States to punish their authors." Dietrich Schindler, *Crimes Against the Law of Nations, in* 8 ENCYCLOPEDIA OF PUB. INT'L L. 109, 109 (Rudolf Bernhardt ed., 1985). As a result, it is now virtually synonymous with the expression "international crime."

The U.S. Constitution, art. I, § 8, confers on Congress the power "[t]o define and punish Piracies and Felonies committed on the high Seas, and Offenses against the Law of Nations." This clause confers two separate powers: first, the power "[t]o define and punish Piracies and Felonies committed on the high Seas"; second, the power to define and punish "Offenses against the Law of Nations." Article IX of the Articles of Confederation of 1777 conferred on the Continental Congress "the sole and exclusive right and power" of "appointing courts for the trial of piracies and felonies committed on the high seas." It did not confer power with respect to offenses against the Law of Nations. A resolution of the Continental Congress recommended that the states enact laws to punish such offenses. The resolution lists four kinds of offenses against the law of nations for which the state legislatures are asked "to provide expeditious, exemplary and adequate punishment":

First. For the Violation of safe conducts or passports, expressly granted under the authority of Congress to the subjects of a foreign power in time of war;

Secondly. For the commission of acts of hostility against such as are in amity, league or truce with the United States, or who are within the same, under a general implied safe conduct;

Thirdly. For the infractions of the immunities of ambassadors and other public ministers, authorized and received as such by the United States in Congress assembled. . . .

Fourthly. For infractions of treaties and conventions to which the United States are a party.

Resolution of the Congress of the United States, Nov. 23, 1781, *in* 21 JOURNALS OF THE CONTINENTAL CONGRESS 1774-1789, at 1136 (Gaillard Hunt ed., 1912), *reprinted in* INTERNATIONAL CRIMINAL LAW 200-01 (Gerhard O.W. Mueller & Edward M. Wise eds., 1965). The reason given for punishing these kinds of offenses against the law of nations is that "a prince, to whom it may be hereafter necessary to disavow any transgression of that law by a citizen of the United States, will receive such disavowal with reluctance and suspicion, if regular and adequate punishment shall not have been provided against the transgressor." Id. 200. *See also* THE FEDERALIST No. 42, at 280-81 (James Madison) (Jacob E. Cooke ed., 1961). Thus, the concept of an "offense against the law of nations" embodies the same ambiguity as the cognate concept of an "international crime."

In one view, such offenses involve a direct personal liability on the part of the perpetrator for a violation of international law. In another, an "offense against the law of nations" is rather (in Sir John Fischer Williams' words) "an act which municipal law treats as an offence because of its influence – real or supposed – upon international relations." It is treated as an offense under municipal law in order to meet a state's obligations under international law to repress such conduct. *See* Howard S. Fredman, Comment, *The Offenses Clause: Congress' International Penal Power*, 8 COLUM. J. TRANSNAT'L L. 279 (1969).

[C] State Criminal Responsibility

States incur international responsibility if they violate international law. At one time it was fashionable to speak of any breach of international law as if it constituted an offense which subjected the offending state to penal sanctions "to be inflicted in open and solemn war by the injured party." 1 JAMES KENT, COMMENTARIES * 181. Since the middle of the nineteenth century, it generally has been recognized that the responsibility of states for acts in violation of international law more closely resembles civil, or more precisely, delictual liability. *See* IAN BROWNLIE, SYSTEM OF THE LAW OF NATIONS: STATE RESPONSIBILITY (Part I) 22-23 (1983). Even so, it has been urged from time to time that, at least for certain acts, states are or should be held criminally responsible. Since the Nuremberg Trial, the principle of individual rather than state responsibility for international crimes has occupied center stage in discussions of international criminal law. But the idea of state criminal responsibility still has its proponents. *See* Otto Triffterer, *Prosecution of States for Crimes of State*, *in* 3 INTERNATIONAL CRIMINAL LAW 99 (M. Cherif Bassiouni ed., 1987); John Dugard, *Criminal Responsibility of States*, *in* 1 INTERNATIONAL CRIMINAL LAW 239 (M. Cherif Bassiouni ed., 2d ed. 1999).

In 1976, the International Law Commission provisionally adopted a draft article on state responsibility which incorporates the idea that there are certain "international crimes" which can give rise to a heightened form of state responsibility. According to Article 19 of the Commission's Draft Articles on State Responsibility:

1. An act of a State which constitutes a breach of an international obligation is an internationally wrongful act, regardless of the subject-matter of the obligation breached.

2. An internationally wrongful act which results from the breach by a State of an international obligation so essential for the protection of fundamental interests of the international community that its breach is recognized as a crime by that community as a whole, constitutes an international crime.

3. Subject to paragraph 2, and on the basis of the rules of international law in force, an international crime may result, *inter alia*, from:

(a) a serious breach of an international obligation of essential importance for maintenance of international peace and security, such as that prohibiting aggression;

(b) a serious breach of an international obligation of essential importance for safeguarding the right of self-determination of peoples, such as that prohibiting the establishment or maintenance by force of colonial domination;

(c) a serious breach on a widespread scale of an international obligation of essential importance for safeguarding the human being, such as those prohibiting slavery, genocide, apartheid;

(d) a serious breach of an international obligation of essential importance for the safeguarding and preservation of the human environment, such as those prohibiting massive pollution of the atmosphere or of the seas.

4. Any internationally wrongful act which is not an international crime in accordance with paragraph 2, constitutes an international delict.

Report of the International Law Commission, U.N. Doc. A/31/10 (1976), *reprinted in* [1976] 2 Y.B. INT'L L. COMM'N pt. 2, U.N. Doc. A/CN.4/SER.4/Add 1 (pt. 2), 73, at 75.

The concept of an "international crime" enunciated by the Commission in 1976 has come in for considerable criticism and, in the intervening years, has lost ground within the International Law Commission itself. It is, perhaps, somewhat less objectionable if it is seen, like the cognate concept of obligations *erga omnes*, as meant only to indicate that certain wrongs are of concern not only to the immediate victim, but to the entire international community. Insofar as it is predicated on wrongs of concern to the whole community, state responsibility might be regarded as analogous to criminal responsibility, which supposedly does involve the community as a whole taking cognizance of law violations. *See* PHILIP JESSUP, A MODERN LAW OF NATIONS 12 (1948).

[D] Violations of *Jus Cogens*

According to the RESTATEMENT (THIRD) OF THE FOREIGN RELATIONS LAW OF THE UNITED STATES (1986), § 102, cmt. (k):

> Some rules of international law are accepted and recognized by the international community of states as peremptory, permitting no derogation, and prevailing over and invalidating international agreements and other rules of international law in conflict with them. Such a peremptory norm is subject to modification only by a subsequent norm of international law having the same character.

Much of the language of this section derives from Article 53 of the Vienna Convention on the Law of Treaties, May 23, 1969, 1155 U.N.T.S. 331, 344, which provides:

> A peremptory norm of general international law is a norm accepted and recognized by the international community of states as a whole as a norm from which no derogation is permitted and which can be modified only by a subsequent norm of general international law having the same character.

The concept of *jus cogens* depends on the idea that there is a hierarchy of international law norms, so that some "trump" others. This idea now seems to be widely accepted, at least in principle. *But see* Prosper Weil, *Towards Normative Relativity in International Law?*, 77 AM. J. INT'L L. 413 (1983). There is less agreement, however, on what norms actually constitute rules of *jus cogens*. According to Reporters' Note 6 to RESTATEMENT § 102:

> There is general agreement that the principles of the United Nations Charter prohibiting the use of force are *jus cogens*. . . It has been suggested that norms that create "international crimes" and obligate all states to proceed against violations are also peremptory. . . Such norms might include rules prohibiting genocide, slave trade and slavery, apartheid and other gross violations of human rights, and perhaps attacks on diplomats.

(Nowadays, the prohibition of torture probably would also place high on most lists of norms that have the status of *jus cogens*.)

[E] Obligations *Erga Omnes*

The classic statement about the nature of obligations *erga omnes* appears in a dictum contained in two paragraphs of the judgment of the International Court of Justice in the *Barcelona Traction* case. Those paragraphs read as follows:

33. When a state admits into its territory foreign investments or foreign nationals, whether natural or juristic persons, it is bound to extend to them the protection of the law and assumes obligations concerning the treatment to be afforded them. These obligations, however, are neither absolute nor unqualified. In particular, an essential distinction should be drawn between the obligations of a State towards the international community as a whole, and those arising vis-à-vis another State in the field of diplomatic protection. By their very nature the former are the concern of all States. In view of the importance of the rights involved, all States can be held to have a legal interest in their protection; they are obligations *erga omnes.*

34. Such obligations derive, for example in contemporary international law, from the outlawing of acts of aggression, and of genocide, as also from the principles and rules concerning the basic rights of the human person, including protection from slavery and racial discrimination. Some of the corresponding rights of protection have entered into the body of general international law; others are conferred by international instruments of a universal or quasi-universal character.

Case Concerning the Barcelona Traction, Light & Power Co., Ltd. (Belgium v. Spain), Second Phase, 1970 I.C.J. 3, 32 (Judgment of Feb. 5). On the concept generally, *see* MAURIZIO RAGAZZI, THE CONCEPT OF INTERNATIONAL OBLIGATIONS *E*RGA *O*MNES (1997).

In the Court's dictum, the concept of an obligation *erga omnes* is concerned with a state's standing to complain about a violation of international law by another state even though it was not particularly affected by the violation. If the other state has violated an obligation owing to "the international community as a whole," presumably any state has a correlative right to complain about the violation. This dictum is not immediately concerned with the criminal liability of individuals. Nonetheless, like the other concepts we are considering, the idea of an obligation *erga omnes* does assume that certain norms of international law have a special importance, a preferred position, because associated with the fundamental interests, or with the common good, of the entire "international community." It has been suggested that, insofar as the norms creating certain "international crimes" and requiring states to proceed against violations are peremptory (*jus cogens*) norms, the obligation to prosecute such crimes may itself be an obligation *erga omnes.* *See* Guy S. Goodwin-Gill, *Crime in International Law: Obligations Erga Omnes and the Duty to Prosecute, in* THE REALITY OF INTERNATIONAL LAW: ESSAYS IN HONOUR OF IAN BROWNLIE 199 (Guy S. Goodwin-Gill & Stefan Talmon eds., 1999).

[F] Crimes Against the Peace and Security of Mankind

Following the Nuremberg Trial, the United Nations embarked on efforts to codify the law applied by the Nuremberg Tribunal. In 1946, the General

Assembly affirmed the principles of international law recognized by the Charter and Judgment of the Nuremberg Tribunal. In 1947, it directed the International Law Commission (ILC) to "formulate" the principles which it had thus affirmed, and also to "prepare a draft code of offenses against the peace and security of mankind." The ILC submitted its formulation of the Nuremberg Principles to the General Assembly in 1950. It also submitted a Draft Code of Offenses Against the Peace and Security of Mankind. A revised version was submitted in 1954. At the same time, the General Assembly had under consideration a Draft Statute for the Establishment of an International Criminal Court. A preliminary version of the statute was submitted in 1951, a revised version in 1953. In the end, however, the General Assembly decided to postpone further consideration of both the code and the statute until it had dealt with the question of defining the crime of aggression. It was not until 1974 that the Assembly agreed on an official definition of aggression. In 1978, it asked the ILC to resume work on the draft code (but not the statute). Work proceeded slowly. In 1991, the ILC provisionally adopted a version of the draft code which included articles on the crimes of aggression, threat of aggression, intervention, colonial domination, genocide, apartheid, systematic or mass violations of human rights, exceptionally serious war crimes, recruitment, financing and training of mercenaries, international terrorism, illicit drug trafficking, and wilful and severe damage to the environment. The draft attracted considerable criticism and underwent further revision. In a version that covered a much narrower range of crimes, it was finally adopted by the ILC in 1996. Meanwhile, the question of establishing an international criminal court had resurfaced on the Commission's agenda. The ILC produced a draft statute in 1993 and a revised version in 1994. This served as a basis for the work which ultimately culminated in the 1998 Rome Statute for an International Criminal Court [chap. 20]. The Rome Statute ended up covering much of the same ground as the ILC's Draft Code. For a full history of these developments, *see* M. Cherif Bassiouni, *The Draft Code of Crimes Against the Peace and Security of Mankind, in* 1 INTERNATIONAL CRIMINAL LAW 293 (M. Cherif Bassiouni ed., 2d ed. 1999); *see also* Rosemary Rayfuse, *The Draft Code of Crimes Against the Peace and Security of Mankind: Eating Disorders at the International Law Commission*, 8 CRIM. L. F. 43 (1997).

DRAFT CODE OF CRIMES AGAINST THE PEACE AND SECURITY OF MANKIND

Report of the International Law Commission on Its Forty-Eighth Session, U.N. GAOR, 51st Sess., Supp. No. 10, at 9, U.N. Doc. A/51/10 (1996)

PART I. GENERAL PROVISIONS

Article 1 Scope and application of the present Code

1. The present Code applies to the crimes against the peace and security of

mankind set out in Part II.

2. Crimes against the peace and security of mankind are crimes under international law and punishable as such, whether or not they are punishable under national law.

Article 2   Individual responsibility

1. A crime against the peace and security of mankind entails individual responsibility.

2. An individual shall be responsible for the crime of aggression in accordance with article 16.

3. An individual shall be responsible for a crime set out in article 17, 18, 19 or 20 if that individual:

(a) intentionally commits such a crime;

(b) orders the commission of such a crime which in fact occurs or is attempted;

(c) fails to prevent or repress the commission of such a crime in the circumstances set out in article 6;

(d) knowingly aids, abets or otherwise assists, directly and substantially, in the commission of such a crime, including providing the means for its commission;

(e) directly participates in planning or conspiring to commit such a crime which in fact occurs;

(f) directly and publicly incites another individual to commit such a crime which in fact occurs;

(g) attempts to commit such a crime by taking action commencing the execution of a crime which does not in fact occur because of circumstances independent of his intentions.

Article 3   Punishment

An individual who is responsible for a crime against the peace and security of mankind shall be liable to punishment. The punishment shall be commensurate with the character and gravity of the crime.

Article 4   Responsibility of States

The fact that the present Code provides for the responsibility of individuals for crimes against the peace and security of mankind is without prejudice to any question of the responsibility of States under international law.

Article 5   Order of a Government or a superior

The fact that an individual charged with a crime against the peace and security of mankind acted pursuant to an order of a Government or a superior does not relieve him of criminal responsibility, but may be considered in mitigation of punishment if justice so requires.

Article 6   Responsibility of the superior

The fact that a crime against the peace and security of mankind was committed by a subordinate does not relieve his superiors of criminal responsibility, if they knew or had reason to know, in the circumstances at the time, that the subordinate was committing or was going to commit such a crime and if they did not take all necessary measures within their power to prevent or repress the crime.

Article 7   Official position and responsibility

The official position of an individual who commits a crime against the peace and security of mankind, even if he acted as head of State or Government, does not relieve him of criminal responsibility or mitigate punishment.

Article 8   Establishment of jurisdiction

Without prejudice to the jurisdiction of an international criminal court, each State Party shall take such measures as may be necessary to establish its jurisdiction over the crimes set out in articles 17, 18, 19 and 20, irrespective of where or by whom those crimes were committed. Jurisdiction over the crime set out in article 16 shall rest with an international criminal court. However, a State referred to in article 16 is not precluded from trying its nationals for the crime set out in that article.

Article 9   Obligation to extradite or prosecute

Without prejudice to the jurisdiction of an international criminal court, the State Party in the territory of which an individual alleged to have committed a crime set out in articles 17, 18, 19 or 20 is found shall extradite or prosecute that individual.

Article 10   Extradition of alleged offenders

1. To the extent that the crimes set out in articles 17, 18, 19 and 20 are not extraditable offences in any extradition treaty existing between States Parties, they shall be deemed to be included as such therein. States Parties undertake to include those crimes as extraditable offences in every extradition treaty to be

concluded between them.

2. If a State Party which makes extradition conditional on the existence of a treaty receives a request for extradition from another State Party with which it has no extradition treaty, it may at its option consider the present Code as the legal basis for extradition in respect of those crimes. Extradition shall be subject to the conditions provided in the law of the requested State.

3. State Parties which do not make extradition conditional on the existence of a treaty shall recognize those crimes as extraditable offences between themselves subject to the conditions provided in the law of the requested State.

4. Each of those crimes shall be treated, for the purpose of extradition between States Parties, as if it had been committed not only in the place in which it occurred but also in the territory of any other State Party.

Article 11   Judicial guarantees

1. An individual charged with a crime against the peace and security of mankind shall be presumed innocent until proved guilty and shall be entitled without discrimination to the minimum guarantees due to all human beings with regard to the law and the facts and shall have the rights:

(a) in the determination of any charge against him, to have a fair and public hearing by a competent, independent and impartial tribunal duly established by law;

(b) to be informed promptly and in detail in a language which he understands of the nature and cause of the charge against him;

(c) to have adequate time and facilities for the preparation of his defence and to communicate with counsel of his own choosing;

(d) to be tried without undue delay;

(e) to be tried in his presence, and to defend himself in person or through legal assistance of his own choosing; to be informed, if he does not have legal assistance, of this right; and to have legal assistance assigned to him and without payment by him if he does not have sufficient means to pay for it;

(f) to examine, or have examined, the witnesses against him and to obtain the attendance and examination of witnesses on his behalf under the same conditions as witnesses against him;

(g) to have the free assistance of an interpreter if he cannot understand or speak the language used in court;

(h) not to be compelled to testify against himself or to confess guilt.

2. An individual convicted of a crime shall have the right to his conviction and sentence being reviewed according to law.

Article 12   Non bis in idem

1. No one shall be tried for a crime against the peace and security of mankind of which he has already been finally convicted or acquitted by an international criminal court.

2. An individual may not be tried again for a crime of which he has been finally convicted or acquitted by a national court except in the following cases:

(a) by an international criminal court, if:

(i) the act which was the subject of the judgement in the national court was characterized by that court as an ordinary crime and not as a crime against the peace and security of mankind; or

(ii) the national court proceedings were not impartial or independent or were designed to shield the accused from international criminal responsibility or the case was not diligently prosecuted;

(b) by a national court of another State, if:

(i) the act which was the subject of the previous judgement took place in the territory of that State; or

(ii) that State was the main victim of the crime.

3. In the case of a subsequent conviction under the present Code, the court, in passing sentence, shall take into account the extent to which any penalty imposed by a national court on the same person for the same act has already been served.

Article 13   Non-retroactivity

1. No one shall be convicted under the present Code for acts committed before its entry into force.

2. Nothing in this article precludes the trial of anyone for any act which, at the time when it was committed, was criminal in accordance with international law or national law.

Article 14   Defences

The competent court shall determine the admissibility of defences in accordance with the general principles of law, in the light of the character of each crime.

Article 15   Extenuating circumstances

In passing sentence, the court shall, where appropriate, take into account extenuating circumstances in accordance with the general principles of law.

PART II.   CRIMES AGAINST THE PEACE AND SECURITY OF MANKIND

Article 16   Crime of aggression

An individual who, as leader or organizer, actively participates in or orders the planning, preparation, initiation or waging of aggression committed by a State shall be responsible for a crime of aggression.

Article 17   Crime of genocide

A crime of genocide means any of the following acts committed with intent to destroy, in whole or in part, a national, ethnic, racial or religious group, as such:

(a) killing members of the group;

(b) causing serious bodily or mental harm to members of the group;

(c) deliberately inflicting on the group conditions of life calculated to bring about its physical destruction in whole or in part;

(d) imposing measures intended to prevent births within the group;

(e) forcibly transferring children of the group to another group.

Article 18   Crimes against humanity

A crime against humanity means any of the following acts, when committed in a systematic manner or on a large scale and instigated or directed by a Government or by any organization or group:

(a) murder;

(b) extermination;

(c) torture;

(d) enslavement;

(e) persecution on political, racial, religious or ethnic grounds;

(f) institutionalized discrimination on racial, ethnic or religious grounds involving the violation of fundamental human rights and freedoms and resulting in seriously disadvantaging a part of the population;

(g) arbitrary deportation or forcible transfer of population;

(h) arbitrary imprisonment;

(i) forced disappearance of persons;

(j) rape, enforced prostitution and other forms of sexual abuse;

(k) other inhumane acts which severely damage physical or mental integrity, health or human dignity, such as mutilation and severe bodily harm.

Article 19   Crimes against United Nations and associated personnel

1. The following crimes constitute crimes against the peace and security of mankind when committed intentionally and in a systematic manner or on a large scale against United Nations and associated personnel involved in a United Nations operation with a view to preventing or impeding that operation from fulfilling its mandate:

(a) murder, kidnapping or other attack upon the person or liberty of any such personnel;

(b) violent attack upon the official premises, the private accommodation or the means of transportation of any such personnel likely to endanger his or her person or liberty.

2. This article shall not apply to a United Nations operation authorized by the Security Council as an enforcement action under Chapter VII of the Charter of the United Nations in which any of the personnel are engaged as combatants against organized armed forces and to which the law of international armed conflict applies.

Article 20   War crimes

Any of the following war crimes constitutes a crime against the peace and security of mankind when committed in a systematic manner or on a large scale:

(a) any of the following acts committed in violation of international humanitarian law:

(i) wilful killing;

(ii) torture or inhuman treatment, including biological experiments;

(iii) wilfully causing great suffering or serious injury to body or health;

(iv) extensive destruction and appropriation of property, not justified by military necessity and carried out unlawfully and wantonly;

(v) compelling a prisoner of war or other protected person to serve in the forces of a hostile Power;

(vi) wilfully depriving a prisoner of war or other protected person of the rights of fair and regular trial;

(vii) unlawful deportation or transfer or unlawful confinement of protected persons;

(viii) taking of hostages;

(b) any of the following acts committed wilfully in violation of international humanitarian law and causing death or serious injury to body or health:

(i) making the civilian population or individual civilians the object of attack;

(ii) launching an indiscriminate attack affecting the civilian population or civilian objects in the knowledge that such attack will cause excessive loss of life, injury to civilians or damage to civilian objects;

(iii) launching an attack against works or installations containing dangerous forces in the knowledge that such attack will cause excessive loss of life, injury to civilians or damage to civilian objects;

(iv) making a person the object of attack in the knowledge that he is hors de combat;

(v) the perfidious use of the distinctive emblem of the red cross, red crescent or red lion and sun or of other recognized protective signs;

(c) any of the following acts committed wilfully in violation of international humanitarian law

(i) the transfer by the Occupying Power of parts of its own civilian population into the territory it occupies;

(ii) unjustifiable delay in the repatriation of prisoners of war or civilians;

(d) outrages upon personal dignity in violation of international humanitarian law, in particular humiliating and degrading treatment, rape, enforced prostitution and any form of indecent assault;

(e) any of the following acts committed in violation of the laws or customs of war:

(i) employment of poisonous weapons or other weapons calculated to cause unnecessary suffering;

(ii) wanton destruction of cities, towns or villages, or devastation not justified by military necessity;

(iii) attack, or bombardment, by whatever means, of undefended towns, villages, dwellings or buildings or of demilitarized zones;

(iv) seizure of, destruction of or wilful damage done to institutions dedicated to religion, charity and education, the arts and sciences, historic monuments and works of art and science;

(v) plunder of public or private property;

(f) any of the following acts committed in violation of international humanitarian law applicable in armed conflict not of an international character:

(i) violence to the life, health and physical or mental well-being of persons, in particular murder as well as cruel treatment such as torture, mutilation or any form of corporal punishment;

(ii) collective punishments;

(iii) taking of hostages;

(iv) acts of terrorism;

(v) outrages upon personal dignity, in particular humiliating and degrading treatment, rape, enforced prostitution and any form of indecent assault;

(vi) pillage;

(vii) the passing of sentences and the carrying out of executions without previous judgement pronounced by a regularly constituted court, affording all the judicial guarantees which are generally recognized as indispensable;

(g) in the case of armed conflict, using methods or means of warfare not justified by military necessity with the intent to cause widespread, long-term and severe damage to the natural environment and thereby gravely prejudice the health or survival of the population and such damage occurs.

Chapter 18
THE NUREMBERG AND TOKYO PRECEDENTS

§ 18.01 The Nuremberg Trial

JUDGMENT OF THE INTERNATIONAL MILITARY TRIBUNAL FOR THE TRIAL OF GERMAN MAJOR WAR CRIMINALS

Nuremberg, Sept. 30 & Oct. 1, 1946
Cmd. 6964

On the 8th August, 1945, the Government of the United Kingdom of Great Britain and Northern Ireland, the Government of the United States of America, the Provisional Government of the French Republic, and the Government of the Union of Soviet Socialist Republics entered into an Agreement establishing this Tribunal for the Trial of War Criminals whose offences have no particular geographical location. . . .

By the Charter annexed to the Agreement, the constitution, jurisdiction and functions of the Tribunal were defined. The Tribunal was invested with power to try and punish persons who had committed crimes against peace, war crimes and crimes against humanity as defined in the Charter. The Charter also provided that at the trial of any individual member of any group or organisation the Tribunal may declare (in connection with any act of which the individual may be convicted) that the group or organisation of which the individual was a member was a criminal organisation. . . .

[I]n accordance with Article 14 of the Charter, an Indictment was lodged against the defendants . . . who had been designated by the Committee of the Chief Prosecutors of the signatory Powers as major war criminals. . . . This Indictment charges the defendants with crimes against peace by the planning, preparation, initiation and waging of wars of aggression, which were also wars in violation of international treaties, agreements and assurances; with war crimes; and with crimes against humanity. The defendants are also charged with participating in the formulation or execution of a common plan or conspiracy to commit all these crimes. The Tribunal was further asked by the Prosecution to declare [certain] named groups or organisations to be criminal within the meaning of the Charter. . . .

The Trial which was conducted in four languages – English, Russian, French and German – began on the 20th November, 1945, and pleas of "Not Guilty" were made by all the defendants except Bormann [who was tried *in absentia*]. The hearing of evidence and the speeches of Counsel concluded on 31st August, 1946. . . .

The Charter Provisions

The individual defendants are indicted under Article 6 of the Charter, which is as follows:

Article 6. The Tribunal established by the Agreement referred to in Article 1 hereof for the trial and punishment of the major war criminals of the European Axis countries shall have the power to try and punish persons who, acting in the interests of the European Axis countries, whether as individuals or as members of organisations, committed any of the following crimes:

The following acts, or any of them, are crimes, coming within the jurisdiction of the Tribunal for which there shall be individual responsibility:

(a) Crimes against Peace: namely, planning, preparation, initiation or waging of a war of aggression, or a war in violation of international treaties, agreements or assurances, or participation in a common plan or conspiracy for the accomplishment of any of the foregoing:

(b) War Crimes: namely, violations of the laws or customs of war. Such violations shall include, but not be limited   to, murder ill-treatment or deportation to slave labour or for any other purpose of civilian population of or in occupied territory, murder or ill-treatment of prisoners of war or persons on the seas, killing of hostages, plunder of public or private property, wanton destruction of cities, towns or villages, or devastation not justified by military necessity:

(c) Crimes against Humanity: namely, murder, extermination, enslavement, deportation, and other inhumane acts   committed against any civilian population, before or during the war, or persecutions on political, racial or religious grounds in execution of or in connection with any crime within the jurisdiction of the Tribunal, whether or not in violation of the domestic law of the country where perpetrated.

Leaders, organisers, instigators and accomplices participating in the formulation or execution of a common plan or conspiracy to commit any of the foregoing crimes are responsible for all acts performed by any persons in execution of such plan.

The Common Plan or Conspiracy and Aggressive War

. . . . Count One of the Indictment charges the defendants with conspiring or having a common plan to commit crimes against peace. Count Two of the Indictment charges the defendants with committing specific crimes against peace by planning, preparing, initiating, and waging wars of aggression against a number of other States. . . .

The charges in the Indictment that the defendants planned and waged aggressive wars are charges of the utmost gravity. War is essentially an evil thing. Its consequences are not confined to the belligerent states alone, but affect the whole world. To initiate a war of aggression, therefore, is not only an international crime; it is the supreme international crime differing only from other war crimes in that it contains within itself the accumulated evil of the whole.

The first acts of aggression referred to in the Indictment are the seizure of Austria and Czechoslovakia and the first war of aggression charged in the Indictment is the war against Poland begun on the 1st September, 1939.

. . . . The war against Poland did not come suddenly out of an otherwise clear sky; the evidence has made it plain that this war of aggression, as well as the seizure of Austria and Czechoslovakia, was pre-meditated and carefully prepared, and was not undertaken until the moment was thought opportune for it to be carried through as a definite part of the pre-ordained scheme and plan. For the aggressive designs of the Nazi Government were not accidents arising out of the immediate political situation in Europe and the world; they were a deliberate and essential part of Nazi foreign policy. . . .

The Law of the Charter

The jurisdiction of the Tribunal is defined in the Agreement and Charter, and the crimes coming within the jurisdiction of the Tribunal, for which there shall be individual responsibility, are set out in Article 6. The law of the Charter is decisive, and binding upon the Tribunal.

The making of the Charter was the exercise of the sovereign legislative power by the countries to which the German Reich unconditionally surrendered; and the undoubted right of these countries to legislate for the occupied territories has been recognised by the civilised world. The Charter is not an arbitrary exercise of power on the part of the victorious nations, but in the view of the Tribunal, as will be shown, it is the expression of international law existing at the time of its creation; and to that extent is itself a contribution to international law.

The Signatory Powers created this Tribunal, defined the law it was to administer, and made regulations for the proper conduct of the Trial. In doing so, they have done together what any one of them might have done singly; for it is not to be doubted that any nation has the right thus to set up special courts to administer law. With regard to the constitution of the court, all that the defendants are entitled to ask is to receive a fair trial on the facts and law.

The Charter makes the planning or waging of a war of aggression or a war in violation of international treaties a crime, and it is therefore not strictly necessary to consider whether and to what extent aggressive war was a crime before the execution of the London Agreement. But in view of the great importance of the questions of law involved, the Tribunal has heard full argument from the Prosecution and the Defence, and will express its view on the matter.

It was urged on behalf of the defendants that a fundamental principle of all law – international and domestic – is that there can be no punishment of crime without a pre-existing law. "*Nullum crimen sine lege. nulla poena sine lege.*" It was submitted that *ex post facto* punishment is abhorrent to the law of all civilised nations, that no sovereign power had made aggressive war a crime at the time the alleged criminal acts were committed, that no statute had defined aggressive war, that no penalty had been fixed for its commission, and no court had been created to try and punish offenders.

In the first place, it is to be observed that the maxim *nullum crimen sine lege* is not a limitation of sovereignty, but is in general a principle of justice. To assert that it is unjust to punish those who in defiance of treaties and assurances have attacked neighbouring states without warning is obviously untrue, for in such circumstances the attacker must know that he is doing wrong, and so far from it being unjust to punish him, it would be unjust if his wrong were allowed to go unpunished. Occupying the positions they did in the government of Germany, the defendants, or at least some of them must have known of the treaties signed by Germany, outlawing recourse to war for the settlement of international disputes; they must have known that they were acting in defiance of all international law when in complete deliberation they carried out the designs of invasion and aggression. On this view of the case alone, it would appear that the maxim has no application to the present facts.

This view is strongly reinforced by a consideration of the state of international law in 1939, so far as aggressive war is concerned. The General Treaty for the Renunciation of War of 27th August, 1928, more generally known as the Pact of Paris or the Kellogg-Briand Pact, was binding on sixty-three nations, including Germany, Italy and Japan at the outbreak of war in 1939.
. . .

[W]hat was the legal effect of this Pact? The nations who signed the Pact or adhered to it unconditionally condemned recourse to war for the future as an instrument of policy, and expressly renounced it. After the signing of the Pact, any nation resorting to war as an instrument of national policy breaks the Pact. In the opinion of the Tribunal, the solemn renunciation of war as an instrument of national policy necessarily involves the proposition that such a war is illegal in international law; and that those who plan and wage such a war, with its inevitable and terrible consequences, are committing a crime in so doing. War for the solution of international controversies undertaken as an instrument of national policy certainly includes a war of aggression, and such a war is therefore outlawed by the Pact. . . .

But it is argued that the Pact does not expressly enact that such wars are crimes, or set up courts to try those who make such wars. To that extent the same is true with regard to the laws of war contained in the Hague Convention. The Hague Convention of 1907 prohibited resort to certain methods of waging war. These included the inhumane treatment of prisoners, the employment of poisoned weapons, the improper use of flags of truce, and similar matters. Many of these prohibitions had been enforced long before the date of the Convention; but since 1907 they have certainly been crimes, punishable as offences against the laws of war; yet the Hague Convention nowhere designates such practices as criminal, nor is any sentence prescribed, nor any mention made of a court to try and punish offenders. For many years past, however, military tribunals have tried and punished individuals guilty of violating the rules of land warfare laid down by this Convention. In the opinion of the Tribunal, those who wage aggressive war are doing that which is equally illegal, and of much greater moment than a breach of one of the rules of the Hague Convention. In interpreting the words of the Pact, it must be remembered that international law is not the product of an international legislature, and that such international agreements as the Pact have to deal with general principles of law, and not with administrative matters of procedure. The law of war is to be found not only in treaties, but in the customs and practices of states which gradually obtained universal recognition, and from the general principles of justice applied by jurists and practiced by military courts. This law is not static, but by continual adaptation follows the needs of a changing world. Indeed, in many cases treaties do no more than express and define for more accurate reference the principles of law already existing.

The view which the Tribunal takes of the true interpretation of the Pact is supported by the international history which preceded it. In the year 1923 the draft of a Treaty of Mutual Assistance was sponsored by the League of Nations. . . . The preamble to the League of Nations 1924 Protocol for the Pacific Settlement of International Disputes ("Geneva Protocol"), after "recognising the solidarity of the members of the international community," declared that "a war of aggression constitutes a violation of this solidarity and is an international crime." . . . Although the Protocol was never ratified, it was signed by the leading statesmen of the world, representing the vast majority of the civilised states and peoples, and may be regarded as strong evidence of the intention to brand aggressive war as an international crime.

At the meeting of the Assembly of the League of Nations on the 24th

September, 1927, all the delegations then present (including the German, the Italian and the Japanese), unanimously adopted a declaration concerning wars of aggression. The preamble to the declaration stated . . . "that a war of aggression . . . is . . . an international crime." The unanimous resolution of the 18th February, 1928, of twenty-one American Republics of the Sixth (Havana) Pan-American Conference, declared that "war of aggression constitutes an international crime against the human species."

All these expressions of opinion, and others that could be cited, so solemnly made, reinforce the construction which the Tribunal placed upon the Pact of Paris, that resort to a war of aggression is not merely illegal, but is criminal. The prohibition of aggressive war demanded by the conscience of the world, finds its expression in the series of pacts and treaties to which the Tribunal has just referred.

It is also important to remember that Article 227 of the Treaty of Versailles provided for the constitution of a special Tribunal, composed of representatives of five of the Allied and Associated Powers which had been belligerents in the first World War opposed to Germany, to try the former German Emperor "for a supreme offence against international morality and the sanctity of treaties." The purpose of this trial was expressed to be "to vindicate the solemn obligations of international undertakings, and the validity of international morality." In Article 228 of the Treaty, the German Government expressly recognised the right of the Allied Powers "to bring before military tribunals persons accused of having committed acts in violation of the laws and customs of war."

It was submitted that international law is concerned with the action of sovereign States, and provides no punishment for individuals; and further, that where the act in question is an act of state, those who carry it out are not personally responsible, but are protected by the doctrine of the sovereignty of the State. In the opinion of the Tribunal, both these submissions must be rejected. That international law imposes duties and liabilities upon individuals as well as upon States has long been recognised. In the recent case of *Ex Parte Quirin,* 317 U.S. 1 (1942), before the Supreme Court of the United States, persons were charged during the war with landing in the United States for purposes of spying and sabotage. The late Justice Stone, speaking for the Court, said: "From the very beginning of its history this Court has applied the law of war as including that part of the law of nations which prescribes for the conduct of war the status, rights and duties of enemy nations as well as enemy individuals." He went on to give a list of cases tried by the Courts, where individual offenders were charged with offences against the laws of nations, and particularly the laws of war. Many other authorities could be quoted, but enough has been said to show that individuals can be punished for violations of international law. Crimes against international law are committed by men, not by abstract entities, and only by punishing individuals who commit such crimes can the provisions of international law be enforced. . . .

The principle of international law, which under certain circumstances, protects the representatives of a state, cannot be applied to acts which are condemned as criminal by international law. The authors of these facts cannot shelter themselves behind their official position in order to be freed from punishment in appropriate proceedings. Article 7 of the Charter expressly declares: "The official position of defendants, whether as Heads of State, or responsible officials in government departments, shall not be considered as freeing them from responsibility, or mitigating punishment."

On the other hand the very essence of the Charter is that individuals have international duties which transcend the national obligations of obedience imposed by the individual State. He who violates the laws of war cannot obtain immunity while acting in pursuance of the authority of the State if the State in authorising action moves outside its competence under international law.

It was also submitted on behalf of most of these defendants that in doing what they did they were acting under the orders of Hitler, and therefore cannot be held responsible for the acts committed by them in carrying out these orders. The Charter specially provides in Article 8: "The fact that the defendant acted pursuant to order of his Government or of a superior shall not free him from responsibility, but may the considered in mitigation of punishment." The provisions of this Article are in conformity with the law of all nations. That a soldier was ordered to kill or torture in violation of the international law of war this never been recognised as a defence to such acts of brutality, though, as the Charter here provides, the order may be urged in mitigation of the punishment. The true test, which is found in varying degrees in the criminal law of most nations, is not the existence of the order, but whether moral choice was in fact possible.

The Law as to the Common Plan or Conspiracy

. . . . Count One . . . charges not only the conspiracy to commit aggressive war, but also to commit war crimes and crimes against humanity. But the Charter does not define as a separate crime any conspiracy except the one to commit acts of aggressive war. Article 6 of the Charter provides: "Leaders, organisers, instigators and accomplices participating in the formulation or execution of a common plan or conspiracy to commit any of the foregoing crimes are responsible for all acts performed by any persons in execution of such plan." In the opinion of the Tribunal these words do not add a new and separate crime to those already listed. The words are designed to establish the responsibility of persons participating in a common plan. The Tribunal will therefore disregard the charges in Count One that the defendants conspired to commit war crimes and crimes against humanity, and will consider only the common plan to prepare, initiate and wage aggressive war.

War Crimes and Crimes Against Humanity

The evidence relating to war crimes has been overwhelming, in its volume and its detail. It is impossible for this Judgment adequately to review it, or to record the mass of documentary and oral evidence that has been presented. The truth remains that war crimes were committed on a vast scale, never before seen in the history of war. They were perpetrated in all the countries occupied by Germany, and on the High Seas, and were attended by every conceivable circumstance of cruelty and horror. There can be no doubt that the majority of them arose from the Nazi conception of "total war," with which the aggressive wars were waged. For in this conception of "total war," the moral ideas underlying the conventions which seek to make war more humane are no longer regarded as having force or validity. Everything is made subordinate to the overmastering dictates of war. Rules, regulations, assurances and treaties all alike are of no moment, and so, freed from the restraining influence of international law, the aggressive war is conducted by the Nazi leaders in the most barbaric way. Accordingly, war crimes were committed when and wherever the Fuehrer and his close associates thought them to be advantageous. They were for the most part the result of cold and criminal calculation.

On some occasions, war crimes were deliberately planned long in advance. In the case of the Soviet Union, the plunder of the territories to be occupied, and the ill-treatment of the civilian population, were settled in minute detail before the attack was begun. . . . Similarly, when planning to exploit the inhabitants of the occupied countries for slave labour on the very greatest scale, the German Government conceived it as an integral part of the war economy, and planned and organised this particular war crime down to the last elaborate detail.

Other war crimes, such as the murder of prisoners of war who had escaped and been recaptured, or the murder of Commandos or captured airmen, or the destruction of the Soviet Commissars, were the result of direct orders circulated through the highest official channels. . . .

Prisoners of war were ill-treated and tortured and murdered, not only in defiance of the well-established rules of international law, but in complete disregard of the elementary dictates of humanity. Civilian populations in occupied territories suffered the same fate. Whole populations were deported to Germany for the purposes of slave labour upon defence works, armament production and similar tasks connected with the war effort. Hostages were taken in very large numbers from the civilian populations in all the occupied countries, and were shot as suited the German purposes. Public and private property was systematically plundered and pillaged in order to enlarge the resources of Germany at the expense of the rest of Europe. Cities and towns and villages were wantonly destroyed without military justification or necessity. .

Murder and Ill-Treatment of Civilian Population

Article 6(b) of the Charter provides that "ill-treatment . . . of civilian population of or in occupied territory . . . killing of hostages . . . wanton destruction of cities, towns or villages" shall be a war crime. In the main these provisions are merely declaratory of the existing laws of war as expressed by the Hague Convention, Article 46 . . .

The territories occupied by Germany were administered in violation of the laws of war. The evidence is quite overwhelming of a systematic rule of violence, brutality and terror. . . . One of the most notorious means of terrorising the people in occupied territories was the use of concentration camps. They were first established in Germany at the moment of the seizure of power by the Nazi Government. Their original purpose was to imprison without trial all those persons who were opposed to the Government, or who were in any way obnoxious to German authority. With the aid of a secret police force, this practice was widely extended and in course of time concentration camps became places of organised and systematic murder, where millions of people were destroyed. In the administration of the occupied territories the concentration camps were used to destroy all opposition groups. . . . A certain number of the concentration camps were equipped with gas chambers for the wholesale destruction of the inmates, and with furnaces for the burning of the bodies. Some of them were in fact used for the extermination of Jews as part of the "final solution" of the Jewish problem. . . .

Slave Labour Policy

Article 6 (b) of the Charter provides that the "ill-treatment, or deportation to slave labour or for any other purpose, of civilian population of or in occupied territory" shall be a war crime. The laws relating to forced labour by the inhabitants of occupied territories are found in Article 52 of The Hague Convention, which provides: "Requisition in kind and services shall not be demanded from municipalities or inhabitants except for the needs of the army of occupation. They shall be in proportion to the resources of the country, and of such a nature as not to involve the inhabitants in the obligation of taking part in military operations against their own country."

The policy of the German occupation authorities was in flagrant violation of the terms of this Convention. . . . [T]he German occupation authorities succeed[ed] in forcing many of the inhabitants of the occupied territories to work for the German war effort, and in deporting at least 5,000,000 persons to Germany to serve German industry and agriculture.

Persecution of the Jews

The persecution of the Jews at the hands of the Nazi Government has been proved in the greatest detail before the Tribunal. It is a record of consistent and systematic inhumanity on the greatest scale.

The anti-Jewish policy was formulated in [the Nazi] Party Programme . . . . With the seizure of power, the persecution of the Jews was intensified. A series of discriminatory laws were passed, which limited the offices and professions permitted to Jews; and restrictions were placed on their family life and their rights of citizenship. By the autumn of 1938, the Nazi policy towards the Jews had reached the stage where it was directed towards the complete exclusion of Jews from German life. Pogroms were organised which included the burning and demolishing of synagogues, the looting of Jewish businesses, and the arrest of prominent Jewish business men. A collective fine of one billion marks was imposed on the Jews, the seizure of Jewish assets was authorised, and the movement of Jews was restricted by regulations to certain specified districts and hours. The creation of ghettoes was carried out on an extensive scale, and by an order of the Security Police Jews were compelled to wear a yellow star to be worn on the breast and back.

It was contended for the Prosecution that certain aspects of this anti-Semitic policy were connected with the plans for aggressive war. The violent measures taken against the Jews in November, 1938, were nominally in retaliation for the killing of an official of the German Embassy in Paris. But the decision to seize Austria and Czechoslovakia had been made a year before. The imposition of a fine of one billion marks was made, and the confiscation of the financial holdings of the Jews was decreed, at a time when German armament expenditure had put the German treasury in difficulties, and when the reduction of expenditure on armaments was being considered. . . .

The Nazi persecution of Jews in Germany before the war, severe and repressive as it was, cannot compare, however, with the policy pursued during the war in the occupied territories. Originally the policy was similar to that which had been in force inside Germany. . . In the summer of 1941, however, plans were made for the "final solution" of the Jewish question in all of Europe. This "final solution " meant the extermination of the Jews, which early in 1939 Hitler had threatened would be one of the consequences of an outbreak of war, and a special section in the Gestapo under Adolf Eichmann, as head of Section B4 of the Gestapo, was formed to carry out the policy. The plan for exterminating the Jews was developed shortly after the attack on the Soviet Union. . . .

Part of the "final solution" was the gathering of Jews from all German occupied Europe in concentration camps. Their physical condition was the test of life or death. All who were fit to work were used as slave labourers in the concentration camps; all who were not fit to work were destroyed in gas chambers and their bodies burnt. Certain concentration camps such as Treblinka and Auschwitz were set aside for this main purpose. . . . Adolf Eichmann, who had been put in charge of this programme by Hitler, has estimated that the policy pursued resulted in the killing of 6,000,000 Jews, of which 4,000,000 were killed in the extermination institutions.

The Law Relating to War Crimes and Crimes Against Humanity

. . . . The Tribunal is of course bound by the Charter, in the definition which it gives both of war crimes and crimes against humanity. With respect to war crimes, however, as has already been pointed out, the crimes defined by Article 6, section (b), of the Charter were already recognised as war crimes under international law. They were covered by Articles 46, 50, 52, and 56 of the Hague Convention of 1907, and Articles 2, 3, 4, 46 and 51 of the Geneva Convention of 1929. That violations of these provisions constituted crimes for which the guilty individuals were punishable is too well settled to admit of argument.

But it is argued that the Hague Convention does not apply in this case, because of the "general participation" clause in Article 2 of the Hague Convention of 1907. That clause provided: "The provisions contained in the regulations (Rules of Land Warfare) referred to in Article 1 as well as in the present Convention do not apply except between contracting powers, and then only if all the belligerents are parties to the Convention." Several of the belligerents in the recent war were not parties to this Convention.

In the opinion of the Tribunal it is not necessary to decide this question. The rules of land warfare expressed in the Convention undoubtedly represented an advance over existing international law at the time of their adoption. But the Convention expressly stated that it was an attempt "to revise the general laws and customs of war," which it thus recognised to be then existing, but by 1939 these rules laid down in the Convention were recognised by all civilised nations, and were regarded as being declaratory of the laws and customs of war which are referred to in Article 6 (b) of the Charter. . . .

With regard to crimes against humanity, there is no doubt whatever that political opponents were murdered in Germany before the war, and that many of them were kept in concentration camps in circumstances of great horror and cruelty. The policy of terror was certainly carried out on a vast scale, and in many cases was organised and systematic. The policy of persecution, repression and murder of civilians in Germany before the war of 1939, who were likely to be hostile to the Government, was most ruthlessly carried out. The persecution of Jews during the same period is established beyond all doubt. To constitute crimes against humanity, the acts relied on before the outbreak of war must have been in execution of, or in connection with, any crime within the jurisdiction of the Tribunal. The Tribunal is of the opinion that revolting and horrible as many of these crimes were, it has not been satisfactorily proved that they were done in execution of, or in connection with, any such crime. The Tribunal therefore cannot make a general declaration that the acts before 1939 were crimes against humanity within the meaning of the Charter, but from the beginning of the war in 1939 war crimes were committed on a vast scale, which were also crimes against humanity; and insofar as the inhumane acts charged in the Indictment, and committed after the beginning of the war, did not constitute war crimes, they were all committed in execution of, or in connection with, the aggressive war, and therefore constituted crimes against humanity.

The Accused Organisations

Article 9 of the Charter provides:

> At the trial of any individual member of any group or organisation the Tribunal may declare (in connection with any act of which the individual may be convicted) that the group or organisation of which the individual was a member was a criminal organisation.

> After receipt of the Indictment the Tribunal shall give such notice as it thinks fit that the prosecution intends to ask the Tribunal to make such declaration and any member of the organisation will be entitled to apply to the Tribunal for leave to be heard by the Tribunal upon the question of the criminal character of the organisation. The Tribunal shall have power to allow or reject the application. If the application is allowed, the Tribunal may direct in what manner the applicants shall be represented and heard.

Article 10 of the Charter makes clear that the declaration of criminality against an accused organisation is final, and cannot be challenged in any subsequent criminal proceeding against a member of that organisation Article 10 is as follows:

> In cases where a group or organisation is declared criminal by the Tribunal, the competent national authority of any Signatory shall have the right to bring individuals to trial for membership therein before national, military or occupation courts. In any such case the criminal nature of the group or organisation is considered proved and shall not be questioned.

The effect of the declaration of criminality by the Tribunal is well illustrated by Law Number 10 of the Control Council of Germany passed on the 20th day of December, 1945, which provides:

Each of the following acts is recognised as a crime:

> (d) Membership in categories of a criminal group or organisation declared criminal by the International Military Tribunal. . . .

> (3) Any person found guilty of any of the crimes above mentioned may upon conviction be punished as shall be determined by the Tribunal to be just. Such punishment may consist of one or more of the following:

(a) Death.

(b) Imprisonment for life or a term of years, with or without hard labour.

(c) Fine, and imprisonment with or without hard labour, in lieu thereof.

In effect, therefore, a member of an organisation which the Tribunal has declared to be criminal may be subsequently convicted of the crime of membership and be punished for that crime by death. This is not to assume that international or military courts which will try these individuals will not exercise appropriate standards of justice. This is a far-reaching and novel procedure. Its application, unless properly safeguarded, may produce great injustice.

Article 9, it should be noted, uses the words "The Tribunal may declare," so that the Tribunal is vested with discretion as to whether it will declare any organisation criminal. This discretion is a judicial one and does not permit arbitrary action, but should be exercised in accordance with well settled legal principles one of the most important of which is that criminal guilt is personal, and that mass punishments should be avoided. If satisfied of the criminal guilt of any organisation or group this Tribunal should not hesitate to declare it to be criminal because the theory of "group criminality" is new, or because it might be unjustly applied by some subsequent tribunals. On the other hand, the Tribunal should make such declaration of criminality so far as possible in a manner to insure that innocent persons will not be punished.

A criminal organisation is analogous to a criminal conspiracy in that the essence of both is cooperation for criminal purposes. There must be a group bound together and organised for a common purpose. The group must be formed or used in connection with the commission of crimes denounced by the Charter. Since the declaration with respect to the organisations and groups will, as has been pointed out, fix the criminality of its members, that definition should exclude persons who had no knowledge of the criminal purposes or acts of the organisation and those who were drafted by the State for membership, unless they were personally implicated in the commission of acts declared criminal by Article 6 of the Charter as members of the organisation. Membership alone is not enough to come within the scope of these declarations. . . .

NOTES AND QUESTIONS

(1) Twenty-four Nazi leaders were indicted before the International Military Tribunal at Nuremberg. One of the twenty-four, Gustav Krupp von Bohlen, was

found to be too ill to be tried. One, Robert Ley, committed suicide while in custody. Martin Bormann was tried and sentenced to death *in absentia*. Of the twenty-one who stood trial in person, three (Hjalmar Schacht, Franz von Papen, and Hans Fritzsche) were acquitted. Seven (Rudolf Hess, Walter Funk, Karl Doenitz, Erich Raeder, Baldur von Schirach, Albert Speer, and Constantin von Neurath) were sentenced to prison terms varying from ten years to life. The remaining eleven (Hermann Goering, Joachim von Ribbentrop, Wilhelm Keitel, Ernest Kaltenbrunner, Alfred Rosenberg, Hans Frank, Wilhelm Frick, Julius Streicher, Fritz Saukel, Alfred Jodl, and Arthur Seyss-Inquart) were sentenced to death. Goering committed suicide before he could be hanged.

The indictment asked for a declaration of criminality against the Leadership Corps of the Nazi Party, the Gestapo, the SS (Black Shirts), its subsidiary the SD, the SA (Brown Shirts), the Reich Cabinet, and the General Staff and High Command of the German Armed Forces. The Leadership Corps, the Gestapo, the SS and SD were declared (with the qualifications set out in the Judgment) to be criminal organizations. The SA, Reich Cabinet, and General Staff and High Command were acquitted.

(2) Following the First World War, a Commission on the Responsibility of the Authors of the War appointed by the Paris Peace Conference recommended establishment of an international tribunal to try both acts which had provoked the war and "violations of the laws and customs of war and the laws of humanity." *See Commission on the Responsibility of the Authors of the War and on Enforcement of Penalties: Report Presented to the Preliminary Peace Conference*, 14 AM. J. INT'L L. 95 (1920). The U.S. representatives on the Commission objected to this proposal as being without precedent in international law. The Commission's report did influence the two provisions of the Versailles Treaty mentioned in the Nuremberg Judgment: Article 227, which provided that the Kaiser should be tried "for a supreme offense against international morality and the sanctity of treaties," and Article 228, which provided for the trial before allied tribunals of Germans accused of violating the laws and customs of war. The Kaiser was never put on trial because the Netherlands, where he had taken refuge, was unwilling to give him up; and the German government resisted the surrender of other German nationals. As a compromise, a dozen defendants accused of war crimes were prosecuted before the German Supreme Court in Leipzig, but given derisory sentences. *See* CLAUDE MULLINS, THE LEIPZIG TRIALS (1921).

(3) On which of the "bases of jurisdiction" considered in chapter 2 did the Nuremberg Tribunal exercise jurisdiction over the defendants? What does the Judgment say about this? Does it accord with the statement in the *Demjanjuk* case (in the next section) that the Tribunal's jurisdiction "necessarily derived from the universality principle"? For analysis of the various possibilities, *see* ROBERT K. WOETZEL, THE NUREMBERG TRIALS IN INTERNATIONAL LAW 58-95 (2d ed. 1962).

(4) In what respects did the law applied by the Tribunal represent a

departure from preexisting international law? Did the Tribunal persuasively answer objections based on the principle that there can be no punishment of crime without a preexisting law? Did the Nuremberg Trial comport with the guarantees with respect to criminal proceedings set out in the International Covenant on Civil and Political Rights (see chap. 16 supra)? Can the trial rationally be justified in terms of its deterrent efficacy? Or does its point lie elsewhere? Was it objectionable as representing "victor's justice"? What were the alternatives in 1946? Consider the following observations in Herbert Wechsler, The Issues of the Nuremberg Trial, 62 POL. SCI. Q. 11, 23-25 (1947):

I have not addressed myself to whether a tribunal of the victors could be impartial, to whether the law of the Charter is ex post facto or whether it is "law" at all. These are, indeed, the issues that are currently mooted. But there are elements in the debate that should lead us to be suspicious of the issues as they are drawn in these terms. For, most of those who mount the attack on one or another of these contentions hasten to assure us that their plea is not one of immunity for the defendants; they argue only that they should have been disposed of politically, that is, dispatched out of hand. This is a curious position indeed. A punitive enterprise launched on the basis of general rules, administered in an adversary proceeding under a separation of prosecutive and adjudicative powers is, in the name of law and justice, asserted to be less desirable than an ex parte execution list or a drumhead court-martial constituted in the immediate aftermath of the war. . . . Those who choose to   do so many view the Nuremberg proceeding as "political" rather than "legal" –   a program calling for the judicial application of principles of liability   politically defined. They cannot view it as less civilized an institution than a program of organized violence against prisoners, whether directed from the respective capitals or by military commanders in the field. . . .

No one who examines the record and the judgment . . . will question the disinterestedness of the Tribunal; and those   who argue that disinterestedness is inherently impossible in this situation   may ask themselves why nations that can procedure such impartial critics should be intrinsically incapable of producing equally impartial judges. The fact is that the judgment of the Tribunal was mainly a judgment of limitation, its principal operation more significantly that of protecting innocence that that of declaring and punishing guilt. . . .

There is . . . too large a disposition   among the defenders of Nuremberg to look for stray tags of international pronouncements and reason therefrom that the law of Nuremberg was previously fully laid down. If the Kellogg-Briand Pact or a general conception of international obligation sufficed to authorize England, and would have authorized us, to declare war on Germany in defense of Poland – and in this enterprise to kill countless thousands of German soldiers and civilians – can it be possible that it failed to authorize punitive action against individual

Germans judicially determined to be responsible for the Polish attack? To be sure, we would demand a more explicit authorization for punishment in domestic law, for we have adopted for the protection of individuals a prophylactic principle absolutely forbidding retroactivity that we can afford to carry to that extreme. International society, being less stable, can afford less luxury. We admit that in other respects. Why should we deny it here?

(5) As mentioned in chapter 17, on December 11, 1946, the U.N. General Assembly adopted a resolution in which it "reaffirm[ed] the principles of international law recognized by the Charter of the Nürnberg Tribunal and the judgment of the Tribunal" and directed the International Law Commission (then called the Committee on the Codification of International Law) to "formulate" those principles. G. A. Res. 95 (I), U.N. Doc. A/64/Add.1, at 188 (1946). The International Law Commission produced its distillation of the Nuremberg Principles in 1950. *See Report of the International Law Commission*, U.N. GAOR, V, Supp. 12 (A/1316), at 11-14 (1950). These read as follows:

Principle I

Any person who commits an act which constitutes a crime under international law is responsible therefor and liable to punishment.

Principle II

The fact that internal law does not impose a penalty for an act which constitutes a crime under international law does not relieve the person who committed the act from responsibility under international law.

Principle III

The fact that a person who committed an act which constitutes a crime under international law acted as Head of State or responsible Government official does not relieve him from responsibility under international law.

Principle IV

The fact that a person acted pursuant to order of his Government or of a superior does not relieve him from responsibility under international law, provided a moral choice was in fact possible to him.

Principle V

Any person charged with a crime under international law has the right to a fair trial on the facts and law.

Principle VI

The crimes hereinafter set out are punishable as crimes under international law:

(a) Crimes against peace:

(i) Planning, preparation, initiation or waging of a war of aggression or a war in violation of international treaties, agreements or assurances;

(ii) Participation in a common plan or conspiracy for the accomplishment of any of the acts mentioned under (i).

(b) War crimes: Violations of the laws or customs of war which include, but are not limited to, murder, ill-treatment or deportation to slave-labour or for any other purpose of civilian population of or in occupied territory; murder or ill-treatment of prisoners of war, of persons on the Seas, killing of hostages, plunder of public or private property, wanton destruction of cities, towns, or villages, or devastation not justified by military necessity.

(c) Crimes against humanity: Murder, extermination, enslavement, deportation and other inhuman acts done against any civilian population, or persecutions on political, racial or religious grounds, when such acts are done or such persecutions are carried on in execution of or in connection with any crime against peace or any war crime.

Principle VII

Complicity in the commission of a crime against peace, a war crime, or a crime against humanity as set forth in   Principle VI is a crime under international   law.

§ 18.02 The Tokyo Trial

The counterpart of the Nuremberg Tribunal in the Far East was the International Military Tribunal for the Far East or the "Tokyo Tribunal." It was composed of eleven judges from eleven countries (Australia, Canada, China, France, Great Britain, India, the Netherlands, New Zealand, the Philippines, the U.S.S.R., and the United States) appointed by General MacArthur, the Supreme Allied Commander for the Far East.

Article 5 of its Charter gave the tribunal "the power to try and punish Far Eastern war criminals who as individuals or members of organizations are charged with offenses which include Crimes against Peace." Thus, the tribunal had jurisdiction only over defendants who were charged with crimes against peace, although it might also try such defendants on charges involving conventional war crimes and crimes against humanity. These three crimes were defined in terms similar to, but also different from, those used in the Article 6 of the Nuremberg Charter:

> a. *Crimes against Peace*: Namely, the planning, preparation, initiation, or waging of a declared or undeclared war of aggression, or a war in violation of international law, treaties, agreements or assurances, or participation in a common plan or conspiracy for the accomplishment of any of the foregoing.

> b. *Conventional War Crimes*: Namely, violations of the laws or customs of war.

> c. *Crimes against Humanity*: Namely, murder, extermination, enslavement, deportation, and other inhumane acts committed before or during the war, or persecutions on political or racial grounds in execution of or in connection with any crime within the jurisdiction of the Tribunal, whether or not in violation of the domestic law of the country where perpetrated.

The trial was conducted in English and Japanese. It began on May 3, 1946. It concluded nearly two years later on April 16, 1948. It took the tribunal another seven months to prepare its 1218-page judgment which was rendered on November 4-12, 1948. All twenty-five defendants were found guilty on one or more counts of the indictment by a vote of 8-3. (The dissenting judges were Henri Bernard of France, Radhabinod Pal of India, and Bernard V. A. Röling of the Netherlands.) Seven defendants were sentenced to death; sixteen to life imprisonment; one to twenty years' and one to seven years' imprisonment. *See* Solis Horwitz, *The Tokyo Trial*, INT'L CONCILIATION No. 465 (1950).

The Tokyo Tribunal never enjoyed the attention and authority accorded to the Nuremberg Tribunal. Even its full judgment remained unpublished until 1977. On source materials for the Tokyo Trial, *see* R. John Pritchard, *The International Military Tribunal for the Far East and the Allied National War Crimes Trials in Asia, in* 3 INTERNATIONAL CRIMINAL LAW 109, 127-31 (M. Cherif Bassiouni ed., 1999).

§ 18.03 Subsequent Trials

Besides the trial before the International Military Tribunal at Nuremberg, other post-war prosecutions in Germany took place under Allied Control Council Law No. 10 (referred to in the Nuremberg Judgment) which authorized the four occupying powers to prosecute German war criminals in their respective zones of occupation. In the American zone, twelve subsequent trials involving 177 individual defendants were held at Nuremberg under this law. *See* Telford Taylor, *Nuremberg Trials: War Crimes and International Law*, INT'L CONCILIATION No. 450 (1949).

The substantive provisions of Control Council Law No. 10 were modeled, more or less, on the Nuremberg Charter. However, in its definition of "crimes against humanity," the Control Council Law did not require a connection to war crimes or crimes against peace. Article II (1)(c) defined "crimes against humanity" as

Atrocities and offenses, including but not limited to murder, extermination, enslavement, deportation, imprisonment, torture, rape or other inhumane acts committed against any civilian population, or persecution on political, racial or religious grounds whether or not in violation of the domestic laws of the country where perpetrated.

U.S. tribunals reached conflicting conclusions about whether this actually permitted prosecution for crimes against humanity unrelated to the war. *See* Telford Taylor, *supra*, at 342-44.

In the Far East, apart from the Tokyo Trial, there also were prosecutions before allied military tribunals. Perhaps the best-known was the trial of General Tomoyuki Yamashita, who was found guilty by a U.S. military commission in the Philippines of failing to take appropriate steps to prevent the troops under his command from committing atrocities against civilians and prisoners of war. *See In re Yamashita*, 327 U.S. 1 (1946).

Other post-war prosecutions took place in Europe before national courts of various countries that had been occupied by Germany during the war and, eventually, before national courts in Germany. Recent examples in France of prosecution for crimes committed during the Second World War are the trials of Klaus Barbie in 1987, Paul Touvier in 1994, and Maurice Papon in 1998. *See* Leila Sadat Wexler, *National Prosecutions for International Crimes: The French Experience, in* 3 INTERNATIONAL CRIMINAL LAW 273 (M. Cherif Bassiouni ed., 1999).

With the passage of time, the question became urgent of whether the prosecution of war crimes was subject to national statutes of limitations. In 1968, the U.N. General Assembly adopted a Convention on the Non-Applicability of Statutory Limitations to War Crimes and Crimes Against Humanity, Nov. 26, 1968, G. A. Res. 2391 (XXIII), 754 U.N.T.S. 75, which entered into force on November 11, 1970. The preamble and first four articles of the convention read as follows:

The States Parties to the present Convention,

Recalling resolutions of the General Assembly of the United Nations 3 (I) of 13 February 1946 and 170 (II) of 31 October 1947 on the extradition and punishment of war criminals, resolution 95 (I) of 11 December 1946 affirming the principles of international law recognized by the Charter of the International Military Tribunal, Nurnberg, and the judgement of the Tribunal, and resolutions   2184(XXI) of 12 December 1966 and 2202(XXI) of 16 December 1966 which expressly condemned as crimes against humanity the violation of the economic and political rights of the indigenous population on the one hand and the policies of apartheid on the other,

Recalling resolutions of the Economic and Social Council of the United Nations 1074 D (XXXIX) of 28 July 1965 and 1158 (XLI) of 5 August 1966 on the punishment of war criminals and of persons who have committed crimes against humanity,

Noting that none of the solemn declarations, instruments or conventions relating to the prosecution and punishment of war crimes and crimes against humanity made provision for a period of limitation,

Considering that war crimes and crimes against humanity are among the gravest crimes in international law,

Convinced that the effective punishment of war crimes and crimes against humanity is an important element in the prevention of such crimes, the protection of human rights and fundamental freedoms, the encouragement of confidence, the furtherance of co-operation among peoples and the promotion of international peace and security,

Noting that the application to war crimes and crimes against humanity of the rules of municipal law relating to the period of limitation for ordinary crimes is a matter of serious concern to world public opinion, since it prevents the prosecution and punishment of persons responsible for those crimes,

Recognizing that it is necessary and timely to affirm in international law, through this Convention, the principle that there is no period of limitation for war crimes and crimes against humanity, and to secure its universal application,

Have agreed as follows:

Article 1

No statutory limitation shall apply to the following crimes, irrespective of the date of their commission:

(a) War crimes as they are defined in the Charter of the International Military Tribunal, Nürnberg, of 8 August 1945 and confirmed by resolutions 3 (1) of 13 February 1946 and 95 (I) of 11

December 1946 of the General Assembly of the United Nations, particularly the "grave breaches" enumerated in the Geneva Conventions of 12 August 1949 for the protection of war victims;

(b) Crimes against humanity whether committed in time of war or in time of peace as they are defined in the Charter of the International Military Tribunal, Nürnberg, of 8 August 1945 and confirmed by resolutions 3 (I) of 13 February 1946 and 95 (I) of 11 December 1946 of the General Assembly of the United Nations, eviction by armed attack or occupation and inhuman acts resulting from the policy of apartheid, and the crime of genocide as defined in the 1948 Convention on the Prevention and Punishment of the Crime of Genocide, even if such acts do not constitute a violation of the domestic law of the country in which they were committed.

Article 2

If any of the crimes mentioned in article I is committed, the provisions of this Convention shall apply to representatives of the State authority and private individuals who, as principals or accomplices, participate in or who directly incite others to the commission of any of those crimes, or who conspire to commit them, irrespective of the degree of completion, and to representatives of the State authority who tolerate their commission.

Article 3

The States Parties to the present Convention undertake to adopt all necessary domestic measures, legislative or otherwise, with a view to making possible the extradition, in accordance with international law, of the persons referred to in article II of this Convention.

Article 4

The States Parties to the present Convention undertake to adopt, in accordance with their respective constitutional processes, any legislative or other measures necessary to ensure that statutory or other limitations shall not apply to the prosecution and punishment of the crimes referred to in articles 1 and 2 of this Convention and that, where they exist, such limitations shall be abolished.

DEMJANJUK v. PETROVSKY

United States Court of Appeals for the Sixth Circuit
776 F.2d 571 (1985)

LIVELY, CHIEF JUDGE:

I

The petitioner, John Demjanjuk, is a native of the Ukraine, one of the republics of the Soviet Union. Demjanjuk was admitted to the United States in 1952 under the Displaced Persons Act of 1948 and became a naturalized United States citizen in 1958. He has resided in the Cleveland, Ohio area since his arrival in this country.

In 1981 the United States District Court for the Northern District of Ohio revoked Demjanjuk's certificate of naturalization and vacated the order admitting him to United States citizenship. . . Chief Judge Battisti of the district court entered extensive findings of fact from which he concluded that the certificate and order "were illegally procured and were procured by willful misrepresentation of material facts under 8 U.S.C. § 1451(a)."

The district court found that Demjanjuk was conscripted into the Soviet Army in 1940 and was captured by the Germans in 1942. After short stays in several German POW camps and a probable tour at the Trawniki SS training camp in Poland, Demjanjuk became a guard at the Treblinka concentration camp, also in Poland, late in 1942. In his various applications for immigration to the United States the petitioner misstated his place of residence during the period 1937-1948 and did not reveal that he had worked for the SS at Treblinka or served in a German military unit later in the war. In the denaturalization proceedings Demjanjuk admitted that his statements concerning residence were false and that he had in fact served in a German military unit. He steadfastly denied that he had been at Trawniki or Treblinka, though documentary evidence placed him at Trawniki and five Treblinka survivors and one former German guard at the camp identified Demjanjuk as a Ukrainian guard who was known as "Ivan or Iwan Grozny," that is, "Ivan the Terrible."

Following the denaturalization order the government began deportation proceedings against Demjanjuk. While these proceedings were underway the State of Israel filed with the United States Department of State a request for the extradition of Demjanjuk. . . . Following a hearing the district court entered an order certifying to the Secretary of State that Demjanjuk was subject to extradition at the request of the State of Israel pursuant to a treaty on extradition between the United States and Israel signed December 10, 1962, effective December 5, 1963. . . .

III

The pertinent portions of the treaty (Convention on Extradition) between the United States and Israel (hereafter the Treaty) found in the first three articles and the thirteenth article are set forth:

Article I

Each Contracting Party agrees, under the conditions and circumstances established by the present Convention, reciprocally to deliver up persons found in its territory who have been charged with or convicted of any of the offenses mentioned in Article II of the present Convention committed within the territorial jurisdiction of the other, or outside thereof under the conditions specified in Article III of the present Convention.

Article II

Persons shall be delivered up according to the provisions of the present Convention for prosecution when they have been charged with, or to undergo sentence when they have been convicted of, any of the following offenses:

1. Murder.

2. Manslaughter.

3. Malicious wounding; inflicting grievous bodily harm. . . .

Article III

When the offense has been committed outside the territorial jurisdiction of the requesting Party, extradition need not be granted unless the laws of the requested Party provide for the punishment of such an offense committed in similar circumstances. . . .

Article XIII

A person extradited under the present Convention shall not be detained, tried or punished in the territory of the requesting Party for any offense other than that for which extradition has been granted nor be extradited by that Party to a third State . . .

The Israeli warrant on which the extradition request was based was issued pursuant to a request which charged Demjanjuk with having "murdered tens of thousands of Jews and non-Jews" while operating the gas chambers to exterminate prisoners at Treblinka. It further asserts that the acts charged were committed "with the intention of destroying the Jewish people and to commit crimes against humanity." The complaint in the district court equated this charge with the crimes of "murder and malicious wounding [and] inflicting grievous bodily harm," listed in the Treaty. The warrant was issued pursuant to a 1950 Israeli statute, the Nazis and Nazi Collaborators (Punishment) Law. This statute made certain acts, including "crimes against the Jewish people," "crimes against humanity" and "war crimes committed during the Nazi period" punishable under Israeli law. The statute defines these crimes as follows:

"crime against the Jewish people" means any of the following acts, committed with intent to destroy the Jewish people in whole or in part:

1. killing Jews;

2. causing serious bodily or mental harm to Jews;

3. placing Jews in living conditions calculated to bring about their physical destruction;

4. imposing measures intended to prevent births among Jews;

5. forcibly transferring Jewish children to another national or religious group;

6. destroying or desecrating Jewish religious or cultural assets or values;

7. inciting to hatred of Jews;

"crime against humanity" means any of the following acts:

murder, extermination, enslavement, starvation or deportation and other inhumane acts committed against any civilian population, and persecution on national, racial, religious or political grounds;

"war crime" means any of the following acts:

murder, ill-treatment or deportation to forced labour or for any other purpose, of civilian population of or in occupied territory; murder or ill-treatment of prisoners of war or persons on the seas; killing of hostages; plunder of public or private property; wanton destruction of cities, towns or villages; and devastation not justified by military necessity.

Demjanjuk contends that the district court had no jurisdiction to consider the request for extradition. He . . . . maintains that the crime he is charged with is not included in the listing of offenses in the treaty. It is his position that "murdering thousands of Jews and non-Jews" is not covered by the treaty designation of "murder." . . . We have no difficulty concluding that "murder" includes the mass murder of Jews. This is a logical reading of the treaty language and is the interpretation given the treaty by the Department of State. That interpretation is entitled to considerable deference. . . .

Demjanjuk also argues that the district court had no jurisdiction because there is a requirement of "double criminality" in international extradition cases. . . We believe the double criminality requirement was met in this case. . . . If the acts upon which the charges of the requesting country are based are also proscribed by a law of the requested nation, the requirement of double criminality is satisfied. Murder is a crime in every state of the United States. The fact that there is no separate offense of mass murder or murder of tens of thousands of Jews in this country is beside the point. The *act* of unlawfully killing one or more persons with the requisite malice is punishable as murder. That is the test. The acts charged are criminal both in Israel and throughout the United States, including Ohio. Demjanjuk's argument that to interpret murder to include murder of Jews would amount to judicial amendment of the Treaty is absurd and offensive.

IV

A separate jurisdictional argument concerns the territorial reach of the statutory law of Israel. Demjanjuk relies on two facts to question the power of the State of Israel to proceed against him. He is not a citizen or resident of Israel and the crimes with which he is charged allegedly were committed in Poland. He also points out that the acts which are the basis of the Israeli arrest warrant allegedly took place in 1942 or 1943, before the State of Israel came into existence. Thus, Demjanjuk maintains that the district court had no jurisdiction because Israel did not charge him with extraditable offenses.

The scope of this nation's international extradition power and the function of the federal courts in the extradition process are set forth in 18 U.S.C. § 3184. . . . Section 3184 clearly provides that the extradition complaint must charge the person sought to be extradited with having committed crimes "within the jurisdiction of any such foreign government," that is, the requesting state. . . The question is whether the murder of Jews in a Nazi extermination camp in Poland during the 1939-1945 war can be considered, for purposes of extradition, crimes within the jurisdiction of the State of Israel.

We look first at the Treaty. Article III provides that when an offense has been committed outside the territorial jurisdiction of the requesting party, "extradition need not be granted unless the laws of the requested party provide for the punishment of such an offense committed in similar circumstances." Demjanjuk maintains that the "need not" language of Article III prohibits extradition in this case because the laws of the United States do not provide punishment for war crimes or crimes against humanity. . . . In our view the treaty language makes two things clear: (1) the parties recognize the right to request extradition for extra territorial crimes, and (2) the requested party has the discretion to deny extradition if its laws do not provide for punishment of offenses committed under similar circumstances. This provision does not affect the authority of a court to certify extraditability; it merely distinguishes between cases where the requested party is required to honor a request and those where it has discretion to deny a request. That the specific offense charged is not a crime in the United States does not necessarily rule out extradition.

The Israeli statute under which Demjanjuk was charged deals with "crimes against the Jewish people," "crimes against humanity" and "war crimes" committed during the Nazi years. It is clear from the language defining the crimes, and other references to acts directed at persecuted persons and committed in places of confinement, that Israel intended to punish under this law those involved in carrying out Hitler's "final solution." This was made explicit in the prosecution of Adolph Eichmann in 1961. *Attorney General v. Eichmann*, 36 I.L.R. 277 (Sup. Ct. Israel 1962). Such a claim of extraterritorial jurisdiction over criminal offenses is not unique to Israel. For example, statutes of the United States provide for punishment in domestic district courts for murder or manslaughter committed within the maritime jurisdiction (18 U.S.C. § 1111) and murder or manslaughter of internationally protected persons wherever they are killed (18 U.S.C. § 1116(c)). We conclude that the reference in 18 U.S.C. § 3184 to crimes committed within the jurisdiction of the requesting government does not refer solely to territorial jurisdiction. Rather, it refers to the authority of a nation to apply its laws to particular conduct. In international law this is referred to as "jurisdiction to prescribe." RESTATEMENT § 401(1).

The law of the United States includes international law. *The Paquete Habana*, 175 U.S. 667, 712, 20 S. Ct. 290, 44 L. Ed. 320 (1900). International law recognizes a "universal jurisdiction" over certain offenses.   .   .   .   This "universality principle" is based on the assumption that some crimes are so universally condemned that the perpetrators are the enemies of all people. Therefore, any nation which has custody of the perpetrators may punish them according to its law applicable to such offenses. This principle is a departure from the general rule that "the character of an act as lawful or unlawful must be determined wholly by the law of the country where the act is done." *American Banana Co. v. United Fruit Co.*, 213 U.S. 347, 356, 53 L. Ed. 826, 29 S. Ct. 511 (1909).

The wartime allies created the International Military Tribunal which tried major Nazi officials at Nuremberg and courts within the four occupation zones of post-war Germany which tried lesser Nazis. All were tried for committing war crimes, and it is generally agreed that the establishment of these tribunals and their proceedings were based on universal jurisdiction.

Demjanjuk argues that the post-war trials were all based on the military defeat of Germany and that with the disestablishment of the special tribunals there are no courts with jurisdiction over alleged war crimes. This argument overlooks the fact that the post-war tribunals were not military courts, though their presence in Germany was made possible by the military defeat of that country. These tribunals did not operate within the limits of traditional military courts. They claimed and exercised a much broader jurisdiction which necessarily derived from the universality principle. Whatever doubts existed prior to 1945 have been erased by the general recognition since that time that there is a jurisdiction over some types of crimes which extends beyond the territorial limits of any nation.

. . . RESTATEMENT § 443 appears to apply to the present case: "A state's courts may exercise jurisdiction to enforce the state's criminal laws which punish universal crimes (§ 404) or other non-territorial offenses within the state's jurisdiction to prescribe (§§ 402-403)." Israel is seeking to enforce its criminal law for the punishment of Nazis and Nazi collaborators for crimes universally recognized and condemned by the community of nations. The fact that Demjanjuk is charged with committing these acts in Poland does not deprive Israel of authority to bring him to trial.

Further, the fact that the State of Israel was not in existence when Demjanjuk allegedly committed the offenses is no bar to Israel's exercising jurisdiction under the universality principle. When proceeding on that jurisdictional premise, neither the nationality of the accused or the victim(s), nor the location of the crime is significant. The underlying assumption is that the crimes are offenses against the law of nations or against humanity and that the prosecuting nation is acting for all nations. This being so, Israel or any other nation, regardless of its status in 1942 or 1943, may undertake to vindicate the interest of all nations by seeking to punish the perpetrators of such crimes.

We conclude that the jurisdictional challenges to the district court's order must fail. The crime of murder is clearly included in the offenses for which extradition is to be granted under the treaty. Murder is a crime both in Israel and in the United States and is included in the specifications of the Nazis and Nazi Collaborators (Punishment) Law; the requirement of "double criminality" is met; and, the State of Israel has jurisdiction to punish for war crimes and crimes against humanity committed outside of its geographic boundaries. . .

V

The remaining inquiry relates to how the "principle of specialty" applies to this case. . . .

The district court clearly certified that Demjanjuk was subject to extradition solely on the charge of murder. Though some of the acts which Demjanjuk is charged with may also constitute other offenses listed in the treaty, he may be tried in Israel only on that charge. However, the particular acts of murder for which he may be tried depend upon Israeli law. Israel may try him under the provisions of the Nazis and Nazi Collaborators (Punishment) Law for "crimes against the Jewish people" ("killing Jews," a species of murder), "crimes against humanity" ("murder . . . committed against any civilian population") and "war crimes" ("murder . . . of civilian population of or in occupied territory"). The principle of specialty does not impose any limitation on the particulars of the charge so long as it encompasses only the offense for which extradition was granted. . . .

The judgment of the district court is affirmed.

———

NOTES AND QUESTIONS

(1) Demjanjuk was extradited to Israel in 1986. He was tried and convicted in 1988. The prosecution was based on his identification as the sadistic guard at Treblinka known as Ivan the Terrible. In 1993, the Israeli Supreme Court reversed his conviction, finding that there was reasonable doubt as to whether he was the Treblinka guard, and the Sixth Circuit vacated the extradition proceedings on the ground that the U.S. government had failed to disclose exculpatory materials in its possession during the earlier litigation. *See Demjanjuk v. Petrovsky*, 10 F.3d 338 (6th Cir. 1993), *cert. denied,* 513 U.S. 914, 130 L. Ed. 2d 205, 115 S. Ct. 295 (1994). In 1998, for the same reason, the district court set aside the 1981 denaturalization order. *See United States v. Demjanjuk*, No. C77-923, 1998 U.S. Dist. LEXIS 4047 (N.D. Ohio, Feb. 20, 1998).

(2) Consider how the concept of double criminality applied in *Demjanjuk* differs from the concept of double criminality applied by the House of Lords in *Pinochet* [chap. 11, *supra*]. Should the Sixth Circuit also have asked whether the offense for which extradition was sought (a) was one over which the U.S. courts were authorized to exercise extraterritorial jurisdiction (b) at the time of the offense?

(3) *Demjanjuk* is an instance of conduct during the Second World War being prosecuted before a national court in a country other than the one in which the conduct occurred. An earlier instance was the trial of Adolf Eichmann in Israel in 1961, which is referred to in the *Demjanjuk* opinion. *See Attorney-General v. Eichmann*, 36 I.L.R. 18 (Dist. Ct. Jerusalem 1961), *aff'd*, 36 I.L.R. 277 (Sup. Ct. Israel 1962). Jurisdiction in such cases depends not only on a permissive rule of international law but also on national legislation authorizing the courts to exercise extraterritorial jurisdiction over war crimes. National legislation, where it exists, may have a narrower scope than international law allows. Very often legislation authorizing the exercise of extraterritorial jurisdiction has been enacted to implement obligations under a particular treaty, such as the Torture Convention or the Geneva Conventions of 1949, and is limited to crimes described in the treaty. Some countries have enacted domestic laws that go

beyond treaty obligations, but these may cover, for instance, only acts committed abroad by or against nationals. In response to concern with the problem of former Nazi collaborators living in Canada, Canada did enact in 1987 a fairly comprehensive statute providing for the prosecution of war crimes and crimes against humanity committed abroad. *See* Criminal Code, R.S.C. 1985, c. 30, §§ 7 (3.71) - 7 (3.77) (Can.); *see also Regina v. Finta*, [1994] 1 S.C.R. 701. The British and Australian war crimes statutes, which were prompted by similar concerns, apply, however, only to acts committed during the Second World War. *See* War Crimes Act, 1991, ch. 13, §1(1) (Eng.); War Crimes Amendment Act, 1989 Austl. Acts No. 3, §9(1). Likewise, the Israeli statute under which Demjanjuk was charged dealt, as the Sixth Circuit notes, only with crimes committed during the Nazi era.

(4) Consider the U.S. War Crimes Act of 1996 (codified at 18 U.S.C. § 2441). Does this appear to be a response to the same problem as the Canadian, British, and Australian war crimes statutes? The act reads as follows:

18 U.S.C. § 2441. War crimes

(a) Offense. Whoever, whether inside or outside the United States, commits a war crime, in any of the circumstances described in subsection (b), shall be fined under this title or imprisoned for life or any term of years, or both, and if death results to the victim, shall also be subject to the penalty of death.

(b) Circumstances. The circumstances referred to in subsection (a) are that the person committing such war crime or the victim of such war crime is a member of the Armed Forces of the United States or a national of the United States (as defined in section 101 of the Immigration and Nationality Act).

(c) Definition. As used in this section the term "war crime" means any conduct –

(1) defined as a grave breach in any of the international conventions signed at Geneva 12 August 1949, or any protocol to such convention to which the United States is a party;

(2) prohibited by Article 23, 25, 27, or 28 of the Annex to the Hague Convention IV, Respecting the Laws and Customs of War on Land, signed 18 October 1907;

(3) which constitutes a violation of common Article 3 of the international conventions signed at Geneva, 12 August 1949, or any protocol to such convention to which the United States is a party and which deals with non-international armed conflict; or

(4) of a person who, in relation to an armed conflict and contrary to

the provisions of the Protocol on Prohibitions or Restrictions on the Use of Mines, Booby-Traps and Other Devices as amended at Geneva on 3 May 1996 (Protocol II as amended on 3 May 1996), when the United States is a party to such Protocol, willfully kills or causes serious injury to civilians.

Chapter 19
THE AD HOC TRIBUNALS FOR THE FORMER YUGOSLAVIA AND RWANDA

§ 19.01 The Ad Hoc Tribunal for the Former Yugoslavia

Beginning in 1991, the U.N. Security Council passed a series of resolutions declaring the ethnic conflict going on in the former Yugoslavia, particularly in Bosnia-Herzegovina, to constitute a breach of international peace and security. It expressed concern about serious violations of international humanitarian law being committed in the area and repeatedly reaffirmed the principle of individual responsibility for those violations. On October 6, 1992, Security Council Resolution 780 (1992) requested the U.N. Secretary-General to appoint a Commission of Experts to investigate violations of international humanitarian law in the former Yugoslavia. In an interim report in January 1993, the Commission recommended the establishment of an international criminal tribunal to try violators. On February 22, 1993, in Resolution 808 (1993), the Security Council decided to establish such a tribunal and asked the Secretary-General to prepare a report on how to implement its decision. The Secretary-General's report (U.N. Doc. S/25704, May 3, 1993) included a draft statute for an international criminal tribunal. On May 25, 1993, the Security Council adopted Resolution 827 (1993), creating the International Criminal Tribunal for the former Yugoslavia, which was to operate under the statute contained in the Secretary-General's report. The Statute and also the Rules of Procedure and Evidence adopted by the Tribunal are readily available on the Tribunal's website: <http://www.un.org/icty>.

The Tribunal initially had eleven judges sitting in two Trial Chambers of three judges each and an Appeals Chamber of five judges. Security Council Resolution 1166 (1998) expanded to number of judges to fourteen, so as to allow for a third Trial Chamber. The judges are elected by the U.N. General Assembly from a list of candidates proposed by the Security Council. The Tribunal's Prosecutor is appointed by the Security Council on nomination by the Secretary General. The Tribunal sits at The Hague. It has jurisdiction over four categories of crime – (1) "grave breaches" of the Geneva Conventions of 1949, (2) "violations of the laws and customs of war," (3) genocide, and (4) "crimes against humanity" – committed in the territory of the former Yugoslavia since January 1, 1991 (and until "a date to be determined by the Security Council upon the restoration of peace"). These four categories of crime comprise the parts of international humanitarian law that the Secretary General's report concluded clearly give rise to individual responsibility as a matter of customary international law.

PROSECUTOR v. TADIC

International Criminal Tribunal for the former Yugoslavia
Case No. IT-95-1-AR72, Appeals Chamber
Decision on the Defense Motion for Interlocutory Appeal on Jurisdiction
(Oct. 2, 1995)

I. INTRODUCTION

1. The Appeals Chamber of the International Tribunal for the Prosecution of Persons Responsible for Serious Violations of International Humanitarian Law Committed in the Territory of Former Yugoslavia since 1991 (hereinafter "International Tribunal") is seized of an appeal lodged by the Defence against a judgement rendered by Trial Chamber II on 10 August 1995. By that judgement, Appellant's motion challenging the jurisdiction of the International Tribunal was denied. . . .

8. [The grounds of appeal relied on by the Appellant] are offered under the following headings:

a) unlawful establishment of the International Tribunal;

b) unjustified primacy of the International Tribunal over competent domestic courts;

c) lack of subject-matter jurisdiction. . . .

II. UNLAWFUL ESTABLISHMENT OF THE INTERNATIONAL TRIBUNAL

9. The first ground of appeal attacks the validity of the establishment of the International Tribunal. . . .

Admissibility of Plea Based on the Invalidity of the Establishment of the Tribunal

13. Before the Trial Chamber, the Prosecutor maintained that: (1) the International Tribunal lacks authority to review its establishment by the Security Council; and that in any case (2) the question whether the Security Council in establishing the International Tribunal complied with the United Nations Charter raises "political questions" which are "non-justiciable." The Trial Chamber approved this line of argument. . . .

(1) *Does the International Tribunal Have Jurisdiction?*

15. To assume that the jurisdiction of the International Tribunal is absolutely limited to what the Security Council "intended" to entrust it with, is to envisage the International Tribunal exclusively as a "subsidiary organ" of the Security Council . . . . But the Security Council not only decided to establish a subsidiary organ . . . it also clearly intended to establish a special kind of "subsidiary organ": a tribunal.

18. [The] power, known as *"la compétence de la compétence"* in French, is part, and indeed a major part, of the incidental or inherent jurisdiction of any judicial or arbitral tribunal, consisting of its "jurisdiction to determine its own jurisdiction." It is a necessary component in the exercise of the judicial function and does not need to be expressly provided for in the constitutive documents of those tribunals. . . .

19. It is true that this power can be limited by an express provision in the arbitration agreement or in the constitutive instruments of standing tribunals. . . . [but since] no such limitative text appears in the Statute of the International Tribunal, the International Tribunal can and indeed has to exercise its *"compétence de la compétence"* and examine the jurisdictional plea of the Defence in order to ascertain its jurisdiction to hear the case on the merits.

(2) *Is The Question At Issue Political And As Such Non-Justiciable?*

24. The doctrines of "political questions" and "non-justiciable disputes" are remnants of the reservations of "sovereignty," "national honour," etc. in very old arbitration treaties. They have receded from the horizon of contemporary international law, except for the occasional invocation of the "political question" argument before the International Court of Justice in advisory proceedings and, very rarely, in contentious proceedings as well. The Court has consistently rejected this argument as a bar to examining a case. It considered it unfounded in law. As long as the case before it or the request for an advisory opinion turns on a legal question capable of a legal answer, the Court considers that it is duty-bound to exercise jurisdiction over it, regardless of the political background or the other political facets of the issue. . . .

25. The Appeals Chamber does not consider that the International Tribunal is barred from examination of the Defence jurisdictional plea by the so-called "political" or "non-justiciable" nature of the issue it raises.

The Issue of Constitutionality

26. Many arguments have been put forward by Appellant in support of the contention that the establishment of the International Tribunal is invalid under the Charter of the United Nations or that it was not duly established by law.

. . . These arguments raise a series of constitutional issues which all turn on the limits of the power of the Security Council under Chapter VII of the Charter of the United Nations [in] determining what action or measures can be taken under this Chapter, particularly the establishment of an international criminal tribunal. . . .

(1) *The Power Of The Security Council To Invoke Chapter VII*

28. Article 39 opens Chapter VII of the Charter of the United Nations and determines the conditions of application of this Chapter. It provides: "The Security Council shall determine the existence of any threat to the peace, breach of the peace, or act of aggression and shall make recommendations, or decide what measures shall be taken in accordance with Articles 41 and 42, to maintain or restore international peace and security." . . .

30. It is not necessary for the purposes of the present decision to examine . . . the question of the limits of the discretion of the Security Council in determining the existence of a "threat to the peace," for two reasons. The first is that an armed conflict (or a series of armed conflicts) has been taking place in the territory of the former Yugoslavia since long before the decision of the Security Council to establish this International Tribunal. If it is considered an international armed conflict, there is no doubt that it falls within the literal sense of the words "breach of the peace" (between the parties or, at the very least, as a "threat to the peace" of others). But even if it were considered merely as an "internal armed conflict," it would still constitute a "threat to the peace" according to the settled practice of the Security Council and the common understanding of the United Nations membership in general. . . .

The second reason, which is more particular to the case at hand, is that Appellant . . . . no longer contests the Security Council's power to determine whether the situation in the former Yugoslavia constituted a threat to the peace, nor the determination itself. . . . But he continues to contest the legality and appropriateness of the measures chosen by the Security Council to that end. . . .

(3) *The Establishment of the International Tribunal as a Measure under Chapter VII*

34. Prima facie, the International Tribunal matches perfectly the description in Article 41 of "measures not involving the use of force." . . .

35. . . . Article 41 reads as follows: "The Security Council may decide what measures not involving the use of armed force are to be employed to give effect to its decisions, and it may call upon the Members of the United Nations to apply such measures. These may include complete or partial interruption of economic relations and of rail, sea, air, postal, telegraphic, radio, and other

means of communication, and the severance of diplomatic relations."

It is evident that the measures set out in Article 41 are merely illustrative examples which obviously do not exclude other measures. All the Article requires is that they do not involve "the use of force." . . . [N]othing in the Article suggests the limitation of the measures to those implemented by States. . . [E]ven a simple literal analysis of the Article shows that the first phrase of the first sentence carries a very general prescription which can accommodate both institutional and Member State action. . . .

36. . . . In sum, the establishment of the International Tribunal falls squarely within the powers of the Security Council under Article 41.

37. The argument that the Security Council, not being endowed with judicial powers, cannot establish a subsidiary organ possessed of such powers is untenable: it results from a fundamental misunderstanding of the constitutional set-up of the Charter.

Plainly, the Security Council is not a judicial organ and is not provided with judicial powers . . . The principal function of the Security Council is the maintenance of international peace and security, in the discharge of which the Security Council exercises both decision-making and executive powers.

38. The establishment of the International Tribunal by the Security Council does not signify, however, that the Security Council has delegated to it some of its own functions or the exercise of some of its own powers. Nor does it mean, in reverse, that the Security Council was usurping for itself part of a judicial function which does not belong to it but to other organs of the United Nations according to the Charter. The Security Council has resorted to the establishment of a judicial organ in the form of an international criminal tribunal as an instrument for the exercise of its own principal function of maintenance of peace and security, i.e., as a measure contributing to the restoration and maintenance of peace in the former Yugoslavia. . . .

39. . . . Article 39 leaves the choice of means and their evaluation to the Security Council, which enjoys wide discretionary powers in this regard; and it could not have been otherwise, as such a choice involves political evaluation of highly complex and dynamic situations. It would be a total misconception of what are the criteria of legality and validity in law to test the legality of such measures *ex post facto* by their success or failure to achieve their ends (in the present case, the restoration of peace in the former Yugoslavia, in quest of which the establishment of the International Tribunal is but one of many measures adopted by the Security Council).

40. For the aforementioned reasons, the Appeals Chamber considers that the International Tribunal has been lawfully established as a measure under Chapter VII of the Charter.

(4) *Was The Establishment Of The International Tribunal Contrary To The General Principle Whereby Courts Must Be "Established By Law"?*

41. Appellant challenges the establishment of the International Tribunal by contending that it has not been established by law. The entitlement of an individual to have a criminal charge against him determined by a tribunal which has been established by law is provided in Article 14, paragraph 1, of the International Covenant on Civil and Political Rights. It provides: "In the determination of any criminal charge against him, or of his rights and obligations in a suit at law, everyone shall be entitled to a fair and public hearing by a competent, independent and impartial tribunal established by law." Similar provisions can be found in Article 6 (1) of the European Convention on Human Rights. . . . and in Article 8 (1) of the American Convention on Human Rights. . . . In support of this assertion, Appellant emphasises the fundamental nature of the "fair trial" or "due process" guarantees afforded in the International Covenant on Civil and Political Rights, the European Convention on Human Rights and the American Convention on Human Rights. Appellant asserts that they are minimum requirements in international law for the administration of criminal justice.

42. . . . . Appellant has not satisfied this Chamber that the requirements laid down in these three conventions must apply not only in the context of national legal systems but also with respect to proceedings conducted before an international court. . . . [T]he principle that a tribunal must be established by law. . . is a general principle of law imposing an international obligation which only applies to the administration of criminal justice in a municipal setting. It follows from this principle that it is incumbent on all States to organize their system of criminal justice in such a way as to ensure that all individuals are guaranteed the right to have a criminal charge determined by a tribunal established by law. This does not entail however that, by contrast, an international criminal court could be set up at the mere whim of a group of governments. Such a court ought to be rooted in the rule of law and offer all guarantees embodied in the relevant international instruments. Then the court may be said to be "established by law."

43. Indeed, there are three possible interpretations of the term "established by law." First, as Appellant argues, "established by law" could mean established by a legislature. Appellant claims that the International Tribunal is the product of a "mere executive order" and not of a "decision making process under democratic control, necessary to create a judicial organization in a democratic society." Therefore Appellant maintains that the International Tribunal not been "established by law."

The case law applying the words "established by law" in the European Convention on Human Rights has favoured this interpretation of the expression. This case law bears out the view that the relevant provision is intended to ensure that tribunals in a democratic society must not depend on the discretion of the executive; rather they should be regulated by law emanating from

Parliament. . . . Or, put another way, the guarantee is intended to ensure that the administration of justice is not a matter of executive discretion, but is regulated by laws made by the legislature.

It is clear that the legislative, executive and judicial division of powers which is largely followed in most municipal systems does not apply to the international setting nor, more specifically, to the setting of an international organization such as the United Nations. Among the principal organs of the United Nations the divisions between judicial, executive and legislative functions are not clear cut. Regarding the judicial function, the International Court of Justice is clearly the "principal judicial organ." There is, however, no legislature, in the technical sense of the term, in the United Nations system and, more generally, no Parliament in the world community. That is to say, there exists no corporate organ formally empowered to enact laws directly binding on international legal subjects.

It is clearly impossible to classify the organs of the United Nations into the above-discussed divisions which exist in the national law of States. . . . Consequently the separation of powers element of the requirement that a tribunal be "established by law" finds no application in an international law setting. The aforementioned principle can only impose an obligation on States concerning the functioning of their own national systems.

44. A second possible interpretation is that the words "established by law" refer to establishment of international courts by a body which, though not a Parliament, has a limited power to take binding decisions. In our view, one such body is the Security Council when, acting under Chapter VII of the United Nations Charter, it makes decisions binding by virtue of Article 25 of the Charter.

According to Appellant, however, there must be something more for a tribunal to be "established by law." Appellant takes the position that, given the differences between the United Nations system and national division of powers, discussed above, the conclusion must be that the United Nations system is not capable of creating the International Tribunal unless there is an amendment to the United Nations Charter. We disagree. It does not follow from the fact that the United Nations has no legislature that the Security Council is not empowered to set up this International Tribunal if it is acting pursuant to an authority found within its constitution, the United Nations Charter. As set out above, we are of the view that the Security Council was endowed with the power to create this International Tribunal as a measure under Chapter VII in the light of its determination that there exists a threat to the peace.

In addition, the establishment of the International Tribunal has been repeatedly approved and endorsed by the "representative" organ of the United Nations, the General Assembly: this body not only participated in its setting up, by electing the Judges and approving the budget, but also expressed its satisfaction with, and encouragement of the activities of the International

Tribunal in various resolutions.

45. The third possible interpretation of the requirement that the International Tribunal be "established by law" is that its establishment must be in accordance with the rule of law. This appears to be the most sensible and most likely meaning of the term in the context of international law. For a tribunal such as this one to be established according to the rule of law, it must be established in accordance with the proper international standards; it must provide all the guarantees of fairness, justice and even-handedness, in full conformity with internationally recognized human rights instruments. . . . The important consideration in determining whether a tribunal has been "established by law" is not whether it was pre-established or established for a specific purpose or situation; what is important is that it be set up by a competent organ in keeping with the relevant legal procedures, and that it observes the requirements of procedural fairness.

This concern about *ad hoc* tribunals that function in such a way as not to afford the individual before them basic fair trial guarantees also underlies United Nations Human Rights Committee's interpretation of the phrase "established by law" contained in Article 14, paragraph 1, of the International Covenant on Civil and Political Rights. While the Human Rights Committee has not determined that "extraordinary" tribunals or "special" courts are incompatible with the requirement that tribunals be established by law, it has taken the position that the provision is intended to ensure that any court, be it "extraordinary" or not, should genuinely afford the accused the full guarantees of fair trial set out in Article 14 of the International Covenant on Civil and Political Rights. . . A similar approach has been taken by the Inter-American Commission. . . .

46. An examination of the Statute of the International Tribunal, and of the Rules of Procedure and Evidence adopted pursuant to that Statute leads to the conclusion that it has been established in accordance with the rule of law. The fair trial guarantees in Article 14 of the International Covenant on Civil and Political Rights have been adopted almost verbatim in Article 21 of the Statute. Other fair trial guarantees appear in the Statute and the Rules of Procedure and Evidence. . . .

47. In conclusion, the Appeals Chamber finds that the International Tribunal has been established in accordance with the appropriate procedures under the United Nations Charter and provides all the necessary safeguards of a fair trial. It is thus "established by law."

48. The first ground of appeal: unlawful establishment of the International Tribunal, is accordingly dismissed.

III. UNJUSTIFIED PRIMACY OF THE INTERNATIONAL TRIBUNAL OVER COMPETENT DOMESTIC COURTS

49. The second ground of appeal attacks the primacy of the International Tribunal over national courts [as an infringement on the sovereignty of the states directly affected]. . .

50. This primacy is established by Article 9 of the Statute of the International Tribunal, which provides:

Concurrent jurisdiction

1. The International Tribunal and national courts shall have concurrent jurisdiction to prosecute persons for serious violations of international humanitarian law committed in the territory of the former Yugoslavia since 1 January 1991.

2. *The International Tribunal shall have primacy over national courts.* At any stage of the procedure, the International Tribunal may formally request national courts to defer to the competence of the International Tribunal in accordance with the present Statute and the Rules of Procedure and Evidence of the International Tribunal. (Emphasis added.)

Appellant's submission is material to the issue, inasmuch as Appellant is expected to stand trial before this International Tribunal as a consequence of a request for deferral which the International Tribunal submitted to the Government of the Federal Republic of Germany on 8 November 1994 and which this Government, as it was bound to do, agreed to honour by surrendering Appellant to the International Tribunal. . . .

Appellant's Brief in support of the motion before the Trial Chamber went into further details which he set down under three headings:

(a) domestic jurisdiction;

(b) sovereignty of States;

(c) *jus de non evocando.* . . .

A. Domestic Jurisdiction

54. Appellant argued in first instance that: "From the moment Bosnia-Herzegovina was recognised as an independent state, it had the competence to establish jurisdiction to try crimes that have been committed on its territory." Appellant added that: "As a matter of fact the state of Bosnia-Herzegovina does exercise its jurisdiction, not only in matters of

ordinary criminal law, but also in matters of alleged violations of crimes against humanity, as for example is the case with the prosecution of Mr Karadzic et al."

This first point is not contested and the Prosecutor has conceded as much. But it does not, by itself, settle the question of the primacy of the International Tribunal. . . .

B. Sovereignty of States

55. . . . In Appellant's view, no State can assume jurisdiction to prosecute crimes committed on the territory of another State, barring a universal interest "justified by a treaty or customary international law or an *opinio juris* on the issue." Based on this proposition, Appellant argues that the same requirements should underpin the establishment of an international tribunal destined to invade an area essentially within the domestic jurisdiction of States. In the present instance, the principle of State sovereignty would have been violated. The Trial Chamber has rejected this plea, holding among other reasons: "In any event, the accused not being a State lacks the *locus standi* to raise the issue of primacy, which involves a plea that the sovereignty of a State has been violated, a plea only a sovereign State may raise or waive and a right clearly the accused cannot take over from the State."

The Trial Chamber relied on the judgement of the District Court of Jerusalem in *Israel v. Eichmann*: "The right to plead violation of the sovereignty of a State is the exclusive right of that State. Only a sovereign State may raise the plea or waive it, and the accused has no right to take over the rights of that State." Consistently with a long line of cases, a similar principle was upheld more recently in the United States of America in the matter of *United States v. Noriega* [chap. 14, *supra*]: "As a general principle of international law, individuals have no standing to challenge violations of international treaties in the absence of a protest by the sovereign involved."

Authoritative as they may be, those pronouncements do not carry, in the field of international law, the weight which they may bring to bear upon national judiciaries. Dating back to a period when sovereignty stood as a sacrosanct and unassailable attribute of statehood, recently this concept has suffered progressive erosion at the hands of the more liberal forces at work in the democratic societies, particularly in the field of human rights. Whatever the situation in domestic litigation, the traditional doctrine upheld and acted upon by the Trial Chamber is not reconcilable, in this International Tribunal, with the view that an accused, being entitled to a full defence, cannot be deprived of a plea so intimately connected with, and grounded in, international law as a defence based on violation of State sovereignty. To bar an accused from raising such a plea is tantamount to deciding that, in this day and age, an international court could not, in a criminal matter where the liberty of an accused is at stake, examine a plea raising the issue of violation of State sovereignty. Such a starling conclusion would imply a contradiction in terms which this Chamber feels it is its duty to refute and lay to rest.

56. That Appellant be recognised the right to plead State sovereignty does not mean, of course, that his plea must be favourably received. . . .

Appellant can call in aid Article 2, paragraph 7, of the United Nations Charter: "Nothing contained in the present Charter shall authorize the United Nations to intervene in matters which are essentially within the domestic jurisdiction of any State. . . " However, one should not forget the commanding restriction at the end of the same paragraph: "but this principle shall not prejudice the application of enforcement measures under Chapter VII." Those are precisely the provisions under which the International Tribunal has been established.

Even without these provisions, matters can be taken out of the jurisdiction of a State. In the present case, the Republic of Bosnia and Herzegovina not only has not contested the jurisdiction of the International Tribunal but has actually approved, and collaborated with, the International Tribunal. . . . As to the Federal Republic of Germany, its cooperation with the International Tribunal is public and has been previously noted. The Trial Chamber was therefore fully justified to write, on this particular issue: "It is pertinent to note that the challenge to the primacy of the International Tribunal has been made against the express intent of the two States most closely affected by the indictment against the accused – Bosnia and Herzegovina and the Federal Republic of Germany. The former, on the territory of which the crimes were allegedly committed, and the latter where the accused resided at the time of his arrest, have unconditionally accepted the jurisdiction of the International Tribunal and the accused cannot claim the rights that have been specifically waived by the States concerned. . ."

57. This is all the more so in view of the nature of the offences alleged against Appellant, offences which, if proven, do not affect the interests of one State alone but shock the conscience of mankind. As early as 1950, in the case of *General Wagener*, the Supreme Military Tribunal of Italy held: "These norms [concerning crimes against laws and customs of war], due to their highly ethical and moral content, have a universal character, not a territorial one" . . . Twelve years later the Supreme Court of Israel in the *Eichmann* case could draw a similar picture: "These crimes constitute acts which damage vital international interests; they impair the foundations and security of the international community; they violate the universal moral values and humanitarian principles that lie hidden in the criminal law systems adopted by civilised nations. . . . They involve the perpetration of an international crime which all the nations of the world are interested in preventing."

58. The public revulsion against similar offences in the 1990s brought about a reaction on the part of the community of nations: hence, among other remedies, the establishment of an international judicial body by an organ of an organization representing the community of nations: the Security Council. This

organ is empowered and mandated, by definition, to deal with transboundary matters or matters which, though domestic in nature, may affect "international peace and security." It would be a travesty of law and a betrayal of the universal need for justice, should the concept of State sovereignty be allowed to be raised successfully against human rights. Borders should not be considered as a shield against the reach of the law and as a protection for those who trample underfoot the most elementary rights of humanity. . . .

Indeed, when an international tribunal such as the present one is created, it must be endowed with primacy over national courts. Otherwise, human nature being what it is, there would be a perennial danger of international crimes being characterised as "ordinary crimes" (Statute of the International Tribunal, art. 10, para. 2(a)), or proceedings being "designed to shield the accused," or cases not being diligently prosecuted (Statute of the International Tribunal, art. 10, para. 2(b)). If not effectively countered by the principle of primacy, any one of those stratagems might be used to defeat the very purpose of the creation of an international criminal jurisdiction, to the benefit of the very people whom it has been designed to prosecute. . . .

60. The plea of State sovereignty must therefore be dismissed.

C. *Jus De Non Evocando*

61. Appellant argues that he has a right to be tried by his national courts under his national laws. No one has questioned that right of Appellant. The problem is elsewhere: is that right exclusive? Does it prevent Appellant from being tried – and having an equally fair trial – before an international tribunal? Appellant contends that such an exclusive right has received universal acceptance: yet one cannot find it expressed either in the Universal Declaration of Human Rights or in the International Covenant on Civil and Political Rights, unless one is prepared to stretch to breaking point the interpretation of their provisions. . . .

62. As a matter of fact – and of law – the principle advocated by Appellant aims at one very specific goal: to avoid the creation of special or extraordinary courts designed to try political offences in times of social unrest without guarantees of a fair trial. This principle is not breached by the transfer of jurisdiction to an international tribunal created by the Security Council acting on behalf of the community of nations. No rights of accused are thereby infringed or threatened; quite to the contrary, they are all specifically spelt out and protected under the Statute of the International Tribunal. No accused can complain. True, he will be removed from his "natural" national forum; but he will be brought before a tribunal at least equally fair, more distanced from the facts of the case and taking a broader view of the matter.

Furthermore, one cannot but rejoice at the thought that, universal jurisdiction being nowadays acknowledged in the case of international crimes, a person suspected of such offences may finally be brought before an international judicial body for a dispassionate consideration of his indictment by impartial, independent and disinterested judges coming, as it happens here, from all continents of the world. . . .

64. For these reasons the Appeals Chamber concludes that Appellant's second ground of appeal, contesting the primacy of the International Tribunal, is ill-founded and must be dismissed.

IV. LACK OF SUBJECT-MATTER JURISDICTION

65. Appellant's third ground of appeal is the claim that the International Tribunal lacks subject-matter jurisdiction over the crimes alleged. The basis for this allegation is Appellant's claim that the subject-matter jurisdiction under Articles 2, 3 and 5 of the Statute of the International Tribunal is limited to crimes committed in the context of an international armed conflict. Before the Trial Chamber, Appellant claimed that the alleged crimes, even if proven, were committed in the context of an internal armed conflict. On appeal an additional alternative claim is asserted to the effect that there was no armed conflict at all in the region where the crimes were allegedly committed. . . .

A. Preliminary Issue: The Existence Of An Armed Conflict

66. . . . Appellant claims that the conflict in the Prijedor region (where the alleged crimes are said to have taken place) was limited to a political assumption of power by the Bosnian Serbs and did not involve armed combat (though movements of tanks are admitted). This argument presents a preliminary issue to which we turn first.

67. International humanitarian law governs the conduct of both internal and international armed conflicts. Appellant correctly points out that for there to be a violation of this body of law, there must be an armed conflict. The definition of "armed conflict" varies depending on whether the hostilities are international or internal but, contrary to Appellant's contention, the temporal and geographical scope of both internal and international armed conflicts extends beyond the exact time and place of hostilities. . . .

70. . . . [A]n armed conflict exists whenever there is a resort to armed force between States or protracted armed violence between governmental authorities and organized armed groups or between such groups within a State. International humanitarian law applies from the initiation of such armed conflicts and extends beyond the cessation of hostilities until a general conclusion of peace is reached; or, in the case of internal conflicts, a peaceful settlement is achieved. Until that moment, international humanitarian law continues to apply in the whole territory of the warring States or, in the case of internal conflicts, the whole territory under the control of a party, whether or

not actual combat takes place there.

Applying the foregoing concept of armed conflicts to this case, we hold that the alleged crimes were committed in the context of an armed conflict. Fighting among the various entities within the former Yugoslavia began in 1991, continued through the summer of 1992 when the alleged crimes are said to have been committed, and persists to this day. Notwithstanding various temporary cease-fire agreements, no general conclusion of peace has brought military operations in the region to a close. These hostilities exceed the intensity requirements applicable to both international and internal armed conflicts. There has been protracted, large-scale violence between the armed forces of different States and between governmental forces and organized insurgent groups. Even if substantial clashes were not occurring in the Prijedor region at the time and place the crimes allegedly were committed – a factual issue on which the Appeals Chamber does not pronounce – international humanitarian law applies. It is sufficient that the alleged crimes were closely related to the hostilities occurring in other parts of the territories controlled by the parties to the conflict. There is no doubt that the allegations at issue here bear the required relationship. The indictment states that in 1992 Bosnian Serbs took control of the Opstina of Prijedor and established a prison camp in Omarska. It further alleges that crimes were committed against civilians inside and outside the Omarska prison camp as part of the Bosnian Serb take-over and consolidation of power in the Prijedor region, which was, in turn, part of the larger Bosnian Serb military campaign to obtain control over Bosnian territory. . . . In light of the foregoing, we conclude that, for the purposes of applying international humanitarian law, the crimes alleged were committed in the context of an armed conflict.

B. Does The Statute Refer Only To International Armed Conflicts?

(1) *Literal Interpretation of the Statute*

71. On the face of it, some provisions of the Statute are unclear as to whether they apply to offences occurring in international armed conflicts only, or to those perpetrated in internal armed conflicts as well. . . . In order better to ascertain the meaning and scope of these provisions, the Appeals Chamber will therefore consider the object and purpose behind the enactment of the Statute.

(2) *Teleological Interpretation of the Statute*

72. In adopting resolution 827, the Security Council established the International Tribunal with the stated purpose of bringing to justice persons responsible for serious violations of international humanitarian law in the former Yugoslavia, thereby deterring future violations and contributing to the re-establishment of peace and security in the region. The context in which the Security Council acted indicates that it intended to achieve this purpose without reference to whether the conflicts in the former Yugoslavia were internal or

international.

As the members of the Security Council well knew, in 1993, when the Statute was drafted, the conflicts in the former Yugoslavia could have been characterized as both internal and international, or alternatively, as an internal conflict alongside an international one, or as an internal conflict that had become internationalized because of external support, or as an international conflict that had subsequently been replaced by one or more internal conflicts, or some combination thereof. The conflict in the former Yugoslavia had been rendered international by the involvement of the Croatian Army in Bosnia-Herzegovina and by the involvement of the Yugoslav National Army ("JNA") in hostilities in Croatia, as well as in Bosnia-Herzegovina at least until its formal withdrawal on 19 May 1992. To the extent that the conflicts had been limited to clashes between Bosnian Government forces and Bosnian Serb rebel forces in Bosnia-Herzegovina, as well as between the Croatian Government and Croatian Serb rebel forces in Krajina (Croatia), they had been internal (unless direct involvement of the Federal Republic of Yugoslavia (Serbia-Montenegro) could be proven). It is notable that the parties to this case also agree that the conflicts in the former Yugoslavia since 1991 have had both internal and international aspects. . . .

74. The Security Council's many statements leading up to the establishment of the International Tribunal reflect an awareness of the mixed character of the conflicts. On the one hand, prior to creating the International Tribunal, the Security Council adopted several resolutions condemning the presence of JNA forces in Bosnia-Herzegovina and Croatia as a violation of the sovereignty of these latter States. On the other hand, in none of these many resolutions did the Security Council explicitly state that the conflicts were international.

In each of its successive resolutions, the Security Council focused on the practices with which it was concerned, without reference to the nature of the conflict. . . . The Security Council was clearly preoccupied with bringing to justice those responsible for these specifically condemned acts, regardless of context. . . .

75. The intent of the Security Council to promote a peaceful solution of the conflict without pronouncing upon the question of its international or internal nature is reflected by the Report of the Secretary-General of 3 May 1993 and by statements of Security Council members regarding their interpretation of the Statute. The Report of the Secretary-General explicitly states that the clause of the Statute concerning the temporal jurisdiction of the International Tribunal was "clearly intended to convey the notion that no judgement as to the international or internal character of the conflict was being exercised." . . .

77. . . . [W]e conclude that the conflicts in the former Yugoslavia have both internal and international aspects, that the members of the Security Council clearly had both aspects of the conflicts in mind when they adopted the Statute of the International Tribunal, and that they intended to empower the

International Tribunal to adjudicate violations of humanitarian law that occurred in either context. To the extent possible under existing international law, the Statute should therefore be construed to give effect to that purpose.

78. With the exception of Article 5 dealing with crimes against humanity, none of the statutory provisions makes explicit reference to the type of conflict as an element of the crime; and, as will be shown below, the reference in Article 5 is made to distinguish the nexus required by the Statute from the nexus required by Article 6 of the London Agreement of 8 August 1945 establishing the International Military Tribunal at Nuremberg. Since customary international law no longer requires any nexus between crimes against humanity and armed conflict (see below, paras. 140 and 141), Article 5 was intended to reintroduce this nexus for the purposes of this Tribunal.   .   . [A]lthough Article 2 does not explicitly refer to the nature of the conflicts, its reference to the grave breaches provisions suggest that it is limited to international armed conflicts. It would however defeat the Security Council's purpose to read a similar international armed conflict requirement into the remaining jurisdictional provisions of the Statute. Contrary to the drafters' apparent indifference to the nature of the underlying conflicts, such an interpretation would authorize the International Tribunal to prosecute and punish certain conduct in an international armed conflict, while turning a blind eye to the very same conduct in an internal armed conflict. . . . .

In light of this understanding of the Security Council's purpose in creating the International Tribunal, we turn below to discussion of Appellant's specific arguments regarding the scope of the jurisdiction of the International Tribunal under Articles 2, 3 and 5 of the Statute.

(3) *Logical And Systematic Interpretation of the Statute*

Article 2

79. Article 2 of the Statute of the International Tribunal provides:

The International Tribunal shall have the power to prosecute persons committing or ordering to be committed grave breaches of the Geneva Conventions of 12 August 1949, namely the following acts against persons or property protected under the provisions of the relevant Geneva Convention:

(a) wilful killing;

(b) torture or inhuman treatment, including biological experiments;

(c) wilfully causing great suffering or serious injury to body or health;

(d) extensive destruction and appropriation of property, not justified by military necessity and carried out unlawfully and wantonly;

(e) compelling a prisoner of war or a civilian to serve in the forces of a hostile power;

(f) wilfully depriving a prisoner of war or a civilian of the rights of fair and regular trial;

(g) unlawful deportation or transfer or unlawful confinement of a civilian;

(h) taking civilians as hostages.

By its explicit terms, and as confirmed in the Report of the Secretary-General, this Article of the Statute is based on the Geneva Conventions of 1949 and, more specifically, the provisions of those Conventions relating to "grave breaches" of the Conventions. Each of the four Geneva Conventions of 1949 contains a "grave breaches" provision, specifying particular breaches of the Convention for which the High Contracting Parties have a duty to prosecute those responsible. In other words, for these specific acts, the Conventions create universal mandatory criminal jurisdiction among contracting States. Although the language of the Conventions might appear to be ambiguous and the question is open to some debate, it is widely contended that the grave breaches provisions establish universal mandatory jurisdiction only with respect to those breaches of the Conventions committed in international armed conflicts. . . .

80. . . . The grave breaches system of the Geneva Conventions establishes a twofold system: there is on the one hand an enumeration of offences that are regarded as so serious as to constitute "grave breaches"; closely bound up with this enumeration a mandatory enforcement mechanism is set up, based on the concept of a duty and a right of all Contracting States to search for and try or extradite persons allegedly responsible for "grave breaches." The international armed conflict element generally attributed to the grave breaches provisions of the Geneva Conventions is merely a function of the system of universal mandatory jurisdiction that those provisions create. The international armed conflict requirement was a necessary limitation on the grave breaches system in light of the intrusion on State sovereignty that such mandatory universal jurisdiction represents. States parties to the 1949 Geneva Conventions did not want to give other States jurisdiction over serious violations of international humanitarian law committed in their internal armed conflicts – at least not the mandatory universal jurisdiction involved in the grave breaches system. . . .

82. The above interpretation is borne out by what could be considered as part of the preparatory works of the Statute of the International Tribunal, namely the Report of the Secretary-General. There, in introducing and explaining the meaning and purport of Article 2 and having regard to the "grave breaches"

system of the Geneva Conventions, reference is made to "international armed conflicts."

83. We find that our interpretation of Article 2 is the only one warranted by the text of the Statute and the relevant provisions of the Geneva Conventions, as well as by a logical construction of their interplay as dictated by Article 2. However, we are aware that this conclusion may appear not to be consonant with recent trends of both State practice and the whole doctrine of human rights – which . . . tend to blur in many respects the traditional dichotomy between international wars and civil strife. . . .

84. [Nevertheless] the Appeals Chamber must conclude that, in the present state of development of the law, Article 2 of the Statute only applies to offences committed within the context of international armed conflicts. . . .

Article 3

86. Article 3 of the Statute declares the International Tribunal competent to adjudicate violations of the laws or customs of war. The provision states:

> The International Tribunal shall have the power to prosecute persons violating the laws or customs of war. Such violations shall include, but not be limited to:
>
> (a) employment of poisonous weapons or other weapons calculated to cause unnecessary suffering;
>
> (b) wanton destruction of cities, towns or villages, or devastation not justified by military necessity;
>
> (c) attack, or bombardment, by whatever means, of undefended towns, villages, dwellings, or buildings;
>
> (d) seizure of, destruction or wilful damage done to institutions dedicated to religion, charity and education, the arts and sciences, historic monuments and works of art and science;
>
> (e) plunder of public or private property.

As explained by the Secretary-General in his Report on the Statute, this provision is based on the 1907 Hague Convention (IV) Respecting the Laws and Customs of War on Land, the Regulations annexed to that Convention, and the Nuremberg Tribunal's interpretation of those Regulations. Appellant argues that the Hague Regulations were adopted to regulate interstate armed conflict, while the conflict in the former Yugoslavia is *in casu* an internal armed conflict; therefore, to the extent that the jurisdiction of the International Tribunal under Article 3 is based on the Hague Regulations, it lacks jurisdiction under Article

3 to adjudicate alleged violations in the former Yugoslavia. Appellant's argument does not bear close scrutiny, for it is based on an unnecessarily narrow reading of the Statute.

(i) The Interpretation of Article 3

87. A literal interpretation of Article 3 shows that: (i) it refers to a broad category of offences, namely all "violations of the laws or customs of war"; and (ii) the enumeration of some of these violations provided in Article 3 are merely illustrative, not exhaustive.

To identify the content of the class of offences falling under Article 3, attention should be drawn to an important fact. The expression "violations of the laws or customs of war" is a traditional term of art used in the past, when the concepts of "war" and "laws of warfare" still prevailed, before they were largely replaced by two broader notions: (i) that of "armed conflict," essentially introduced by the 1949 Geneva Conventions; and (ii) the correlative notion of "international law of armed conflict," or the more recent and comprehensive notion of "international humanitarian law," which has emerged as a result of the influence of human rights doctrines on the law of armed conflict. As stated above, it is clear from the Report of the Secretary-General that the old-fashioned expression referred to above was used in Article 3 of the Statute primarily to make reference to the 1907 Hague Convention (IV) Respecting the Laws and Customs of War on Land and the Regulations annexed thereto (Report of the Secretary-General, at para. 41). However, as the Report indicates, the Hague Convention, considered *qua* customary law, constitutes an important area of humanitarian international law. In other words, the Secretary-General himself concedes that the traditional laws of warfare are now more correctly termed "international humanitarian law" and that the Hague Regulations constitute an important segment of such law. Furthermore, the Secretary-General has also correctly admitted that the Hague Regulations have a broader scope than the Geneva Conventions, in that they cover not only the protection of victims of armed violence (civilians) or of those who no longer take part in hostilities (prisoners of war), but also the conduct of hostilities; in the words of the Report: "The Hague Regulations cover aspects of international humanitarian law which are also covered by the 1949 Geneva Conventions." These comments suggest that Article 3 is intended to cover both Geneva and Hague law. On the other hand, the Secretary-General's subsequent comments indicate that the violations explicitly listed in Article 3 relate to Hague law not contained in the Geneva Conventions. As pointed out above, this list is, however, merely illustrative: indeed, Article 3, before enumerating the violations provides that they "shall include but not be limited to" the list of offences. Considering this list in the general context of the Secretary-General's discussion of the Hague Regulations and international humanitarian law, we conclude that this list may be construed to include other infringements of international humanitarian law. The only limitation is that such infringements must not be already covered by Article 2 (lest this latter provision should become superfluous). Article 3 may be taken to cover all violations of international humanitarian law other than the "grave breaches" of the four Geneva Conventions falling under Article 2 (or, for that matter, the violations covered by Articles 4 and 5, to the extent that Articles 3, 4 and 5 overlap).

88. That Article 3 does not confine itself to covering violations of Hague law, but is intended also to refer to all violations of international humanitarian law (subject to the limitations just stated), is borne out by the debates in the Security Council that followed the adoption of the resolution establishing the International Tribunal. . . .

89. In light of the above remarks, it can be held that Article 3 is a general clause covering all violations of humanitarian law not falling under Article 2 or covered by Articles 4 or 5, more specifically: (i) violations of the Hague law on international conflicts; (ii) infringements of provisions of the Geneva Conventions other than those classified as "grave breaches" by those Conventions; (iii) violations of common Article 3 and other customary rules on internal conflicts; (iv) violations of agreements binding upon the parties to the conflict, considered *qua* treaty law, i.e., agreements which have not turned into customary international law.

90. The Appeals Chamber would like to add that, in interpreting the meaning and purport of the expressions "violations of the laws or customs of war" or "violations of international humanitarian law," one must take account of the context of the Statute as a whole. A systematic construction of the Statute emphasises the fact that various provisions, in spelling out the purpose and tasks of the International Tribunal or in defining its functions, refer to "serious violations of international humanitarian law." It is therefore appropriate to take the expression "violations of the laws or customs of war" to cover serious violations of international humanitarian law.

91. Article 3 thus confers on the International Tribunal jurisdiction over any serious offence against international humanitarian law not covered by Article 2, 4 or 5. Article 3 is a fundamental provision laying down that any "serious violation of international humanitarian law" must be prosecuted by the International Tribunal. In other words, Article 3 functions as a residual clause designed to ensure that no serious violation of international humanitarian law is taken away from the jurisdiction of the International Tribunal. Article 3 aims to make such jurisdiction watertight and inescapable. . . .

(ii) The Conditions that must be Fulfilled for a Violation of International Humanitarian Law to be Subject to Article 3

94. The Appeals Chamber deems it fitting to specify the conditions to be fulfilled for Article 3 to become applicable. The following requirements must be met for an offence to be subject to prosecution before the International Tribunal under Article 3:

(i) the violation must constitute an infringement of a rule of international humanitarian law;

(ii) the rule must be customary in nature or, if it belongs to treaty law, the required conditions must be met;

(iii) the violation must be "serious," that is to say, it must constitute a breach of a rule protecting important values, and the breach must involve grave consequences for the victim. Thus, for instance, the fact of a combatant simply appropriating a loaf of bread in an occupied village would not amount to a "serious violation of international humanitarian law" although it may be regarded as falling foul of the basic principle laid down in Article 46, paragraph 1, of the Hague Regulations (and the corresponding rule of customary international law) whereby "private property must be respected" by any army occupying an enemy territory;

(iv) the violation of the rule must entail, under customary or conventional law, the individual criminal responsibility of the person breaching the rule.

It follows that it does not matter whether the "serious violation" has occurred within the context of an international or an internal armed conflict, as long as the requirements set out above are met.

[The Judgment goes on to consider at length two of these requirements, namely (i) the existence of customary international rules governing internal strife, and (ii) the question of whether the violation of such rules may entail individual criminal responsibility, "because of the paucity of authoritative judicial pronouncements and legal literature on this matter." It concludes, *inter alia*, that violations of common Article 3 of the 1949 Geneva Conventions can give rise to individual criminal liability under customary international law.]

(v) Conclusion

137. In the light of the intent of the Security Council and the logical and systematic interpretation of Article 3 as well as customary international law, the Appeals Chamber concludes that, under Article 3, the International Tribunal has jurisdiction over the acts alleged in the indictment, regardless of whether they occurred within an internal or an international armed conflict. Thus, to the extent that Appellant's challenge to jurisdiction under Article 3 is based on the nature of the underlying conflict, the motion must be denied.

Article 5

138. Article 5 of the Statute confers jurisdiction over crimes against

humanity. More specifically, the Article provides:

> The International Tribunal shall have the power to prosecute persons responsible for the following crimes when committed in armed conflict, whether international or internal in character, and directed against any civilian population: (a) murder; (b) extermination; (c) enslavement; (d) deportation; (e) imprisonment; (f) torture; (g) rape; (h) persecutions on political, racial and religious grounds; (i) other inhumane acts.

As noted by the Secretary-General in his Report on the Statute, crimes against humanity were first recognized in the trials of war criminals following World War II. The offence was defined in Article 6, paragraph 2(c) of the Nuremberg Charter and subsequently affirmed in the 1948 General Assembly Resolution affirming the Nuremberg principles.

139. . . . [B]oth of these formulations of the crime limited it to those acts committed "in the execution of or in connection with any crime against peace or any war crime." . . .

140. [But] the nexus between crimes against humanity and either crimes against peace or war crimes, required by the Nuremberg Charter, was peculiar to the jurisdiction of the Nuremberg Tribunal. Although the nexus requirement in the Nuremberg Charter was carried over to the 1948 General Assembly resolution affirming the Nuremberg principles, there is no logical or legal basis for this requirement and it has been abandoned in subsequent State practice with respect to crimes against humanity. Most notably, the nexus requirement was eliminated from the definition of crimes against humanity contained in Article II(1)(c) of Control Council Law No. 10 of 20 December 1945. The obsolescence of the nexus requirement is evidenced by international conventions regarding genocide and apartheid, both of which prohibit particular types of crimes against humanity regardless of any connection to armed conflict. (Convention on the Prevention and Punishment of the Crime of Genocide, 9 December 1948, art. 1, 78 U.N.T.S. 277, (providing that genocide, "whether committed in time of peace or in time of war, is a crime under international law"); International Convention on the Suppression and Punishment of the Crime of Apartheid, 30 November 1973, 1015 U.N.T.S. 243, arts. 1-2.)

141. It is by now a settled rule of customary international law that crimes against humanity do not require a connection to international armed conflict. Indeed. . . customary international law may not require a connection between crimes against humanity and any conflict at all. Thus, by requiring that crimes against humanity be committed in either internal or international armed conflict, the Security Council may have defined the crime in Article 5 more narrowly than necessary under customary international law. . . .

142. We conclude, therefore, that Article 5 may be invoked as a basis of jurisdiction over crimes committed in either internal or international armed conflicts. In addition, for the reasons stated above (paras. 66-70), we conclude

that in this case there was an armed conflict. Therefore, the Appellant's challenge to the jurisdiction of the International Tribunal under Article 5 must be dismissed. . . .

145. For the reasons stated above, the third ground of appeal, based on lack of subject-matter jurisdiction, must be dismissed.

NOTES AND QUESTIONS

(1) Tadic was tried on thirty one counts alleging "grave breaches" of the Geneva Conventions, "violations of the laws and customs of war," and "crimes against humanity." The charges involved murder, torture, and sexual violence committed against Muslims and Croats in northwestern Bosnia during the summer of 1992. On May 7, 1997, Tadic was found guilty on eleven counts involving the brutal mistreatment of prisoners at the Omarska prison camp and of civilians in the nearby village of Kozarac. *See Prosecutor v. Tadic*, Opinion & Judgment, Case No. IT-94-1-T (May 7, 1997). On July 14, 1997, he was sentenced to twenty years' imprisonment, with a recommended minimum term of ten years. The most controversial aspect of the Trial Chamber's judgment was its finding that Tadic could not be found guilty of "grave breaches" of the Geneva Conventions, since his victims were no longer "protected persons" under those Conventions after May 19, 1992, when the Yugoslav National Army supposedly withdrew from Bosnia and the conflict therefore ceased to be "international." On July 15, 1999, on appeal by the prosecution, this aspect of the Trial Chamber's judgment was reversed by the Appeals Chamber and the case remanded for resentencing. *See Prosecutor v. Tadic*, Judgment on Appeal against Opinion & Judgment, Case No. IT-94-1-A (July 15, 1999). On November 11, 1999, Tadic was resentenced to a maximum term of twenty-five years' imprisonment. On January 26, 2000, the Appeals Chamber reduced his sentence to a maximum term of twenty years. *See Prosecutor v. Tadic*, Judgment on Sentencing Appeals, Case No. IT-94-1-A (Jan. 26, 2000).

(2) How persuasive is the reasoning by which the Appeals Chamber concluded that the Yugoslavia Tribunal indeed was "established by law"? Did the Chamber necessarily have to conclude that armed conflict in Bosnia had *both* international and internal aspects? *See* Theodor Meron, *Classification of Armed Conflict in the Former Yugoslavia: Nicaragua's Fallout*, 92 AM. J. INT'L L. 236 (1998), *reprinted in* THEODOR MERON, WAR CRIMES LAW COMES OF AGE 286 (1998). This has left it to the trial chambers to decide in each case whether the specific conflict in which the accused was engaged was international or non-international in character. It also has "diminished the likelihood of the prosecutor's seeking to stigmatize heinous acts against protected persons as grave breaches of international humanitarian law." Sean D. Murphy, *Progress*

and Jurisprudence of the International Criminal Tribunal for the Former Yugoslavia, 93 AM. J. INT'L L. 57, 70 (1999).

(3) Article 20(1) of the Yugoslavia Tribunal's Statute provides that trials shall be conducted "with full respect for the rights of the accused and due regard for the protection of victims and witnesses." Protection of witnesses has taken various forms, some of them quite controversial. These include the use of pseudonyms, distortion of voice and video images, *in camera* testimony, and full witness anonymity, *i.e.*, withholding the witness's identity from the accused. *See* Sean D. Murphy, *supra* Note (2), at 83-85.

(4) Under Article 29 of the Tribunal's Statute, states are required "to cooperate with the International Tribunal in the investigation and prosecution of persons accused of committing serious violations of international humanitarian law." This is a directive backed by the authority of the Security Council. Does it authorize the Tribunal to issue subpoenas to state officials? In *Prosecutor v. Blaskic*, Judgement on the Request of the Republic of Croatia for Review of the Decision of Trial Chamber II, Case No. IT-95-14-AR 108 *bis* (Oct. 29, 1997), where Judge McDonald had issued a *subpoena duces tecum* against Croatia and its defense minister, the Appeals Chamber held that the Tribunal could address orders to states, but was barred from addressing them to specific state officials as such, since it was up to the state itself to determine which officials are responsible for the requested documents.

The failure of states to enforce warrants of arrest issued by the Tribunal appears to be one of the central obstacles to its effective functioning. Is this simply the result of a "failure of will" on the part of the states concerned?

(5) Do the objections raised by the defense in *Tadic* to the jurisdiction of the ICTY have greater (or less) validity when applied to the ICTR? In *Prosecutor v. Kanyabashi*, Case No. ICTR-96-15-T, Decision on Jurisdiction (Jun. 18, 1997), Trial Chamber II of the Rwanda Tribunal confronted a similar set of objections to its jurisdiction. In rejecting those objections, it referred to the "persuasive authority" of the Appeals Chamber decision on jurisdiction in *Tadic*. *See* Virginia Morris, *International Decisions: Prosecutor v. Kanyabashi*, 92 AM. J. INT'L L. 66 (1998).

19.02 The Ad Hoc Tribunal for Rwanda

PROSECUTOR v. AKAYESU

International Criminal Tribunal for Rwanda
Case No. ICTR-96-4-T, Trial Chamber I
Judgement (Sept. 2, 1998)

1. INTRODUCTION

1.1. The International Tribunal

1. This judgment is rendered by Trial Chamber I of the International Tribunal for the prosecution of persons responsible for genocide and other serious violations of international humanitarian law committed in the territory of Rwanda and Rwandan citizens responsible for genocide and other such violations committed in the territory of neighbouring States, between 1 January and 31 December 1994 (the "Tribunal"). The judgment follows the indictment and trial of Jean Paul Akayesu, a Rwandan citizen who was *bourgmestre* of Taba commune, Prefecture of Gitarama, in Rwanda, at the time the crimes alleged in the indictment were perpetrated.

2. The Tribunal was established by the United Nations Security Council by its Resolution 955 of 8 November 1994. After having reviewed various official United Nations reports which indicated that acts of genocide and other systematic, widespread and flagrant violations of international humanitarian law had been committed in Rwanda, the Security Council concluded that the situation in Rwanda in 1994 constituted a threat to international peace and security within the meaning of Chapter VII of the United Nations Charter. Determined to put an end to such crimes and "convinced that . . . the prosecution of persons responsible for such acts and violations . . . would contribute to the process of national reconciliation and to the restoration and maintenance of peace," the Security Council, acting under the said Chapter VII established the Tribunal. . . .

3. The Tribunal is governed by its Statute, annexed to the Security Council Resolution 955, and by its Rules of Procedure and Evidence, adopted by the Judges on 5 July 1995 and amended subsequently. The two Trial Chambers and the Appeals Chamber of the Tribunal are composed of eleven Judges in all,

three sitting in each Trial Chamber and five in the Appeals Chamber.* They are elected by the United Nations General Assembly and represent, in accordance with Article 12(3) (c) of the Statute, the principal legal systems of the world. The Statute stipulates that the members of the Appeals Chamber of the other special international criminal tribunal, namely the Tribunal for the prosecution of persons responsible for serious violations of international humanitarian law committed in the territory of the former Yugoslavia since 1991 ("the Tribunal for the former Yugoslavia"), shall also serve as members of the Appeals Chamber of the Tribunal for Rwanda.

4. Under the Statute, the Tribunal has the power to prosecute persons responsible for serious violations of international human law committed in the territory of Rwanda and Rwandan citizens responsible for genocide and other such violations committed in the territory of neighbouring States, between 1 January and 31 December 1994. According to Articles 2 to 4 of the Statute relating to its *ratione materiae* jurisdiction, the Tribunal has the power to prosecute persons who committed genocide as defined in Article 2 of the Statute, persons responsible for crimes against humanity as defined in Article 3 of the Statute and persons responsible for serious violations of Article 3 Common to the Geneva Conventions of 12 August 1949 on the protection of victims of war, and of Additional Protocol II thereto of 8 June 1977, a crime defined in Article 4 of the Statute. Article 8 of the Statute provides that the Tribunal has concurrent jurisdiction with national courts over which it, however, has primacy.

5. The Statute stipulates that the Prosecutor, who acts as a separate organ of the Tribunal, is responsible for the investigation and prosecution of the perpetrators of such violations. . . . Under the Statute, the Prosecutor of the Tribunal for the former Yugoslavia shall also serve as the Prosecutor of the Tribunal for Rwanda. However, the two Tribunals maintain separate Offices of the Prosecutor and Deputy Prosecutors. The Prosecutor of the Tribunal for Rwanda is assisted by a team of investigators, trial attorneys and senior trial attorneys, who are based in Kigali, Rwanda. These officials travel to Arusha [the seat of the Tribunal in Tanzania] whenever they are expected to plead a case before the Tribunal. . . .

1.4. The Trial

10. On 13 February 1996, the then Prosecutor, Richard Goldstone, submitted an Indictment against Akayesu, which was subsequently amended on 17 June 1997. It contains a total of 15 counts covering genocide, crimes against humanity and violations of Article 3 Common to the 1949 Geneva Conventions

---

* Security Council Resolution 1165 (1998) added three judges to the Tribunal, so as to allow for a third Trial Chamber. The Tribunal's Statute and Rules of Evidence and Procedure, as well as the relevant Security Council resolutions, are available on the Tribunal's website: <http://www.ictr.org>. – Eds.

and Additional Protocol II of 1977 thereto. More specifically, Akayesu was individually charged with genocide, complicity in genocide, direct and public incitement to commit genocide, extermination, murder, torture, cruel treatment, rape, other inhumane acts and outrages upon personal dignity, which he allegedly committed in Taba commune of which he was the *bourgmestre* at the time of the alleged acts.

[The first part of Akayesu's trial took place between January 9 and May 24, 1997. The prosecution sought to show that, as the official in charge of maintaining law and order in the commune, Akayesu was responsible for the deaths of at least 2000 Tutsi killed in Taba between April 7 and the end of June 1994. A number of these killing were shown to have taken place in his presence and on his orders. The trial was then adjourned to allow the Prosecutor's office to investigate Akayesu's responsibility for rape and other crimes of sexual violence against Tutsi women, evidence of which had emerged during the first phase of the trial. The amended indictment of June 17, 1997, added charges of sexual violence. When trial resumed on October 23, 1997, testimony concerning these charges was presented. The court ordered protective measures for witnesses. No information that could identify the witnesses was given. Letters of the alphabet were used as pseudonyms to refer to protected witnesses. Screens isolated them from the public, although not from the accused or his counsel. The trial concluded on March 26, 1998.]

6. THE LAW

6.1 Cumulative Charges

461. In the amended Indictment, the accused is charged cumulatively with more than one crime in relation to the same sets of facts. . . .

462. The question which arises at this stage is whether . . . the Chamber . . . may find the accused guilty of all of the crimes charged in relation to those facts or only one. The reason for posing this question is that it might be argued that the accumulation of criminal charges offends against the principle of double jeopardy or a substantive *non bis in idem* principle in criminal law. Thus an accused who is found guilty of both genocide and crimes against humanity in relation to the same set of facts may argue that he has been twice judged for the same offence, which is generally considered impermissible in criminal law.

463. The Chamber notes that this question has been posed, and answered, by the Trial Chamber of the ICTY in the first case before that Tribunal, *The Prosecutor v. Dusko Tadic*. Trial Chamber II, confronted with this issue, stated:

> In any event, since this is a matter that will only be relevant insofar as it might affect penalty, it can best be dealt with if and when matters of penalty fall for consideration. What can, however, be said with certainty is that penalty cannot be made to depend upon whether offences arising

from the same conduct are alleged cumulatively or in the alternative. What is to be punished by penalty is proven criminal conduct and that will not depend upon technicalities of pleading.

464. In that case, when the matter reached the sentencing stage, the Trial Chamber dealt with the matter of cumulative criminal charges by imposing *concurrent* sentences for each cumulative charge. Thus, for example, in relation to one particular beating, the accused received 7 years' imprisonment for the beating as a crime against humanity, and a 6 year concurrent sentence for the same beating as a violation of the laws or customs of war.

465. The Chamber takes due note of the practice of the ICTY. This practice was also followed in the *Barbie* case, where the French *Cour de Cassation* held that a single event could be qualified both as a crime against humanity and as a war crime.

466. It is clear that the practice of concurrent sentencing ensures that the accused is not twice punished for the same acts. Notwithstanding this absence of prejudice to the accused, it is still necessary to justify the prosecutorial practice of accumulating criminal charges. . . .

468. On the basis of national and international law and jurisprudence, the Chamber concludes that it is acceptable to convict the accused of two offences in relation to the same set of facts in the following circumstances: (1) where the offences have different elements; or (2) where the provisions creating the offences protect different interests; or (3) where it is necessary to record a conviction for both offences in order fully to describe what the accused did. However, the Chamber finds that it is not justifiable to convict an accused of two offences in relation to the same set of facts where (a) one offence is a lesser included offence of the other, for example, murder and grievous bodily harm, robbery and theft, or rape and indecent assault; or (b) where one offence charges accomplice liability and the other offence charges liability as a principal, e.g. genocide and complicity in genocide.

469. Having regard to its Statute, the Chamber believes that the offences under the Statute – genocide, crimes against humanity, and violations of article 3 common to the Geneva Conventions and of Additional Protocol II – have different elements and, moreover, are intended to protect different interests. The crime of genocide exists to protect certain groups from extermination or attempted extermination. The concept of crimes against humanity exists to protect civilian populations from persecution. The idea of violations of article 3 common to the Geneva Conventions and of Additional Protocol II is to protect non-combatants from war crimes in civil war. These crimes have different purposes and are, therefore, never co-extensive. Thus it is legitimate to charge these crimes in relation to the same set of facts. It may, additionally, depending on the case, be necessary to record a conviction for more than one of these offences in order to reflect what crimes an accused committed. If, for example, a general ordered that all prisoners of war belonging to a particular ethnic

group should be killed, with the intent thereby to eliminate the group, this would be both genocide and a violation of common article 3, although not necessarily a crime against humanity. Convictions for genocide and violations of common article 3 would accurately reflect the accused general's course of conduct.

470. Conversely, the Chamber does not consider that any of genocide, crimes against humanity, and violations of article 3 common to the Geneva Conventions and of Additional Protocol II are lesser included forms of each other. The ICTR Statute does not establish a hierarchy of norms, but rather all three offences are presented on an equal footing. While genocide may be considered the gravest crime, there is no justification in the Statute for finding that crimes against humanity or violations of common article 3 and additional protocol II are in all circumstances alternative charges to genocide and thus lesser included offences. As stated, and it is a related point, these offences have different constituent elements. Again, this consideration renders multiple convictions for these offences in relation to the same set of facts permissible.

6.2. Individual criminal responsibility (Article 6 of the Statute)

471. The Accused is charged under Article 6(1) of the Statute of the Tribunal with individual criminal responsibility for the crimes alleged in the Indictment. With regard to Counts 13, 14 and 15 on sexual violence, the Accused is charged additionally, or alternatively, under Article 6(3) of the Statute. . . . Article 6(1) sets forth the basic principles of individual criminal liability, which are undoubtedly common to most national criminal jurisdictions. Article 6(3), by contrast, constitutes something of an exception to the principles articulated in Article 6(1), as it derives from military law, namely the principle of the liability of a commander for the acts of his subordinates or "command responsibility."

472. Article 6(1) provides that: "A person who planned, instigated, ordered, committed or otherwise aided and abetted in the planning, preparation or execution of a crime referred to in articles 2 to 4 of the present Statute, shall be individually responsible for the crime." Thus, in addition to responsibility as principal perpetrator, the Accused can be held responsible for the criminal acts of others where he plans with them, instigates them, orders them or aids and abets them to commit those acts. . . .

473. Thus, Article 6(1) covers various stages of the commission of a crime, ranging from its initial planning to its execution, through its organization. However, the principle of individual criminal responsibility as provided for in Article 6(1) implies that the planning or preparation of the crime actually leads to its commission. Indeed, the principle of individual criminal responsibility for an attempt to commit a crime obtained only in case of genocide. Conversely, this would mean that with respect to any other form of criminal participation and, in particular, those referred to in Article 6(1), the perpetrator would incur criminal responsibility only if the offence were completed.

476. The elements of the offences or, more specifically, the forms of participation in the commission of one of the crimes under Articles 2 to 4 of the Statute, as stipulated in Article 6(1) of the said Statute, their elements are inherent in the forms of participation *per se* which render the perpetrators thereof individually responsible for such crimes. The moral element is reflected in the desire of the Accused that the crime be in fact committed.

479. Therefore, as can be seen, the forms of participation referred to in Article 6(1), cannot render their perpetrator criminally liable where he did not act knowingly, and even where he should have had such knowledge. This greatly differs from Article 6(3) . . . which does not necessarily require that the superior acted knowingly to render him criminally liable; it suffices that he had reason to know that his subordinates were about to commit or had committed a crime and failed to take the necessary or reasonable measures to prevent such acts or punish the perpetrators thereof. In a way, this is liability by omission or abstention.

487. Article 6 (3) stipulates that:

> The fact that any of the acts referred to in Articles 2 to 4 of the present Statute was committed by a subordinate does not relieve his or her superior of criminal responsibility if he or she knew or had reason to know that the subordinate was about to commit such acts or had done so and the superior failed to take the necessary and reasonable measures to prevent such acts or to punish the perpetrators thereof.

488. There are varying views regarding the *mens rea* required for command responsibility. According to one view it derives from a legal rule of strict liability, that is, the superior is criminally responsible for acts committed by his subordinate, without it being necessary to prove the criminal intent of the superior. Another view holds that negligence which is so serious as to be tantamount to consent or criminal intent, is a lesser requirement. . . .

489. The Chamber holds that it is necessary to recall that criminal intent is the moral element required for any crime and that, where the objective is to ascertain the individual criminal responsibility of a person Accused of crimes falling within the jurisdiction of the Chamber, such as genocide, crimes against humanity and violations of Article 3 Common to the Geneva Conventions and of Additional Protocol II thereto, it is certainly proper to ensure that there has been malicious intent, or, at least, ensure that negligence was so serious as to be tantamount to acquiescence or even malicious intent.

490. As to whether the form of individual criminal responsibility referred to Article 6 (3) of the Statute applies to persons in positions of both military and civilian authority, it should be noted that during the Tokyo trials, certain civilian authorities were convicted of war crimes under this principle. Hirota, former Foreign Minister of Japan, was convicted of atrocities – including mass rape – committed in the "rape of Nanking," under a count which charged that

he had "recklessly disregarded their legal duty by virtue of their offices to take adequate steps to secure the observance and prevent breaches of the law and customs of war." The Tokyo Tribunal held that:

> Hirota was derelict in his duty in not insisting before the Cabinet that immediate action be taken to put an end to the atrocities, failing any other action open to him to bring about the same result. He was content to rely on assurances which he knew were not being implemented while hundreds of murders, violations of women, and other atrocities were being committed daily. His inaction amounted to criminal negligence.

It should, however, be noted that Judge Röling strongly dissented from this finding, and held that Hirota should have been acquitted. Concerning the principle of command responsibility as applied to a civilian leader, Judge Röling stated that:

> Generally speaking, a Tribunal should be very careful in holding civil government officials responsible for the behaviour of the army in the field. Moreover, the Tribunal is here to apply the general principles of law as they exist with relation to the responsibility for omissions. Considerations of both law and policy, of both justice and expediency, indicate that this responsibility should only be recognized in a very restricted sense.

491. The Chamber therefore finds that in the case of civilians, the application of the principle of individual criminal responsibility, enshrined in Article 6 (3), to civilians remains contentious. Against this background, the Chamber holds that it is appropriate to assess on a case by case basis the power of authority actually devolved upon the Accused in order to determine whether or not he had the power to take all necessary and reasonable measures to prevent the commission of the alleged crimes or to punish the perpetrators thereof.

6.3. Genocide (Article 2 of the Statute)

6.3.1. Genocide

492. Article 2 of the Statute stipulates that the Tribunal shall have the power to prosecute persons responsible for genocide, complicity to commit genocide, direct and public incitement to commit genocide, attempt to commit genocide and complicity in genocide.

493. In accordance with the said provisions of the Statute, the Prosecutor has charged Akayesu with the crimes legally defined as genocide (count 1), complicity in genocide (count 2) and incitement to commit genocide (count 4).

Crime of Genocide, punishable under Article 2(3)(a) of the Statute

494. The definition of genocide, as given in Article 2 of the Tribunal's Statute, is taken verbatim from Articles 2 and 3 of the Convention on the Prevention and Punishment of the Crime of Genocide [chap. 21, *infra*]. . . .

495. The Genocide Convention is undeniably considered part of customary international law. . . . The Chamber notes that Rwanda acceded, by legislative decree, to the Convention on Genocide on 12 February 1975. Thus, punishment of the crime of genocide did exist in Rwanda in 1994, at the time of the acts alleged in the Indictment, and the perpetrator was liable to be brought before the competent courts of Rwanda to answer for this crime.

497. Contrary to popular belief, the crime of genocide does not imply the actual extermination of [a] group in its entirety, but is understood as such once any one of the acts mentioned in Article 2(2)(a) through 2(2)(e) is committed with the specific intent to destroy "in whole or in part" a national, ethnical, racial or religious group.

498. Genocide is distinct from other crimes inasmuch as it embodies a special intent or *dolus specialis*. Special intent of a crime is the specific intention, required as a constitutive element of the crime, which demands that the perpetrator clearly seeks to produce the act charged. Thus, the special intent in the crime of genocide lies in "the intent to destroy, in whole or in part, a national, ethnical, racial or religious group, as such."

499. Thus, for a crime of genocide to have been committed, it is necessary that one of the acts listed under Article 2(2) of the Statute be committed, that the particular act be committed against a specifically targeted group, it being a national, ethnical, racial or religious group. Consequently, in order to clarify the constitutive elements of the crime of genocide, the Chamber will first state its findings on the acts provided for under Article 2(2)(a) through Article 2(2)(e) of the Statute, the groups protected by the Genocide Convention, and the special intent or *dolus specialis* necessary for genocide to take place.

Killing members of the group (paragraph (a)):

500. With regard to Article 2(2)(a) of the Statute, like in the Genocide Convention, the Chamber notes that the said paragraph states "*meurtre*" in the French version while the English version states "killing." The Trial Chamber is of the opinion that the term "killing" used in the English version is too general, since it could very well include both intentional and unintentional homicides, whereas the term "*meurtre*" used in the French version, is more precise. It is accepted that there is murder when death has been caused with the intention to do so . . . .

Causing serious bodily or mental harm to members of the group (paragraph b)

502. Causing serious bodily or mental harm to members of the group does not necessarily mean that the harm is permanent and irremediable.

503. In the Adolf Eichmann case, who was convicted of crimes against the Jewish people, genocide under another legal definition, the District Court of Jerusalem stated in its judgment of 12 December 1961, that serious bodily or mental harm of members of the group can be caused

> by the enslavement, starvation, deportation and persecution . . . and by their detention in ghettos, transit camps and concentration camps in conditions which were designed to cause their degradation, deprivation of their rights as human beings, and to suppress them and cause them inhumane suffering and torture.

504. For purposes of interpreting Article 2 (2)(b) of the Statute, the Chamber takes serious bodily or mental harm, without limiting itself thereto, to mean acts of torture, be they bodily or mental, inhumane or degrading treatment, persecution.

Deliberately inflicting on the group conditions of life calculated to bring about its physical destruction in whole or in part (paragraph c):

505. The Chamber holds that the expression deliberately inflicting on the group conditions of life calculated to bring about its physical destruction in whole or in part, should be construed as the methods of destruction by which the perpetrator does not immediately kill the members of the group, but which, ultimately, seek their physical destruction.

506. For purposes of interpreting Article 2(2)(c) of the Statute, the Chamber is of the opinion that the means of deliberate inflicting on the group conditions of life calculated to bring about its physical destruction, in whole or part, include, *inter alia*, subjecting a group of people to a subsistence diet, systematic expulsion from homes and the reduction of essential medical services below minimum requirement.

Imposing measures intended to prevent births within the group (paragraph d):

507. For purposes of interpreting Article 2(2)(d) of the Statute, the Chamber holds that the measures intended to prevent births within the group, should be construed as sexual mutilation, the practice of sterilization, forced birth control, separation of the sexes and prohibition of marriages. In patriarchal societies, where membership of a group is determined by the identity of the father, an example of a measure intended to prevent births within a group is the case where, during rape, a woman of the said group is deliberately impregnated by a man of another group, with the intent to have her give birth to a child who

will consequently not belong to its mother's group.

508. Furthermore, the Chamber notes that measures intended to prevent births within the group may be physical, but can also be mental. For instance, rape can be a measure intended to prevent births when the person raped refuses subsequently to procreate, in the same way that members of a group can be led, through threats or trauma, not to procreate.

Forcibly transferring children of the group to another group (paragraph e)

509. With respect to forcibly transferring children of the group to another group, the Chamber is of the opinion that, as in the case of measures intended to prevent births, the objective is not only to sanction a direct act of forcible physical transfer, but also to sanction acts of threats or trauma which would lead to the forcible transfer of children from one group to another.

510. Since the special intent to commit genocide lies in the intent to "destroy, in whole or in part, a national, ethnical, racial or religious group, as such," it is necessary to consider a definition of the group as such. Article 2 of the Statute, just like the Genocide Convention, stipulates four types of victim groups, namely national, ethnical, racial or religious groups.

511. On reading through the *travaux préparatoires* of the Genocide Convention, it appears that the crime of genocide was allegedly perceived as targeting only "stable" groups, constituted in a permanent fashion and membership of which is determined by birth, with the exclusion of the more "mobile" groups which one joins through individual voluntary commitment, such as political and economic groups. Therefore, a common criterion in the four types of groups protected by the Genocide Convention is that membership in such groups would seem to be normally not challengeable by its members, who belong to it automatically, by birth, in a continuous and often irremediable manner. . . .

516. [T]he Chamber considered whether the groups protected by the Genocide Convention, echoed in Article 2 of the Statute, should be limited to only the four groups expressly mentioned and whether they should not also include any group which is stable and permanent like the said four groups. In other words, the question that arises is whether it would be impossible to punish the physical destruction of a group as such under the Genocide Convention, if the said group, although stable and membership is by birth, does not meet the definition of any one of the four groups expressly protected by the Genocide Convention. In the opinion of the Chamber, it is particularly important to respect the intention of the drafters of the Genocide Convention, which according to the *travaux préparatoires*, was patently to ensure the protection of any stable and permanent group.

520. With regard to the crime of genocide, the offender is culpable only when

he has committed one of the offences charged under Article 2(2) of the Statute with the clear intent to destroy, in whole or in part, a particular group. The offender is culpable because he knew or should have known that the act committed would destroy, in whole or in part, a group.

521. In concrete terms, for any of the acts charged under Article 2 (2) of the Statute to be a constitutive element of genocide, the act must have been committed against one or several individuals, because such individual or individuals were members of a specific group, and specifically because they belonged to this group. Thus, the victim is chosen not because of his individual identity, but rather on account of his membership of a national, ethnical, racial or religious group. The victim of the act is therefore a member of a group, chosen as such, which, hence, means that the victim of the crime of genocide is the group itself and not only the individual.

522. The perpetration of the act charged therefore extends beyond its actual commission, for example, the murder of a particular individual, for the realisation of an ulterior motive, which is to destroy, in whole or part, the group of which the individual is just one element.

523. On the issue of determining the offender's specific intent, the Chamber considers that intent is a mental factor which is difficult, even impossible, to determine. This is the reason why, in the absence of a confession from the accused, his intent can be inferred from a certain number of presumptions of fact. The Chamber considers that it is possible to deduce the genocidal intent inherent in a particular act charged from the general context of the perpetration of other culpable acts systematically directed against that same group, whether these acts were committed by the same offender or by others. Other factors, such as the scale of atrocities committed, their general nature, in a region or a country, or furthermore, the fact of deliberately and systematically targeting victims on account of their membership of a particular group, while excluding the members of other groups, can enable the Chamber to infer the genocidal intent of a particular act.

6.3.2. Complicity in Genocide

The Crime of Complicity in Genocide, punishable under Article 2(3)e) of the Statute

525. Under Article 2(3)e) of the Statute, the Chamber shall have the power to prosecute persons who have committed complicity in genocide. The Prosecutor has charged Akayesu with such a crime under count 2 of the Indictment.

527. The Chamber notes that complicity is viewed as a form of criminal participation by all criminal law systems, notably, under the Anglo-Saxon system (or Common Law) and the Roman-Continental system (or Civil Law).

Since the accomplice to an offence may be defined as someone who associates himself in an offence committed by another, complicity necessarily implies the existence of a principal offence.

530. Consequently, the Chamber is of the opinion that in order for an accused to be found guilty of complicity in genocide, it must, first of all, be proven beyond a reasonable doubt that the crime of genocide has, indeed, been committed.

531. The issue thence is whether a person can be tried for complicity even where the perpetrator of the principal offence himself has not being tried. . . . As far as the Chamber is aware, all criminal systems provide that an accomplice may also be tried, even where the principal perpetrator of the crime has not been identified, or where, for any other reasons, guilt could not be proven.

538. The intent or mental element of complicity implies in general that, at the moment he acted, the accomplice knew of the assistance he was providing in the commission of the principal offence. In other words, the accomplice must have acted knowingly.

540. As far as genocide is concerned, the intent of the accomplice is thus to knowingly aid or abet one or more persons to commit the crime of genocide. Therefore, the Chamber is of the opinion that an accomplice to genocide need not necessarily possess the *dolus specialis* of genocide, namely the specific intent to destroy, in whole or in part, a national, ethnic, racial or religious group, as such.

541. Thus, if for example, an accused knowingly aided or abetted another in the commission of a murder, while being unaware that the principal was committing such a murder, with the intent to destroy, in whole or in part, the group to which the murdered victim belonged, the accused could be prosecuted for complicity in murder, and certainly not for complicity in genocide. However, if the accused knowingly aided and abetted in the commission of such a murder while he knew or had reason to know that the principal was acting with genocidal intent, the accused would be an accomplice to genocide, even though he did not share the murderer's intent to destroy the group.

542. This finding by the Chamber comports with the decisions rendered by the District Court of Jerusalem on 12 December 1961 and the Supreme Court of Israel on 29 May 1962 in the case of Adolf Eichmann. Since Eichmann raised the argument in his defence that he was a "small cog" in the Nazi machine, both the District Court and the Supreme Court dealt with accomplice liability and found that "even a small cog, even an insignificant operator, is under our criminal law liable to be regarded as an accomplice in the commission of an offence, in which case he will be dealt with as if he were the actual murderer or destroyer."

543. The District Court accepted that Eichmann did not personally devise the "Final Solution" himself, but nevertheless, as the head of those engaged in carrying out the "Final Solution" – "acting in accordance with the directives of

his superiors, but [with] wide discretionary powers in planning operations on his own initiative," he incurred individual criminal liability for crimes against the Jewish people, as much as his superiors. Likewise, with respect to his subordinates who actually carried out the executions, "the legal and moral responsibility of he who delivers up the victim to his death is, in our opinion, no smaller, and may be greater, than the responsibility of he who kills the victim with his own hands." The District Court found that participation in the extermination plan with knowledge of the plan rendered the person liable "as an accomplice to the extermination of all . . . victims from 1941 to 1945, irrespective of the extent of his participation."

544. The findings of the Israeli courts in this case support the principle that the *mens rea*, or special intent, required for complicity in genocide is *knowledge* of the genocidal plan, coupled with the *actus reus* of participation in the execution of such plan. Crucially, then, it does not appear that the specific intent to commit the crime of genocide, as reflected in the phrase "with intent to destroy, in whole or in part, a national, ethnical, racial or religious group, as such," is required for complicity or accomplice liability.

545. In conclusion, the Chamber is of the opinion that an accused is liable as an accomplice to genocide if he knowingly aided or abetted or instigated one or more persons in the commission of genocide, while knowing that such a person or persons were committing genocide, even though the accused himself did not have the specific intent to destroy, in whole or in part, a national, ethnical, racial or religious group, as such. . . .

6.3.3. Direct and Public Incitement to Commit Genocide

The Crime of Direct and Public Incitement to Commit Genocide, punishable under Article 2(3)(c) of the Statute

549. Under count 4, the Prosecutor charges Akayesu with direct and public incitement to commit genocide, a crime punishable under Article 2(3)(c) of the Statute.

550. Perhaps the most famous conviction for incitement to commit crimes of international dimension was that of Julius Streicher by the Nuremberg Tribunal for the virulently anti-Semitic articles which he had published in his weekly newspaper *Der Stürmer*. The Nuremberg Tribunal found that: "Streicher's incitement to murder and extermination, at the time when Jews in the East were being killed under the most horrible conditions, clearly constitutes persecution on political and racial grounds in connection with War Crimes, as defined by the Charter, and constitutes a Crime against Humanity."

551. At the time the Convention on Genocide was adopted, the delegates agreed to expressly spell out direct and public incitement to commit genocide as

a specific crime, in particular, because of its critical role in the planning of a genocide. . . .

554. Under the Statute, direct and public incitement is expressly defined as a specific crime, punishable as such, by virtue of Article 2(3)(c). With respect to such a crime, the Chamber deems it appropriate to first define the three terms: incitement, direct and public.

555. Incitement is defined in Common law systems as encouraging or persuading another to commit an offence. One line of authority in Common law would also view threats or other forms of pressure as a form of incitement. . . .Civil law systems punish direct and public incitement assuming the form of provocation, which is defined as an act intended to directly provoke another to commit a crime or a misdemeanour through speeches, shouting or threats, or any other means of audiovisual communication. Such a provocation, as defined under Civil law, is made up of the same elements as direct and public incitement to commit genocide covered by Article 2 of the Statute, that is to say it is both direct and public.

556. The public element of incitement to commit genocide may be better appreciated in light of two factors: the place where the incitement occurred and whether or not assistance was selective or limited. A line of authority commonly followed in Civil law systems would regard words as being public where they were spoken aloud in a place that were public by definition. According to the International Law Commission, public incitement is characterized by a call for criminal action to a number of individuals in a public place or to members of the general public at large by such means as the mass media, for example, radio or television. It should be noted in this respect that at the time Convention on Genocide was adopted, the delegates specifically agreed to rule out the possibility of including private incitement to commit genocide as a crime, thereby underscoring their commitment to set aside for punishment only the truly public forms of incitement.

557. The "direct" element of incitement implies that the incitement assume a direct form and specifically provoke another to engage in a criminal act, and that more than mere vague or indirect suggestion goes to constitute direct incitement. Under Civil law systems, provocation, the equivalent of incitement, is regarded as being direct where it is aimed at causing a specific offence to be committed. The prosecution must prove a definite causation between the act characterized as incitement, or provocation in this case, and a specific offence. However, the Chamber is of the opinion that the direct element of incitement should be viewed in the light of its cultural and linguistic content. Indeed, a particular speech may be perceived as "direct" in one country, and not so in another, depending on the audience. The Chamber further recalls that incitement may be direct, and nonetheless implicit. Thus, at the time the Convention on Genocide was being drafted, the Polish delegate observed that it was sufficient to play skillfully on mob psychology by casting suspicion on certain groups, by insinuating that they were responsible for economic or other

difficulties in order to create an atmosphere favourable to the perpetration of the crime.

558. The Chamber will therefore consider on a case-by-case basis whether, in light of the culture of Rwanda and the specific circumstances of the instant case, acts of incitement can be viewed as direct or not, by focusing mainly on the issue of whether the persons for whom the message was intended immediately grasped the implication thereof.

559. In light of the foregoing, it can be noted in the final analysis that whatever the legal system, direct and public incitement must be defined for the purposes of interpreting Article 2(3)(c), as directly provoking the perpetrator(s) to commit genocide, whether through speeches, shouting or threats uttered in public places or at public gatherings, or through the sale or dissemination, offer for sale or display of written material or printed matter in public places or at public gatherings, or through the public display of placards or posters, or through any other means of audiovisual communication.

560. The *mens rea* required for the crime of direct and public incitement to commit genocide lies in the intent to directly prompt or provoke another to commit genocide. It implies a desire on the part of the perpetrator to create by his actions a particular state of mind necessary to commit such a crime in the minds of the person(s) he is so engaging. That is to say that the person who is inciting to commit genocide must have himself the specific intent to commit genocide, namely, to destroy, in whole or in part, a national, ethnical, racial or religious group, as such.

561. Therefore, the issue before the Chamber is whether the crime of direct and public incitement to commit genocide can be punished even where such incitement was unsuccessful. It appears from the *travaux préparatoires* of the Convention on Genocide that the drafters of the Convention considered stating explicitly that incitement to commit genocide could be punished, whether or not it was successful. In the end, a majority decided against such an approach. Nevertheless, the Chamber is of the opinion that it cannot thereby be inferred that the intent of the drafters was not to punish unsuccessful acts of incitement. In light of the overall *travaux*, the Chamber holds the view that the drafters of the Convention simply decided not to specifically mention that such a form of incitement could be punished.

562. There are under Common law so-called inchoate offences, which are punishable by virtue of the criminal act alone, irrespective of the result thereof, which may or may not have been achieved. The Civil law counterparts of inchoate offences are known as *infractions formelles* (acts constituting an offence *per se* irrespective of their results), as opposed to *infractions matérielles* (strict liability offences). Indeed, as is the case with inchoate offenses, in *infractions formelles*, the method alone is punishable. Put another way, such offenses are "deemed to have been consummated regardless of the result achieved," contrary to *infractions matérielles*. . . . It should be noted, however,

that such offences are the exception, the rule being that in theory, an offence can only be punished in relation to the result envisaged by the lawmakers. In the opinion of the Chamber, the fact that such acts are in themselves particularly dangerous because of the high risk they carry for society, even if they fail to produce results, warrants that they be punished as an exceptional measure. The Chamber holds that genocide clearly falls within the category of crimes so serious that direct and public incitement to commit such a crime must be punished as such, even where such incitement failed to produce the result expected by the perpetrator.

6.4. Crimes against Humanity (Article 3 of the Statute) *

Crimes against Humanity – Historical development

563. Crimes against humanity were recognized in the Charter and Judgment of the Nuremberg Tribunal, as well as in Law No. 10 of the Control Council for Germany [see chap. 18, supra] . . . .

565. Crimes against humanity are aimed at any civilian population and are prohibited regardless of whether they are committed in an armed conflict, international or internal in character. In fact, the concept of crimes against humanity had been recognised long before Nuremberg. On 28 May 1915, the Governments of France, Great Britain and Russia made a declaration regarding the massacres of the Armenian population in Turkey, denouncing them as "crimes against humanity and civilisation for which all the members of the Turkish government will be held responsible together with its agents implicated in the massacres." The 1919 Report of the Commission on the Responsibility of the Authors of the War and on Enforcement of Penalties formulated by representatives from several States and presented to the Paris Peace Conference also referred to "offences against . . . the laws of humanity."

566. These World War I notions derived, in part, from the Martens clause of the Hague Convention (IV) of 1907, which referred to "the usages established among civilised peoples, from the laws of humanity, and the dictates of the public conscience." . . .

567. The Chamber notes that, following the Nuremberg and Tokyo trials, the concept of crimes against humanity underwent a gradual evolution in the

---

*Article 3 ("Crimes Against Humanity") of the Statute of the Rwanda Tribunal provides: "The International Tribunal for Rwanda shall have the power to prosecute persons responsible for the following crimes when committed as part of a widespread or systematic attack against any civilian population on national, political, ethnic, racial or religious grounds: (a) murder; (b) extermination, (c) enslavement; (d) deportation; (e) imprisonment; (f) torture; (g) rape; (h) persecutions on political, racial and religious grounds; (i) other inhumane acts." – Eds.

Eichmann, Barbie, Touvier and Papon cases.

568. In the *Eichmann* case, the accused, Otto Adolf Eichmann, was charged with offences under Nazi and Nazi Collaborators (punishment) Law, 5710/1950, for his participation in the implementation of the plan know as "the Final Solution of the Jewish problem." Pursuant to Section I (b) of the said law: "Crime against humanity means any of the following acts: murder, extermination, enslavement, starvation or deportation and other inhumane acts committed against any civilian population, and persecution on national, racial, religious or political grounds." The district court in the Eichmann stated that crimes against humanity differs from genocide in that for the commission of genocide special intent is required. This special intent is not required for crimes against humanity. Eichmann was convicted by the District court and sentenced to death. Eichmann appealed against his conviction and his appeal was dismissed by the supreme court.

569. In the *Barbie* case, the accused, Klaus Barbie, who was the head of the Gestapo in Lyons from November 1942 to August 1944, during the wartime occupation of France, was convicted in 1987 of crimes against humanity for his role in the deportation and extermination of civilians. Barbie appealed in cassation, but the appeal was dismissed. For the purposes of the present Judgment, what is of interest is the definition of crimes against humanity employed by the Court. The French Court of Cassation, in a Judgment rendered on 20 December 1985, stated:

> Crimes against humanity, within the meaning of Article 6(c) of the Charter of the International Military Tribunal annexed to the London Agreement of 8 August 1945, which were not subject to statutory limitation of the right of prosecution, even if they were crimes which could also be classified as war crimes within the meaning of Article 6(b) of the Charter, *were inhumane acts and persecution committed in a systematic manner in the name of a State practising a policy of ideological supremacy, not only against persons by reason of their membership of a racial or religious community, but also against the opponents of that policy, whatever the form of their opposition* (words italicized by the Court). 78 I.L.R. 136, at 137.

570. This was affirmed in a Judgment of the Court of Cassation of 3 June 1988, in which the Court held that:

> The fact that the accused, who had been found guilty of one of the crimes enumerated in Article 6(c) of the Charter of the Nuremberg Tribunal, in perpetrating that crime took part in the execution of a common plan to bring about the deportation or extermination of the civilian population during the war, or persecutions on political, racial or religious grounds, constituted not a distinct offence or an aggravating circumstance but rather *an essential element of the crime against humanity, consisting of the fact that the acts charged were performed in a systematic manner*

in the name of a State practising by those means a policy of ideological supremacy." I.L.R. at 332 & 336 (emphasis added). . .

571. The definition of crimes against humanity developed in *Barbie* was further developed in the *Touvier* case. In that case, the accused, Paul Touvier, had been a high-ranking officer in the Militia (*Milice*) of Lyons, which operated in "Vichy" France during the German occupation. He was convicted of crimes against humanity for his role in the shooting of seven Jews at Rillieux on 29 June 1994 as a reprisal for the assassination by members of the Resistance, on the previous day, of the Minister for Propaganda of the "Vichy" Government.

572. The Court of Appeal applied the definition of crimes against humanity used in *Barbie*, stating that:

> The specific intent necessary to establish a crime against humanity was the intention to take part in the execution of a common plan by committing, in a systematic manner, inhuman acts or persecutions in the name of a State practising a policy of ideological supremacy.

573. Applying this definition, the Court of Appeal held that Touvier could not be guilty of crimes against humanity since he committed the acts in question in the name of the "Vichy" State, which was not a State practising a policy of ideological supremacy, although it collaborated with Nazi Germany, which clearly did practice such a policy.

574. The Court of Cassation allowed appeal from the decision of the Court of Appeal, on the grounds that the crimes committed by the accused had been committed at the instigation of a Gestapo officer, and to that extent were linked to Nazi Germany, a State practising a policy of ideological supremacy against persons by virtue of their membership of a racial or religious community. Therefore the crimes could be categorised as crimes against humanity. Touvier was eventually convicted of crimes against humanity by the *Cour d'Assises des Yvelines* on 20 April 1994.

575. The definition of crimes against humanity used in *Barbie* was later affirmed by the ICTY in its *Vukovar* Rule 61 Decision of 3 April 1996 (IT-95-13-R61), to support its finding that crimes against humanity applied equally where the victims of the acts were members of a resistance movement as to where the victims were civilians . . . .

Crimes against Humanity in Article 3 of the Statute of the Tribunal

578. The Chamber considers that Article 3 of the Statute confers on the Chamber the jurisdiction to prosecute persons for various inhumane acts which constitute crimes against humanity. This category of crimes may be broadly broken down into four essential elements, namely:

(i) the act must be inhumane in nature and character, causing great suffering, or serious injury to body or to mental or physical health;

(ii) the act must be committed as part of a wide spread or systematic attack;

(iii) the act must be committed against members of the civilian population;

(iv) the act must be committed on one or more discriminatory grounds, namely, national, political, ethnic, racial or religious grounds. . . .

585. Article 3 of the Statute sets out various acts that constitute crimes against humanity, namely: murder; extermination; enslavement; deportation; imprisonment; torture; rape; persecution on political, racial and religious grounds; and; other inhumane acts. Although the category of acts that constitute crimes against humanity are set out in Article 3, this category is not exhaustive. Any act which is inhumane in nature and character may constitute a crime against humanity, provided the other elements are met. This is evident in (i) which caters for all other inhumane acts not stipulated in (a) to (h) of Article 3. . . .

586. The Chamber notes that the accused is indicted for murder, extermination, torture, rape and other acts that constitute inhumane acts. . .

596. Considering the extent to which rape constitute crimes against humanity, pursuant to Article 3(g) of the Statute, the Chamber must define rape, as there is no commonly accepted definition of this term in international law. While rape has been defined in certain national jurisdictions as non-consensual intercourse, variations on the act of rape may include acts which involve the insertion of objects and/or the use of bodily orifices not considered to be intrinsically sexual.

597. The Chamber considers that rape is a form of aggression and that the central elements of the crime of rape cannot be captured in a mechanical description of objects and body parts. The Convention against Torture and Other Cruel, Inhuman and Degrading Treatment or Punishment does not catalogue specific acts in its definition of torture, focusing rather on the conceptual frame work of state sanctioned violence. This approach is more useful in international law. Like torture, rape is used for such purposes as intimidation, degradation, humiliation, discrimination, punishment, control or destruction of a person. Like torture, rape is a violation of personal dignity, and rape in fact constitutes torture when inflicted by or at the instigation of or with the consent or acquiescence of a public official or other person acting in an official capacity.

598. The Chamber defines rape as a physical invasion of a sexual nature, committed on a person under circumstances which are coercive. Sexual violence,

which includes rape, is considered to be any act of a sexual nature which is committed on a person under circumstances which are coercive. This act must be committed (a) as part of a widespread or systematic attack;(b) on a civilian population; (c) on certain catalogued discriminatory grounds, namely: national, ethnic, political, racial, or religious grounds.

6.5. Violations of Common Article 3 and Additional Protocol II (Article 4 of the Statute)

Article 4 of the Statute

599. Pursuant to Article 4 of the Statute, the Chamber "shall have the power to prosecute persons committing or ordering to be committed serious violations of Article 3 common to the four Geneva Conventions of 12 August 1949 for the Protection of War Victims, and of Additional Protocol II thereto of 8 June 1977. These violations shall include, but shall not be limited to: (a) violence to life, health and physical or mental well-being of persons, in particular murder as well as cruel treatment such as torture, mutilation or any form of corporal punishment; (b) collective punishments; (c) taking of hostages; (d) acts of terrorism; (e) outrages upon personal dignity, in particular humiliating and degrading treatment, rape, enforced prostitution and any form of indecent assault; (f pillage; (g) the passing of sentences and the carrying out of executions without previous judgment pronounced by a regularly constituted court, affording all the judicial guarantees which are recognised as indispensable by civilised peoples; (h) threats to commit any of the foregoing acts."

Applicability of Common Article 3 and Additional Protocol II

601. The four 1949 Geneva Conventions and the 1977 Additional Protocol I thereto generally apply to international armed conflicts only, whereas Article 3 common to the Geneva Conventions extends a minimum threshold of humanitarian protection as well to all persons affected by a non-international conflict, a protection which was further developed and enhanced in the 1977 Additional Protocol II. In the field of international humanitarian law, a clear distinction as to the thresholds of application has been made between situations of international armed conflicts, in which the law of armed conflicts is applicable as a whole, situations of non-international (internal) armed conflicts, where Common Article 3 and Additional Protocol II are applicable, and non-international armed conflicts where only Common Article 3 is applicable. Situations of internal disturbances are not covered by international humanitarian law.

604. The Security Council, when delimiting the subject-matter jurisdiction of the ICTR, incorporated violations of international humanitarian law which may be committed in the context of both an international and an internal armed

conflict:

> Given the nature of the conflict as non-international in character, the Council has incorporated within the subject-matter jurisdiction of the Tribunal violations of international humanitarian law which may either be committed in both international and internal armed conflicts, such as the crime of genocide and crimes against humanity, or may be committed only in internal armed conflicts, such as violations of article 3 common to the four Geneva Conventions, as more fully elaborated in article 4 of Additional Protocol II.

In that latter respect, the Security Council has elected to take a more expansive approach to the choice of the applicable law than the one underlying the Statute of the Yugoslav Tribunal, and included within the subject-matter jurisdiction of the Rwanda Tribunal international instruments regardless of whether they were considered part of customary international law or whether they have customarily entailed the individual criminal responsibility of the perpetrator of the crime. Article 4 of the Statute, accordingly, includes violations of Additional Protocol II, which, as a whole, has not yet been universally recognized as part of customary international law, for the first time criminalizes common article 3 of the four Geneva Conventions.

605. Although the Security Council elected to take a more expansive approach to the choice of the subject-matter jurisdiction of the Tribunal than that of the ICTY, by incorporating international instruments regardless of whether they were considered part of customary international law or whether they customarily entailed the individual criminal responsibility of the perpetrator of the crime, the Chamber believes, an essential question which should be addressed at this stage is whether Article 4 of the Statute includes norms which did not, at the time the crimes alleged in the Indictment were committed, form part of existing international customary law. [T]he Chamber recalls the establishment of the ICTY, during which the UN Secretary General asserted that in application of the principle of *nullum crimen sine lege* the International Tribunal should apply rules of International Humanitarian law which are *beyond any doubt part* of customary law. . . .

608. It is today clear that the norms of Common Article 3 have acquired the status of customary law in that most States, by their domestic penal codes, have criminalized acts which if committed during internal armed conflict, would constitute violations of Common Article 3. . . .

609. . . . Additional Protocol II as a whole was not deemed by the Secretary-General to have been universally recognized as part of customary international law. . . . "[M]any provisions of this Protocol [II] can now be regarded as declaratory of existing rules or as having crystallised in emerging rules of customary law," but not all.

610. [However,] it should be recalled that the relevant Article in the context

of the ICTR is Article 4(2) (Fundamental Guarantees) of Additional Protocol II. All of the guarantees, as enumerated in Article 4 reaffirm and supplement Common Article 3 and, as discussed above, Common Article 3 being customary in nature, the Chamber is of the opinion that these guarantees did also at the time of the events alleged in the Indictment form part of existing international customary law.

Individual Criminal Responsibility

611. For the purposes of an international criminal Tribunal which is trying individuals, it is not sufficient merely to affirm that Common Article 3 and parts of Article 4 of Additional Protocol II – which comprise the subject-matter jurisdiction of Article 4 of the Statute – form part of international customary law. . . . [I]t must also be shown that an individual committing serious violations of these customary norms incurs, as a matter of custom, individual criminal responsibility thereby. Otherwise, it might be argued that these instruments only state norms applicable to States and Parties to a conflict, and that they do not create crimes for which individuals may be tried.

612. As regards individual criminal responsibility for serious violations of Common Article 3, the ICTY has already affirmed this principle in the *Tadic* case.

613. Basing itself on rulings of the Nuremberg Tribunal, on "elements of international practice which show that States intend to criminalise serious breaches of customary rules and principles on internal conflicts," as well as on national legislation designed to implement the Geneva Conventions, the ICTY Appeals Chamber reached the conclusion: "All of these factors confirm that customary international law imposes criminal liability for serious violations of common Article 3, as supplemented by other general principles and rules on protection of victims of internal armed conflict, and for breaching certain fundamental principles and rules regarding means and methods of combat in civil strife."

615. The Chamber considers this finding of the ICTY Appeals Chamber convincing and dispositive of the issue, both with respect to serious violations of Common Article 3 and of Additional Protocol II. . . .

[On the counts of the indictment charging Akayesu, under Article 4 of the Statute, with violations of Common Article 3 of the Geneva Conventions or of Additional Protocol II, the Trial Chamber found that, while there was an "armed conflict not of an international character" taking place in Rwanda at the time of the events in question, it had not been proved that Akayesu's acts were committed in conjunction with that armed conflict. He therefore could not be found guilty on those counts. He was found guilty under Article 3 on seven counts alleging crimes against humanity (involving murder, extermination, torture, rape, and other inhumane acts). He also was found guilty under Article 2 on two counts alleging genocide and direct and public incitement to commit genocide, but not guilty on a count alleging complicity in genocide, on the ground that the same person cannot be both a principal and an accomplice to the same offense. On October 2, 1998, Akayesu was sentenced to life imprisonment.]

NOTES AND QUESTIONS

(1) In the three months between April 7 and July 17, 1994, over a half million and perhaps closer to a million Rwandans were killed by their neighbors. Most of the killers were members of the majority Hutu ethnic group; most of the victims were minority Tutsi. On July 17, the Tutsi-led Rwandan Patriotic Front achieved military victory and took over the government of Rwanda. In September 1994, the new government of Rwanda asked the U.N. to set up an International Criminal Tribunal for Rwanda on the model of the Yugoslav Tribunal. But, ironically, on November 8, 1994, Rwanda, then a member of the Security Council, cast the sole vote opposing establishment of the ICTR – in part on the ground that, just as Nazi war criminals had been tried in Germany and, if convicted, faced execution, so those guilty of genocide in Rwanda should be tried in Rwanda (rather than Arusha) and also face the death penalty.

The ICTR is not expected to deal with the bulk of the 100,000 criminal cases arising from the Rwandan genocide. These will be dealt with in the Rwandan courts. *See* Madeline H. Morris, *The Trials of Concurrent Jurisdiction: The Case of Rwanda*, 7 DUKE J. COMP. & INT'L L. 349 (1997), *reprinted in* 3 INTERNATIONAL CRIMINAL LAW 567 (M. Cherif Bassiouni ed., 1999). Would it have made more sense to pour the money that has gone into the ICTR into rebuilding the Rwandan judicial system? Or are there special reasons why it is important to establish an international tribunal to deal with large-scale human rights atrocities?

(2) The Yugoslav Tribunal was established in 1993, the Rwanda Tribunal in 1994. The fact that the Security Council had acted to set up a criminal court not once, but twice, began to make a permanent international criminal court look feasible. The Rome Statute to establish a permanent court [*see* chap. 20] was adopted in 1998. Will this mean an end of special *ad hoc* tribunals? In fact, plans to set up two more *ad hoc* tribunals are presently under consideration.

First, on May 24, 2000, the U.N. and Cambodian officials reached a tentative agreement to establish an international court to try former leaders of the Khmer Rouge who killed more than a million Cambodians between 1975 and 1979. For an account of the options and difficulties connected with bringing the Khmer Rouge to justice, *see* STEVEN R. RATNER & JASON S. ABRAMS, ACCOUNTABILITY FOR HUMAN RIGHTS ATROCITIES IN INTERNATIONAL LAW: BEYOND THE NUREMBERG LEGACY 227-89 (1997). The agreement still has to be approved by the Cambodian legislature. It calls for the tribunal to have two prosecutors, one appointed by Cambodia, one by the U.N.; and five judges, three from Cambodia, two nominated by the U.N. Either prosecutor can proceed with an indictment, provided it is not blocked by a vote of four of the five judges. *See* Barbara Crossette, *Cambodian Will Prosecute Khmer Rouge*, N.Y. TIMES, May 25, 2000, at A12.

Second, on August 14, 2000, the Security Council adopted Resolution 1315 (2000), in which it asked the Secretary-General "to negotiate an agreement with the Government of Sierra Leone to create an independent special court" to try "crimes against humanity, war crimes and other serious violations of international humanitarian law, as well as crimes under relevant Sierra Leonean law committed within the territory of Sierra Leone." The Council left it to the Secretary-General to address "lingering questions about how authority should be shared between Sierra Leone's judicial system and neutral international experts." Barbara Crossette, *U.N. to Establish a War Crimes Panel to Hear Sierra Leone Atrocity Cases*, N.Y. TIMES, Aug. 15, 2000, at A6. The resolution did emphasize "the importance of ensuring the impartiality, independence and credibility of the process, in particular with regard to the status of the judges and the prosecutors"; and it requested "the Secretary-General to address in his report the questions of the temporal jurisdiction of the special court, an appeals process including the advisability, feasibility, and appropriateness of an appeals chamber in the special court or of sharing the Appeals Chamber of the International Criminal Tribunals for the Former Yugoslavia and Rwanda or other effective options, and a possible alternative host State, should it be necessary to convene the special court outside the seat of the court in Sierra Leone, if circumstances so require. . . ."

Chapter 20
THE ROME STATUTE FOR AN INTERNATIONAL CRIMINAL COURT

THE ROME STATUTE FOR AN
INTERNATIONAL CRIMINAL COURT

Adopted by the United Nations Diplomatic Conference of Plenipotentiaries on the Establishment of an International Criminal Court on July 17, 1998. U.N. GAOR, 53d Sess., U.N. Doc. A/CONF. 183/9 (1998) [*]

PREAMBLE

The States Parties to this Statute,

Conscious that all peoples are united by common bonds, their cultures pieced together in a shared heritage, and concerned that this delicate mosaic may be shattered at any time,

Mindful that during this century millions of children, women and men have been victims of unimaginable atrocities that deeply shock the conscience of humanity,

Recognizing that such grave crimes threaten the peace, security and well-being of the world,

Affirming that the most serious crimes of concern to the international community as a whole must not go unpunished and that their effective prosecution must be ensured by taking measures at the national level and by enhancing international cooperation,

Determined to put an end to impunity for the perpetrators of these crimes and thus to contribute to the prevention of such crimes,

Recalling that it is the duty of every State to exercise its criminal jurisdiction over those responsible for international crimes,

---

[*] With corrections of November 10, 1998, and July 12, 1999.

Reaffirming the Purposes and Principles of the Charter of the United Nations, and in particular that all States shall refrain from the threat or use of force against the territorial integrity or political independence of any State, or in any other manner inconsistent with the Purposes of the United Nations,

Emphasizing in this connection that nothing in this Statute shall be taken as authorizing any State Party to intervene in an armed conflict or in the internal affairs of any State,

Determined to these ends and for the sake of present and future generations, to establish an independent permanent International Criminal Court in relationship with the United Nations system, with jurisdiction over the most serious crimes of concern to the international community as a whole,

Emphasizing that the International Criminal Court established under this Statute shall be complementary to national criminal jurisdictions,

Resolved to guarantee lasting respect for and the enforcement of international justice,

Have agreed as follows

PART 1. ESTABLISHMENT OF THE COURT

Article 1 – The Court

An International Criminal Court ("the Court") is hereby established. It shall be a permanent institution and shall have the power to exercise its jurisdiction over persons for the most serious crimes of international concern, as referred to in this Statute, and shall be complementary to national criminal jurisdictions. The jurisdiction and functioning of the Court shall be governed by the provisions of this Statute.

Article 2 – Relationship of the Court with the United Nations

The Court shall be brought into relationship with the United Nations through an agreement to be approved by the Assembly of States Parties to this Statute and thereafter concluded by the President of the Court on its behalf.

Article 3 – Seat of the Court

1. The seat of the Court shall be established at The Hague in the Netherlands ("the host State").

2. The Court shall enter into a headquarters agreement with the host State, to be approved by the Assembly of States Parties and thereafter concluded by the President of the Court on its behalf.

3. The Court may sit elsewhere, whenever it considers it desirable, as provided in this Statute.

Article 4 – Legal status and powers of the Court

1. The Court shall have international legal personality. It shall also have such legal capacity as may be necessary for the exercise of its functions and the fulfilment of its purposes.

2. The Court may exercise its functions and powers, as provided in this Statute, on the territory of any State Party and, by special agreement, on the territory of any other State.

PART 2. JURISDICTION, ADMISSIBILITY AND APPLICABLE LAW

Article 5 – Crimes within the jurisdiction of the Court

1. The jurisdiction of the Court shall be limited to the most serious crimes of concern to the international community as a whole. The Court has jurisdiction in accordance with this Statute with respect to the following crimes:

   (a) The crime of genocide;

   (b) Crimes against humanity;

   (c) War crimes;

   (d) The crime of aggression.

2. The Court shall exercise jurisdiction over the crime of aggression once a provision is adopted in accordance with articles 121 and 123 defining the crime and setting out the conditions under which the Court shall exercise jurisdiction with respect to this crime. Such a provision shall be consistent with the relevant provisions of the Charter of the United Nations.

Article 6 – Genocide

For the purpose of this Statute, "genocide" means any of the following acts committed with intent to destroy, in whole or in part, a national, ethnical, racial or religious group, as such:

(a) Killing members of the group;

(b) Causing serious bodily or mental harm to members of the group;

(c) Deliberately inflicting on the group conditions of life calculated to bring about its physical destruction in whole or in part;

(d) Imposing measures intended to prevent births within the group;

(e) Forcibly transferring children of the group to another group.

Article 7 – Crimes against humanity

1. For the purpose of this Statute, "crime against humanity" means any of the following acts when committed as part of a widespread or systematic attack directed against any civilian population, with knowledge of the attack:

(a) Murder;

(b) Extermination;

(c) Enslavement;

(d) Deportation or forcible transfer of population;

(e) Imprisonment or other severe deprivation of physical liberty in violation of fundamental rules of international law;

(f) Torture;

(g) Rape, sexual slavery, enforced prostitution, forced pregnancy, enforced sterilization, or any other form of sexual violence of comparable gravity;

(h) Persecution against any identifiable group or collectivity on political, racial, national, ethnic, cultural, religious, gender as defined in paragraph 3, or other grounds that are universally recognized as impermissible under international law, in connection with any act referred to in this paragraph or any crime within the jurisdiction of the Court;

(i) Enforced disappearance of persons;

(j) The crime of apartheid;

(k) Other inhumane acts of a similar character intentionally causing great suffering, or serious injury to body or to mental or physical health.

2. For the purpose of paragraph 1:

(a) "Attack directed against any civilian population" means a course of conduct involving the multiple commission of acts referred to in paragraph 1 against any civilian population, pursuant to or in furtherance of a State or organizational policy to commit such attack;

(b) "Extermination" includes the intentional infliction of conditions of life, inter alia the deprivation of access to food and medicine, calculated to bring about the destruction of part of a population;

(c) "Enslavement" means the exercise of any or all of the powers attaching to the right of ownership over a person and includes the exercise of such power in the course of trafficking in persons, in particular women and children;

(d) "Deportation or forcible transfer of population" means forced displacement of the persons concerned by expulsion or other coercive acts from the area in which they are lawfully present, without grounds permitted under international law;

(e) "Torture" means the intentional infliction of severe pain or suffering, whether physical or mental, upon a person in the custody or under the control of the accused; except that torture shall not include pain or suffering arising only from, inherent in or incidental to, lawful sanctions;

(f) "Forced pregnancy" means the unlawful confinement of a woman forcibly made pregnant, with the intent of affecting the ethnic composition of any population or carrying out other grave violations of international law. This definition shall not in any way be interpreted as affecting national laws relating to pregnancy;

(g) "Persecution" means the intentional and severe deprivation of fundamental rights contrary to international law by reason of the identity of the group or collectivity;

(h) "The crime of apartheid" means inhumane acts of a character similar to those referred to in paragraph 1, committed in the context of an institutionalized regime of systematic oppression and domination by one racial group over any other racial group or groups and committed with the intention of maintaining that regime;

(i) "Enforced disappearance of persons" means the arrest, detention or abduction of persons by, or with the authorization, support or acquiescence of, a State or a political organization, followed by a refusal to acknowledge that deprivation of freedom or to give information on the fate or whereabouts of those persons, with the intention of removing them from the protection of the law for a prolonged period of time.

3. For the purpose of this Statute, it is understood that the term "gender" refers to the two sexes, male and female, within the context of society. The term "gender" does not indicate any meaning different from the above.

Article 8 – War crimes

1. The Court shall have jurisdiction in respect of war crimes in particular when committed as part of a plan or policy or as part of a large-scale commission of such crimes.

2. For the purpose of this Statute, "war crimes" means:

(a) Grave breaches of the Geneva Conventions of 12 August 1949, namely, any of the following acts against persons or property protected under the provisions of the relevant Geneva Convention:

(i) Wilful killing;

(ii) Torture or inhuman treatment, including biological experiments;

(iii) Wilfully causing great suffering, or serious injury to body or health;

(iv) Extensive destruction and appropriation of property, not justified by military necessity and carried out unlawfully and wantonly;

(v) Compelling a prisoner of war or other protected person to serve in the forces of a hostile Power;

(vi) Wilfully depriving a prisoner of war or other protected person of the rights of fair and regular trial;

(vii) Unlawful deportation or transfer or unlawful confinement;

(viii) Taking of hostages.

(b) Other serious violations of the laws and customs applicable in international armed conflict, within the established framework of international law, namely, any of the following acts:

(i) Intentionally directing attacks against the civilian population as such or against individual civilians not taking direct part in hostilities;

(ii) Intentionally directing attacks against civilian objects, that is, objects which are not military objectives;

(iii) Intentionally directing attacks against personnel, installations, material, units or vehicles involved in a humanitarian assistance or peacekeeping mission in accordance with the Charter of the United Nations, as long as they are entitled to the protection given to civilians or civilian objects under the international law of armed conflict;

(iv) Intentionally launching an attack in the knowledge that such attack will cause incidental loss of life or injury to civilians or damage to civilian objects or widespread, long-term and severe damage to the natural environment which would be clearly excessive in relation to the concrete and direct overall military advantage anticipated;

(v) Attacking or bombarding, by whatever means, towns, villages, dwellings or buildings which are undefended and which are not military objectives;

(vi) Killing or wounding a combatant who, having laid down his arms or having no longer means of defence, has surrendered at discretion;

(vii) Making improper use of a flag of truce, of the flag or of the military insignia and uniform of the enemy or of the United Nations, as well as of the distinctive emblems of the Geneva Conventions, resulting in death or serious personal injury;

(viii) The transfer, directly or indirectly, by the Occupying Power of parts of its own civilian population into the territory it occupies, or the deportation or transfer of all or parts of the population of the occupied territory within or outside this territory;

(ix) Intentionally directing attacks against buildings dedicated to religion, education, art, science or charitable purposes, historic monuments, hospitals and places where the sick and wounded are collected, provided they are not military objectives;

(x) Subjecting persons who are in the power of an adverse party to physical mutilation or to medical or scientific experiments of any kind which are neither justified by the medical, dental or hospital treatment of the person concerned nor carried out in his or her interest, and which cause death to or seriously endanger the health of such person or persons;

(xi) Killing or wounding treacherously individuals belonging to the hostile nation or army;

(xii) Declaring that no quarter will be given;

(xiii) Destroying or seizing the enemy's property unless such destruction or seizure be imperatively demanded by the necessities of war;

(xiv) Declaring abolished, suspended or inadmissible in a court of law the rights and actions of the nationals of the hostile party;

(xv) Compelling the nationals of the hostile party to take part in the operations of war directed against their own country, even if they were in the belligerent's service before the commencement of the war;

(xvi) Pillaging a town or place, even when taken by assault;

(xvii) Employing poison or poisoned weapons;

(xviii) Employing asphyxiating, poisonous or other gases, and all analogous liquids, materials or devices;

(xix) Employing bullets which expand or flatten easily in the human body, such as bullets with a hard envelope which does not entirely cover the core or is pierced with incisions;

(xx) Employing weapons, projectiles and material and methods of warfare which are of a nature to cause superfluous injury or unnecessary suffering or which are inherently indiscriminate in violation of the international law of armed conflict, provided that such weapons, projectiles and material and methods of warfare are the subject of a comprehensive prohibition and are included in an annex to this Statute, by an amendment in accordance with the relevant provisions set forth in articles 121 and 123;

(xxi) Committing outrages upon personal dignity, in particular humiliating and degrading treatment;

(xxii) Committing rape, sexual slavery, enforced prostitution, forced pregnancy, as defined in article 7, paragraph 2 (f), enforced sterilization, or any other form of sexual violence also constituting a grave breach of the Geneva Conventions;

(xxiii) Utilizing the presence of a civilian or other protected person to render certain points, areas or military forces immune from military operations;

(xxiv) Intentionally directing attacks against buildings, material, medical units and transport, and personnel using the distinctive emblems of the Geneva Conventions in conformity with international law;

(xxv) Intentionally using starvation of civilians as a method of warfare by depriving them of objects indispensable to their survival, including wilfully impeding relief supplies as provided for under the Geneva Conventions;

(xxvi) Conscripting or enlisting children under the age of fifteen years into the national armed forces or using them to participate actively in hostilities.

(c) In the case of an armed conflict not of an international character, serious violations of article 3 common to the four Geneva Conventions of 12 August 1949, namely, any of the following acts committed against persons taking no active part in the hostilities, including members of armed forces who have laid down their arms and those placed hors de combat by sickness, wounds, detention or any other cause:

(i) Violence to life and person, in particular murder of all kinds, mutilation, cruel treatment and torture;

(ii) Committing outrages upon personal dignity, in particular humiliating and degrading treatment;

(iii) Taking of hostages;

(iv) The passing of sentences and the carrying out of executions without previous judgement pronounced by a regularly constituted court, affording all judicial guarantees which are generally recognized as indispensable.

(d) Paragraph 2 (c) applies to armed conflicts not of an international character and thus does not apply to situations of internal disturbances and tensions, such as riots, isolated and sporadic acts of violence or other acts of a similar nature.

(e) Other serious violations of the laws and customs applicable in armed conflicts not of an international character, within the established framework of international law, namely, any of the following acts:

(i) Intentionally directing attacks against the civilian population as such or against individual civilians not taking direct part in hostilities;

(ii) Intentionally directing attacks against buildings, material, medical units and transport, and personnel using the distinctive emblems of the Geneva Conventions in conformity with international law;

(iii) Intentionally directing attacks against personnel, installations, material, units or vehicles involved in a humanitarian assistance or peacekeeping mission in accordance with the Charter of the United Nations, as long as they are entitled to the protection given to civilians or civilian objects under the international law of armed conflict;

(iv) Intentionally directing attacks against buildings dedicated to religion, education, art, science or charitable purposes, historic monuments, hospitals and places where the sick and wounded are collected, provided they are not military objectives;

(v) Pillaging a town or place, even when taken by assault;

(vi) Committing rape, sexual slavery, enforced prostitution, forced pregnancy, as defined in article 7, paragraph 2 (f), enforced sterilization, and any other form of sexual violence also constituting a serious violation of article 3 common to the four Geneva Conventions;

(vii) Conscripting or enlisting children under the age of fifteen years into armed forces or groups or using them to participate actively in hostilities;

(viii) Ordering the displacement of the civilian population for reasons related to the conflict, unless the security of the civilians involved or imperative military reasons so demand;

(ix) Killing or wounding treacherously a combatant adversary;

(x) Declaring that no quarter will be given;

(xi) Subjecting persons who are in the power of another party to the conflict to physical mutilation or to medical or scientific experiments of any kind which are neither justified by the medical, dental or hospital treatment of the person concerned nor carried out in his or her interest, and which cause death to or seriously endanger the health of such person or persons;

(xii) Destroying or seizing the property of an adversary unless such destruction or seizure be imperatively demanded by the necessities of the conflict;

(f) Paragraph 2 (e) applies to armed conflicts not of an international character and thus does not apply to situations of internal disturbances and tensions, such as riots, isolated and sporadic acts of violence or other acts of a similar nature. It applies to armed conflicts that take place in the territory of a State when there is protracted armed conflict between governmental authorities and organized armed groups or between such groups.

3. Nothing in paragraph 2 (c) and (e) shall affect the responsibility of a Government to maintain or re-establish law and order in the State or to defend the unity and territorial integrity of the State, by all legitimate means.

Article 9 – Elements of Crimes

1. Elements of Crimes shall assist the Court in the interpretation and application of articles 6, 7 and 8. They shall be adopted by a two-thirds majority of the members of the Assembly of States Parties.

2. Amendments to the Elements of Crimes may be proposed by:

(a) Any State Party;

(b) The judges acting by an absolute majority;

(c) The Prosecutor.

Such amendments shall be adopted by a two-thirds majority of the members of the Assembly of States Parties.

.3. The Elements of Crimes and amendments thereto shall be consistent with this Statute.

Article 10

Nothing in this Part shall be interpreted as limiting or prejudicing in any way existing or developing rules of international law for purposes other than this Statute.

Article 11 – Jurisdiction ratione temporis

1. The Court has jurisdiction only with respect to crimes committed after the entry into force of this Statute.

2. If a State becomes a Party to this Statute after its entry into force, the Court may exercise its jurisdiction only with respect to crimes committed after the entry into force of this Statute for that State, unless that State has made a declaration under article 12, paragraph 3.

Article 12 – Preconditions to the exercise of jurisdiction

1. A State which becomes a Party to this Statute thereby accepts the jurisdiction of the Court with respect to the crimes referred to in article 5.

2. In the case of article 13, paragraph (a) or (c), the Court may exercise its jurisdiction if one or more of the following States are Parties to this Statute or have accepted the jurisdiction of the Court in accordance with paragraph 3:

(a) The State on the territory of which the conduct in question occurred or, if the crime was committed on board a vessel or aircraft, the State of registration of that vessel or aircraft;

(b) The State of which the person accused of the crime is a national.

3. If the acceptance of a State which is not a Party to this Statute is required under paragraph 2, that State may, by declaration lodged with the Registrar, accept the exercise of jurisdiction by the Court with respect to the crime in question. The accepting State shall cooperate with the Court without any delay

or exception in accordance with Part 9.

Article 13 – Exercise of jurisdiction

The Court may exercise its jurisdiction with respect to a crime referred to in article 5 in accordance with the provisions of this Statute if:

(a) A situation in which one or more of such crimes appears to have been committed is referred to the Prosecutor by a State Party in accordance with article 14;

(b) A situation in which one or more of such crimes appears to have been committed is referred to the Prosecutor by the Security Council acting under Chapter VII of the Charter of the United Nations; or

(c) The Prosecutor has initiated an investigation in respect of such a crime in accordance with article 15.

Article 14 – Referral of a situation by a State Party

1. A State Party may refer to the Prosecutor a situation in which one or more crimes within the jurisdiction of the Court appear to have been committed requesting the Prosecutor to investigate the situation for the purpose of determining whether one or more specific persons should be charged with the commission of such crimes.

2. As far as possible, a referral shall specify the relevant circumstances and be accompanied by such supporting documentation as is available to the State referring the situation.

Article 15 – Prosecutor

1. The Prosecutor may initiate investigations proprio motu on the basis of information on crimes within the jurisdiction of the Court.

2. The Prosecutor shall analyse the seriousness of the information received. For this purpose, he or she may seek additional information from States, organs of the United Nations, intergovernmental or non-governmental organizations, or other reliable sources that he or she deems appropriate, and may receive written or oral testimony at the seat of the Court.

3. If the Prosecutor concludes that there is a reasonable basis to proceed with an investigation, he or she shall submit to the Pre-Trial Chamber a request for authorization of an investigation, together with any supporting material collected. Victims may make representations to the Pre-Trial Chamber, in

accordance with the Rules of Procedure and Evidence.

4. If the Pre-Trial Chamber, upon examination of the request and the supporting material, considers that there is a reasonable basis to proceed with an investigation, and that the case appears to fall within the jurisdiction of the Court, it shall authorize the commencement of the investigation, without prejudice to subsequent determinations by the Court with regard to the jurisdiction and admissibility of a case.

5. The refusal of the Pre-Trial Chamber to authorize the investigation shall not preclude the presentation of a subsequent request by the Prosecutor based on new facts or evidence regarding the same situation.

6. If, after the preliminary examination referred to in paragraphs 1 and 2, the Prosecutor concludes that the information provided does not constitute a reasonable basis for an investigation, he or she shall inform those who provided the information. This shall not preclude the Prosecutor from considering further information submitted to him or her regarding the same situation in the light of new facts or evidence.

Article 16 – Deferral of investigation or prosecution

No investigation or prosecution may be commenced or proceeded with under this Statute for a period of 12 months after the Security Council, in a resolution adopted under Chapter VII of the Charter of the United Nations, has requested the Court to that effect; that request may be renewed by the Council under the same conditions.

Article 17 – Issues of admissibility

1. Having regard to paragraph 10 of the Preamble and article 1, the Court shall determine that a case is inadmissible where:

(a) The case is being investigated or prosecuted by a State which has jurisdiction over it, unless the State is unwilling or unable genuinely to carry out the investigation or prosecution;

(b) The case has been investigated by a State which has jurisdiction over it and the State has decided not to prosecute the person concerned, unless the decision resulted from the unwillingness or inability of the State genuinely to prosecute;

(c) The person concerned has already been tried for conduct which is the subject of the complaint, and a trial by the Court is not permitted under article 20, paragraph 3;

(d) The case is not of sufficient gravity to justify further action by the Court.

2. In order to determine unwillingness in a particular case, the Court shall consider, having regard to the principles of due process recognized by international law, whether one or more of the following exist, as applicable:

(a) The proceedings were or are being undertaken or the national decision was made for the purpose of shielding the person concerned from criminal responsibility for crimes within the jurisdiction of the Court referred to in article 5;

(b) There has been an unjustified delay in the proceedings which in the circumstances is inconsistent with an intent to bring the person concerned to justice;

(c) The proceedings were not or are not being conducted independently or impartially, and they were or are being conducted in a manner which, in the circumstances, is inconsistent with an intent to bring the person concerned to justice.

3. In order to determine inability in a particular case, the Court shall consider whether, due to a total or substantial collapse or unavailability of its national judicial system, the State is unable to obtain the accused or the necessary evidence and testimony or otherwise unable to carry out its proceedings.

Article 18 – Preliminary rulings regarding admissibility

1. When a situation has been referred to the Court pursuant to article 13 (a) and the Prosecutor has determined that there would be a reasonable basis to commence an investigation, or the Prosecutor initiates an investigation pursuant to articles 13 (c) and 15, the Prosecutor shall notify all States Parties and those States which, taking into account the information available, would normally exercise jurisdiction over the crimes concerned. The Prosecutor may notify such States on a confidential basis and, where the Prosecutor believes it necessary to protect persons, prevent destruction of evidence or prevent the absconding of persons, may limit the scope of the information provided to States.

2. Within one month of receipt of that notification, a State may inform the Court that it is investigating or has investigated its nationals or others within its jurisdiction with respect to criminal acts which may constitute crimes referred to in article 5 and which relate to the information provided in the notification to States. At the request of that State, the Prosecutor shall defer to the State's investigation of those persons unless the Pre-Trial Chamber, on the application of the Prosecutor, decides to authorize the investigation.

3. The Prosecutor's deferral to a State's investigation shall be open to review by

the Prosecutor six months after the date of deferral or at any time when there has been a significant change of circumstances based on the State's unwillingness or inability genuinely to carry out the investigation.

4. The State concerned or the Prosecutor may appeal to the Appeals Chamber against a ruling of the Pre-Trial Chamber, in accordance with article 82. The appeal may be heard on an expedited basis.

5. When the Prosecutor has deferred an investigation in accordance with paragraph 2, the Prosecutor may request that the State concerned periodically inform the Prosecutor of the progress of its investigations and any subsequent prosecutions. States Parties shall respond to such requests without undue delay.

6. Pending a ruling by the Pre-Trial Chamber, or at any time when the Prosecutor has deferred an investigation under this article, the Prosecutor may, on an exceptional basis, seek authority from the Pre-Trial Chamber to pursue necessary investigative steps for the purpose of preserving evidence where there is a unique opportunity to obtain important evidence or there is a significant risk that such evidence may not be subsequently available.

7. A State which has challenged a ruling of the Pre-Trial Chamber under this article may challenge the admissibility of a case under article 19 on the grounds of additional significant facts or significant change of circumstances.

Article 19 – Challenges to the jurisdiction of the Court or the admissibility of a case

1. The Court shall satisfy itself that it has jurisdiction in any case brought before it. The Court may, on its own motion, determine the admissibility of a case in accordance with article 17.

2. Challenges to the admissibility of a case on the grounds referred to in article 17 or challenges to the jurisdiction of the Court may be made by:

(a) An accused or a person for whom a warrant of arrest or a summons to appear has been issued under article 58;

(b) A State which has jurisdiction over a case, on the ground that it is investigating or prosecuting the case or has investigated or prosecuted; or

(c) A State from which acceptance of jurisdiction is required under article 12.

3. The Prosecutor may seek a ruling from the Court regarding a question of jurisdiction or admissibility. In proceedings with respect to jurisdiction or admissibility, those who have referred the situation under article 13, as well as victims, may also submit observations to the Court.

4. The admissibility of a case or the jurisdiction of the Court may be challenged only once by any person or State referred to in paragraph 2. The challenge shall take place prior to or at the commencement of the trial. In exceptional circumstances, the Court may grant leave for a challenge to be brought more than once or at a time later than the commencement of the trial. Challenges to the admissibility of a case, at the commencement of a trial, or subsequently with the leave of the Court, may be based only on article 17, paragraph 1 (c).

5. A State referred to in paragraph 2 (b) and (c) shall make a challenge at the earliest opportunity.

6. Prior to the confirmation of the charges, challenges to the admissibility of a case or challenges to the jurisdiction of the Court shall be referred to the Pre-Trial Chamber. After confirmation of the charges, they shall be referred to the Trial Chamber. Decisions with respect to jurisdiction or admissibility may be appealed to the Appeals Chamber in accordance with article 82.

7. If a challenge is made by a State referred to in paragraph 2 (b) or (c), the Prosecutor shall suspend the investigation until such time as the Court makes a determination in accordance with article 17.

8. Pending a ruling by the Court, the Prosecutor may seek authority from the Court:

(a) To pursue necessary investigative steps of the kind referred to in article 18, paragraph 6;

(b) To take a statement or testimony from a witness or complete the collection and examination of evidence which had begun prior to the making of the challenge; and

(c) In cooperation with the relevant States, to prevent the absconding of persons in respect of whom the Prosecutor has already requested a warrant of arrest under article 58.

9. The making of a challenge shall not affect the validity of any act performed by the Prosecutor or any order or warrant issued by the Court prior to the making of the challenge.

10. If the Court has decided that a case is inadmissible under article 17, the Prosecutor may submit a request for a review of the decision when he or she is fully satisfied that new facts have arisen which negate the basis on which the case had previously been found inadmissible under article 17.

11. If the Prosecutor, having regard to the matters referred to in article 17, defers an investigation, the Prosecutor may request that the relevant State make available to the Prosecutor information on the proceedings. That information shall, at the request of the State concerned, be confidential. If the

Prosecutor thereafter decides to proceed with an investigation, he or she shall notify the State to which deferral of the proceedings has taken place.

Article 20 – Ne bis in idem

1. Except as provided in this Statute, no person shall be tried before the Court with respect to conduct which formed the basis of crimes for which the person has been convicted or acquitted by the Court.

2. No person shall be tried by another court for a crime referred to in article 5 for which that person has already been convicted or acquitted by the Court.

3. No person who has been tried by another court for conduct also proscribed under article 6, 7 or 8 shall be tried by the Court with respect to the same conduct unless the proceedings in the other court:

(a) Were for the purpose of shielding the person concerned from criminal responsibility for crimes within the jurisdiction of the Court; or

(b) Otherwise were not conducted independently or impartially in accordance with the norms of due process recognized by international law and were conducted in a manner which, in the circumstances, was inconsistent with an intent to bring the person concerned to justice.

Article 21 – Applicable law

1. The Court shall apply:

(a) In the first place, this Statute, Elements of Crimes and its Rules of Procedure and Evidence;

(b) In the second place, where appropriate, applicable treaties and the principles and rules of international law, including the established principles of the international law of armed conflict;

(c) Failing that, general principles of law derived by the Court from national laws of legal systems of the world including, as appropriate, the national laws of States that would normally exercise jurisdiction over the crime, provided that those principles are not inconsistent with this Statute and with international law and internationally recognized norms and standards.

2. The Court may apply principles and rules of law as interpreted in its previous decisions.

3. The application and interpretation of law pursuant to this article must be consistent with internationally recognized human rights, and be without any

adverse distinction founded on grounds such as gender as defined in article 7, paragraph 3, age, race, colour, language, religion or belief, political or other opinion, national, ethnic or social origin, wealth, birth or other status.

PART 3. GENERAL PRINCIPLES OF CRIMINAL LAW

Article 22 – Nullum crimen sine lege

1. A person shall not be criminally responsible under this Statute unless the conduct in question constitutes, at the time it takes place, a crime within the jurisdiction of the Court.

2. The definition of a crime shall be strictly construed and shall not be extended by analogy. In case of ambiguity, the definition shall be interpreted in favour of the person being investigated, prosecuted or convicted.

3. This article shall not affect the characterization of any conduct as criminal under international law independently of this Statute.

Article 23 – Nulla poena sine lege

A person convicted by the Court may be punished only in accordance with this Statute.

Article 24 – Non-retroactivity ratione personae

1. No person shall be criminally responsible under this Statute for conduct prior to the entry into force of the Statute.

2. In the event of a change in the law applicable to a given case prior to a final judgement, the law more favourable to the person being investigated, prosecuted or convicted shall apply.

Article 25 – Individual criminal responsibility

1. The Court shall have jurisdiction over natural persons pursuant to this Statute.

2. A person who commits a crime within the jurisdiction of the Court shall be individually responsible and liable for punishment in accordance with this Statute.

3. In accordance with this Statute, a person shall be criminally responsible and liable for punishment for a crime within the jurisdiction of the Court if that

person:

(a) Commits such a crime, whether as an individual, jointly with another or through another person, regardless of whether that other person is criminally responsible;

(b) Orders, solicits or induces the commission of such a crime which in fact occurs or is attempted;

(c) For the purpose of facilitating the commission of such a crime, aids, abets or otherwise assists in its commission or its attempted commission, including providing the means for its commission;

(d) In any other way contributes to the commission or attempted commission of such a crime by a group of persons acting with a common purpose. Such contribution shall be intentional and shall either:

(i) Be made with the aim of furthering the criminal activity or criminal purpose of the group, where such activity or purpose involves the commission of a crime within the jurisdiction of the Court; or

(ii) Be made in the knowledge of the intention of the group to commit the crime;

(e) In respect of the crime of genocide, directly and publicly incites others to commit genocide;

(f) Attempts to commit such a crime by taking action that commences its execution by means of a substantial step, but the crime does not occur because of circumstances independent of the person's intentions. However, a person who abandons the effort to commit the crime or otherwise prevents the completion of the crime shall not be liable for punishment under this Statute for the attempt to commit that crime if that person completely and voluntarily gave up the criminal purpose.

4. No provision in this Statute relating to individual criminal responsibility shall affect the responsibility of States under international law.

Article 26 – Exclusion of jurisdiction over persons under eighteen

The Court shall have no jurisdiction over any person who was under the age of 18 at the time of the alleged commission of a crime.

Article 27 – Irrelevance of official capacity

1. This Statute shall apply equally to all persons without any distinction based on official capacity. In particular, official capacity as a Head of State or Government, a member of a Government or parliament, an elected representative or a government official shall in no case exempt a person from criminal responsibility under this Statute, nor shall it, in and of itself, constitute a ground for reduction of sentence.

2. Immunities or special procedural rules which may attach to the official capacity of a person, whether under national or international law, shall not bar the Court from exercising its jurisdiction over such a person.

Article 28 – Responsibility of commanders and other superiors

In addition to other grounds of criminal responsibility under this Statute for crimes within the jurisdiction of the Court:

1. A military commander or person effectively acting as a military commander shall be criminally responsible for crimes within the jurisdiction of the Court committed by forces under his or her effective command and control, or effective authority and control as the case may be, as a result of his or her failure to exercise control properly over such forces, where:

(a) That military commander or person either knew or, owing to the circumstances at the time, should have known that the forces were committing or about to commit such crimes; and

(b) That military commander or person failed to take all necessary and reasonable measures within his or her power to prevent or repress their commission or to submit the matter to the competent authorities for investigation and prosecution.

2. With respect to superior and subordinate relationships not described in paragraph 1, a superior shall be criminally responsible for crimes within the jurisdiction of the Court committed by subordinates under his or her effective authority and control, as a result of his or her failure to exercise control properly over such subordinates, where:

(a) The superior either knew, or consciously disregarded information which clearly indicated, that the subordinates were committing or about to commit such crimes;

(b) The crimes concerned activities that were within the effective responsibility and control of the superior; and

(c) The superior failed to take all necessary and reasonable measures within his or her power to prevent or repress their commission or to submit the matter to the competent authorities for investigation and prosecution.

Article 29 – Non-applicability of statute of limitations

The crimes within the jurisdiction of the Court shall not be subject to any statute of limitations.

Article 30 – Mental element

1. Unless otherwise provided, a person shall be criminally responsible and liable for punishment for a crime within the jurisdiction of the Court only if the material elements are committed with intent and knowledge.

2. For the purposes of this article, a person has intent where:

(a) In relation to conduct, that person means to engage in the conduct;

(b) In relation to a consequence, that person means to cause that consequence or is aware that it will occur in the ordinary course of events.

3. For the purposes of this article, "knowledge" means awareness that a circumstance exists or a consequence will occur in the ordinary course of events. "Know" and "knowingly" shall be construed accordingly.

Article 31 – Grounds for excluding criminal responsibility

1. In addition to other grounds for excluding criminal responsibility provided for in this Statute, a person shall not be criminally responsible if, at the time of that person' conduct:

(a) The person suffers from a mental disease or defect that destroys that person's capacity to appreciate the unlawfulness or nature of his or her conduct, or capacity to control his or her conduct to conform to the requirements of law;

(b) The person is in a state of intoxication that destroys that person's capacity to appreciate the unlawfulness or nature of his or her conduct, or capacity to control his or her conduct to conform to the requirements of law, unless the person has become voluntarily intoxicated under such circumstances that the person knew, or disregarded the risk, that, as a result of the intoxication, he or she was likely to engage in conduct constituting a crime within the jurisdiction of the Court;

(c) The person acts reasonably to defend himself or herself or another person or, in the case of war crimes, property which is essential for the survival of the person or another person or property which is essential for accomplishing a military mission, against an imminent and unlawful use of force in a manner proportionate to the degree of danger to the person or the other person or property protected. The fact that the person was involved in a defensive operation conducted by forces shall not in itself constitute a ground for excluding criminal responsibility under this subparagraph;

(d) The conduct which is alleged to constitute a crime within the jurisdiction of the Court has been caused by duress resulting from a threat of imminent death or of continuing or imminent serious bodily harm against that person or another person, and the person acts necessarily and reasonably to avoid this threat, provided that the person does not intend to cause a greater harm than the one sought to be avoided. Such a threat may either be:

(i) Made by other persons; or

(ii) Constituted by other circumstances beyond that person's control.

2. The Court shall determine the applicability of the grounds for excluding criminal responsibility provided for in this Statute to the case before it.

3. At trial, the Court may consider a ground for excluding criminal responsibility other than those referred to in paragraph 1 where such a ground is derived from applicable law as set forth in article 21. The procedures relating to the consideration of such a ground shall be provided for in the Rules of Procedure and Evidence.

Article 32 – Mistake of fact or mistake of law

1. A mistake of fact shall be a ground for excluding criminal responsibility only if it negates the mental element required by the crime.

2. A mistake of law as to whether a particular type of conduct is a crime within the jurisdiction of the Court shall not be a ground for excluding criminal responsibility. A mistake of law may, however, be a ground for excluding criminal responsibility if it negates the mental element required by such a crime, or as provided for in article 33.

Article 33 – Superior orders and prescription of law

1. The fact that a crime within the jurisdiction of the Court has been committed by a person pursuant to an order of a Government or of a superior, whether military or civilian, shall not relieve that person of criminal responsibility unless:

(a) The person was under a legal obligation to obey orders of the Government or the superior in question;

(b) The person did not know that the order was unlawful; and

(c) The order was not manifestly unlawful.

2. For the purposes of this article, orders to commit genocide or crimes against humanity are manifestly unlawful.

PART 4. COMPOSITION AND ADMINISTRATION OF THE COURT

Article 34 – Organs of the Court

The Court shall be composed of the following organs:

(a) The Presidency;

(b) An Appeals Division, a Trial Division and a Pre-Trial Division;

(c) The Office of the Prosecutor;

(d) The Registry.

Article 35 – Service of judges

1. All judges shall be elected as full-time members of the Court and shall be available to serve on that basis from the commencement of their terms of office.

2. The judges composing the Presidency shall serve on a full -time basis as soon as they are elected.

3. The Presidency may, on the basis of the workload of the Court and in consultation with its members, decide from time to time to what extent the remaining judges shall be required to serve on a full-time basis. Any such arrangement shall be without prejudice to the provisions of article 40.

4. The financial arrangements for judges not required to serve on a full-time basis shall be made in accordance with article 49.

Article 36 – Qualifications, nomination and election of judges

1. Subject to the provisions of paragraph 2, there shall be 18 judges of the Court.

2.(a) The Presidency, acting on behalf of the Court, may propose an increase in the number of judges specified in paragraph 1, indicating the reasons why this is considered necessary and appropriate. The Registrar shall promptly circulate any such proposal to all States Parties.

(b) Any such proposal shall then be considered at a meeting of the Assembly of States Parties to be convened in accordance with article 112. The proposal shall be considered adopted if approved at the meeting by a vote of two-thirds of the members of the Assembly of States Parties and shall enter into force at such time as decided by the Assembly of States Parties.

(c) (i) Once a proposal for an increase in the number of judges has been adopted under subparagraph (b), the election of the additional judges shall take place at the next session of the Assembly of States Parties in accordance with paragraphs 3 to 8 inclusive, and article 37, paragraph 2;

(ii) Once a proposal for an increase in the number of judges has been adopted and brought into effect under subparagraphs (b) and (c) (i), it shall be open to the Presidency at any time thereafter, if the workload of the Court justifies it, to propose a reduction in the number of judges, provided that the number of judges shall not be reduced below that specified in paragraph 1. The proposal shall be dealt with in accordance with the procedure laid down in subparagraphs (a) and (b). In the event that the proposal is adopted, the number of judges shall be progressively decreased as the terms of office of serving judges expire, until the necessary number has been reached.

3. (a) The judges shall be chosen from among persons of high moral character, impartiality and integrity who possess the qualifications required in their respective States for appointment to the highest judicial offices.

(b) Every candidate for election to the Court shall:

(i) Have established competence in criminal law and procedure, and the necessary relevant experience, whether as judge, prosecutor, advocate or in other similar capacity, in criminal proceedings; or

(ii) Have established competence in relevant areas of international law such as international humanitarian law and the law of human rights, and extensive experience in a professional legal capacity which is of relevance to the judicial work of the Court;

(c) Every candidate for election to the Court shall have an excellent knowledge of and be fluent in at least one of the working languages of the

Court.

4. (a) Nominations of candidates for election to the Court may be made by any State Party to this Statute, and shall be made either:

(i) By the procedure for the nomination of candidates for appointment to the highest judicial offices in the State in question; or

(ii) By the procedure provided for the nomination of candidates for the International Court of Justice in the Statute of that Court.

Nominations shall be accompanied by a statement in the necessary detail specifying how the candidate fulfils the requirements of paragraph 3.

(b) Each State Party may put forward one candidate for any given election who need not necessarily be a national of that State Party but shall in any case be a national of a State Party.

(c) The Assembly of States Parties may decide to establish, if appropriate, an Advisory Committee on nominations. In that event, the Committee's composition and mandate shall be established by the Assembly of States Parties.

5. For the purposes of the election, there shall be two lists of candidates:
List A containing the names of candidates with the qualifications specified in paragraph 3 (b) (i); and

List B containing the names of candidates with the qualifications specified in paragraph 3 (b) (ii).

A candidate with sufficient qualifications for both lists may choose on which list to appear. At the first election to the Court, at least nine judges shall be elected from list A and at least five judges from list B. Subsequent elections shall be so organized as to maintain the equivalent proportion on the Court of judges qualified on the two lists.

6. (a) The judges shall be elected by secret ballot at a meeting of the Assembly of States Parties convened for that purpose under article 112. Subject to paragraph 7, the persons elected to the Court shall be the 18 candidates who obtain the highest number of votes and a two-thirds majority of the States Parties present and voting.

(b) In the event that a sufficient number of judges is not elected on the first ballot, successive ballots shall be held in accordance with the procedures laid down in subparagraph (a) until the remaining places have been filled.

7. No two judges may be nationals of the same State. A person who, for the purposes of membership in the Court, could be regarded as a national of more

than one State shall be deemed to be a national of the State in which that person ordinarily exercises civil and political rights.

8. (a) The States Parties shall, in the selection of judges, take into account the need, within the membership of the Court, for:

(i) The representation of the principal legal systems of the world;

(ii) Equitable geographical representation; and

(iii) A fair representation of female and male judges.

(b) States Parties shall also take into account the need to include judges with legal expertise on specific issues, including, but not limited to, violence against women or children.

9. (a) Subject to subparagraph (b), judges shall hold office for a term of nine years and, subject to subparagraph (c) and to article 37, paragraph 2, shall not be eligible for re-election.

(b) At the first election, one third of the judges elected shall be selected by lot to serve for a term of three years; one third of the judges elected shall be selected by lot to serve for a term of six years; and the remainder shall serve for a term of nine years.

(c) A judge who is selected to serve for a term of three years under subparagraph (b) shall be eligible for re-election for a full term.

10. Notwithstanding paragraph 9, a judge assigned to a Trial or Appeals Chamber in accordance with article 39 shall continue in office to complete any trial or appeal the hearing of which has already commenced before that Chamber.

Article 37 – Judicial vacancies

1. In the event of a vacancy, an election shall be held in accordance with article 36 to fill the vacancy.

2. A judge elected to fill a vacancy shall serve for the remainder of the predecessors term and, if that period is three years or less, shall be eligible for re-election for a full term under article 36.

Article 38 – The Presidency

1. The President and the First and Second Vice-Presidents shall be elected by an absolute majority of the judges. They shall each serve for a term of three

years or until the end of their respective terms of office as judges, whichever expires earlier. They shall be eligible for re-election once.

2. The First Vice-President shall act in place of the President in the event that the President is unavailable or disqualified. The Second Vice-President shall act in place of the President in the event that both the President and the First Vice-President are unavailable or disqualified.

3. The President, together with the First and Second Vice-Presidents, shall constitute the Presidency, which shall be responsible for:

(a) The proper administration of the Court, with the exception of the Office of the Prosecutor; and

(b) The other functions conferred upon it in accordance with this Statute.

4. In discharging its responsibility under paragraph 3 (a), the Presidency shall coordinate with and seek the concurrence of the Prosecutor on all matters of mutual concern.

Article 39 – Chambers

1. As soon as possible after the election of the judges, the Court shall organize itself into the divisions specified in article 34, paragraph (b). The Appeals Division shall be composed of the President and four other judges, the Trial Division of not less than six judges and the Pre-Trial Division of not less than six judges. The assignment of judges to divisions shall be based on the nature of the functions to be performed by each division and the qualifications and experience of the judges elected to the Court, in such a way that each division shall contain an appropriate combination of expertise in criminal law and procedure and in international law. The Trial and Pre-Trial Divisions shall be composed predominantly of judges with criminal trial experience.

2. (a) The judicial functions of the Court shall be carried out in each division by Chambers.

(b) (i) The Appeals Chamber shall be composed of all the judges of the Appeals Division;

ii) The functions of the Trial Chamber shall be carried out by three judges of the Trial Division;

(iii) The functions of the Pre -Trial Chamber shall be carried out either by three judges of the Pre -Trial Division or by a single judge of that division in accordance with this Statute and the Rules of Procedure and Evidence;

(c) Nothing in this paragraph shall preclude the simultaneous constitution of more than one Trial Chamber or Pre - Trial Chamber when the efficient management of the Court's workload so requires.

3. (a) Judges assigned to the Trial and Pre -Trial Divisions shall serve in those divisions for a period of three years, and thereafter until the completion of any case the hearing of which has already commenced in the division concerned.

(b) Judges assigned to the Appeals Division shall serve in that division for their entire term of office.

4. Judges assigned to the Appeals Division shall serve only in that division. Nothing in this article shall, however, preclude the temporary attachment of judges from the Trial Division to the Pre-Trial Division or vice versa, if the Presidency considers that the efficient management of the Court's workload so requires, provided that under no circumstances shall a judge who has participated in the pre-trial phase of a case be eligible to sit on the Trial Chamber hearing that case.

Article 40 – Independence of the judges

1. The judges shall be independent in the performance of their functions.

2. Judges shall not engage in any activity which is likely to interfere with their judicial functions or to affect confidence in their independence.

3. Judges required to serve on a full-time basis at the seat of the Court shall not engage in any other occupation of a professional nature.

4. Any question regarding the application of paragraphs 2 and 3 shall be decided by an absolute majority of the judges. Where any such question concerns an individual judge, that judge shall not take part in the decision.

Article 41 – Excusing and disqualification of judges

1. The Presidency may, at the request of a judge, excuse that judge from the exercise of a function under this Statute, in accordance with the Rules of Procedure and Evidence.

2. (a) A judge shall not participate in any case in which his or her impartiality might reasonably be doubted on any ground. A judge shall be disqualified from a case in accordance with this paragraph if, inter alia, that judge has previously been involved in any capacity in that case before the Court or in a related criminal case at the national level involving the person being investigated or prosecuted. A judge shall also be disqualified on such other grounds as may be provided for in the Rules of Procedure and Evidence.

(b) The Prosecutor or the person being investigated or prosecuted may request the disqualification of a judge under this paragraph.

(c) Any question as to the disqualification of a judge shall be decided by an absolute majority of the judges. The challenged judge shall be entitled to present his or her comments on the matter, but shall not take part in the decision.

Article 42 – The Office of the Prosecutor

1. The Office of the Prosecutor shall act independently as a separate organ of the Court. It shall be responsible for receiving referrals and any substantiated information on crimes within the jurisdiction of the Court, for examining them and for conducting investigations and prosecutions before the Court. A member of the Office shall not seek or act on instructions from any external source.

2. The Office shall be headed by the Prosecutor. The Prosecutor shall have full authority over the management and administration of the Office, including the staff, facilities and other resources thereof. The Prosecutor shall be assisted by one or more Deputy Prosecutors, who shall be entitled to carry out any of the acts required of the Prosecutor under this Statute. The Prosecutor and the Deputy Prosecutors shall be of different nationalities. They shall serve on a full-time basis.

3. The Prosecutor and the Deputy Prosecutors shall be persons of high moral character, be highly competent in and have extensive practical experience in the prosecution or trial of criminal cases. They shall have an excellent knowledge of and be fluent in at least one of the working languages of the Court.

4. The Prosecutor shall be elected by secret ballot by an absolute majority of the members of the Assembly of States Parties. The Deputy Prosecutors shall be elected in the same way from a list of candidates provided by the Prosecutor. The Prosecutor shall nominate three candidates for each position of Deputy Prosecutor to be filled. Unless a shorter term is decided upon at the time of their election, the Prosecutor and the Deputy Prosecutors shall hold office for a term of nine years and shall not be eligible for re-election.

5. Neither the Prosecutor nor a Deputy Prosecutor shall engage in any activity which is likely to interfere with his or her prosecutorial functions or to affect confidence in his or her independence. They shall not engage in any other occupation of a professional nature.

6. The Presidency may excuse the Prosecutor or a Deputy Prosecutor, at his or her request, from acting in a particular case.

7. Neither the Prosecutor nor a Deputy Prosecutor shall participate in any matter in which their impartiality might reasonably be doubted on any ground.

They shall be disqualified from a case in accordance with this paragraph if, inter alia, they have previously been involved in any capacity in that case before the Court or in a related criminal case at the national level involving the person being investigated or prosecuted.

8. Any question as to the disqualification of the Prosecutor or a Deputy Prosecutor shall be decided by the Appeals Chamber.

(a) The person being investigated or prosecuted may at any time request the disqualification of the Prosecutor or a Deputy Prosecutor on the grounds set out in this article;

(b) The Prosecutor or the Deputy Prosecutor, as appropriate, shall be entitled to present his or her comments on the matter;

9. The Prosecutor shall appoint advisers with legal expertise on specific issues, including, but not limited to, sexual and gender violence and violence against children.

Article 43 – The Registry

1. The Registry shall be responsible for the non-judicial aspects of the administration and servicing of the Court, without prejudice to the functions and powers of the Prosecutor in accordance with article 42.

2. The Registry shall be headed by the Registrar, who shall be the principal administrative officer of the Court. The Registrar shall exercise his or her functions under the authority of the President of the Court.

3. The Registrar and the Deputy Registrar shall be persons of high moral character, be highly competent and have an excellent knowledge of and be fluent in at least one of the working languages of the Court.

4. The judges shall elect the Registrar by an absolute majority by secret ballot, taking into account any recommendation by the Assembly of States Parties. If the need arises and upon the recommendation of the Registrar, the judges shall elect, in the same manner, a Deputy Registrar.

5. The Registrar shall hold office for a term of five years, shall be eligible for re-election once and shall serve on a full-time basis. The Deputy Registrar shall hold office for a term of five years or such shorter term as may be decided upon by an absolute majority of the judges, and may be elected on the basis that the Deputy Registrar shall be called upon to serve as required.

6. The Registrar shall set up a Victims and Witnesses Unit within the Registry. This Unit shall provide, in consultation with the Office of the Prosecutor, protective measures and security arrangements, counselling and other

appropriate assistance for witnesses, victims who appear before the Court and others who are at risk on account of testimony given by such witnesses. The Unit shall include staff with expertise in trauma, including trauma related to crimes of sexual violence.

Article 44 – Staff

1. The Prosecutor and the Registrar shall appoint such qualified staff as may be required to their respective offices. In the case of the Prosecutor, this shall include the appointment of investigators.

2. In the employment of staff, the Prosecutor and the Registrar shall ensure the highest standards of efficiency, competency and integrity, and shall have regard, mutatis mutandis, to the criteria set forth in article 36, paragraph 8.

3. The Registrar, with the agreement of the Presidency and the Prosecutor, shall propose Staff Regulations which include the terms and conditions upon which the staff of the Court shall be appointed, remunerated and dismissed. The Staff Regulations shall be approved by the Assembly of States Parties.

4. The Court may, in exceptional circumstances, employ the expertise of gratis personnel offered by States Parties, intergovernmental organizations or non-governmental organizations to assist with the work of any of the organs of the Court. The Prosecutor may accept any such offer on behalf of the Office of the Prosecutor. Such gratis personnel shall be employed in accordance with guidelines to be established by the Assembly of States Parties.

Article 45 – Solemn undertaking

Before taking up their respective duties under this Statute, the judges, the Prosecutor, the Deputy Prosecutors, the Registrar and the Deputy Registrar shall each make a solemn undertaking in open court to exercise his or her respective functions impartially and conscientiously.

Article 46 – Removal from office

1. A judge, the Prosecutor, a Deputy Prosecutor, the Registrar or the Deputy Registrar shall be removed from office if a decision to this effect is made in accordance with paragraph 2, in cases where that person:

(a) Is found to have committed serious misconduct or a serious breach of his or her duties under this Statute, as provided for in the Rules of Procedure and Evidence; or

(b) Is unable to exercise the functions required by this Statute.

2. A decision as to the removal from office of a judge, the Prosecutor or a Deputy Prosecutor under paragraph 1 shall be made by the Assembly of States Parties, by secret ballot:

(a) In the case of a judge, by a two-thirds majority of the States Parties upon a recommendation adopted by a two-thirds majority of the other judges;

(b) In the case of the Prosecutor, by an absolute majority of the States Parties;

(c) In the case of a Deputy Prosecutor, by an absolute majority of the States Parties upon the recommendation of the Prosecutor.

3. A decision as to the removal from office of the Registrar or Deputy Registrar shall be made by an absolute majority of the judges.

4. A judge, Prosecutor, Deputy Prosecutor, Registrar or Deputy Registrar whose conduct or ability to exercise the functions of the office as required by this Statute is challenged under this article shall have full opportunity to present and receive evidence and to make submissions in accordance with the Rules of Procedure and Evidence. The person in question shall not otherwise participate in the consideration of the matter.

Article 47 – Disciplinary measures

A judge, Prosecutor, Deputy Prosecutor, Registrar or Deputy Registrar who has committed misconduct of a less serious nature than that set out in article 46, paragraph 1, shall be subject to disciplinary measures, in accordance with the Rules of Procedure and Evidence.

Article 48 – Privileges and immunities

1. The Court shall enjoy in the territory of each State Party such privileges and immunities as are necessary for the fulfilment of its purposes.

2. The judges, the Prosecutor, the Deputy Prosecutors and the Registrar shall, when engaged on or with respect to the business of the Court, enjoy the same privileges and immunities as are accorded to heads of diplomatic missions and shall, after the expiry of their terms of office, continue to be accorded immunity from legal process of every kind in respect of words spoken or written and acts performed by them in their official capacity.

3. The Deputy Registrar, the staff of the Office of the Prosecutor and the staff of the Registry shall enjoy the privileges and immunities and facilities necessary for the performance of their functions, in accordance with the agreement on the privileges and immunities of the Court.

4. Counsel, experts, witnesses or any other person required to be present at the seat of the Court shall be accorded such treatment as is necessary for the proper functioning of the Court, in accordance with the agreement on the privileges and immunities of the Court.

5. The privileges and immunities of:

(a) A judge or the Prosecutor may be waived by an absolute majority of the judges;

(b) The Registrar may be waived by the Presidency;

(c) The Deputy Prosecutors and staff of the Office of the Prosecutor may be waived by the Prosecutor;

(d) The Deputy Registrar and staff of the Registry may be waived by the Registrar.

Article 49 – Salaries, allowances and expenses

The judges, the Prosecutor, the Deputy Prosecutors, the Registrar and the Deputy Registrar shall receive such salaries, allowances and expenses as may be decided upon by the Assembly of States Parties. These salaries and allowances shall not be reduced during their terms of office.

Article 50 – Official and working languages

1. The official languages of the Court shall be Arabic, Chinese, English, French, Russian and Spanish. The judgements of the Court, as well as other decisions resolving fundamental issues before the Court, shall be published in the official languages. The Presidency shall, in accordance with the criteria established by the Rules of Procedure and Evidence, determine which decisions may be considered as resolving fundamental issues for the purposes of this paragraph.

2. The working languages of the Court shall be English and French. The Rules of Procedure and Evidence shall determine the cases in which other official languages may be used as working languages.

3. At the request of any party to a proceeding or a State allowed to intervene in a proceeding, the Court shall authorize a language other than English or French to be used by such a party or State, provided that the Court considers such authorization to be adequately justified.

Article 51 – Rules of Procedure and Evidence

1. The Rules of Procedure and Evidence shall enter into force upon adoption by a two - thirds majority of the members of the Assembly of States Parties.

2. Amendments to the Rules of Procedure and Evidence may be proposed by:

(a) Any State Party;

(b) The judges acting by an absolute majority; or

(c) The Prosecutor.

Such amendments shall enter into force upon adoption by a two-thirds majority of the members of the Assembly of States Parties.

3. After the adoption of the Rules of Procedure and Evidence, in urgent cases where the Rules do not provide for a specific situation before the Court, the judges may, by a two - thirds majority, draw up provisional Rules to be applied until adopted, amended or rejected at the next ordinary or special session of the Assembly of States Parties.

4. The Rules of Procedure and Evidence, amendments thereto and any provisional Rule shall be consistent with this Statute. Amendments to the Rules of Procedure and Evidence as well as provisional Rules shall not be applied retroactively to the detriment of the person who is being investigated or prosecuted or who has been convicted.

5. In the event of conflict between the Statute and the Rules of Procedure and Evidence, the Statute shall prevail.

Article 52 – Regulations of the Court

1. The judges shall, in accordance with this Statute and the Rules of Procedure and Evidence, adopt, by an absolute majority, the Regulations of the Court necessary for its routine functioning.

2. The Prosecutor and the Registrar shall be consulted in the elaboration of the Regulations and any amendments thereto.

3. The Regulations and any amendments thereto shall take effect upon adoption unless otherwise decided by the judges. Immediately upon adoption, they shall be circulated to States Parties for comments. If within six months there are no objections from a majority of States Parties, they shall remain in force.

PART 5. INVESTIGATION AND PROSECUTION

Article 53– Initiation of an investigation

1. The Prosecutor shall, having evaluated the information made available to him or her, initiate an investigation unless he or she determines that there is no reasonable basis to proceed under this Statute. In deciding whether to initiate an investigation, the Prosecutor shall consider whether:

(a) The information available to the Prosecutor provides a reasonable basis to believe that a crime within the jurisdiction of the Court has been or is being committed;

(b) The case is or would be admissible under article 17; and

(c) Taking into account the gravity of the crime and the interests of victims, there are nonetheless substantial reasons to believe that an investigation would not serve the interests of justice.

If the Prosecutor determines that there is no reasonable basis to proceed and his or her determination is based solely on subparagraph (c) above, he or she shall inform the Pre-Trial Chamber.

2. If, upon investigation, the Prosecutor concludes that there is not a sufficient basis for a prosecution because:

(a) There is not a sufficient legal or factual basis to seek a warrant or summons under article 58;

(b) The case is inadmissible under article 17; or

(c) A prosecution is not in the interests of justice, taking into account all the circumstances, including the gravity of the crime, the interests of victims and the age or infirmity of the alleged perpetrator, and his or her role in the alleged crime;

The Prosecutor shall inform the Pre-Trial Chamber and the State making a referral under article 14 or the Security Council in a case under article 13, paragraph (b), of his or her conclusion and the reasons for the conclusion.

3. (a) At the request of the State making a referral under article 14 or the Security Council under article 13, paragraph (b), the Pre-Trial Chamber may review a decision of the Prosecutor under paragraph 1 or 2 not to proceed and may request the Prosecutor to reconsider that decision.

(b) In addition, the Pre-Trial Chamber may, on its own initiative, review a decision of the Prosecutor not to proceed if it is based solely on paragraph 1 (c) or 2 (c). In such a case, the decision of the Prosecutor shall be effective only if confirmed by the Pre-Trial Chamber.

4. The Prosecutor may, at any time, reconsider a decision whether to initiate an investigation or prosecution based on new facts or information.

Article 54 – Duties and powers of the Prosecutor with respect to investigations

1. The Prosecutor shall:

(a) In order to establish the truth, extend the investigation to cover all facts and evidence relevant to an assessment of whether there is criminal responsibility under this Statute, and, in doing so, investigate incriminating and exonerating circumstances equally;

(b) Take appropriate measures to ensure the effective investigation and prosecution of crimes within the jurisdiction of the Court, and in doing so, respect the interests and personal circumstances of victims and witnesses, including age, gender as defined in article 7, paragraph 3, and health, and take into account the nature of the crime, in particular where it involves sexual violence, gender violence or violence against children; and

(c) Fully respect the rights of persons arising under this Statute.

2. The Prosecutor may conduct investigations on the territory of a State:

(a) In accordance with the provisions of Part 9; or

(b) As authorized by the Pre-Trial Chamber under article 57, paragraph 3 (d).

3. The Prosecutor may:

(a) Collect and examine evidence;

(b) Request the presence of and question persons being investigated, victims and witnesses;

(c) Seek the cooperation of any State or intergovernmental organization or arrangement in accordance with its respective competence and/or mandate;

(d) Enter into such arrangements or agreements, not inconsistent with this Statute, as may be necessary to facilitate the cooperation of a State, intergovernmental organization or person;

(e) Agree not to disclose, at any stage of the proceedings, documents or information that the Prosecutor obtains on the condition of confidentiality and solely for the purpose of generating new evidence, unless the provider of the information consents; and

(f) Take necessary measures, or request that necessary measures be taken, to ensure the confidentiality of information, the protection of any person or the preservation of evidence.

Article 55– Rights of persons during an investigation

1. In respect of an investigation under this Statute, a person:

(a) Shall not be compelled to incriminate himself or herself or to confess guilt;

(b) Shall not be subjected to any form of coercion, duress or threat, to torture or to any other form of cruel, inhuman or degrading treatment or punishment; and

(c) Shall, if questioned in a language other than a language the person fully understands and speaks, have, free of any cost, the assistance of a competent interpreter and such translations as are necessary to meet the requirements of fairness;

(d) Shall not be subjected to arbitrary arrest or detention; and shall not be deprived of his or her liberty except on such grounds and in accordance with such procedures as are established in the Statute.

2. Where there are grounds to believe that a person has committed a crime within the jurisdiction of the Court and that person is about to be questioned either by the Prosecutor, or by national authorities pursuant to a request made under Part 9 of this Statute, that person shall also have the following rights of which he or she shall be informed prior to being questioned:

(a) To be informed, prior to being questioned, that there are grounds to believe that he or she has committed a crime within the jurisdiction of the Court;

(b) To remain silent, without such silence being a consideration in the determination of guilt or innocence;

(c) To have legal assistance of the person's choosing, or, if the person does not have legal assistance, to have legal assistance assigned to him or her, in any case where the interests of justice so require, and without payment by the person in any such case if the person does not have sufficient means to pay for it;

(d) To be questioned in the presence of counsel unless the person has voluntarily waived his or her right to counsel.

Article 56 – Role of the Pre-Trial Chamber in relation to a unique investigative opportunity

1. (a) Where the Prosecutor considers an investigation to present a unique opportunity to take testimony or a statement from a witness or to examine, collect or test evidence, which may not be available subsequently for the purposes of a trial, the Prosecutor shall so inform the Pre-Trial Chamber.

(b) In that case, the Pre-Trial Chamber may, upon request of the Prosecutor, take such measures as may be necessary to ensure the efficiency and integrity of the proceedings and, in particular, to protect the rights of the defence.

(c) Unless the Pre-Trial Chamber orders otherwise, the Prosecutor shall provide the relevant information to the person who has been arrested or appeared in response to a summons in connection with the investigation referred to in subparagraph (a), in order that he or she may be heard on the matter.

2. The measures referred to in paragraph 1 (b) may include:

(a) Making recommendations or orders regarding procedures to be followed;

(b) Directing that a record be made of the proceedings;

(c) Appointing an expert to assist;

(d) Authorizing counsel for a person who has been arrested, or appeared before the Court in response to a summons, to participate, or where there has not yet been such an arrest or appearance or counsel has not been designated, appointing another counsel to attend and represent the interests of the defence;

(e) Naming one of its members or, if necessary, another available judge of the Pre-Trial or Trial Division to observe and make recommendations or orders regarding the collection and preservation of evidence and the questioning of persons;

(f) Taking such other action as may be necessary to collect or preserve evidence.

3. (a) Where the Prosecutor has not sought measures pursuant to this article but the Pre-Trial Chamber considers that such measures are required to preserve evidence that it deems would be essential for the defence at trial, it shall consult with the Prosecutor as to whether there is good reason for the Prosecutor's failure to request the measures. If upon consultation, the Pre-Trial Chamber concludes that the Prosecutor's failure to request such measures is unjustified, the Pre-Trial Chamber may take such measures on

its own initiative.

(b) A decision of the Pre -Trial Chamber to act on its own initiative under this paragraph may be appealed by the Prosecutor. The appeal shall be heard on an expedited basis.

4. The admissibility of evidence preserved or collected for trial pursuant to this article, or the record thereof, shall be governed at trial by article 69, and given such weight as determined by the Trial Chamber.

Article 57– Functions and powers of the Pre-Trial Chamber

1. Unless otherwise provided for in this Statute, the Pre -Trial Chamber shall exercise its functions in accordance with the provisions of this article.

2. (a) Orders or rulings of the Pre -Trial Chamber issued under articles 15, 18, 19, 54, paragraph 2, 61, paragraph 7, and 72 must be concurred in by a majority of its judges.

(b) In all other cases, a single judge of the Pre -Trial Chamber may exercise the functions provided for in this Statute, unless otherwise provided for in the Rules of Procedure and Evidence or by a majority of the Pre-Trial Chamber.

3. In addition to its other functions under this Statute, the Pre -Trial Chamber may:

(a) At the request of the Prosecutor, issue such orders and warrants as may be required for the purposes of an investigation;

(b) Upon the request of a person who has been arrested or has appeared pursuant to a summons under article 58, issue such orders, including measures such as those described in article 56, or seek such cooperation pursuant to Part 9 as may be necessary to assist the person in the preparation of his or her defence;

(c) Where necessary, provide for the protection and privacy of victims and witnesses, the preservation of evidence, the protection of persons who have been arrested or appeared in response to a summons, and the protection of national security information;

(d) Authorize the Prosecutor to take specific investigative steps within the territory of a State Party without having secured the cooperation of that State under Part 9 if, whenever possible having regard to the views of the State concerned, the Pre-Trial Chamber has determined in that case that the State is clearly unable to execute a request for cooperation due to the unavailability of any authority or any component of its judicial system competent to execute the request for cooperation under Part 9.

(e) Where a warrant of arrest or a summons has been issued under article 58, and having due regard to the strength of the evidence and the rights of the parties concerned, as provided for in this Statute and the Rules of Procedure and Evidence, seek the cooperation of States pursuant to article 93, paragraph 1 (j), to take protective measures for the purpose of forfeiture in particular for the ultimate benefit of victims.

Article 58 – Issuance by the Pre-Trial Chamber of a warrant of arrest or a summons to appear

1. At any time after the initiation of an investigation, the Pre-Trial Chamber shall, on the application of the Prosecutor, issue a warrant of arrest of a person if, having examined the application and the evidence or other information submitted by the Prosecutor, it is satisfied that:

(a) There are reasonable grounds to believe that the person has committed a crime within the jurisdiction of the Court; and

(b) The arrest of the person appears necessary:

(i) To ensure the person's appearance at trial,

(ii) To ensure that the person does not obstruct or endanger the investigation or the court proceedings, or

(iii) Where applicable, to prevent the person from continuing with the commission of that crime or a related crime which is within the jurisdiction of the Court and which arises out of the same circumstances.

2. The application of the Prosecutor shall contain:

(a) The name of the person and any other relevant identifying information;

(b) A specific reference to the crimes within the jurisdiction of the Court which the person is alleged to have committed;

(c) A concise statement of the facts which are alleged to constitute those crimes;

(d) A summary of the evidence and any other information which establish reasonable grounds to believe that the person committed those crimes; and

(e) The reason why the Prosecutor believes that the arrest of the person is necessary.

3. The warrant of arrest shall contain:

(a) The name of the person and any other relevant identifying information;

(b) A specific reference to the crimes within the jurisdiction of the Court for which the person's arrest is sought; and

(c) A concise statement of the facts which are alleged to constitute those crimes.

4. The warrant of arrest shall remain in effect until otherwise ordered by the Court.

5. On the basis of the warrant of arrest, the Court may request the provisional arrest or the arrest and surrender of the person under Part 9.

6. The Prosecutor may request the Pre-Trial Chamber to amend the warrant of arrest by modifying or adding to the crimes specified therein. The Pre-Trial Chamber shall so amend the warrant if it is satisfied that there are reasonable grounds to believe that the person committed the modified or additional crimes.

7. As an alternative to seeking a warrant of arrest, the Prosecutor may submit an application requesting that the Pre-Trial Chamber issue a summons for the person to appear. If the Pre-Trial Chamber is satisfied that there are reasonable grounds to believe that the person committed the crime alleged and that a summons is sufficient to ensure the person's appearance, it shall issue the summons, with or without conditions restricting liberty (other than detention) if provided for by national law, for the person to appear. The summons shall contain:

(a) The name of the person and any other relevant identifying information;

(b) The specified date on which the person is to appear;

(c) A specific reference to the crimes within the jurisdiction of the Court which the person is alleged to have committed; and

(d) A concise statement of the facts which are alleged to constitute the crime.

The summons shall be served on the person.

Article 59– Arrest proceedings in the custodial State

1. A State Party which has received a request for provisional arrest or for arrest and surrender shall immediately take steps to arrest the person in question in accordance with its laws and the provisions of Part 9.

2. A person arrested shall be brought promptly before the competent judicial authority in the custodial State which shall determine, in accordance with the law of that State, that:

(a) The warrant applies to that person;

(b) The person has been arrested in accordance with the proper process; and

(c) The person's rights have been respected.

3. The person arrested shall have the right to apply to the competent authority in the custodial State for interim release pending surrender.

4. In reaching a decision on any such application, the competent authority in the custodial State shall consider whether, given the gravity of the alleged crimes, there are urgent and exceptional circumstances to justify interim release and whether necessary safeguards exist to ensure that the custodial State can fulfil its duty to surrender the person to the Court. It shall not be open to the competent authority of the custodial State to consider whether the warrant of arrest was properly issued in accordance with article 58, paragraph 1 (a) and (b).

5. The Pre-Trial Chamber shall be notified of any request for interim release and shall make recommendations to the competent authority in the custodial State. The competent authority in the custodial State shall give full consideration to such recommendations, including any recommendations on measures to prevent the escape of the person, before rendering its decision.

6. If the person is granted interim release, the Pre-Trial Chamber may request periodic reports on the status of the interim release.

7. Once ordered to be surrendered by the custodial State, the person shall be delivered to the Court as soon as possible.

Article 60 – Initial proceedings before the Court

1. Upon the surrender of the person to the Court, or the person's appearance before the Court voluntarily or pursuant to a summons, the Pre-Trial Chamber shall satisfy itself that the person has been informed of the crimes which he or she is alleged to have committed, and of his or her rights under this Statute, including the right to apply for interim release pending trial.

2. A person subject to a warrant of arrest may apply for interim release pending trial. If the Pre-Trial Chamber is satisfied that the conditions set forth in article 58, paragraph 1, are met, the person shall continue to be detained. If it is not so satisfied, the Pre-Trial Chamber shall release the person, with or without conditions.

3. The Pre -Trial Chamber shall periodically review its ruling on the release or detention of the person, and may do so at any time on the request of the Prosecutor or the person. Upon such review, it may modify its ruling as to detention, release or conditions of release, if it is satisfied that changed circumstances so require.

4. The Pre-Trial Chamber shall ensure that a person is not detained for an unreasonable period prior to trial due to inexcusable delay by the Prosecutor. If such delay occurs, the Court shall consider releasing the person, with or without conditions.

5. If necessary, the Pre -Trial Chamber may issue a warrant of arrest to secure the presence of a person who has been released.

Article 61– Confirmation of the charges before trial

1. Subject to the provisions of paragraph 2, within a reasonable time after the person's surrender or voluntary appearance before the Court, the Pre -Trial Chamber shall hold a hearing to confirm the charges on which the Prosecutor intends to seek trial. The hearing shall be held in the presence of the Prosecutor and the person charged, as well as his or her counsel.

2. The Pre-Trial Chamber may, upon request of the Prosecutor or on its own motion, hold a hearing in the absence of the person charged to confirm the charges on which the Prosecutor intends to seek trial when the person has:

(a) Waived his or her right to be present; or

(b) Fled or cannot be found and all reasonable steps have been taken to secure his or her appearance before the Court and to inform the person of the charges and that a hearing to confirm those charges will be held.

In that case, the person shall be represented by counsel where the Pre-Trial Chamber determines that it is in the interests of justice.

3. Within a reasonable time before the hearing, the person shall:

(a) Be provided with a copy of the document containing the charges on which the Prosecutor intends to bring the person to trial; and

(b) Be informed of the evidence on which the Prosecutor intends to rely at the hearing.

The Pre-Trial Chamber may issue orders regarding the disclosure of information for the purposes of the hearing.

4. Before the hearing, the Prosecutor may continue the investigation and may

amend or withdraw any charges. The person shall be given reasonable notice before the hearing of any amendment to or withdrawal of charges. In case of a withdrawal of charges, the Prosecutor shall notify the Pre-Trial Chamber of the reasons for the withdrawal.

5. At the hearing, the Prosecutor shall support each charge with sufficient evidence to establish substantial grounds to believe that the person committed the crime charged. The Prosecutor may rely on documentary or summary evidence and need not call the witnesses expected to testify at the trial.

6. At the hearing, the person may:

(a) Object to the charges;

(b) Challenge the evidence presented by the Prosecutor; and

(c) Present evidence.

7. The Pre-Trial Chamber shall, on the basis of the hearing, determine whether there is sufficient evidence to establish substantial grounds to believe that the person committed each of the crimes charged. Based on its determination, the Pre-Trial Chamber shall:

(a) Confirm those charges in relation to which it has determined that there is sufficient evidence; and commit the person to a Trial Chamber for trial on the charges as confirmed;

(b) Decline to confirm those charges in relation to which it has determined that there is insufficient evidence;

(c) Adjourn the hearing and request the Prosecutor to consider:

(i) Providing further evidence or conducting further investigation with respect to a particular charge; or

(ii) Amending a charge because the evidence submitted appears to establish a different crime within the jurisdiction of the Court.

8. Where the Pre-Trial Chamber declines to confirm a charge, the Prosecutor shall not be precluded from subsequently requesting its confirmation if the request is supported by additional evidence.

9. After the charges are confirmed and before the trial has begun, the Prosecutor may, with the permission of the Pre-Trial Chamber and after notice to the accused, amend the charges. If the Prosecutor seeks to add additional charges or to substitute more serious charges, a hearing under this article to confirm those charges must be held. After commencement of the trial, the Prosecutor may, with the permission of the Trial Chamber, withdraw the

charges.

10. Any warrant previously issued shall cease to have effect with respect to any charges which have not been confirmed by the Pre-Trial Chamber or which have been withdrawn by the Prosecutor.

11. Once the charges have been confirmed in accordance with this article, the Presidency shall constitute a Trial Chamber which, subject to paragraph 8 and to article 64, paragraph 4, shall be responsible for the conduct of subsequent proceedings and may exercise any function of the Pre-Trial Chamber that is relevant and capable of application in those proceedings.

PART 6. THE TRIAL

Article 62 – Place of trial

Unless otherwise decided, the place of the trial shall be the seat of the Court.

Article 63 – Trial in the presence of the accused

1. The accused shall be present during the trial.

2. If the accused, being present before the Court, continues to disrupt the trial, the Trial Chamber may remove the accused and shall make provision for him or her to observe the trial and instruct counsel from outside the courtroom, through the use of communications technology, if required. Such measures shall be taken only in exceptional circumstances after other reasonable alternatives have proved inadequate, and only for such duration as is strictly required.

Article 64 – Functions and powers of the Trial Chamber

1. The functions and powers of the Trial Chamber set out in this article shall be exercised in accordance with this Statute and the Rules of Procedure and Evidence.

2. The Trial Chamber shall ensure that a trial is fair and expeditious and is conducted with full respect for the rights of the accused and due regard for the protection of victims and witnesses.

3. Upon assignment of a case for trial in accordance with this Statute, the Trial Chamber assigned to deal with the case shall:

(a) Confer with the parties and adopt such procedures as are necessary to facilitate the fair and expeditious conduct of the proceedings;

(b) Determine the language or languages to be used at trial; and

(c) Subject to any other relevant provisions of this Statute, provide for disclosure of documents or information not previously disclosed, sufficiently in advance of the commencement of the trial to enable adequate preparation for trial.

4. The Trial Chamber may, if necessary for its effective and fair functioning, refer preliminary issues to the Pre -Trial Chamber or, if necessary, to another available judge of the Pre -Trial Division.

5. Upon notice to the parties, the Trial Chamber may, as appropriate, direct that there be joinder or severance in respect of charges against more than one accused.

6. In performing its functions prior to trial or during the course of a trial, the Trial Chamber may, as necessary:

(a) Exercise any functions of the Pre -Trial Chamber referred to in article 61, paragraph 11;

(b) Require the attendance and testimony of witnesses and production of documents and other evidence by obtaining, if necessary, the assistance of States as provided in this Statute;

(c) Provide for the protection of confidential information;

(d) Order the production of evidence in addition to that already collected prior to the trial or presented during the trial by the parties;

(e) Provide for the protection of the accused, witnesses and victims; and

(f) Rule on any other relevant matters.

7. The trial shall be held in public. The Trial Chamber may, however, determine that special circumstances require that certain proceedings be in closed session for the purposes set forth in article 68, or to protect confidential or sensitive information to be given in evidence.

8. (a) At the commencement of the trial, the Trial Chamber shall have read to the accused the charges previously confirmed by the Pre-Trial Chamber. The Trial Chamber shall satisfy itself that the accused understands the nature of the charges. It shall afford him or her the opportunity to make an admission of guilt in accordance with article 65 or to plead not guilty.

(b) At the trial, the presiding judge may give directions for the conduct of proceedings, including to ensure that they are conducted in a fair and impartial manner. Subject to any directions of the presiding judge, the parties may submit evidence in accordance with the provisions of this Statute.

9. The Trial Chamber shall have, inter alia, the power on application of a party or on its own motion to:

(a) Rule on the admissibility or relevance of evidence; and

(b) Take all necessary steps to maintain order in the course of a hearing.

10. The Trial Chamber shall ensure that a complete record of the trial, which accurately reflects the proceedings, is made and that it is maintained and preserved by the Registrar.

Article 65 – Proceedings on an admission of guilt

1. Where the accused makes an admission of guilt pursuant to article 64, paragraph 8 (a), the Trial Chamber shall determine whether:

(a) The accused understands the nature and consequences of the admission of guilt;

(b) The admission is voluntarily made by the accused after sufficient consultation with defence counsel; and

(c) The admission of guilt is supported by the facts of the case that are contained in:

(i) The charges brought by the Prosecutor and admitted by the accused;

(ii) Any materials presented by the Prosecutor which supplement the charges and which the accused accepts; and

(iii) Any other evidence, such as the testimony of witnesses, presented by the Prosecutor or the accused.

2. Where the Trial Chamber is satisfied that the matters referred to in paragraph 1 are established, it shall consider the admission of guilt, together with any additional evidence presented, as establishing all the essential facts that are required to prove the crime to which the admission of guilt relates, and may convict the accused of that crime.

3. Where the Trial Chamber is not satisfied that the matters referred to in paragraph 1 are established, it shall consider the admission of guilt as not having been made, in which case it shall order that the trial be continued under the ordinary trial procedures provided by this Statute and may remit the case

to another Trial Chamber.

4. Where the Trial Chamber is of the opinion that a more complete presentation of the facts of the case is required in the interests of justice, in particular the interests of the victims, the Trial Chamber may:

(a) Request the Prosecutor to present additional evidence, including the testimony of witnesses; or

(b) Order that the trial be continued under the ordinary trial procedures provided by this Statute, in which case it shall consider the admission of guilt as not having been made and may remit the case to another Trial Chamber.

5. Any discussions between the Prosecutor and the defence regarding modification of the charges, the admission of guilt or the penalty to be imposed shall not be binding on the Court.

Article 66 – Presumption of innocence

1. Everyone shall be presumed innocent until proved guilty before the Court in accordance with the applicable law.

2. The onus is on the Prosecutor to prove the guilt of the accused.

3. In order to convict the accused, the Court must be convinced of the guilt of the accused beyond reasonable doubt.

Article 67 – Rights of the accused

1. In the determination of any charge, the accused shall be entitled to a public hearing, having regard to the provisions of this Statute, to a fair hearing conducted impartially, and to the following minimum guarantees, in full equality:

(a) To be informed promptly and in detail of the nature, cause and content of the charge, in a language which the accused fully understands and speaks;

(b) To have adequate time and facilities for the preparation of the defence and to communicate freely with counsel of the accused's choosing in confidence;

(c) To be tried without undue delay;

(d) Subject to article 63, paragraph 2, to be present at the trial, to conduct the defence in person or through legal assistance of the accused's choosing, to be informed, if the accused does not have legal assistance, of this right and to have legal assistance assigned by the Court in any case where the interests of justice so require, and without payment if the accused lacks sufficient means to pay for it;

(e) To examine, or have examined, the witnesses against him or her and to obtain the attendance and examination of witnesses on his or her behalf under the same conditions as witnesses against him or her. The accused shall also be entitled to raise defences and to present other evidence admissible under this Statute;

(f) To have, free of any cost, the assistance of a competent interpreter and such translations as are necessary to meet the requirements of fairness, if any of the proceedings of or documents presented to the Court are not in a language which the accused fully understands and speaks;

(g) Not to be compelled to testify or to confess guilt and to remain silent, without such silence being a consideration in the determination of guilt or innocence;

(h) To make an unsworn oral or written statement in his or her defence; and

(i) Not to have imposed on him or her any reversal of the burden of proof or any onus of rebuttal.

2. In addition to any other disclosure provided for in this Statute, the Prosecutor shall, as soon as practicable, disclose to the defence evidence in the Prosecutor's possession or control which he or she believes shows or tends to show the innocence of the accused, or to mitigate the guilt of the accused, or which may affect the credibility of prosecution evidence. In case of doubt as to the application of this paragraph, the Court shall decide.

Article 68 – Protection of the victims and witnesses and their participation in the proceedings

1. The Court shall take appropriate measures to protect the safety, physical and psychological well-being, dignity and privacy of victims and witnesses. In so doing, the Court shall have regard to all relevant factors, including age, gender as defined in article 2, paragraph 3, and health, and the nature of the crime, in particular, but not limited to, where the crime involves sexual or gender violence or violence against children. The Prosecutor shall take such measures particularly during the investigation and prosecution of such crimes. These measures shall not be prejudicial to or inconsistent with the rights of the accused and a fair and impartial trial.

2. As an exception to the principle of public hearings provided for in article 67, the Chambers of the Court may, to protect victims and witnesses or an accused, conduct any part of the proceedings in camera or allow the presentation of evidence by electronic or other special means. In particular, such measures shall

be implemented in the case of a victim of sexual violence or a child who is a victim or a witness, unless otherwise ordered by the Court, having regard to all the circumstances, particularly the views of the victim or witness.

3. Where the personal interests of the victims are affected, the Court shall permit their views and concerns to be presented and considered at stages of the proceedings determined to be appropriate by the Court and in a manner which is not prejudicial to or inconsistent with the rights of the accused and a fair and impartial trial. Such views and concerns may be presented by the legal representatives of the victims where the Court considers it appropriate, in accordance with the Rules of Procedure and Evidence.

4. The Victims and Witnesses Unit may advise the Prosecutor and the Court on appropriate protective measures, security arrangements, counselling and assistance as referred to in article 43, paragraph 6.

5. Where the disclosure of evidence or information pursuant to this Statute may lead to the grave endangerment of the security of a witness or his or her family, the Prosecutor may, for the purposes of any proceedings conducted prior to the commencement of the trial, withhold such evidence or information and instead submit a summary thereof. Such measures shall be exercised in a manner which is not prejudicial to or inconsistent with the rights of the accused and a fair and impartial trial.

6. A State may make an application for necessary measures to be taken in respect of the protection of its servants or agents and the protection of confidential or sensitive information.

Article 69 – Evidence

1. Before testifying, each witness shall, in accordance with the Rules of Procedure and Evidence, give an undertaking as to the truthfulness of the evidence to be given by that witness.

2. The testimony of a witness at trial shall be given in person, except to the extent provided by the measures set forth in article 68 or in the Rules of Procedure and Evidence. The Court may also permit the giving of viva voce (oral) or recorded testimony of a witness by means of video or audio technology, as well as the introduction of documents or written transcripts, subject to this Statute and in accordance with the Rules of Procedure and Evidence. These measures shall not be prejudicial to or inconsistent with the rights of the accused.

3. The parties may submit evidence relevant to the case, in accordance with article 64. The Court shall have the authority to request the submission of all evidence that it considers necessary for the determination of the truth.

4. The Court may rule on the relevance or admissibility of any evidence, taking into account, inter alia, the probative value of the evidence and any prejudice that such evidence may cause to a fair trial or to a fair evaluation of the testimony of a witness, in accordance with the Rules of Procedure and Evidence.

5. The Court shall respect and observe privileges on confidentiality as provided for in the Rules of Procedure and Evidence.

6. The Court shall not require proof of facts of common knowledge but may take judicial notice of them.

7. Evidence obtained by means of a violation of this Statute or internationally recognized human rights shall not be admissible if:

(a) The violation casts substantial doubt on the reliability of the evidence; or

(b) The admission of the evidence would be antithetical to and would seriously damage the integrity of the proceedings.

8. When deciding on the relevance or admissibility of evidence collected by a State, the Court shall not rule on the application of the State's national law.

Article 70 – Offences against the administration of justice

1. The Court shall have jurisdiction over the following offences against its administration of justice when committed intentionally:

(a) Giving false testimony when under an obligation pursuant to article 69, paragraph 1, to tell the truth;

(b) Presenting evidence that the party knows is false or forged;

(c) Corruptly influencing a witness, obstructing or interfering with the attendance or testimony of a witness, retaliating against a witness for giving testimony or destroying, tampering with or interfering with the collection of evidence;

(d) Impeding, intimidating or corruptly influencing an official of the Court for the purpose of forcing or persuading the official not to perform, or to perform improperly, his or her duties;

(e) Retaliating against an official of the Court on account of duties performed by that or another official;

(f) Soliciting or accepting a bribe as an official of the Court in conjunction with his or her official duties.

2. The principles and procedures governing the Court's exercise of jurisdiction over offences under this article shall be those provided for in the Rules of Procedure and Evidence. The conditions for providing international cooperation to the Court with respect to its proceedings under this article shall be governed by the domestic laws of the requested State.

3. In the event of conviction, the Court may impose a term of imprisonment not exceeding five years, or a fine in accordance with the Rules of Procedure and Evidence, or both.

4. (a) Each State Party shall extend its criminal laws penalizing offences against the integrity of its own investigative or judicial process to offences against the administration of justice referred to in this article, committed on its territory, or by one of its nationals;

(b) Upon request by the Court, whenever it deems it proper, the State Party shall submit the case to its competent authorities for the purpose of prosecution. Those authorities shall treat such cases with diligence and devote sufficient resources to enable them to be conducted effectively.

Article 71 – Sanctions for misconduct before the Court

1. The Court may sanction persons present before it who commit misconduct, including disruption of its proceedings or deliberate refusal to comply with its directions, by administrative measures other than imprisonment, such as temporary or permanent removal from the courtroom, a fine or other similar measures provided for in the Rules of Procedure and Evidence.

2. The procedures governing the imposition of the measures set forth in paragraph 1 shall be those provided for in the Rules of Procedure and Evidence.

Article 72 – Protection of national security information

1. This article applies in any case where the disclosure of the information or documents of a State would, in the opinion of that State, prejudice its national security interests. Such cases include those falling within the scope of article 56, paragraphs 2 and 3, article 61, paragraph 3, article 64, paragraph 3, article 67, paragraph 2, article 68, paragraph 6, article 87, paragraph 6 and article 93, as well as cases arising at any other stage of the proceedings where such disclosure may be at issue.

2. This article shall also apply when a person who has been requested to give information or evidence has refused to do so or has referred the matter to the State on the ground that disclosure would prejudice the national security interests of a State and the State concerned confirms that it is of the opinion that disclosure would prejudice its national security interests.

3. Nothing in this article shall prejudice the requirements of confidentiality applicable under article 54, paragraph 3 (e) and (f), or the application of article 73.

4. If a State learns that information or documents of the State are being, or are likely to be, disclosed at any stage of the proceedings, and it is of the opinion that disclosure would prejudice its national security interests, that State shall have the right to intervene in order to obtain resolution of the issue in accordance with this article.

5. If, in the opinion of a State, disclosure of information would prejudice its national security interests, all reasonable steps will be taken by the State, acting in conjunction with the Prosecutor, the Defence or the Pre-Trial Chamber or Trial Chamber, as the case may be, to seek to resolve the matter by cooperative means. Such steps may include:

(a) Modification or clarification of the request;

(b) A determination by the Court regarding the relevance of the information or evidence sought, or a determination as to whether the evidence, though relevant, could be or has been obtained from a source other than the requested State;

(c) Obtaining the information or evidence from a different source or in a different form; or

(d) Agreement on conditions under which the assistance could be provided including, among other things, providing summaries or redactions, limitations on disclosure, use of in camera or ex parte proceedings, or other protective measures permissible under the Statute and the Rules.

6. Once all reasonable steps have been taken to resolve the matter through cooperative means, and if the State considers that there are no means or conditions under which the information or documents could be provided or disclosed without prejudice to its national security interests, it shall so notify the Prosecutor or the Court of the specific reasons for its decision, unless a specific description of the reasons would itself necessarily result in such prejudice to the State's national security interests.

7. Thereafter, if the Court determines that the evidence is relevant and necessary for the establishment of the guilt or innocence of the accused, the Court may undertake the following actions:

(a) Where disclosure of the information or document is sought pursuant to a request for cooperation under Part 9 or the circumstances described in paragraph 2, and the State has invoked the ground for refusal referred to in article 93, paragraph 4:

(i) The Court may, before making any conclusion referred to in subparagraph 7 (a) (ii), request further consultations for the purpose of considering the State's representations, which may include, as appropriate, hearings in camera and ex parte;

(ii) If the Court concludes that, by invoking the ground for refusal under article 93, paragraph 4, in the circumstances of the case, the requested State is not acting in accordance with its obligations under the Statute, the Court may refer the matter in accordance with article 87, paragraph 7, specifying the reasons for its conclusion; and

(iii) The Court may make such inference in the trial of the accused as to the existence or non-existence of a fact, as may be appropriate in the circumstances; or

(b) In all other circumstances:

(i) Order disclosure; or

(ii) To the extent it does not order disclosure, make such inference in the trial of the accused as to the existence or non-existence of a fact, as may be appropriate in the circumstances.

Article 73 – Third-party information or documents

If a State Party is requested by the Court to provide a document or information in its custody, possession or control, which was disclosed to it in confidence by a State, intergovernmental organization or international organization, it shall seek the consent of the originator to disclose that document or information. If the originator is a State Party, it shall either consent to disclosure of the information or document or undertake to resolve the issue of disclosure with the Court, subject to the provisions of article 72. If the originator is not a State Party and refuses consent to disclosure, the requested State shall inform the Court that it is unable to provide the document or information because of a pre-existing obligation of confidentiality to the originator.

Article 74 – Requirements for the decision

1. All the judges of the Trial Chamber shall be present at each stage of the trial and throughout their deliberations. The Presidency may, on a case-by-case basis, designate, as available, one or more alternate judges to be present at each stage of the trial and to replace a member of the Trial Chamber if that member is unable to continue attending.

2. The Trial Chamber's decision shall be based on its evaluation of the evidence and the entire proceedings. The decision shall not exceed the facts and

circumstances described in the charges and any amendments to the charges. The Court may base its decision only on evidence submitted and discussed before it at the trial.

3. The judges shall attempt to achieve unanimity in their decision, failing which the decision shall be taken by a majority of the judges.

4. The deliberations of the Trial Chamber shall remain secret.

5. The decision shall be in writing and shall contain a full and reasoned statement of the Trial Chamber's findings on the evidence and conclusions. The Trial Chamber shall issue one decision. When there is no unanimity, the Trial Chamber's decision shall contain the views of the majority and the minority. The decision or a summary thereof shall be delivered in open court.

Article 75 – Reparations to victims

1. The Court shall establish principles relating to reparations to, or in respect of, victims, including restitution, compensation and rehabilitation. On this basis, in its decision the Court may, either upon request or on its own motion in exceptional circumstances, determine the scope and extent of any damage, loss and injury to, or in respect of, victims and will state the principles on which it is acting.

2. The Court may make an order directly against a convicted person specifying appropriate reparations to, or in respect of, victims, including restitution, compensation and rehabilitation. Where appropriate, the Court may order that the award for reparations be made through the Trust Fund provided for in article 79.

3. Before making an order under this article, the Court may invite and shall take account of representations from or on behalf of the convicted person, victims, other interested persons or interested States.

4. In exercising its power under this article, the Court may, after a person is convicted of a crime within the jurisdiction of the Court, determine whether, in order to give effect to an order which it may make under this article, it is necessary to seek measures under article 93, paragraph 1.

5. A State Party shall give effect to a decision under this article as if the provisions of article 109 were applicable to this article.

6. Nothing in this article shall be interpreted as prejudicing the rights of victims under national or international law.

Article 76 – Sentencing

1. In the event of a conviction, the Trial Chamber shall consider the appropriate sentence to be imposed and shall take into account the evidence presented and submissions made during the trial that are relevant to the sentence.

2. Except where article 65 applies and before the completion of the trial, the Trial Chamber may on its own motion and shall, at the request of the Prosecutor or the accused, hold a further hearing to hear any additional evidence or submissions relevant to the sentence, in accordance with the Rules of Procedure and Evidence.

3. Where paragraph 2 applies, any representations under article 75 shall be heard during the further hearing referred to in paragraph 2 and, if necessary, during any additional hearing.

4. The sentence shall be pronounced in public and, wherever possible, in the presence of the accused.

PART 7. PENALTIES

Article 77 – Applicable penalties

1. Subject to article 110, the Court may impose one of the following penalties on a person convicted of a crime under article 5 of this Statute:

(a) Imprisonment for a specified number of years, which may not exceed a maximum of 30 years; or

(b) A term of life imprisonment when justified by the extreme gravity of the crime and the individual circumstances of the convicted person.

2. In addition to imprisonment, the Court may order:

(a) A fine under the criteria provided for in the Rules of Procedure and Evidence;

(b) A forfeiture of proceeds, property and assets derived directly or indirectly from that crime, without prejudice to the rights of bona fide third parties.

Article 78 – Determination of the sentence

1. In determining the sentence, the Court shall, in accordance with the Rules of Procedure and Evidence, take into account such factors as the gravity of the crime and the individual circumstances of the convicted person.

2. In imposing a sentence of imprisonment, the Court shall deduct the time, if any, previously spent in detention in accordance with an order of the Court. The Court may deduct any time otherwise spent in detention in connection with conduct underlying the crime.

3. When a person has been convicted of more than one crime, the Court shall pronounce a sentence for each crime and a joint sentence specifying the total period of imprisonment. This period shall be no less than the highest individual sentence pronounced and shall not exceed 30 years' imprisonment or a sentence of life imprisonment in conformity with article 77, paragraph 1 (b).

Article 79 – Trust Fund

1. A Trust Fund shall be established by decision of the Assembly of States Parties for the benefit of victims of crimes within the jurisdiction of the Court, and of the families of such victims.

2. The Court may order money and other property collected through fines or forfeiture to be transferred, by order of the Court, to the Trust Fund.

3. The Trust Fund shall be managed according to criteria to be determined by the Assembly of States Parties.

Article 80 – Non-prejudice to national application of penalties and national laws

Nothing in this Part of the Statute affects the application by States of penalties prescribed by their national law, nor the law of States which do not provide for penalties prescribed in this Part.

PART 8. APPEAL AND REVISION

Article 81 – Appeal against decision of acquittal or conviction or against sentence

1. A decision under article 74 may be appealed in accordance with the Rules of Procedure and Evidence as follows:

(a) The Prosecutor may make an appeal on any of the following grounds:

(i) Procedural error,

(ii) Error of fact, or

(iii) Error of law;

(b) The convicted person or the Prosecutor on that person's behalf may make an appeal on any of the following grounds:

(i) Procedural error,

(ii) Error of fact,

(iii) Error of law, or

(iv) Any other ground that affects the fairness or reliability of the proceedings or decision.

2. (a) A sentence may be appealed, in accordance with the Rules of Procedure and Evidence, by the Prosecutor or the convicted person on the ground of disproportion between the crime and the sentence;

(b) If on an appeal against sentence the Court considers that there are grounds on which the conviction might be set aside, wholly or in part, it may invite the Prosecutor and the convicted person to submit grounds under article 81, paragraph 1 (a) or (b), and may render a decision on conviction in accordance with article 83;

(c) The same procedure applies when the Court, on an appeal against conviction only, considers that there are grounds to reduce the sentence under paragraph 2 (a).

3. (a) Unless the Trial Chamber orders otherwise, a convicted person shall remain in custody pending an appeal;

(b) When a convicted person's time in custody exceeds the sentence of imprisonment imposed, that person shall be released, except that if the Prosecutor is also appealing, the release may be subject to the conditions under subparagraph (c) below;

(c) In case of an acquittal, the accused shall be released immediately, subject to the following:

(i) Under exceptional circumstances, and having regard, inter alia, to the concrete risk of flight, the seriousness of the offence charged and the probability of success on appeal, the Trial Chamber, at the request of the Prosecutor, may maintain the detention of the person pending appeal;

(ii) A decision by the Trial Chamber under subparagraph (c) (i) may be appealed in accordance with the Rules of Procedure and Evidence.

4. Subject to the provisions of paragraph 3 (a) and (b), execution of the decision or sentence shall be suspended during the period allowed for appeal and for the duration of the appeal proceedings.

Article 82– Appeal against other decisions

1. Either party may appeal any of the following decisions in accordance with the Rules of Procedure and Evidence:

(a) A decision with respect to jurisdiction or admissibility;

(b) A decision granting or denying release of the person being investigated or prosecuted;

(c) A decision of the Pre-Trial Chamber to act on its own initiative under article 56, paragraph 3;

(d) A decision that involves an issue that would significantly affect the fair and expeditious conduct of the proceedings or the outcome of the trial, and for which, in the opinion of the Pre-Trial or Trial Chamber, an immediate resolution by the Appeals Chamber may materially advance the proceedings.

2. A decision of the Pre-Trial Chamber under article 57, paragraph 3 (d), may be appealed against by the State concerned or by the Prosecutor, with the leave of the Pre-Trial Chamber. The appeal shall be heard on an expedited basis.

3. An appeal shall not of itself have suspensive effect unless the Appeals Chamber so orders, upon request, in accordance with the Rules of Procedure and Evidence.

4. A legal representative of the victims, the convicted person or a bona fide owner of property adversely affected by an order under article 73 may appeal against the order for reparations, as provided in the Rules of Procedure and Evidence.

Article 83 – Proceedings on appeal

1. For the purposes of proceedings under article 81 and this article, the Appeals Chamber shall have all the powers of the Trial Chamber.

2. If the Appeals Chamber finds that the proceedings appealed from were unfair in a way that affected the reliability of the decision or sentence, or that the decision or sentence appealed from was materially affected by error of fact or law or procedural error, it may:

(a) Reverse or amend the decision or sentence; or

(b) Order a new trial before a different Trial Chamber.

For these purposes, the Appeals Chamber may remand a factual issue to the original Trial Chamber for it to determine the issue and to report back accordingly, or may itself call evidence to determine the issue. When the decision or sentence has been appealed only by the person convicted, or the Prosecutor on that person's behalf, it cannot be amended to his or her detriment.

3. If in an appeal against sentence the Appeals Chamber finds that the sentence is disproportionate to the crime, it may vary the sentence in accordance with Part 7.

4. The judgement of the Appeals Chamber shall be taken by a majority of the judges and shall be delivered in open court. The judgement shall state the reasons on which it is based. When there is no unanimity, the judgement of the Appeals Chamber shall contain the views of the majority and the minority, but a judge may deliver a separate or dissenting opinion on a question of law.

5. The Appeals Chamber may deliver its judgement in the absence of the person acquitted or convicted.

Article 84 – Revision of conviction or sentence

1. The convicted person or, after death, spouses, children, parents or one person alive at the time of the accused's death who has been given express written instructions from the accused to bring such a claim, or the Prosecutor on the person's behalf, may apply to the Appeals Chamber to revise the final judgement of conviction or sentence on the grounds that:

(a) New evidence has been discovered that:

(i) Was not available at the time of trial, and such unavailability was not wholly or partially attributable to the party making application; and

(ii) Is sufficiently important that had it been proved at trial it would have been likely to have resulted in a different verdict;

(b) It has been newly discovered that decisive evidence, taken into account at trial and upon which the conviction depends, was false, forged or falsified;

(c) One or more of the judges who participated in conviction or confirmation of the charges has committed, in that case, an act of serious misconduct or serious breach of duty of sufficient gravity to justify the removal of that judge or those judges from office under article 46.

2. The Appeals Chamber shall reject the application if it considers it to be unfounded. If it determines that the application is meritorious, it may, as appropriate:

(a) Reconvene the original Trial Chamber;

(b) Constitute a new Trial Chamber; or

(c) Retain jurisdiction over the matter, with a view to, after hearing the parties in the manner set forth in the Rules of Procedure and Evidence, arriving at a determination on whether the judgement should be revised.

Article 85 – Compensation to an arrested or convicted person

1. Anyone who has been the victim of unlawful arrest or detention shall have an enforceable right to compensation.

2. When a person has by a final decision been convicted of a criminal offence, and when subsequently his or her conviction has been reversed on the ground that a new or newly discovered fact shows conclusively that there has been a miscarriage of justice, the person who has suffered punishment as a result of such conviction shall be compensated according to law, unless it is proved that the non-disclosure of the unknown fact in time is wholly or partly attributable to him or her.

3. In exceptional circumstances, where the Court finds conclusive facts showing that there has been a grave and manifest miscarriage of justice, it may in its discretion award compensation, according to the criteria provided in the Rules of Procedure and Evidence, to a person who has been released from detention following a final decision of acquittal or a termination of the proceedings for that reason.

PART 9. INTERNATIONAL COOPERATION AND JUDICIAL ASSISTANCE

Article 86 – General obligation to cooperate

States Parties shall, in accordance with the provisions of this Statute, cooperate fully with the Court in its investigation and prosecution of crimes within the jurisdiction of the Court.

Article 87 – Requests for cooperation: general provisions

1. (a) The Court shall have the authority to make requests to States Parties for cooperation. The requests shall be transmitted through the diplomatic channel or any other appropriate channel as may be designated by each State Party upon ratification, acceptance, approval or accession.

Subsequent changes to the designation shall be made by each State Party in accordance with the Rules of Procedure and Evidence.

(b) When appropriate, without prejudice to the provisions of subparagraph (a), requests may also be transmitted through the International Criminal Police Organization or any appropriate regional organization.

2. Requests for cooperation and any documents supporting the request shall either be in or be accompanied by a translation into an official language of the requested State or in one of the working languages of the Court, in accordance with the choice made by that State upon ratification, acceptance, approval or accession.

Subsequent changes to this choice shall be made in accordance with the Rules of Procedure and Evidence.

3. The requested State shall keep confidential a request for cooperation and any documents supporting the request, except to the extent that the disclosure is necessary for execution of the request.

4. In relation to any request for assistance presented under Part 9, the Court may take such measures, including measures related to the protection of information, as may be necessary to ensure the safety or physical or psychological well – being of any victims, potential witnesses and their families. The Court may request that any information that is made available under Part 9 shall be provided and handled in a manner that protects the safety and physical or psychological well – being of any victims, potential witnesses and their families.

5. The Court may invite any State not party to this Statute to provide assistance under this Part on the basis of an ad hoc arrangement, an agreement with such State or any other appropriate basis.

Where a State not party to this Statute, which has entered into an ad hoc arrangement or an agreement with the Court, fails to cooperate with requests pursuant to any such arrangement or agreement, the Court may so inform the Assembly of States Parties or, where the Security Council referred the matter to the Court, the Security Council.

6. The Court may ask any intergovernmental organization to provide information or documents. The Court may also ask for other forms of cooperation and assistance which may be agreed upon with such an organization and which are in accordance with its competence or mandate.

7. Where a State Party fails to comply with a request to cooperate by the Court contrary to the provisions of this Statute, thereby preventing the Court from exercising its functions and powers under this Statute, the Court may make a finding to that effect and refer the matter to the Assembly of States Parties or, where the Security Council referred the matter to the Court, to the Security Council.

Article 88 – Availability of procedures under national law

States Parties shall ensure that there are procedures available under their national law for all of the forms of cooperation which are specified under this Part.

Article 89 – Surrender of persons to the Court

1. The Court may transmit a request for the arrest and surrender of a person, together with the material supporting the request outlined in article 91, to any State on the territory of which that person may be found and shall request the cooperation of that State in the arrest and surrender of such a person. States Parties shall, in accordance with the provisions of this Part and the procedure under their national law, comply with requests for arrest and surrender.

2. Where the person sought for surrender brings a challenge before a national court on the basis of the principle of ne bis in idem as provided in article 20, the requested State shall immediately consult with the Court to determine if there has been a relevant ruling on admissibility. If the case is admissible, the requested State shall proceed with the execution of the request. If an admissibility ruling is pending, the requested State may postpone the execution of the request for surrender of the person until the Court makes a determination on admissibility.

3. (a) A State Party shall authorize, in accordance with its national procedural law, transportation through its territory of a person being surrendered to the Court by another State, except where transit through that State would impede or delay the surrender.

   (b) A request by the Court for transit shall be transmitted in accordance with article 87. The request for transit shall contain:

   (i) A description of the person being transported;

   (ii) A brief statement of the facts of the case and their legal characterization; and

   (iii) The warrant for arrest and surrender;

   (c) A person being transported shall be detained in custody during the period of transit;

   (d) No authorization is required if the person is transported by air and no landing is scheduled on the territory of the transit State;

   (e) If an unscheduled landing occurs on the territory of the transit State, that State may require a request for transit from the Court as provided for in subparagraph (b). The transit State shall detain the person being transported until the request for transit is received and the transit is effected; provided that detention for purposes of this subparagraph may not be extended beyond 96 hours from the unscheduled landing unless the request is received within that time.

4. If the person sought is being proceeded against or is serving a sentence in the requested State for a crime different from that for which surrender to the Court is sought, the requested State, after making its decision to grant the request, shall consult with the Court.

Article 90 – Competing requests

1. A State Party which receives a request from the Court for the surrender of a person under article 89 shall, if it also receives a request from any other State for the extradition of the same person for the same conduct which forms the basis of the crime for which the Court seeks the person's surrender, notify the Court and the requesting State of that fact.

2. Where the requesting State is a State Party, the requested State shall give priority to the request from the Court if:

(a) The Court has, pursuant to articles 18 and 19, made a determination that the case in respect of which surrender is sought is admissible and that determination takes into account the investigation or prosecution conducted by the requesting State in respect of its request for extradition; or

(b) The Court makes the determination described in subparagraph (a) pursuant to the requested State's notification under paragraph 1.

3. Where a determination under paragraph 2 (a) has not been made, the requested State may, at its discretion, pending the determination of the Court under paragraph 2 (b), proceed to deal with the request for extradition from the requesting State but shall not extradite the person until the Court has determined that the case is inadmissible. The Court's determination shall be made on an expedited basis.

4. If the requesting State is a State not Party to this Statute the requested State, if it is not under an international obligation to extradite the person to the requesting State, shall give priority to the request for surrender from the Court, if the Court has determined that the case is admissible.

5. Where a case under paragraph 4 has not been determined to be admissible by the Court, the requested State may, at its discretion, proceed to deal with the request for extradition from the requesting State.

6. In cases where paragraph 4 applies except that the requested State is under an existing international obligation to extradite the person to the requesting State not Party to this Statute, the requested State shall determine whether to surrender the person to the Court or extradite the person to the requesting State. In making its decision, the requested State shall consider all the relevant factors, including but not limited to:

(a) The respective dates of the requests;

(b) The interests of the requesting State including, where relevant, whether the crime was committed in its territory and the nationality of the victims and of the person sought; and

(c) The possibility of subsequent surrender between the Court and the requesting State.

7. Where a State Party which receives a request from the Court for the surrender of a person also receives a request from any State for the extradition of the same person for conduct other than that which constitutes the crime for which the Court seeks the person's surrender:

(a) The requested State shall, if it is not under an existing international obligation to extradite the person to the requesting State, give priority to the request from the Court;

(b) The requested State shall, if it is under an existing international obligation to extradite the person to the requesting State, determine whether to surrender the person to the Court or extradite the person to the requesting State. In making its decision, the requested State shall consider all the relevant factors, including but not limited to those set out in paragraph 6, but shall give special consideration to the relative nature and gravity of the conduct in question.

8. Where pursuant to a notification under this article, the Court has determined a case to be inadmissible, and subsequently extradition to the requesting State is refused, the requested State shall notify the Court of this decision.

Article 91 – Contents of request for arrest and surrender

1. A request for arrest and surrender shall be made in writing. In urgent cases, a request may be made by any medium capable of delivering a written record, provided that the request shall be confirmed through the channel provided for in article 87, paragraph 1 (a).

2. In the case of a request for the arrest and surrender of a person for whom a warrant of arrest has been issued by the Pre - Trial Chamber under article 58, the request shall contain or be supported by:

(a) Information describing the person sought, sufficient to identify the person, and information as to that person's probable location;

(b) A copy of the warrant of arrest; and

(c) Such documents, statements or information as may be necessary to meet the requirements for the surrender process in the requested State, except that those requirements should not be more burdensome than those applicable to requests for extradition pursuant to treaties or arrangements between the requested State and other States and should, if possible, be less burdensome, taking into account the distinct nature of the Court.

3. In the case of a request for the arrest and surrender of a person already convicted, the request shall contain or be supported by:

(a) A copy of any warrant of arrest for that person;

(b) A copy of the judgement of conviction;

(c) Information to demonstrate that the person sought is the one referred to in the judgement of conviction; and

(d) If the person sought has been sentenced, a copy of the sentence imposed and, in the case of a sentence for imprisonment, a statement of any time already served and the time remaining to be served.

4. Upon the request of the Court, a State Party shall consult with the Court, either generally or with respect to a specific matter, regarding any requirements under its national law that may apply under paragraph 2 (c). During the consultations, the State Party shall advise the Court of the specific requirements of its national law.

Article 92 – Provisional arrest

1. In urgent cases, the Court may request the provisional arrest of the person sought, pending presentation of the request for surrender and the documents supporting the request as specified in article 91.

2. The request for provisional arrest shall be made by any medium capable of delivering a written record and shall contain:

(a) Information describing the person sought, sufficient to identify the person, and information as to that person's probable location;

(b) A concise statement of the crimes for which the person's arrest is sought and of the facts which are alleged to constitute those crimes, including, where possible, the date and location of the crime;

(c) A statement of the existence of a warrant of arrest or a judgement of conviction against the person sought; and

(d) A statement that a request for surrender of the person sought will follow.

3. A person who is provisionally arrested may be released from custody if the requested State has not received the request for surrender and the documents supporting the request as specified in article 91 within the time limits specified in the Rules of Procedure and Evidence. However, the person may consent to surrender before the expiration of this period if permitted by the law of the requested State. In such a case, the requested State shall proceed to surrender the person to the Court as soon as possible.

4. The fact that the person sought has been released from custody pursuant to paragraph 3 shall not prejudice the subsequent arrest and surrender of that person if the request for surrender and the documents supporting the request are delivered at a later date.

Article 93 – Other forms of cooperation

1. States Parties shall, in accordance with the provisions of this Part and under procedures of national law, comply with requests by the Court to provide the following assistance in relation to investigations or prosecutions:

(a) The identification and whereabouts of persons or the location of items;

(b) The taking of evidence, including testimony under oath, and the production of evidence, including expert opinions and reports necessary to the Court;

(c) The questioning of any person being investigated or prosecuted;

(d) The service of documents, including judicial documents;

(e) Facilitating the voluntary appearance of persons as witnesses or experts before the Court;

(f) The temporary transfer of persons as provided in paragraph 7;

(g) The examination of places or sites, including the exhumation and examination of grave sites;

(h) The execution of searches and seizures;

(i) The provision of records and documents, including official records and documents;

(j) The protection of victims and witnesses and the preservation of evidence;

(k) The identification, tracing and freezing or seizure of proceeds, property and assets and instrumentalities of crimes for the purpose of eventual forfeiture, without prejudice to the rights of bona fide third parties; and

(l) Any other type of assistance which is not prohibited by the law of the requested State, with a view to facilitating the investigation and prosecution of crimes within the jurisdiction of the Court.

2. The Court shall have the authority to provide an assurance to a witness or an expert appearing before the Court that he or she will not be prosecuted, detained or subjected to any restriction of personal freedom by the Court in respect of any act or omission that preceded the departure of that person from the requested State.

3. Where execution of a particular measure of assistance detailed in a request presented under paragraph 1, is prohibited in the requested State on the basis of an existing fundamental legal principle of general application, the requested State shall promptly consult with the Court to try to resolve the matter. In the consultations, consideration should be given to whether the assistance can be rendered in another manner or subject to conditions. If after consultations the matter cannot be resolved, the Court shall modify the request as necessary.

4. In accordance with article 72, a State Party may deny a request for assistance, in whole or in part, only if the request concerns the production of any documents or disclosure of evidence which relates to its national security.

5. Before denying a request for assistance under paragraph 1 (l), the requested State shall consider whether the assistance can be provided subject to specified conditions, or whether the assistance can be provided at a later date or in an alternative manner, provided that if the Court or the Prosecutor accepts the assistance subject to conditions, the Court of the Prosecutor shall abide by them.

6. If a request for assistance is denied, the requested State Party shall promptly inform the Court or the Prosecutor of the reasons for such denial.

7. (a) The Court may request the temporary transfer of a person in custody for purposes of identification or for obtaining testimony or other assistance. The person may be transferred if the following conditions are fulfilled:

(i) The person freely gives his or her informed consent to the transfer; and

(ii) The requested State agrees to the transfer, subject to such conditions as that State and the Court may agree.

(b) The person being transferred shall remain in custody. When the purposes of the transfer have been fulfilled, the Court shall return the person without delay to the requested State.

8. (a) The Court shall ensure the confidentiality of documents and information, except as required for the investigation and proceedings described in the request.

(b) The requested State may, when necessary, transmit documents or information to the Prosecutor on a confidential basis. The Prosecutor may then use them solely for the purpose of generating new evidence;

(c) The requested State may, on its own motion or at the request of the Prosecutor, subsequently consent to the disclosure of such documents or information. They may then be used as evidence pursuant to the provisions of Parts 5 and 6 and in accordance with the Rules of Procedure and Evidence.

9. (a) (i) In the event that a State Party receives competing requests, other than for surrender or extradition, from the Court and from another State pursuant to an international obligation, the State Party shall endeavour, in consultation with the Court and the other State, to meet both requests, if necessary by postponing or attaching conditions to one or the other request.

(ii) Failing that, competing requests shall be resolved in accordance with the principles established in article 90.

(b) Where, however, the request from the Court concerns information, property or persons which are subject to the control of a third State or an international organization by virtue of an international agreement, the requested States shall so inform the Court and the Court shall direct its request to the third State or international organization.

10. (a) The Court may, upon request, cooperate with and provide assistance to a State Party conducting an investigation into or trial in respect of conduct which constitutes a crime within the jurisdiction of the Court or which constitutes a serious crime under the national law of the requesting State.

(b) (i) The assistance provided under subparagraph (a) shall include, inter alia:

(1) The transmission of statements, documents or other types of evidence obtained in the course of an investigation or a trial conducted by the Court; and

(2) The questioning of any person detained by order of the Court;

(ii) In the case of assistance under subparagraph (b) (i) (1):

(1) If the documents or other types of evidence have been obtained with the assistance of a State, such transmission shall require the consent of

that State;

(2) If the statements, documents or other types of evidence have been provided by a witness or expert, such transmission shall be subject to the provisions of article 68.

(c) The Court may, under the conditions set out in this paragraph, grant a request for assistance under this paragraph from a State which is not a Party to the Statute.

Article 94 – Postponement of execution of a request in respect of ongoing investigation or prosecution

1. If the immediate execution of a request would interfere with an ongoing investigation or prosecution of a case different from that to which the request relates, the requested State may postpone the execution of the request for a period of time agreed upon with the Court. However, the postponement shall be no longer than is necessary to complete the relevant investigation or prosecution in the requested State. Before making a decision to postpone, the requested State should consider whether the assistance may be immediately provided subject to certain conditions.

2. If a decision to postpone is taken pursuant to paragraph 1, the Prosecutor may, however, seek measures to preserve evidence, pursuant to article 93, paragraph 1 (j).

Article 95 – Postponement of execution of a request in respect of an admissibility challenge

Without prejudice to article 53, paragraph 2, where there is an admissibility challenge under consideration by the Court pursuant to articles 18 or 19, the requested State may postpone the execution of a request under this Part pending a determination by the Court, unless the Court has specifically ordered that the Prosecutor may pursue the collection of such evidence pursuant to articles 18 or 19.

Article 96 – Contents of request for other forms of assistance under article 93

1. A request for other forms of assistance referred to in article 93 shall be made in writing. In urgent cases, a request may be made by any medium capable of delivering a written record, provided that the request shall be confirmed through the channel provided for in article 87, paragraph 1 (a).

2. The request shall, as applicable, contain or be supported by the following:

(a) A concise statement of the purpose of the request and the assistance sought, including the legal basis and the grounds for the request;

(b) As much detailed information as possible about the location or identification of any person or place that must be found or identified in order for the assistance sought to be provided;

(c) A concise statement of the essential facts underlying the request;

(d) The reasons for and details of any procedure or requirement to be followed;

(e) Such information as may be required under the law of the requested State in order to execute the request; and

(f) Any other information relevant in order for the assistance sought to be provided.

3. Upon the request of the Court, a State Party shall consult with the Court, either generally or with respect to a specific matter, regarding any requirements under its national law that may apply under paragraph 2 (e). During the consultations, the State Party shall advise the Court of the specific requirements of its national law.

4. The provisions of this article shall, where applicable, also apply in respect of a request for assistance made to the Court.

Article 97 – Consultations

Where a State Party receives a request under this Part in relation to which it identifies problems which may impede or prevent the execution of the request, that State shall consult with the Court without delay in order to resolve the matter. Such problems may include, inter alia:

(a) Insufficient information to execute the request;

(b) In the case of a request for surrender, the fact that despite best efforts, the person sought cannot be located or that the investigation conducted has determined that the person in the custodial State is clearly not the person named in the warrant; or

(c) The fact that execution of the request in its current form would require the requested State to breach a pre-existing treaty obligation undertaken with respect to another State.

Article 98 – Cooperation with respect to waiver of immunity and consent to surrender

1. The Court may not proceed with a request for surrender or assistance which would require the requested State to act inconsistently with its obligations under international law with respect to the State or diplomatic immunity of a person or property of a third State, unless the Court can first obtain the cooperation of that third State for the waiver of the immunity.

2. The Court may not proceed with a request for surrender which would require the requested State to act inconsistently with its obligations under international agreements pursuant to which the consent of a sending State is required to surrender a person of that State to the Court, unless the Court can first obtain the cooperation of the sending State for the giving of consent for the surrender.

Article 99 – Execution of requests under articles 93 and 96

1. Requests for assistance shall be executed in accordance with the relevant procedure under the law of the requested State and, unless prohibited by such law, in the manner specified in the request, including following any procedure outlined therein or permitting persons specified in the request to be present at and assist in the execution process.

2. In the case of an urgent request, the documents or evidence produced in response shall, at the request of the Court, be sent urgently.

3. Replies from the requested State shall be transmitted in their original language and form.

4. Without prejudice to other articles in this Part, where it is necessary for the successful execution of a request which can be executed without any compulsory measures, including specifically the interview of or taking evidence from a person on a voluntary basis, including doing so without the presence of the authorities of the requested State Party if it is essential for the request to be executed, and the examination without modification of a public site or other public place, the Prosecutor may execute such request directly on the territory of a State as follows:

(a) When the State Party requested is a State on the territory of which the crime is alleged to have been committed, and there has been a determination of admissibility pursuant to articles 18 or 19, the Prosecutor may directly execute such request following all possible consultations with the requested State Party;

(b) In other cases, the Prosecutor may execute such request following consultations with the requested State Party and subject to any reasonable conditions or concerns raised by that State Party. Where the requested State

Party identifies problems with the execution of a request pursuant to this subparagraph it shall, without delay, consult with the Court to resolve the matter.

5. Provisions allowing a person heard or examined by the Court under article 72 to invoke restrictions designed to prevent disclosure of confidential information connected with national defence or security shall also apply to the execution of requests for assistance under this article.

Article 100 – Costs

1. The ordinary costs for execution of requests in the territory of the requested State shall be borne by that State, except for the following, which shall be borne by the Court:

(a) Costs associated with the travel and security of witnesses and experts or the transfer under article 93 of persons in custody;

(b) Costs of translation, interpretation and transcription;

(c) Travel and subsistence costs of the judges, the Prosecutor, the Deputy Prosecutors, the Registrar, the Deputy Registrar and staff of any organ of the Court;

(d) Costs of any expert opinion or report requested by the Court;

(e) Costs associated with the transport of a person being surrendered to the Court by a custodial State; and

(f) Following consultations, any extraordinary costs that may result from the execution of a request.

2. The provisions of paragraph 1 shall, as appropriate, apply to requests from States Parties to the Court. In that case, the Court shall bear the ordinary costs of execution.

Article 101 – Rule of speciality

1. A person surrendered to the Court under this Statute shall not be proceeded against, punished or detained for any conduct committed prior to surrender, other than the conduct or course of conduct which forms the basis of the crimes for which that person has been surrendered.

2. The Court may request a waiver of the requirements of paragraph 1 from the State which surrendered the person to the Court and, if necessary, the Court shall provide additional information in accordance with article 91. States

Parties shall have the authority to provide a waiver to the Court and should endeavour to do so.

Article 102 – Use of terms

For the purposes of this Statute:

(a) "surrender" means the delivering up of a person by a State to the Court, pursuant to this Statute.

(b) "extradition" means the delivering up of a person by one State to another as provided by treaty, convention or national legislation.

PART 10. ENFORCEMENT

Article 103 – Role of States in enforcement of sentences of imprisonment

1. (a) A sentence of imprisonment shall be served in a State designated by the Court from a list of States which have indicated to the Court their willingness to accept sentenced persons.

(b) At the time of declaring its willingness to accept sentenced persons, a State may attach conditions to its acceptance as agreed by the Court and in accordance with this Part.

(c) A State designated in a particular case shall promptly inform the Court whether it accepts the Court's designation.

2. (a) The State of enforcement shall notify the Court of any circumstances, including the exercise of any conditions agreed under paragraph 1, which could materially affect the terms or extent of the imprisonment. The Court shall be given at least 45 days' notice of any such known or foreseeable circumstances. During this period, the State of enforcement shall take no action that might prejudice its obligations under article 110.

(b) Where the Court cannot agree to the circumstances referred to in subparagraph (a), it shall notify the State of enforcement and proceed in accordance with article 104, paragraph 1.

3. In exercising its discretion to make a designation under paragraph 1, the Court shall take into account the following:

(a) The principle that States Parties should share the responsibility for enforcing sentences of imprisonment, in accordance with principles of equitable distribution, as provided in the Rules of Procedure and Evidence;

(b) The application of widely accepted international treaty standards governing the treatment of prisoners;

(c) The views of the sentenced person; and

(d) The nationality of the sentenced person;

(e) Such other factors regarding the circumstances of the crime or the person sentenced, or the effective enforcement of the sentence, as may be appropriate in designating the State of enforcement.

4. If no State is designated under paragraph 1, the sentence of imprisonment shall be served in a prison facility made available by the host State, in accordance with the conditions set out in the headquarters agreement referred to in article 3, paragraph 2. In such a case, the costs arising out of the enforcement of a sentence of imprisonment shall be borne by the Court.

Article 104 – Change in designation of State of enforcement

1. The Court may, at any time, decide to transfer a sentenced person to a prison of another State.

2. A sentenced person may, at any time, apply to the Court to be transferred from the State of enforcement.

Article 105 – Enforcement of the sentence

1. Subject to conditions which a State may have specified in accordance with article 103, paragraph 1 (b), the sentence of imprisonment shall be binding on the States Parties, which shall in no case modify it.

2. The Court alone shall have the right to decide any application for appeal and revision. The State of enforcement shall not impede the making of any such application by a sentenced person.

Article 106 – Supervision of enforcement of sentences and conditions of imprisonment

1. The enforcement of a sentence of imprisonment shall be subject to the supervision of the Court and shall be consistent with widely accepted international treaty standards governing treatment of prisoners.

2. The conditions of imprisonment shall be governed by the law of the State of enforcement and shall be consistent with widely accepted international treaty standards governing treatment of prisoners; in no case shall such conditions be

more or less favourable than those available to prisoners convicted of similar offences in the State of enforcement.

3. Communications between a sentenced person and the Court shall be unimpeded and confidential.

Article 107 – Transfer of the person upon completion of sentence

1. Following completion of the sentence, a person who is not a national of the State of enforcement may, in accordance with the law of the State of enforcement, be transferred to a State which is obliged to receive him or her, or to another State which agrees to receive him or her, taking into account any wishes of the person to be transferred to that State, unless the State of enforcement authorizes the person to remain in its territory.

2. If no State bears the costs arising out of transferring the person to another State pursuant to paragraph 1, such costs shall be borne by the Court.

3. Subject to the provisions of article 108, the State of enforcement may also, in accordance with its national law, extradite or otherwise surrender the person to the State which has requested the extradition or surrender of the person for purposes of trial or enforcement of a sentence.

PART 11. ASSEMBLY OF STATES PARTIES

Article 112 – Assembly of States Parties

1. An Assembly of States Parties to this Statute is hereby established. Each State Party shall have one representative in the Assembly who may be accompanied by alternates and advisers. Other States which have signed the Statute or the Final Act may be observers in the Assembly.

2. The Assembly shall:

(a) Consider and adopt, as appropriate, recommendations of the Preparatory Commission;

(b) Provide management oversight to the Presidency, the Prosecutor and the Registrar regarding the administration of the Court;

(c) Consider the reports and activities of the Bureau established under paragraph 3 and take appropriate action in regard thereto;

(d) Consider and decide the budget for the Court;

(e) Decide whether to alter, in accordance with article 36, the number of judges;

(f) Consider pursuant to article 87, paragraphs 5 and 7, any question relating to non-cooperation;

(g) Perform any other function consistent with this Statute or the Rules of Procedure and Evidence.

3. (a) The Assembly shall have a Bureau consisting of a President, two Vice-Presidents and 18 members elected by the Assembly for three-year terms.

(b) The Bureau shall have a representative character, taking into account, in particular, equitable geographical distribution and the adequate representation of the principal legal systems of the world.

(c) The Bureau shall meet as often as necessary, but at least once a year. It shall assist the Assembly in the discharge of its responsibilities.

4. The Assembly may establish such subsidiary bodies as may be necessary, including an independent oversight mechanism for inspection, evaluation and investigation of the Court, in order to enhance its efficiency and economy.

5. The President of the Court, the Prosecutor and the Registrar or their representatives may participate, as appropriate, in meetings of the Assembly and of the Bureau.

6. The Assembly shall meet at the seat of the Court or at the Headquarters of the United Nations once a year and, when circumstances so require, hold special sessions. Except as otherwise specified in this Statute, special sessions shall be convened by the Bureau on its own initiative or at the request of one third of the States Parties.

7. Each State Party shall have one vote. Every effort shall be made to reach decisions by consensus in the Assembly and in the Bureau. If consensus cannot be reached, except as otherwise provided in the Statute:

(a) Decisions on matters of substance must be approved by a two-thirds majority of those present and voting provided that an absolute majority of States Parties constitutes the quorum for voting;

(b) Decisions on matters of procedure shall be taken by a simple majority of States Parties present and voting.

8. A State Party which is in arrears in the payment of its financial contributions towards the costs of the Court shall have no vote in the Assembly and in the Bureau if the amount of its arrears equals or exceeds the amount of the contributions due from it for the preceding two full years. The Assembly may, nevertheless, permit such a State Party to vote in the Assembly and in the

Bureau if it is satisfied that the failure to pay is due to conditions beyond the control of the State Party.

9. The Assembly shall adopt its own rules of procedure.

10. The official and working languages of the Assembly shall be those of the General Assembly of the United Nations.

PART 12. FINANCING

Article 113 – Financial Regulations

Except as otherwise specifically provided, all financial matters related to the Court and the meetings of the Assembly of States Parties, including its Bureau and subsidiary bodies, shall be governed by this Statute and the Financial Regulations and Rules adopted by the Assembly of States Parties.

Article 114 – Payment of expenses

Expenses of the Court and the Assembly of States Parties, including its Bureau and subsidiary bodies, shall be paid from the funds of the Court.

Article 115 – Funds of the Court and of the Assembly of States Parties

The expenses of the Court and the Assembly of States Parties, including its Bureau and subsidiary bodies, as provided for in the budget decided by the Assembly of States Parties, shall be provided by the following sources:

(a) Assessed contributions made by States Parties;

(b) Funds provided by the United Nations, subject to the approval of the General Assembly, in particular in relation to the expenses incurred due to referrals by the Security Council.

Article 116 – Voluntary contributions

Without prejudice to article 115, the Court may receive and utilize, as additional funds, voluntary contributions from Governments, international organizations, individuals, corporations and other entities, in accordance with relevant criteria adopted by the Assembly of States Parties.

Article 117 – Assessment of contributions

The contributions of States Parties shall be assessed in accordance with an agreed scale of assessment, based on the scale adopted by the United Nations for its regular budget and adjusted in accordance with the principles on which that scale is based.

Article 118 – Annual audit

The records, books and accounts of the Court, including its annual financial statements, shall be audited annually by an independent auditor.

PART 13. FINAL CLAUSES

Article 119 – Settlement of disputes

1. Any dispute concerning the judicial functions of the Court shall be settled by the decision of the Court.

2. Any other dispute between two or more States Parties relating to the interpretation or application of this Statute which is not settled through negotiations within three months of their commencement shall be referred to the Assembly of States Parties. The Assembly may itself seek to settle the dispute or make recommendations on further means of settlement of the dispute, including referral to the International Court of Justice in conformity with the Statute of that Court.

Article 120 – Reservations

No reservations may be made to this Statute.

Article 121 – Amendments

1. After the expiry of seven years from the entry into force of this Statute, any State Party may propose amendments thereto. The text of any proposed amendment shall be submitted to the Secretary-General of the United Nations, who shall promptly circulate it to all States Parties.

2. No sooner than three months from the date of notification, the next Assembly of States Parties shall, by a majority of those present and voting, decide whether to take up the proposal. The Assembly may deal with the proposal directly or convene a Review Conference if the issue involved so warrants.

3. The adoption of an amendment at a meeting of the Assembly of States Parties or at a Review Conference on which consensus cannot be reached shall require a two - thirds majority of States Parties.

4. Except as provided in paragraph 5, an amendment shall enter into force for all States Parties one year after instruments of ratification or acceptance have been deposited with the Secretary-General of the United Nations by seven-eighths of them.

5. Any amendment to article 5 of this Statute shall enter into force for those States Parties which have accepted the amendment one year after the deposit of their instruments of ratification or acceptance. In respect of a State Party which has not accepted the amendment, the Court shall not exercise its jurisdiction regarding a crime covered by the amendment when committed by that State Party's nationals or on its territory.

6. If an amendment has been accepted by seven-eighths of States Parties in accordance with paragraph 4, any State Party which has not accepted the amendment may withdraw from the Statute with immediate effect, notwithstanding paragraph 1 of article 127, but subject to paragraph 2 of article 127, by giving notice no later than one year after the entry into force of such amendment.

7. The Secretary-General of the United Nations shall circulate to all States Parties any amendment adopted at a meeting of the Assembly of States Parties or at a Review Conference.

Article 122 – Amendments to provisions of an institutional nature

1. Amendments to provisions of the Statute which are of an exclusively institutional nature, namely, article 35, article 36, paragraphs 8 and 9 article 37, article 38, article 39, paragraphs 1 (first two sentences), 2 and 4, article 42, paragraphs 4 to 9, article 43, paragraphs 2 and 3, and articles 44, 46, 47 and 49, may be proposed at any time, notwithstanding article 121, paragraph 1, by any State Party. The text of any proposed amendment shall be submitted to the Secretary-General of the United Nations or such other person designated by the Assembly of States Parties who shall promptly circulate it to all States Parties and to others participating in the Assembly.

2. Amendments under this article on which consensus cannot be reached shall be adopted by the Assembly of States Parties or by a Review Conference, by a two - thirds majority of States Parties. Such amendments shall enter into force for all States Parties six months after their adoption by the Assembly or, as the case may be, by the Conference.

Article 123 – Review of the Statute

1. Seven years after the entry into force of this Statute the Secretary-General of the United Nations shall convene a Review Conference to consider any amendments to this Statute. Such review may include, but is not limited to, the list of crimes contained in article 5. The Conference shall be open to those participating in the Assembly of States Parties and on the same conditions.

2. At any time thereafter, at the request of a State Party and for the purposes set out in paragraph 1, the Secretary-General of the United Nations shall, upon approval by a majority of States Parties, convene a Review Conference.

3. The provisions of article 121, paragraphs 3 to 7, shall apply to the adoption and entry into force of any amendment to the Statute considered at a Review Conference.

Article 124 – Transitional Provision

Notwithstanding article 12 paragraph 1, a State, on becoming a party to this Statute, may declare that, for a period of seven years after the entry into force of this Statute for the State concerned, it does not accept the jurisdiction of the Court with respect to the category of crimes referred to in article 8 when a crime is alleged to have been committed by its nationals or on its territory. A declaration under this article may be withdrawn at any time. The provisions of this article shall be reviewed at the Review Conference convened in accordance with article 123, paragraph 1.

Article 125 – Signature, ratification, acceptance, approval or accession

1. This Statute shall be open for signature by all States in Rome, at the headquarters of the Food and Agriculture Organization of the United Nations, on 17 July 1998. Thereafter, it shall remain open for signature in Rome at the Ministry of Foreign Affairs of Italy until 17 October 1998. After that date, the Statute shall remain open for signature in New York, at United Nations Headquarters, until 31 December 2000.

2. This Statute is subject to ratification, acceptance or approval by signatory States. Instruments of ratification, acceptance or approval shall be deposited with the Secretary-General of the United Nations.

3. This Statute shall be open to accession by all States. Instruments of accession shall be deposited with the Secretary-General of the United Nations.

Article 126 – Entry into force

1. This Statute shall enter into force on the first day of the month after the 60th day following the date of the deposit of the 60th instrument of ratification, acceptance, approval or accession with the Secretary-General of the United Nations.

2. For each State ratifying, accepting, approving or acceding to the Statute after the deposit of the 60th instrument of ratification, acceptance, approval or accession, the Statute shall enter into force on the first day of the month after the 60th day following the deposit by such State of its instrument of ratification, acceptance, approval or accession.

Article 127 – Withdrawal

1. A State Party may, by written notification addressed to the Secretary-General of the United Nations, withdraw from this Statute. The withdrawal shall take effect one year after the date of receipt of the notification, unless the notification specifies a later date.

2. A State shall not be discharged, by reason of its withdrawal, from the obligations arising from this Statute while it was a Party to the Statute, including any financial obligations which may have accrued. Its withdrawal shall not affect any cooperation with the Court in connection with criminal investigations and proceedings in relation to which the withdrawing State had a duty to cooperate and which were commenced prior to the date on which the withdrawal became effective, nor shall it prejudice in any way the continued consideration of any matter which was already under consideration by the Court prior to the date on which the withdrawal became effective.

Article 128 – Authentic texts

The original of this Statute, of which the Arabic, Chinese, English, French, Russian and Spanish texts are equally authentic, shall be deposited with the Secretary-General of the United Nations, who shall send certified copies thereof to all States.

NOTES AND QUESTIONS

(1) The Rome Statute was adopted at the conclusion of a five-week diplomatic conference by a vote of 120 to 7, with 21 abstentions. The vote was taken electronically, but not recorded, so there is no official tally of how particular

states voted. The United States is known to have been one of the seven states voting against the Statute. As of October 2, 2000, the Statute had been signed by 114 countries. It had been ratified by twenty-one: Senegal, Trinidad and Tobago, San Marino, Italy, Fiji, Ghana, Norway, Belize, Tajikistan, Iceland, Venezuela, France, Belgium, Canada, Mali, Lesotho, New Zealand, Botswana, Luxembourg, Sierra Leone, and Gabon. It therefore had just over one-third of the sixty ratifications needed to bring it into force (*see* Art. 126). Current information regarding signatures and ratifications can be found on the website maintained by the NGO Coalition for an International Criminal Court, at <http://www.iccnow.org>.

(2) The Rome Conference, in addition to the Statute, adopted several resolutions which are annexed to the "Final Act" of the Conference (U.N. Doc. A/CONF./183/10). One of these resolutions (Resolution F) established the Preparatory Commission for the International Criminal Court, composed of representatives of states which signed the Final Act and of others invited to participate. The Preparatory Commission ("PrepCom") is to "prepare proposals for practical arrangements for the establishment and coming into operation of the Court," including, among other things, draft texts of the Court' s Rules of Procedure and Evidence, the Elements of Crimes referred to in Article 9 of the Statute, and "proposals for a provision on aggression" (*see* Art. 5(2)). The Preparatory Commission will "remain in existence until the *conclusion* of the first meeting of the Assembly of States Parties." It held its first five sessions between February 1999 and June 2000. Completed drafts of the Rules of Procedure and Evidence (U.N. Doc. PCNICC/2000/INF/3/Add. 1) and Elements of Crimes (U.N. Doc. PCNICC/2000/INF/3/Add. 2) were approved by the Preparatory Commission at the end of the fifth session, on June 30, 2000. These documents are available on the U.N.'s ICC website: <http://www. un.org/law/icc>.

What is the purpose of the Elements of Crimes? Will they be binding on the Court?

Article 9(1) of the Statute says that these Elements "shall assist the Court in the interpretation and application of articles 6, 7 and 8." Article 21(1) says: "The Court shall apply: (a) In the first place, this Statute, Elements of Crimes and its Rules of Procedure and Evidence. . ." In light of this language, could the Court properly refuse the "assistance" provided by the Elements of Crimes?

What is the earliest date on which the provision on aggression can come into effect? Article 5(2) contemplates that the provision on aggression will be adopted in accordance with the procedures for amending the Statute set out in Articles 121 and 123. Articles 121 and 123 indicate that amendments to the Statute can only be adopted after it has been in force for seven years. Is adoption of an amendment defining aggression subject to the seven-year waiting period prescribed in Articles 121 and 123; or is the reference to those articles in Article 5(2) "limited to the *ways of adoption* mentioned therein but not to the time limit contained in those articles"? Otto Triffterer, *Preliminary Remarks: The*

Permanent International Criminal Court — Ideal and Reality, in COMMENTARY ON THE ROME STATUTE OF THE INTERNATIONAL CRIMINAL COURT: OBSERVERS' NOTES, ARTICLE BY ARTICLE 17, 40 (Otto Triffterer ed., 1999).

(4) Should the Statute have given the Court jurisdiction over "international crimes" other than genocide, crimes against humanity, war crimes, and aggression? Consider Resolution E, adopted at the conclusion of the Conference:

> *The United Nations Diplomatic Conference of Plenipotentiaries on the Establishment of an International Criminal Court,*
>
> *Having adopted* the Statute of an International Criminal Court,
>
> *Recognizing* that terrorists acts, by whomever and wherever perpetrated and whatever their forms, methods or motives, are serious crimes of concern to the international community,
>
> *Recognizing* that the international trafficking of illicit drugs is a very serious crime, sometimes destabilizing the political and social and economic order in States,
>
> *Deeply alarmed* at the persistence of these scourges, which pose serious threats to international peace and security,
>
> *Regretting* that no generally acceptable definition of the crimes of terrorism and drug crimes could be agreed upon for the[ir] inclusion, within the jurisdiction of the Court,
>
> *Affirming* that the Statute of the International Criminal Court provides for a review mechanism, which allows for an expansion in the future of the jurisdiction of the Court,
>
> *Recommends* that a Review Conference pursuant to article 123 of the Statute of the International Criminal Court consider the crimes of terrorism and drug crimes with a view to arriving at an acceptable definition and their inclusion in the list of crimes within the jurisdiction of the Court.

(5) Except in cases referred by the Security Council, the Court's jurisdiction depends on the consent of the state on whose territory an offense took place or of the state of which the accused is a national (*see* Art. 12). The Rome Conference did not adopt a proposal to give the Court jurisdiction whenever a state having custody of the accused is a party to the Statute. Can the jurisdiction conferred by the Statute fairly be described, then, as "universal jurisdiction"? *See* Edward M. Wise, *The International Criminal Court: A Budget of Paradoxes*, 8 TULANE J. INT'L & COMP. LAW 261, 270-71 (2000). How far do the limitations imposed on its jurisdiction seriously weaken the potential effectiveness of the ICC?

Article 86 imposes on the parties an obligation to "cooperate fully with the Court in its investigation and prosecution of crimes within the jurisdiction of the Court." What precisely does that obligation entail? Is it true that "the articles that follow so riddled with exceptions and qualifications" as to suggest the states "are not willing to make the concessions to international cooperation that are needed to make the Court a success in practice"? Leila Nadya Sadat & S. Richard Carden, *The New International Criminal Court: An Uneasy Revolution*, 88 GEO. L. J. 381, 444 (2000). Is there any way to enforce the obligation imposed by Article 86?

(5) "What are the advantages and disadvantages of the International Criminal Court? Are the disadvantages based upon particular details in the Statute or fundamental conceptual concerns?" Ellen S. Podgor, in *Panel Discussion: Association of American Law Schools Panel on the International Criminal Court*, 36 AM. CRIM. L. REV. 223, 230 (1999).

Consider the controversial answer given in Alfred P. Rubin, *A Critical View of the Proposed International Criminal Court*, 23 FLETCHER F. WORLD AFF. 139 (1999):

> In my opinion, the ICC as outlined in the Statute cannot possibly work as envisaged. This is not because technical problems have been carelessly handled, although there do seem to be some questions, as must be expected in such a work. It is because the ICC is based on a model of international legal order that seems unrealistic. In concentrating on using the positive law to provide a tribunal intended to enforce the "moral law," the framers of the ICC have created an organization that cannot do what is expected of it.

Why did the United States oppose adoption of the Statute at the Rome Conference? *See* David J. Scheffer, *The United States and the International Criminal Court*, 93 AM. J. INT'L L. 12 (1999); *see also* Bartram S. Brown, *U.S. Objections to the Statute of the International Criminal Court: A Brief Response*, 31 N.Y.U. J. INT'L L. & POL. 855 (1999); John F. Murphy, *The Quivering Gulliver: U.S. Views on a Permanent International Criminal Court*, 34 INT'L LAW. 45 (2000); Michael P. Scharf, *The Politics Behind U.S. Opposition to the International Criminal Court*, 6 BROWN J. WORLD AFF. 97 (1999). On other occasions, the United States has strongly supported the creation of international criminal tribunals. What makes the ICC different? The stated objections boil down, in large part, to concern that U.S. officials and military personnel, who are involved in peace-keeping and humanitarian interventions throughout the world, will be uniquely vulnerable to prosecution on trumped-up charges of having committed war crimes. The United States therefore proposed in Rome that any prosecution before the Court should be authorized by the U.N. Security Council, in which the United States has a veto; or else that a government's consent be required before one of its nationals can be prosecuted. The Conference was not prepared to adopt a rule allowing a country, once it adhered to the Statute, completely to veto the prosecution of its nationals in a particular case. But a number of provisions in the final text were designed to take account of anxieties voiced by the United States. These include the language of Article 8 limiting the Court's jurisdiction over war crimes to those that are "committed as part of a plan or policy or as part of the large-scale commission of such crimes," thus excluding jurisdiction over random acts of individual soldiers; the provision in Article 15, by which the Prosecutor's decision to investigate a particular case requires the approval of a three-judge pre-trial chamber, which in turn is subject to an interlocutory appeal to the Appeals Chamber; the provision of Article 16 allowing the U.N. Security Council to request that an investigation or prosecution be deferred for a year at a time; and the "complementarity" provisions in Articles 17 and 18, by which a case is inadmissible if it is being dealt with by national authorities, unless there is evidence that those authorities are "unwilling or unable genuinely" to prosecute. Do these compromises represent an adequate response to the objections raised by the United States?

(6) Might U.S. military personnel be subject to the Court's jurisdiction even though the United States is not a party to the Statute? Possibly, if they commit crimes under the Statute on the territory of a state which is a party or has otherwise consented to the Court's jurisdiction (*see* Art. 12). On the effect of the Rome Statute on non-parties generally, *see* Gennady M. Danilenko, *The Statute of the International Criminal Court and Third States*, 21 MICH. J. INT'L L. 445 (2000).

Concern with this possibility led the U.S. delegation to propose during the last days of the Rome Conference that the Court should not have jurisdiction over nationals of a non-party state without that state's consent in cases involving "acts of officials or agents of a state in the course of official duties acknowledged by the state as such." *See* Theodor Meron, *The Court We Want*, WASH. POST, Oct. 13, 1998, at A15. Some observers have suggested that had this been the U.S opening position, it might have been adopted; but, given all the other compromises made along the way, there was great reluctance to consider it at the end of the Conference.

Along the same lines, the United States has proposed to the Preparatory Commission that the following provision be contained in a supplemental agreement between the U.N. and the ICC:

The United Nations and the International Criminal Court agree that the Court may seek the surrender or accept custody of a national who acts within the overall direction of a U.N. Member State, and such directing State has so acknowledged, only in the event (a) the directing State is a State Party to the Statute or the Court obtains the consent of the directing State, or (b) measures have been authorized pursuant to Chapter VII of the U.N. Charter against the directing State in relation to the situation or actions giving rise to the alleged crime or crimes, provided that in connection with such authorization the Security Council has determined that this subsection shall apply.

(7) More fundamental objections to the ICC appear to stem from (a) a mistrust of international institutions in general, as posing a threat to full U.S. sovereignty; and (b) the view that the U.S. government lacks constitutional authority to participate in a tribunal that will not afford U.S. citizens all of the procedural guarantees contained in the Bill of Rights. How far are these objections valid? On the constitutional issues involved in U.S. participation, *see* Paul D. Marquardt, *Law Without Borders: The Constitutionality of an International Criminal Court*, 33 COLUM. J. TRANSNAT'L L. 73 (1995). In this connection, consider the proposed legislative findings recited in section 2 of a bill entitled the "American Servicemembers' Protection Act of 2000," S. 2726, 106th Cong., introduced by Senator Helms on June 14, 2000 (and the identical text of the contemporaneous H.R. 4652):

Congress makes the following findings . . . .

(6) Any Americans prosecuted by the International Criminal Court will, under the Rome Statute, be denied many of the procedural protections to which all Americans are entitled under the Bill of Rights to the United States Constitution, including, among others, the right to trial by jury, the right not to be compelled to provide self-incriminating testimony, and the right to confront and cross-examine all witnesses for the prosecution.

(7) American servicemen and women deserve the full protection of the United States Constitution when they are deployed around the world to protect the vital national interests of the United States. The United States Government has an obligation to protect American servicemen and women, to the maximum extent possible, against criminal prosecutions carried out by United Nations officials under procedures that deny them their constitutional rights.

(8) In addition to exposing American servicemen and women to the risk of international criminal prosecution, the Rome Statute creates a risk that the President and other senior elected and appointed officials of the United States Government may be prosecuted by the International Criminal Court. Particularly if the Preparatory Commission agrees on a definition of the Crime of Aggression, senior United States officials may be at risk of criminal prosecution for national security decisions involving such matters as responding to acts of terrorism, preventing the proliferation of weapons of mass destruction, and deterring aggression. No less than American servicemen and women, senior officials of the United States Government deserve the full protection of the United States Constitution with respect to official actions taken by them to protect the national interests of the United States.

Chapter 21

THE SUBSTANTIVE LAW OF INTERNATIONAL CRIMES

§ 21.01 Specific Offenses

[A] Aggression

DEFINITION OF AGGRESSION

General Assembly Resolution 3314 (XXIX), Dec. 14, 1974
U.N. GAOR, Supp. 31, at 143, U.N.Doc. A/9631 (1974)

The General Assembly,

Basing itself on the fact that one of the fundamental purposes of the United Nations is to maintain international peace and security and to take effective collective measures for the prevention and removal of threats to the peace, and for the suppression of acts of aggression or other breaches of the peace,

Recalling that the Security Council, in accordance with Article 39 of the Charter of the United Nations, shall determine the existence of any threat to the peace, breach of the peace or act of aggression and shall make recommendations, or decide what measures shall be taken in accordance with Articles 41 and 42, to maintain or restore international peace and security,

Recalling also the duty of States under the Charter to settle their international disputes by peaceful means in order not to endanger international peace, security and justice,

Bearing in mind that nothing in this Definition shall be interpreted as in any way affecting the scope of the provisions of the Charter with respect to the functions and powers of the organs of the United Nations,

Considering also that, since aggression is the most serious and dangerous form of the illegal use of force, being fraught, in the conditions created by the existence of all types of weapons of mass destruction, with the possible threat of a world conflict and all its catastrophic consequences, aggression should be defined at the present stage,

Reaffirming the duty of States not to use armed force to deprive peoples of their right to self-determination, freedom and independence, or to disrupt territorial Integrity,

Reaffirming also that the territory of a State shall not be violated by being the object, even temporarily, of military occupation or of other measures of force taken by another State in contravention of the Charter, and that it shall not be the object of acquisition by another State resulting from such measures or the threat thereof,

Reaffirming also the provisions of the Declaration on Principles of International Law concerning Friendly Relations and Cooperation among States in accordance with the Charter of the United Nations,

Convinced that the adoption of a definition of aggression ought to have the effect of deterring a potential aggressor, would simplify the determination of acts of aggression and the implementation of measures to suppress them and would also facilitate the protection of the rights and lawful interests of, and the rendering of assistance to, the victim,

Believing that, although the question whether an act of aggression has been committed must be considered in the light of all the circumstances of each particular case, it is nevertheless desirable to formulate basic principles as guidance for such determination,

Adopts the following Definition of Aggression:

Article I

Aggression is the use of armed force by a State against the sovereignty, territorial integrity or political independence of another State, or in any other manner inconsistent with the Charter of the United Nations, as set out in this Definition.

Article 2

The first use of armed force by a State in contravention of the Charter shall constitute *prima facie* evidence of an act of aggression although the Security Council may, in conformity with the Charter, conclude that a determination that an act of aggression has been committed would not be justified in the light of other relevant circumstances, including the fact that the acts concerned or their consequences are not of sufficient gravity.

Article 3

Any of the following acts, regardless of a declaration of war, shall, subject to and in accordance with the provisions of article 2, qualify as an act of aggression:

(a) The invasion or attack by the armed forces of a State of the territory of another State, or any military occupation, however temporary, resulting from such invasion or attack, or any annexation by the use of force of the territory of another State or part thereof,

(b) Bombardment by the armed forces of a State against the territory of another State or the use of any weapons by a State against the territory of another State;

(c) The blockade of the ports or coasts of a State by the armed forces of another State;

(d) An attack by the armed forces of a State on the land, sea or air forces, or marine and air fleets of another State;

(e) The use of armed forces of one State which are within the territory of another State with the agreement of the receiving State, in contravention of the conditions provided for in the agreement or any extension of their presence in such territory beyond the termination of the agreement;

(f) The action of a State in allowing its territory, which it has placed at the disposal of another State, to be used by that other State for perpetrating an act of aggression against a third State;

(g) The sending by or on behalf of a State of armed bands, groups, irregulars or mercenaries, which carry out acts of armed force against another State of such gravity as to amount to the acts listed above, or its substantial involvement therein.

Article 4

The acts enumerated above are not exhaustive and the Security Council may determine that other acts constitute aggression under the provisions of the Charter.

Article 5

1. No consideration of whatever nature, whether political, economic, military or otherwise, may serve as a justification for aggression.

2. A war of aggression is a crime against international peace. Aggression gives

rise to international responsibility.

3. No territorial acquisition or special advantage resulting from aggression is or shall be recognized as lawful.

Article 6

Nothing in this Definition shall be construed as in any way enlarging or diminishing the scope of the Charter, including its provisions concerning cases in which the use of force is lawful.

Article 7

Nothing in this Definition, and in particular article 3, could in any way prejudice the right to self-determination, freedom and independence, as derived from the Charter, of peoples forcibly deprived of that right and referred to in the Declaration on Principles of International Law concerning Friendly Relations and Cooperation among States in accordance with the Charter of the United Nations, particularly peoples under colonial and racist regimes or other forms of alien domination: nor the right of these peoples to struggle to that end and to seek and receive support, in accordance with the principles of the Charter and in conformity with the above-mentioned Declaration.

Article 8

In their interpretation and application the above provisions are interrelated and each provision should be construed in the context of the other provisions.

NOTES AND QUESTIONS

(1) The General Assembly adopted Resolution 3314 by consensus, without taking a vote. An explanatory note to Article 1 added that: "In this definition, the term 'State' (a) Is used without prejudice to questions of recognition or to whether a State is a Member of the United Nations; (b) Includes the concept of a 'group of States' where appropriate." This was meant, in part, to indicate that the term covered divided territories such as Germany, Korea, and China.

(2) Compare the General Assembly's definition of aggression with the definition of "crimes against peace" in the Charters of the Nuremberg and Tokyo Tribunals [see chap. 18, supra]. On the problem of defining aggression, and for further references, see generally M. Cherif Bassiouni & Benjamin B. Ferencz,

The Crime Against Peace, in 1 INTERNATIONAL CRIMINAL LAW 313 (M. Cherif Bassiouni ed., 2d ed. 1999).

(3) Over the opposition of the United States, Article 5 of the Rome Statute [*see* chap. 20] gives the International Criminal Court jurisdiction over "the crime of aggression," but goes on the provide that the Court can assume jurisdiction over this crime only after an amendment to the Statute is adopted defining the crime and the conditions under which the Court is to exercise jurisdiction over it. Article 5 further stipulates that "[s]uch a provision shall be consistent with the relevant provisions of the Charter of the United Nations."

In devising the definition called for by Article 5, what weight should be given to General Assembly Resolution 3314 (1974)? Does it represent an authoritative statement of international law? Note that, in the *Nicaragua* case [*Military and Paramilitary Activities in and against Nicaragua (Nicar. v. U.S.)*, Merits, 1986 I.C.J. REP. 14, 103, para. 195 (June 27)], the International Court of Justice indicated that Article 3(g) of the General Assembly's Definition "may be taken to reflect customary international law." But even if the Declaration is a statement of existing international law, is it necessarily binding on the Security Council? Recall that Article 39 of the U.N. Charter provides: "The Security Council shall determine the existence of any threat to the peace, breach of the peace, or act of aggression and shall make recommendations, or decide what measures shall be taken . . . to maintain or restore international peace and security." Under the system established by the Charter, is it possible to produce a definition of aggression that does not leave the final decision as to whether aggression occurred to the Security Council? If the Security Council has the decisive word as to whether aggression occurred, is it possible to devise a definition of aggression for purposes of imposing criminal sanctions on individuals that will not make liability directly depend on the decision of a political body? Can doing so be reconciled with ordinary understandings of how criminal law is supposed to operate?

[B] Genocide and Crimes Against Humanity

CONVENTION ON THE PREVENTION AND PUNISHMENT OF THE CRIME OF GENOCIDE

General Assembly Resolution 260 A (III), Dec. 9, 1948
78 U.N.T.S. 277

The Contracting Parties,

Having considered the declaration made by the General Assembly of the United Nations in its resolution 96 (I) dated 11 December 1946 that genocide is a crime under international law, contrary to the spirit and aims of the United Nations and condemned by the civilized world;

Recognizing that at all periods of history genocide has inflicted great losses on humanity; and

Being convinced that, in order to liberate mankind from such an odious scourge, international co-operation is required,

Hereby agree as hereinafter provided:

Article I

The Contracting Parties confirm that genocide, whether committed in time of peace or in time of war, is a crime under international law which they undertake to prevent and to punish.

Article II

In the present Convention, genocide means any of the following acts committed with intent to destroy, in whole or in part, a national, ethnical, racial or religious group, as such:

   (a) Killing members of the group;

   (b) Causing serious bodily or mental harm to members of the group;

   (c) Deliberately inflicting on the group conditions of life calculated to bring about its physical destruction in whole or in part;

   (d) Imposing measures intended to prevent births within the group;

   (e) Forcibly transferring children of the group to another group.
   Article III

The following acts shall be punishable:

   (a) Genocide;

   (b) Conspiracy to commit genocide;

   (c) Direct and public incitement to commit genocide;

   (d) Attempt to commit genocide;

   (e) Complicity in genocide.

Article IV

Persons committing genocide or any of the other acts enumerated in article III shall be punished, whether they are constitutionally responsible rulers, public officials or private individuals.

Article V

The Contracting Parties undertake to enact, in accordance with their respective Constitutions, the necessary legislation to give effect to the provisions of the present Convention, and, in particular, to provide effective penalties for persons guilty of genocide or any of the other acts enumerated in article III.

Article VI

Persons charged with genocide or any of the other acts enumerated in article III shall be tried by a competent tribunal of the State in the territory of which the act was committed, or by such international penal tribunal as may have jurisdiction with respect to those Contracting Parties which shall have accepted its jurisdiction.

Article VII

Genocide and the other acts enumerated in article III shall not be considered as political crimes for the purpose of extradition.

The Contracting Parties pledge themselves in such cases to grant extradition in accordance with their laws and treaties in force.

Article VIII

Any Contracting Party may call upon the competent organs of the United Nations to take such action under the Charter of the United Nations as they consider appropriate for the prevention and suppression of acts of genocide or any of the other acts enumerated in article III.

Article IX

Disputes between the Contracting Parties relating to the interpretation, application or fulfilment of the present Convention, including those relating to the responsibility of a State for genocide or for any of the other acts enumerated in article III, shall be submitted to the International Court of Justice at the request of any of the parties to the dispute.

Notes and Questions

(1) The Genocide Convention contains nineteen articles. Articles 10 to 19 are "final clauses." The Convention came into force on January 12, 1951. It was not ratified by the United States until 1986. The Convention was given effect as part of U.S. law through the Genocide Convention Implementation Act of 1987, Pub. L. 100-106, 102 Stat. 3045, enacted on November 5, 1988. The act is codified at 18 U.S. Code §§ 1091-1093. It reads as follows:

§ 1091. Genocide

(a) Basic offense. Whoever, whether in time of peace or in time of war, in a circumstance described in subsection (d) and with the specific intent to destroy, in whole or in substantial part, a national, ethnic, racial, or religious group as such –

(1) kills members of that group;

(2) causes serious bodily injury to members of that group;

(3) causes the permanent impairment of the mental faculties of members of the group through drugs, torture, or similar techniques;

(4) subjects the group to conditions of life that are intended to cause the physical destruction of the group in whole or in part;

(5) imposes measures intended to prevent births within the group; or

(6) transfers by force children of the group to another group;
or attempts to do so, shall be punished as provided in subsection (b).

(b) Punishment for basic offense. The punishment for an offense under subsection (a) is –

(1) in the case of an offense under subsection (a)(1), where death results, by death or imprisonment for life and a fine of not more than $1,000,000, or both; and

(2) a fine of not more than $1,000,000 or imprisonment for not more than twenty years, or both, in any other case.

(c) Incitement offense. Whoever in a circumstance described in subsection (d) directly and publicly incites another to violate subsection (a) shall be fined not more than $500,000 or imprisoned not more than five years, or both.

(d) Required circumstance for offense. The circumstance referred to in subsections (a) and (c) is that –

(1) the offense is committed within the United States; or

(2) the alleged offender is a national of the United States (as defined in section 101 of the Immigration and Nationality Act (8 U.S.C. § 1101)).

(e) Nonapplicability of certain limitation. Notwithstanding section 3282 of this title, in the case of an offense under subsection (a)(1), an indictment may be found, or information   instituted, at any time without limitation.

§ 1092. Exclusive remedies

Nothing in this chapter [18 USCS §§ 1091 et seq.] shall be construed as precluding the application of State or local laws to the conduct proscribed by this chapter, nor shall anything in this chapter be construed as creating any substantive or procedural right enforceable by law by any party in any proceeding.

§ 1093. Definitions

As used in this chapter [18 USCS §§ 1091 et seq.] –

(1) the term "children" means the   plural and means individuals who have not attained the age of eighteen years;

(2) the term "ethnic group" means a set of individuals whose identity as such is distinctive in terms of common cultural traditions or heritage;

(3) the term "incites" means urges another to engage imminently in conduct in circumstances under which there is a substantial likelihood of imminently causing such conduct;

(4) the term "members" means the plural;

(5) the term "national group" means a set of individuals whose identity as such is distinctive in terms of nationality or national origins;

(6) the term "racial group" means a set of individuals whose identity as such is distinctive in terms of physical characteristics or biological descent;

(7) the term "religious group" means a set of individuals whose identity as such is distinctive in terms of common religious creed, beliefs, doctrines, practices, or rituals; and

(8) the term "substantial part" means a part of a group of such numerical significance that the destruction or loss of that part would cause the destruction of the group as a viable entity within the nation of which such group is a part.

How does the definition of "genocide" in the U.S. statute differ from that in the Genocide Convention? Note that in ratifying the Convention, the U.S. expressed the interpretive "understanding" that, as used in the Convention, (1) the phrase intent to destroy a group "in whole or in part" means the specific intent to destroy it "in whole or substantial part"; and (2) the term "mental harm" means "permanent impairment of mental facilities through drugs, torture or similar techniques."

(2) Does either the Convention or the U.S. statute contemplate the possibility of courts exercising "universal jurisdiction" in cases of genocide? Does that necessarily preclude the exercise of such jurisdiction?

(3) One of the most controversial aspects of the definition of "genocide" in the Convention is its exclusion of political and social groups from the list of those protected. The term "genocide" was coined by Raphael Lemkin in his book, AXIS RULE IN OCCUPIED EUROPE (1944), to describe Nazi efforts to reconstruct social and economic structure, to Aryanize, and to destroy a sense of separate national identity, in German-occupied territories. *See also* Raphael Lemkin, *Genocide as a Crime Under International Law*, 41 AM J. INT'L L. 145 (1947). General Assembly Resolution 96(1), Dec. 11, 1946, which is referred to in the preamble to the Genocide Convention, declared that "genocide is a crime under international law" and is punishable "whether the crimes is committed on religious, racial, political or any other grounds." Two years later, the Convention dropped the possibility that genocide could be committed against a political group. Under the Convention's definition, would the murder of a million or more Cambodians by the Khmer Rouge between 1975 and 1979, as part of an effort to reconstruct the country's social and economic structure, constitute genocide? Nevertheless, the definition of "genocide" in international instruments has remained remarkably stable since 1948. There is an obvious reluctance to tamper with the canonical statement contained in a widely-ratified agreement.

(4) Compare, by contrast, the different definitions of "crimes against humanity" contained in Article 6(c) of the Charter of the Nuremberg Tribunal, in Article 5(c) of the Charter of the Tokyo Tribunal, in Article II(1)(c) of Allied Control Council Law No. 10 [chap. 18, *supra*], in Article 5 of the ICTY Statute, in Article 3 of the ICTR Statute [chap. 19, *supra*], in Article 18 of the International Law Commission's 1996 Draft Code of Crimes Against the Peace and Security of Mankind [chap. 17, *supra*], and in Article 7 of the Rome Statute [chap. 20, *supra*]. What precisely are the differences between these various

definitions? What seems to account for these differences? Assuming (as is generally believed to be the case) that "crimes against humanity" constitute a violation of customary international law, which definition more accurately reflects customary international law? How would one tell? What is the case for requiring, for instance, that "crimes against humanity" must occur during an international armed conflict, or during armed conflict, or be committed on "discriminatory grounds," or be "widespread and systematic"? What is the relationship between "crimes against humanity" under one or another of these definitions and genocide or war crimes? For comprehensive discussion of the concept of "crimes against humanity," *see* M. CHERIF BASSIOUNI, CRIMES AGAINST HUMANITY IN INTERNATIONAL LAW (2d ed. 1999).

[C] War Crimes

The first Hague Peace Conference of 1899 sought to codify the rules governing permissible and impermissible methods for the conduct of war in a series of declarations and conventions. It was followed by a second Hague Peace Conference in 1907. The Regulations attached to Hague Convention IV of 1907 still constitute the basic statement of the rules of land warfare. These are now generally regarded as amounting to rules of customary international law. No conference has been called since to revise or update the laws of war as a whole; but there have been subsequent conventions directed toward specific problems, such as the 1954 Convention for the Protection of Cultural Property in the Event of Armed Conflict, or the 1976 Convention on the Prohibition of Military or Any Other Hostile Use of Environmental Modification Techniques. For the texts of the various conventions defining what are now considered "war crimes," *see* THE LAWS OF ARMED CONFLICTS (Dietrich Schindler & Jiri Toman eds., 3d ed. 1988).

No provision of the Hague Conventions actually uses the term "war crime" or refers to individual responsibility for breaches of those conventions. It seems to have been assumed that the parties would punish violations under their own municipal law. They were required to do so when violations were committed by their own forces and permitted to do so when violations were committed by the enemy. Punishing violations committed by captured members of enemy forces constituted, in effect, a species of reprisal, which was tolerated on the ground that strong, individualized reprisals are virtually the only means available during the course of hostilities to insure that parties to the conflict continue to observe the rules of war. But, at least since Nuremberg, at least certain violations of the Hague Conventions have been widely understood as not only conduct that belligerents are required or permitted to punish, but also as conduct that give rise to individual criminal responsibility under international law.

The Hague Conventions cover methods for the conduct of war. Another part of the law of war is contained in a series of Geneva Conventions, culminating in the four Geneva Conventions of 1949, supplemented by two Additional

Protocols in 1977. The four conventions of 1949 respectively set out rules (1) for the Amelioration of the Condition of the Wounded and Sick in Armed Forces in the Field; (2) for the Amelioration of the Condition of the Wounded, Sick and Shipwrecked Members of the Armed Forces at Sea, (3) Relative to the Treatment of Prisoners of War, and (4) Relative to the Protection of Civilians in Time of War (especially in occupied territory). Common provisions in all four conventions single out certain violations as constituting "grave breaches" and require each party "to enact any legislation necessary to provide effective penal sanctions" for such "grave breaches," and "to search for persons alleged to have committed, or to have ordered" them, and to "bring such persons, regardless of their nationality, before its own courts" or, "if it prefers . . .[to] hand such persons over for trial to another High Contracting Party concerned. . ." These obligations are imposed on states; but, again, the substance of the provisions of the Geneva Convention with respect to "grave breaches" are widely regarded as having been transmuted into rules of customary international law that give rise to individual criminal responsibility.

Common Article 3, which appears in each of the four Geneva Conventions (and is quoted in *Kadic v. Karadzic*, chap. 9, *supra*), applies in cases of "armed conflict not of an international character" which occurs in the territory of one of the parties. It sets out a basic code of humanitarian rules to be followed in such a conflict. Additional Protocol II likewise applies to non-international armed conflicts and supplements common Article 3. The *Tadic* and *Akayesu* opinions [*see* chap.19, *supra*] consider the question of how far customary international law imposes individual criminal responsibility for the violation of these rules.

§21.02 The General Part

A system of criminal law does more than proscribe specific offenses: it also contains principles and rules about what constitutes culpable conduct, about what mental states are required for criminal liability, about when particular results can be attributed to a particular actor, about responsibility for the conduct of others and for inchoate crimes, about general justifications for otherwise wrongful conduct, about excuses that entirely or partially exclude culpability, and about the grading of offenses and sanctions according to different levels and degrees of culpability and harm. The rules pertaining to all of these matters vary as between different national systems. So long as the prosecution of international crimes takes place in national courts, one has to expect that there will be national differences in the general concepts and rules of criminal law applied in such prosecutions. *See* Edward M. Wise, *War Crimes and Criminal Law, in* STUDIES IN COMPARATIVE CRIMINAL LAW 35 (Edward M. Wise & Gerhard O. W. Mueller eds., 1975).

At the same time, in part because the concepts and principles of criminal law have a normative dimension that serves to promote a just as well as effective system of law enforcement, there are, notwithstanding national differences, considerable similarities in basic principles of criminal law throughout the world. It is this measure of commonality that made possible agreement on Part 3 of the Rome Statute [*see* chap. 20, *supra*], which sets out the "General Principles of Criminal Law" to be applied by the International Criminal Court. *See* OBSERVATIONS ON THE CONSOLIDATED ICC TEXT BEFORE THE FINAL SESSION OF THE PREPARATORY COMMITTEE 45 (Association Internationale de Droit Pénal, Nouvelles Études Pénales No. 13 *bis*, Leila Sadat Wexler ed., 1998). For commentary on the Statute's treatment of these general principles, *see* COMMENTARY ON THE ROME STATUTE OF THE INTERNATIONAL CRIMINAL COURT: OBSERVERS' NOTES, ARTICLE BY ARTICLE 447-588 (Otto Triffterer ed., 1999); Kai Ambos, *General Principles of Criminal Law in the Rome Statute*, 10 CRIM. L. F. 1 (1999); William A. Schabas, *General Principles of Criminal Law in the International Criminal Court Statute (Part III)*, 6 EUR. J. CRIME, CRIM. L. & CRIM. JUST. 400 (1998).

Meanwhile, as illustrated by the following case, the *ad hoc* tribunals for the former Yugoslavia and Rwanda also have been confronted with the need to resolve differences with respect to general principles of criminal law.

PROSECUTOR v. ERDEMOVIC

International Criminal Tribunal for the former Yugoslavia
Case No. IT-96-22-A, Appeals Chamber, Judgement, Oct. 7, 1997

[Before Trial Chamber I, Erdemovic, a Bosnian Croat, pleaded guilty to a charge of committing "crimes against humanity" by participating, as a member of the Bosnian Serb army, in the massacre of Bosnian Muslims that followed the fall of the U.N. "safe area" of Srebrenica in 1995. There were, however, certain equivocal elements in his admission of guilt, since he claimed to have acted on superior orders and under duress. In accepting his plea, the Trial Chamber felt obliged to ask whether, on the facts of the case, he actually was guilty. It concluded that acting under superior orders or duress had no bearing on liability, although it might serve to mitigate the sentence. Erdemovic was sentenced to ten years' imprisonment. *See Prosecutor v. Erdemovic*, Case No. IT-96-22-T, Sentencing Judgement (Nov. 29, 1996).

Erdemovic appealed against his sentence, in part on procedural grounds, in part on the ground that the Trial Chamber had erred in rejecting duress as a complete defense. The five judges constituting the Appeals Chamber were Antonio Cassese (Italy), Gabrielle Kirk McDonald (U.S.A.), Haopei Li (China), Ninian Stephen (Australia), and Lal Chand Vohrah (Malaysia). The Appeals Chamber, by a majority of four to one (Judge Li dissenting), held that, under the circumstances of the case, Erdemovic's plea was not fully informed. It remanded the matter to another Trial Chamber to allow Erdemovic to replead. The Appeals Chamber also held, by three votes to two (Judges Cassese and Stephen dissenting), that duress cannot be a complete defense to a charge of "crimes against humanity" or of war crimes which involve the killing of innocent human beings. Each of the five judges in the Appeals Chamber appended to the judgment a lengthy separate opinion. The following extracts from the opinions delivered in the Appeals Chamber concern the issue of whether duress can ever afford a complete defense.]

JUDGEMENT

19. For the reasons set out in the Joint Separate Opinion of Judge McDonald and Judge Vohrah and in the Separate and Dissenting Opinion of Judge Li, the majority of the Appeals Chamber finds that duress does not afford a complete defence to a soldier charged with a crime against humanity and/or a war crime involving the killing of innocent human beings. Consequently, the majority of the Appeals Chamber finds that the guilty plea of the Appellant was not equivocal. Judge Cassese and Judge Stephen dissent from this view for the reasons set out in their Separate and Dissenting Opinions.

JOINT SEPARATE OPINION OF JUDGE MCDONALD AND JUDGE VOHRAH:

43. [T]he only express affirmation of the availability of duress as a defence to the killing of innocent persons in post-World War Two military tribunal cases appears in the *Einsatzgruppen* case before a United States military tribunal. . . . [H]owever, the value of this authority is cast into some considerable doubt by the fact that the United States military tribunal in the *Einsatzgruppen* case did not cite any authority for its opinion that duress may constitute a complete defence to killing an innocent individual. . . .

44. [Moreover,] the *Einsatzgruppen* decision is in discord with the preponderant view of international authorities. There is no other precedent in the case-law of international post-World War Two military tribunals which could be cited as authority for the proposition that duress is a complete defence to the killing of innocent persons in international law. . . .

47. A number of war crimes cases have been brought to our attention as supporting the position that duress is a complete defence to the killing of innocent persons in international law . . . .

48. . . . In our view, however, these cases are insufficient to support the finding of a customary rule providing for the availability of the defence of duress to the killing of innocent persons. . . . [A] number of the cases are of questionable relevance and authority. . . .

49. Although some of the above mentioned cases may clearly represent the positions of national jurisdictions regarding the availability of duress as a complete defence to the killing of innocent persons, neither they nor the

principles on this issue found in decisions of the post-World War Two military tribunals are, in our view, entitled to be given the status of customary international law. . . . To the extent that the domestic decisions and national laws of States relating to the issue of duress as a defence to murder may be regarded as state practice, it is quite plain that this practice is not at all consistent.

52. . . . [I]n addition . . . the above mentioned cases were decisions of national military tribunals or national courts which applied national law, not international law. . . .

53. In relation to the post-World War Two military tribunals constituted under the London Charter or Control Council Law No. 10, doubt remains as to whether any of these military tribunals were truly "international in character."
. . . .

54. . . . [T]o the extent that the post-World War Two military tribunals constituted under the London Charter or Control Council Law No.10 were held to be international, this was merely with regard to their constitution, character and competence. . . . [T]hese tribunals . . . invariably drew on the jurisprudence of their own national jurisdictions. This is evidenced by the fact that British military tribunals followed British law and the United States military tribunals followed United States law.

55. In light of the above discussion, it is our considered view that no rule may be found in customary international law regarding the availability or the non-availability of duress as a defence to a charge of killing innocent human beings. The post-World War Two military tribunals did not establish such a rule. We do not think that the decisions of these tribunals or those of other national courts and military tribunals constitute consistent and uniform state practice . . . .

66. [The opinion goes on to survey the treatment of duress in various legal systems and concludes that it is] a general principle of law recognised by civilised nations that an accused person is less blameworthy and less deserving of the full punishment when he performs a certain prohibited act under duress.
. . .

67. The rules of the various legal systems of the world are, however, largely inconsistent regarding the specific question whether duress affords a complete defence to a combatant charged with a war crime or a crime against humanity involving the killing of innocent persons. . . . [C]ivil law systems in general would theoretically allow duress as a complete defence to all crimes including murder and unlawful killing. On the other hand, there are laws of other legal systems which categorically reject duress as a defence to murder. . . .

72. It is clear from the differing positions of the principal legal systems of the world that there is no consistent concrete rule which answers the question

whether or not duress is a defence to the killing of innocent persons. It is not possible to reconcile the opposing positions and, indeed, we do not believe that the issue should be reduced to a contest between common law and civil law. We would therefore approach this problem bearing in mind the specific context in which the International Tribunal was established, the types of crimes over which it has jurisdiction, and the fact that the International Tribunal's mandate is expressed in the Statute as being in relation to "serious violations of international humanitarian law."

75. [T]he law should not be the product or slave of logic or intellectual hair-splitting, but must serve broader normative purposes in light of its social, political and economic role. . . . The purview of the International Tribunal relates to war crimes and crimes against humanity committed in armed conflicts of extreme violence with egregious dimensions. . . . We are concerned that, in relation to the most heinous crimes known to humankind, the principles of law to which we give credence have the appropriate normative effect upon soldiers bearing weapons of destruction and upon the commanders who control them in armed conflict situations. The facts of this particular case, for example, involved the cold-blooded slaughter of 1200 men and boys by soldiers using automatic weapons. We must bear in mind that we are operating in the realm of international humanitarian law which has, as one of its prime objectives, the protection of the weak and vulnerable in such a situation where their lives and security are endangered. Concerns about the harm which could arise from admitting duress as a defence to murder were sufficient to persuade a majority of the House of Lords and the Privy Council to categorically deny the defence in the national context to prevent the growth of domestic crime and the impunity of miscreants. Are they now insufficient to persuade us to similarly reject duress as a complete defence in our application of laws designed to take account of humanitarian concerns in the arena of brutal war, to punish perpetrators of crimes against humanity and war crimes, and to deter the commission of such crimes in the future? If national law denies recognition of duress as a defence in respect of the killing of innocent persons, international criminal law can do no less than match that policy since it deals with murders often of far greater magnitude. If national law denies duress as a defence even in a case in which a single innocent life is extinguished due to action under duress, international law, in our view, cannot admit duress in cases which involve the slaugher of innocent human beings on a large scale. . . .

78. We do not think our reference to considerations of policy are improper. It would be naive to believe that international law operates and develops wholly divorced from considerations of social and economic policy. There is the view that international law should distance itself from social policy . . . . We are of the opinion that this separation of law from social policy is inapposite in relation to the application of international humanitarian law to crimes occurring during times of war. It is clear to us that whatever is the distinction between the international legal order and municipal legal orders in general, the distinction is imperfect in respect of the criminal law which, both at the international and the municipal level, is directed towards consistent aims. At the municipal level,

criminal law and criminal policy are closely intertwined. There is no reason why this should be any different in international criminal law. . . .

79. . . . It has been argued that . . . . in a situation where the victim or victims would have died in any event, such as in the present case where the victims were to be executed by firing squad, there would be no reason for the accused to have sacrificed his life. The accused could not have saved the victim life by giving his own and thus, according to this argument, it is unjust and illogical for the law to expect an accused to sacrifice his life in the knowledge that the victim/s will die anyway. The argument, it is said, is vindicated in the Italian case of *Masetti* which was decided by the Court of Assize in L'Aquila. The accused in that case raised duress in response to the charge of having organised the execution of two partisans upon being ordered to do so by the battalion commander. The Court of Assize acquitted the accused on the ground of duress . . .

80.The *Masetti* approach proceeds from the starting point of strict utilitarian logic based on the fact that if the victim will die anyway, the accused is not at all morally blameworthy for taking part in the execution; there is absolutely no reason why the accused should die as it would be unjust for the law to expect the accused to die for nothing. It should be immediately apparent that the assertion that the accused is not morally blameworthy where the victim would have died in any case depends entirely again upon a view of morality based on utilitarian logic. This does not, in our opinion, address the true rationale for our rejection of duress as a defence to the killing of innocent human beings. The approach we take does not involve a balancing of harms for and against killing but rests upon an application in the context of international humanitarian law of the rule that duress does not justify or excuse the killing of an innocent person. Our view is based upon a recognition that international humanitarian law should guide the conduct of combatants and their commanders. There must be legal limits as to the conduct of combatants and their commanders in armed conflict. In accordance with the spirit of international humanitarian law, we deny the availability of duress as a complete defence to combatants who have killed innocent persons. In so doing, we give notice in no uncertain terms that those who kill innocent persons will not be able to take advantage of duress as a defence and thus get away with impunity for their criminal acts in the taking of innocent lives. . . .

88. After the above survey of authorities in the different systems of law and exploration of the various policy considerations which we must bear in mind, we take the view that duress cannot afford a complete defence to a soldier charged with crimes against humanity or war crimes in international law involving the taking of innocent lives. We do so having regard to our mandated obligation under the Statute to ensure that international humanitarian law, which is concerned with the protection of humankind, is not in any way undermined. .

SEPARATE AND DISSENTING OPINION OF JUDGE LI:

2. With regard to this question [of whether duress can be a complete defence to the massacre of innocent civilians], there is neither applicable conventional nor customary international law for its solution.

3. National laws and practices of various States on this question are also divergent, so that no general principle of law recognised by civilised nations can be deduced from them. . . .

4. As no general principle of law can be found on the question, recourse is to be had to the decisions of Military Tribunals, both international and national, which apply international law. . . .

5. From a study of these decisions the following principles can be obtained: as a general rule, duress can be a complete defence if the following requirements are met, (a) the act was done to avoid an immediate danger both serious and irreparable, (b) there was no other adequate means to escape, and (c) the remedy was not disproportionate to evil. To this general rule there is an important exception: if the act was a heinous crime, for instance, the killing of innocent civilians or prisoners of war, duress cannot be a complete defence, but can only be a ground of mitigation of punishment if justice requires. . . .

8. In my view, both the rule and the exception are reasonable and sound, and should be applied by this International Tribunal. In the first place, the main aim of international humanitarian law is the protection of innocent civilians, prisoners of war and other persons *hors de combat*. As the life of an innocent human being is the *sine qua non* of his existence, so international humanitarian law must strive to ensure its protection and to deter its destruction. Admission of duress as a complete defence or justification in the massacre of innocent persons is tantamount to both encouraging the subordinate under duress to kill such persons with impunity instead of deterring him from committing such a horrendous crime, and also helping the superior in his attempt to kill them. Such an anti-human policy of law the international community can never tolerate, and this International Tribunal can never adopt.

Second, the present municipal laws of various countries regarding the propriety or necessity of recognising the exception to the rule, as shown above, are divergent. On the one hand, the legal systems of the British Commonwealth and some civil-law systems admit the exception. On the other hand, some other civil-law systems do not provide for it. In such circumstances, this International Tribunal cannot but opt for the solution best suited for the protection of innocent persons.

9. In support of the argument that duress can be a complete defence to the massacre of innocent civilians the *Einsatzgruppen* case is referred to. The facts of this case are that the accused Ohlendorf and 23 other persons were commanders or subordinate officers of special SS units called *Einsatzgruppen*,

who accompanied the German Army in its invasion of Soviet Russia during the Second World War and exterminated Jews, gypsies, insane people, communist functionaries and so-called "Asiatic inferiors and asocials," who were civilians or prisoners of war. These SS Units caused the death of approximately one million of such persons in the German-occupied territories of Russia. The principal charge of this case was murder to which the plea of duress was raised by the accused.

10. In its Judgement the United States Military Tribunal at Nürnberg stated the following:

> But it is stated that in military law even if the subordinate realises that the act he is called upon to perform is a crime, he may not refuse its execution without incurring serious consequences, and that this, therefore, constitutes duress. Let it be said at once that there is no law which requires that an innocent man must forfeit his life or suffer serious harm in order to avoid committing a crime which he condemns. The threat, however, must be imminent, real, and inevitable. No court will punish a man who, with a loaded pistol at his head, is compelled to pull a lethal lever. Nor need the peril be that imminent in order to escape punishment.

However, the above statement is merely a dictum. Further, the plea of duress was rejected on the grounds that "if the mental and moral capacities of the superior and subordinate are pooled in the planning and execution of an illegal act, the subordinate may not subsequently protest that he was forced into the performance of an illegal undertaking." As a result all the accused were convicted. Ohlendorf and many others were sentenced to death by hanging, while others were sentenced to life or 10 to 20 years' imprisonment. So this case does not settle the law concerning duress in cases of heinous crimes.

11. Furthermore, it is argued that in the present case even if the Appellant had refused to execute the order under the threat of death, all the innocent Muslims would also have been exterminated by all the other members of his Unit, so that his act should be justified on this ground. The absurdity of this argument is apparent, because it would justify every one of the criminal group who participated in the joint massacre of innocent persons. Moreover, there is absolutely no authority for such a proposition.

12. From the above considerations my conclusion on this question is that duress can only be a mitigating circumstance and is not a defence to the massacre of innocent persons. This view agrees with and is in support of the Joint Separate Opinion of Judges McDonald and Vohrah.

SEPARATE AND DISSENTING OPINION OF JUDGE CASSESE:

11. [T]he majority of the Appeals Chamber has embarked upon a detailed

investigation of "practical policy considerations" and has concluded by upholding "policy considerations" substantially based on English law. I submit that this examination is *extraneous to the task of our Tribunal*. This International Tribunal is called upon to apply international law, in particular our Statute and principles and rules of international humanitarian law and international criminal law. Our International Tribunal is a court of law; it is bound only by international law. It should therefore refrain from engaging in meta-legal analyses. In addition, it should refrain from relying exclusively on notions, policy considerations or the philosophical underpinnings of common-law countries, while disregarding those of civil-law countries or other systems of law. What is even more important, a policy-oriented approach in the area of criminal law runs contrary to the fundamental customary principle *nullum crimen sine lege*. . . .

12. I consider that: (1) under international criminal law duress may be generally urged as a defence, provided certain strict requirements are met; when it cannot be admitted as a defence, duress may nevertheless be acted upon as a mitigating circumstance; (2) with regard to war crimes or crimes against humanity whose underlying offence is murder or more generally the taking of human life, no special rule of customary international law has evolved on the matter; consequently, even with respect to these offences the *general rule on duress* applies; it follows that duress may amount to a defence provided that its stringent requirements are met. For offences involving killing, it is true, however, that one of the requirements – proportionality – would usually not be fulfilled. Nevertheless, in exceptional circumstances this requirement might be met, for example, when the killing would be *in any case* perpetrated by persons other than the one acting under duress (since then it is not a question of saving your own life by killing another person, but of simply saving your own life when the other person will inevitably die, which may not be disproportionate as a remedy); (3) the Appeals Chamber should therefore remit the case to a Trial Chamber on the issue of duress (as well as on the issue that the plea was not informed), directing the Trial Chamber to enter a not-guilty plea on behalf of Drazen Erdemovic (the "Appellant") and then to satisfy itself, in trial proceedings, whether or not the Appellant acted under duress and consequently, whether or not he is excused. . . .

19. The Prosecution has submitted that there exists a "sufficiently clear norm" of customary international law which specifically precludes duress as a defence to violations of humanitarian law involving the taking of innocent life. The Prosecution has based this conclusion on the following reasoning:

(i) the authoritative source on which one can draw to determine whether an international rule has evolved on the matter is the case-law of military tribunals of the occupying powers sitting in judgement after the Second World War. This case-law has greater precedential value than national case-law since those military tribunals were established under Control Council Law No. 10 of 20 December 1945, which has become part of customary international law;

(ii) three cases brought before these courts have decisive weight, because the issue of duress was not decided upon as an *obiter dictum* but by way of *ratio decidendi* and in addition the ruling of these courts was supported by legal authorities. These cases are *Stalag Luft III* and *Feurstein*, both decided by British courts in Germany, plus *Hölzer et al*, decided by a Canadian court in Germany.

Two other cases, which took a contrary position, namely *Jepsen*, decided by a British court sitting in Germany and *Einsatzgruppen*, decided by a United States Court sitting at Nürnberg, should, according to the Prosecution, be disregarded. The former, because it did not provide any authority and in addition preceded in time the other two aforementioned British cases, hence was overruled by them as *lex posterior*; the latter case because the American court did not take account of the previous British and Canadian cases, provided no authority for its *ratio decidendi* and hence substantially made an "arbitrary statement" of law.

(iii) The three aforementioned cases reflect customary international law as well as general principles of law; consequently it is warranted to conclude that there exists a customary rule of international law barring duress as a defence to killing.

I respectfully find that the Prosecution's argument is wholly lacking in merit.

20. My objections to the Prosecution's submissions are based (i) on the case-law invoked by the Prosecution and (ii) on the case-law it does not invoke.

21. As for the case-law relied upon by the Prosecution, let me start with a minor objection. It is simply not correct to contend that the military tribunals of the Occupying Powers referred to by the Prosecutor "were jurisdictions of equal authority" constituted under Control Council Law No. 10, which has acquired customary international law status; consequently, that their decisions would have more weight than those of national jurisdictions on the issue at stake. Contrary to the Prosecution's submissions, the three British military tribunals were instituted under the Royal Warrant of 14 June 1945 and the Regulations for the Trial of War Criminals appended thereto. They consequently were of national jurisdiction. Similarly, the Canadian military tribunal which decided *Hölzer et al.* was set up under the War Crimes Regulations (Canada) and was, therefore, also of national jurisdiction. Both the British and Canadian tribunals applied *their own national law* on matters not covered by international criminal law, such as duress. By contrast, the United States Military Tribunal II, sitting at Nürnberg – which heard the *Einsatzgruppen* case – was established under Control Council Law No. 10. Therefore, of the Tribunals referred to, this alone can be regarded as having an international character – at least, as far as its origin was concerned. . . .

22. My major objection, however, is that a careful perusal of the cases at issue (the original records of which I consulted in the British Public Record Office in

Kew, Richmond) shows that they have been misinterpreted by the Prosecution [and fail to support the proposition that a defense of duress is unavailable to an accused charged with unlawful killing.]

27. The opposite view was . . . taken in the *Einsatzgruppen* case by the United States Military Tribunal II sitting at Nürnberg. As I have pointed out before, this Tribunal, unlike all the other ones cited so far, acted under Control Council Law No. 10, and therefore its decisions carry more weight than the ones by national courts acting under national legislation. Indeed, as Control Council Law No. 10 can be regarded as an international agreement among the four Occupying Powers (subsequently transformed, to a large extent, into customary law), the action of the courts established or acting under that Law acquires an international relevance that cannot be attributed to national courts pronouncing solely on the strength of national law. . . .

28. It appears from the above survey of the case-law cited by the Prosecution that it is unwarranted to contend that an exception to the customary rule that duress is a defence to a criminal charge has evolved on the matter, removing offences involving unlawful killing from the ambit of duress. This alleged exception would only be supported by one case, *Hölzer et al.*, and would run counter to a case of greater authority, *Einsatzgruppen*. . . .

29. Admittedly, the view propounded in *Hölzer et al.* is also upheld in the provisions of two military manuals. One is the British Military Manual . . . The other . . . is the United States Manual for Courts-Martial, of 1984, whereby duress is a defence "to any offence except killing an innocent person." The view upheld in the case-law and military manuals just mentioned is clearly under the strong influence of English criminal law, which has traditionally rejected the notion that duress may ever excuse the killing of an innocent person, largely on the strength of the old authorities Hale, Blackstone and Stephen. However, recent trends suggest fluctuations in this area of English law. Besides, as has been cogently emphasised by Judge Stephen in his Separate and Dissenting Opinion, the case-law of common-law countries only envisages situations where an accused has a choice between his own life and the life of another, as distinct from cases where instead the choice was either death for another or death for both. This may be because the latter situation, which in its typical form arises where the accused is an unwilling member of a squad engaged in mass execution, almost never arises in a nation during peacetime, but only when the nation is at war. Be that as it may, it would clearly be unwarranted to infer, on the basis of one case decided under Canadian law (*Hölzer et al.*) and the international military regulations of two States, that a customary rule excepting murder-type offences from the ambit of duress has evolved in international criminal law.

30. In addition to the paucity of "evidentiary" material supporting the Prosecution's contention, there is an even more compelling reason for dismissing it. The Prosecution has failed to mention many other cases of violations of international law involving killing where the defence of duress was raised by

the accused and which support a contrary conclusion. According to these cases, which are consistent with the penal law of the relevant States, if some basic conditions . . . are met, duress can be regarded as a defence even when it entails the taking of innocent human life. [The many cases cited by Judge Cassese include the *Masetti* case, which is referred to in the joint opinion of Judges McDonald and Vohrah.]

40. I referred above to the Prosecution's contention that *an exception has evolved in customary international law excluding duress* as an admissible defence in offences involving the taking of innocent lives. This contention can only find support in one Canadian case (*Hölzer et al.*), as well as the military regulations of the United Kingdom and the United States. With these elements of practice one should contrast the contrary, copious case-law I have just surveyed as well as the legislation to the contrary of so many civil-law countries. In my opinion, this manifest inconsistency of State practice warrants the *dismissal* of the Prosecution's contention: *no special customary rule has evolved in international law* on whether or not duress can be admitted as a defence in case of crimes involving the killing of persons.

41. [T]he majority of the Appeals Chamber has reached this same conclusion, although through different arguments. However . . . the Appeals Chamber majority does not draw from the absence of that special rule the only conclusion logically warranted: that one must apply, on a case-by-case basis, the *general rule* on duress to *all* categories of crime, whether or not they involve killing. . . . [Thus,] even in case of war crimes and crimes against humanity involving killing, if confronted with the defence of duress, an international criminal court must apply, as a minimum, the four criteria [that almost universally have to be met for duress to be upheld as a defense], namely (1) a severe threat to life or limb; (2) no adequate means to escape the threat; (3) proportionality in the means taken to avoid the threat; (4) the situation of duress should not have been self-induced.

42. The third criterion – proportionality (meaning that the remedy should not be disproportionate to the evil or that the lesser of two evils should be chosen) – will, in practice, be the hardest to satisfy where the underlying offence involves the killing of innocents. . . . The important point, however – and this is the fundamental source of my disagreement with the majority – is that this question should be for the Trial Chamber to decide with all the facts before it. The defence should not be cut off absolutely and *a priori* from invoking the excuse of duress by a ruling of this International Tribunal whereby, in law, the fact of acting under duress can *never* be a defence to killing innocents. This is altogether too dogmatic and, moreover, it is a stance unsupported by international law, where there is no rule to this effect; in international law there only exists a general rule stating that duress may be a defence when certain requirements are met. . . .

44. Thus the case-law seems to make an exception for those instances where – on the facts – it is highly probable, if not certain, that if the person acting

under duress had refused to commit the crime, the crime would in any event have been carried out by persons other than the accused. The commonest example of such a case is where an execution squad has been assembled to kill the victims, and the accused participates, in some form, in the execution squad, either as an active member or as an organiser, albeit only under the threat of death. In this case, if an individual member of the execution squad first *refuses to obey* but has then to comply with the order as a result of duress, he may be excused: indeed, whether or not he is killed or instead takes part in the execution, the civilians, prisoners of war, etc., *would be shot anyway*. Were he to comply with his legal duty not to shoot innocent persons, he would forfeit his life *for no benefit to anyone and no effect whatsoever* apart from setting a heroic example for mankind (which the law cannot demand him to set): his sacrifice of his own life would be to no avail. In this case the evil threatened (the menace to his life and his subsequent death) would be greater than the remedy (his refraining from committing the crime, *i.e.*, from participating in the execution).

In sum, the customary rule of international law on duress, as evolved on the basis of case-law and the military regulations of some States, *does not exclude* the applicability of duress to war crimes and crimes against humanity whose underlying offence is murder or unlawful killing. However, as the right to life is the most fundamental human right, the rule demands that the general requirements for duress be applied *particularly strictly* in the case of killing of innocent persons. . . .

47. I contend that the international legal regulation of duress in case of murder, as I have endeavoured to infer it from case-law and practice, is both realistic and flexible. It also takes account of social expectations more than the rule suggested by the Prosecution and that propounded by the majority. Law is based on what society can reasonably expect of its members. It should not set *intractable* standards of behaviour which require mankind to perform acts of martyrdom, and brand as criminal any behaviour falling below those standards. . . .

49. What I have argued so far leads me to the conclusion that international criminal law on duress is not ambiguous or uncertain. Here lies the main point of my disagreement with the Appeals Chamber's majority. Admittedly, when duress is urged as a defence for a war crime or a crime against humanity where the underlying offence is the killing of innocent persons, it proves particularly difficult for the international judge to establish whether the relevant facts are present and the necessary high requirements laid down in law are satisfied. But this is a matter for the trial judge to look into. However difficult and tricky his judicial investigation, he is not left empty-handed by law: on the contrary, he can draw from international law fairly accurate guidelines, spelled out in a number of national cases dealing with war crimes and crimes against humanity . . . (some of these cases were based on Control Council Law No. 10 and are therefore endowed with a more authoritative weight).

It should therefore be no surprise that I do not share the views of the majority of the Appeals Chamber, according to which, since international criminal law is ambiguous or uncertain on this matter, it is warranted to make a policy-directed choice and thus rely on "considerations of social and economic policy." I disagree not only because, as I have already repeatedly stated, in my view international law is not ambiguous or uncertain, but also because to uphold in this area of criminal law the concept of recourse to a policy-directed choice is tantamount to running foul of the customary principle *nullum crimen sine lege.* An international court must apply *lex lata,* that is to say, the existing rules of international law as they are created through the sources of the international legal system. If it has instead recourse to policy considerations or moral principles, it acts *ultra vires.* . . .

SEPARATE AND DISSENTING OPINION OF JUDGE STEPHEN:

24. . . . What the decisions do in my view demonstrate is that in relation to duress the strong tendency has been to apply principles of criminal law derived from analogous municipal law rules of the particular tribunal . . . . The post-Second World War military tribunals do not appear to have acted in relation to duress in conscious conformity with the dictates of international law, as, for example, they have in their treatment of the doctrine of superior orders. It appears to me that it cannot be said that, in applying one principle or another to particular cases, the necessary *opinio iuris sine necessitatis* was present so as to establish any rule of customary international law.

25. I accordingly turn to those "general principles of law recognised by civilised nations," referred to in Article 38(1)(c) of the Statute of the International Court of Justice as a further source of international law. . . . The detailed examination of national criminal codes which has been made in the Joint and Separate Opinion of Judges McDonald and Vohrah shows duress to be an available defence to a charge of murder in the great majority of those legal systems, other than those of the common law, which it examines. . . .

26. Were it not for the common law exceptional exclusion of murder . . . there would, I think, accordingly be little doubt that duress, albeit hedged around with appropriate qualifications, should likewise be treated in international law as a general principle of law recognized by civilized nations as available as a defence to all crimes. . . .

29. If, then, it is the common law exception of duress in case of murder that gives rise to doubt concerning duress in international law, what is, I believe, at least clear is the absence in the common law of any satisfying and reasoned principle governing the exclusion of duress in the case of very serious crimes including murder. . . .

52. . . . [I]t has generally been supposed by those opposing duress as any defence to murder "that there is a direct choice between the life of the person

under duress and the life of the victim," [but this] is by no means always the case. . ." It is not. . . the case in the present instance. . . . [T]he altogether different situation which faced the Appellant in the present case, according to his account of events, was one in which he believed, in all probability correctly, that no choice of his would alter the fate of the Muslim victims. . . .

64. While it seems clear that the principles underlying the defence of duress and necessity "have been accepted as a fundamental rule of justice by most nations in their municipal law" the extent of their application in international law is, as I have said, only in doubt by reason of the common law's exception in cases involving the taking of innocent life. No doubt, in identifying a general principle, an international tribunal must not, as one author has put it, be "doing violence to the fundamental concepts of any of those systems." However, the exception of murder apart, duress as a defence is now a "fundamental concept" of the common law and the grounds for exception in the case of murder have been aptly described . . . as being the concern of common law judges with the supreme importance that the law affords to the protection of human life and their repugnance that the law "should recognize in any individual in any circumstances, however extreme, the right to choose that one innocent person should be killed rather than another." Neither this concern nor this repugnance can have any application to a case in which nothing that an accused can do can save the life which the law seeks to protect, so that no question of choice concerning an innocent life is left to an accused. In such a case the foundation upon which rests the exception at common law to its otherwise well-accepted recognition of duress as a defence disappears and what remains is the role of duress in freeing an accused from criminal responsibility when the stringent conditions for its application are satisfied. In such a case, too, there is nothing either in the principles of the common law or in the cases in which those principles have been applied which would exclude duress as a defence; the principle which supports its exclusion in the case of the taking of innocent lives is absent. No violence is done to the fundamental concepts of the common law by the recognition in international law of duress as a defence in such cases. Whether it may be raised as a defence in international law in other circumstances in crimes involving the taking of innocent lives is a matter for another day and another case. . . .

66. It is for the foregoing reasons that I conclude that, despite the exception which the common law makes to the availability of duress in cases of murder where the choice is truly between one life or another, the defence of duress can be adopted into international law as deriving from a general principle of law recognized by the world's major legal systems, at least where that exception does not apply.

NOTES AND QUESTIONS

(1) On remand, Erdemovic pleaded guilty to a charge of violating the laws and customs of war, and was sentenced to five years' imprisonment. *See Prosecutor v. Erdemovic*, Case No. IT-96-22-T *bis*, Sentencing Judgement (Mar. 5, 1998).

(2) Recall that in *Prosecutor v. Furundzija*, Case No. IT-95-17/1-T, Judgement (Dec. 10, 1998), portions of which are reproduced in chap. 9, *supra*, the accused was charged with torture and outrages upon personal dignity including rape, but had not directly committed the acts of sexual violence himself. A long section of the judgment (paras. 190-249) deals with the law governing the liability of an accomplice and takes up a number of questions (on which there are divisions between and within legal systems), such as whether an aider and abettor must provide tangible assistance, or whether encouragement or moral support will suffice; whether the accomplice has to be causally responsible for the principal's actions, or need simply in some way facilitate commission of the offense; and whether the accomplice must have the same intent as the principal, or whether knowledge that his action will assist the perpetration of an offense is sufficient. The judgment relies primarily on "international case law." Its discussion of the cases considered relevant is introduced by the statement:

> 194. For a correct appraisal of this case law, it is important to bear in mind, with each of the cases to be examined, the forum in which the case was heard, as well as the law applied, as these factors determine its authoritative value. In addition, one should constantly be mindful of the need for great caution in using national case law for the purpose of determining whether customary rules of international criminal law have evolved in a particular matter.

(3) The proper treatment of superior orders has been a matter of great controversy. A part of the controversy goes, however, to words, not substance. It is clear that a crime cannot be justified on the ground that the person who committed it was acting under orders. A superior order does not in itself exclude criminal responsibility. In this respect, there is no defense of superior orders *per se*. But the order may form an element of another defense – a defense along the lines of mistake of law in cases in which the accused was entirely unaware of the illegality of the order, or along the lines of duress or compulsion in cases in which the accused's life would have been at risk were the order not obeyed, *i.e.*, where he had no "moral choice" but to follow the order. Insofar as an excuse along one or both of these lines is allowed, it might be said that the law recognizes a defense of superior orders. But it also might be said that there is still no special defense: the real ground of exculpation is the broader one that someone who could not reasonably be expected to know that his conduct was illegal, or who could not reasonably be expected to have disobeyed an order, acts without culpability. Whether a defense should be allowed on either of these grounds is controversial as well. But it helps to recognize that this – not the question of whether the law permits a defense of superior orders *per se* – is the

crucial question. *See* MODEL DRAFT STATUTE FOR THE INTERNATIONAL CRIMINAL COURT BASED ON THE PREPARATORY COMMITTEE'S TEXT TO THE DIPLOMATIC CONFERENCE, ROME, June 15-July 17, 1988, at 58 (Association Internationale de Droit Pénal, Nouvelles Études Pénales No. 13 *ter*, Leila Sadat Wexler ed., 1998). To what extent is Article 33 of the Rome Statute problematic precisely because it fails to recognize this distinction? *See* Kai Ambos, *General Principles of Criminal Law in the Rome Statute*, 10 CRIM. L. F. 1, 30-32 (1999).

(4) For extensive discussion of the converse problem of the responsibility of a military or civilian superior for acts of subordinates, *see Prosecutor v. Delalic*, Case No. IT-96-21-T, Judgement (Nov. 16, 1998), paras. 333-63. This is the so-called "Celebici case" noted in chap. 9, *supra. See also Prosecutor v. Akayesu*, [chap. 19, *supra*], paras. 487-91. While Article 28 of the Rome Statute makes provision for the responsibility of civilian as well as military superiors, it also distinguishes between the conditions under which the two will be liable for acts of subordinates. Is the distinction drawn in Article 28 the same as that drawn in para. 491 of the judgment in *Akayesu*?

SELECTED REFERENCES

International Law in General

American Law Institute, *Restatement (Third) of the Foreign Relations Law of the United States* (1986).

Brownlie, Ian, *Principles of International Law* (5th ed. 1998).

Janis, Mark W., *An Introduction to International Law* (3d ed. 1999).

Jennings, Sir Robert, & Sir Arthur Watts, *Oppenheim's International Law: Peace* (9th ed. 1992).

Malanczuk, Peter, *Akehurst's Modern Introduction to International Law* (7th ed. 1997).

International Criminal Law in General

Bassiouni, M. Cherif, ed., *International Criminal Law* (3 vols., 2d ed. 1999).

Bassiouni, M. Cherif, & Ved Nanda, eds., *A Treatise on International Criminal Law* (2 vols., 1973).

Dugard, John, & Christine Van den Wyngaert, eds., *International Criminal Law and Procedure* (1996).

Mueller, Gerhard O. W., & Edward M. Wise, eds., *International Criminal Law* (1965).

Paust, Jordon J., M. Cherif Bassiouni, Sharon A. Williams, Michael Scharf, Jimmy Gurulé & Bruce Zagaris, eds., *International Criminal Law: Cases and Materials* (1996).

International Aspects of Criminal Law

Bassiouni, M.Cherif, *International Extradition: United States Law and Practice* (3d ed. 1996).

Blakesley, Christopher L., *Terrorism, Drugs, International Law, and the Protection of Human Liberty* (1992).

Cruver, Donald R., *Complying with the Foreign Practices Act – A Guide for U.S. Firms Doing Business in the International Marketplace* (2d ed. 1999).

Lillich, Richard, ed., *International Aspects of Criminal Law* (1981).

Nadelmann, Ethan A., *Cops Across Borders: The Internationalization of U.S. Criminal Law Enforcement* (1993).

Ristau, Bruno A., & Michael Abbell, *International Judicial Assistance* (6 vols., looseleaf, 1984-).

Shearer, I. A., *Extradition in International Law* (1971).

The Prosecution of International Crimes

Askin, Kelley D., & Dorean M. Koenig, *Women and International Human Rights Law* (3 vols., 1999).

Askin, Kelley D., *War Crimes Against Women: Prosecution in International War Crimes Tribunals* (1997).

Bassiouni, M. Cherif, *Crimes Against Humanity in International Law* (2d ed. 1999).

Bassiouni, M. Cherif, ed., *The Statute of the International Criminal Court: A Documentary History* (1998).

Bassiouni, M. Cherif, & Peter Manikas, *The Law of the International Criminal Tribunal for the Former Yugoslavia* (1996).

Bassiouni, M.Cherif, & Edward M. Wise, *Aut Dedere aut Judicare: The Duty to Extradite or Prosecute in International Law* (1994).

Cooper, Belinda, ed., *War Crimes: The Legacy of Nuremberg* (1999).

Ferencz, Benjamin, *An International Criminal Court: A Step Toward World Peace – A Documentary History and Analysis* (2 vols. 1980).

Ginsburgs, George, & V. N. Kudriavtsev, eds., *The Nuremberg Trial and International Law* (1990).

Klip, André, & Göran Sluiter, eds., *Annotated Leading Cases of International Tribunals: The International Criminal Tribunal for the former Yugoslavia 1993-1998* (1999).

Morris, Virginia, & Michael Scharf, *An Insider's Guide to the International Criminal Tribunal for the former Yugoslavia: A Documentary History & Analysis* (1994).

Neier, Aryeh, *War Crimes – Brutality, Genocide, Terror, & the Struggle for Justice* (1998).

Ratner, Steven R., & Jason S. Abrams, *Accountability for Human Rights Atrocities in International Law: Beyond the Nuremberg Legacy* (1997).

Taylor, Telford, *The Anatomy of the Nuremberg Trials: A Personal Memoir* (1992).

Taylor, Telford, *Nuremberg and Vietnam: An American Tragedy* (1970).

Triffterer, Otto, ed., *Commentary on the Rome Statute of the International Criminal Court: Observers' Notes, Article by Article* (1999).

Woetzel, Robert K., *The Nuremberg Trials in International Law* (2d ed. 1962).

Websites

ASIL Guide to Electronic Resources for International Law – International Criminal Law: <http://www.asil.org/resource/home.htm>.

United Nations: <http://www.un.org>.

U.S. Department of Justice: <http://www.usdoj.gov>.

TABLE OF CASES

[Principal cases appear in capitals; References are to pages.]

TABLE OF STATUTES AND INTERNATIONAL AGREEMENTS

[References are to casebook sections.]

INDEX

[References are to casebook pages.]

I-1

U

UNIVERSAL JURISDICTION

U.S. CONSTITUTION (SEE SPECIFIC AMENDMENT)

W

WAR CRIMES

Y

YUGOSLAVIA (AD HOC TRIBUNAL FOR THE FORMER)